ST. MN
ST. MARY W9-ADF-636

Volume II
National Revolution and Social Revolution
December 1920–June 1927

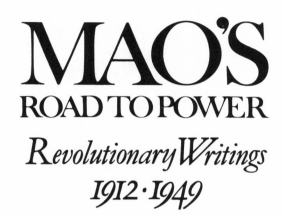

MAO'S
ROAD TO POWER
Revolutionary Writings
1912·1949

This volume was prepared under the auspices of
the John King Fairbank Center for East Asian Research,
Harvard University

The project for the translation of Mao Zedong's pre-1949 writings has been supported by a grant from the National Endowment for the Humanities, an independent federal agency.

The Cover

The calligraphy on the cover reproduces the complete manuscript of Mao's letter of March 7, 1923, to the secretary of the Socialist Youth League. Our English translation can be found below, on p. 155.

Volume II
National Revolution and Social Revolution
December 1920–June 1927

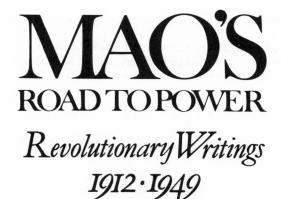

MAO'S
ROAD TO POWER
Revolutionary Writings
1912·1949

Stuart R. Schram, Editor

Nancy J. Hodes, Associate Editor

An East Gate Book

M.E. Sharpe
Armonk, New York
London, England

An East Gate Book

Translations copyright © 1994 John King Fairbank Center for East Asian Research

Introductory materials copyright © 1994 Stuart R. Schram

All rights reserved. No part of this book may be reproduced in any form without written permission from the publisher, M. E. Sharpe, Inc., 80 Business Park Drive, Armonk, New York 10504.

Library of Congress Cataloging-in-Publication Data

(Revised for vol. 2)

Mao, Tse-tung, 1893–1976.
[Selections. English. 1992]
Mao's road to power.

"East gate book."
Includes bibliographical references and index.
Contents: v. 1. The pre-Marxist period, 1912–1920—
v. 2. National revolution and social revolution, December 1920–June 1927.
I. Schram, Stuart R.
II. Title.
DS778.M3A25   1992
951.04   92-26783
ISBN 1-56324-049-1 (v. 1 : acid-free)
ISBN 1-56324-430-6 (v. 2)
CIP

Printed in the United States of America

The paper used in this publication meets the minimum requirements of American National Standard for Information Sciences— Permanence of Paper for Printed Library Materials, ANSI Z 39.48-1984.

BM (c)   10   9   8   7   6   5   4   3   2   1

Contents

1922

1923

1924

1925

1926

1927

Acknowledgments

Major funding for this project has been provided by the National Endowment for the Humanities, from which we have received three generous grants, for the periods 1989-1991, 1991-1993, and 1993-1995. In addition, many individual and corporate donors have contributed substantially toward the cost-sharing element of our budget. These include, in alphabetical order: Mrs. H. Ahmanson; Ambassador Kwang S. Choi; Phyllis Collins and the Dillon Fund; the Harvard-Yenching Institute; James R. Houghton, the CBS Foundation, the Corning, Inc. Foundation, J.P. Morgan & Co., and the Metropolitan Life Foundation; the Kandell Fund for Dr. Alice Kandell; Robert H. Morehouse; Dr. Park Un-Tae; James O. Welch, Jr., RJR Nabisco, and the Vanguard Group; Ambassador Yangsoo Yoo; and William S. Youngman. We also wish to thank the Committee on Scholarly Communication with China, which provided the grant (paid by the U.S. Information Agency) for a visit to China in September-November 1991 by the editor of these volumes, Stuart Schram, to consult Chinese scholars and obtain information relevant to the work of the project.

Translations of the materials included in this volume have been drafted by many different hands. Our team of translators has included, in alphabetical order, Hsuan Delorme, Gu Weiqun, Li Jin, Li Yuwei, Li Zhuqing, Lin Chun, Pei Minxin, Shen Tong, Su Weizhou, Tian Dongdong, Wang Xisu, Wang Zhi, Bill Wycoff, Ye Yang, Zhang Aiping, and Zheng Shiping. Michele Grant, Research Assistant in 1990-1991, drafted some of the notes.

Nancy Hodes, Research Assistant since mid-1991, and associate editor of the present volume, has participated extensively in the revision and annotation of the translations. Her contribution to the checking of the final translations against the Chinese originals has been of exceptional value. She has also drafted some translations, as has Stuart Schram. In particular, she has prepared the initial versions of all Mao's poems, which were then revised in collaboration with Stuart Schram. Final responsibility for the accuracy and literary quality of the work as a whole rests with him as editor.

We are grateful to Eugene Wu, the Director of the Harvard-Yenching Library, for obtaining from the Guomindang archives a number of manuscript items translated here, and for locating several other texts in the rare periodical holdings of the library. We also extend our sincere thanks to Professor C. Martin Wilbur for kindly allowing us to make use of the documentation on the land question in 1927 which he obtained from the Guomindang archives in the 1960s, and to Dr. Jean Ashton, the Librarian of the Columbia University Rare Book and Manu-

script Library where the C. Martin Wilbur Papers are now deposited, for author-
izing us to publish our translations of items from this source. (Further details can
be found below, in the source notes accompanying the relevant texts.)

This project was launched with the active participation of Roderick
MacFarquhar, Director of the Fairbank Center until June 30, 1992. Without his
organizing ability and continuing wholehearted support, it would never have
come to fruition. His successor, Professor James L. Watson, has continued to
take a keen and sympathetic interest in our work.

The general introduction to the series, and the introduction to Volume II, were
written by Stuart Schram, who wishes to acknowledge his very great indebted-
ness to Benjamin Schwartz, a pioneer in the study of Mao Zedong's thought.
Professor Schwartz read successive drafts of these two introductions, and made
stimulating and thoughtful comments which have greatly improved the final
versions. For any remaining errors and inadequacies, the fault lies once again
with the editor.

GENERAL INTRODUCTION

Mao Zedong and the Chinese Revolution, 1912-1949

Mao Zedong stands out as one of the dominant figures of the twentieth century. Guerrilla leader, strategist, conqueror, ruler, poet, and philosopher, he placed his imprint on China, and on the world. This edition of Mao's writings provides abundant documentation in his own words regarding both his life and his thought. Because of the central role of Mao's ideas and actions in the turbulent course of the Chinese revolution, it thus offers a rich body of historical data about China in the first half of the twentieth century.

The process of change and upheaval in China which Mao sought to master had been going on for roughly a century by the time he was born in 1893. Its origins lay in the incapacity of the old order to cope with the population explosion at the end of the eighteenth century, and with other economic and social problems, as well as in the shock administered by the Opium War of 1840 and further European aggression and expansion thereafter.

Mao's native Hunan Province was crucially involved both in the struggles of the Qing dynasty to maintain its authority, and in the radical ferment which led to successive challenges to the imperial system. Thus on the one hand, the Hunan Army of the great conservative viceroy Zeng Guofan was the main instrument for putting down the Taiping Rebellion and saving the dynasty in the middle of the nineteenth century. But on the other hand, the most radical of the late nineteenth-century reformers, and the only one to lay down his life in 1898, Tan Sitong, was also a Hunanese, as was Huang Xing, whose contribution to the Revolution of 1911 was arguably as great as that of Sun Yatsen.[1] In his youth, Mao profoundly admired all three of these men, though they stood for very different things: Zeng for the empire and the Confucian values which sustained it, Tan for defying tradition and seeking inspiration in the West, Huang for Western-style constitutional democracy.

---

1. Abundant references to all three of these figures are to be found in Mao's writings, especially those of the early period contained in Volume I of this series. See, regarding Zeng, pp. 10, 72, and 131. On Tan, see "Zhang Kundi's Record of Two Talks with Mao Zedong," September 1917, p. 139. On Huang, see "Letter to Miyazaki Tōten," March 1917, pp. 111–12.

Apart from Mao's strong Hunanese patriotism, which inclined him to admire eminent figures from his own province, he undoubtedly saw these three as forceful and effective leaders who, each in his own way, fought to assure the future of China. Any sense that they were contradictory symbols would have been diminished by the fact that from an early age Mao never advocated exclusive reliance on either Chinese or Western values, but repeatedly sought a synthesis of the two. In August 1917, Mao Zedong expressed the view that despite the "antiquated" and otherwise undesirable traits of the Chinese mentality, "Western thought is not necessarily all correct either; very many parts of it should be transformed at the same time as Oriental thought."[2] In a sense, this sentence sums up the problem he sought to resolve throughout his whole career: How could China develop an advanced civilization, and become rich and powerful, while remaining Chinese?

As shown by the texts contained in Volume I, Mao's early exposure to "Westernizing" influences was not limited to Marxism. Other currents of European thought played a significant role in his development. Whether he was dealing with liberalism or Leninism, however, Mao tenaciously sought to adapt and transform these ideologies, even as he espoused them and learned from them.

Mao Zedong played an active and significant role in the movement for political and intellectual renewal which developed in the aftermath of the patriotic student demonstrations of May 4, 1919, against the transfer of German concessions in China to Japan. This "new thought tide," which had begun to manifest itself at least as early as 1915, dominated the scene from 1919 onward, and prepared the ground for the triumph of radicalism and the foundation of the Chinese Communist Party in 1921. But though Mao enthusiastically supported the call of Chen Duxiu, who later became the Party's first leader, for the Western values incarnated by "Mr. Science" and "Mr. Democracy," he never wholly endorsed the total negation of Chinese culture advocated by many people during the May Fourth period. His condemnations of the old thought as backward and slavish are nearly always balanced by a call to learn from both Eastern and Western thought and to develop something new out of these twin sources.

In 1919 and 1920, Mao leaned toward anarchism rather than socialism. Only in January 1921 did he at last draw the explicit conclusion that anarchism would not work, and that Russia's proletarian dictatorship represented the model which must be followed.[3] Half the remaining fifty-five years of his life were devoted to creating such a dictatorship, and the other half to deciding what to do with it, and how to overcome the defects which he perceived in it. From beginning to end of this process, Mao drew upon Chinese experience and Chinese civilization in revising and reforming this Western import.

To the extent that, from the 1920s onward, Mao was a committed Leninist, his

2. Letter of August 1917 to Li Jinxi, Volume 1, p. 132.
3. See below, in this volume, his letter of January 21, 1921, to Cai Hesen.

understanding of the doctrine shaped his vision of the world. But to the extent that, although he was a communist revolutionary, he always "planted his backside on the body of China,"[4] ideology alone did not exhaustively determine his outlook. One of Mao Zedong's most remarkable attributes was the extent to which he linked theory and practice. He was in some respects not a very good Marxist, but few men have ever applied so well Marx's dictum that the vocation of the philosopher is not merely to understand the world, but to change it.

It is reliably reported that Mao's close collaborators tried in vain, during the Yan'an period, to interest him in writings by Marx such as *The 18 Brumaire of Louis Bonaparte*. To such detailed historical analyses based on economic and social facts, he preferred *The Communist Manifesto*, of which he saw the message as "*Jieji douzheng, jieji douzheng, jieji douzheng!*" (Class struggle, class struggle, class struggle!) In other words, for Mao the essence of Marxism resided in the fundamental idea of the struggle between oppressor and oppressed as the motive force of history.

Such a perspective offered many advantages. It opened the door to the immediate pursuit of revolutionary goals, since even though China did not have a very large urban proletariat, there was no lack of oppressed people to be found there. It thus eliminated the need for the Chinese to feel inferior, or to await salvation from without, just because their country was still stuck in some precapitalist stage of development (whether "Asiatic" or "feudal"). And, by placing the polarity "oppressor/oppressed" at the heart of the revolutionary ideology itself, this approach pointed toward a conception in which landlord oppression, and the oppression of China by the imperialists, were perceived as the two key targets of the struggle.

Mao displayed, in any case, a remarkably acute perception of the realities of Chinese society, and consistently adapted his ideas to those realities, at least during the struggle for power. In the early years after its foundation in 1921, the Chinese Communist Party sought support primarily from the working class in the cities and adopted a strategy based on a "united front" or alliance with Sun Yatsen's Guomindang. Mao threw himself into this enterprise with enthusiasm, serving first as a labor union organizer in Hunan in 1922-1923, and then as a high official within the Guomindang organization in 1923-1924. Soon, however, he moved away from this perspective, and even before urban-based revolution was put down in blood by Chiang Kaishek in 1927, he asserted that the real center of gravity of Chinese society was to be found in the countryside. From this fact, he drew the conclusion that the decisive blows against the existing reactionary order must be struck in the countryside by the peasants.

By August 1927, Mao had concluded that mobilizing the peasant masses was

---

4. Mao Zedong, "Ruhe yanjiu Zhonggong dangshi" (How to study the history of the Chinese Communist Party), lecture of March 1942, published in *Dangshi yanjiu* (Research on Party History), No. 1, 1980, pp. 2–7.

not enough. A red army was also necessary to serve as the spearhead of revolution, and so he put forward the slogan: "Political power comes out of the barrel of a gun." In the mountain fastness of the Jinggangshan base area in Jiangxi Province, to which he retreated at the end of 1927 with the remnants of his forces, he began to elaborate a comprehensive strategy for rural revolution, combining land reform with the tactics of guerrilla warfare. In this he was aided by Zhu De, a professional soldier who had joined the Chinese Communist Party, and soon became known as the "commander-in-chief." These tactics rapidly achieved a considerable measure of success. The "Chinese Soviet Republic," established in 1931 in a larger and more populous area of Jiangxi, survived for several years, though when Chiang Kaishek finally devised the right strategy and mobilized his crack troops against it, the Communists were defeated and forced to embark in 1934 on the Long March.

By this time, Mao Zedong had been reduced virtually to the position of a figurehead by the Moscow-trained members of the so-called "Internationalist" faction, who dominated the leadership of the Chinese Communist Party. At a conference held at Zunyi in January 1935, in the course of the Long March, Mao began his comeback. Soon he was once again in effective charge of military operations, though he became chairman of the Party only in 1943.

Mao's vision of the Chinese people as a whole as the victim of oppression now came decisively into play. Japanese aggression led in 1936 to the Xi'an Incident, in which Chiang Kaishek was kidnapped in order to force him to oppose the invader. This event was the catalyst which produced a second "united front" between the Communists and the Guomindang. Without it, Mao Zedong and the forces he led might well have remained a side current in the remote and backward region of Shaanxi, or even been exterminated altogether. As it was, the collaboration of 1937-1945, however perfunctory and opportunistic on both sides, gave Mao the occasion to establish himself as a patriotic national leader. Above all, the resulting context of guerrilla warfare behind the Japanese lines allowed the Communists to build a foundation of political and military power throughout wide areas of Northern and Central China.

During the years in Yan'an, from 1937 to 1946, Mao Zedong also finally consolidated his own dominant position in the Chinese Communist Party, and in particular his role as the ideological mentor of the Party. Beginning in November 1936, he seized the opportunity to read a number of writings by Chinese Marxists, and Soviet works in Chinese translation, which had been published while he was struggling for survival a few years earlier. These provided the stimulus for the elaboration of his own interpretation of Marxism-Leninism, and in particular for his theory of contradictions. Another of the main features of his thought, the emphasis on practice as the source of knowledge, had long been in evidence and had found expression in the sociological surveys in the countryside which he himself carried out beginning as early as 1926.

In 1938, Mao called for the "Sinification of Marxism," that is, the modification not only of its language but of its substance in order to adapt it to Chinese culture and Chinese realities. By 1941, he had begun to suggest that he himself had carried out this enterprise, and to attack those in the Party who preferred to translate ready-made formulas from the Soviet Union. The "Rectification Campaign" of 1942-43 was designed in large measure to change the thinking of such "Internationalists," or to eliminate them from positions of influence.

When Mao was elected chairman of the Politburo and of the Secretariat in March 1943, the terms of his appointment to this second post contained a curious provision: Mao alone, as chairman, could out-vote the other two members of the Secretariat in case of disagreement. This was the first step toward setting Mao above and apart from all other Party members and thereby opening the way to the subsequent cult. At the Seventh Party Congress in April 1945 came apotheosis: Mao Zedong's thought was written into the Party statutes as the guide to all work, and Mao was hailed as the greatest theoretical genius in China's history for his achievement in creating such a remarkable doctrine.

In 1939-1940, Mao had put forward the slogan of "New Democracy" and defined it as a régime in which proletariat (read Communist Party) and bourgeoisie (read Guomindang) would jointly exercise dictatorship over reactionary and pro-Japanese elements in Chinese society. Moreover, as late as 1945, when the Communists were still in a weaker position than the Guomindang, Mao indicated that this form of rule would be based on free elections with universal suffrage. Later, when the Communist Party had military victory within its grasp and was in a position to do things entirely in its own way, Mao would state forthrightly, in "On People's Democratic Dictatorship," that such a dictatorship could in fact just as well be called a "People's Democratic Autocracy." In other words, it was to be democratic only in the sense that it served the people's interests; in form, it was to exercise its authority through a "powerful state apparatus."

In 1946, when the failure of General George Marshall's attempts at mediation led to renewed civil war, Mao and his comrades revived the policy of land reform, which had been suspended during the alliance with the Guomindang, and thereby recreated a climate of agrarian revolution. Thus national and social revolution were interwoven in the strategy which ultimately brought final victory in 1949.

In March 1949, Mao declared that though the Chinese revolution had previously taken the path of surrounding the cities from the countryside, henceforth the building of socialism would take place in the orthodox way, with leadership and enlightenment radiating outward from the cities to the countryside. Looking at the twenty-seven years under Mao's leadership after 1949, however, the two most striking developments—the chiliastic hopes of instant plenty which characterized the Great Leap Forward of the late 1950s, and the anxiety about the corrupting effects of material progress, coupled with a nostalgia for "military communism," which underlay the Cultural Revolution—both bore the mark of rural utopianism. Thus Mao's road to power, though it led to total victory over the Nationalists, also cultivated in Mao himself, and in the Party, attitudes which would subsequently engender great problems.

Revolution in its Leninist guise has loomed large in the world for most of the twentieth century, and the Chinese revolution has been, with the Russian revolution, one of its two most important manifestations. The Bolshevik revolution set a pattern long regarded as the only standard of communist orthodoxy, but the revolutionary process in China was in some respects even more remarkable. Although communism now appears bankrupt throughout much of the world, the impact of Mao is still a living reality in China two decades after his death. Particularly since the Tiananmen events of June 1989, the continuing relevance of Mao's political and ideological heritage has been stressed ever more heavily by the Chinese leadership. Interest in Mao Zedong has been rekindled in some sectors of the population, and elements of a new Mao cult have even emerged.

Though the ultimate impact of these recent trends remains uncertain, the problem of how to come to terms with the modern world, while retaining China's own identity, still represents perhaps the greatest challenge facing the Chinese. Mao did not solve it, but he boldly grappled with the political and intellectual challenge of the West as no Chinese ruler before him had done. If Lenin has suffered the ultimate insult of being replaced by Peter the Great as the symbol of Russian national identity, it could be argued that Mao cannot, like Lenin, be supplanted by a figure analogous to Peter because he himself played the role of China's first modernizing and Westernizing autocrat. However misguided many of Mao's ideas, and however flawed his performance, his efforts in this direction will remain a benchmark to a people still struggling to define their place in the community of nations.

INTRODUCTION

The Writings of Mao Zedong, 1920-1927

The texts from 1912 to November 1920 contained in Volume I of this edition shed light primarily on the life and intellectual development of the young Mao. Though several of the more important documents in that volume emanate from organizations, such as the New People's Study Society or the Cultural Book Society, Mao's imprint on these bodies was so profound that the views expressed in them can be taken as corresponding in large part to his own thinking. The present volume, covering the period December 1920–June 1927, introduces a new theme: Mao's activity as a member of two parties, the Chinese Communist Party and the Guomindang, neither of which he controlled, though he played an important role in both. Many of his reports and speeches at this time were therefore produced within an institutional framework that led him, or required him, to adapt his own standpoint to the position of the party or parties concerned. Thus, to the biographical framework of the first volume is added a further dimension: that of "party history." The constraints of party orthodoxy were not, however, so rigid during this early period as they subsequently became, and Mao's status was sufficiently high to allow him substantial freedom of expression. In addition, the materials translated here include some texts of a more personal character. Consequently, despite the changing historical context, there remains a large element of continuity between this volume and its predecessor.

Before the First Congress of the Chinese Communist Party

Volume I of this edition is subtitled "The Pre-Marxist Period" because as of November 1920 Mao had not yet, despite his increasingly radical political stance, explicitly declared his allegiance to Marxist socialism. The first document in the present volume, dated December 1, 1920, did place him on record to this effect. Writing to Cai Hesen and other members of the New People's Study Society then studying in France, Mao endorsed the view that Cai had put forward in a letter of August 13, 1920, according to which a proletarian dictatorship on the Russian model constituted the only solution for China.[1] In January 1921, he

---

1. See below, "Letter to Xiao Xudong, Cai Linbin, and the Other Members in France," December 1, 1920.

went a step farther, accepting Marx's materialist conception of history as "the philosophical basis of our Party," and explicitly repudiating the anarchist ideas for which he had previously shown so much sympathy.[2]

Although the Chinese Communist Party held its First Congress only in July 1921, Mao could refer in this letter to "our Party" as an existing entity because "Communist Small Groups" constituting nuclei of the Party had been formed in August 1920 in Shanghai and in October 1920 in Beijing, and similar groups would shortly emerge elsewhere. Unfortunately, no writings by Mao himself are available regarding his role in the process of founding the Party, either in Hunan or at the national level. In a sense, this is not surprising, since even the Chinese texts of the key documents from the First Congress have been lost, so that the Chinese Communist Party has been obliged to retranslate them from English and Russian versions. It does, however, seem slightly odd that not a single inner-Party communication signed by Mao should exist for the period of nearly two years from the late summer of 1920 to the early summer of 1922, though various sources indicate that he was active at that time in establishing both the Communist Party and the Socialist Youth League in Changsha.[3]

The reason may lie in the tentative and informal character of such organizations in their early stages. Thus Mao's achievements in establishing the Youth League in early 1921 apparently consisted primarily in fostering a nucleus of like-minded comrades within the New People's Study Society. These efforts are illustrated by the materials translated in the early part of this volume, documenting Mao's involvement with the New People's Study Society[4] and the Cultural Book Society.[5] The political context in which these activities took place was, however, significantly modified as a result of the changes in the governorship of Hunan in the latter part of 1920.

In June 1920, the brutal and repressive governor, Zhang Jingyao, had fled the province after a campaign in which Mao had played a leading part.[6] Though the mobilization of public opinion had been a significant factor, Zhang had been put to flight in the first instance by military defeat at the hands of former governor

---

2. See Mao's "Letter to Cai Hesen," January 21, 1921, translated below. Regarding his preference for Kropotkin over Marx in 1919, see Volume I, p. 380.

3. See, in English, Li Jui [Li Rui], *The Early Revolutionary Activities of Comrade Mao Tse-tung* (hereafter Li Jui, *Early Mao*) (White Plains: M. E. Sharpe, 1977), pp. 162–67. This version has been translated from the first Chinese edition, published in 1957. The third edition of this book draws on a wide range of recently published sources, and presents a more balanced picture. See Li Rui, *Zaonian Mao Zedong* (The Young Mao Zedong) (Shenyang: Liaoning renmin chubanshe, 1991); the corresponding passage appears on pp. 366–81.

4. See below, in addition to Mao's letter of December 1, 1920, mentioned previously, the two reports on the affairs of the New People's Study Society.

5. See below, "Business Report of the Cultural Book Society" No. 2, May 1921.

6. See Volume I, pp. 457–523 *passim*, for an abundant documentation in Mao's own words regarding this "movement to expel Zhang."

Tan Yankai and his trusted subordinate Zhao Hengti. At the time, Mao declared that Tan and Zhao had "become heroes among their [Hunanese] compatriots."[7] Tan Yankai, having resumed the governorship, convened in September a "Hunan self-government conference"; Mao regarded this as a "manifestly revolutionary act," and added that, as a result, Tan's government was "indeed a revolutionary government."[8] Mao reiterated this view in a letter of November 25, 1920,[9] but at that very moment the rivalry between Tan and Zhao culminated in Tan's forced departure and his replacement by Zhao Hengti.

Tan Yankai was a holder of the *jinshi* degree and a former Hanlin compiler who had written the signboard for Mao's Cultural Book Society in his own calligraphy. Zhao Hengti was in no sense a savage like Zhang Jingyao, but he was a military man in education and experience (even though he had been regarded as relatively leftist at the time of the 1911 Revolution). Henceforth, therefore, Mao was confronted by a sterner and less urbane figure in the governor's residence.

On October 10, 1921, Mao participated in the setting up of the Hunan branch office of the Chinese Communist Party in Changsha. (He had attended the First Congress as a delegate of the "Hunan organization" of the Party, but this, as already noted, may have been somewhat tenuous.)[10] As for the Socialist Youth League, on June 17, 1922, Mao chaired a meeting of the Executive Committee of the Changsha branch, which adopted a set of regulations, drafted by Mao, for reorganizing the branch. Three days later he wrote a letter requesting that he be allowed to serve as secretary, even though he was over the age limit of twenty-eight.[11]

Another of Mao's activities in 1921 that demonstrated significant continuity with the May Fourth period was the establishment of the Hunan Self-Study University.[12] Even though the name had originally been suggested to Mao by Hu Shi,[13] this institution undoubtedly served as a cadre school for the Chinese Communist Party. At the same time, the documents concerning it develop themes prominent in Mao's earlier writings: the importance of making culture more widely available to all classes of society, the need to take account of the

---

7. See the letter dated June 23, 1920, in Volume I, p. 530.

8. See the proposal of October 5–6, 1920, by Mao and others, in Volume I, pp. 567–68.

9. See his letter to Xiang Jingyu, Volume I, pp. 595–96.

10. See, in particular, Pang Xianzhi (ed.), *Mao Zedong nianpu. 1893–1949* (Chronological Biography of Mao Zedong, 1893–1949) (hereafter *Nianpu*) (Beijing: Zhongyang wenxian chubanshe, 1993), Vol. I, pp. 85, 89.

11. See below, "To Shi Fuliang and the Central Committee of the Socialist Youth League," June 20, 1922. These events are also summarized in *Nianpu*, Vol. 1, pp. 95–96.

12. See below, "Statement on the Founding of the Hunan Self-Study University" and "Outline of the Organization of the Hunan Self-Study University," August 1921; and "Admissions Notice of the Hunan Self-Study University," December 1921.

13. See Mao's letter of March 14, 1920, to Zhou Shizhao, Volume I, p. 506, where it is stated: "Mr. Hu Shizhi coined this term."

students' individual natures, and the value of self-reliance and of developing a "strong personality."

Mao Zedong as a Labor Organizer, 1922-1923[14]

As late as December 1921, Mao stated that education was his chosen lifelong vocation.[15] Meanwhile, however, he had also become involved in the labor movement. In earlier years he had come into contact with the workers through the night school he organized for them in 1917.[16] In August 1921, he was named head of the Hunan office of the Secretariat of Chinese Labor Organizations, set up by the Chinese Communist Party at its First Congress.[17] Despite the objections of Sneevliet, the representative of the International, the First Congress had adopted a sectarian and closed-door policy, ruling out cooperation with other parties and organizations and making even membership in the Party itself secret. The Labor Secretariat was thus particularly important as a channel through which Communists could enter into contact with the working class.

Once again, as in the case of the Party, there are no writings by Mao himself relating explicitly to the activities of the secretariat until the summer of 1922. In November 1921, at the request of the anarchist labor leaders Huang Ai and Pang Renquan, Mao contributed an article to the organ of the Labor Association they had organized a year earlier expressing his sympathy for it.[18] Mao had sought to maintain good relations with these two men and to work with them despite ideological differences. Writing in their paper, he stressed that the purpose of a labor organization was "not merely to rally the laborers to get better pay and shorter working hours by means of strikes," but that it "should also nurture

---

14. On this phase of Mao's career, see Lynda Shaffer, *Mao and the Workers. The Hunan Labor Movement, 1920–1923* (hereafter Shaffer, *Mao and the Workers*) (Armonk, N.Y.: M. E. Sharpe, 1982); Li Jui, *Early Mao, passim*; and Angus W. McDonald, Jr., *The Urban Origins of Rural Revolution. Elites and the Masses in Hunan Province, China, 1911–1927* (hereafter McDonald, *Urban Origins*) (Berkeley: University of California Press, 1978), pp. 142–217.

15. See below, "Answers to the Questionnaire Regarding Lifetime Aspirations for Members of the Young China Association," December 1921. (Mao had belonged to this organization since December 1919.)

16. See the materials in Volume I, pp. 143–56.

17. For a recent and well-documented account of the First Congress, see the introduction to Tony Saich (ed.), *The Origins of the First United Front in China. The Role of Sneevliet (Alias Maring)* (hereafter Saich, *Origins*) (Leiden: E. J. Brill, 1991, 2 vols.), pp. 52–69. The 1924 M.A. essay of Chen Gongbo, a founding member of the Party, remains an important source for the materials adopted at the Congress. See Ch'en Kung-po, *The Communist Movement in China*, edited with an introduction by C. Martin Wilbur (hereafter Ch'en, *Communist Movement*) (New York: Columbia University East Asian Institute, 1960).

18. See below, "My Hopes for the Labor Association," November 21, 1921.

class consciousness." He added that unions required effective organization, so as to avoid "too much dispersion of authority." At the same time, he refrained from any mention of Marxism and from more explicit criticism of anarchist views.

Many sources state that by late 1921 Mao had succeeded in persuading Huang and Pang to join the Socialist Youth League, and Sneevliet believed this to be true.[19] The two labor leaders were, however, executed by Zhao Hengti in January 1922 because of their role in mobilizing the cotton workers for a strike.[20] The governor proceeded to dissolve the Labor Association and close down its newspaper, effectively putting an end to its activity.

On May Day of 1922, Mao wrote an article in which he first laid down the apparently benign principle of the right of the workers to the "full fruits of their labor" and then added that "of course" this right could be exercised "only after Communism is put into effect." He went on to warn the employers that the fate of Russia's "capitalist class and nobility" might await them.[21]

The Second Congress of the Chinese Communist Party in July 1922 gave a new impetus to participation in the labor movement. On this occasion, a resolution was adopted concerning "The Labor Union Movement and the Communist Party."[22] This document explained that the difference between the Communist Party and the labor unions was that the Communist Party was an organization of proletarian elements endowed with class consciousness, while the labor unions were organizations of all workers, regardless of their political views. Thus the Party was the brain and the unions were the body. In order to impose its leadership, the Party should set up strong groups in labor unions created by the Guomindang, the anarchists, or Christian organizations.

Mao himself, for reasons that remain obscure, did not attend the congress, but for approximately nine months after it was held he devoted himself, for the first and only time in his career, primarily to work in the unions. He did so in the first instance as head of the Hunan Office of the Secretariat of Chinese Labor Organizations, and the present volume contains a substantial number of documents to

---

19. See his article, originally published in May 1922, reprinted in Saich, *Origins*, p. 747.

20. Regarding the course of the strike at the First Textile Mill and the execution of Huang and Pang, see McDonald, *Urban Origins*, pp. 157–65, and Shaffer, *Mao and the Workers*, pp. 47–48, 54–57. See also below, the record of discussions between representatives of Hunan labor organizations, including Mao, and Governor Zhao, December 14, 1922, and the notes thereto.

21. See below, "Some Issues That Deserve More Attention," May 1, 1922.

22. For the text, see *Zhonggong zhongyang wenjian xuanji* (Selected Documents of the Central Committee of the Chinese Communist Party) (hereafter *Central Committee Documents*) (Beijing: Zhonggong zhongyang dangxiao chubanshe, 1989), Vol. I (1921–1925), pp. 76–82. A complete English translation can be found in Tony Saich, *The Rise to Power of the Chinese Communist Party. Documents and Analysis, 1920–1949* (hereafter Saich, *Rise to Power*) (Armonk, N.Y.: M. E. Sharpe, 1995), Doc. A.16, pp. 50–54.

which he put his name in that capacity.[23] In November 1922, building in part on the foundation laid earlier by the Labor Association of Huang Ai and Pang Renquan, Mao and others established the All-Hunan Federation of Labor Organizations. At the first meeting of that organization on November 5, 1922, Mao was elected head or general secretary (*zong ganshi*). Thus he had henceforth two bases for his activity among the workers.

All of the texts written or signed by Mao in 1922-1923 must, of course, be interpreted in the context of the overall development of the labor movement.[24] In June 1922, the office of the Labor Secretariat in Shanghai was closed down by the authorities of the International Settlement. In the same month, Wu Peifu, following his victory in the war against Zhang Zuolin, restored Li Yuanhong to the presidency, and recalled the "Old Parliament" of 1913. Wu also declared himself in favor of attaching labor-protection legislation to the new constitution which the parliament had been asked to draft.[25] The Labor Secretariat thereupon transferred its headquarters from Shanghai to Beijing, both to escape repression and to take advantage of the relatively favorable situation in the North, and proceeded in July 1922 to draft the "Petition for a Labor Law" translated below. These circumstances serve to explain the moderate tone of the document.

There is no way of knowing whether Mao played a significant role in drafting this text, or whether he merely contributed his name. It is interesting to note, however, that like some pieces by Mao of late 1920 which appear in Volume I, this petition places the labor problem in the context of an international trend that emerged following the Industrial Revolution, adding that "only the advanced nations of Europe and America" had drawn significant lessons from this experience. "The example of Soviet Russia" is mentioned in a positive light, but is not presented as a norm. While the resolution of the Second Congress of the Chinese Communist Party on labor unions stressed that there could be nothing in common between the capitalists and the workers, and that the unions should advance quickly toward the ultimate goal of overthrowing the capitalist system of wage

---

23. The first of these, translated below, "Petition for a Labor Law and a General Outline for Labor Legislation," July 1922, is signed by him using this title, together with the overall head, Deng Zhongxia, and the heads of the four other regional offices in Shanghai, Wuhan, Guangdong, and Shandong.

24. The standard work on this topic is that of Jean Chesneaux, *Le mouvement ouvrier chinois de 1919 à 1927* (hereafter *Chesneaux, Mouvement ouvrier*) (Paris: Mouton, 1962). It is complemented by a useful research guide, *Les syndicats chinois 1919–1927* (Paris: Mouton, 1965), containing a chronology, a list of the principal workers' organizations by province (including those for Hunan), and 31 texts in Chinese, with French translations. Saich, *Origins*, also contains a great deal of information about the Communist Party and the labor unions, in the form of Sneevliet's notes and correspondence regarding events as they took place.

25. In the text of the petition, Wu Peifu is referred to by his *zi*, Ziyu.

slavery, the petition spoke rather of "justifiable self-defense" of the workers, to which they had been forced by "problems between labor and capital."

Though the language of this petition was relatively moderate, it served as the vehicle for a campaign that played a significant role in raising the political consciousness of the workers. A telegram of September 1922 almost certainly drafted by Mao declared that the movement to establish a labor law "now reverberates throughout the land."[26] Here "the establishment of a worker-peasant state in Soviet Russia" was characterized as "a model for all other countries in the world," and the parliamentarians were warned that if they did not act quickly to pass the proposed labor law, they would no longer be recognized as representing the will of the people.

Mao Zedong was involved at this time in the affairs of many different unions.[27] Texts emanating from a large number of these are included in the Tokyo edition of Mao's works, but there are reasons to believe that in many cases he did not actually play a role in drafting them. We are persuaded, however, that his name can legitimately be attached to the materials of the Masons' and Carpenters' Union, the Guangzhou-Hankou Railroad Workers' Union, and the Typesetters' Union translated below.

The texts for the last four months of 1922 date from a time when, broadly speaking, the labor movement in Hunan was on the offensive, and when it conducted, with Mao's participation and guidance, a number of victorious strikes. The long and detailed account of negotiations held in December 1922 between labor leaders and the provincial authorities reflects this favorable climate. In it, Governor Zhao Hengti himself, while defending the execution of Huang and Pang, declared his intention of "protecting all workers," and even went so far as to state that socialism might be realized in the future, though it could not be put into practice today.[28]

Looking back on the period from late 1922 to early 1923, in his own retrospective overview of July 1923, Mao listed ten strikes, nine of which were "victorious or semivictorious," while only one ended in defeat.[29] That one defeat was, however, of crucial and decisive importance and helped usher in a whole new era in the history of the Chinese revolution.

In the spring of 1922, an agreement had been concluded between the Secretar-

---

26. See below, "Telegram from Labor Groups to the Upper and Lower Houses of Parliament," September 6, 1922, to which the first signatory was Mao's Hunan Branch of the Labor Secretariat.

27. For details regarding the labor movement in Hunan and Mao's role in it, see Li Jui, *Early Mao*; McDonald, *Urban Origins*; and Shaffer, *Mao and the Workers*.

28. See below, "The True Circumstances of the Negotiations between the Representatives of Various Labor Organizations and Provincial Governor Zhao . . . ," December 14, 1922. On this occasion, Mao signed in his capacity as a representative of the All-Hunan Federation of Labor Organizations, rather than on behalf of the Labor Secretariat.

29. See below, Section D of "Hunan Under the Provincial Constitution," July 1, 1923.

iat of Chinese Labor Organizations, which was then actively engaged in setting up unions of railroad workers, and Wu Peifu. It provided for the appointment of six "secret inspectors," who were given free passes for travel throughout the rail network. Wu Peifu was described by the Second Congress of the Chinese Communist Party in June 1922 as a "comparatively progressive militarist,"[30] and at about the same time, Wu called (as already noted) for labor-protection legislation. From Wu's point of view, the Communists could be useful in undercutting the influence of his pro-Japanese rivals of the Communications clique on the railroads, from which he derived revenues to maintain the Zhili army and finance his plans to unify China. In the autumn of 1922, during the first rail strikes, Wu Peifu had required the management to adopt a conciliatory attitude. In January 1923, when workers on the Beijing-Hankou line announced their intention of forming a General Union of the Beijing-Hankou Railway, which would be an amalgamation of the various local rail workers' clubs, Wu decided, however, that things had gone too far. He announced the prohibition of the inaugural meeting, which was to take place in Zhengzhou, and when the meeting was held nonetheless on February 1, he sent troops to break it up.

As a result, a full-scale strike of railroad workers was called on February 4. The workers demanded punishment of the troops involved in the action, dismissal of some railroad managers, and pay increases. On February 7, 1923, Cao Kun in Beijing, Wu Peifu in Luoyang, and Xiao Yaonan in Wuchang sent troops to attack the strikers. Thirty to thirty-five workers were killed and many more were seriously wounded.[31]

This incident, which became known as the February 7 Massacre, was an important turning point in the political situation, as well as in the history of the labor movement. It occurred at a crucial stage in the reorientation of the Chinese Communist Party's attitude toward the Guomindang, which had been going on since the spring of 1922. In April of that year, Sneevliet had met with Chen Duxiu and other leaders of the Chinese Party and urged on them the advantages of cooperating with the Guomindang, and even of joining it. Fearful that such tactics would compromise their independence, the Chinese rejected this formula, which became known as the "bloc within." Thereupon, Sneevliet traveled to Moscow, presented a detailed report on the situation in China to the Executive Committee of the Communist International in July, and was given formal written instructions from the International endorsing his idea of working within the

---

30. See Section 2.1 of the "Manifesto of the Communist Party of China" adopted by the Second Congress, in Ch'en, *Communist Movement*, p. 118.

31. Accounts of these events in Mao's own words appear below in the telegrams to Xiao Yaonan and Wu Peifu of February 20, 1923, and the first and second open telegrams in support of fellow workers of the Beijing-Wuhan Railroad, dated February 1923. For a detailed discussion of the policy of cooperation with Wu Peifu, the relations between Wu and Sun Yatsen, and disagreements about this matter in Moscow, see Saich, *Origins*, pp. 119–64, and Chesneaux, *Mouvement ouvrier*, pp. 272–78, 299–303.

Guomindang. Meanwhile, at its Second Congress in July, the Chinese Communist Party had abandoned its earlier sectarianism and decided on a policy of cooperation with the Guomindang, but the Chinese leaders still rejected the idea of actually joining the rival Nationalist Party. Armed with the document from Moscow, Sneevliet convened a Plenum of the Central Committee at Hangzhou in August, and forced the acceptance of the "bloc within" by the Chinese Communist Party.[32]

Despite this decision and a Comintern directive of January 1923 ordering them to "remain within the Guomindang,"[33] some Chinese Communists continued to resist the idea of joining the rival party. On the whole, the February 7 Massacre, by underscoring the weakness of the emerging Chinese labor movement, strengthened the view that the Communist Party could not operate in isolation and needed the support of Sun Yatsen. Though he had achieved significant victories in Hunan, Mao himself pointed out in conversations with Sneevliet that in the country as a whole, no more than 30,000 workers, out of a total of 3 million, had as yet been organized in a modern way. The two main factors in the political situation were, in his view, military force and the influence of the foreign powers. Mao was, according to Sneevliet's notes, "at the end of his Latin with labor organization" and was so pessimistic that he saw the only salvation of China in diplomatic and military intervention by Russia.[34]

Nevertheless, not everyone in the Chinese Communist Party drew the same conclusions from the February defeat, and there was a sharp confrontation between partisans and adversaries of Sneevliet's policy at the Third Congress of the Chinese Communist Party, June 12–20, 1923, where the matter was finally settled. Zhang Guotao, the principal opponent of working through the Guomindang, wrote in his memoirs that Mao Zedong had originally been on his side during the debates at the Third Congress, but that Mao later shifted his position and accepted the line of the International.[35] This seems unlikely in view of the fact that, as early as April 1923, Mao had written that the Guomindang constituted "the main body of the revolutionary democratic faction" in Chinese politics, and that the Communist Party had "temporarily abandoned its most radical views" in order to cooperate with it.[36]

It is true that in this text, Mao did not explicitly refer to participation by Communists in the Guomindang. At the Third Congress, he did call for this step.

---

32. The literature on these historical questions is extensive. The facts are summed up on the basis of the most authoritative documentation by Saich in *Origins*, pp. 87–120.

33. For the text, see Saich, *Origins*, pp. 565–66.

34. See Saich, *Origins*, pp. 448–49 and 589–90.

35. *The Rise of the Chinese Communist Party, 1921–1927*. Vol. I of the Autobiography of Chang Kuo-t'ao (hereafter Chang, *Autobiography*) (Lawrence, Kansas: The University Press of Kansas, 1971), pp. 299–312.

36. See below, "The Foreign Powers, the Warlords, and the Revolution," April 10, 1923.

The issue is of such central importance that it seems appropriate to reproduce here the full text of Sneevliet's notes on Mao's remarks.

1. Whether Guomindang cannot develop is a question.
2. No bourgeoisie revolution is possible in China. All antiforeign movements were (are) carried on by those who have empty stomach, but not bourgeoisie.
3. Bourgeoisie cannot lead the movement. National revolution cannot appear when capitalist class in the capitalist countries is not overthrown. Therefore national revolution in China must be after the world revolution.
4. Expects the international cooperation in China, a period of peace will come, then capitalism will develop very rapidly, Chinese proletariat increase a great quantity.
5. Guomindang is dominated by petty bourgeoisie. He believes petty bourgeoisie can for the present time to lead. That is why we should join Guomindang.
6. We should not be afraid of joining.
7. Peasants and small merchants are good material for Guomindang.[37]

Thus, at the Third Congress, Mao unequivocally endorsed the policy of joining the Guomindang in order to pursue the "national revolution." Turning aside from his activities in the labor movement, he threw himself beginning in the spring of 1923 into the struggle to mobilize the Chinese people against the domination of the warlords and their imperialist backers under the Guomindang banner. This by no means implied that he had lost interest in social revolution, but it did involve the temporary sacrifice or attenuation of certain goals in order not to offend the Party's nationalist allies.

The exact date on which Mao joined the Guomindang is unknown. Chen Duxiu, Li Dazhao, and Zhang Tailei had joined on September 4, 1922, immediately after the Hangzhou Plenum.[38] It seems likely that Mao had done so before the Third Congress.[39] In any case, immediately after the Third Congress, Mao was a member of the Guomindang, for it was in that capacity that on June 25, 1923, he signed a letter to Sun Yatsen, together with Chen Duxiu, Li Dazhao, Cai Hesen, and Tan Pingshan. The main burden of this communication was that, in order to oppose and overcome the "feudal warlords," the Guomindang must

---

37. Saich, *Origins*, p. 580. Spelling, capitalization, and Romanization in this passage have been changed, and obvious grammatical errors corrected. In a few instances, clumsy or incorrect modes of expression have been let stand, to avoid imposing one interpretation of Sneevliet's possible meaning.

38. See Sneevliet's notes in Saich, *Origins*, p. 338.

39. See Li Yongtai, *Mao Zedong yu da geming* (Mao Zedong and the Great Revolution) (hereafter Li Yongtai, *Mao and the Great Revolution*) (Chengdu: Sichuan renmin chubanshe, 1991), pp. 156–57.

establish a new-style "centralized national-revolutionary army" to fight them.[40] This letter thus signals a turning point in Mao's discovery of the role of military force in the Chinese revolution.

Mao Zedong and the United Front, 1923-1924

Following the Third Congress of the Chinese Communist Party, Mao was elected to the Central Executive Committee and to its standing organ, the Central Bureau. He also became secretary of the Central Executive Committee and head of the Organization Department. One further point that should be raised about Mao's line at this time concerns the extent to which he had already turned his attention, in June 1923, to the peasantry as a force which might prove more effective than the workers. The Manifesto of the Second Party Congress in July 1922 had declared that China's 300 million peasants were "the most important factor in the revolutionary movement," adding that, when this great number of poor peasants joined hands with the workers, the victory of the Chinese revolution would be assured.[41] Mao, as already noted, had been absent on that occasion. Subsequently, Chen Duxiu had stated in a report of November 1922 on the tactics of the Party: "The working class movement in the economically backward countries of the East cannot achieve its revolutionary tasks unless it is assisted by the poor peasant masses."[42]

On May 24, 1923, the Comintern had dispatched a directive to the Third Congress of the Chinese Communist Party devoted in large part to the peasant question. This document did not reach Shanghai until July 18, well after the proceedings of the congress had ended, but it obviously carried weight in subsequent discussions within the Chinese Communist Party. The directive from Moscow asserted that the national revolution in China could be successful only if it was possible "to induce the fundamental mass of the Chinese population—the peasant small holders—to take part in it." Thus, "the central question in our whole policy is the peasant question." Consequently, the Communist Party, as the party of the working class, must strive to bring about an alliance between the workers and the peasants by promoting the confiscation of large estates and the distribution of the land among the peasantry. "It goes without saying," the directive added, "that leadership must be vested in the party of the working class." Drawing from the recent strikes the conclusion not that the workers' movement was weak, but that it was strong, the Comintern ordered Chinese comrades to turn their Party into "a mass party of the proletariat."[43]

---

40. See below, the translation of extracts from this text.
41. *Central Committee Documents*, Vol. I, p. 113.
42. See Saich, *Rise to Power*, Doc. A.18, p. 58.
43. For an English text, see Saich, *Origins*, pp. 567–69. The translation of the extracts quoted here has been revised on the basis of the Russian original in P. Mif (ed.), *Strategiya*

At the Third Congress, Mao spoke up forcefully regarding the importance of the peasant movement. His remarks attracted such attention that he was one of two delegates appointed to draft the brief resolution regarding the peasants adopted at the congress. This document called on the Party to "gather together small peasants, sharecroppers, and farm laborers to resist the imperialists who control China, to overthrow the warlords and corrupt officials, and to resist the local ruffians and bad gentry, so as to protect the interests of the peasants and to promote the national revolutionary movement."[44]

At this time, Mao had as yet no direct experience of organizing the peasants, so the resolution was rather abstract and general in character.[45] His language during the debates at the Third Congress was more concrete and forceful. Zhang Guotao summarizes it as follows in his memoirs:

> [Mao] did point out to the Congress that in Hunan there were few workers and even fewer Guomindang and Chinese Communist Party members, whereas the peasants there filled the mountains and fields. Thus he reached the conclusion that in any revolution the peasant problem was the most important problem. He substantiated his thesis by pointing out that throughout the successive ages of Chinese history all rebellions and revolutions had peasant insurrections as their mainstay. The reason that the Guomindang has a foundation in Guangdong is quite simply that it has armies composed of these peasants. If the Chinese Communist Party also lays stress on the peasant movement and mobilizes the peasants, it will not be difficult to create a situation similar to that in Guangdong.[46]

Several well-documented works published recently in China reproduce verbatim much of this paragraph, as it appears in the Chinese version of Zhang's memoirs, changing only one or two characters.[47] In substance, Zhang's account is clearly regarded as accurate.

If we compare Mao's remarks regarding relations with the Guomindang and

---

i *Taktika Kominterna v Natsional'no-kolonial'noi Revolyutsii na Primere Kitaya* (The Strategy and Tactics of the Comintern in the National-Colonial Revolution, on the Basis of the Chinese Example) (hereafter, Mif, *Strategy and Tactics*) (Moscow: Institute of International Economics and International Politics, 1934), pp. 114–16.

44. See below, "Resolution on the Peasant Question," June 1923.

45. For a similar judgment by a Chinese scholar, see Li Yongtai, *Mao and the Great Revolution*, p. 282.

46. Chang, *Autobiography*, p. 309. The translation has been modified to correspond more closely to the Chinese version, cited in the following note.

47. Compare Zhang Guotao, "Wode huiyi" (My Memoirs), Chapter 6, *Ming bao* Vol.I, no. 10, October 1966, p. 79, with *Zhongguo Gongchandang huiyi gaiyao* (A Summary Account of Chinese Communist Party Meetings) (hereafter *Party Meetings*) (Shenyang: Shenyang chubanshe, 1991), p. 21; Ma Yuqing and Zhang Wanlu, *Mao Zedong gemingde daolu* (Mao Zedong's Revolutionary Way) (hereafter Ma and Zhang, *Mao's Way*) (Xi'an: Shaanxi renmin chubanshe, 1991), p. 51; and Li Yongtai, *Mao and the Great Revolution*, pp. 281–82.

his comments on the peasant problem, there appears to be a certain contradiction between the optimism of his call to "create a situation similar to that in Guangdong" by mobilizing the peasants, and the pessimism of his conclusion, noted by Sneevliet, that no successful national revolution will really be possible in China until after the overthrow of the capitalist class in Europe and America. His article of April 1923, already cited, suggests an answer to this dilemma. On the one hand, Mao argues, "there is no way in which the various influential factions within the country can be made to unite at present." But "in the future, . . . the most advanced Communist faction, and the moderate Research clique, intellectual faction, and commercial faction, will all cooperate with the Guomindang to form a great democratic faction," which will ultimately triumph over the warlord faction, though perhaps only in eight or ten years. Thus, in the short run, the imperialists will remain strong and will keep the warlords in power. But in the long run, reaction will stimulate the growth of revolutionary thought and action on the part of the people, and thus lead to its own negation.[48]

The idea that extremes engender one another, and in particular that oppression leads to revolt, is highly characteristic of Mao's thinking. In his article of 1919, "The Great Union of the Popular Masses," he wrote: "Our Chinese people possesses great inherent capacities! The more profound the oppression, the more powerful its reaction. . . ."[49] In similar vein, Mao concluded his April 1923 article with the argument that reaction and confusion would surely lead to peace and unification. This situation, he argued, "is the mother of revolution, it is the magic potion of democracy and independence." As to how, and how rapidly, this potion would do its work, Mao's ideas shifted repeatedly during the four years of the "First United Front" between the Chinese Communist Party and the Guomindang.

Mao Zedong's first contribution after the Third Congress was a long article, already cited, reviewing the situation in his native province.[50] This contains much concrete information but little in the way of ideas. The piece he published ten days later is far more provocative and has been the subject of some controversy.

On June 13, 1923, while the Third Congress was in session, Cao Kun, leader of the Zhili clique and military governor of the northern provinces, forced the resignation of President Li Yuanhong with the intention of supplanting him. In the end, it took Cao until October to achieve this goal and required the payment of bribes of 5,000 *yuan* each to the members of the Old Parliament, specially reconvened for the purpose, to persuade them to elect him. Meanwhile, the reaction of public opinion to his action was extremely hostile, and the Shanghai General Chamber of Commerce, at an extraordinary meeting on June 23, "de-

---

48. See below, "The Foreign Powers, the Warlords, and the Revolution," April 10, 1923.
49. See Volume I, p. 389.
50. See, below, "Hunan under the Provincial Constitution," July 1, 1923.

clared its independence," with the goal of establishing "merchant power."[51]

It was in this context that Mao published his article of July 11, 1923.[52] Hailing the declaration of the Chamber of Commerce as "the first instance of merchant involvement in politics," Mao went on to assert that "because of historical necessity and the trend of current realities, the task that the merchants should shoulder in the national revolution" was "more urgent and more important than the work that the rest of the Chinese people should take upon themselves." The merchants, he argued, suffered more from the "dual oppression of the warlords and foreign powers" than any other segment of the population. The merchants themselves, he declared, must unite, for the broader their unity, "the greater their strength to lead the people of the entire nation." At the same time, he added that only a closely knit united front including not only the merchants, but also the workers, peasants, students, and teachers of the whole country could assure the victory of "the great enterprise of revolution."

Efforts have been made to explain away these clear statements regarding merchant leadership of the revolution as referring merely to the fact that the Chinese revolution was in its "bourgeois-democratic stage." Such an argument can scarcely be sustained. There remains the problem of exactly how Mao understood the united front of all democratic forces at this time. His article appeared in the context of a special issue of the Communist Party organ *Xiangdao*, edited by his close friend Cai Hesen. The introductory piece by Chen Duxiu, entitled "The Beijing Coup d'État and the Guomindang," asserted forcefully that only the Guomindang could save the country at this juncture and called on the Guomindang to "arise and take command of the citizens, to carry out the revolutionary movement." The article on "The Beijing Coup d'État and the Laboring Class" hailed the merchants for "raising the banner of resistance," and called on the workers to support them as the only way to take vengeance on the warlords for the February 7 Massacre.[53] Maring, too, summing up the problem of the relations between the Chinese Communist Party and the Guomindang in the aftermath of the Third Congress, declared that the demands of the Chambers of Commerce were "pure revolutionary demands."[54]

Thus Mao Zedong was not the only one in the Chinese Communist Party impressed by the action of the Chamber of Commerce, even though its initiative ultimately came to nothing and was abandoned a few weeks later. Mao, who had declared at the Third Congress that the bourgeoisie could not lead the movement,

---

51. On the reaction of the Chamber of Commerce, see Marie-Claire Bergère's chapter in the *Cambridge History of China*, Vol. 12, pp. 782–83.

52. See below, "The Beijing Coup d'État and the Merchants."

53. Chen Duxiu, "Beijing zhengbian yu Guomindang" (The Beijing Coup d'État and the Guomindang), *Xiangdao zhoubao* (The Guide Weekly) no. 31/32, July 11, 1923, pp. 229–30; "Jingren," "Beijing zhengbian yu laodong jieji" (The Beijing Coup d'État and the Laboring Class), *Ibid.*, pp. 234–35.

54. See Saich, *Rise to Power*, Doc. A.20, p. 65.

though the petty bourgeoisie could do so "for the present time," had been sufficiently struck by the dramatic gesture of the merchants to modify that position. Though he would never again write of the commercial bourgeoisie in quite these terms, there is no reason to assume that his enthusiasm at the time was not sincere.

Mao's next two articles in *The Guide Weekly* took up once again the theme of imperialist crimes against China which was so close to his heart. Already in his article on Cao Kun's coup, he had stigmatized America in passing as "the most murderous of hangmen." Now he denounced the "naked invasion of China by the British pirates" during the negotiations over Weihaiwei, and the general subservience to Britain, America, and Japan, which made of the Chinese government "the countinghouse of our foreign masters."[55]

The two letters of September 1923 translated here reflect the dual nature of Mao's political activity at this time, in the Chinese Communist Party and in the Guomindang. The first, to the Socialist Youth League, is of little interest except as an illustration of the fact that he drafted such documents on behalf of the Central Committee of the Party.[56] The second confirms, as already noted, Mao's role in reestablishing a Guomindang organization in Hunan after a decade's interruption resulting from repression by successive governors. These efforts were to begin in the capital, Changsha, and then extend to other cities in the province.[57]

The remaining text of 1923 is a poem addressed to his wife, Yang Kaihui.[58] This is the only item for the whole period from 1922 to 1927 that is of a purely personal character. Two other poems, written in 1925 and 1927, though they express Mao's feelings, do so in terms of his political aspirations. This one, deploring a lovers' quarrel that had led to estrangement between Mao and Yang Kaihui, is of particular poignancy because of their final separation following the defeat of the revolution in the summer of 1927 and Yang Kaihui's execution by the Guomindang in 1930.

In October 1923, a new Soviet emissary, Michael Borodin, had arrived in China as adviser to Sun Yatsen and the Guomindang. Three months later, his efforts bore fruit in the form of a new-style Guomindang, reorganized on Leninist principles, which held its first congress in January 1924. At this gathering, Mao spoke on a number of occasions and was elected an alternate member of the Central Executive Committee.[59] We have included in this volume all of Mao's

---

55. See below, "The British and Liang Ruhao" and "The Cigarette Tax," both published in *The Guide Weekly* on August 29, 1923.

56. See below, "Reply to the Central Executive Committee of the Youth League," September 6, 1923.

57. See below, "Letter to Lin Boqu and Peng Sumin," September 28, 1923.

58. See below, "Poem to the Tune of 'Congratulate the Groom,' " probably written in December.

59. See below, the extracts from the minutes of the Congress for the sessions of January 20, 25, 28, and 29, 1924.

contributions, even when the substance of what he said was not of great interest, because they are part of the record of his political career. On January 20, Mao urged that the congress approve in principle the organization of a new government in opposition to that of Cao Kun in Beijing, rather than arguing about the precise name for the revolutionary government. On January 25, he once again pressed for a vote in order to get on with the proceedings. On January 28, responding to a demand that Guomindang members be barred from joining any other party, Mao intervened in favor of the view, put forward by Li Dazhao and supported by Hu Hanmin, that Communists who entered the Guomindang would in any case be bound by its discipline. No special restrictions need therefore be applied to them, and Mao demanded once again that a vote be taken to settle the point.

On January 29, Mao made statements of greater substantive interest. He opposed the establishment of a specialized Research Department because, he declared, "its basic idea is to separate application from research. This, however, is something that our party, as a revolutionary party, cannot do." On the same day, Mao opposed the call for a system of proportional representation in future parliamentary elections. "Our party," he argued, "being a revolutionary party, should adopt measures conducive to the revolution, but reject those detrimental to revolution. The proportional representation system is detrimental to the revolutionary party because once a minority gets elected they will have the power to sabotage the revolutionary cause. . . . Once freedom is given to the opposition party, it will put the cause of revolution in great danger." The chairman of the meeting, Lin Sen, suggested that proportional representation conflicted with Sun Yatsen's view that periods of military government and of political tutelage must precede the period of constitutional government, and the proposal was put aside until the next congress.

After the congress, Mao attended the first four meetings of the Central Party Bureau. At the fourth of these, on February 9, 1924, he put forward several resolutions for discussion. The main thrust of these was that the available funds should not be used only for party offices at the central and provincial levels (which were "hollow offices"), but should be channeled to the city and *xian* offices and the district offices (which were the "real party offices"). The city, *xian*, and district offices, he argued, were "the most decisive organs by which our party directs the activities of party members." And among the cities, resources should be concentrated on the most important ones, where circumstances were most favorable.[60] This insistence on "real" offices, rather than empty bureaucratic formalism, was to remain characteristic of Mao.

Working with the "Center-Left" Guomindang, 1924-1925

In mid-February, Mao left Guangzhou to take up a position with the Shanghai Executive Bureau of the Guomindang, with a mandate from the Central Commit-

---

60. See below, "Fourth Meeting of the Central Party Bureau of the Chinese Guomindang," February 9, 1924.

tee of the Chinese Communist Party. At the first meeting of the Shanghai Bureau, which took place on February 25, 1924, Mao was appointed secretary of the Organization Department and acting head of the documents section of the Secretariat, in which capacity he kept the minutes of this and subsequent meetings.[61] Since he retained the posts to which he had been elected at the Third Congress of the Chinese Communist Party in the previous year, he was called upon to exercise simultaneously important responsibilities in both parties. Balancing the objectives and the susceptibilities of the two groups of comrades did not always prove an easy task.

In March 1924, Mao Zedong attended a plenum of the Central Committee of the Communist Youth League in Shanghai. According to the memoirs of the representative of the Youth International at the time, S. A. Dalin, Mao put forward on this occasion the view that the Guomindang, guided by the new Three People's Principles, was a revolutionary workers' party and should be admitted to the Comintern. Dalin further states that Mao regarded the whole of the peasantry, rich and poor, as a single class opposed to capitalism and foreign imperialism, and completely ignored the importance of organizing the workers.[62] There is no confirmation of Dalin's report from other sources, but if such was indeed Mao's attitude in March 1924, it soon changed. By the late spring of 1924, slightly less than a year after the decision at the Third Congress to join the Guomindang, considerable tensions had developed in the relationship between the two parties. From the beginning, a substantial minority of old Guomindang members had opposed the admission of Communists, and with the passage of time these elements became more vocal both inside and outside the party.

At the First Enlarged Session of the new Central Executive Committee of the Chinese Communist Party, held May 10–15, 1924, a "Resolution Concerning the Problem of Work by the Communist Party within the Guomindang" was adopted. It noted that a large number of Guomindang members had long shown their affinity with the possessing classes and were not inclined to struggle against imperialism. As a result, on questions such as anti-imperialism, democracy, reforms in the interest of the peasantry, and concessions for the workers, "two factions" could be identified within the Guomindang. The task of the Communists was not to expand the Guomindang indiscriminately, but to support and strengthen the democratic and anti-imperialist left within it.[63]

Although Mao was present in Shanghai when this meeting was held, there is no record of his role in it. An authoritative Soviet account identifies Mao, to-

---

61. *Nianpu*, 1, p. 123. See also Li Yongtai, *Mao and the Great Revolution*, pp. 178–79.

62. See S. A. Dalin, *Kitayskie Memuary 1921–1927* (Chinese Memoirs 1921–1927) (Moscow: Izdatel'stvo "Nauka," 1975), pp. 164–65.

63. For the Chinese text of this document, see *Central Committee Documents*, Vol. I, pp. 230–33. An English translation can be found in Saich, *Rise to Power*, Doc. B.1, pp. 119–21.

gether with his close friend Cai Hesen and Chen Duxiu, as one of the main protagonists of a trend in favor of breaking with the Guomindang that emerged in the Chinese Communist Party in the summer of 1924.[64] In any case, Mao did sign, as secretary of the Central Executive Committee, circular no. 15 of July 21, 1924, which, without actually calling for withdrawal from the Guomindang, urged Communists to prepare for such a contingency.[65]

This document lays bare in striking fashion the dilemma that, from beginning to end, remained at the heart of the relationship between the Guomindang and the Chinese Communist Party. Only a very few Guomindang leaders, wrote Chen and Mao, had not yet made up their minds to separate from the Communists, and even Sun Yatsen did not wish to offend the right-wing elements in his own party. In the face of "overt and covert attacks" by a majority of Guomindang members, the Communists regarded it as their duty to grasp "the real power of leading all organizations of workers, peasants, students, and citizens" in order to consolidate their strength within the left wing of the Guomindang. Further measures were to include not recommending for membership in the Guomindang anyone who did not manifest a left-wing orientation, and establishing the "People's Association for Foreign Affairs" to "prepare the ground for the crystallization of the Guomindang left or a possible new Guomindang in the future." Even though this circular was to be kept secret, and Communists were to do their best to "be tolerant and cooperate with" the Guomindang, it was hardly likely that these policies would remain entirely unknown to those against whom they were directed. A cycle of action and reaction therefore appeared inevitable.

Tensions between the two parties were further increased when, following the overthrow of Cao Kun on November 2, 1924, the organizers of this coup—Feng Yuxiang, Duan Qirui, and Zhang Zuolin—invited Sun Yatsen to come to Beijing to discuss plans for national reconciliation. In a postscript dated November 6, 1924, to their circular of November 1, Chen Duxiu and Mao Zedong stated that the Central Bureau had "slightly changed its policy," and now had "no fundamental objection" to Sun's participation in such a conference, though they would "seriously admonish" him to speak in conformity with the Political Program (drawn up by Borodin) adopted at the First Guomindang Congress.[66]

However skeptical they may have been about Sun's intentions, his death from illness in March 1925 left the Communists in the presence of leaders with whom long-term collaboration was even more problematic. Both before and after Sun's

---

64. V.I. Glunin, "The Comintern and the Rise of the Communist Movement in China (1920–1927)," in *The Comintern and the East* (Moscow: Progress Publishers, 1979), p. 314.

65. See below, "The Struggle against the Right Wing of the Guomindang," July 21, 1924.

66. See below, "Strengthening Party Work and Our Position on Sun Yatsen's Attendance at the Northern Peace Conference," November 1, 1924.

demise, the Comintern advisers Borodin and Voitinsky urged the Chinese Communist Party to prepare for a split in the Guomindang, and even to promote such a split, because it would serve to purge the Guomindang of rightist elements. In May 1925, Stalin provided an authoritative justification for such policy, declaring that "in countries like . . . China, . . . Communists must pass from a united national front policy to the policy of a revolutionary bloc of the workers and the petty bourgeoisie. This bloc . . . can take the form of a single party, a workers' and peasants' party of the Guomindang type." Thus the bourgeoisie as a whole was effectively excluded from the national revolution.[67]

The present volume contains no documentation about developments from November 1924 to October 1925 because no texts by Mao are available to us for this period, apart from one poem written in the autumn of 1925. As early as May 1924, Mao had asked to be relieved from one of his offices under the Guomindang because of excessive pressure of work.[68] At the end of December he requested and obtained from the Chinese Communist Party a leave of absence to recuperate from exhaustion, and went to rest first in Changsha and then in his native village of Shaoshan, to which he returned on February 6, 1925. As a result, when the Fourth Congress of the Chinese Communist Party was held in Shanghai January 11–22, 1925, Mao once again failed to attend, and ceased to be a member of the Central Executive Committee.

While Mao was in Shaoshan, the May 30th Incident of 1925 gave a new impulsion to revolutionary activity. Thereupon he emerged from his period of repose and spent several months investigating and organizing the peasantry in Hunan, returning to Guangzhou only at the beginning of October.

The Chinese Communist Party resolution of May 1924 had stressed that propaganda was the key to pushing the Guomindang in a leftward direction and had stated explicitly: "To achieve this objective, we must, in practice, be able to join the Guomindang Propaganda Department."[69] On October 5, 1925, Wang Jingwei, who was too busy running the national government in Guangzhou to exercise his functions as head of the Propaganda Department of the Guomindang Central Executive Committee, recommended that Mao be appointed acting head. This proposal was duly endorsed by the Central Executive Committee, and Mao assumed his new functions the same day. For the next eight months, until the end of May 1926, Mao was indeed able to play an influential role in Guomindang affairs.

Mao's first opportunity to take the stage in this new capacity came with the Congress of Guangdong Party Organizations that took place later in October

---

67. For a clear summary of these developments, critical of Stalin's "subjectivism," see Glunin, "The Comintern and the Rise of the Communist Movement," pp. 323–36. Stalin's speech of May 18, 1925, is quoted from S. Schram and H. Carrère d'Encausse, *Marxism and Asia* (London: Allen Lane the Penguin Press, 1969), pp. 226–27.

68. See below, the letter of May 26, 1924.

69. For this passage, see Saich, *Rise to Power*, p. 120.

1925. In an October 20 editorial for the *Daily Bulletin* of the Congress, Mao interpreted the "revolutionary Three People's Principles" of "our great leader, Mr. Sun Yatsen," as a call for a national liberation struggle against the imperialists, a democratic struggle against the warlords, and resistance to the "feudal-patriarchal forces" of the compradors and the landlords, in order to secure prosperity for the people.[70]

A few days later, in a manifesto that he co-authored, and in a speech to the congress, Mao adopted once again a resolutely bipolar view. The "revolutionary forces of the whole world," including the movements of the oppressed nations in the East and the movements of social revolution in the West, were, he declared, already mustered against the forces of reaction, led by British and Japanese imperialism. All those in the Guomindang who sought to take up an intermediate position would end up, like the German Social Democrats or the British Labor Party, on the side of imperialism.[71]

The following month, responding yet again to a survey by the Young China Association, Mao gave a concise summary of his political credo at the time:

> I believe in communism and advocate the social revolution of the proletariat. The present domestic and foreign oppression cannot, however, be overthrown by the forces of one class alone. I advocate making use of the national revolution in which the proletariat, the petty bourgeoisie, and the left wing of the middle bourgeoisie cooperate to carry out the Three People's Principles of the Chinese Guomindang in order to overthrow imperialism, overthrow the warlords, and overthrow the comprador and landlord classes (that is to say, the Chinese big bourgeoisie and the right wing of the middle bourgeoisie, who have close ties to imperialism and the warlords), and to realize the joint rule of the proletariat, the petty bourgeoisie, and the left wing of the middle bourgeoisie, that is, the rule of the revolutionary popular masses.[72]

Thus Mao, unlike Stalin, was prepared to divide the bourgeoisie in half and to include its left wing in the revolutionary united front.

Almost at the same time, in November 1925, those elements in the Guomindang most hostile to cooperation with the Communists broke away, as Borodin had predicted and hoped they would do, and convened a meeting of like-minded members of the Central Executive Committee in the Western Hills near Beijing. At its Fourth Congress in January 1925, the Chinese Communist Party had adopted a "Resolution on the National Revolutionary Movement," which distinguished a small "center" in the Guomindang made up of "revolutionary elements" among the "petty bourgeois intellectual class."[73] The emer-

---

70. See below, the editorial of October 20, 1925.

71. See below, the documents dated October 26 and October 27, 1925.

72. See below, "A Filled-out Form for the Survey Conducted by the Reorganization Committee of the Young China Association," November 21, 1925.

73. See Doc. B.6, Section 5, in Saich, *Rise to Power*, pp. 134–36.

gence at the end of 1925 of a right-wing opposition within the Guomindang, henceforth referred to as the "Western Hills Faction," temporarily encouraged cooperation between what might be called, in the resulting new circumstances, the "Center-Left" faction (including Chiang Kaishek), and the Communists. The thirty-odd texts dated between November 27, 1925, and January 19, 1926, that appear below were all, without exception, written by Mao in this context and in his capacity as a member of the Guomindang.

Throughout this period Wang Jingwei continued to be occupied with other matters, and Mao, as acting head, ran the Propaganda Department of the Guomindang Central Executive Committee and edited its official publication, the *Political Weekly.* Understandably, most of the articles and documents produced by Mao at this time were devoted to attacking the Western Hills Faction.[74] Another main theme was the depradations of imperialism, especially British, Japanese, and American imperialism.[75] These two topics were, of course, frequently linked together in his writings, since the rightists were regarded as tools of imperialism.

Other texts dealt in broader terms with the strategy of the Chinese revolution and its social basis. These include "Analysis of All the Classes in Chinese Society," the first item in the official canon of the *Selected Works,* previously dated March 1, 1926, but which is now known to have been published on December 1, 1925, in *Geming* (Revolution), the semimonthly organ of the Guomindang's National Revolutionary Army.[76] The version included here, like all other texts from the *Selected Works* that appear in this and subsequent volumes of our edition, is presented in such a way as to show all significant variants between what Mao originally wrote and the text as he revised it in the 1950s.[77]

As might have been expected, given the auspices under which the article originally appeared, the "enemies" and "friends" around whom Mao's analysis revolves are the enemies and friends of the Guomindang. In terms of class, Mao's view is not unlike that which he had stated two and a half years earlier at the Third Congress of the Chinese Communist Party: the petty bourgeoisie is revolutionary; the middle bourgeoisie vacillates and may be either a friend or an enemy. No doubt Mao regarded Chiang Kaishek at this time as a representative of the left wing of the middle bourgeoisie, which was a friend of the revolution,

---

74. For the first such document, see below, "The Central Executive Committee of the Chinese Guomindang Sternly Repudiates the Illegal Meeting of Beijing Party Members," November 27, 1925.

75. For the first such item, see below, "Propaganda Guidelines of the Chinese Guomindang in the War against the Fengtian Clique," November 27, 1925, proposed by "Department Head Mao Zedong" and passed at a meeting of the Central Executive Committee on that date.

76. See below, "Analysis of All the Classes in Chinese Society," December 1, 1925.

77. For details regarding the way in which this is done, see the "Note on Sources and Conventions," which follows this Introduction.

but not a true friend, and against which it was necessary to remain on guard.

In his editorial for the first issue of the *Political Weekly*, Mao refuted the notion that Guangdong was "Communist."[78] This was obviously the view he had to put, as a loyal member of both parties, to defend the Guomindang against accusations of radicalism and at the same time to defend the Communists against the charge that they were trying to take it over. A number of other pieces in the magazine were devoted to the same theme.[79] Seeking guidance and support in Moscow was presented as the attitude not of Communists alone, but of all enlightened Chinese patriots.[80] Thus Mao seized on a newspaper dispatch from Beijing declaring, "The diplomatic corps has received detailed reports from Guangdong that although the ideology of Chiang Kaishek manifests Bolsheviza-tion, he cares for the people, while on the other hand when the troops of the anti-Communist forces . . . reach a locality, they are guilty of many Communist activities."[81]

Mao Zedong played a leading role at the Second Congress of the Guomindang, and continued, as he had done at the First Congress, to speak on questions of organization and discipline. The points he addressed included the status of Communists in the Guomindang and the treatment to be meted out to conservative elements in the party. On at least one occasion, he and Chiang Kaishek succeeded one another on the platform. Immediately following Mao's report of January 18 on the resolution regarding propaganda, Chiang put forward a motion to improve the economic conditions of the soldiers.[82]

In addition to the report on propaganda and the resolution regarding it, Mao made another important contribution to the proceedings in the shape of the resolution concerning the peasant movement. The two topics as Mao presented them were not unrelated, for at the end of the report on propaganda he listed among the shortcomings of Guomindang propaganda in the past the fact that "we have concentrated too much on urban dwellers and neglected the peasantry."[83] Mao would not commit such an error again.

When Mao drafted the resolution on the peasant problem for the Third Con-gress of the Chinese Communist Party in June 1923, he had no concrete experi-ence of organizing peasants. Now he had acquired such experience. The resolution on the peasant movement that he presented to the congress on January

---

78. See below, "Reasons for Publishing the *Political Weekly*," December 5, 1925.

79. See, for example, "The 3–3–3–1 System," "If They Share the Aim of Exterminat-ing the Communists, Even Enemies Are Our Friends," "The 'Communist Program' and 'Not Really Communist,' " and other articles dated December 5, 1925.

80. See below, "Students are Selected by the Chinese Guomindang to Go to Sun Yatsen University in Moscow," December 13, 1925.

81. See below, "That's What Bolshevization Has Always Been," December 13, 1925.

82. See below, "Statements Made at the Second National Congress of the Chinese Guomindang," January 18 and 19, 1926.

83. See below, the "Report on Propaganda," submitted on January 8, 1926.

19 emphasized the central importance of the peasantry in the national revolution.[84] The opening passage clearly conveyed the message:

> China now has not yet gone beyond the agricultural economy and peasant production, and the peasants account for as much as 90 percent of the total productive output. If we wish to carry out the Director General's Three People's Principles, the first thing is to liberate the peasants. . . . China's national revolution is, to put it plainly, a peasant revolution. . . . The Chinese Guomindang should always and everywhere consider the peasant movement as its foundation.

The political measures envisaged, though formulated in moderate terms, were relatively far-reaching. They called for guiding the peasants to organize and take part in the national revolution, eliminating the warlords, compradors, local bullies, and bad gentry who harmed the peasants, and dissolving the landlord militia. The economic measures included forbidding usurious loans, setting limits to land rent, reducing farm laborers' working hours, and abolishing exorbitant taxes. Guomindang branches everywhere were urged to set up "Peasant Movement Training Institutes," like that in Guangzhou at which Mao had taught the previous fall and of which he would become principal in May 1926.

Although it was lively and vivid, the article on the attitudes of various strata among the peasantry, which Mao published in January 1926, was likewise prudent in calling for revolutionary action. Mao's analysis in this piece is patterned on that in the article of December 1925 on all the classes in Chinese society, but the discussion of conditions in the countryside is more detailed and more concrete. There are, to begin with, eight categories instead of five: big landlords, small landlords, owner-peasants, semiowner peasants, sharecroppers, poor peasants, farm laborers, and vagrants. The first four of these represent the rural components in the first four categories of the December 1925 article: big bourgeoisie, middle bourgeoisie, petty bourgeoisie, and semiproletariat. The sharecroppers, who were part of the semiproletariat in the "Analysis of All the Classes," here become a separate category, while the poor peasants, farm laborers, and vagrants, who were all lumped together as part of the proletariat, are treated separately.

In this article on the peasants, the "militant participation of the proletariat" is mentioned only in passing as a factor that frightens and antagonizes the small landlords. In the "Analysis of All the Classes," it is stated explicitly that "the industrial proletariat has become the leading force in the revolutionary movement." This fact is not further elaborated on, however, and there is no reference at all in either of the articles to land reform or any social change in the country-

---

84. Mao was not originally the drafter of this resolution, but he headed a subcommittee that drastically revised an earlier version. For the text, see below, "Resolution Concerning the Peasant Movement," January 19, 1926.

side. It is true that these writings were addressed to a Guomindang audience, but Sun Yatsen had long ago put forward the slogan of "land to the tiller" (*gengzhe youqitian*). The Chinese Communist Party as a whole had long lagged behind the Guomindang in the importance it attached to the peasant question. Only at the Second Enlarged Plenum of the Central Executive Committee in October 1925 had the Party, in an "Address to the Peasants," called for giving the peasants land, while emphasizing that this could only take place after the workers, peasants, and other people had seized political power.[85]

One trait in Mao's analysis that is highly characteristic of his approach remained the same in both articles: the tendency to distinguish social categories, not in terms of their relationship to the means of production, but on the basis of the amount of deprivation from which they suffer. Thus the owner-peasants in the article on the peasantry, like the petty bourgeoisie as a whole in "All the Classes," were sliced into strata defined by whether they had a surplus, could just make ends meet, or had an annual deficit and were constantly slipping further into debt. In both cases, Mao postulated a direct relationship between poverty and revolutionary spirit. This approach was criticized at the time as of dubious Marxist orthodoxy in the commentary published, together with a Russian translation of Mao's article, in the organ of the Soviet advisers working in Guangzhou. Mao's main error, they argued, was to treat Chinese society as though it were a developed capitalist system and to classify vast numbers of peasants as "proletarians."[86]

Orthodox or not, this perspective was to remain characteristic of Mao's approach to revolution from this time forward. Another point, much more prominent in the article on the peasantry than in that of December, was Mao's emphasis on the revolutionary potential of the vagrants or lumpenproletarians. He wrote of them with considerable sympathy, noting that the five subcategories of soldiers, bandits, thieves, beggars, and prostitutes had different ways of making a living, but that they were all human beings leading a precarious existence. "These people," he commented, "are capable of fighting very bravely, and if a method can be found for leading them, they can become a revolutionary force." The nature and role of this class was to become a burning issue beginning in 1928, when Mao allied himself with two bandit leaders on the Jinggangshan.

---

85. The term used in this Communist Party document was *gengdi nongyou*, literally "peasant ownership of cultivated land," and was interpreted to mean that peasants who had long rented a certain parcel of land from a landlord should be given title to it. For the Chinese text of the address of October 10, 1925, see *Central Committee Documents*, Vol. I, pp. 509–17, especially pp. 512–13. A partial English translation can be found in Saich, *Rise to Power*, Doc. B.13, pp. 163–66. For confirmation of the fact that this was the first time the Chinese Communist Party had put forward such a concrete proposal for solving the land problem of the peasants, see *Party Meetings*, p. 41. The resolution of the Third Congress in 1923, drafted by Mao, was as already noted rather anodine.

86. See the article of M. Volin in *Kanton* (Canton), no. 8/9, 1926; reprinted in *Voprosy Filosofii* no. 6, 1969, especially pp. 130 and 134–36.

These later developments are abundantly illustrated by the materials translated in Volume III.

Toward Radical Agrarian Revolution

In mid-February, Mao requested two weeks' leave from his duties in the Guomindang Secretariat, once again on grounds of mental strain.[87] According to the testimony of Mao Dun, who was his closest collaborator in the Propaganda Department at this time, Mao was not really ill, but had gone on a secret mission to inspect the peasant movement on the Hunan-Guangdong border.[88] In any case, he was rapidly back in action, drafting resolutions for a meeting of the Standing Committee of the Guomindang Central Executive Committee on March 16. On March 18, he delivered a lecture on the anniversary of the Paris Commune, in which he laid primary emphasis on the importance of turning the Guomindang into a "united, centralized and disciplined party," in order to pursue class struggle against the imperialists and the domestic reactionaries, and avoid the fate of the Commune.[89]

Shortly afterward, there occurred the so-called *Zhongshan* gunboat incident of March 20, 1926. These events, in which Chiang Kaishek arrested the Communist chief of the Naval Bureau and disarmed the guards protecting the residences of the Russian advisers in Guangzhou, marked a sharp turning point in relations between the Chinese Communist Party and the Guomindang. Some sources indicate that a majority of Communists, including Mao Zedong and Zhou Enlai, were in favor of fighting back, arguing that few other Guomindang generals supported Chiang. The Soviet military advisers opposed this, however, and their Chinese comrades were obliged to compromise.[90]

Though the immediate conflict was smoothed over by the deportation of the three Russian advisers Chiang most disliked and the parallel expulsion of several conservative Guomindang officials, the situation was irrevocably altered. Among the points that Borodin was obliged to accept as part of the price for the resolution of this affair was Soviet support for the forthcoming Northern Expedition, about which Moscow and the Chinese Communists had previously expressed great skepticism. Accordingly, on March 30, 1926, Mao advocated taking advantage of the political awakening which would be brought about by the arrival of the revolutionary forces to push the development of the peasant associations in

---

87. See below, the letter of February 14, 1926.

88. See *Nianpu*, Vol. 1, p. 156, and the note to the letter of February 14, 1926.

89. See below, "Some Points for Attention in Commemorating the Paris Commune," March 12, 1926.

90. See, in particular, *Nianpu*, 1, pp. 159–60. For an overview of this complicated affair, see the succinct account in C. Martin Wilbur, *The Nationalist Revolution in China, 1923–1928* (hereafter Wilbur, *Nationalist Revolution*), pp.47–49 (originally published in the *Cambridge History of China*, Vol. 12, pp. 573–75).

the areas traversed by Chiang's armies.[91] He did so at a meeting of a Guomindang organ, but he undoubtedly intended that the trend he sought to promote should benefit primarily the Communists and their allies on the left.

For his part, Chiang Kaishek called a plenary meeting of the Guomindang Central Executive Committee May 15–25, 1926, and imposed the adoption of severe restrictions on the role that could be played by Communists in the Guomindang apparatus. On May 19, 1926, in his capacity as acting head of the Propaganda Department, Mao Zedong delivered the report on propaganda to this very Plenum.[92] Although he knew that his tenure as a leading member of the Guomindang bureaucracy was about to come to an end, Mao described with gusto the wide-ranging initiatives he had taken during the previous three months to expand the influence of the Guomindang. A centerpiece of this report was a plan for a series of writings on the national movement in five subseries, each comprising twelve brochures of approximately 10,000 characters. This compilation was to begin with Wang Jingwei's *History of the Guomindang*, and was to feature accounts of "the Jewish national liberation movement" and of national struggles in Morocco, Egypt, Syria, Mexico, and Persia, as well as "recent colonial revolutionary movements." The Russian revolution and labor movements throughout the world would not be neglected, but five of the sixty pieces were to deal with peasant movements.

Mao made this proposal while he was engaged in running the Sixth Session of the Guomindang Peasant Movement Training Institute in Guangzhou, which had begun on May 3. Although, like other Communists, he was obliged to resign as a department head of the Central Executive Committee following the Plenum, he retained his position as principal of the Peasant Institute.[93] During his tenure at the institute, Mao compiled *Collected Writings on the Peasant Problem*. His introduction to this series, written in September, brought together in particularly striking form the two themes of nationalism and peasant revolution that dominated his thinking in 1926.[94]

The core of Mao's argument on this occasion was that "in an economically backward semicolony, the feudal class in the countryside constitutes the only solid basis for the ruling class at home and for imperialism abroad." The Chinese warlords, he asserted, were "merely the chieftains of this rural feudal class." Unless this basis were shaken, it would be "absolutely impossible to shake the

---

91. See below, the relevant extracts from the proceedings of this meeting.

92. See below, "Report on the Work of the Propaganda Department from February 1 to May 15."

93. His resignation as acting head of the Propaganda Department was formally accepted on May 28, together with those of the other two Communist department heads, Tan Pingshan and Lin Zuhan. See Li Yongtai, *Mao and the Great Revolution*, pp. 271–72, and *Nianpu*, Vol. 1, p. 165.

94. See below, "The National Revolution and the Peasant Movement," September 1, 1926.

superstructure built upon it." To be sure, the warlords also used the comprador class in the cities to dally with the imperialists, but the compradors were neither so numerous nor so powerful as the landlords. Because the landlord class was the main basis of warlord rule and imperialist domination, the decisive blows in the Chinese national revolution could only be struck in the countryside, and it was the peasants who were there to strike them. Hence, Mao concluded:

> Although we are all aware that the workers, students, and middle and small merchants in the cities should rise and strike fiercely at the comprador class, and directly resist imperialism, and although we know that the progressive working class in particular is the leader of all the revolutionary classes, yet if the peasants do not rise and fight in the villages to overthrow the privileges of the feudal-patriarchal landlord class, the power of the warlords and of imperialism can never be hurled down root and branch.

Mao went on to argue that the peasants were more unyieldingly revolutionary than the workers. "The peasant movement in China," he wrote, "is a movement of class struggle that combines political and economic struggle. In this respect, it is somewhat different in nature from the workers' movement in the cities." And he added, spelling out his meaning:

> At present, the political objectives of the urban working class are merely to seek complete freedom of assembly and of association; this class does not yet seek to destroy immediately the political position of the bourgeoisie. As for the peasants in the countryside, on the other hand, as soon as they rise up, they run into the political power of those local bullies, bad gentry, and landlords who have been crushing the peasants for several thousand years. . . . If they do not overthrow this political power that is crushing them, there can be no place for the peasants. This is a very important peculiarity of the peasant movement in China today.

In other words, the workers were endowed only with what Lenin called "trade-union consciousness," namely the desire to struggle for an immediate improvement in their material conditions. The peasants, thanks to their decisive position in Chinese society, had developed a higher level of political awareness and were prepared to fight to the end against their oppressors. Describing the impact of rural revolution in Hailufeng, where Peng Pai had already been organizing peasant associations for five years, Mao stated flatly: "The Chinese revolution has only this form, and no other."

Never again would Mao go so far in exalting the role of the peasants over that of the workers. Indeed, in a speech to the Agricultural Association of China in August 1926, he had called on those present to go to the countryside to arouse the peasants from their "bad conservative natures."[95] Moreover, as indicated by the passing reference to working-class leadership in the previous quotation, Mao's praise of the peasants did not in itself demonstrate that he was unaware of

---

95. See below, Mao's "Address to the Ninth Congress of the Agricultural Association of China," August 14, 1926.

the basic axioms of Marxism. Emotionally, if not intellectually, the peasants would nevertheless remain at the center of his revolutionary vision.

As Mao had predicted in March, the victorious progress of the Northern Expedition, which had reached Changsha in August 1926 and captured Nanchang and Wuhan by December, led to the rapid expansion and increasing radicalization of the peasant associations. Though the final split between Chiang Kaishek and his rivals in Wuhan did not take place until March 1927, from October 1926 onward Mao carried out his activities in the context of the Left Guomindang, and of the Chinese Communist Party organization.

In late October 1926, Mao participated in a "Joint Session" of members of the Guomindang Central Executive Committee and delegates of provincial and local party organizations from various parts of China. This was, in fact, a major initiative to lay down new and more radical policies in the light of the victories achieved by the Northern Expedition, and to encourage Wang Jingwei to return from his self-imposed exile in Europe and serve as a rallying point for the Guomindang left. Formally, it might be regarded as comparable to the Western Hills meeting in the sense that a group of Central Executive Committee members, enlarged in this instance to include representatives from lower levels, sought to speak and act in the name of the Guomindang as a whole. The issues thus raised were hotly debated at a session devoted explicitly to the issue of the nature and powers of this hybrid body, at which Mao forcefully defended the validity of the decisions taken.[96]

Once again questions involving the peasants were raised, and once again Mao gave clear expression to his growing conviction that revolution in the countryside was the central problem in China's national revolution. In the course of a discussion as to whether taxes should be collected in advance from the peasants of Guangdong, as had so often been done by the warlords in the past in order to meet pressing financial needs, Mao declared: "Our party's most important policy is the policy toward the peasants. To levy . . . taxes in advance is sure to arouse suspicion on the part of the peasants towards our party. It would be more feasible to obtain revenue from the wealthy minority through the issuance of bonds."[97] The Basic Program adopted at the Joint Session, which Mao had helped to draft, contained eight provisions dealing with rural problems, including a 25 percent reduction in land rents and a prohibition of interest rates exceeding 20 percent.[98]

As for the Communist Party, Mao had ceased, as already noted, to be a member of the Central Executive Committee in January 1925. At its Second enlarged meeting in October 1925, apart from the "Address to the Peasantry" mentioned above, the Central Executive Committee adopted a "Resolution on

---

96. See below, the record of the discussion of the nature of the Joint Session on October 28, 1926.

97. See below, the record of the session devoted to this topic on October 27, 1926.

98. See below, "Basic Program of the National Union of People's Organizations," October 27, 1926.

the Question of Organization" providing for the establishment of a commission on the peasant movement.[99] A year later, in November 1926, Mao became secretary of this commission. A resolution of the Chinese Communist Party Central Bureau dated November 15, 1926, and drafted by Mao stated that this organ began to function effectively only after Comrade Mao took charge.[100] Once again, Mao called in this text for concentrating on a few areas where conditions were particularly favorable. He stressed the importance of cooperating with the Left Guomindang and urged the establishment of a peasant movement training institute (like that which he had just been running in Guangzhou) in Wuchang. Such an institute was effectively set up in March 1927.[101]

Later in November 1926, Mao wrote an article, based no doubt largely on the reports that crossed his desk in Shanghai, but perhaps also in part on personal observation, regarding the sufferings of the peasants in the two nearby provinces of Jiangsu and Zhejiang.[102] It contains some vivid vignettes, but little regarding the policies that should be followed, except a strong emphasis on the need for the peasants to organize effectively in order to avoid being crushed by the landlords and the warlords who stand back of them.

By December, Mao Zedong had arrived in Hunan to undertake what would become perhaps the most celebrated piece of fieldwork in modern times. Addressing a joint session of the provincial Peasants' and Workers' Congresses in Changsha on December 20, he declared once again that the central problem of the national revolution was the peasant problem. Since the peasants provided both raw materials and a market for manufactured goods, their well-being was vital to the merchants as well as to the workers. The students, too, had no choice but to make revolution if they wanted an opportunity to make use of what they had learned. "The time for us to overthrow the landlords" had not yet come, but they should be asked to reduce rents and interest.[103]

When he returned in early February 1927 from a thirty-two-day trip to the Hunanese countryside, Mao took a far bolder position. Only in his brief report to the Central Committee of the Chinese Communist Party did he explicitly call for land reform. The poor peasants, he wrote, had two problems, "the problem of

---

99. See the translation in Saich, *Rise to Power*, Doc. B.11, pp. 158–61.

100. See below, "Plan for the Current Peasant Movement," November 15, 1926.

101. The steps leading to its establishment are outlined in "Zhongyang nongmin yundong jiangxisuo chenglizhi jingguo" (The Process of Establishing the Central Peasant Movement Training Institute) in *Bujuan 9*, pp. 207–13. This document, and several others regarding the Institute in Wuhan, are attributed to Mao in the Tokyo edition, but there are reasons to believe he did not write them, and they are therefore not translated in this volume. For one text that does refer to the Institute, see below, "Remarks at the Meeting to Welcome Peasant Representatives from Hunan and Hubei Provinces," March 18, 1927.

102. See below, "The Bitter Sufferings of the Peasants in Jiangsu and Zhejiang, and Their Movements of Resistance," November 25, 1926.

103. See below, "Speech at the Welcome Meeting Held by the Provincial Peasants' and Workers' Congresses," December 20, 1926.

capital, and the problem of the land." "Both these problems," he added, "are no longer problems of propaganda, but require immediate action."[104] His longer and better-known report, which addresses itself simply to "revolutionary comrades," but was obviously meant primarily for the Guomindang, abstained from making this point, but otherwise its tone was no less radical.[105]

The substance of the two documents had to be substantially the same, since in the report to the Communist Party he stressed that the problems in the country-side "must all be resolved under the banner of the Guomindang" and that the Communist Party should "absolutely not raise immediately" its own banner. Mao's powerful revolutionary message could therefore not be concealed from the Guomindang, and Mao was probably too exhilarated by what he had witnessed in Hunan to wish to conceal it. Indeed, he went so far as to declare that a united front with the Guomindang had never really existed hitherto, and that one could be set up only after a period of revolutionary struggle in which the power of the feudal landlords was overthrown. "Today," he added, "the masses are going to the left, and in many places our Party, not to mention the Guomindang, . . . has not reached the same level of revolutionary feeling as the masses."

The celebrated "Hunan Peasant Report" is too long and its content too rich for any kind of comprehensive summary here. Mao's own text is eminently reada-ble, and this document has, in any case, been exhaustively analyzed in the literature. One or two points should be made, however, about the variants be-tween what Mao wrote in 1927 and the *Selected Works* text. Perhaps the most important statement edited out in 1950 is the following:

> To give credit where credit is due, if we allot ten points to the accomplish-ments of the democratic revolution, then the achievements of the city dwellers and the military rate only three points, while the remaining seven points should go to the achievements of the peasants in their rural revolution.[106]

By implication, Mao here reiterated the view he had expressed in September 1926 to the effect that the peasants were pursuing political goals more resolutely and effectively than the urban workers. His perspective on the rural revolution also comprised the attribution of leadership to the poor peasants. This point is more strongly made in the original text than in the *Selected Works* version, but is present even in the revised text, though Mao in 1950 added that the poor peas-ants were "most responsive to Communist Party leadership." In neither version is there any mention of proletarian leadership.[107] As noted above in another con-

---

104. See below, "Report to the Central Committee on Observations Regarding the Peasant Movement in Hunan," February 16, 1927.
105. See below, "Report on the Peasant Movement in Hunan," February 1927.
106. See below, Section I.4 of the report, "It's Terrible and It's Fine."
107. See below, Section II.2 of the report, "Vanguard of the Revolution or Outstanding Contributors to the Revolution."

text, he had not necessarily rejected this Marxist axiom, but it was obviously not uppermost in his mind in the spring of 1927.

In the final paragraph of the report, Mao remarked ironically: "Curiously enough, it is reported from Nanchang that Chiang Kaishek . . . and other such gentlemen do not altogether approve of the activities of the Hunan peasants." Very soon afterward, on April 12, 1927, Chiang made very clear just how much he disapproved of these and any other revolutionary activities by massacring on a large scale in Shanghai the organized workers who had helped him to take the city.

This action put an end to one equivocal situation, but brought about another one. In early 1927, Stalin had persisted in the face of all the evidence in regarding Chiang Kaishek as a "revolutionary military man." Now that the Guomindang was clearly split into the Left in Wuhan and the Right in Shanghai, with no pretense of unity between them, a situation was created in which Guomindang leaders less fearful of revolution than Chiang began nonetheless to ask themselves whether or not they wished to remain in an intimate alliance with the Communists. The materials in this volume for the period down to June 1927 illustrate the difficulties encountered by Mao and his comrades in seeking to keep faith with the peasants and maintain the forward progress of the revolution, while not offending too gravely their remaining Nationalist allies. Finally, in July 1927, the Left Guomindang would also turn against the Chinese Communist Party and its Soviet backers, thus inaugurating an entirely different period documented in Volume III of this edition.

An important step toward the final rupture between Chiang Kaishek and the Left was represented by the Third Plenum of the Second Central Executive Committee of the Guomindang, which met March 10–17, 1927, in Wuhan. On this occasion, the key posts occupied by Chiang as head of the party and of the national government were abolished in favor of a collective leadership. The resolution on the peasant question drafted by Mao called forcefully for action to protect the peasant associations against the feudal power holders in the countryside. It demanded that a start be made on land reform, beginning with the property of temples, corrupt officials, local bullies, and bad gentry, and that the rent and interest reduction called for in the program adopted in October 1926 by the Joint Session be carried out immediately.[108] A message to the peasants adopted at the same Plenum echoed Mao's argument of September 1926 that the peasants, because they suffered the most, were most revolutionary. Recalling Sun Yatsen's slogan of "land to the tiller," it declared that the Guomindang was "determined to support the peasants in their struggle for the land until the land problem is completely solved."[109]

The problem was that most of the officers, even in the armies loyal to Wuhan

---

108. See below, "Resolution on the Peasant Question," March 16, 1927.
109. See below, "Declaration to the Peasants," March 16, 1927, put forward by Mao Zedong, Deng Yanda, and Chen Kewen.

rather than to Chiang Kaishek, belonged precisely to the "feudal landlord class" which Mao was bent on overthrowing. To push actual land reform, in any significant degree, was therefore incompatible with the maintenance of even that semblance of a united front which remained. The paradoxical nature of the situation at this time is reflected in the composition of the interim executive committee of the All-China Peasant Association elected in early April. It included, in addition to Mao, Peng Pai, and other Communists, former governor of Hunan (and Hanlin scholar) Tan Yankai and the "progressive military man" Tang Shengzhi, the current governor of Hunan.[110]

Mao sought to square this circle, in the course of meetings of the Land Committee under the Left Guomindang National Government in April and May, by suggesting that for the time being land reform be limited to "political confiscation" in which small landlords and rich peasants would be spared, and land belonging to officers and soldiers of the National Revolutionary Army would also be exempt.[111]

The Land Committee had been established by the Standing Committee of the Central Executive Committee at its Fifth Enlarged Session on April 2, 1927. The other members, apart from Mao, were Deng Yanda, Xu Qian, Gu Mengyu, and Tan Pingshan. Its purpose was to be "deciding on measures for giving land to the peasants" and "creating a revolutionary phenomenon throughout the countryside, so as to permit the subsequent overthrow of the feudal system."[112] It soon became apparent that the complex and controversial issues involved would require a range of experience and knowledge, so in addition to the meetings of the five-man committee, six "enlarged sessions" were convened, with the participation of up to forty provincial and lower-level leaders, and of military officials. The materials translated below, while they do not give a complete picture of this process as a whole, do provide a vivid image of the discussions and of Mao's participation in them.

---

110. See below, "Telegram from the Executive Committee of the All-China Peasant Association on Taking Office," April 9, 1927. Shortly afterward, Mao added his signature to those of these gentlemen, and of Wang Jingwei, Chen Gongbo, Zhang Fakui, and others, on a circular telegram denouncing Chiang Kaishek as a traitor, scum, and swindler of the people. See below, the text of April 22, 1927.

111. The most complete and accurate account of these discussions can be found in Wilbur, *Nationalist Revolution*, pp. 117–24. Professor Wilbur's account is based, in particular, on copies and summaries of the relevant materials from the Guomindang Archives in Taiwan, which we have been privileged to use in preparing this volume. (For details, see the "Acknowledgments" which precede this introduction.) A somewhat different interpretation is presented in Roy Hofheinz, Jr., *The Broken Wave. The Chinese Communist Peasant Movement, 1922–1928* (Cambridge, Massachusetts: Harvard University Press, 1977), pp. 35–45. In Chinese, see Jiang Yongjing, *Baoluoting yu Wuhan zhengquan* (Borodin and the Wuhan Régime) (Taibei: Zhongguo xueshu zhuzuo jiangzhu weiyuanhui, 1963), pp. 276–310, which also reproduces lengthy extracts from the primary sources.

112. See *Nianpu*, 1, p. 191.

At the Second Meeting of the original Land Committee, on April 12, 1927, Mao adopted a rather cavalier attitude toward the framework within which land reform should be carried out, declaring:

> What we call land confiscation consists in not paying rent; there is no need for any other method. At the present time, there is already a high tide of the peasant movement in Hunan and Hubei, and on their own initiative the peasants have refused to pay rent and have seized political power. In solving the land question in China, we must first have the reality, and it will be all right if legal recognition of this reality comes only later.[113]

At the First Enlarged Meeting of the Land Committee on April 19, Mao asserted that political power in the countryside could reside for the time being in the Peasant Associations. But at the same time, he also stressed the importance of productivity. "If the land question is not resolved," he declared, "the economically backward countries will not be able to increase their productive force, will be unable to resolve the problem of the misery of the peasants' lives, and will be unable to improve the land." He also stressed the importance of creating a sound basis for raising revenue.[114]

"Political confiscation" restricted to the land of local bullies, bad gentry, warlords, and those big landlords who did not have relatives in the Revolutionary Army offered only limited hope to the peasants. Mao therefore went farther, at the Third Enlarged Meeting on April 22, declaring that "if five out of ten households are rich peasants, we must redistribute the land of the rich peasants to the other five households." This led Wang Jingwei to remark that, while Mao was talking about political confiscation in words, he was in fact advocating economic confiscation.[115]

Two days later, at the Fourth Enlarged Meeting, Mao stated that, for the time being, it was appropriate only to use the slogan "public ownership of land," not that of "land nationalization." But he also observed, "Distribution is a continuous process of change, not a matter of one distribution which then lasts forever."[116]

This open-ended perspective inspired enthusiasm in Mao Zedong and others involved in organizing the peasants. The proceedings, translated below, of a special Committee on the Peasant Movement that met on April 26, 1927, show him advocating the creation of a "Peasant Movement Committee for the War Zone" to push forward the mobilization of the peasants in the wake of the Northern

---

113. See *Nianpu*, 1, p. 193, which gives the date of the meeting at which this statement was made. The identical extract appears in Jiang Yongjing, *Borodin*, p. 282.

114. See below, Mao's remarks at the First Enlarged Meeting of the Land Committee on April 19, 1927.

115. See below, "Explanations at the Third Meeting of the Wuhan Land Committee," April 22, 1927.

116. A complete translation of the proceedings of this meeting can be found in the Wilbur Papers in the Columbia University Rare Book and Manuscript Library.

Expedition and to "solve the problem of the peasants' political power."[117] Land-lords and moderate elements in the Wuhan Guomindang were, however, frightened rather than enthusiastic. In the end, Mao was obliged to put his name to a vague and moderate compromise which offered the peasants relatively little,[118] and even these recommendations were set aside "temporarily" by the Guomindang Political Council on May 12, 1927, on the grounds that they would adversely affect the chances of victory for the National Revolution.[119] Thus, the problem of satisfying both constituencies—the "haves" in the Guomindang political and military elite and the "have-nots" in the countryside—ultimately proved insoluble.

From April 27 to May 10, 1927, while these deliberations of the Land Committee were going on, the Chinese Communist Party held its Fifth Congress, likewise in Wuhan. Mao was one of eighty delegates to the congress, but did not play a major role in it. According to the Comintern delegate M. N. Roy, Mao criticized the "compromising attitude" of Chen Duxiu (in fact, the attitude of Stalin) toward the bourgeoisie and the Party's failure to take a decision regarding the peasant question, but no actual text of this or any other speech by Mao during the congress is available. In any case, his views did not find acceptance, and Mao soon gave expression to his frustration by ceasing to attend the sessions. At the end of the congress, he was not even elected a full member of the Central Committee.[120]

On May 30, 1927, in his capacity as one of the five members of the standing committee of the All-China Peasant Association, Mao signed a directive that stressed the role of the peasants as "the main force of the national revolution." The goal of the revolution was overthrowing imperialism and the feudal forces and creating a democratic political power; to achieve it, the principle of "land to the tiller" must "ultimately" be put into practice. Observing that "a few peasants' actions sometimes unavoidably hurt the interests of the revolutionary soldiers," the directive urged the peasants to cooperate with small landlords, middle and small merchants, and the families of revolutionary officers and direct their attacks primarily against the village bullies and bad gentry.[121]

On the same day, in Moscow, the Comintern had adopted a decision calling for continued "energetic participation" in the government of the Left Guomindang, which in class terms represented "not only the peasants, the workers, and the artisans, but a part of the middle bourgeoisie." At the same time, the Guomindang should be reorganized so as to turn it into a loose federation of mass

---

117. See below, "Remarks at the Enlarged Meeting of the Committee on the Peasant Movement," April 26, 1927.

118. See below, "Report of the Land Committee," May 9, 1927.

119. Wilbur, *National Revolution*, p. 124.

120. Regarding the Fifth Congress and Mao's role in it, see *Party Meetings*, pp. 54–60. There were thirty-one members of the new Central Committee; Mao was listed first among the fourteen alternate members.

121. See below, "Important Directive of the All-China Peasant Association to the Peasant Associations of Hunan, Hubei, and Jiangxi Provinces," May 30, 1927.

organizations, which could be more easily manipulated. The agrarian revolution must be carried forward, though only the land of the "landlords, the mandarinate, and the monasteries" should be confiscated.[122] The telegram that Stalin proceeded to send to his Chinese comrades likewise called for combating "excesses" in the countryside through the medium of the peasant associations, but stressed even more heavily the importance of taking over and transforming the Guomindang.[123]

Faced with such contradictory orders, which it would have been impossible to carry out completely, the Chinese Communists chose to avoid an immediate crisis in relations with the Left Guomindang and to place the emphasis on "reining in" the peasants. In early June, Mao proceeded to call once again, in directives of the Peasant Association, for the elimination of the "primitive manifestations of the early stage of the peasant movement" through heightened revolutionary discipline.[124]

A few weeks earlier, on May 21, 1927, hundreds of peasant militiamen had been massacred near Changsha, and scarcely a month later, on July 15, 1927, the leader of the Wuhan Left, Wang Jingwei, expelled the Communists from his faction of the Guomindang, thereby bringing to an end the experiment of the First United Front. Many of the texts regarding the peasant movement authored by Mao from April to June 1927 remain thus, in large measure, a footnote to history, but some of them reflected more than others his true sentiments at this time. One in particular, his address at a banquet for delegates to the Pacific Labor Conference at the end of May, can serve as a fitting conclusion to this introduction, and a harbinger of things to come:

> The Chinese revolution is a part of the world revolution. . . . The international imperialists, in an attempt to oppose the Chinese revolution, have already fabricated the Second World War. The workers along the Pacific Rim are the first to raise the banner of righteousness and to oppose this cruel massacre. . . . The Chinese peasant movement is the main force in the revolutionary process. They should especially go hand in hand with the working class of the whole world and rely deeply on the influence and guidance of the workers' movement. This demonstrates that the workers have quite naturally become the leaders of the peasants.[125]

Mao did indeed believe in the need to rely on the influence and guidance of the international workers' movement, in other words, of Moscow. But in China itself, he regarded the peasant movement as "the main force in the revolutionary process," and would continue to do so for a long time to come.

---

122. For the full text of the Resolution on the Chinese Question adopted at the Eighth Plenum of the Executive Committee of the Communist International on May 30, 1927, see Mif, *Strategy and Tactics*, pp. 167–79, especially pp. 172, 174–75. Extracts in English can be found in Eudin and North, *Soviet Russia and the East 1920–1927* (Stanford: Stanford University Press, 1957), pp. 369–76.

123. See Eudin and North, *Soviet Russia and the East*, pp. 379–80.

124. See below, the directives dated June 7 and June 13, 1927.

125 See below, Mao's "Opening Address at the Welcome Banquet for Delegates to the Pacific Labor Conference," May 31, 1927.

Note on Sources and Conventions

This edition of Mao Zedong's writings in English translation aims to serve a dual audience, comprising not only China specialists, but those interested in Mao from other perspectives. In terms of content and presentation, we have done our best to make it useful and accessible to both these groups.

Scope. This is a complete edition, in the sense that it will include a translation of every item of which the Chinese text can be obtained. It cannot be absolutely complete, because some materials are still kept under tight control in the archives of the Chinese Communist Party. The situation has, however, changed dramatically since Mao's death, as a result of the publication in China, either openly or for restricted circulation (*neibu*), of a number of important texts.

Although the *Zhongyang wenxian yanjiushi* (Department for Research on Party Literature), which is the organ of the Central Committee of the Chinese Communist Party responsible for the publication of Mao's writings, has always disclaimed any intention of producing his complete pre-1949 works, it appeared in early 1989 that such an edition was in fact on the way, at least for a part of his early career. An advertising leaflet dated December 20, 1988, announced the appearance, in the spring of 1989, of two volumes, *Mao Zedong zaoqi zhuzuo ji* (Collected Writings by Mao Zedong from the Early Period), and *Jiandang he da geming shiqi Mao Zedong zhuzuo ji* (Collected Writings by Mao Zedong during the Period of Establishing the Party and of the Great Revolution [of 1924– 1927]), and invited advance orders for both volumes. The events of June 4, 1989, led first to the postponement of publication, and then to the decision to issue only the first of these volumes, for internal circulation, under the new title of *Mao Zedong zaoqi wengao, 1912.6–1920.11* (Draft Writings by Mao Zedong for the Early Period, June 1912–November 1920).

Prior to June 1989, further volumes in the same format were in preparation, at least down to the early 1930s. These plans have now been set aside, and no complete Chinese edition can be expected unless there is a radical change in the political situation. But, as forecast in Volume I, the corpus of available materials has now been substantially expanded by the publication in Beijing in December 1993 of two major series to commemorate the hundredth anniversary of Mao's birth. These are the *Mao Zedong wenji* (Collected Writings of Mao Zedong), of which the first two volumes, for the period 1921–1942, have now appeared, and the third volume is in press; and a six-volume edition of Mao's military writings, *Mao Zedong junshi wenji* (Collected Military Writings of Mao Zedong). We are therefore resuming the publication of our edition, after the pause for the centenary announced in Volume I.

Sources. More than 90 percent of the 169 texts included in Volume I were taken from the internal Chinese edition for the corresponding period. We therefore limited ourselves to listing, in the "Note on Sources and Conventions" for that volume, the sources from which we had translated the remaining sixteen items. That solution is not available to us here, because there is no complete, or nearly complete, Chinese edition of Mao's writings from December 1920 onward. This and future volumes must therefore be drawn from a variety of materials.

The twenty volumes of the *Mao Zedong ji* (Collected Writings of Mao Zedong) and the *Mao Zedong ji. Bujuan* (Collected Writings of Mao Zedong. Supplement), edited by Professor Takeuchi Minoru and published in Tokyo in the 1970s and 1980s, still constitute the most important single collection available of Mao's pre-1949 writings. (For details on this, and other sources cited below, see the Bibliography at the end of this volume.) Then there are the centenary materials listed above. The various specialized volumes issued a decade ago to commemorate Mao's ninetieth birthday also contain a number of previously unavailable items from the pre-1949 period. These include a collection of Mao's correspondence, *Mao Zedong shuxin xuanji* (Selected Correspondence of Mao Zedong), as well as a volume on journalism, *Mao Zedong xinwen gongzuo wenxuan* (Selected Writings by Mao Zedong on Journalistic Work), both of which appeared in 1983, and one on rural surveys, *Mao Zedong nongcun diaocha wenji* (Collected Writings by Mao Zedong on Rural Surveys), published in 1982.

As already indicated, all of these recent official publications are selective. Fortunately, we have been able to supplement them with materials drawn from an extremely wide range of sources, including individual texts published in China for restricted circulation, contemporary newspapers and periodicals of the 1920s, and documents from the Guomindang archives. In these circumstances, it would be cumbersome, and inconvenient for the reader, to present details regarding the provenance of every item in a single table here. This information is therefore given in an unnumbered footnote at the beginning of each text. We have also included in these source notes information about the first publication, or the earliest known version, of the writing in question. To avoid ambiguity, all works referred to in these notes are designated by their Chinese titles, sometimes in a shortened version. (For indications regarding short titles, and for full bibliographical details regarding all works cited, including those mentioned above, see once again the Bibliography at the end of this volume.)

Other things being equal, we have referred the reader who wishes to consult the Chinese text to the *Mao Zedong ji* and the *Bujuan* whenever the item in question appears there, because this series offers the convenience of a large quantity of materials in compact form. There are, however, instances in which the version contained in recent official Chinese publications is more accurate or more complete, and we have accordingly taken it as the basis for our translation. In such cases, the nature of the more significant differences is indicated in notes to the text in question, but we have not sought to show the variants systemati-cally. That has been done only in dealing with changes made in the original text of Mao's writings of the 1920s when they were revised in 1950 for inclusion in the official edition of his *Selected Works*.

Variants. While there are some differences between the various versions of texts by Mao published in the 1930s and 1940s, these are on the whole minor. Systematic revision of his pre-1949 writings was undertaken only from 1950 onward, in preparing the four-volume edition of the *Mao Zedong xuanji*, trans-lated into English as the *Selected Works of Mao Tse-tung*. This problem did not arise in our Volume I, because its coverage ended in 1920, and the earliest item in the *Selected Works* is the "Analysis of All the Classes in Chinese Society," written in 1925. Apart from this text, the present volume contains the well-known "Report on the Peasant Movement in Hunan" of February 1927. (The second edition of the *Xuanji*, which appeared in 1991, amends the date of "Analy-sis of All the Classes" from March 1926 to December 1, 1925, and corrects a few minor typographical errors, but the texts of Mao's writings that it contains are basically identical with those of the original edition of the 1950s.)

Much ink has been spilled regarding the question of which version of the texts included in the official canon is more authentic, or more authoritative. Despite the passions formerly aroused by this issue, the answer seems rather obvious. For purposes of the historical record, only the text as originally written (when it is available) can tell us what Mao actually said in the 1920s and thereafter. For the study of Mao Zedong's thought, both versions have their uses in documenting how his ideas evolved over time. For purposes of defining ideological orthodoxy under the People's Republic, the *Selected Works* version is, of course, the ulti-mate standard.

In any case, the purpose of this edition is not to lay down which was the "real" Mao, but to enable the reader to distinguish between what Mao wrote at any given moment in his life, and the revised texts which were produced in the 1950s under Mao's close supervision, and often with his own active participa-tion. We have endeavored to do this in the following manner:

1. The translations that appear here correspond to the earliest available ver-sion of the text in question.
2. Words and passages from this original version that have been deleted in the *Xuanji* are printed in italics.
3. Substantive and significant changes in the text, including additions made by Mao, or under his authority, in the 1950s, are shown in the footnotes. The *Mao Zedong ji* indicates meticulously *all* changes, including those that involve only matters of punctuation or style (such as the frequent replacement of the somewhat more literary conjunction *yu* by the more colloquial *he*, both meaning "and.") We have shown in the English ver-sion only those changes that appeared to us to have a significant impact on

the meaning of the text. Any such judgement is, of course, in some degree subjective. We have sought to err on the side of showing too many variants, rather than too few, even when there was monotonous repetition in the changes, but we have not hesitated to leave out of account variants we regarded as trivial.

In footnotes of this kind, the words that appear *before* the arrow reproduce enough of the original text to identify what has been changed. The words that appear *after* the arrow correspond to what has been added or revised in the *Xuanji*. Because, in the rewriting of the 1950s, sentences and whole passages have often been substantially recast, it would take up far too much space, and make our text unreadable, to show every variant in detail. In some instances, it has been possible to show the new version in the form of complete sentences, but frequently we include only enough of the new wording to make plain the main thrust of the changes. Because the official translation has been available for four decades, and has been widely quoted in the literature, we have taken this version as our starting-point whenever it corresponds to the original Chinese text, but have modified or corrected it as we judged appropriate.

Annotation. So that any attentive reader will be able to follow the details of Mao's argument in each case, we have assumed no knowledge of anything relating to China. Persons, institutions, places, and events are briefly characterized at the point where Mao first refers to them. Some individuals of secondary importance, especially those who appear only as names in a long list, are not included in the notes. We have also ruled out, with rare exceptions, annotations regarding people or events in the West. Despite these limitations, the reader will soon discover that the personages who do merit identification are as numerous as the characters in a traditional Chinese novel.

To keep the notes within reasonable compass, we have generally restricted those regarding Mao's contemporaries to their lives down to the period covered by each volume. To make it easier to locate information, frequent references have been inserted indicating where the first note about a given individual appears in the volume. In a few instances, notes about Mao's contemporaries have been split into two, so that the reader will not be confronted in reading a text regarding the early 1920s with information relating to later events which might themselves require explanation.

In each biographical note dates of birth and death, separated by a hyphen, are given immediately after the name. A blank following the hyphen should, in principle, signify that the person in question is still living. In the case of individuals born in the 1870s and 1880s, this is obviously unlikely, but in many instances even the editors working in Beijing have not been able to ascertain the facts. We have done our best to fill these gaps, but have not always succeeded. Sometimes a Chinese source ends with the word "deceased" (*yigu*), without giving the date of death. Here we have inserted a question mark after the hyphen, and have mentioned the fact in the note. It should not be assumed that all those born in the 1890s for whom no second date is given are already dead; some of them are in fact very much alive as of 1994.

The introductions, including that to the present volume, should be considered in a very real sense as an extension of the notes. These texts will, we hope, help readers unfamiliar with Mao Zedong, or with early twentieth-century China, find their *own* way through Mao's writings of the early period. Any controversial or provocative statements which they may contain are intended to stimulate reflection, not to impose a particular interpretation on the reader. This is a collection of historical source material, not a volume of interpretation.

Use of Chinese terms. On the whole, we have sought to render all Chinese expressions into accurate and readable English, but in a few cases it has seemed simpler and less ambiguous to use the Chinese word. These instances include, to begin with, *zi* (courtesy name) and *hao* (literary name). Because both Mao, and the authors he cited, frequently employ these alternative appellations instead of the *ming* or given name of the individual to whom they are referring, information regarding them is essential to the intelligence of the text. The English word "style" is sometimes used here, but because it may stand either for *zi* or for *hao*, it does not offer a satisfactory solution. The Chinese terms have, in any case, long been used in Western-language biographical dictionaries of China, as well as in Chinese works.

Similarly, in the case of second or provincial-level, and third or metropolitan-level graduates of the old examination system, we have chosen to use the Chinese terms, respectively *juren* and *jinshi*. The literal translations of "recommended man" and "presented scholar" would hardly have been suitable for expressions which recur constantly in Mao's writings, nor would Western parallels (such as "doctorate" for *jinshi*) have been adequate. We have also preferred *xian* to "county" for the administrative subdivision which constituted the lowest level of the imperial bureaucracy, and still exists in China today. Apart from the Western connotations of "county," there is the problem that *xian* is also often translated "district" (as in the expression "district magistrate"), and "district" itself is ambiguous in the Chinese context. We have also preferred to use the Chinese word *li* rather than to translate "Chinese league" (or simply "league"), or to give the equivalent in miles or kilometers.

In one instance we have, on the contrary, used an English translation instead of a Chinese term. The main subdivisions in older writings, commonly referred to by their Chinese name of *juan*, are here called simply "volume" (abbreviated as "Vol."). Readers who consult the Chinese texts should have no difficulty in determining when this refers to the physically separate volumes of modern editions, and when it means *juan*.

In two other respects, finally, we have been guided by the presentation of our Chinese sources. Mao frequently emphasized words or phrases by placing dots or circles next to each of the characters involved. In this edition, the corresponding text has been set in bold. Usually we have also added a note explicitly pointing this out, but it should be clearly stated that all such highlighting is Mao's, not ours. Also, some of the Chinese texts we have translated contain omissions, because the editors in Tokyo, or even those in Beijing, did not have access to a complete version of the document in question, or could not read a few characters. When the number of missing characters is small, each one is commonly represented in the printed Chinese text by a hollow square occupying the space which would normally be taken up by a single character. In our English version, each such square has been represented by the symbol [X], so the reader of the translation can see how much is missing. Where the gap is a long one, we have dispensed with this procedure, and conveyed the necessary information in a footnote.

Volume II
National Revolution and Social Revolution
December 1920–June 1927

MAO'S
ROAD TO POWER
Revolutionary Writings
1912·1949

—1920—

Letter to Xiao Xudong,[1] Cai Linbin,[2] and the Other Members in France

(December 1, 1920)

Dear Hesen and Zisheng, as well as all the other members in France,

I was extremely glad to receive the letters from you two brothers. The Montargis Conference and the several letters from the two of you mark the beginning of concrete plans for the Study Society.[3] I have very great hopes for the future of the Society and, in consequence, I also have a few plans. I have long thought about drafting a proposal and presenting it to the members for consultation. Now that I have received your letters, I do not think it necessary for me to write up my own proposal any more. I only hope that each of us seventy-odd members will seriously consider the plans outlined in your letters and then give a thorough evaluation, taking a stand either for or against, or adding any other plans and ideas to yours. I often feel that the development of each of us individuals, or that of the Society, requires a clear approach. Without such an approach, the individ-

---

This letter was first published in January 1921 in Vol. 3 of the *Xinmin xuehui huiyuan tongxinji* (Collected Correspondence of Members of the New People's Study Society). The source for our translation is the Chinese text in the documentary collection *Xinmin xuehui ziliao* (Materials on the New People's Study Society), pp. 144–52, reproduced in *Mao Zedong ji. Bujuan*, Vol. 1, pp. 289–96. (For further details regarding these and other sources see the Note on Sources and Conventions at the beginning of this volume, and the Bibliography at the end.)

1. Xiao Zisheng (1894–1976), also known as Xiao Xudong, was one of Mao's closest friends during the years 1915–1920, as evidenced by the numerous letters and references to him contained in Volume I of this edition. Xiao's book, published under the name of Siao-yu, *Mao Tse-tung and I Were Beggars* (Syracuse: Syracuse University Press, 1959), reflects this intimacy as well as the hostility generated by their subsequent political differences. Xiao Zisheng went to France in 1919 on the work-study program, but returned to China in the winter of 1920 and met with Mao in March 1921 in Changsha.

2. Cai Hesen (1895–1931), alternative name Cai Linbin, was a native of Xiangxiang *xian*, Hunan. With Xiao Zisheng, he was one of Mao's two best friends during the years at First Normal School in Changsha. The New People's Study Society was founded at a meeting in his house, and unlike Xiao, he later followed the same political course as Mao. Indeed, as indicated by Mao's letter to him of January 21, 1921, translated below, he played an important role in convincing Mao Zedong that China should follow a Marxist and a Leninist path.

3. I.e., the New People's Study Society.

ual or the Society can only advance blindly, ruining in the end not only each individual but also this Society, which is full of promise. Would that not be a shame? Before the Society was founded, we already had some plans. Indeed, this Society was founded as the result of mutual discussions and study that took place among a few people two years ago. Once the Society was founded, it immediately formulated a common ideology, which has had considerable influence in transforming the thinking and improving the lives of individuals. At the same time, there has been some study of our collective existence and of our common progress. The fact is, however, that no concrete programs were put forward, and there were no publications that could serve as organs for public discussion. Furthermore, for the last two years members have been scattered to different locations, and those in Changsha have been unable to meet for discussions because of political obstacles. As a result, even though there were plans and ideas, they have been kept inside each individual's heart, have been mentioned when a few people got together, or appear in the correspondence among individuals. In sum, these plans and ideas have been known only to some members. You have now had a big gathering in Montargis[4] and have decided on a common program. In addition, you two brothers have expressed your own ideas, based on your own ideals and observations. We members who are not in France must naturally study and evaluate the views that all of you have put forward and then come to some decisions about them. But before the members in Changsha meet for joint study, criticism, and decisions, let me first give you my own personal ideas about your letters.

I proceed to discuss them point by point.

I. *The question of the guiding principle of our Society.* In the last analysis, what guiding principle should we adopt to serve as the common objective of our Society? Zisheng says in his letter that the Montargis Conference adopted the following position regarding the orientation which the Society should pursue: "The conference resolves that our Society's guiding principle is to reform China and the world." To adopt "reforming China and the world" as the guiding principle of our Society is entirely in harmony with what I have been advocating, and I expect the majority of the members will agree with this. According to my contacts and observations, most members of the Society incline toward cosmopolitanism.[5] As evidence, consider the fact that a majority reject patriotism; they reject the pursuit of the interests of one group or nation while disregarding the

---

4. This meeting was held in July 1920 at Montargis, a town some sixty miles south of Paris where Cai, Xiao, Xiang Jingyu, and many members of the New People's Study Society had gone with other work-study students to improve their French in the hope of subsequently entering universities.

5. *Shijiezhuyi*, literally "world-ism."

happiness of all mankind. The majority feel that each of us is a member of the human race, and do not want to complicate the matter by belonging to some meaningless country, family, or religion and becoming slaves to these. This type of cosmopolitanism is a doctrine of universal brotherhood, it is an ism that seeks to benefit not only oneself but also others. This is precisely what is called socialism. All socialisms are international in nature and should not have any patriotic coloration. Hesen said in his August 13 letter, "I will draw up a clear and definite proposal, stressing two points—the dictatorship of the proletariat and internationalism. Since most of the clear-thinking young people I have seen have some middle-class values mixed in with an internationalist coloration, we must not fail to take a clear stand on these two points." Apart from proletarian dictatorship, which I will discuss under the following heading, the point about internationalism really needs to be solemnly emphasized now. True, we who are born in this place, China, should naturally work in this locality, both because it is more convenient to act here, and because China is more immature and more corrupt than any other place in the world, and reform should therefore start here. But our feelings should be universal; we must not love only this place and not other places. This is one level. At the same time, our activities should in no way be limited to China. In my opinion, even though there must be people working in China, it is even more important to have people working throughout the world. For example, there should be people helping Russia complete her social revolution, helping Korea gain independence, helping the countries of Southeast Asia become independent, and helping Mongolia, Xinjiang, Tibet, and Qinghai to become autonomous and enjoy self-determination. All these causes are very important. Next I shall discuss the question of methods.

II. *The question of methods*. Our goal—to reform China and the world—having been determined, the next question which arises is that of methods. When it comes right down to it, what methods should we use to reach our goal "to reform China and the world"? Hesen says in his letter, "I now see clearly that socialism is a reaction to capitalism. Its main mission is to destroy the capitalist economic system, and its method lies in the dictatorship of the proletariat." He also says, "I don't think anarchism will work in the world today, because obviously there exist two antagonistic classes in this world. In overthrowing the dictatorship of the bourgeoisie,[6] there is no way the reactionary forces can be suppressed save by the dictatorship of the proletariat. Russia is a clear illustration. Therefore I think that in the future reform of China, the principles and methods of socialism will be entirely appropriate. . . . I think we must first organize a Communist Party, because it is the initiator, propagandist, vanguard, and operational headquarters of the revolutionary movement." Hesen's view is that we should apply

---

6. Cai's term here is *youchan jieji* (literally "propertied class"), but the renderings of Marxist terms were not yet clearly established in 1920, and plainly it is the bourgeoisie (*zichan jieji*) he has in mind.

Russian methods to reform China and the world. He is in favor of Marxist methods. But Zisheng says, "The evolution of the world has no time limit, nor does revolution. We do not regard it as permissible to sacrifice part of the people in exchange for the welfare of the majority. I advocate a moderate revolution, a revolution with education as its instrument, which seeks to promote the general welfare of the people and carries out reforms through the medium of trade unions and cooperatives. I do not think the Russian-style Marxist revolution is justified, but am inclined to favor the new-style revolution of anarchism, or antiauthoritarianism,[7] in the manner of Proudhon. It is milder and more gradual; although gradual, it is mild." Meanwhile Li Hesheng,[8] in a letter to me, has expressed ideas similar to Zisheng's. He says, "To reform society, I do not approve of sweeping reform. I feel it would be an excellent thing to transform society from within by means of the division of labor and mutual aid. The diseases of each society have their own particular background. I doubt very much that one prescription can cure all the world's ills. I have some fundamental reservations about Russian-style revolution." In principle, I agree with Zisheng and Hesheng's ideas (to seek the welfare of all by peaceful means), but I do not believe they will work in reality. Russell, speaking in Changsha,[9] advocated ideas similar to those of Zisheng and Hesheng. He took a position in favor of communism, but against the dictatorship of the workers and peasants. He said that one should employ the method of education to make the propertied classes conscious [of their failings], and that in this way it would not be necessary to limit freedom or to have recourse to war and bloody revolution. After Russell's speech, I argued in depth with Yinbo,[10] Lirong,[11] and others. My assessment of Russell's position can be summed up in two sentences: "This is all very well in theory; in reality it can't be done." The crux of Russell's, Zisheng's and Hesheng's arguments is "use the method of education." But education requires: (1) money, (2) people, and (3) institutions. In today's world, money is entirely in the hands of the capitalists; those in charge of education are all

---

7. Xiao Zisheng, as quoted here, treats anarchist (*wuzhengfu*) and antiauthoritarian (*wuqiangquan*, literally "no oppressive power") as synonyms that characterize the new type of revolution advocated by Proudhon.

8. Li Hesheng (1897–), also known as Li Weihan, Luo Mai, and Luo Man, was a native of Liling *xian*, Hunan. He was a student of the First Normal School, who joined the New People's Study Society shortly after its founding in 1918. In mid-1919 he went to France on the work-study program and while there was an active sponsor and organizer of the Socialist Youth League. Upon his return to China he became a teacher in the Preparatory Class of the Self-Study University set up in September 1922.

9. Bertrand Russell attended a conference on the subject of constitutions sponsored by official organizations in Changsha on November 1, 1920, and lectured on self-government.

10. On Peng Huang, *zi* Yinbo, see below, the note to Mao's letter to him dated January 28, 1921.

11. Yi Lirong. See below, the relevant note to Mao's letter of January 28, 1921, to Peng Huang.

either capitalists or slaves of capitalists. The schools and the press, the two most important instruments of education, are also under the exclusive control of the capitalists. In short, education in today's world is capitalist education. If you teach capitalism to children, these children, when they grow up, will in turn teach capitalism to a second generation of children. If education has thus fallen into the hands of the capitalists, it is because they have "parliaments" to pass laws protecting the capitalists and handicapping the proletariat. They have "governments" to execute these laws and to enforce actively the advantages and prohibitions they contain. They have "armies" and "police" to provide passive guarantees for the safety and happiness of the capitalists and to repress the demands of the proletariat. They have "banks" as their treasury to ensure the circulation of their wealth. They have factories, which are the instruments by which they monopolize the commodities produced. Consequently, unless the Communists seize political power, they will not be able to find refuge in a place under their own control; how, then, could they take charge of education? Thus the capitalists have long been in control of education and go on praising their capitalism to the skies, so that the number of converts to the Communist propaganda of the Communist Party diminishes day by day. That is why I believe that the method of education is not feasible. A Russian-style revolution, it seems to me, is a last resort when all other means have been exhausted. It is not that some other better means are rejected and we only want to use this terrorist tactic. This constitutes the first argument. The second argument is that, on the basis of the principle of mental habits, and of observations on the course of human history, I feel it is quite impossible to expect the capitalists to be converted to communism. Human life is marked by habit, which is a psychological force just like the force that causes an object to roll down a slope. To prevent the object from rolling, according to the principles of mechanics, an equally strong force is needed to counter it. In order to change a person's mind, a force of the same strength is also needed to counter it. If we try to transform them by the power of education, we will not be able to take over all or a large part of the two instruments of education, the schools and the newspapers. Thus, even though we have mouths and tongues, publications, and one or two schools as propaganda organs, it will be as Master Zhu[12] has said, "Teaching is like helping a drunkard: when you help him up on one side, he falls down on the other side." This is really not enough to change the mentality of the adherents of capitalism even slightly; how, then, can one hope that they will repent and turn toward the good? So much from a psychological standpoint. If we turn to

---

12. Zhu Xi, the Song dynasty neo-Confucian philosopher whose works Mao had studied under Yang Changji. In fact, Mao's paraphrase of this saying is closer to the original statement of the Cheng brothers (see *Er Cheng ji. Henan Chengshi yishu*, Vol. 18) than to Zhu Xi's adaptation, in *Jinsilu. Weixue.*

the historical standpoint, human life is nothing but the expansion of men's real desires. These real desires only expand, and assuredly never diminish. Small capitalists necessarily want to be bigger capitalists; big capitalists necessarily want to be among the biggest. This is a definite psychological pattern. Historically, no despot, imperialist, or militarist has ever stepped down of his own free will without waiting for people to overthrow him. Napoleon I proclaimed himself emperor and failed, but Napoleon III once again took the title of emperor. Yuan Shikai failed; then, once again, there was Duan Qirui.[13] Zhang Taiyan,[14] when lecturing in Changsha, urged everyone to read history. He said that Yuan, Duan, and the like had all failed because they never read history. I would argue that to read history is an act of intelligence. To pursue one's desires is an act of impulse. Intelligence can direct impulse effectively only within certain boundaries. Once beyond those boundaries, impulse will prevail over the intellect, advance boldly, and not be stopped until confronted with forces greater than itself. There are popular sayings that bear this out, such as: "Unless a man reaches the Yellow River, he will never give up," "The next mountain always seems higher," and "Man is never satisfied; once he gets Gansu, he wants Sichuan too." In the light of what I have just said, from both the psychological and the historical standpoints, we can see that capitalism cannot be overthrown by the force of a few feeble efforts at education. This is the second argument. Now I turn to the third argument. Ideals are certainly important, but reality is even more important. If we use peaceful means to attain the goal of communism, when will we finally achieve it? Let us assume it will take a hundred years. How, during these hundred years, are we going to deal with the unceasing groans of the proletariat (who are in fact ourselves)? The proletariat is actually several times more numerous than the bourgeoisie. If we assume that the proletariat constitutes two-thirds of humanity, then 1 billion of the 1.5 billion members of the human race are proletarians (I fear the figure is even higher), who during this century will be cruelly exploited by the remaining third of capitalists. How can we bear this? Moreover, the proletariat has already become conscious of the fact that it, too, should possess property, and that its present sufferings, caused by the absence of property,

---

13. Duan Qirui (1865–1936), *zi* Zhiquan, was one of Yuan Shikai's chief lieutenants. As premier for most of the time from April 1916 to October 1918, he did not seek to restore the monarchy, as Yuan had done in 1915–1916, but he did strive to unify the country by military means. Many critical references by Mao to his activities are to be found in Volume I of this edition. A native of Hefei in Anhui Province, he was the leader of the Anhui clique during the struggles among rival factions of northern militarists. For an analysis of these events, see below, the text of April 10, 1923, "The Foreign Powers, the Warlords, and the Revolution."

14. For details regarding Zhang Binglin (1869–1936), *zi* Meishu, *hao* Taiyan, see in Volume I, p. 106, the note to Mao's letter of December 9, 1916, to Li Jinxi. In 1918 Zhang broke with Sun Yatsen and thereafter evolved in a conservative direction. He had always been a strong admirer of the Legalists, Han Feizi and Shang Yang, stressing the importance of an effective centralized administration.

are unjustified. Because they are dissatisfied at having no property,[15] they have put forward a demand for communism,[16] which has already become a fact. This fact confronts us, we cannot make it disappear. It is a thing that makes you want to act as soon as you become aware of it. Therefore, in my opinion, the Russian Revolution, and the fact that radical Communists in various countries are daily growing more numerous and more tightly organized, represent simply the natural course of events. This is the third argument. There is yet a further reason, namely that I am skeptical about anarchism. My reasons for this do not lie simply in the impossibility of a society without power or organization, but in the difficulties that would result from creating such a society. For such a social state will certainly decrease the death rate and increase the birth rate, thus necessarily leading to overpopulation. Unless it is possible to create a situation in which there is (1) no need to eat, (2) no need for clothing, (3) no need for housing, and (4) climates and soil conditions all over the world are the same, or (5) new lands are constantly being discovered to accomodate people, in the end the predicament of overpopulation cannot be avoided. For all the reasons just stated, my present view of absolute liberalism, anarchism, and even democracy,[17] is that these things sound very good in theory, but are not feasible in reality. Therefore, I do not agree with the views of Zisheng and Hesheng, but express my profound approbation for Hesen's views.

III. *The question of attitude.* There are two kinds of attitudes: that of the Society, and that of the individual members. In my opinion, the attitude of the Society should first of all be "low-key."[18] This was discusssed at Bansong Park, in Shanghai,[19] and has now been approved as well by the members in France, so it should be regarded as settled. It is important that we should "not rely on old authorities." Our society is new and creative, and absolutely should not allow old authorities to sneak in. We should ask everyone to pay attention to this point. As for the attitudes of members toward each other, and of members individually, I think they should comprise: (1) "mutual aid and exhortation" (mutual help such as help in emergencies, studies, and careers; mutual exhortation such as encouraging each other positively to do good and

---

15. *Wuchan*, literally "propertyless."

16. *Gongchan*, literally "common property."

17. Here Mao writes "democracy-ism" (*demokelaxizhuyi*), using (as was common at the time) a phonetic transcription of the English word democracy, and adding *zhuyi* (ism) at the end of it.

18. *Qianzai.* This compound commonly has the meaning of "latent," "hidden," or "secret." Here the idea is that the members of the Society should not put themselves forward too much for the time being.

19. Regarding the Bansong Park conference of May 1920, at which a "low-key and realistic" attitude was decided on, see below, the "Report on the Activities of the New People's Study Society," winter 1920–1921.

passively to avoid evil), (2) sincerity (not craftiness), (3) openheartedness (in character), and (4) seeking improvement (having the ability to transform one's nature and the will to improve oneself). The first point applies to mutual relationships; the last three to individuals. The above two attitudes of the Society, and four attitudes of the members, are relevant to the spirit of the Society and its members and are exceedingly important.

IV. *The question of studies.* I strongly agree with your two approaches of joint studies and specialized studies. You all feel that living in scattered quarters is not convenient, and want to live together so that you can both work and have opportunities to meet for frequent discussions. This is excellent. The Changsha comrades are already in one location, and your example should definitely be copied here. As for specializing in different subjects, there is no better way than to take ideology as the key link and books and periodicals as the net;[20] to read first individually and then exchange ideas. I suggest that wherever there are two members, things should be organized in this way. Zisheng pointed out that we must study hard and remarked that our general knowledge is still insufficient, that none of us comrades have specialized learning, and that China has an insignificant number of scholars at present. This is indeed the truth! Progress in thought is the foundation for progress in life and career. The only way to advance one's thinking is through study and research. I am very unhappy about my neglect of my own studies. I must follow your example from now on, and strive harder in my studies.

V. *Questions relating to the operations of the Society.* It is on this issue that Zisheng and Hesen have most to say. I agree with all of Zisheng's eighteen items in "My Views of the Society." Under the heading of "The Basic Plans," the three paragraphs "determining the goals of the operation of the Society," "preparing talent," and "preparing funds" are particularly outstanding. As to designating the period before 1936 as the purely preparatory stage, I suggest that it be extended five more years so the preparatory stage will last until 1941. Among the items listed by Zisheng concerning Changsha, three of them—"building a firm foundation based on the main guidelines of the Society," "setting up primary schools," and "recruiting rank-and-file members"—are most important. But a fourth one should be added: "setting up various kinds of new and valuable enterprises." The most important overseas headquarters as listed by Zisheng are France, Russia, and Southeast Asia. I think the movements of the Society can be roughly summed up, for the time being, under four headings: (1) the Hunan movement, (2) the South East Asian movement, (3) the movement of going to France to study, and (4) the movement of going to Russia to study. We do not now need to

---

20. *Yi zhuyi wei gang, yi shubao wei mu.* This metaphor of the "key link" and the net is one that Mao would employ constantly down to the end of his life, for example in the slogans "grain as the key link" and "steel as the key link" at the time of the Great Leap Forward, and "class struggle as the key link" during the Cultural Revolution.

seek further expansion; if we can develop these four existing movements and make it our goal to see them achieve results, this will be more practical. What do you gentlemen think? As for the "primary school education," "labor education," "cooperative movement," "pamphlets," "gathering relatives to live together," and "helping various bodies" that Hesen wants me to undertake, I am willing to do all these things. The only point I do not understand is "sticking stamps."[21] Please instruct me further. Now that the Cultural Book Society has been established, its foundation can be consolidated, and the business end can also move ahead. It appears that the present plan to establish a branch society in every *xian* can be carried out within two years. If so, the effect will be considerable.

VI. *The question of maintaining liaison among comrades.* This is extremely important. I think all of us seventy-odd members should, with sincerest hearts, be in touch individually with comrades near us all the time about everything, and embark hand-in-hand on the road to world reform. Man or woman, old or young, intellectual, peasant, worker, or merchant, whoever is sincere of heart, open and frank in character, with thoughts turned toward self-improvement, and able to benefit from mutual help and mutual encouragement, can be brought in and become one of us.

This was discussed in detail in Hesen's letter, and was also mentioned by Zisheng. I think the great enterprise of creating a special environment and reforming China and the world can definitely not be carried out by a mere handful. I hope each of our seventy-odd people will take this to heart.

I have more or less explained my ideas. I hear that Zisheng has already returned to China and reached Beijing.[22] Soon we can talk face-to-face. I

---

21. "Sticking stamps" (*tie youhua*) had been advocated by Cai Hesen in his letter of May 28, 1920, to Mao (*Cai Hesen wenji* [Beijing: Renmin chubanshe, 1980], p. 29). The general idea, which Cai attributed to Li Shizeng, was plain enough: in order to husband its own scarce resources, the New People's Study Society should find ways to make use of the channels provided by other organizations in order to propagate its views. Three channels should be used: normal schools, primary schools, and existing periodicals. Cai's explanation was not, however, altogether lucid, so it was not surprising that Mao did not understand. In the case of other publications, the "stamps" were apparently small printed documents to be stuck on, or inserted in, the periodical in question before it was distributed. In the case of schools, however, while such leaflets might have been used, "sticking stamps" may also have been a metaphor for incorporating the ideas of the Society into oral or written communications of the "host" organization.

22. The first report of the New People's Study Society, dated winter 1920, confirms (Section IX) that Xiao Zisheng did indeed return to China in October 1920. Why, if Mao was aware of this fact, did he include Xiao among the addressees of a letter sent to France? The most likely explanation is that, since Xiao had chaired the meeting in Montargis at which the Society's objectives were discussed, Mao used his name and that of Cai Hesen as representative of the two main tendencies expressed on that occasion.

would like to ask the friends in France to criticize my ideas once again in order to seek a joint decision. This would be fortunate indeed for me and for the Society.

> Your younger brother Zedong
> December 1, ninth year [of the Republic][23]
> Cultural Book Society
> 12 midnight

---

23. During the years covered by this volume, Mao employed both the Western and the Chinese calendars. In the dates which appear at the head of each text, we have used the Western form. Where Mao himself gives a date, either within a text, or at the end of a letter or other document, we have translated it in accordance with the form he used in Chinese. For further details on the treatment of dates see above, the Note on Sources and Conventions.

Advertisement of the Cultural Book Society in Changsha

(December 1, 1920)

(I) Our Book Society has been organized jointly by a group of comrades. Its capital is held in common; money once invested is not returned, nor do we pay any dividends. The Book Society specializes in selling new publications, both foreign and domestic. The price is extremely reasonable, since we aim only to cover shipping and handling expenses. The head office is located in the capital of Hunan Province; branch offices are located in every *xian*. This arrangement facilitates the dissemination of all sorts of worthwhile new publications throughout the whole province so that everyone can avail himself of the opportunity to read them.

(II) We sell the following three categories of publications:

1. Books (series and individual volumes, more than 160 titles at present).
2. Magazines (monthly, semimonthly, magazines appearing once every ten days, weekly, yearly, and quarterly, more than 40 titles at present).
3. Daily newspapers (We distribute only three titles at present).

(III) We would gladly distribute all worthwhile new publications. We always pay on time; our bills are never in arrears. We sincerely hope that authors and publishers all over the country will contact us immediately whenever they have new works so that we can make arrangements for their distribution.

(IV) Our address is 56 Chaozong Street, Changsha.

This advertisement originally appeared in *Xin qingnian*, Vol. 8, No. 4, December 1920. Our translation has been made from the text as reproduced in *Mao Zedong ji. Bujuan*, Vol. 1, p. 287.

Mao Zedong's Letter Refuting Unjust Accusations

(With Reference to the Incident of Tearing Down the Flag at the Last Meeting of the Provincial Assembly)

(December 3, 1920)

Mao Zedong has been falsely accused by some resentful people of the incident of tearing down the flag at a meeting of the Assembly.[1] Yesterday Mr. Mao wrote to the police to refute the false charges. The text of the letter is as follows:

To Chief of Police Tang for His Excellency's Inspection:

Yesterday I received a summons to come to your honorable Station for a meeting with Section Chief He Shaoyuan of your Station. At the meeting, Section Chief He brought up a note from the Provincial Assembly stating that informed sources had sent a letter to the Assembly. The letter accused me, Zedong, of inviting representatives of all civic groups to a meeting at the library in order to incite a certain army to smash up the Provincial Assembly. The letter was said to be signed by four people, who called themselves Cao Ren, Wang Fuxing, Long Jianxun, and Wang Ren. If you examine the previous incident, when someone tore down the flag at the Provincial Assembly, some people who bore me a grudge tried to blame it on me. (A detailed report was submitted to Section Chief He. He will provide you with the facts at your request.) Now they are seizing an opportunity to defame my reputation. This time they have further alleged that I, Zedong, want to destroy the Provincial Assembly. I have devoted

---

This letter was published in the Changsha *Dagongbao*, December 5, 1920. Our source is the text as reproduced in *Mao Zedong ji. Bujuan,* Vol. 1, pp. 297–98.

1. The incident of the tearing down of the flag occured on October 10, 1920, the day the "Petition for the Hunan Self-Government Movement," translated in Volume I, pp. 577–78, was to be presented to Governor Tan Yankai by representatives of numerous Changsha organizations. Some ten thousand people marched to the Provincial Assembly shouting slogans in support of the proposal. The flag was torn down because it was regarded as the symbol of the old Assembly, and more broadly of the continuing dominance of the old elite. Tan Yankai (1880–1930), *zi* Zu'an, a native of Chaling, Hunan Province, was a *jinshi* of the Guangxu period, and drew political support from the gentry. He served as governor of Hunan from October 1911 to October 1913, from August 1916 to August 1917, and then from July to November 1920, when he was replaced by his subordinate Zhao Hengti.

myself to teaching, and I am busily engaged in study in order to broaden my learning. I have no interest in participating in senseless and fleeting public whims. Regarding autonomy for Hunan, which I regard as a matter of life or death, of glory or disgrace, for the people of Hunan, I have indeed made statements on an intellectual plane. I have also, following in the wake of many others, sought to promote its realization by what is known as the "Proposal for Enacting a Constitution."[2] All this I have done in a manner completely open and above board; there is nothing in the slightest degree secret about it. There is, however, a group of muddle-headed people who seek to confuse the Proposal for Enacting a Constitution with the October 10 street demonstrations by the people of Changsha and the mass meeting held at that time. Those who are hostile to me, seeking to find some trivial pretext, have used this occasion to frame me. They failed the first time, and now they are trying a second time. I, Zedong, adopting a responsible attitude, now make the following two solemn public statements:

I. Have I, Zedong, been unhappy with the Provincial Assembly in the past over the question of enacting a constitution? The answer is, "Yes."

II. Did I, Zedong, tear down the flag and plot to smash the Provincial Assembly? The answer is, "No."

In the past, I have been unhappy with the Provincial Assembly over the question of enacting a constitution for good reasons, which I would not hesitate to declare even in front of the gentlemen of the assembly. As for tearing down the flag and plotting to smash the assembly, I did no such thing, and it should not be said that I did. Recently, some sinister and underhanded people have been trying to confuse right and wrong. They love to spread irresponsible rumors, but do not have the courage to show the public who they really are. It is the duty of your honorable Station to uphold proper conduct and discipline, to rid society of criminals and false accusers—a duty you cannot ignore. I must request you to see that the slanderers are arrested and punished severely and speedily as a warning to others of the same ilk. Moreover, Zedong is a free citizen of our New Hunan; no one should be allowed to damage either my body or my reputation, except in accordance with the law. Since those people have tried twice already to frame me, they are likely to do it a third or fourth time. Or they may seek to achieve their ends by other means. I earnestly entreat your honorable Station to enforce police regulations strictly and to remove the thugs in order to reassure the law-abiding citizens. I, Zedong, would not be the only one to benefit from it. I beg your favorable consideration for this plea.

> Mao Zedong
> Principal of the primary school attached to
> the First Normal School
> December 3, ninth year [of the Republic]

---

2. I.e., the document of October 5–6, 1920, which appears in Volume I of this edition, pp. 565–71.

Report on the Affairs of the New People's Study Society (No. 1)

(Winter of 1920)

Winter Issue of the Ninth Year of the Republic

(I)

The report on the affairs of the New People's Study Society is the history of its life. The New People's Study Society is a living organism; its members are its cells. The New People's Study Society has already been alive for three years now. Its membership has grown from about a dozen to over fifty people. Its members have spread out from its birthplace to many other locations, both at home and abroad. Its activities have also increased from just one to several. Although for most of the members this is a time of life for pursuing their studies and nurturing their abilities, this is also a very precious time. These three years have brought a new environment for the Society and a new life for its members. The most meaningful thing for the dozens of us is that, whether in groups or alone, we have led, in this new environment, a life different from that before. The function of this first report on the affairs of the Society is to relate selected important parts of the life of the Society and its members, as the opening section in the complete history of the Society and its members.

(II)

The New People's Study Society was launched in the winter of the sixth year of the Republic. Its birthplace was Changsha. All its founders were students who had graduated from, or were still studying in, the schools of Changsha. They all shared a common ideal at that time, namely: "To improve the life of the individual and of the whole human race." Consequently, "How can we improve the life of the individual and of the whole human race?" became a question which was urgently discussed. At that time, they were especially aware of the problem of "improving individual life," and above all of the problem of "improving one's own life." Generally speaking, there were about fifteen people who participated in discussions of such questions. Whenever they met they held discussions, and their discussions always touched on questions like these. The atmosphere of

---

This report was originally published as a separate pamphlet in 1920. Our source is the version in *Xinmin xuehui ziliao*, pp. 1–14, which incorporates some manuscript corrections on the copy available to the editors; this text is reproduced in *Mao Zedong ji. Bujuan*, Vol. 1, pp. 299–315.

these discussions was extremely intimate, and in all there were probably more than a hundred of them. The discussion of questions such as these goes back as far as the fourth and fifth years of the Republic. In the winter of the sixth year of the Republic, the conclusion was reached that we must "gather together comrades, and create a new environment, for the sake of common activities." It was at this point that a motion was put forward to organize a Study Society, and was immediately approved by all. At that time, the intention of the initiators was very simple. They just felt that they wanted to improve their own personal qualities and to progress in their studies, and hence were extremely enthusiastic about seeking friends and mutual aid. That was indeed the first basic reason for the establishment of the Society. Also, at that time the new thought and new literature had already sprung up in the country, and we all felt that in our minds the old thought, the old ethics, and the old literature had been totally swept away. We came to a sudden realization that it was all wrong to lead a quiet and solitary life, and that on the contrary it was necessary to seek an active and collective life. This was also one of the reasons for launching the Society. Yet another reason was that most of us were Mr. Yang Huaizhong's[1] students. Listening to Mr. Yang Huaizhong's presentations, we formed a view of life that emphasizes continual striving and improvement. From this, the New People's Study Society was born.

(III)

Now let us give an account of the first meeting of the New People's Study Society, i.e., its inaugural meeting. The New People's Study Society was founded on April 17, in the seventh year of the Republic, at a meeting in the home of Cai Hesen, situated in Liujia Taizi on Mount Yuelu, across the river from the provincial capital of Hunan. The following people attended the meeting: Cai Hesen, Xiao Zisheng, Xiao Zizhang, Chen Zanzhou, Luo Zhanglong, Mao Runzhi, Zou Dingcheng, Zhang Zhipu,[2] Zhou Xiaosan,[3] Chen Qimin, Ye Zhaozhen,[4] and Luo Yunxi. The statutes of the Society were adopted. Dingcheng and Runzhi had drafted the statutes, of which the provisions were rather detailed. Zisheng opposed the inclusion of articles relating to activities not to be carried out at present, and suggested they be deleted. After discussion, the majority favored Zisheng's opinion. The articles of the statutes passed by the meeting are as follows:

---

1. Yang Changji, Mao's ethics teacher at First Normal School. Regarding Yang and his profound influence on the young Mao, see Volume I of this edition, *passim*.

2. Zhang Zhipu is Zhang Kundi. See the note to his record of two talks with Mao dated September 1917, in Volume I of this edition, pp. 137–40.

3. Zhou Xiaosan was an alternative name for Zhou Mingdi. See the note to the *Evening School Journal*, November 1917, in Volume I of this edition, p. 151.

4. Ye Zhaozhen (1893–1918), *zi* Ruiling, was a native of Yiyang in Hunan Province. He was a student at Hunan First Normal School and a teacher of Chinese at the Workers' Evening School in 1917. On his death, see below, par. V.

Article 1: The name of this society shall be the New People's Study Society.

Article 2: The main goals of the Society are to reform academic studies, to temper the character of its members, and to ameliorate the human heart and customs.

Article 3: Anyone who is recommended by five or more members of the Society, and wins the approval of more than half of the total membership, can become a member.

Article 4: All members must abide by the following rules:

1. Do not be hypocritical;
2. Do not be lazy;
3. Do not be wasteful;
4. Do not gamble;
5. Do not consort with prostitutes.

Article 5: Every member is obligated to write at least once a year to the Society to report on what he has been doing, as well as on conditions in his locality and on the results he has obtained from his research, as a form of mutual aid.

Article 6: There shall be one general secretary, who will be in charge of all the activities of the Society. There will be several executive secretaries who assist the general secretary in managing the affairs of the Society. The term shall be three years, and they shall be elected by the members.

Article 7: The Society shall hold an annual meeting every autumn. Ad hoc meetings may be called when necessary.

Article 8: Each member shall pay one silver *yuan* admission fee on being admitted to the Society. Annual membership dues shall be one silver *yuan*. Should there be unusual expenses, a general vote shall be required to collect special contributions.

Article 9: The Society is located in Changsha.

Article 10: Should a member engage in improper behavior or willfully violate these statutes, he may be expelled from the Society after a majority vote against him.

Article 11: When anything in these statutes is found inappropriate, they may be revised by a majority vote of the members.

After voting to pass the statutes, the members elected Zisheng as General Secretary. The members had lunch together. After lunch, they discussed various procedural questions concerning members going to other provinces or going abroad. The meeting came to a close in the afternoon. The weather was bright and clear. Gentle breezes caressed the azure waters of the river and the emerald grass along its banks. This left an indelible impression on all those who attended the meeting.

(IV)

In the four months from the founding of the Study Society on April 17 of the seventh year of the Republic to August of the same year, there were two events that are worth recording. First, there was the admission of new members. After the inaugural meeting, the following nine people in succession joined the Society: Zhou Dunyuan, He Shuheng,[5] Li Hesheng, Zou Pangeng, Xiong Jinding,[6] Xiong Kunfu,[7] Chen Zhangfu,[8] Fu Changyu,[9] Zeng Xinghuang.[10] Secondly, there was the launching of a movement to study in France. People had tried to launch one before, but without success. This time, the first two initiators in Changsha were Cai Hesen and Xiao Zisheng. Zisheng was teaching at Chuyi, and Hesen was living at Chuyi.[11] They talked it over every day. He Shuheng, Mao Runzhi, and Chen Zanzhou participated frequently in the discussions as well. Several other members of the Society were also planning to go abroad, so at the end of June, a meeting was held at the residence of Chen Zanzhou and Xiao Zizhang at the primary school attached to First Normal School (Chen and Xiao being teachers there). Those who had planned to participate were: He Shuheng, Xiao Zisheng, Xiao Zizhang, Chen Zanzhou, Zhou Dunyuan, Cai Hesen, Mao Runzhi, Zou Dingcheng, Zhang Zhipu, Chen Qimin, Li Hesheng, and others. A few of these were absent because of other engagements. This discussion focused on one point, "members going abroad." It was considered essential to have a movement to study in France and to make every effort to promote it. Then they had a meal together. From then on, Hesen and Zisheng assumed responsibility for making arrangements relating to study in France. Hesen left for Beijing shortly after.

The political situation in Hunan was extremely chaotic at that time. Tang Xiangming, Liu Renxi,[12] Tan Yankai, Fu Liangzuo, Tan Haoming,[13] and Zhang

5. He Shuheng (1870–1935) was a native of Hunan. In 1917 he was one of Mao's teachers in the Training Department of the First Normal School. He was the oldest of the thirteen founding members of the New People's Study Society in 1918 and was also involved with Mao in the Cultural Book Society. He was chosen, together with Mao, from the Hunan Marxist group to attend the First Congress of the Chinese Communist Party in Shanghai in July 1921.

6. Xiong Chuxiong (1886–1973), alternative name Jinding, was a native of Changsha. A graduate of First Normal School, he went on to become an elementary school teacher. He was a contributor to the Cultural Book Society and editor of the Education Association's journal Tongsu bao (Popular Newspaper).

7. Xiong Guangchu. For details see the note to Mao's letter of August 1915 to Xiao Zisheng in Volume I of this edition, p. 74.

8. Chen Chang (1894–1930), alternative name Zhangfu, was born in Liuyang, Hunan Province. He was a graduate of First Normal School and later a student of the Self-Study University. For a time he was head of the Shuikoushan Workers' Union.

9. Fu Changyu (1896–), alternative name Haitao, was a native of Liuyang, Hunan Province, and had studied at the Tokyo Institute of Technology.

10. Zeng Yilu. For details see the note to the Evening School Journal, November 1917, in Volume I of this edition, p. 151.

11. Chuyi refers to the Chuyi Primary School in Changsha. Both the Strengthen Learning Society and the Cultural Book Society had been founded there. See Volume I, pp. 373, 583.

12. Liu Renxi was interim governor of Hunan July–August 1916 after Tang Xiangming was ousted. For more detail see note 14 to Mao's letter of July 18, 1916, to Xiao Zisheng, in Volume I of this edition, p. 97.

13. Tan Haoming was the commander-in-chief of the Hunan-Guangxi-Guangdong Army responsible for driving out Fu Liangzuo in November 1917. Tan was military governor of Hunan until March 1918.

Jingyao took turns in power. Education was completely ruined, to the point that there were almost no schools to go to. When Hesen arrived in Beijing, he learned from contacts with Messrs. Li Shizeng and Cai Jiemin[14] that the prospects for a study program or a work-study program in France were rather good. He thereupon wrote to Zisheng, Runzhi, Zanzhou, Dingcheng,[15] and others, telling them to go ahead and gather together comrades wishing to study in France. At the outset, very few wanted to go. It was not until August 19 that twenty-five people arrived in Beijing from Hunan. After that, the number gradually increased. Members who went north were: Hesen, Zisheng, Zizhang, Zanzhou, Kunfu, Zhipu, Xinghuang, Dingcheng, Hesheng, Yunxi, Runzhi, and Zhanglong—twelve in all. Except for Zhanglong, who was in the humanities at Beijing University, and Runzhi, who was in the library there, all the rest joined the preparatory class for studying in France. (Zhipu, Hesheng, and Xinghuang were in the Baoding section; Hesen was in the Bulicun section; Zisheng, Zizhang, Zanzhou, Kunfu, Dingcheng, and Yunxi were in the Beijing section.)[16] When we first planned this, we did not foresee all the difficulties that subsequently arose. With all eyes fixed on the happy land ahead, and spurred on by our impulses and by the oppressive environment, all of us forged ahead courageously. No matter what the outcome, this undertaking was bound to produce some positive results. Although in the midst of it members were assailed by numerous unexpected attacks and difficulties, in the end not a single one was disheartened.

---

14. Li Shizeng (1881–1973), original name Yuying, a native of Hebei, and Cai Yuanpei (1868–1940), *zi* Heqing, *hao* Jiemin, a native of Zhejiang, Chancellor of Peking University from 1916 to 1926, had joined in founding the Sino-French Educational Society in 1916. They were both engaged in 1920 in promoting the work-study program under which many Hunan students, including Cai Hesen, subsequently went to France.

15. For convenience, a list of the full names of people whose courtesy names (*zi*) or other names are used throughout this text follows: Boling is Zhang Huai; Chiyu is Luo Zonghan; Dingcheng is Zou Yiding; Dunxiang is Zhou Dunxiang; Dunyuan is Zhou Shizhao; Hesen is Cai Hesen; Hesheng is Li Weihan; Jixu is Jiang Zhuru; Junzhan is Lao Junzhan; Kunfu is Xiong Guangchu; Qimin is Chen Qimin; Qinwen is Li Si'an; Runzhi is Mao Zedong; Shuheng is He Shuheng; Siyong is Tao Yi; Wangcheng is Liu Mingyan; Wenfu is Tang Yaozhang; Xinghuang is Zeng Yilu; Yinbo is Peng Huang; Yunchan is Wei Bi; Yunxi is Luo Xuezan; Yusheng is Ouyang Ze; Zanzhou is Chen Zanzhou; Zhipu is Zhang Kundi; Zhunru is Zhou Dunxiang; Zisheng is Xiao Zisheng; Zizhang is Xiao Zizhang.

16. The preparatory classes for study in France organized by Mao Zedong, Cai Hesen and others in the autumn of 1918 were divided into three sections. One of these was located in Beijing, another in Baoding (approximately 80 miles southwest of the capital), and the third in the village of Bulicun, in Li *xian*, just south of Baoding. The elementary section, located in Bulicun, had less stringent entrance requirements than the other two. Cai Hesen had spent some time there initially serving as a teacher, as well as studying French. For a brief account, see Li Jui [Rui], *The Early Revolutionary Activities of Comrade Mao Tse-tung* (M. E. Sharpe: White Plains, 1977), pp. 90–91. (Hereafter Li Jui, *Early Mao*.) A fuller discussion can be found in the third Chinese edition of his book, Li Rui, *Zaonian Mao Zedong* (Shenyang: Liaoning renmin chubanshe, 1991), p. 181.

While the members were in Beijing, they invited Messrs. Cai Jiemin, Tao Menghe, and Hu Shizhi[17] each to talk to them on one occasion. All the meetings were held in the humanities building at Beijing University. The form of these talks was that the members raised questions and asked them to respond. The questions raised were mostly about scholarship and about the philosophy of life.

In the beginning, members lived separately in Beijing. Later they all lived together in one place, at 7 Sanyanjing Lane, Houmennei. Those who lived there together were: Zisheng, Yunxi, Zanzhou, Runzhi, Kunfu, Zhanglong, Yushan (Ouyang Yushan joined the Society one year later); Hesen moved in, too, from Bulicun. The eight of them huddled together in three very small rooms, sharing huge blankets on high *kangs*.[18] Zizhang and Wangcheng (Liu Wangcheng joined the Society one year later) lived at no. 8 of the same lane. Zisheng left for France in January of the eighth year of the Republic. In February, Runzhi went back to Hunan and Xiao Zizhang left for Shanghai. Zanzhou and others had to change their living quarters because their French class was moved from the Beijing University science department in the Mashen Temple to the Yijiao Temple French Building in the western district of the city. Zhanglong moved to another place, too. Thus the communal life in Sanyanjing Lane came to an end. Zanzhou and those who studied in the western district moved to the rear wing of Fuyou Temple, 99 Beichang Street, where they had a new communal life. At this time, Zizhang had already returned from Shanghai, so the number of people living together was still eight, the only difference as compared to Sanyanjing Lane being the absence of Runzhi, Zhanglong, and Zisheng. At the same time in Baoding, Zhipu, Hesheng, and Xinghuang were living together at the Yude Middle School with some forty other people who were preparing to study in France. After the preparation period was completed, the members of the Society in Beijing and Baoding left successively for France.

---

17. Tao Menghe (1887–1960), *zi* Lügong, a native of Tianjin, had graduated in sociology from the University of London. At this time, he was a professor at Beijing University. Hu Shi (1891–1962), *zi* Shizhi, a native of Anhui, had taken a Ph.D. at Columbia under John Dewey, and was likewise a professor at Beijing University. Regarding his considerable influence on Mao during the May Fourth period, see Volume I, especially the statutes of the Problem Study Society, pp. 407–13, and Mao's letter to him, p. 531. After Mao became a Communist, he was increasingly critical of Hu, but as late as 1923 he characterized Hu as the leader of "the faction of the rising intellectual class." See below, "The Foreign Powers, the Warlords, and the Revolution," April 10, 1923.

18. A *kang* is a flat brick oven on which people commonly slept in North China in order to keep warm. In recounting his life at this time to Edgar Snow, Mao recalled, "When we were all packed fast on the *kang*, there was scarcely room enough for any of us to breathe. I used to have to warn people on each side of me when I wanted to turn over" (Snow, *Red Star over China* [London: Gollancz, 1937], p. 149).

(V)

Here we must record two most unfortunate events: the death of member Ye Ruiling in July of the seventh year of the Republic, and the death of member Zou Dingcheng in April of the eighth year of the Republic.

Mr. Ye's name was Zhaozhen. Born in Yiyang, he graduated from Hunan First Provincial Normal School. He was a peaceful and righteous man and a highly motivated student. On his way home after graduation, he suffered heat stroke and died immediately after arriving.

Mr. Zou, named Yiding, was born in Xiangyin and was in the same class as Mr. Ye. He was eager to study and had high aspirations; he was also a self-disciplined man of strong character. He went to Beijing in October of the seventh year of the Republic to attend the preparatory class for study in France. He had become ill as a result of years of overwork, and his health deteriorated further at that time. He went back to Hunan in January of the eighth year of the Republic and finally died in April. He left several dozen notebooks containing his diaries and essays. His friends wish to publish the best of these, but nothing has appeared in print as yet. There is probably no one who came into contact with him who did not consider him a person worthy of respect and love. He had a fiancée whom he greatly loved. He wrote her a letter immediately before his death, but unfortunately no third person has read it, so his last words cannot be preserved. He was one of the important founders of the Society. At the time the Society was founded, he considered it as indispensable and never wavered in the slightest. He had very great hopes for the Society. He never expected that he himself would unfortunately die a premature death. Everyone who had ever met him or spent some time with him knows that he followed the good effortlessly; that he mended his mistakes unhesitatingly; that he never kept anything back; that he loved his neighbor as himself; that he was frank and straightforward, courageous, and sincere; that he was eager to learn; and that he had a passion for moral justice.

(VI)

In the eighth year of the Republic, the main activities of the Society and its members in Changsha were as follows:

The first half year was rather uneventful. Dunyuan taught at Xiuye; Shuheng taught at Chuyi. Runzhi ran the weekly organ of the United Students' Association, the *Xiang River Review*, and had quite a bit of success.[19] The second half

---

19. This newspaper, which Mao edited in July–August 1919, did indeed enjoy a considerable measure of success. For Mao's own contributions to the issues now extant, see Volume I, pp. 318–68 and 377–95.

year saw the following people join the Society: Luo Chiyu (Zonghan), Zhang Yisheng (Guoji), Xia Manbo (Xi),[20] Jiang Jixu (Zhuru), Yi Yuehui (Kexun),[21] Xiang Jingyu, Tao Siyong (Yi),[22] Peng Yinbo (Huang), Li Chengde (Zhenpian), Zhang Boling (Huai), Tang Wenfu (Yaozhang),[23] Shen Junyi (Jun),[24] Li Qinwen (Si'an), Zhou Dunxiang,[25] Wei Yunchan (Bi), Lao Junzhan (Qirong), Xie Weixin (Nanling),[26] Xu Ying,[27] Liu Jizhuang (Xiuzhi),[28] Zhong Chusheng (Guotao), Zhang Quanshan (Chao),[29] Jiang Zhulin (Huiyu).[30] A meeting was held at Zhounan Girls' School, which began with a proposal from the Changsha members that the statutes be amended on the grounds that they were too sketchy. They moved a resolution establishing two departments, "Deliberative" and "Executive," and further providing, under the Executive Department, for subdepartments of "Schools," "Editorial Work," "Women," and "Study Abroad."

From that time on, the Changsha members began to use the new statutes. They elected Shuheng and Qinwen[31] as chairman and deputy chairman of the Executive Committee, and Siyong, Dunyuan, Runzhi, Dunxiang, Yunchang, Qimin, Wenfu,

---

20. Xia Xi (1902–1936), *zi* Manbo, born in Yiyang, Hunan Province, studied at the First Normal School and was an early member of the New People's Study Society. In 1920 he helped found both the Russia Studies Society and the Hunan branch of the Socialist Youth League, and in the fall of the following year he joined the Chinese Communist Party. In January 1922, he was a delegate to the Congress of Communist and Revolutionary Organizations of the Far East in Moscow. Regarding Xia Xi's later activities, see the note to the text of January 29, 1924.

21. Yi Yuehui (1899–1950[?]), besides using the name Kexun, was also known as Yuewei. A native of Changsha, he was a graduate of First Normal School and one of the founders of the Xupu Cultural Book Society. He was executed as a counter-revolutionary after 1949.

22. Tao Yi (1896–1930), *zi* Siyong, a native of Xiangtan, Hunan Province, was Mao's first sweetheart. She was active in the Hunan self-government movement and helped Mao organize the Cultural Book Society. She and Mao later drifted apart, and in the winter of 1920–1921 he married Yang Kaihui. Though at the January 1921 meeting of the New People's Study Society, of which the record is translated below, Tao voted in favor of Bolshevism as the answer to China's problems, she subsequently rejected communism.

23. Tang Yaozhang (1900–1973), also known as Tang Wenfu, was a native of Changsha and a student of Mingde Middle School.

24. Shen Junyi, also known as Shen Jun, was a native of Changsha. He studied at the Mingde University at Hankou from September 1920.

25. Zhou Dunxiang (1898–1980), alternative name Zhunru, a native of Changsha, had studied at Zhounan Girls' School. In 1921 she went to teach in Singapore.

26. Xie Nanling (1901–1928), also known as Weixin, was a native of Ningxiang, Hunan Province, and a graduate of First Normal.

27. Xu Ying, also born in Ningxiang, was one of the earliest female members.

28. Liu Xiuzhi (1895–), alternative name Jizhuang, a native of Xiangtan, Hunan Province, was a graduate of First Normal School.

29. For details on Zhang Chao, see note 11 to the *Evening School Journal* of November 1917, in Volume I of this edition, p. 151.

30. Jiang Huiyu (1899–1925), alternative names Zhulin and Ruiyu, a native of Ningxiang, Hunan Province, was a graduate of First Normal.

31. I.e., He Shuheng and Li Si'an.

and Jixu as members of the Deliberative Department. Immediately after the meeting, however, the movement to expel Zhang began, many members left the city, and the activities of the Society stopped for a full year. Although the statutes had been amended and people elected to office, this was nothing but an empty formality. Members in Paris were rather critical of the actions taken in Changsha. At that time, Runzhi, Chiyu, Zanzhou, Boling, and others established a People's News Agency in Beijing, devoted wholly to the purpose of expelling Zhang. Prior to going abroad in summer, Cai Hesen founded a "Hunan Artistic Embroidery Company" in Changsha, but it is not easy to set such a thing up all at once, and nothing concrete has come of it yet. Three people joined the Society at this time: Liu Wangcheng (Mingyan), Ouyang Yusheng (Ze), and Yang Runyu.

(VII)

In the spring and summer of the ninth year of the Republic, Mao Runzhi, Li Qinwen, and others left Beijing for Shanghai because of the Hunan problem;[32] Zanzhou, Kunfu, Zizhang, Wangcheng, Yusheng, and Boling arrived one after the other in Shanghai from Beijing, Tianjin, and Changsha to wait for the ship to France. Yunchang, Junzhan, and Zhunru left Hunan for Shanghai to practice French and to get ready to go to France. There were twelve members in Shanghai at that time. Because Zanzhou and four others were soon to leave for France, a farewell meeting was held at Bansong Park in Shanghai on May 8. All members in Shanghai attended. The discussions were very long; the main points are summarized below.

1. The attitude of the Society:
Be low-key and realistic. Do not strive for vain glory or seek to cut a figure. Runzhi proposed that the Society as such should not do too many things, but that its members as individuals should create all kinds of things in many different areas.
2. Scholarly research:
All participants felt that members engaged in too little in-depth research. They advocated that from now on, whenever three or more members get together, meetings for scholarly discussion be organized so as to exchange knowledge and to create an atmosphere of love for learning.
3. Publishing a Society newsletter:
Zanzhou and Zizhang both said that if members are to have an instrument for maintaining contact and communication with one another, a newsletter is extremely important. They suggested that it be published as soon as possible. It

---

32. The "Hunan problem" referred to is the struggle to drive out Governor Zhang Jingyao, in which Mao and his friends played a prominent role. On this campaign, which culminated when Zhang fled the province in mid-June 1920, see the extensive documentation in Volume I of this edition.

would not, however, be for sale and would be sent to no one outside the Society save teachers and close friends. This won universal approval. It was tentatively decided that it should be published in Shanghai; Zanzhou was chosen to take responsibility for collecting articles from members in France, and Runzhi to be responsible for its printing in Shanghai. Then, however, members went back to Hunan, because the situation in Hunan had been resolved, and publication was consequently suspended.

4. Admission of new members:

Everyone felt that from now on, it is advisable to be more cautious in introducing new members. Otherwise it will be disadvantageous not only to the existing members, but to new members. It was resolved that there should be four requirements for new members: (1) purity, (2) sincerity, (3) willingness to strive, and (4) obeying the truth. (Changsha members later merged "willingness to strive" and "obeying the truth" into "striving for improvement.") The procedures for becoming a member of the Society are as follows: (1) recommendation by five existing members; (2) examination and approval by the Deliberative Department; (3) an official letter to all members informing them of its decision, to see whether anyone objects.

5. The attitude of members:

Generally speaking, members should be truthful with each other. They should be frank and correct each other's mistakes. They should not be indifferent to fellow members' mistakes and sufferings, or ignore them. They should listen with open minds to the exhortations of others. They should study hard.

6. No branch Societies should be established:

In the past, the Society had considered setting up branch Societies in places where there was a fairly large number of members. In the discussions held that day, members felt that it was not necessary to establish branch Societies, and that doing so would have the negative effect of dissipating the unified strength of the whole body of members. In places such as Paris, where there is a relatively large number of members, academic symposia may be organized on a regular basis.

On this occasion, the farewell party had turned into a regular discussion meeting. Night fell, so we continued by lamplight. And yet everyone felt he had not said all he wanted to say. At noon, we took pictures in the rain. Nearby, we could look upon the Song River. The green grass and emerald waters extended as far as we could see.

(VIII)

Six people left Shanghai for France on May 11, in the ninth year of the Republic: Zanzhou, Zizhang, Kunfu, Wangcheng, Boling, and Yusheng. The members in Shanghai shook hands and waved kerchiefs to bid them farewell from the banks of the Huangpu River.

Zhang Jingyao was still occupying Hunan at that time. Members founded two organizations, the "Association for Promoting Reform in Hunan," to work out plans to reform Hunan after the expulsion of Zhang, and the "Self-study Society," to make it possible for comrades to study together. Both were located in Minhou Lane, Shanghai. Zhang Jingyao was expelled by the Hunan Army in June. Members who had fled to Beijing, Shanghai, Hengyang, and Yongzhou gradually returned to [the capital of] Hunan. The following is a list of what the Changsha members were doing as of the winter of this year.

Chen Qimin—teaching at Zhounan [women's school]
Tao Siyong—working at Zhounan
Zhong Chusheng—teaching at Zhounan
He Shuheng—working in the Editorial Department of Popular Books and Papers
Zhou Dunyuan—working as an editor at the *Popular Newspaper*
Xiong Jinding—working in the Editorial Department of Popular Books and Papers
Mao Runzhi—working at the primary school attached to First Normal School[33]
Zhang Quanshan—teaching at the primary school attached to First Normal School
Liu Jizhuang—teaching at the primary school attached to First Normal School
Jiang Jixu—studying at First Normal School
Yi Yuehui—same as the above
Xia Manbo—same as the above
Jiang Zhulin—same as the above
Xie Weixin—same as the above
Li Chengde—studying full-time at Hunan-Yale Medical School
Tang Wenfu—studying at Mingde Middle School
Zou Pangeng[34]—teaching at Xiuye
Peng Yinbo—engaging in self-study at the Cultural Book Society
Yi Lirong—working at the Cultural Book Society
Ren Peidao—working at the Cultural Book Society.

At present, Changsha members are working on the following concrete projects: Jiang Jixu, Yi Yuehui, Xia Manbo, and others are working hard on reforming the First Normal School; He Shuheng, Zhou Dunyuan, Xiong Jinding, and others are working hard on popular education and on running the *Popular Newspaper,* which has an excellent content; Chen Qimin, Tao Siyong, Zhong Chusheng, and others are working hard to reform the Zhounan Women's School.

At present, members of the Society in Changsha are devoting their efforts on the one hand to establishing the Cultural Book Society and on the other to

---

33. As indicated above in his letter of December 3, 1920, Mao was at this time principal of the primary school attached to First Normal School.

34. Zou Yunzhen (1894–1985), alternative names Panqin, Panqing, and Pangeng, graduated from First Normal, and was involved in the foundation of the Self-Study University.

launching the autonomy movement. Both enterprises have received moral support from comrades everywhere. During the same period, the Society has accepted
five new members. They are: Cai Xianxi (Chang), Xiong Zuoying (Jiguang), Xiong
Zuolin (Shubin), Ren Zhenyu (Peidao), and Wu Dezhuang (Jiaying).[35]

(IX)

In the previous pages we have briefly related the circumstances of members
in Beijing, Shanghai, and Changsha. Now we shall give an account of members
in France.[36]

In all, eighteen members have gone to France: first Xiao Zisheng, who went
to France in the spring of the eighth year; then Luo Rongxi, Zhang Zhipu, Li
Hesheng, and Zeng Xinghuang, who went to France in the autumn of the
same year; then Cai Hesen, Cai Xianxi, Xiang Jingyu, Xiong Zuoying, and
Xiong Zuolin, who went to France in the spring of the ninth year; next Xiao
Zizhang, Chen Zanzhou, Xiong Kunfu, Zhang Bailing, Liu Wangcheng, and
Ouyang Yusheng, who went to France that autumn; and then finally Lao
Junzhan and Wei Yunchan, who went in the winter of the ninth year. Except for
Zisheng, who returned to China in October 1920, the location and circumstances
of the remaining seventeen members at the end of 1920 were as follows:

Luo Rongxi—working as an electrician in a factory located in [Le] Creusot in
central France[37]

---

35. All of these new members were female. Xiong Zuoying and Xiong Zuolin were
born in Liuyang, Hunan Province; Wu Dezhuang was a native of Xupu, Hunan. Ren
Peidao (1894–), *zi* Zhenyu, was a native of Xiangyin, Hunan. She was a graduate of
Hunan First Women's Normal School and Beijing Normal University. Cai Chang (1900–
1990), also known as Xianxi, a native of Xiangxiang, Hunan, was the younger sister of Cai
Hesen. She was an active organizer of the Socialist Youth Corps during her stay in France
and joined the Chinese Communist Party in 1923. After 1949, she became one of the most
important women's leaders.

36. Articles regarding the Chinese students in France that provide useful background
to Mao's account include those of Paul Bailey, "The Chinese Work-Study Movement in
France," *The China Quarterly* no. 115, September 1988, pp. 441–61, and Geneviève
Barman and Nicole Dulioust, "La France au miroir chinois," *Les Temps modernes* no. 498,
January 1988, pp. 32–67. Extensive documentation can be found in Zhang Yunhou et al.
(eds.), *Liufa qingong jianxue yundong* (The Work-Study Movement in France), 2 vols.
(Shanghai: Shanghai renmin chubanshe, 1980, 1986). This last source contains, on pp.
222–23, an annotated text of the passage on France translated here, with notes indicating
the correct Chinese transcription of place-names that appear in Mao's report in wrong or
outdated forms, and other tables listing the cities where the Chinese students were located
in late 1921. These materials have been drawn on in preparing the version that appears
below.

37. The reference is to the Schneider engineering works in Le Creusot, between Paris
and Lyon. A number of Chinese students were employed there in 1920–21, including
Deng Xiaoping, for a few weeks in April 1921, and Li Lisan for a longer period.

Zhang Zhipu—working in a factory located in Champagne in northern France[38]

Li Hesheng—moved from the western suburbs of Paris to stay with Zhang Zhipu during his convalesence

Zeng Xinghuang—working in a factory located in southwest France

Cai Hesen—learning French in a boys' school in Montargis, France

Cai Xianxi—learning French in a girls' school in Montargis, France

Xiang Jingyu—same as the above

Xiong Jiguang—same as the above

Xiong Shubin—same as the above

Xiao Zizhang—lived at Colombe in the western suburbs of Paris;[39] later moved to [Le] Creusot to live with Luo Rongxi

Chen Zanzhou—employed as an unskilled worker in a factory in a place called Firminy in France[40]

Xiong Kunfu—studying French at a school in St. Maixent in northwestern France[41]

Zhang Bailing—studying French at a school in Tours, France

Liu Wangcheng—studying French at Fontainebleau School in France

Ouyang Yusheng—studying French at a school in St. Maixent in northwestern France

Lao Junzhan—just arrived in France and entered a girls' school in southern France to study French

Wei Yunchan—same as the above.

(X)

The circumstances of those members who have gone to Southeast Asia, Japan, and other parts of China are as follows:

In Beijing:

Luo Zhanglong—entered the Humanities Department of Beijing University in September of the seventh year. He has been there for two and a half years now

Luo Chiyu—beginning in April of the ninth year, he ran the People's News Agency all by himself.[42] At the end of the year, he wrapped up the affairs of the News Agency and returned to Hunan via Nanjing.

---

38. The reference is presumably to the Scheider electrical works in Champagne-sur-Seine, between Paris and Melun.

39. La Garenne-Colombe is a working-class suburb northwest of Paris.

40. Firminy, near St. Etienne, was the location of another large engineering factory.

41. Saint Maixent is located some 200 miles west of Paris, between Poitiers and La Rochelle.

42. On the People's News Agency (*Pingmin tongxinshe*), which had been set up in Beijing by Mao and others at the end of 1919 in the context of the struggle against Zhang Jingyao, see the materials in Volume I, especially pp. 457-59, 469-71, and 496-97.

In Hankou:

Shen Junyi—entered Mingde University in September of the ninth Year.

In Nanjing:

Zhou Zhunru—studying in the Extension Department of Nanjing Higher Normal School. When Nangao introduced the coeducational system, Zhou entered through the Shanghai YWCA.

In Shanghai:

Yang Runyu—studying English at the YWCA on Kunshan Road; went to Shanghai from Changsha to study in July of the ninth year.

In Japan:

Fu Changyu—at Tokyo Higher Technical School. Left Changsha for Japan in the sixth year and entered the School in the seventh year

Zhou Xiaosan—at Tokyo Teachers' College. Left Changsha for Japan in the seventh Year and entered the college in the eighth year.

In Southeast Asia:

Zhang Yisheng—teaching at Daonan School and Overseas Chinese Middle School in Singapore. Left Changsha for Singapore in February of the ninth year.

Li Qinwen—teaching at Kuncheng Girls' School in Singapore. Left Changsha for Singapore in August of the ninth year.[43]

(XI)

We have roughly covered the "concrete" circumstances of the Society for the three years from its establishment in the seventh year to the end of the ninth year. There are also some "abstract" circumstances, which will be dealt with here.

Our Society has many strong points; nevertheless, it also has some shortcomings. What are the strong points? We have several unwritten articles of belief, such as "Do not show off," "Do not seek publicity," "Do not seek instant results," and "Do not rely upon the old authorities."

These articles of belief, being unwritten, exist only in our mutual relationships and discussions and have never been spelled out.

Because we "do not show off," most members do not flatter each other when they meet; because "the words must correspond to the meaning," self-criticism and encouragement always outweigh pleasantries and self-congratulation. Because we "do not seek publicity," even though our Society has been in existence for three years, its name is not yet known in society, except to a very few friends

---

43. The Chinese text in the *Bujuan* reads "eighth month of the ninth month" (*jiu yue ba yue*); this is an obvious misprint.

we know well. Because we "do not seek instant results," members have the sense that whether they study or work, we are only "laying a foundation," and the results lie in the future. If we want to achieve much and be successful in the future, we need to lay a large and solid foundation. Because we "do not rely upon the old authorities," members all feel that our Society is creative, not imitative. The contributions of the various members of this Society in many different domains, both now and in the future, will also be creative, and not imitative. It is for this reason that our Society has never established any ties with the old authorities and has never invited people from the old authorities to join our Society. Furthermore, members of our Society have several other virtues. First of all, we have fresh minds. Most members do not have old-fashioned ideas and are able to accept the new thought. Secondly, we are full of fighting spirit. Most members are able to fight, too. On the positive side, we can unite good people to achieve worthy ends; on the negative side, we reject evil people and eliminate evil things. The fighting spirit of the members is everywhere manifest, in reforming life styles, pursuing knowledge, and promoting progress outside. Thirdly, we have a spirit of mutual aid and self-sacrifice. Members are usually able to help each other and have a spirit of sacrifice.

For all its various strong points, mentioned above, the Society also has many shortcomings. First, our scholarship is weak and superficial. Most of the members are middle-school graduates, or are still studying in middle schools. Very few have gone on to study at specialized schools, or those at a higher level, or have graduated from such schools, so their level of scholarship is naturally very superficial. Second, there is childishness both in thought and in behavior. As a whole, the thinking of our members is inevitably somewhat immature. Some members are apt to launch or support causes rashly, thus falling into childishness. Third, some members are working more than they are studying. It is not time yet for members to devote all of their efforts to work. Both our plans and the requirements of the real situation dictate that at present we work toward laying a relatively solid foundation. The present situation is, however, that some members are working full time, and the resulting sacrifice is inevitably too great. Fourth, there is a lack of close contact and understanding among some of the members. This goes against the spirit of the Society. From now on, we cannot be satisfied unless ways can be found to enable members to move from not knowing each other and not understanding each other very well to both knowing and understanding each other.

————————————————————————————

Letter to Cai Hesen

(January 21, 1921)

Dear Elder Brother Hesen:

Your letter was forwarded to me by Zisheng[1] only at the end of last year. The materialist conception of history is the philosophical basis of our Party. It is all facts, and is not like rationalism, which cannot be substantiated and is easily undermined. I had not studied this question previously, but there are substantial reasons for my present refusal to recognize that the principles of anarchism can be verified. The political organization of a factory (the arrangement, management, etc. of production in the factory) differs only in size, not in nature, from that of a nation or of the world. Syndicalism regards the political organization of a nation as qualitatively different from the political organization of a factory; it claims this is a different matter, which should be handed over to a different kind of people. This is either a deliberate attempt to make lame excuses for being resigned to circumstances, or evidence of stupidity and lack of common sense. Furthermore, there is an extremely important argument [against this view] in terms of method: without achieving political power, it is impossible to launch, maintain, and carry through the revolution! The view put forward in this letter of yours[2] is entirely appropriate, there is not a single word with which I disagree. As far as the Party is concerned, Mr. Chen Zhongfu and others have already started organizing it. In the matter of publications, I expect *The Communist*,[3] published in Shanghai, is available to you there [in France]. It really merits the

---

This letter was first published in January 1921 in Vol. 3 of the *Xinmin xuehui huiyuan tongxinji*. Our source is the version in *Xinmin xuehui ziliao*, pp. 162–63, reproduced in *Mao Zedong ji. Bujuan*, Vol. 2, pp. 13–14.

1. Xiao Zisheng.
2. Cai Hesen had asserted that the only solution for China lay in a proletarian dictatorship, exactly like that in Soviet Russia. For the text of his letter, dated September 16, 1920, see *Cai Hesen wenji*, pp. 63–72.
3. *Gongchandang*, literally "The Communist Party," but more commonly rendered as "The Communist."

description "to take a clear-cut stand" (Zhongfu was the author of the Manifesto).[4] I'll write you in more detail later.

Your younger brother Zedong
January 21, tenth year, in the southern part
of the city

---

4. Zhongfu was the *zi* of Chen Duxiu (1879–1942), original name Chen Qiansheng, *hao* Shi'an, who had been the prime mover in the foundation of the first Communist Group in Shanghai in August 1920. (For more details regarding Chen, see, in Volume I, pp. 325–30, Mao's article of July 14, 1919, "The Arrest and Rescue of Chen Duxiu," especially note 1, p. 325.) The Shanghai group had prepared a "Manifesto of the Chinese Communist Party" in November 1920, calling for the abolition of the state and the creation of a new Communist society. "The whole world," it declared, "can be viewed as a single capitalist institution. Therefore class struggle in one country can have repercussions in others." For the full text, see Tony Saich, *The Rise to Power of the Chinese Communist Party: Documents and Analysis, 1920–1949* (hereafter Saich, *Rise to Power*), Doc. A.2, pp. 11–13.

Letter to Peng Huang[1]

(January 28, 1921)

Elder Brother Yinbo,

Thank you very much for your letter, and for the pass![2] There is more to say about the topic of how to treat people, which we discussed the other day. As I think you know very well, I, your Younger Brother, am unwilling to work together with evil persons. At the same time, I do not allow myself to hate evil like an enemy. First of all, an evil person does not consider himself evil; second, our detestation of him may be not without bias; third, evil may in the last analysis turn out not to be evil; fourth, every person has both strengths and weaknesses, both bad and good points with regard to his talents and disposition, and we must not seize only on one aspect and ignore the other. You, Elder Brother, have also often mentioned the last two points. The first point is an objective matter, while the second is a subjective matter. Neither should be neglected in observing people. In the past two and a half years virtually all the time I have spent in self-cultivation has been wasted. I have gone to extremes in reasoning, I have tended to be overcritical in viewing people, and my attempts at thorough self-examination have been almost completely useless. Today, regardless of how regretful I am, I cannot return to two and a half years ago and start over. I have long been wanting to tell you my humble opinion of you, but never had the chance. Now I would like to give you a word of advice and shall be honored if you would condescend to listen to me. Few of our friends are like you in having lofty aspirations, courage, and physical strength. You also have, however, a number of shortcomings: (1) your way of speaking is lacking in frankness and straightforwardness, and your attitude is lacking in lucidity and decisiveness, showing too much modesty while revealing too little of your true features;

This letter is translated from the text in *Mao Zedong shuxin xuanji*, pp. 17–19, where the text is followed by the indication "based on a manuscript copy." It does not appear to have been published previously.

1. Peng Huang (1896–1921), *zi* Yinbo, was a native of Xiangxiang, Hunan. A close friend of Mao from an early date, he was a student leader in Hunan during the May Fourth movement and helped organize the Cultural Book Society, the Russia Studies Society, and other progressive groups. He had participated in the Bansong Park meeting of the New People's Study Society in May 1920.

2. It has not been possible to determine to what meeting or other guarded premises this may have granted admission.

(2) you are preoccupied with personal emotions and feelings, leaving no room for reason in dealing with problems; (3) you are suspicious at times and yet unwilling to explain things openly; (4) you are subjective rather than objective in your observations and criticisms; (5) you have a slight tendency to refuse to recognize others' merits; (6) you have a bit of vanity; (7) you display a certain arrogance; (8) you rarely conduct a self-examination and are clear in blaming others but unclear about your own weaknesses; (9) you are good at big talk, but weak in systematic analysis; (10) you think too highly of yourself and are too facile in your judgements. I always feel that every person must have his defects; the superior man (*junzi*) can only mend his ways but certainly cannot be innately without faults. My observations regarding your shortcomings may not be appropriate. Anyway, except points (1) and (3) and also point (5) by which I believe I am not much affected all the rest fit me too. We have the desire to save the world, but we have not adequately cultivated and disciplined ourselves. If the trunk is not solidly rooted, how can branches and leaves be luxuriant? Without excellent tools, how can the job be properly done? I have a very great defect, which I feel ashamed to reveal to others: I am weak-willed. You often say that my will is strong, but in fact I have clear self-knowledge: there is nothing weaker than my will! I constantly have the wrong attitude and always argue, so that people detest me. You might call this my strong will, but in fact it is a manifestation of my weakness. I have long since learned that on earth only those who attain complete gentleness can be most firm. I myself, however, am not capable of practicing this truth, so I knowingly violate it and do exactly the opposite without hesitation. How dreadful it is to think of this! What nevertheless gives me a little consolation is that I cherish my ideal sincerely (just to have that ideal) and am responsible for what I say and what I do. I do not want to sacrifice my true self, I do not wish **myself**[3] to turn myself into a puppet. As for how to treat friends, we should deal with affairs in terms of affairs, and personal relationships in terms of personal relationships. Doing things is a matter of principles and laws, while personal friendship is a matter of sentiment. I feel your treatment of Lirong[4] is rather improper, since your intention is not fully sincere, and you are

---

3. Here and elsewhere in this volume words and passages set in bold correspond (unless otherwise specified) to Mao's own emphasis, by placing dots or circles next to the characters. Mao was rather fond of this rhetorical device, which therefore occurs frequently.

4. The reference is to Yi Lirong (1898–), alternative names Runsan, Runsheng, and Yunshan, a native of Xiangtan, Hunan. A close friend of Mao and a member of the New People's Study Society, he was also one of the organizers of the Cultural Book Society and the first manager of the society's store in 1920. In a letter of January 6, 1921, Mao had written to Peng Huang: "I have been rather dissatisfied with [your] attitude toward Lirong during the past month. It is greatly at variance with the broadminded attitude you regularly adopt. . . . Both flattering people to their faces and vilifying them to their faces are entirely unbecoming to human beings." (*Nianpu*, Vol. 1, p. 79.) No further information is available about the substance of the quarrel between Peng and Yi.

more concerned with giving vent to your anger than with kindly helping him. You say that the way to treat me is to resist. What kind of a person am I then in your eyes? For example, if someone invites me to an entertainment, it is perfectly proper for me "not to accept," but what is this talk about "resistance"? As for saying that so-and-so and Lirong should be "subjugated," that is truly, truly excessive! How can any person be subjugated? Subjugation must rely on "force," but force can only be effective when it is based on the law; force does not apply to personal relations, and if used in that area would be absolutely ineffective. Not only that, but reaction would follow. I think we only have arguments about isms, and have no personal arguments. Arguments over isms arise from unavoidable conflicts between them, but the struggle is between isms, and not between private individuals. There are many personal quarrels in this world, but actually **by and large they can be reconciled.** Most of them are caused by the "impulse to dominate" and "affronts to one's will." I would say that the argument between you and Lirong belongs to the latter kind. (I have had similar experiences quite often, and also treat others like this.) It is most difficult to bear an affront to one's will. Once people like us, whose self-cultivation is not yet perfect, encounter such a situation, few can endure it without rising up vehemently. Only those who have "broad vision" and are "great of heart" can bear it. What do you think? It was already twelve o'clock when I came back from the city tonight. I then sat and talked with the children for an hour before writing this letter. I have just written what came to mind. Pray forgive me for the incoherence in my writing as well as in my ideas!

With best wishes,

Your younger brother Zedong
Night, January 28

The Greatest Defects of the Draft Provincial Constitution

(April 25–26, 1921)

What are the greatest defects of the draft Provincial Constitution? Let us now discuss them in the order of the articles. The first and greatest defect is that the rights of the people are not sufficiently defined. In my opinion, the following three extremely important articles must absolutely be added to the Provincial Constitution.

(1) All the people, regardless of gender, have the right to inherit their relatives' property.

If, however, the relative wishes to give part or all of the property to the cause of public welfare, that right should not be restricted by this article.

(2) All the people have the right freely to decide on their own marriages.

With the sole exception of the legally defined marriageable age, the freedom of marriage is not to be restricted by parents or anyone else.

Divorce among the people is not to be restricted except in accordance with legal provisions.

(3) All the people have the right to seek legitimate occupations in accordance with their own free will.

All occupations not detrimental to the peace and happiness of society, such as education, agriculture, industry, commerce, journalism, lawyer, doctor, writer, and artist are legitimate occupations.

Of the above three articles, the first aims to remove the disadvantage of women having no property. If women have no property, then attempts by women to solve problems such as those of education, occupation, participation in politics, and marriage are nothing but empty talk. Property is the root; education, occupation, marriage, and so on are all branches and leaves. Those in the Women's Association[1] who attack not the root, but rather the branches and

---

This proposal originally appeared in the Changsha *Dagongbao* on April 25–26, 1921. Our source is the text as reproduced in *Mao Zedong ji. Bujuan*, Vol. 2, pp. 15–17.

1. The Hunan Women's Association was formally established in February 1921. It began what became known as the "five-proposal movement," proposing equal rights for women with regard to property inheritance, voting and right to hold office, education, occupation, and self-determination in marriage. The association was successful in December 1921 in obtaining provision for women's suffrage and personal freedom in the Hunan Provincial Constitution.

leaves, are indeed mistaken in their view. This article for changing the Chinese inheritance system will have very great influence, and must therefore be laid down in the constitution. As for the second article, in China sons and daughters have no right to determine their own marriage. Creating disaster in the family, this does further harm to society as well; the roots of evil in many different domains lie here. That sons and daughters should have the right to determine their own marriage has, moreover, been accepted as a universal truth. While fixing the marriageable age of men and women, and a minimal requirement for divorce (such as bilateral consent) should be left to the civil law, the transfer of the right of betrothal from the fathers and mothers to their sons and daughters is a major element in changing the marriage system of our country, and should therefore be laid down in the constitution. I think this is truly important. The third article is especially important. At present, there are so very many jobless and unemployed people. It is truly preposterous that the constitution has not provided any means to solve such a momentous social problem. Here it is stipulated that the people have the right freely to seek a legitimate occupation, thus providing constitutional protection for the people's "right of existence" by having it defined in the constitution. In my view, this is of a higher order of importance than defining "the freedom of the person." Immediately afterward, what is meant by legitimate occupation is also defined. In this way, politics in the future may become a kind of politics of the legitimately employed, not the idlers' politics[2] it is now.

The first great defect of the Provincial Constitution has been set forth above. What, then, is its second greatest defect? It is that people who do not have any legitimate occupation also have the right to be elected to office, and that there is no stipulation whatever about issues relating to labor. That a general election is not sufficient to solve social problems has been made known to us through concrete examples in the advanced countries of Europe and America. Now if we move one step backward and allow people who do not have any legitimate occupation the right to vote, then the right to be elected can by no means be unrestricted. Note that formerly restrictions were based on property, and now the restrictions are to be based on occupation. Those who own property may perhaps find themselves among those who are restricted; I call this reverse restriction. If we do not have occupational restrictions on the assemblymen, then once again only rich people will in fact be elected, and poor people will lose out. If the society of idlers has parliamentary representatives, and the society of the legitimately employed does

---

2. *Youmin zhengzhi.* For the most part, in this edition we have translated *youmin* as "vagrants." Here, however, where Mao is placing primary emphasis on the fact that these people have no "legitimate occupation" rather than on their low class status, "idlers" seems more appropriate.

not have parliamentary representatives, the result will continue to be a type of politics unfavorable to the common people. Therefore I propose that:

In article 29, in addition to the three kinds of people who do not have the right to be elected as assemblymen—"soldiers," "officials," and "students"—one more kind should be added: "people who do not have legitimate occupations." (The definitions of legitimate occupations have already been given above.)

Thus, those who sit idly and live on interest or on inheritance, and those who are nothing but politicians, may not be elected. Those who are to be elected will all have legitimate occupations. The politics of the legitimately employed will then take shape.

Business Report of the Cultural Book Society (No. 2)

(April 1921)

I

Last year, we issued a business report of our Society, dealing with affairs during the "preparatory" and "interim business" periods.[1] Now this "Second Business Report of the Society" covers activities during our "first half year," that is, from the inauguration of the Society in September of last year to the end of March this year. The Changsha Cultural Book Society opened at the beginning of last September, and seven months have elapsed from then until the end of March this year, or one month more than was stipulated in the "Outline of the Organization of Our Society," which provided for "one report every six months."[2] This has been done for the sake of greater convenience in the accounting process. From now on, the rule of "one report every six months" laid down in our Organizational Outline will be observed.

II

There are several reasons why we issue this report. First of all, as part of our duties, those of us who are managing the affairs of the Society should, together with those members of the Society directly involved in its affairs, report to everyone on all aspects of how books and periodicals are sold. Only if we see to it that every member is informed about the actual circumstances of the Society will we be doing our duty. Secondly, Chinese always believe in the practice of secrecy in doing business. Except for his own cronies, no one else can get a single word of information out of a Chinese businessman. Such secrecy is truly a fault. If a man is doing his business in an open and upright way, why can't he announce all the details openly? The Cultural Book Society is a publicly owned

---

So far as is known, this report was first published in *Xinmin xuehui ziliao*, pp. 279–97. Our translation is made from that text, as reproduced in *Mao Zedong ji. Bujuan*, Vol. 2, pp. 19–43.

1. For this report, dated October 22, 1920, see Volume I of this edition, pp. 583–87.

2. Actually, the "Outline of the Organization of the Cultural Book Society" dated August 25, 1920, referred to an audit every six months, to be reported to the Council of the Society, but a notice for the attention of branch offices issued at about the same time called for reports from each branch every six months, which would be edited and distributed as a "Report on Book Society Activities." For these documents, see Volume I of this edition, pp. 540–42.

institution. It is by no means a business in the pursuit of private profit. In order to avoid such a fault, we oppose secrecy and are completely open, announcing everything about the society outside our own membership. Thirdly, the task of our Society, as already explained in the "Account of Our Founding," is that "we wish to introduce, through the fastest and easiest channels, all kinds of new Chinese and foreign books, newspapers, and magazines, which will serve as the source materials for new research by the young, and by the Hunanese people as a whole."[3] The organizational outline also calls for "ensuring that all sorts of worthwhile new publications may circulate throughout the whole province, and everyone will have the opportunity to read them." A great mission like this cannot be shouldered by our few dozen members alone. In order to fulfill the goal that "everyone has a chance to read," we believe that the most important thing is to set up a branch in every *xian*. If we make an estimate on the assumption that there is a branch of the Society in each of the 75 *xian*, and each branch has 10 members, we need 750 members. Consequently, it is only by making the affairs of the Society open and public, and seeing to it that comrades both far and near understand the advantages of the Society, set up branches everywhere, and help us by word and deed in our mission of disseminating [books and periodicals], that we can achieve our goal of "province-wide circulation." Fourthly, what we have in our Society is books and periodicals; what we lack is capital. Why is this? Because the books and periodicals come from outside, and we can get as many as we want, but the capital is contributed by our members, who are not all rich men. Also, our members have many things to do, apart from the business of the Society, so how could they have a lot of money for us to use as capital? Furthermore, the Society's capital has the character of "public wealth." It cannot be withdrawn, nor does it pay any interest. How can our impoverished members provide all that much? Nevertheless, a thing like the Cultural Book Society is truly worthy of note. It has two main advantages:

1. Running the business is simple.
2. It does not waste capital.

Everybody knows that among all the urgent tasks at present, none is more important than spreading culture. To promote the spread of culture effectively, there is no better way than setting up book societies like our "Cultural Book Society." If the business is properly managed, will not the efficacy of a book society exceed that of several schools? Therefore, for the purpose of enlarging the business of our Society and expanding it to include a branch in every *xian*, we hope that those comrades who have the means will help us with a somewhat larger contribution. (We are planning to raise 3,000 *yuan* as public capital for the

---

3. See "The Founding of the Cultural Book Society" (July 31, 1920), in Volume I of this edition, pp. 534–35.

Book Society within 2 years.) We do not know who is willing to help us, and naturally it would not be a good idea to go around asking everyone. Only by making public the affairs of our Society can we hope that those who sympathise with us will come forward of their own accord to offer assistance. Fifthly, all we have done hitherto has been to sell books; we have not published anything ourselves. But now we are planning to organize an "editing and translating company" and a "printing shop," which will be fully integrated into the "distribution" side of the Book Society. Then our Society will have its own independent publications. It will be impossible to expand even more the business of our Society in this way unless we attract even more comrades and even more capital (the editing and translating company will require 3,000 *yuan*, while the printing shop will require 5,000 *yuan*). For this reason, too, our Society's affairs must be made public, for only thus can we win the sympathy and interest of the public. There is a final reason, which concerns the business interests of the staff of the Society. This sixth point is that, if we want our business to flourish, we must keep the accounts in good order. In our Society, we have three types of accounts, namely, the "daily accounts," the "monthly accounts," and the "semi-annual accounts." The "daily account" refers to the summing up of the daily business accounts every evening; the "monthly account" is the summing up of the accounts of the entire previous month on the first day of each month; the "semi-annual account" is the summing up of the accounts for the previous half year. The "business situation" presented in this business report of the Society[4] is the result of the first "semi-annual account." Because we have such accounts, procedures are available and our concepts are clear; we can correct our old mistakes and work out new plans, thus making it easier to progress.

III

Those things that have been reported in the "First Business Report of the Society" will not be reported again here. The noteworthy events that have occurred during the several months since the Cultural Book Society was founded at a meeting held in Chuyi Elementary School on August 1 of last year,[5] signed a lease on August 20 to rent part of a building in Chaozong Street belonging to the Hunan-Yale Medical School as the location of the Society, opened for business on September 9, and convened the first meeting of the board of directors in the Changsha *xian* office on October 22, can be briefly summarized as follows:

1. The extraordinary meeting of the board of directors. The extraordinary meeting of the board of directors was held in the Changsha *xian* office on

---

4. I.e., Section V below.
5. The first report gives this date as August 2, 1920. (See Volume I, p. 583.) The reason for the discrepancy is not known.

December 29. The meeting was attended by Jiang Yonghong,[6] He Shouqian, Wang Jifan, Zhou Dunyuan, Guo Taoseng, Peng Yinbo, Xiong Jinding, Yi Lirong, Zhao Yunwen, Liu Yujie[7] and Mao Runzhi. Mr. Jiang Yonghong chaired the meeting. Two issues were discussed: "looking for a new location for the Society" and "raising more capital." First of all, the problem of the Society's location was discussed. Because the Society is currently located in an out-of-the-way corner near the Caochao Gate, and it is felt that there is not enough room space, it would be desirable, with a view to the further development of the Society's activities, to find somewhat larger and more centrally located accomodation. It was resolved that the Society should move to a new location, but that the issue should be handled with caution. Once we have moved, it may earnestly be hoped that things will be more settled and stable, but the Society should remain at its original location at Hunan-Yale until suitable premises are found and everything is clearly arranged. Just two days before the meeting, the director of the Chuanshan Study Society,[8] Mr. Qiu Yishan, agreed to lend part of their building to our Society. Everyone thought this was a very good idea, but that it was necessary to have a clear contract with them so that we could hold to our goal of "stable progression." Consequently, it was decided that there should be further concrete negotiations between our Society and the Chuanshan Study Society. Next, the issue of expenditure was discussed. As of now, we are still 530 *yuan* short of the fund-raising goal of 1,000 *yuan* that the first meeting of the board of directors fixed for the end of the year. For everyone to make small donations is not an effective method. Mr. Jiang Yonghong offered to collect these 530 *yuan* all by himself. The meeting was then dismissed.

2. Signing contracts with the Commercial Press and other publishers. The following transactions took place after January of this year. Before January, we had signed a series of contracts for selling books with publishers in other cities, such as "Zhonghua," "East Asia," "Taidong," "New Youth," "Beijing University Press," and the "Society for Academic Lectures." Beginning in January of this year, thanks to an introduction from Mr. Yang Duanliu, we signed a contract with the Commercial Press in Shanghai to act as their retail distributors. As such,

---

6. Jiang Yonghong was the secretary general of the newly founded Russia Studies Society at this time.

7. Liu Yujie was a major investor in the Cultural Book Society and was very active in the movement for a new constitution for Hunan.

8. The Chuanshan Study Society, or Society for the Study of Wang Fuzhi, was originally founded in 1898 by Hunanese gentry. It was devoted to the study of the writings of Wang Fuzhi (1619–1692), *zi* Ernong, *hao* Chuanshan, one of the most celebrated of the patriotic scholars of the Ming-Qing transition period. It took its name from the style of Chuanshan ("Boat Mountain") adopted by Wang when he retired there after the fall of the Ming. The society was relaunched in 1911, and Mao had often attended the weekly public lectures given there. It was a well-established and prestigious institution with its own spacious premises on the outskirts of Changsha.

we have received discounts varying from 10 to 30 percent. In February, we also negotiated a retail contract with the Evans Book Company in Shanghai. Evans is, however, a Western book company, which has very few books in Chinese. At present, there is not a great demand for Western books in Hunan, so we cannot sell many of their books. In March, the "New Knowledge Book Society" was founded in Beijing. This is a newly established book society, of which the aims are broadly similar to those of our Cultural Book Society. It has produced a volume, *Five Major Lectures by Russell*, and has approached our Society about a contract to distribute this book; our Society has already agreed to do so. There is something in Sichuan called the "Huayang Books and Periodicals Circulation Agency," which wants to hand over to our Society to sell as its agents those books that have not been sold out in Sichuan. There is also the "Asian Civilization Association" in Beijing, which has asked our Society to act as agent for its newly reorganized *Current Affairs Monthly*. Our company has already agreed to both of these proposals. In addition, several newly established magazine publishers have approached our Society during this period about acting as their agents.

3. Brisk sales of books and periodicals. From the time when our Society opened for business last year to the end of this March, the more than 160 books, more than 40 periodicals, and 3 newspapers that our Society offers have been selling very briskly all the time, except for the one month of the winter vacation, and our Society has not been able to keep up with the demand. On the one hand, this is because our company does not have enough capital to buy books in large quantities from publishers outside the province, and small quantities are sold out as soon as they arrive. On the other hand, a sudden and urgent need has arisen in society for new publications. Under the positive stimulus of the New Thought Tide, and the negative stimulus of the old ideas, people are suddenly moved to buy and to read as many books as they can. This is indeed a gratifying phenomenon. Naturally, most of the book buyers are intellectuals, but some booklets, such as *Laboring Circles*, have been sold in substantial quantities among the toilers. In terms of age, most book buyers are naturally young people; those who are middle-aged and older come second.

4. Setting up branches. If our society wants to give the people in every *xian* the opportunity to buy new books, the only way to do so is to set up a branch in all the 75 *xian*. As regards branches, the policy of our Society is by no means to set them up itself, but rather to help comrades in the various *xian* to set up branches in their respective *xian*. Those who do not have a detailed knowledge of our Society may suppose that it is very difficult to set up a branch, but in fact it is an extremely easy thing to do. First of all, as far as capital is concerned, all they need is enough money to buy the first and second batches of books, a minimum of 50 *yuan* and a maximum of 100. Beginning with the third batch, they can use the receipts from the sale of the first two batches of books to purchase them. Secondly, if business is good in a given *xian*, there will certainly be no problem. If business is slow in some *xian*, it does not matter. Branches are

to be set up opposite some public place; they do not require their own independent shop fronts, and expenses need not be great. In remote *xian* and impoverished towns, it does not matter if no more than a few tens of *yuan*, or even a few *yuan*, worth of books can be sold in a year. Thirdly, in dealing with the branches, our Society will charge them for each book received and will not earn even a single penny of profit. All preferential prices and discounts will be passed on directly to the branches. Thus, even if the branch cannot make a great deal of profit because business is slow, it will never lose its capital. Fourthly, the management of [such a] subsidiary business does not require many people. Fifthly, books that have not been sold may be returned to the Society, so that [a branch] will not waste its funds because of overstocking unsalable books. Given the existence of these five factors, we say it is "extremely easy" to set up a branch. Up to the end of March of this year, seven branches in all have been set up by our Society: "Pingjiang," "Liuxi," "Wugang," "Baoqing," "Hengyang," "Ningxiang," and "Xupu." Apart from the branches, there are seven "sales departments." What is the difference between a "branch" and a "sales department"? (1) Branches receive the full benefit of the preferential price, that is to say that they receive the original book supplier's full discount; sales departments get somewhat less, they can only get a 5 percent commission. (2) Branches are located in other *xian*, while sales departments are by run schools or individuals in this city. (Individuals who sell only pamphlets among the common people and laboring circles are allowed the preferential prices.)

IV

The above-mentioned seven branches and seven sales departments are listed below in the order of their establishment, with brief particulars under the four headings of "date of establishment," "location," "founders," and "amount of book sales." As for their detailed situation, the Society has already collected data from each branch and will report on this subsequently. The cutoff date for the following list is the end of March; branches and sales departments established on or after April 1 are not included.

Branches

Pingjiang Cultural Book Society—Founded on November 3, 1920; located in the Rescuing the Poor Factory in Pingjiang *xian* town. Founders: Zhang Zimou, Li Liuru, Yu Jihun, Wu Dazhuo, Fang Weixia, and others. The amount of book sales is about 60 *yuan*.

Liuxi Cultural Book Society—Founded on November 10, 1920; located in Jinjiang Higher Primary School, Xixiang, Liuyang. Founders: Song Xianjue, Chen Zhangfu, and others. The amount of book sales is about 60 *yuan*.

Wugang Cultural Book Society—Founded on December 22, 1920; located in Wugang Middle School. Founders: Deng Zongyu, Xia Dalun, Dai Huasheng, Xia Changyan, Dai Yuanzhang, Ouyang Gangzhong, and others. The amount of book sales is about 40 *yuan*.

Baoqing Cultural Book Society—Founded on January 8, 1921; located in the Third Wumiao District National Primary School in the town of Baoqing. Founders: Kuang Rixiu, Huang Lin, He Minfan, and others. The amount of book sales is about 120 *yuan*.

Hengyang Cultural Book Society—Founded on March 20, 1921; located in the Third Normal School. Founders: Qu Zijian, He Shu, and others. The amount of book sales is about 80 *yuan*.

Ningxiang Cultural Book Society—Founded on March 27, 1921; located in the Encourage Learning Institute. Founders: Xiao Shuwei, Jiang Xiaoyan, He Shuheng, and others. The amount of book sales is about 50 *yuan*.

Xupu Cultural Book Society—Founded on March 28, 1921; located in the Encourage Learning Institute. Founders: Zou Shizhen, Jiang Zhuru, Zhou Xianhuai, Guan Kun, Hu Jianfeng, Wu Jiaying, Shu Xiuyu, Yi Kexun, Gong Boan, and others. The amount of book sales is about 70 *yuan*.

Sales Departments

Sales Department of the First Normal School—Managers: Huang Tiehe and others.

Sales Department of the Primary School Attached to the First Normal School—Managers: Xiong Keyi, Li Yunhong, and others.

Sales Department of Chuyi Primary School—Managers: Tan Xiewu, Liu Zhongkai, Yao Jiawen, and others.

Sales Department of Xiuye School—Managers: Liu Yujie, Zhang Ziren, Li Zhenyu, and others.

Yang Shicai.

He Yuqiu.

Cai Zengzhun.

V

The business situation of the Cultural Book Society during the seven months from September, the ninth year of the Republic of China to March 31, the tenth year of the Republic of China, can be broken down under the following headings:

1. Income

The Society sold books, magazines, and daily newspapers during these seven months. Here is the total income from retail sales. (Each item is based on the detailed accounts.)

A. Books and Magazines

1) Cash income from retail sales: 869.868 silver dollars and 366,780 copper cash
2) Income from customers' accounts: 1415.875 silver dollars and 233,830 copper cash
3) Income from the seven branches: 342.15648 silver dollars and 20,210 copper cash
4) Income from the seven sales departments: 195.47345 silver dollars and 66,230 copper cash
5) Income from magazine subscriptions (refers to payments already received for magazines at the prepaid subscription price): 159.013 silver dollars and 5,980 copper cash
6) Income from books that the Society returned to the original suppliers and treated as sold: 50.145 silver dollars and 2,100 copper cash

Total for item A: 3,032.53093 silver dollars, and 695 strings of copper cash, plus 130 cash[9]

B. Newspapers

1) *China Times*: 333.4444 silver dollars and 31,230 copper cash
2) *Morning Post*: 202.397 silver dollars and 25,350 copper cash
3) *Dagongbao* (L'Impartial): 9.494 silver dollars
4) *Hunan Daily*: 4.40 silver dollars
5) *Shihuabao* (True Talk News): 3.691 silver dollars

Total for item B: 553.4264 silver dollars and 56 strings of copper cash, plus 580 cash

Total income from items A and B:
3,585.95733 silver dollars and 751,710 copper cash, which correspond to 464.018 silver dollars
The sum of these is 4,049.97533 silver dollars in all, representing the total income for seven months.

2. Expenditures

Expenditures of the Society during the seven-month period for books and periodicals bought from publishers outside the province, and for the operating

---

9. One string of copper cash was made up of 1,000 coins.

expenses of the Society. (Each item is based on the detailed accounts.)

Payments for books and periodicals

A. Book Publishers and Magazine Companies

1) Shanghai Taidong Library: 798.955 silver dollars
2) Guangzhou *New Youth* Society: 536.55 silver dollars
3) Shanghai East Asia Book Company: 453.64 silver dollars
4) Beijing University Press: 230.628 silver dollars
5) Shanghai China Book Company: 203.18 silver dollars
6) Wuchang Liqun Book Company: 157.745 silver dollars
7) Beijing *Morning Post* Society: 155.015 silver dollars
8) Beijing Society for Academic Lectures: 124.37625 silver dollars
9) Changsha Qunyi Book Company: 97.55 silver dollars
10) Chengdu Huayang Book and Periodical Distribution Agency: 59.70 silver dollars and 3,600 copper cash
11) Shanghai Commercial Press: 69.285 silver dollars
12) Shanghai New Woman Society: 53.257 silver dollars
13) Shanghai New Education and Common Progress Society: 42.464 silver dollars
14) Beijing New Life Society: 41.33 silver dollars
15) Jiangsu Provincial Council on Education: 30.085 silver dollars
16) Luo Zonghan, in Beijing: 28.65 silver dollars
17) Changsha *Mining Journal* Society: 20 silver dollars
18) Yi Jiayue, in Beijing: 19.20 silver dollars
19) Xiong Jinding, in Changsha: 40 strings of copper cash
20) Nanjing Ji'nan School: 16.46 silver dollars
21) Shanghai Chinese Science Company: 12.48 silver dollars
22) Beijing *New China Magazine* Society: 11.90 silver dollars
23) Lin Yulan, in Beijing: 10.20 silver dollars
24) Tangshan Press of the Tangshan Specialized Industrial Science Society: 10.08 silver dollars
25) Changsha New People's Study Society: 15 strings of copper cash, plus 900 cash
26) Beijing Higher Normal School *Journal of Education* Society: 9.20 silver dollars
27) Beijing Higher Normal School *Popular Education* Society: 8.75 silver dollars
28) Beijing University *Journal of Painting* Society: 8.75 silver dollars
29) Overseas New Voice Society: 13 strings of copper cash, plus 600 cash
30) Beijing *Labor Voice Weekly* Society: 8.178 silver dollars
31) Beijing *Dawn Magazine* Society: 8 silver dollars

32) Beijing University *Music Journal* Society: 7.80 silver dollars
33) Suzhou *Women's Review* Society: 7.68 silver dollars
34) Beijing *Studies of the Family* Society: 7.20 silver dollars
35) Shanghai *Academic Studies* Society: 6.45 silver dollars
36) Shanghai Guangwen Publishing House: 6 silver dollars
37) Ren Ceqi, in Changsha: 5.70 silver dollars
38) Shanghai Industry and Commerce Friendship Association: 5.57 silver dollars
39) Guangzhou *The Toiler* Society: 4.80 silver dollars
40) Beijing *Popular Medicine Monthly* Society: 4.80 silver dollars
41) Luo Yi, in Changsha: 4.675 silver dollars
42) Wuchang Higher Normal School Educational Studies Research Society: 4 silver dollars
43) Li Ruosong, in Shanghai: 4 silver dollars
44) Huang Hejun, in Changsha: 6,000 copper cash
45) Beijing University *Journal of Mathematical Theory* Society: 3.80 silver dollars
46) Shanghai Fudan University *Common People's Weekly* Society: 3.50 silver dollar.
47) Paris *Chinese Workers' Thrice-monthly Review* Society: 5 strings of copper cash, plus 580 cash
48) *Beijing Women's Higher Normal School Weekly* Society: 3.145 silver dollars
49) Beijing Asian Civilization Association: 3 silver dollars
50) New Young People's Society: 2.73 silver dollars
51) Wuchang Higher Normal School Society for Mathematical Theory: 2.64 silver dollars
52) Hunan Provincial Council on Education: 2.50 silver dollars
53) Beijing Higher Normal School English Language Society: 2.40 silver dollars
54) Fuzhou Popular Hygiene Society: 2.40 silver dollars
55) Nanjing Ji'nan School *China and South East Asia Magazine* Society: 2.16 silver dollars
56) Beijing Higher Normal School Society for Mathematical Theory: 2.10 silver dollars
57) Shanghai *Youshi Illustrated* Society: 2 silver dollars
58) *Youth Society Magazine* Society: 2 silver dollars
59) Changsha Huitong Printing House: 1.68 silver dollars
60) Shanghai *Minxin Weekly* Society: 1.60 silver dollars
61) Beijing Higher Normal School Engineering Society: 0.96 silver dollar
62) Beijing *Humanist Monthly* Society: 0.70 silver dollar
63) Beijing *Struggle Weekly* Society: 0.63 silver dollar
64) Beijing *Business Weekly* Society: 0.50 silver dollar
65) Beijing *Weekly Critic* Society: 0.40 silver dollar

Total for Item A:

3,335.12825 silver dollars and 84 strings of copper cash, plus 680 cash, equivalent to 52.27 silver dollars amounting in all to 3,387.39825 silver dollars, including 560.82675 silver dollars for "merchandise in stock."

The actual payments made under Item A amount to 2,826.5715 silver dollars.

B. Newspaper Publishers

China Times: 217.35 silver dollars
Morning Post: 150.04 silver dollars
Dagongbao: 8.83 silver dollars
Hunan Daily: 3.50 silver dollars
Shihuabao: 5.95 silver dollars

The total amount under Item B is 385.67 silver dollars.

The total for Items A and B is 3,212.2415 silver dollars in all.

Payments for Business Expenses

A. Salaries

(One manager; three assistants—one in charge of books, one in charge of accounts who also deals with newspapers, and one in charge of newspapers; one cook, who also does other chores; one special negotiator).
Total: 390.24 silver dollars

B. Miscellaneous expense

(Postage, loss on exchange,[10] printing costs, advertising, paper, rent, and other miscellaneous expenses)
Total: 340.513 silver dollars
The sum total of Items A and B is 730.753 silver dollars.
The total of all payments listed above is 3,942.9945 silver dollars.

Balancing income and expenditure gives a favorable balance of 106.98083 silver dollars in "pure profit"—the actual surplus for our business over the period of seven months.

VI

The financial circumstances of our business, as reported above, should be clear to all. There should also be statistics regarding the books and periodicals sold by

---

10. This presumably refers to the cost of changing copper cash into silver dollars or the equivalent.

our Society. First of all, the number of copies of a particular book sold in Hunan will indicate its impact upon the people of Hunan. Secondly, by preparing statistics every six months, we may compare the semi-annual increase or decrease in the sales of a particular book. It would, however, be a lot of trouble to list all the books and periodicals. Here we have excluded those that are not so important. Those listed below are relatively more important in terms of their content. Those that are referred to as "sets" are titles consisting of two or more volumes, while those that are referred to as "copies" consist of one volume only.[11]

1. Important books:

Five Major Lectures by Dewey	220 sets
Introduction to Marx's *Capital*	200 copies
History of Socialism	100 sets
The Road to Freedom	60 copies
Syndicalism	60 copies
Dewey, *Trends in Modern Education*	160 copies
The New Zoology	150 copies
Society and Education	150 copies
Pragmatism	100 copies
Society and Ethics	50 copies
Dewey, *On The Development of Democracy in America*	70 copies
The Relationship between Science and Human Evolution[12]	80 copies
The Words and Deeds of Cai Jiemin[13]	100 copies
Superstition and Psychology	100 copies
Drops of Water	80 sets
Basic Problems in Ethics	50 sets
Yang Changji, *History of Western Ethics*	40 sets
Russell, *Principles of Social Reconstruction*	100 sets
Morning Post Fiction, Volume 1	200 copies
The Thought of Kropotkin	200 copies
Studies of the New Russia	80 copies
The Worker-Peasant Government and China	80 copies
Wu Zhihui, *Talks with Guests at the New Moon Temple*	40 sets

---

11. Like the lists in the "First Business Report" of October 22, 1920, and the "Cultural Book Society Announcement" of November 10, 1920, with which it overlaps to a considerable extent, this enumeration mixes precise titles with somewhat approximate descriptions of the volumes in question. Explanations regarding individual titles given in the notes to these two texts, which appear in Volume I, pp. 583–87 and 589–91, are not repeated here.

12. This book was by Wang Xinggong.

13. Cai Yuanpei.

Life of Tolstoy	100 copies
The Philosophy of Education	150 copies
Pragmatic Ethics	250 copies
The Political Economy of Cooperativism	40 sets
The History of Philosophy	150 copies
Hu Shi, *Outline of the History of Chinese Philosophy*	80 copies
A General Survey of Chinese Grammar	60 sets
The Islands of South East Asia	30 sets
South East Asia	40 copies
A Newly Punctuated *The Scholars*	140 sets
A Newly Punctuated *Water Margin*	100 sets
Letters Written in the Vernacular	180 sets
Short Stories[14]	130 copies
Hu Shi, *A Book of Experiments*	140 copies
Darwin's *Origin of Species*	30 sets
Haeckel's *Monism*	35 sets
Russell, *Political Ideals*	70 copies
On Women	70 copies
The Structure of the National Language	80 copies
A General Survey of Social Issues	40 sets
The Art of Thinking	40 copies
The European Economy after the Peace Conference[15] . .	60 copies
The Meaning and Value of Human Life	70 copies
Problems in Philosophy[16]	20 copies

2. Important magazines:

New Youth (monthly)	2,000 copies
Labor World (weekly)	5,000 copies
New Tide (monthly)	200 copies
Popular Education (weekly)	300 copies
New Life (fortnightly)	2,400 copies
New Education (monthly)	300 copies
Young China (monthly)	600 copies
Young World (monthly)	280 copies

---

14. A volume of stories translated by Hu Shi.

15. This was a translation of John Maynard Keynes' *The Economic Consequences of the Peace*.

16. This is, in fact, the volume of lectures by Bertrand Russell, published by the Beijing University Xinzhi shushe (New Knowledge Book Society), referred to in section III of this report. The title given there, *Five major lectures by Russell*, appears on the book as a subtitle. (The text of the lectures was established by Zhao Yuanren.)

Science (monthly) . . . .   100 copies
Chinese Education Circles (monthly) . . . .   200 copies
Reform . . . .   180 copies
Popular Translations . . . .   250 copies

3. Important newspapers:

China Times . . . .   75 copies per day
Morning Post . . . .   45 copies per day

VII

Below we publish the capital investments of members of the Society, in the order in which their contributions were received:

August 8:
    Mr. Zhao Yunwen—10 silver dollars

August 24:
    Mr. Zhu Jianfan—1 silver dollar and 9 *yuan* in paper currency

August 25:
    Mr. Yi Peiji—10 silver dollars

August 28:
    Mr. Guo Kaidi—5 silver dollars

August 31:
    Mr. Wang Jifan—5 silver dollars
    Mr. Wu Xiaoshan—10 *yuan* in paper currency

September 3:
    Mr. Pan Shicen—8,100 copper cash
    Mr. Fang Weixia—7,800 copper cash
    Mr. Yi Lirong—10 silver dollars

September 4:
    Mr. Liu Yujie—5 *yuan* in paper currency

September 8:
    Mr. Jiang Jihuan—28 silver dollars, and 12 *yuan* in paper currency
    Mr. Lin Yunyuan—5 *yuan* in paper currency

September 9:
    Mr. Jiang Jihuan—59.30 *yuan* in small bills of paper currency, 100 copper cash, and 6 *yuan* in paper currency

September 24:
    Miss Tao Yi—10 silver dollars

Mr. Zhou Shizhao—2 *yuan* in paper currency, and 200 copper cash
Mr. He Shuheng—2 *yuan* in paper currency, and 200 copper cash
Mr. Xiong Chuxiong—2 *yuan* in paper currency, and 200 copper cash

September 27:
Mr. Guo Kaidi—5 silver dollars
Mr. Lin Yunyuan—5 *yuan* in paper currency

October 2:
Mr. Xiong Chuxiong—8 *yuan* in paper currency

October 4:
Mr. Pan Shicen—5 *yuan* in paper currency

October 5:
Mr. Wang Jifan—5 silver dollars

October 17:
Mr. Mao Zedong—10 silver dollars

October 20:
Mr. Zou Yunzhen—3 *yuan* in paper currency
Dagongbao—8.83 silver dollars

October 23:
Mr. Liu Yujie—5 *yuan* in paper currency

October 29:
Mr. Xiong Mengfei—4 silver dollars

November 1:
Mr. Zhou Shizhao—1 silver dollar, and 3 *yuan* in paper currency

November 4:
Mr. Kuang Rixiu—6 silver dollars
Mr. Tang Jijie—10 silver dollars
Mr. He Shuheng—8 *yuan* in paper currency
Mr. Zhou Shizhao—4 *yuan* in paper currency

November[17] 13:
Mr. Zuo Xueqian—148,500 copper cash and 100 *yuan* in paper currency

---

17. The text reads *shi* (tenth month, i.e., October), rather than *shiyi* (eleventh month, or November), but this must be a printing error.

November 5:
  Mr. He Minfan—5 silver dollars
  Mr. Qiu Ao—10 silver dollars

November 8:
  Mr. Chen Shunong—10 *yuan* in paper currency

November 15:
  Mr. Peng Huang—3 silver dollars

November 21:
  Mr. Ren Muyao—2 silver dollars

December 9:
  Dagongbao—1.17 silver dollars

December 21:
  Mr. Fang Weixia—5 silver dollars

January 18 of the tenth year[18]
  Mr. Zuo Shimin—10 silver dollars

February 27:
  Mr. Wang Linsu—2 silver dollars
  Mr. Jiang Jihuan—200 silver dollars

After converting the paper currency into silver dollars, the total amount is 692.635 silver dollars and 149 strings of copper cash, plus 200 cash.

VIII

The staff of the Society:

Yi Lirong (manager)
Mao Zedong (special negotiator)
Li Xiang (assistant, in charge of books)
Tang Ziguang (assistant, in charge of newspapers and books)
Wang Xianmei (assistant, in charge of newspapers)
Huang De'an (cook and janitor)

The above constitute the present staff. In addition, during the period covered by this report, Mr. Chen Zibo and Mr. Ren Peidao each worked as assistants for about two months. (The end.)

The Society is located at 56 Chaozong Street, Changsha.

---

18. 1921.

Report on the Affairs of the New People's Study Society (No.2)

(Summer of 1921)

Summer Issue of the Tenth Year of the Republic

This report on the affairs of the Society is devoted exclusively to a record of three meetings of Society members held in Changsha in January of the tenth year. The first of these three meetings was a New Year's meeting, held from January 1 to January 3; the second meeting was the regular monthly meeting for January of this year and took place on January 16; the third meeting was the regular monthly meeting for February of this year and took place on February 20. The discussion on each of these three occasions was extremely detailed and exhaustive. It is recorded separately below.

As a result of the political situation in Hunan, the members of the New People's Study Society in Changsha had not had a meeting for a very long time. At the end of the ninth year, the political situation in Changsha was somewhat more stable, and more than twenty members were in Changsha, so a meeting was planned.[1] At this time, the term of the members of the Deliberative Department (one year) had expired, so they could not call a meeting. Consequently, preliminary arrangements for a meeting were first worked out by He Shuheng, Zhou Dunyuan, Mao Runzhi, Xiong Jinding, Tao Siyong, and other staff members, who issued the following announcement:

The Society should have held a meeting long ago, but for various reasons this was not done. It has now been decided that a three-day meeting will be held beginning on January 1 of the tenth year. It will be a fairly long meeting, to discuss the various issues listed below:

Like the first report of the society, this document was first published as a separate pamphlet in 1921. Our source is the version in *Xinmin xuexui ziliao*, pp. 15–41, which incorporates some manuscript corrections on the copy available to the editors; this text is reproduced in *Mao Zedong ji. Bujuan*, Vol. 2, pp. 45–73.

1. On November 27, 1920, Tan Yankai, who had been governor since Zhang Jingyao was driven out of Hunan in June 1920, was succeeded by his subordinate Zhao Hengti. While Mao may not have welcomed this change, it did usher in a period of relative stability.

1) What should be the common goal of the New People's Study Society?
2) What methods must be adopted in order to achieve that goal?
3) How shall we begin to apply these methods immediately?
4) Individual members' plans of action (each person speaks for himself).
5) Individual members' means of livelihood (each person speaks for himself).
6) What attitudes should the Study Society as such and each individual member adopt?
7) How should members conduct their academic study and research?
8) Revising the Society's statutes, and increasing the dues.
9) The conditions and procedures for admitting new members (including the question of expulsion from the Society).
10) The question of members' domestic concerns.
11) The presentation and criticism of [members'] individual characters.
12) The question of the members' health and recreation.
13) The question of commemorating the anniversary of the Society's founding.
14) Impromptu motions.

Some of the aforementioned questions have been raised by our members in Paris; others represent problems that our local members wish to see resolved as soon as possible. Everyone is requested to think about these issues in advance and prepare himself so as to be ready to express his views at the meeting, with a view to finding appropriate solutions. The meeting will take place at the Cultural Book Society in Chaozong Street. The schedule for the meeting is: first day, from 9:30 A.M. to 11:30 A.M.; second day, from 9:00 A.M. to 2:00 P.M. (every member should bring twenty cents for lunch); third day, from 9:30 A.M. to 11:30 A.M. We earnestly hope that every member will arrange his schedule and come to the meeting, which will be held rain or shine. And please be strictly punctual.

The New People's Study Society

The meeting was held at the Cultural Book Society on January 1 of the tenth year. It was attended by more than ten people. On this day, the whole city was covered with snow, resplendent in the winter light, a bright and fresh scene. The meeting started at ten o'clock, and was chaired by Mr. He Shuheng. The chairman asked Mao Runzhi to make a report on the purpose of the meeting and the history of the Study Society. Mr. Mao said: Our Study Society should have met long ago. Because of all sorts of calamities, it was impossible to hold a meeting before last year. Now the meeting cannot be postponed any longer. Taking advantage of the New Year's holiday, when people everywhere are on vacation, we are holding a relatively long meeting to discuss all the various issues that our fellow members regard as most urgent. As for the history of our Study Society, it can be summarized in broad outline. He then gave a brief report on various aspects of the work and study of members of the Study Society, both at home and abroad, during the past two years. After Mr. Mao had finished his report, the chairman raised all the issues to be discussed at the meeting. Chen Qimin proposed that, because the substance of the first three questions was extremely important, they should be held over for discussion on the following day. He singled out several of the remaining issues for discussion that day. Mao Runzhi declared that because of their great importance, these issues should be briefly discussed on that day, but without being voted on. Everyone agreed, and so discussion began on the following three questions:

"What should be the common goal of the New People's Study Society?"
"What methods must be adopted in order to achieve that goal?"
"How shall we begin to apply these methods immediately?"

Since the three issues are interrelated, they were discussed together. Mao Runzhi said: I can inform all of you regarding the results of a discussion of these issues by members of the Society in Paris. The result of the discussion by members in Paris was, concerning the first question, to advocate that our common goal should be "to transform China and the world." As regards the second question, some members favored radical methods, while others favored gradual methods. With reference to the third question, some members proposed organizing a Communist Party, while others wanted to practice a work-study philosophy and to transform education. All these points are covered in the correspondence from Paris. Xiong Jinding declared that since the New People's Study Society has hitherto always embraced the goal of transforming China and the world, it was not necessary to discuss this issue further. Mao Runzhi disagreed, saying: The first issue must be discussed further, because manifestly there are two schools of thought in China today about how to resolve the problems of society. One advocates transformation, while the other wants reform.[2] The former is that of Chen Duxiu and others; the latter is that of Liang Qichao, Zhang Dongsun[3] and others. Peng Yinbo said: The idea of transforming the world is too broad and general. However great our force, the transformation of which we speak can touch only a part of the world. China can be objected to as too small a sphere, so I advocate transforming East Asia. As regards the material aspect, we shall

---

2. Mao, who two years earlier had treated the various terms meaning, loosely, "reform," as virtually interchangeable, now distinguishes very sharply indeed between *gaizao* (transformation, literally reconstruction) and *gailiang* (reform, literally changing for the better).

3. Zhang Dongsun (1886–1973), *zi* Shengxin, a native of Zhejiang, was a philosopher specializing in Western thought and an advocate of the constitutionalist theories of Liang Qichao. In 1920 he was editor of the Shanghai *Shishi xinbao* (China Times).

create a world of machines;[4] as regards the spiritual aspect, we exert our utmost efforts to help the great majority of the people to attain happiness. Chen Qimin endorsed the idea of transforming East Asia. He said that Europe has its own European method of transformation, and we cannot act on their behalf. It would, however, be appropriate to include Australia in East Asia, and we should also be responsible for Africa. As to the two terms, "transformation" and "reform," I prefer the former. The reason is that capitalism is strongly entrenched and hard to overcome. If it is not overthrown root and branch, no new construction will be possible; therefore, I believe in the worker-peasant dictatorship. One cannot speak of transformation if there is too much freedom, because, if you emphasize freedom, the result will be, on the contrary, the absence of freedom. As regards method, this goal is not something that can be realized within twenty years. At present, we should devote our energies not to the immediate establishment of some hybrid[5] worker-peasant government, but to propaganda. In the case of East Asia, it is particularly important to bring about the industrial revolution. Mao Runzhi stated: Reform is a patchwork method. We should advocate large-scale transformation. As for [the formulation] "transforming East Asia," it is not so good as "transforming China and the world." By referring to "the world," we show that our perspective is international; by referring to "China," we clearly signify the starting point of our endeavor. "East Asia" has no clear meaning. The China problem is in fact a world problem. Hence, if we merely set out to transform China, and pay no heed to transforming the world, any transformation we carry out will inevitably be so narrow in scope as to constitute an obstacle to world [transformation]. As for method, I agree entirely with [Chen] Qimin's suggestion that we should follow the Russian model. For the Russian method represents a road newly discovered after all the other roads had turned out to be dead ends. This method alone contains greater potential, as compared to other methods of transformation. Since the discussion had gone on for quite a long time, the chairman announced that discussion of these three issues (goal, methods, and application) should be suspended temporarily for that day.

The chairman invited everyone at the meeting to discuss the next issue:

"What attitudes should the Society as such and each individual member adopt?"

---

4. "World of machines" is a literal translation of *jiqi shijie.* Peng's idea was presumably to create a mechanized, industrialized, and technologically advanced China, as a part of the modern world.

5. Chen's metaphor is *feilüfeima,* "neither donkey nor horse." A rough English equivalent would be "neither fish nor fowl," but the Chinese expression has other overtones, because the union of a donkey and a horse results in a mule, which (as Wang Fuzhi pointed out long ago) is sterile. Mao Zedong nonetheless declared in his "Talk to Music Workers" of August 1956: "You can produce some things which are neither Chinese nor Western. If what comes out is neither a donkey nor a horse but a mule, that would not be bad at all." (Schram, *Mao Tse-tung Unrehearsed,* p. 88.)

Mao Runzhi reported on the results of a discussion that was held among our members at Bansong Park in Shanghai. They advocated that our Society adopt an attitude of latent action. What is referred to as "latent action" by no means signifies "inaction" (the letter from Paris says that our Society's strong point is its stability of purpose, and its weak point is inaction), but rather means guarding against creating a reputation not founded on reality. As to our members' attitudes toward one another, they advocate "mutual aid" and "mutual encouragement." Everyone agreed with the Shanghai resolution (the question of attitude was thus resolved). The chairman raised the question, "How should members conduct their academic study and research?" Mao Runzhi reported on the views of our Paris members about collective versus individual ways of proceeding with study and research (see the letters from Xiao Zisheng). They also propose setting definite topics for our studies and suggest that it would be useful to investigate several isms (such as communism, anarchism, pragmatism, etc.), each for a specified period of time. This would be far more profitable than just reading widely at random. Chen Qimin declared: I feel that the environment often drags us down, so it is necessary for the members of our Society to gather together in one place, to live and study together. This would make it somewhat easier to concentrate more manpower in order to transform the environment. Xiong Jinding said: To live together and to have meetings are two methods. Both are necessary. He Shuheng suggested that we run a restaurant for the common people. Yi Lirong declared: Provided only that we are able to live together, we can still get together frequently, even though we follow different professions. Mao Runzhi said: Only if we organize a common occupation can we possibly live together. But we are now discussing the question of how we should conduct our research and study. Li Chengde declared: We should not limit our study to socialism alone; we should also study philosophy, science, literature, esthetics, and so on. There is a saying of Master Zhu:[6] "Keep the larger things in mind even while taking the smaller tasks in hand." Our members must also adopt such an attitude. There is nothing to prevent us from using all sorts of methods to achieve our goal. Mao Runzhi said: Our members should be free to pursue various kinds of general or specialized study. The subject to which particular attention is paid at present in the research of our Society must be one that all our members find of interest and consider extremely urgent at this time. He proposed that our research should be concentrated on "isms" alone, such as socialism, pragmatism, etc. Chen Qimin advocated establishing a plan for the study of

---

6. Zhu Xi (1130–1200), the famous philosopher of the Song dynasty and founder of one of the two schools of neo-Confucianism. For Mao's encounter with his thought at an early age, see the "Classroom Notes" of 1913, in Volume I of this edition. The sentence that follows is not a direct quotation from any of his writings, and appears to be Li's summary or paraphrase of a central idea in Zhu Xi's thought. While asserting the fundamental importance of *li* or principle, which transcended the real world, Zhu Xi also stressed the value of investigating concrete things (*ge wu*) in daily practice.

several isms between now and the end of the year, with results to be achieved by the end of this time period. Mao Runzhi proposed that, as a provisional measure, a schedule be drawn up for the next half year, providing for the study of five or six isms. Mr. He Shuheng suggested that we should have a meeting every month, at which those who had obtained some results from their research could come and talk, while the others could come and listen. Peng Yinbo declared that socialism, philosophy, literature, politics and economics all need to be studied, so he did not approve of the idea that our study should be focused on doctrines only. Mao Runzhi explained: What we refer to as doing research on isms means studying isms as they appear in philosophy, literature, politics, economics and all the other academic fields. There are, of course, no other isms apart from these.

The discussion moved on to the issue of how to read books. Some proposed that members read individually first and give lectures on the lessons they had personally derived from their reading. Others suggested that all should read the same book, and that each person should present his impressions of it at meetings. No firm decision on this issue has as yet been taken. It was resolved, however, that one meeting be held each month devoted solely to academic discussion. It was proposed that the remaining unresolved issues be held over to the next meeting, and not considered at the New Year's conference (the issue of research and study was, by and large, resolved).

Members then proceeded to discuss "revising the Society's statutes and increasing the dues."

In reality, the statutes of our Society should have been revised much earlier. Previously, many people have suggested that the statutes be simplified somewhat. The letters from Paris also support this view. But busily engaged as we are every day in discussing various problems, it has really been impossible to revise the charter immediately. Mao Runzhi proposed that a drafting committee be appointed, and that once the draft had been established it should be voted on and adopted at a meeting of members of the Society in Changsha, after which the approval of the members in Paris and other places could be sought. Everyone agreed that the task of preparing the draft should be entrusted to the members of the staff. As for increasing the dues, it was decided that the annual dues should be increased by one *yuan* to cover the cost of printing the *Business Report of the Society* and the *Collected Correspondence*. (The questions of the Society's statutes and the membership dues were thus resolved).

Regarding the question, "The conditions and procedures for admitting new members and for expulsion from the Society," the following decisions were reached after discussion on that day:

The conditions for the admission of new members to the Society (that is to say, the articles of faith for members of the Society) are (1) integrity, (2) sincerity, and (3) the aspiration to improve oneself.

The procedures for the admission of new members are that they be introduced by five members, and that a circular notice be sent to all members. (The provision that they should be approved by the board of appraisers was omitted, because it had been decided that day not to establish a board of appraisers.)

As for the question of expelling members from the Society, because there are some who are members only in name, but not members in their essential nature, it was decided: (1) to insert an announcement in the business report of the Society (see below), (2) to drop their names from the membership list, and (3) not to invite such persons to meetings of the Society. The announcement adopted was as follows:[7]

To whom it may concern:

The members of this Society have come together with the goal of mutual aid and encouragement. It has now been almost three years since the Society was founded in the early summer of the seventh year of the Republic. Even though in form the Society has not yet fully taken shape, it has been consistent in spirit. There may, however, be individual members of the Society who fail to understand its spirit. There are those who are so involved in other matters that they cannot devote their attention to the Society; there are those who are so strongly attached to other organizations that they have no feelings for our Society; there are those who lack an interest in collective living; there are those who do not aspire in the least to perfect themselves; there are those whose conduct is unacceptable to the majority of the members. This Society considers that, even though people in the circumstances indicated above were formerly listed as our members, there is no real possibility of mutual aid and encouragement from them. If we are to maintain the spirit of the Society as a whole, there is no alternative but to cease recognizing them as members. It is also hoped that in future, in recommending new members to the Society, a strenuous effort will be made not to include people of the type mentioned above. This would be fortunate indeed for the future of the Society.

> The New People's Study Society
> January 2, tenth year

(The question of the admission and expulsion of members was thus resolved.)

---

7. This "Urgent Notice," which was drafted by Mao, also appears separately under the date of January 2, 1921, in the *Mao Zedong ji. Bujuan*. Since the text as it occurs here is word-for-word identical with that version, with one or two inconsequential exceptions, it does not seem necessary to print the document twice.

January 2 was the second day of the meeting. The snow was even deeper, but more than ten people were present at the meeting (everyone present at the meeting on the previous day came again on this day). Because there were those not present on the previous day who came on this day, the chairman (He Shuheng) presented a brief summary of the issues that had been discussed and resolved the day before. The discussion of the first question, which had been left unresolved on the previous day, was resumed:

"What should be the common goal of the Study Society?"
Everyone spoke in turn, from left to right, beginning with the chairman.
He Shuheng: The common goal of the Society should be "to transform the world."
Mao Runzhi: It should be "to transform China and the world."
Ren Peidao: Ditto.
Tao Siyong: Ditto.
Yi Yuehui: Ditto.
Yi Lirong: Ditto.
Zou Panqing: I am extremely dubious about the word, "to transform." In general, people assume that we want to carry out a fundamental transformation and to overturn completely everything that has existed in the past, in order to build anew. In reality, this cannot be done. Nothing in the world can be accomplished at one leap; rather, things evolve gradually. It is not appropriate for the New People's Study Society to adopt an attitude of transforming things. It is better for us to adopt the approach of research, and to study thoroughly the methods of the various isms, so as to see which ism's methods are most appropriate. There is a difference between the Eastern and Western nations, and the maladies which afflict humankind are so multifarious that they certainly cannot be cured by a single prescription. Mr. Zou's intervention was extremely long.

Chen Zhangfu: The scope of the expression, "to transform the world," is rather vast. It allows us to regard the world as our family, and is a much more pleasing idea. For this reason, I am in favor of using "to transform China and the world."

Zhang Quanshan: I have yet another proposal, but I need not present it to you today. I point out simply, with reference to our discussion just now, that it does not seem proper to place China and the world side by side. It would be better to use "to transform China and extend [this transformation] to the world."

Chen Zibo: The present society is extremely evil. The expression "reform"[8] is too mild to be effective, and we must adopt a radical attitude. Therefore, I advocate "transformation." China is, however, a part of the world; hence I suggest deleting the word "China," and using "to transform the world."

Zhong Chusheng: There is no reason why we should not have a somewhat larger goal. I advocate using "to transform the world."

---

8. *Gailiang.*

He Yangu: I agree with Zhong.

Peng Yinbo: I am in favor of using "to transform China and the world," and I want to take back what I said yesterday about "transforming East Asia."

Xiong Jinding: I am for "to transform the world."

Liu Jizhuang: I agree with Xiong.

Li Chengde: I advocate that we use "to promote the evolution of society."

Zhou Dunyuan: I agree with Li.

After everyone had spoken, there were some exchanges of criticism. The chairman said: Yesterday, we decided not to put any resolutions to the vote, but in fact, it appears impossible, without a vote, to distinguish clearly which of the proposals enjoys majority or minority support. Everyone agreed with the idea of taking a vote. The chairman said: Those who endorse "to transform China and the world" as our common goal please stand up! The following people stood up: Tao Siyong, Yi Lirong, Mao Runzhi, Zhong Chusheng, Zhou Dunyuan, Ren Peidao, Chen Qimin, Yi Yuehui, Chen Zhangfu, and Peng Yinbo (ten people). The chairman said: Those who endorse "to transform the world" as our common goal please stand up! The following people stood up: Xiong Jinding, Liu Jizhuang, Chen Zibo, He Shuheng, and He Yangu (five people). The above two proposals are essentially of the same nature, despite minor verbal differences. Then, the chairman said once again: Those who endorse "to promote the evolution of society" please stand up! The following people stood up: Li Chengde and Zhou Dunyuan (two people). Zhou Dunyuan explained: I endorse both "to transform China and the world" and "to promote the evolution of society." In addition, two people, Zou Panqing and Zhang Quanshan, declared that they abstained. (Thus the question of the goal was resolved.)

The discussion on the question of methods.

"What methods must be adopted in order to achieve that goal?"

First of all, a report was made by Mao Runzhi about the proposal from Paris by Mr. Cai Hesen. He also said: Broadly speaking, the following are the methods employed in the world to solve the problems of society:

1. Social policy;
2. Social democracy;
3. The radical type of communism (the doctrine of Lenin);
4. The moderate type of communism (the doctrine of Russell);
5. Anarchism.

We may use them for reference in working out our own method.

Then, everyone spoke in turn (Chen Qimin had now arrived at the meeting):

He Shuheng: I advocate radicalism. One moment of upheaval is worth twenty years of education. I firmly believe in these words.

Mao Runzhi: My view is broadly the same as Mr. He's. Social policy is no method at all, because all it does is patch up some leaks. Social democracy resorts to a parliament as its tool for transforming things, but in reality the laws passed by a parliament always protect the propertied class. Anarchism rejects all authority, and I fear that such a doctrine can never be realized. The moderate type of communism, such as the extreme freedom advocated by Russell, lets the capitalists run wild, and therefore it will never work either. The radical type of communism, or the ideology of the workers and the peasants, which employs the method of class dictatorship, can be expected to achieve results. Hence it is the best method for us to use.

Ren Peidao: I agree with the views of He and Mao. But the basic starting point is education. If the people have all received an education, it will naturally be easier to transform them.

Tao Siyong: I, too, used to have this dream of starting with education, but given the present economic conditions in China, it is utterly impossible to educate people properly. In my view, we should approach the soldiers and propagate our ideology, causing them to change spontaneously and to carry out a radical transformation.

Chen Qimin: I approve of the Russian method, because many people in the world at present have put forward different methods of transformation, but only the method adopted by Russia has been put to the test of experience. None of the others, such as anarchism, syndicalism, and guild socialism, have been able to be put into general practice.

Yi Lirong: If we want to transform society, this cannot be done without revolution. After revolution, a dictatorship of the leaders is absolutely indispensable. This dictatorship is not, however, what is commonly called a dictatorship. It must be a dictatorship with a purpose. But today, we must prepare ourselves and carry out much study and discussion. We cannot blindly issue orders to others.

Yi Yuehui: Let me state that I have not studied this at all.

Zou Panqing: In theory anarchism is the best, but in reality it simply does not work. Democracy is, after all, the most feasible. I advocate making the medicine fit the illness. We should advance gradually, both in time and in space. Material relief should be brought about by industrialization, and spiritual relief by universalizing and improving education. How, though, can the effects of education be increased more rapidly, and how can industry not increase the concentration of capital? These are still problems.

Chen Zhangfu: In the past, I thought that, from the perspective of the common people alone, social policy might also work. Later, however, I came to realize that social policy would not work from any perspective. Therefore, I too now endorse Bolshevism.

Zhang Quanshan: The first step is to adopt radicalism, but because the Russians sacrificed freedom to equality, we should then, as our second step, adopt the socialism of Russell and the Guild Socialists.

Chen Zibo: The first step is violent revolution; the second step is the worker-peasant dictatorship.

Zhong Chusheng: I advocate radicalism. In China, society is apathetic and human nature is degenerate. Therefore, a radical method must be adopted. Since Chinese society lacks organization and training, we must employ authoritarianism. Afterward, however, adjustments can be made from time to time.

He Yangu:[9] I advocate overthrowing all the capitalists and bureaucrats.

Peng Yinbo: I believe in the superiority of Bolshevism and in adopting revolutionary methods. We must talk about isms. To talk about isms is not just empty chatter. China has hitherto never had the ism of democracy, but this ism is already outmoded and cannot be applied. I am not fundamentally opposed to anarchism, but anarchism is subjective, and not everyone in the world is a Kropotkin or a Tolstoy. A low level of material civilization is not necessarily an obstacle to the application of socialism. Let's compare conditions in China to those in countries like Germany, England, America, and France. We know that neither French syndicalism, nor English guild socialism, nor the I.W.W.[10] of America, nor German social democracy, can be applied in China. National conditions in China, such as social organization, the industrial situation, and the nature of the people, are very close to those in Russia. Therefore, Russian radicalism can be implemented in China. At the same time, we need not copy radicalism indiscriminately. What we need is simply to have the same spirit, or in other words, to apply revolutionary socialism. Within the Study Society there should be a consistent spirit, study in common, and a relatively practical attitude.

Xiong Chuxiong: I take the view that right now we should only destroy, not construct. We need not talk about isms, but should simply carry on the work of destruction.

Liu Jizhuang: I have nothing to say about isms, for I have not studied them. I agree with what Mr. Xiong said about destruction, except that we should also prepare for construction.

Li Chengde: I have grave doubts about employing the methods of the Russian worker-peasant government. I advocate the moderate methods of Russell, taking education as the starting point and transforming the individual personality. Once the majority of the people have acquired understanding, transformation of the whole body can be undertaken.

Zhou Dunyuan: Anarchism will not work, because not everyone is good by nature. Current conditions in China must absolutely be smashed. I cannot but

---

9. He Yangu (1898–1978), a woman, was a native of Changsha and a graduate of Zhounan Girls' School.

10. The Industrial Workers of the World, or I.W.W., was the main radical workers' organization in the United States during the First World War and in its immediate aftermath. The initials appear here in the Chinese text.

have doubts, however, about radicalism, which places trammels on freedom beyond what human nature can bear. It is right to start with education, to progress gradually, and to carry out transformation step by step. It is appropriate that we take destruction as our first task. After destruction, the work of construction should basically start from the lower levels.

Chen Qimin: When we speak of education and industry, we must have an ism; we must make use of the doctrine of the workers and peasants. To cure a disease, one must start with the root cause; then bit by bit, and very slowly, the results will come.

After everyone had taken the floor in turn, there was free discussion. Peng Yinbo said: Step-by-step transformation should also tend toward our common goal. Ren Peidao supported what Chen Qimin had said about curing a disease by starting with the root cause, though he suggested that a supplementary remedy was needed even after the disease had been cured, and that this supplementary remedy was education. Zou Panqing continued to oppose the argument for transformation. Quoting the words: "The mind of the body is precarious, the mind of the spirit is subtle,"[11] he said that since people had a mixture of the mind of the body and the mind of the spirit, and could not be entirely good, transformation must be carried out step by step. He Shuheng said: Construction should also be started at any time, and modified at any time. I do not agree with Xiong Jinding's theory of destruction alone. He added that there was no need to talk about isms, but everyone should work. Mao Runzhi declared: That everyone should work is in fact an ism, called universal-toil-ism. Zhou Dunyuan did not approve of universal-toil-ism, saying that under the power of the workers and peasants, talent would be crushed. He advocated that there should be freedom to engage in science or the arts, and everyone need not work.

The discussion on the question of method had lasted until two o'clock. The chairman put it to the vote. Twelve people voted in favor of Bolshevism: He Shuheng, Mao Runzhi, Tao Siyong, Yi Kexun, Yi Lirong, Chen Zhangfu, Zhang Quanshan, Chen Zibo, Zhong Chusheng, He Yangu, Peng Yinbo, and Chen Qimin. Two people voted for democracy: Ren Peidao and Zou Panqing. One person voted for the moderate method of communism: Li Chengde. Three people had still not made up their minds: Zhou Dunyuan, Liu Jizhuang, and Xiong Jinding. (The issue of method was, by and large, resolved.)

---

11. This quotation from the *Book of Historical Documents*, chapter on the Great Yu, was frequently commented on by the Song and Ming neo-Confucians. Legge's version (Vol. III, p. 61) does not fit the interpretation placed on it by Zou Panqing, so we give that in Derk Bodde's translation of Fung Yu-lan, *History of Chinese Philosophy*, Vol. 2 (Princeton: Princeton University Press, 1952), p. 559. The passage reads: "The mind of the body [*renxin*] is precarious; the mind of the spirit [*daoxin*] is subtle. Be discriminating, be undivided, that you may sincerely hold fast to the mean."

The discussion recorded above brought the second day to a close. Everyone had lunch together.

January 3 was the third day of the meeting. First of all, the question "How shall we begin to apply these methods immediately?" was discussed. Again, everyone expressed his opinion in turn:

He Shuheng: On the one hand, we must perfect ourselves and study more. On the other hand, we must stress propagating [our ideas], starting with the workers and soldiers. We must make known, as fully as possible, the corruption and privileges of the militarists, politicians, and plutocrats; we must exalt the sacredness of labor and promote conflicts and uprisings. In addition, we should have more links with the Russians. It is also appropriate to consult with people like Chen Jiongming.[12]

Chen Qimin: In our research, we should emphasize comparison, selecting and applying the best and finest. Our propaganda should also be aimed at the intellectual class, so that no talent will be wasted. Whenever there is the opportunity we must push things forward, in order to lay down a solid foundation for the party which we must organize.

Zhou Dunyuan: Let's start from the bottom and advance gradually, stress universalization, plant our feet firmly on the ground, and proceed step by step. We can start with a school and a restaurant. Our study must be done in depth.

Xiong Jinding: We should first carry out research before proceeding with a method of action. Our method of action should stress propagating [our ideas]. A school can best be run by the participants themselves. Another practical way to spread our views widely is to run a newspaper. We really must organize a party. We must strengthen liaison and must not be afraid to make great sacrifices. Sufficient funds should be prepared ahead of time. If we obtain wealth, it will not be for ourselves, provided only that we have a goal and an organization.

Peng Yinbo: Four things are indispensable: research, propagating [our ideas], organization, and liaison. The scope of research should be many-sided; science, literature, philosophy, economics, and politics should not be neglected. What each of us has learned should be shared with the others. In propagating our ideas,

---

12. Chen Jiongming (1878–1933), original name Jie, *zi* Jingcun and Cansan, was a native of Guangdong. A member of the Tongmenghui from 1909, he enjoyed a long association with Sun Yatsen, who had appointed him governor of Guangdong in 1920. In January 1921, he invited Chen Duxiu to become chairman of the provincial Education Committee, a post that Chen Duxiu used as a base for his efforts to organize the Communist movement in South China. It was therefore not surprising that He Shuheng should have regarded him at this time as a person with whom the New People's Study Society should consult. In 1922, Chen Jiongming broke with Sun Yatsen, and the materials in this volume for the years 1925–1927 are filled with Mao's attacks on him.

we should also emphasize the intellectual class. We must organize a party of the toilers, because a great cause can hardly be accomplished by a small number of people. The more people we have, the easier our task will be. The Socialist Youth League[13] is a spirited organization, which we should support. In terms of liaison, it is important to maintain contact with both individuals and organizations, such as the Young China Association.[14]

He Yangu: Research and propagating our views are extremely important. It is even more necessary that we personally immerse ourselves in laboring circles.

Chen Zibo: When we go to the working class, we should distribute many pamphlets, and there is no reason why these should not be written in fairly radical language. In organizing the Party, we should distinguish between the cities and the villages. We can make use of the Hong Society.[15]

Yi Yuehui: We can learn from the methods of the Socialist Youth League.

Jiang Ruiyu: We should develop each person's special abilities and make use of every opportunity. Priority should be given to education.

Zhang Quanshan: The subjective and objective aspects must both be emphasized. On the objective side, there are three methods: (1) propaganda, which has three subdivisions—(a) schools, (b) pamphlets, and (c) secret speeches; (2) organization; and (3) liaison, which has three subdivisions—(a) individuals, (b) small collective bodies, and (c) large collective bodies, such as Russia. On the subjective side, we should increase our individual capacities.

Chen Zhangfu: We should begin our study right away. Propaganda like that of the Cultural Book Society is the most effective. The fact that the educators in my *xian* have felt extremely guilty since the Liuxi Cultural Book Society[16] was established is an example of this. We should start with a movement of the townspeople, making more speeches and increasing links with people. In estab-

---

13. The Socialist Youth League, the youth organization of the Chinese Communist Party then in the course of organization, was set up in Hunan in October 1920. Many members of the New People's Study Society subsequently joined it, and it became a large and powerful organization in Hunan by early 1923.

14. The Young China Association was organized in Beijing in mid-1918 by Li Dazhao, Wang Guangqi, and other intellectuals and returned students from Japan. Its goal was to promote nationalism and the rejuvenation of China. It was formally established on July 1, 1919, in the wake of the May Fourth movement, with membership drawing largely from students and educationalists, and took an active role in political movements of the time. Mao became a member in December 1919 and remained one for several years, even though the Society evolved toward a moderate or centrist position.

15. The term *Honghui* was used loosely for a variety of secret societies related to the White Lotus, including the *Gelaohui* or Elder Brother Society, of which Mao had first-hand knowledge from his youth in rural Hunan, and the Green Gang in the cities. Here it may refer simply to the secret societies in general.

16. The Liuxi branch of the Cultural Book Society was founded on November 10, 1920. See the "Second Business Report of the Cultural Book Society," dated April 1921, above.

lishing links, we can copy Yan Xizhai's[17] method of educating the patient while curing his disease. Restaurants and tea houses are the best places to start. Organize vegetable gardens, starting with the laboring people. Set up more evening schools. To establish links, we must go ourselves to working-class circles, and we should also get in touch with women's circles.

Zou Panqing: The world is evolving gradually. It is appropriate, therefore, to transform it step by step, in a moderate way, starting from the here and now. Special attention must be paid to educational enterprises. Running an educational enterprise requires capital, but we should oppose borrowing money from outside. Propaganda should emphasize the working class and should be long-term propaganda. Education is a fundamental task, because comrades produced in the schools are the firmest and strongest. One real comrade is worth more than several ordinary people. Raise money by donations to run schools. Start with elementary school, proceeding to middle school and college; start in Changsha, proceeding then to other provinces and other countries. Advance gradually, and in due course solid results will be obtained. In running newspapers, we must emphasize adapting them for popular consumption.

Jiang Jixu: To do things requires money. Fund-raising should come from running a business. Everyone will be expected to do his share.

Yi Lirong: There is nothing inherently frightening in extremism. If you have not studied it, naturally you will be afraid of it. Such research must be thorough. Propaganda, if it is presented with a sincere attitude, will certainly be effective. Propaganda and organization should be integrated. When you organize, conduct propaganda; and when you conduct propaganda, organize. We must create an extremist faction of ten thousand people and propagate our message everywhere. Artists can do this by the method of suggestion.

Tao Siyong: What I want to say can be put as follows: "How shall I myself get started right now?" My answer is, "I want to start reading right away."

Ren Peidao: Take our own reading as the starting point.

Mao Runzhi: I agree with the various methods for getting started you gentlemen have proposed: study, organization, propaganda, establishing links, fund raising, and business. I would merely add that "self-cultivation"[18] should be

---

17. Xizhai was the *hao* of Yan Yuan (1635–1704), *zi* Yuzhi, one of the most original thinkers of the late Ming and early Qing period. As suggested by the name he took, which means "Studio of Practical Knowledge," he opposed mere contemplation and maintained that the true way of study was to be found in the practical arts of mathematics, astronomy, and mechanics, and especially in military training. For his influence on the young Mao see the essay of 1917, "A Study of Physical Education," in Volume I of this edition, p. 116. In his youth, Yan Yuan had studied medicine in order to support his family; hence the reference here to educating and curing people at the same time.

18. *Xiuyang*, the self-cultivation, originally of Confucian inspiration, that Mao had studied beginning in 1913 with Yang Changji. See the "Classroom Notes" in Volume I of this edition, especially pp. 14–28 and 38–39.

included under study. Establishing links might be called "establishing links with comrades," for it is useless to have contacts with those, whether they be individuals or organizations, who are not comrades. To raise funds, we could first organize a savings association for members of the Society. We must run various kinds of basic enterprises, such as schools, vegetable gardens, popular newspapers, lecture groups, printing houses, editing and translating companies, etc. Among these, the Cultural Book Society is most economical and effective. I hope all of you will find ways to promote and spread it.

After everyone had spoken in turn, there was an exchange of views as to the various methods for getting started that had been proposed. Most people said we should concentrate on those that are both necessary and can realistically be carried out. The chairman then put together the following composite list of the methods for getting started that had been formulated by everyone.

Methods for getting started:

1. Study and self-cultivation
   a. isms
   b. various fields of study
2. Organization
   a. organizing a Socialist Youth League
3. Propaganda
   a. education
   b. newspapers and pamphlets
   c. talks
4. Links among comrades
5. Capital funds
   a. organizing a savings association
6. Basic enterprises
   a. schools (including evening schools)
   b. promoting and spreading the Cultural Book Society
   c. printing shop
   d. editing company
   e. popular newspapers
   f. lecture groups
   g. vegetable gardens

The chairman then took a vote on whether or not the above-listed six items, with the subheadings, should be approved as the methods by which the members of the Society would proceed to get started. Everyone present stood up. (The issue of the method for getting started was thus resolved.)

The next subject for the discussion was the domestic concerns of members.

Chen Zhangfu reported on the content of the letters from our members in Paris. He added that many members had known the suffering of domestic problems, and it was urgent to find a remedy for these. Mao Runzhi said that this was a very great problem. Currently, an extremely large number of young people had domestic troubles, and the majority of our members also had such troubles. If we did not seek to resolve them now, it would be even more difficult to find a solution in future. A number of people proceeded in turn to relate their own family problems. Some people proposed organizing a "school for the transformation of wives," some wanted to organize "factories," and some advocated setting up a "women's work-study school." Finally, it was decided, in accordance with the letters from Paris, to begin by organizing a "Women's Society for Self-Perfectionment." Tao Siyong, Yi Lirong, Chen Zhangfu, and Ren Peidao were nominated as members of a preparatory committee. These four were asked to explore what means of relief might be adopted; after they had reached some conclusions, the issue would be further considered. (The issue of domestic concerns was thus resolved.)

The next subject for the discussion was "The question of the anniversary of the Study Society."

It was unanimously agreed that April 17 would be the anniversary of the founding of the Study Society, and that members in each locality should get together separately for a dinner on this day.

The next subject for the discussion was "The question of the members' health and recreation."

Everyone considered that this was an important question, but felt that it was not appropriate to vote on regulations regarding matters falling under the heading of "improving our health," such as getting up early, exercising, taking baths, avoiding exhaustion, and giving up smoking and drinking, because these were matters for careful consideration and effort on the part of individual members. A vote was, however, taken to approve the following sorts of gatherings for "improving our recreational activities":

1. River cruises: Specific dates will be chosen for at least three cruises in the fifth, seventh, and eighth months of the lunar calendar.
2. Mountain excursions: Three trips to be scheduled in spring, summer, and autumn.
3. Spring outing to visit graves: On March 3.
4. Dinner meetings: Once a month, on the day of the regular monthly meeting, the cost for each dinner to be twenty copper cash.
5. Frolics in the snow: Arrangements to be made whenever it snows.
6. Ball games: Arrangements to be made at the discretion of the members.
(The question of health and recreation was thus resolved.)

There remained three further issues: "Individual members' plans of action," "Individual members' means of livelihood," and "The presentation and criticism of individual character," which could not be discussed for lack of time. They would be resolved at this year's regular January meeting.

On the third day, the discussion was resumed at 10:00 A.M., and the meeting lasted until 2:00 P.M. On this day, everyone went to the river bank outside the Caochao Gate for a photo session. The snow storm was so heavy that none of the pictures came out.

January 16 was the day of the regular monthly meeting of Changsha members for January, the tenth year of the Republic. As usual, the meeting took place at the Cultural Book Society. Twenty-one people came to the meeting. The chairman, He Shuheng, said: I report that today, we are going to resume our discussion of the questions that were not resolved during our New Year's meeting. There are three issues: (1) Individual members' plans of action, (2) Individual members' means of livelihood, and (3) The presentation and criticism of individual characters. I invite you all to begin by discussing the first question:

"Individual members' plans of action."

Each of the twenty-one people present spoke in turn.

He Shuheng: My plan is a narrow one. In the future, I will remain an elementary-school teacher. I would like to open a school in my native village. Within three years, I want to travel to different parts of the country to conduct surveys. At the same time, I will not neglect reading and study. In the past, I was interested in learning foreign languages, but now I feel that I am too old to learn them well. Nevertheless, I still want to study Japanese, primarily in order to read Japanese books. In doing something, one should start on a very small scale.

Zhou Dunyuan: My aim is to do some academic research. I intend to devote some effort to literature and philosophy, but my future career will be in education. My current plan of action is to master English in two years. Formerly, I wanted to go to school, but now it seems to me that there are no schools in China worth attending. I intend to raise some money in the near future to go to Japan, but this is not easy. Although going to Japan may not be all that wonderful, it still has two advantages: first, I can isolate myself from the outside world and avoid being entangled in the current turmoil in China; secondly, even though Japan does not have its own independent culture, it is very quick to assimilate things and is not lacking in things worthy of study. In case I have difficulty in raising the money, I may have to seek a government loan.

Peng Yinbo: Formerly, I planned to spend my life in the business world, and so I went to business school. Later, when I found out that my personality was not suited to business, I quit. I used to have an ambition to master several foreign languages, to acquire something of a general understanding of metaphysics, to make a contribution to business, and to engage in international trade. Now, however, this has all changed. I feel that if you want to transform society, you cannot do so unless there is economic and political transformation. First, I intended to study in America but was prevented by lack of money. Then, I also thought of going to France. Beginning last year, I wanted to go to Russia as well. Now, I would still like to go to Russia via France. I will stay in Changsha only for another two years at most. While in Changsha, apart from making a living for myself, I also wish to aid the labor organizations. As for what to study, my mind has not changed, but now I want to learn only two foreign languages, English and Russian.

Zhong Chusheng: I feel that I can live only in the field of education, and moreover, I wish to live only there. For this reason, having in the past already entered middle school, I switched to normal school. Because the higher normal school in our province is no good, I did not want to go there after graduating from normal school and consequently became a teacher. Several years have somehow elapsed since then. I would like to continue to devote my efforts to education and get together enough money to make a visit to Japan.

Chen Zibo: I won't make definite plans until after I graduate from middle school. During my stay in Changsha, I shall on the one hand make a contribution to society by propagating our doctrines among the soldiers and workers, and on the other hand prepare my own lessons.

Xie Nanling: In transforming society, we should, I believe, start from the lowest level—that is, from the villages. Consequently, I would like very much to devote all my energies to education in the countryside. After graduation from normal school, I have decided to pursue further study, either at the Southwest University, or at the higher normal school, or at the advanced institute of engineering. After finishing my advanced studies, I will definitely work in the countryside. I want to change the prevailing psychological attitudes toward what are petty and what are noble occupations.

Zhang Quanshan: Formerly, I only had a plan for my studies. Since last year, I have also had a plan for my career. As far as learning is concerned, I want to begin with mathematics, physics, and chemistry. Right now, I study English whenever I have the leisure. In addition to supporting myself, I have to pay the tuition for a young friend. For this reason, I will have to stay in Changsha for another year and a half and continue to work as a teacher.

Jiang Jixu: I would like to become an educator, with a career in elementary and middle-school education. After graduating from normal school, I shall teach and save money so I can enter the higher normal school and then study abroad. While making my career in education, I would like to gather together some comrades and run a school of our own.

Mao Runzhi: I feel that general knowledge is very important. At present, the learning of those who are called specialists is really only general, if that. For myself, I have decided to study only general knowledge until I reach the age of thirty, because I lack knowledge of the basic natural sciences such as mathematics, physics, and chemistry, and I want to find a way to remedy this deficiency. In literature, though I am not good at creative writing, I sometimes have an inspiration. I enjoy studying philosophy. As regards applied learning, I am studying educational theory and teaching methods. In the realm of work, I have come to realize that the method of "everyone does his own thing" is wholly ineffectual and extremely uneconomical. I would like to do my part in carrying out an enterprise that we have all decided to pursue, so that some years later, when my contribution is combined with the parts for which others have taken responsability, something will have been achieved. Last year, when I was in Shanghai, I decided to stay in Changsha for two years and then to go to Russia. Now, half a year has already passed, and in another year and a half I shall leave this province. While in Changsha, in addition to my educational work, I plan to concentrate on building and expanding the Cultural Book Society. In these two years of study, I intend to obtain a broad understanding of scholarly thinking throughout the world by reading translations and periodicals. The only problem is that one cannot concentrate on study while working at the same time. The second half of last year was totally sacrificed (this was a most painful sacrifice). From now on, I want to make sure I devote one hour every day to reading books and another hour to reading newspapers.

Luo Chiyu: My lifelong career is education. Education is for the benefit of mankind and of society, so I want to do some research in sociology. I cannot decide how to conduct my research, whether by self-study, or by going to school, at home or abroad. As regards my plan for the immediate future, I am going to learn English beginning with the first month of the next lunar year. I want to learn English well enough to read books within five years.

Xia Manbo: I firmly believe in the principle of carrying on work and study at the same time, and using mind and body together. I want to study education while learning a craft. This is my goal. My method is, first of all, that I have decided to graduate from normal school and, after graduation, to work as a teacher for a few years. While teaching, I will, at the same time, devote myself both to research and to the practice of my craft. Only after ten years will I go abroad.

Zou Pangeng: I have been pondering over my plan for many years. After revising it several times, I now seem to have something of a grasp on it. A person's career, as I see it, is composed of just two aspects, study and publication.[19] My personal intention is to study literature and philosophy (in the broad

---

19. The Chinese expression *fabiao* is the common term for "to publish," especially in the case of an article. It seems plain from Zou Pangeng's statement as a whole that he has in mind making known the results of his studies in due course, either in print or in other ways.

sense). I plan to spend one year reviewing all the natural sciences that I have already learned, two more years studying literature, and then one more year studying English. During these four years, I will also do some part-time teaching (but not be in charge of a class). I will pursue my own studies whenever I am not in class. After four years, I am going to Japan, where I shall stay for at least a year. I do not, however, want to go to school there, because I have always been against it. After that, I shall pursue learning for another five years, but I do not have any detailed idea about this yet. I may even go to the West, it is hard to say. This is my ten-year plan of study. Once it is accomplished, I will devote myself to publication. As for the reason why I do not approve of schools, it is that you cannot really learn anything in school.

Yi Yuehui: Recently, I have come to the definite realization that ultimately I want to become an educator. During my period of preparation, I shall first study foreign languages. At the very least, I will master English, French, and Japanese, the primary emphasis being on English. By reading books on education in English, I will combine my study of education with my study of foreign languages. I, too, believe that there is no need to go to school. Therefore, I have decided to start working in education within six months. Every day, I will spend four hours working and six hours reading.

Chen Qimin's intervention was very long. Here only the main points are recorded. Chen said: My individual plans comprise, first of all, my lifelong plan, which is a plan to read all my life. This plan has been fixed on the basis of my own world view and personality. The universe, I believe, is made up of two components: space and time. Time is a straight line, while space is a whole. Neither of them is fragmented. It is my nature to enjoy diversity. Consequently, I feel that whatever people in the universe want to study, I want to study, and whatever people in the universe have discoursed upon, I want to discourse upon. Literature, philosophy, and science—all these I want to study. I want to become a "trust" in academic circles. I cannot lay down a systematic course of study for the time being. Whether or not to pursue further studies in school, and whether or not to go abroad, are not, I feel, real problems for me. Because schools cannot confine me, I can make use of the schools. So perhaps I may go back to school. As for going abroad, knowledge in the world is divided into two major branches; one belongs to Asia and the other to Europe. Formerly, I took the view that in studying Asia one could concentrate on Chinese learning, with some attention to India and Japan. As for Europe, it was hard to say which country one should concentrate on, so I thought I would first study Asian learning. That used to be my way of thinking. Subsequently, I thought I would use Western methods to pursue Eastern learning. Now I want to study East and West simultaneously. If in future I go abroad, I will live mostly in one country but travel around to different countries, playing the role of a hunter in the academic world. As for advanced study, I have not yet decided in what year or in which school I will undertake it. There is no end to study; it is never complete and ends only with death. What I have talked about thus far is my lifelong plan. Now, I would like to say something about my immediate plans. Economic pressures keep me from going abroad, but this is truly to my advantage because I plan to make use of the time to study Chinese learning. In approaching Chinese learning, I shall concentrate on the Zhou and the Qin, for there is no learning to speak of from all the dynasties that follow the Zhou and the Qin. The Song dynasty may be an exception in that it was influenced by Buddhism. The Qing dynasty, which was an era of return to the ancients, is of course worth studying. I intend to use a historical method in mastering Chinese learning, putting the emphasis on two subjects—literature and philosophy. It is my belief that the study of the cool and dispassionate subjects should be reserved until later and that those dealing with human affairs, such as politics and economics, should come first. Now, in the West, both politics and economics are organized on a large scale. Consequently, my study of the West will probably focus on the political and economic aspects. Formerly, I had a plan for mastering three foreign languages in two years, but, because of the real obstacles, I have now established a new plan for mastering two foreign languages in three years. In addition to English, I would like to learn French and Japanese.

He Yangu: My plan is changing all the time. Formerly, when I was a student at the normal school, I had no particular plan in my mind. After graduation, I taught for a few years. I thought of going to higher normal school, but that didn't happen. Now I intend to study medicine and, to this end, I want to learn English, chemistry, physiology, and so on. Since I am not financially independent, I plan to go to medical school only after I have put aside some money by working for two years. Medicine is a profession that saves people. During this period of work, I will study English and chemistry at the same time.

Wu Yuzhen:[20] I would like to join the work-study program in France, but I am afraid that I will not be able to go because I do not have any money. Right now I am still trying to save the money and at the same time learn a bit of English.

Tao Siyong: If Mr. Chen wants to be a "trust" in the field of learning, I can only be a little coal-picker.[21] After graduation from normal school, I could not go on to advanced studies because of my financial situation. I thought that if I taught for a few years, I would be able to save the money for further study. Contrary to my expectations, my circumstances have remained the same down to the present. I have long thought about finding a partner for self-study, but several attempts have been unsuccessful. Last year, I wanted to enter Beijing Higher Normal School, but this came to nothing. Last summer I went to Nanjing Higher

---

20. Wu Yuzhen (1899–), a woman, was a native of Xiangtan, Hunan, and a graduate of Zhounan Girls' School.

21. The reference is to the practice, common at the time among the poor, of sending children to factory yards to pick up bits of coal for use at home.

Normal School in the hope of being admitted but was again unsuccessful. Since then, I have simply stayed at Zhounan, working and also studying, starting with psychology, pedagogy, and English. At the same time, I want to forge links with women friends in the provincial capital and elsewhere. I feel that in seeking friends, they need not necessarily be better than oneself. Anyone who has high aspirations should be contacted.

Ren Peidao: Many of my plans have failed in the past. Originally, I wanted to pursue advanced studies, but afterward this proved impossible because of difficulties caused by the cost and by the location. Under the circumstances, I made a plan to become an elementary-school teacher, with the twin objectives of accumulating experience and saving for future needs. Several years in Xupu have also led to no useful result. Last year I wanted to go to France but was once again unsuccessful for lack of money. I have made an effort, quitting my teaching job with the intention of devoting myself exclusively to learning in Changsha, but since coming to Changsha I have not been able to do what I wanted to do. Now all I can do is seek a way to support myself while at the same time studying English and awaiting once again the opportunity for further study.

Wu Jiaying: During my student years, I had very great plans and hopes. But after entering society and spending a few years there, the scope of my former plans has been considerably diminished! Now I do not even have any concrete plan worth speaking of. I am left only with the general idea, which I have maintained all along, of somehow advancing in both respects, learning and a career.

Tang Wenfu: Mr. Chen sees the universe as a whole, and in the light of this has elaborated his world outlook and then in turn established his plans. My plan is also based on my world outlook. In my view, the universe is only "beauty." To me, there is nothing in the world that is not beautiful. I am happy to study anything that stirs my sense of beauty. Literature can express beauty, and poetry in particular is a major literary form for expressing beauty. Therefore, I would like to study and create poetry. I seek neither fame nor profit, nor do I care about the praise and blame of others. I seek to satisfy my own needs and that is all. Philosophy is also something I want to study. Those who seek learning need, first, discrimination and, second, courage. Courage, however, is the most important; without courage you cannot succeed in your studies. I am willing to stand up and attack everything, to become a "reckless fool" in learning. For the next eighteen months I am not going to leave the province, but will work a little to earn a living while studying English and Japanese. After eighteen months, I will go either to Beijing University or to Nanjing Higher Normal School—I have not yet decided which. In any case, I know that my personality is inclined toward literature, and I want to devote myself entirely to it in the future.

Xiong Jinding: In my opinion, if you want to do anything, you must have money. That is why I have long had the idea of making a fortune. I often looked for and read books like *Ten Rich Men* and *The Money-Makers*,[22] and so on. I have often felt that when you live under a society like that of China, there are two roads to wealth: becoming an official or going into business. To get an official position, you have to curry favor, and that is something I am not willing to do. As for business, I have also given it a try but stopped for various reasons. Now, I am thinking of making a start in production. Formerly, I talked with Xiao Zisheng and others about cultivating wasteland in the three eastern provinces, but because of various difficulties we did not go ahead with this project. Just now, we are discussing other methods. I believe that while we do not require personal profit, collective capital is indispensable. Only by increasing our capital can we expand our enterprise. We need not be overly fastidious about our methods, so long as they serve to make money.

This ended the foregoing presentations of individual members' plans of action. In the past, most of our friends tended to keep their own plans secret and were unwilling to reveal them publicly. Thus, other people did not know about their plans, and they did not know about other people's plans either. Everyone was left in the dark. As a result, it was impossible to engage in mutual aid or to cooperate on a common project with others sharing the same goal, even if we wanted to. The results of such a phenomenon of "everyone thinking his own thoughts," and "everyone doing his thing" are: First, if your plan is faulty or wrong, it will remain faulty or wrong to the day you die, because you have no chance to be corrected. You will not achieve what you desired, and you will be left with nothing but remorse. We often observe such a situation. Second, even if your plan is not faulty or wrong, in the end you cannot fulfill it because you work on it all by yourself without any help from others. This is also a common occurrence. It is because our colleagues in Changsha were aware of such failures that they decided each one should describe his own plans. If our colleagues in different places can follow suit, talking about their plans and recording them in the business report of the Society, everyone who reads that report will surely benefit in many ways.

When the above presentations of individual plans were over, there was a twenty-minute break. The discussion then moved on to the second question:

"Individual members' means of livelihood."

---

22. The reference is to Vol. 129 of the *Shiji* (and the corresponding section of various dynastic histories) entitled *Huozhi zhuan*, or *Huozhi liezhuan*. This was rendered as "The Money-Makers" by Burton Watson in his translation of excerpts from the work, *Records of the Grand Historian of China* (New York: Columbia University Press, 1961), Vol. II, pp. 476–99, and also by Yang Hsien-yi and Gladys Yang in their version, *Records of the Historian* (Hong Kong: The Commercial Press, 1974), pp. 410–28.

This is also a very important issue. In the past, scholars on the whole never studied methods for making a living. As a result, a situation was created in which every community of scholars was a community of scoundrels who would stop at nothing. In reality, the problem of getting food to eat is never easy to solve. If, on top of that, it is not studied, efforts will unavoidably be made to solve it by some foolish means. The result of the discussion of this question by the members of the New People's Study Society in Changsha was that all of them, with the exception of one or two persons who, for different reasons, were not in favor of stressing the question of making a living, believed that this was an extremely important issue. The following is a record of this discussion.

He Shuheng: My own way of life is very simple and therefore I can handle it easily. The only thing is that I must also get the money for my children's educational expenses. I plan to make a career in education and hope that I can live on this modest income. As for other, improper ways of enriching oneself, I will not indulge in them no matter what happens.

Peng Yinbo: There are three common problems, namely, study, work, and making a living, none of which is easy to resolve. In my opinion, however, as long as a person has courage he need not be concerned about making a living. Russell says, "We should think about things other than making a living." I am deeply convinced of this. Once we have solved the problems of study and work, making a living will be no problem. We must, however, choose a direction for earning our living. There are many ways of making a living, such as being an official, that we should not choose. We can only choose the field of education (apart from other new organizations and new means of livelihood) or labor. Working as a laborer also has its difficulties because the laborers are too ignorant. Consequently, if we want to work, the only really satisfactory solution is to have a new organization.

Tang Wenfu: If in the course of our studies our minds are entirely focused on trying to solve the problem of earning a living, I fear that we may fall behind, and if we fail to solve it we will become frustrated. Currently, I am helping to edit the news for *The People's Rule Daily*. The job is not very time-consuming, and at the same time I get a little pay, enough to support myself and to buy books and newspapers. In the future, I plan to have a job like this, which gives me a living on the one hand but allows me to study on the other.

Chen Zibo: Although I have a small inheritance, my father controls it entirely and does not let me manage it myself. There is no way I can get out of this painful situation except by living independently. Since I am still in school, this is very difficult. I intend to work at the Cultural Book Society during my winter and summer vacations so that I will be able to pay the tuition from my wages. My means of livelihood after graduation will be decided when the time comes.

Zhou Dunyuan: For the time being, I am working for a newspaper to support myself. I would like very much not to work at all in the future and to devote myself entirely to my studies. But I have to make some extra money.

Zhang Quanshan: My profession is teaching.

Zhong Chusheng: My profession is teaching.

Xie Nanling: My family is poor, but I can endure suffering. My material livelihood can very easily be dealt with. But I do not have any money to buy books, so to pursue advanced studies in future will also be very difficult. Recently, I have thought of opening a small workshop, or a printing plant, as a means of making a living.

Xia Manbo: At present, I am a parasite; and not only am I myself a parasite, but I am carrying with me two other parasites, my wife and my daughter. In the future, I would like to engage in a handicraft as the means for earning my living. At present, I have still not graduated from the normal school, but I intend to open a small printing shop within the year so as to cover my expenses with the income from it. After graduation, I would like to make a living by working as a teacher. My family includes my father, two younger sisters, my wife, and my daughter. None of them, except my father, are producers. Thus, the family's livelihood is extremely precarious.

Yi Yuehui: As regards consumption, I advocate maintaining a proper standard, neither too luxurious nor too austere, with tasty food, clothing to cover our bodies, and a house that is clean, light, and airy. As for the method of making a living, for the time being it is my monthly pay as a teacher. My major expense, I fear, is the money spent on books.

He Yangu: At present, I do not have a means of livelihood. As for my plans, I would like to study medicine. So long as that is not possible, I will continue to work in education, on a part-work, part-study basis. I think our standard of consumption should not be too simple. Food and housing should meet the requirements of hygiene, and what we wear should keep us warm.

Xiong Chuxing: Our individual livelihoods alone pose no problem. What makes the problem of earning a living difficult to resolve lies in the fact that, apart from ourselves, we have to take care of others—our juniors. We have to explore new means, such as the two small jobs of "delivering lime"[23] and "supplying kerosene," which no one did before, but which, once launched, have become very good means of earning a living. If we have no work at all to do, we too can explore new avenues. I do not like to be too stingy when it comes to spending money on living expenses. For if life is a bit more comfortable, your expectations will surely be somewhat greater, and you will definitely be somewhat more courageous in doing things.

Mao Runzhi: The work I would like to do is on the one hand to teach and on the other hand to be a reporter. Most likely, my future livelihood will depend on the salaries from these two jobs. At present, I feel that work relying solely on brainpower is very difficult, so I want to learn to do some form of manual labor,

---

23. For plaster and cement.

such as knitting socks or baking bread. With the ability to do this kind of job, one can go anywhere in the world and make enough to eat. With regard to consumption, I am all for a simple, rather than luxurious, way of life.

Luo Chiyu: As far as production is concerned, I am making a living in the field of education. As regards consumption, my income and expenditure are balanced; there is no need to be too frugal. In addition to myself, I must also support my family.

Jiang Jixu: One's material livelihood has only three components: clothing, food, and shelter. I have now decided that I do not want any of my family's property. After my graduation from normal school I will work as a teacher and will live together with some close friends, helping each other by sharing living expenses and taking turns in pursuing advanced studies. I have decided to wear only cotton clothes for the next ten years, and one meal a day will provide sufficient food. I shall be even less particular about housing. As to spiritual life, I have an urgent desire to study. I used to believe that human life was meaningless, nothing but a process of endless evolution which made people confused, and gave them a feeling of boredom. Now, under the influence of Dewey and Russell, I don't think constantly of the hopeless, dark, and evil side of things. I keep my mind fixed only on the hopeful and bright side of things. Thus, I feel some joy in life.

Zou Pangeng: Because I want to study, I have to take the problem of making a living into consideration. My family is basically self-supporting, but it would be even better if I could pay for books and periodicals myself. When, in future, I devote myself full time to study, things will be more difficult.

Tao Siyong: At present, my livelihood is dependent on my teaching and my job in the school administration. When I cannot totally rely on these two sources of income, I resort to cooking, tailoring, and crocheting. Although earning my material livelihood presents no difficulties, I am not good at managing my finances, and when I have money I cannot save it. The life of the spirit is a difficult matter because it requires learning. The spirit is like a fish, and knowledge is like water. The spirit can only be happy if it has learning.

Chen Qimin: Regarding the life of the spirit, my views will be plain to you in broad outline from my previous remarks, and I will not repeat what I said then. The problem of material livelihood cannot be solved by the individual, and therefore, both socialism and communism revolutionize life. Too dry and hard a life will inevitably affect one's psyche. So we should definitely not deliberately deprive ourselves of the satisfaction of our bodily needs. We should maintain appropriate standards for our food and drink, clothing, and shelter. Although they should not be luxurious, they must always be "sufficient." The individual cannot solve all the problems of his livelihood; the individual can only try to do everything that does lie within his power.

Ren Peidao: Right now I can make a living by teaching and I am content with simple clothing and food.

At this moment, Wu Dezhuang left the meeting to attend to other business. The presentation by each person in turn of his means for earning a living was at an end. There was discussion among members. Zhou Dunyuan said: The most important thing is to encourage virtue and admonish faults. I often have the impression that, though friends frequently get together to converse, their talk is often idle talk, and they seldom sincerely address the issues of how to cultivate one's character through study. It is my hope that our members will pay attention to this point, and that when we meet it will not be for the purpose of idle talk, but to encourage virtue and admonish faults, and to discuss issues. I also feel that, at the present time, we should emphasize "transformation of the self," and that we must not join too many organizations, or get involved in too many activites, which might hamper our self-cultivation. Jiang Jixu strongly agreed with what Zhou had said, remarking, "This is exactly what we should do." Tao Siyong declared: I have joined seven or eight organizations in all. In future, I should withdraw from four or five of them. He Shuheng said: When friends meet, they should criticize one another extensively. As to the actual means for making a living, it is still necessary to do a lot more research. Mao Runzhi did not approve of Xiong Jinding's views regarding consumption and declared that a life of luxury was not just without benefit, it was harmful. He advocated that, under the guidance of science, we should maintain the level of nutrition necessary for our bodies, keep our bodies warm, and live in adequate housing. That is "sufficiency"; anything more than "sufficiency" would bring harm. At this point, He Shuheng made a proposal: In thinking about collective means of production, the suggestion made just now to run a print shop is, I think, worth discussing and putting into practice. Mao Runzhi said: The Cultural Book Society has such a plan. Since the "Book Society" has only a distribution department, it also needs to set up a print shop and an editing and translation office. Xia Manbo said: If others are willing to help organize it, I am willing to take responsibility for carrying this out. It was unanimously agreed that this was a most urgent task, and as a result it was decided that the matter should be discussed again at another time. "The presentation and criticism of individual character" was not discussed because of the lateness of the hour, and the meeting was adjourned.

Dear Members:

It is estimated that report no. 3 on the affairs of the Society can be edited and printed only about the end of this year. The draft of the fourth volume of *Collected Correspondence* is, however, complete, and the volume will come out in August of this year. We hope that draft materials for the fifth volume will continue to arrive. Please send your letters, no matter how casual or short they are (including post cards). All mail should be addressed to the Changsha Cultural Book Society.

A Couplet for the Hero Yi Baisha[1]

(1921)

The useless one died not, the useful one died in anger; I weep
for the future of the Republic.

Last year I mourned Mr. Chen,[2] this year I mourn Mr. Yi;
what can be done now about Changsha's backwardness?

We have translated this text from *Shici duilian*, p. 160. It was first published in 1987 in
Duilian, Vol. 3, No. 2.

1. Yi Baisha (1886–1921), a native of Changsha, had been a teacher at First Normal
School, Nankai University in Tianjin, and Fudan University in Shanghai. In May 1921, he
went to Beijing with the intention of killing the leader of the warlord government, but
failed. He then went south to organize an army for a northern expedition but was not
successful in this either. Thereupon, he committed suicide by drowning himself in the sea
off the coast of Guangdong, on the day of the Dragon Boat Festival, in the hope of
arousing the masses.

2. Mr. Chen (*Chen gong*) refers to Chen Tianhua (1875–1905), who like Yi Baisha
had committed suicide for patriotic reasons by throwing himself into the sea. Mao's only
known writing in praise of him is a passage in the "Overall Account of the Hunan United
Students' Association," translated in Volume I, pp. 402–3. This text was published not
"last year," i.e., in 1920, but on August 4, 1919. Perhaps a poem in his memory has been
lost; perhaps Mao was using *qu nian* loosely to mean "in recent years."

Statement on the Founding of the Hunan Self-Study University

(August 1921)

Hunanese have recently founded a "Self-Study University," the primary aim of which is to adopt the form of the old-style academies and infuse it with the content of the modern schools, in the hope that all of the students enrolled will read on their own and study together. In the midst of China's present tide of "university mania," this may be considered the most practical system of education. This school has recently issued a statement explaining the principles underlying its establishment:

Man cannot but seek learning, and the search for learning requires both a place and an organization. In the past, the place to pursue learning was the academies.[1] When the academies were abolished and turned into schools, everyone strove to censure the academies and praise the schools. In fact, there are things about both the academies and the schools that may be censured and things about both that may be praised. What the academies should be censured for is the fact that the content of their studies was wrong: it consisted of such instruments of official employment as the "eight-legged essay."[2] These were merely play-

---

This manifesto was first published in *Dongfang zazhi* Vol. 20, No. 6, March 1923. Our translation has been made from the version in *Mao Zedong ji*, Vol. 1, pp. 81–84, where it is dated April 17, 1921. Chinese sources, including the *Nianpu*, confirm that Mao actually drafted this document in August 1921.

1. Academies, or *shuyuan*, which had first appeared in the tenth century, remained the most important institutions of higher education in China down to the early twentieth century. Supported by the gentry and the officials, they existed at various levels, mainly in *xian* and prefectural seats. Following the Reform Movement of 1895, Western learning came to occupy a small place in their curriculum, but their focus remained essentially, as Mao indicates in this passage, on preparing young scholars for official careers. They lost their *raison d'être* with the abolition of the imperial examination system in 1905.

2. The stereotyped form of writing required for all imperial examinations from the Chenghua reign (1465–87) in the mid-Ming to the abolition of the system in the late Qing. As the term suggests, the essays had to be written according to a rigid eight-part schema. *Bagu*, or eight-legged essays, remained a favorite target of Mao's, and a synonym for all sorts of pedantry, to the end of his life. The most celebrated instance is no doubt his second keynote speech of February 8, 1942, for the Rectification Campaign, attacking *dang bagu* or "Party formalism."

things; how can they be regarded as genuine learning? If we base ourselves on this point, we may say that the academies were greatly in error. But the academies had their extremely good points. If we want to understand the good points of the academies, we must first understand the bad points of the schools. As a matter of fact, the schools have many good points, but they also have not a few bad points. **The first bad point of the schools is that there is no personal relationship between teachers and students. The teachers mainly think about making money and the students think mainly about getting a diploma. The exchange is made and they leave, each getting what he is after, so that the giving and receiving of learning becomes nothing more than a commercial transaction.**[3] The second bad point of the schools is a kind of mechanical uniformity of teaching methods and management methods that is destructive to human life. Each person has different qualities. They differ in their abilities and understanding, but the schools ignore these aspects totally and know only how to stuff the same thing down everyone's throat. If human beings are to respect the personality, we must not say that someone "administers" someone else. Carrying on the legacy of the despotic emperors, the schools ignore the personality of the students and openly "administer" them. Because the faculty treat everyone the same way, the human nature of the students is not fulfilled; because the students are administered mechanically, their personalities are not fulfilled. This is the gravest defect of the schools, and one that persons concerned about education must absolutely not overlook. The third bad point of the schools is that there are too many hours and a complicated curriculum so that students' heads are buried in class all day long, and no one knows that there is also a world outside of the classroom. The students' spirits are so exhausted they cannot think, and they are totally unable to apply their minds to spontaneous self-motivated study. In generalizing about these bad points, we do not mean, of course, that all schools are like this, and where these faults do exist there is usually still hope that they may be reformed in the future. But in general it is like this, and there is no way to conceal it, even if you wanted to. The general root of this problem is that the students are put in a passive position, where their personalities are ground down and their spirits annihilated, where the weak sink or swim as usual and the talented are hobbled. If we take another look at the academies, although their form also has its bad points, it has none of the bad points of the schools listed above. First, the teachers and students have strong feelings for each other. Second, there is no faculty management but rather a spirit of communication and free research. Third, the curriculum is simple, the research and study are thorough, and it is possible to relax and enjoy life. Thus, in regard to the "form of study," the academies are far superior to the schools. The modern schools do, however, have one especially strong point, which is that their "study content" is

---

3. The passage in bold is emphasized in the Chinese by the use of dots next to the characters.

entirely scientific, or that they use the scientific method to study philosophy and literature. On this point, the academies are inferior to the schools. What makes the Self-Study University a new type of system is that it adopts the form of the old-style academies and fills them with the content of the modern schools, so that it is a special kind of organization that is suited to human nature and facilitates study.

Above, we have discussed the various strengths and weaknesses of the academies versus the schools and the fact that the Self-Study University borrows from the strengths of each and discards their weaknesses. Now let us speak of an advantage that is unique to the Self-Study University and a defect shared by the academies and the schools: democratic[4] versus undemocratic. First, the academies and the official universities all demand very strict qualifications, and it goes without saying that those who do not meet these qualifications cannot enroll. Someone who in fact is qualified but for some reason does not meet the qualifications, that is, someone who is really highly talented but misses out on the entrance examination, is thereupon cut off from the road to learning. Today there are indeed quite a few ambitious young people who have not had a chance to seek learning, and this is truly a shame. Second, the academies and official universities treat academic studies as excessively mysterious. They think that only a very small group of very special people can come to study, that the great majority of the common people are by nature unable to participate in learning. As a result, learning is monopolized by a small number of "academic lords"[5] and becomes widely separated from the society of ordinary people, thus giving rise to that strange phenomenon of the intellectual class enslaving the class of ordinary people. Third, poor people cannot enter the academies. Unless your family is rich, it is even more impossible to attend the official universities. In order to graduate from an official university it takes over one thousand and up to two thousand *yuan*. For a person without money, the university is truly a case of "the wild cat dreaming of eating the flesh of the swan." The Self-Study University makes every effort to overcome these defects. First of all, while considerations of space make it necessary to place some slight limitation on the number of students residing at the university, anyone residing elsewhere who is dedicated to learning may enroll. Secondly, learning is treated like a simple homemade meal that you eat when you are hungry. We will strive to smash the mystery of learning and to make it open and public so that everyone can get a portion.

---

4. *Pingminzhuyi*, literally "common people-ism," one of the terms then used for democracy.

5. *Xuefa*. The character *fa*, which meant originally a classification according to rank, also has the sense of a powerful person, and has been used since the 1920s primarily in the expression *junfa*, "warlord." It also occurs in the compound *caifa*, "financial magnate." In the present context, *xuefa* might also be translated "scholar clique," but that would not convey the emphasis on oppressive individuals. Decades later, during the Cultural Revolution, Mao used this term to castigate the intellectuals who opposed him.

Thirdly, although in this present age in which "money is life," the Self-Study University cannot make it possible for every member of the so-called "proletariat"[6] to attain a high level of education, in our hearts we cherish the goal of striving to change the situation in the direction of "it does not require a lot of money to get an education." The students of the Self-Study University can come to the school to study, or they can study at home, or they can also study in the shops, in groups, in public institutions, making it much more convenient than the official universities, and naturally less expensive.

The Self-Study University is, as stated above, a democratic university. What, then, is the content of the Self-Study University like? Let us now make some general points: First, the main idea of education for students of the Self-Study University is "to read and think on one's own." The "library" within the Self-Study University is set up solely for this purpose. Second, aside from reading and thinking on their own, the students of the Self-Study University also "discuss and study together." Various research groups are set up specifically for this purpose. Third, although the Self-Study University does not want teachers who stuff learning down the students' throats, it does want those who can give guidance at any time and assist the students with their self-study. Fourth, the Self-Study University takes fields of study as the unit. Students may study a single field of study or they may also study in several fields. The time and scope of each field is determined according to the student's own wishes and level. Fifth, the students of the Self-Study University are not only engaged in studying. They should also have the desire to perfect themselves, to develop a strong personality, and to wash away bad habits, in order to prepare for reforming society.

Finally, we want to say something about the need for a Self-Study University in Hunan. Gentlemen, has not Hunan been until now without a single institution of higher learning? The reasons for the fact that a provincial university could not be founded in the most recent years, and that if it had, it would simply have been an official-type university, are clearly understood by everyone. But how are the thirty million Hunanese people living in the regions washed by the Xiang, Yuan, Zi, and Li Rivers[7] to express and develop their spiritual needs and cultural instincts? Even though the Hunan people are as outstanding and full of vitality as the just-risen sun, and even though they are full of hope, unless there is a way for them to satisfy their spiritual needs and develop their cultural instincts, how can being Hunanese be meaningful? At this point, we feel that a great task has fallen on the shoulders of the Hunanese people. What responsibility? That of themselves perfecting, developing, and creating their individual and collective natures

---

6. The fact that Mao put quotation marks around the Chinese term for proletariat, *wuchanjieji*, underscores the fact that he was still not very clear about what it meant in Marxist terms. As in his writings of the May Fourth era, he appears to have in mind something like the literal meaning of the Chinese, "propertyless class."

7. The Xiang, Yuan, Zi, and Li are all rivers in Hunan, flowing in a north-easterly direction and emptying into Lake Dongting.

and personalities. The Hunan Self-Study University has been founded with this idea in mind. Although it cannot have ties to every individual Hunanese, in spirit it must become an institution of learning for the whole of Hunanese society. Although we cannot say that it will definitely achieve excellent results, if we work hard and press forward over the months and years we are confident that we shall one day attain our goals.

This school at present has two faculties, arts and law. Within the faculty of arts, the courses include Chinese literature, Western literature, English, logic, psychology, ethics, education, sociology, history, geography, journalism, philosophy, etc. In the faculty of law, the curriculum includes jurisprudence, political studies, economics, etc. All these are listed in the university's outline of organization, which is published simultanously with the above statement.

An Outline of the Organization of the Hunan Self-Study University

(August 16, 1921)

Section One: Guiding Principles and Name

Article 1. As there are defects in the current educational system, this university draws upon the strengths of the traditional academies and modern schools and applies self-motivational methods to the study of the various fields of learning, in the hope of finding truth and training human talents so that culture may be universally available to ordinary people and learning may be widely disseminated in society. It is founded by the Chuanshan Study Society[1] of Hunan and has been given the name "Hunan Self-Study University."

Section Two: University Board of Trustees

Article 2. This university establishes a University Board of Trustees composed of fifteen trustees to be responsible for the finances of the university and to execute the charter of this university. They are to be elected by the members of the society. The number of university trustees may be increased when necessary.

Article 3. The board of trustees may convene board meetings when more than half of those trustees who are present at the location of the university are in attendance. Those trustees who are not present at the location of the university may communicate their views to the board at any time, and may also delegate other trustees to represent their views.

Article 4. The board of trustees elects one person as the "resident trustee" to exercise general supervision over the affairs of the university.

This document was first published in the Changsha *Dagongbao* on August 16, 17, 18, 19, and 20, 1921. Our source is the version in *Mao Zedong ji. Bujuan*, Vol. 2, pp. 75–84.

1. On the Chuanshan Study Society, or Society for the Study of Wang Fuzhi, see above, the note to the business report of the Cultural Book Society of April 1, 1921. He Shuheng was appointed head of the Chuanshan Academy after his dismissal as head of the Hunan Education Association in May 1921. The Hunan government gave the society a stipend of 400 *yuan* monthly, and with the agreement of the society, Mao used its headquarters and the money to help launch the Self-Study University as a center for Communist Party activities.

Article 5. The board of trustees of the university appoints an unspecified number of honorary trustees. The board of trustees may elect persons with the following qualifcations to be honorary trustees:

1. Those who have donated more than 5,000 *yuan* to the university
2. Those who have made great contributions to supporting the university
3. Presidents of domestic and foreign universities and specialized schools.

Section Three: Dean and Administrators

Article 6. The university has one dean for academic affairs who is appointed by the board of trustees, and who is responsible for directing the self-studies of the students and evaluating their progress. However, when necessary, instructors in special subjects may be appointed to assist the dean in carrying out his responsibilities for instruction and evaluation.

Article 7. The university temporarily appoints the following administrators:

1. One secretary who is entrusted by the trustee-in-residence with the administration of such affairs as relate to letters, documents, communications, and the facilities of the university
2. One treasurer, who is entrusted by the trustee-in-residence with the administration of matters relating to the disbursement and use of the university's funds
3. One librarian, who is entrusted by the trustee-in-residence with the administration of the library of the university
4. One laboratory director, who is entrusted by the trustee-in-residence with the administration of the university's laboratory.

Article 8. In addition to the administrators listed above, the university may add appropriate administrators when necessary. Their responsibilities and number may be determined at the time.

Section Four: Correspondents

Article 9. The university appoints correspondents to major universities, specialized schools, and scholarly organizations both at home and abroad. Their responsibility is to maintain communication between this university and other schools and bodies, as well as to monitor and report to this university on the conditions and main results of scholarly research by these schools and bodies.

Article 10. The university appoints correspondents in those areas, both at home and abroad, where scholarship is thriving (such as Beijing, Shanghai, Guangzhou, Nanjing, Wuchang, Paris, London, Berlin, New York, Moscow, and Tokyo) to maintain communications between the university and these cultural regions, as well as to monitor and report to the university all the important cultural and scholarly developments in these regions.

Article 11. The university appoints correspondents to the major post-secondary schools and scholarly groups in Hunan Province (in the provincial capital and individual *xian*) to maintain communication between the university and other schools and groups, and to promote scholarly exchange.

Article 12. In addition to the above-mentioned responsibilities, correspondents may be given other special tasks on an ad hoc basis.

Section Five: Students

Article 13. All those who have graduated from secondary schools and above, irrespective of sex or age, provided they have self-study abilities and are willing to use the method of self-study to pursue advanced scholarship, may register to enter the university after certification and acceptance by the university. Those who are not graduates of secondary schools and above, but have comparable foundations in various subjects, may also enroll after certification and acceptance by the university. Students in the various special classes at the university need not, however, meet the above qualifications.

Article 14. Students of this university are of the following two types:

1. residents—who live at the school
2. nonresidents—who live outside.

Resident students must pass examinations in order to be admitted into the university; moreover, they themselves are responsible for room and board, and for miscellaneous fees. Both resident and nonresident students enjoy the privileges of using the university library, taking correspondence courses, attending lectures and gatherings, and other opportunities for study offered by the university. All students must pay an appropriate deposit at the beginning of each semester, which will be returned to them at the end of the semester. Whether students should pay tuition and how much tuition they should pay will be determined at the time, according to the circumstances of their studies.

Article 15. The number of students will be determined according to the condition of the university's housing, library, and other facilities at the time.

Article 16. A student at this university will be ordered to leave the school at any time should one of the following conditions apply:

1. Those who do not have the ability to study on their own, or fail to devote themselves completely to the study of the subjects they have chosen, or fail to show any results
2. Those who, under the pretext of self-study, divert their attention to improper affairs outside of the school
3. Those who do not have the ability to control themselves or have no aspiration to self-improvement

4. Those who disturb public order and damage the reputation of other students and of the university.

Section Six: Research

Article 17. The university, at present, has established two faculties, humanities and law. The subjects for study are as follows:

Faculty of Humanities:
Chinese literature
Western literature
English
logic
psychology
ethics
education
sociology
history
geography
journalism
philosophy

Faculty of Law:
legal studies
political science
economics

The details of each of the above subjects will be spelled out elsewhere. Students must select at least one of the above subjects.

Article 18. The methods of study at the university are divided into the following two types:

1. Individual research—Students design their own curricula and study the selected subjects individually.
2. Group research—All kinds of study groups will be organized. For example, in the natural sciences, a "Mathematics Study Group," a "Psychological Study Group," an "Economics Study Group," and others. In philosophy, a "Group for the Study of the Philosophers of the Zhou and Qin Dynasties," a "Group for the Study of Indian Philosophy," and a "Group for the Study of Russell's Philosophy." In literature, a "Chinese Literature Study Group," an "English Literature Study Group," a "Poetry, Fiction, and Drama Study Group," and so on. These will be organized individually by the students of the university on the basis of similar interests, with a fixed period to complete the research. During the period of study, meet-

ings, debates, and discussions may be called at any time. The organization of each study group will be defined separately.

Article 19. To facilitate research, this university will institute the following three supplementary measures:

1. Guidance by correspondence: The university will hire professors from the national universities and other scholars at home and abroad to provide scheduled guidance by correspondence. Their guidance shall include the following items:

   a. Providing reading lists
   b. Guidance in research methods
   c. Answering questions

2. Special courses: For example, in a field like foreign languages, the university should be prepared, depending on circumstances, to offer special classes in English, French, and Russian. In addition, the university should also provide various forms of popular education, such as workers' evening classes, to be organized separately.

3. Special lectures: The university will establish special lectures and will periodically invite well-known persons to come to the school to lecture.

Article 20. As cultural links, and to introduce new knowledge, the university will organize various translation groups, such as a "French translation group," an "English translation group," a "Japanese translation group," and so on.

Section Seven: Labor

Article 21. To put an end to the legacy of intellectual weaklings, the students of the university will seek parallel development in both physique and intellect, and will also attempt to bring together the intellectual class and the working class. We should pay attention to labor. To realize this goal of [participation in] labor, the university should possess suitable facilities, such as a horticultural garden, a printing shop, an ironworks, etc.

Section Eight: Library and Laboratory

Article 22. The university will build a library on the school premises to house important Chinese and foreign books, journals, and newspapers to be used by students for research and reference.

Article 23. The university will build a physics and chemistry laboratory on the premises to be used for actual experiments by the students.

Section Nine: The Presentation of Results

Article 24. Students of the university may present their results in the following three ways:

1. Notes taken and papers done during the term
2. Papers written at the end of each semester
3. Papers written at the completion of each course.

Article 25. There is no fixed time limit on a student's course of study at this university. The completion of each course constitutes one unit. Those who pass a course will be given a certificate for that course. (For example, those who have completed and passed the course on mathematics will be given certificates in mathematics.) But those students who do not want certificates may audit courses. Students may be granted permission to conduct long-term research at the university.

Section Ten: Funds

Article 26. Most of the funds for the university are to be used for building and equipping the library and the laboratory. The sources are as follows:

1. Subsidies from the Study Society
2. Public and private donations.

Section Eleven: University Accomodation

Article 27. The university uses the buildings of the Chuanshan Study Society of Hunan as its accomodation (Xiaowumenzheng Street in Changsha). In the future, the premises will be enlarged or new buildings constructed as required.

Section Twelve: Branches and Overseas Offices

Article 28. To facilitate the students' research, the university will establish branches in key areas of Hunan. The main school in Changsha is the first branch; the second and subsequent branches will be opened when there are sufficient funds.

Article 29. Students of the university may open overseas offices when necessary.

Section Thirteen: Rules for Self-Government and Amendments to this Charter

Article 30. Life within the university is governed by the "Rules of Self-Government." These rules are drawn up jointly by the trustee-in-residence, the dean for academic affairs, the administrative staff, and the students.

Article 31. Amendments to this charter must be approved by the board of trustees of the university.

Letter to Yang Zhongjian[1]

(September 29, 1921)

Mr. Zhongjian:

A few days ago I received an announcement informing me that you had been elected director of the Executive Board. Today I have again received a notice, requesting that I fill out retroactively a form for admission to the association. I am now enclosing the completed form, with photo attached. My sponsor was Mr. Wang Guangqi,[2] who had collected five other [sponsors] for me, of whom I can remember only three. The only way you can find out about the other two is to ask Mr. Wang. Please be so kind as to mail any future correspondence to the Cultural Book Society, Chaozong Street, Changsha.

Your younger brother,
Zedong

This letter is translated from the text in *Mao Zedong shuxin xuanji*, p. 20, which is followed by the indication "based on a manuscript copy." It does not appear to have been published previously.

1. Yang Zhongjian (1897–1979), a native of Hua *xian*, Shaanxi Province, was a paleontologist. At this time he was the director of the Executive Board of the Young China Association.

2. Wang Guangqi (1892–1936) was a native of Wenjiang, Sichuan Province. An intellectual reformer who had studied in Japan, he was one of the initiators of the Young China Association in Beijing in 1918 and was the first director of the Executive Board. He also sponsored the Work-Study Mutual Aid Society.

My Hopes for the Labor Association[1]

(November 21, 1921)

The Labor Association is now one year old, and I have been sympathizing with it for one year as well. Why do I have such particular sympathy for the Labor Association? Labor is sacred,[2] all things are made by laborers, and the Labor Association is a united body of laborers, so everyone should be sympathetic to it. During the past year, the association's difficulties in establishing itself have already written the first page in the history of the Hunan labor movement. Now it's time to begin writing the second page. I hope that what is written on this second page will be very different from what is on the first page: that the material will be richer, the meaning fresher, the style and organization further approaching perfection. Therefore, on the basis of my own thoughts, I want to contribute some hopes for the future:

1. The purpose of a labor organization is not merely to rally the laborers to get better pay and shorter working hours by means of strikes. It should also nurture class consciousness so as to unite the whole class and seek the basic interests of the whole class. I hope that every member of the Labor Association will pay special attention to this very basic goal.
2. As far as organization is concerned, it is best to follow the pattern of the Western trade unions: a body of representatives from the members should elect a certain number of people to form a committee with full powers to oversee the administration of the association. We certainly do not want the

---

This article appeared on November 21, 1921, in a special issue of *Laogong zhoukan* commemorating the first anniversary of the establishment of the Labor Association. Our source is *Mao Zedong wenji*, Vol. 1, pp. 6–7, which gives these particulars regarding first publication more clearly than the text in *Mao Zedong ji. Bujuan*, Vol. 9, pp. 115–16.

1. The Labor Association Mao is referring to is that organized in November 1920 by two Hunanese anarchists, Huang Ai and Pang Renquan. Huang and Pang were graduates of the Hunan First Industrial School. At the outset most of the members were students from industrial schools, but membership quickly expanded to include tradesmen and factory workers. Until this time, its largest action has been the organization of 2,000-odd workers in April 1921 to demonstrate at the No. 1 Cotton Mill in opposition to the selling of the factory to interests outside the province. Its organ was called *Labor Weekly*. Regarding the subsequent careers of Huang and Pang and their execution in 1922 see below, the note to the document dated December 14, 1922.

2. "Labor is sacred" (*laogong shensheng*) was one of the key slogans of the nascent labor and communist movement in this early period.

old guild system, but neither do we want a system that has too many staff members, too many departments, or too much dispersion of authority.

3. The Labor Association has been organized by the workers, so it should be financed by the workers themselves. Furthermore, it should raise funds for strikes and elections. Of course, we cannot accomplish these goals immediately, but I feel the first step should be that whatever the circumstances, each member pays minimal monthly dues, even if it is as little as one copper cash a month. The second step should be that the association be self-supporting. This is very important. I hope every member of the Labor Association will pay attention to it.

My hopes are limited to these three. In conclusion, I want to address a few simple words by way of a toast to my friends the laborers, to stir their ardor:

"Those who do not labor shall not eat!"

"Laborers should have the right to strike!"

"Labor is sacred!"

"From each according to his ability, to each according to his deserts!"

"The whole world belongs to the laborers!"

"Workers of the world, unite!"

A Couplet Written with Li Lisan[1]

(November 1921)

A guest has returned to Lake Dongting,
On the banks of the Xiao and the Xiang I encountered my old friend.

This couplet was first published in *Minjian duilian gushi*, No. 6, 1986. We have taken it, like all of Mao's poems and couplets, from *Shici duilian*, p. 161.

1. Li Lisan (1899–1967), original name Li Longzhi, a native of Liling, Hunan Province, was also known under the aliases of Bai Shan and Li Minran. After studying at the Changjun Middle School in Changsha, Li went to France in 1919 on the work-study scheme. There he was an active sponsor of the Socialist Youth League and was deported by the French government in 1921 for related activities. Li Lisan had met Mao Zedong during his student days, but Mao remarked later to Edgar Snow that their friendship "never developed." Nonetheless, when Li returned to Hunan in 1921, he called on Mao at his home in Changsha. According to a note in *Shici duilian*, Mao, summoned to the door by his wife Yang Kaihui, exclaimed, "A guest has returned to Lake Dongting." Thereupon Li Lisan responded, "On the banks of the Xiao and the Xiang I encountered my old friend." It had long been a custom among the Chinese literati to compose a line and invite another person to complete the couplet. Mao's contribution to this literary dialogue might be described as noncommittal.

Answers to the Questionnaire Regarding Lifetime Aspirations for Members of the Young China Association

(December 1921)

Name	Mao Zedong
Prospective lifelong academic interest	Pedagogics
Prospective lifelong career	Education
Date and place for starting career	Already started in July, 1919, in Hunan[1]
Prospective lifelong means of livelihood	Monthly salary for educational work, and income from writing
Further comments	I have only started preparing for my desired career. After three or four years' preparation, I must go abroad to study for at least five years; the place will be Russia. Afterwards, on return, I will set about the career I want to undertake.

Mao's reply was included in the results of this survey as reported in December 1921 by the Executive of the Young China Association. We have taken as our source the version reproduced in *Mao Zedong ji. Bujuan*, Vol. 2, p. 87.

1. Mao was in fact appointed a history teacher at the Xiuye Primary School in Changsha immediately after his return from Shanghai on April 6, 1919, and held this post until December of the same year.

————————————1922————————————

Some Issues That Deserve More Attention

(May 1, 1922)

Would it not be a joke if the autonomous province of Hunan, the Hunan that loudly proclaims the politics of all the people, were to turn aside completely from the workers? If we believe that one should not turn aside from the workers, then "May Day," the only holiday there is to commemorate the workers, surely deserves at least some attention from everyone!

If people are going to pay attention, then please pay attention to the following three matters concerning the workers: (1) the workers' right to existence, (2) the workers' right to work, (3) the workers' right to the full fruits of their labor.

Except for those who practice usury, those who live on an inheritance, and those who have investments in some business enterprise, most people are workers who work with their hands or their minds. From their bodies these workers produce "labor power," which alone makes it possible for them to support themselves on the one hand and, on the other hand, for the capitalists to make a profit. This assuredly depends on one thing, namely, the "existence" of the workers. If they were unable to "exist," there would naturally be no "labor power." In that case the result would inevitably be "death" for the workers, but how could the capitalists "live" on their own? According to this line of reasoning, it is imperative to provide food adequate to maintain the lives of young workers who are now under the age of eighteen but are going to become older workers over the age of eighteen, so that they will eventually have some labor power to sell. This is truly a point to which astute capitalists should pay attention. As for workers who have sold their labor power throughout their lives, once they are over sixty and have exhausted their labor power and cannot sell it any more they should be put in a position to live out their allotted span, just like the plants in autumn that can soak up the rain and dew and thus live out their allotted time. According to this reasoning, those over sixty who cannot sell their labor power should be given a bit of life-sustaining food. A person should have the right to receive the food necessary to preserve his existence during the "old" and "young" stages when he is not able to work. This is the right to existence.

Except for those too lazy to work, who may be left to starve, all healthy persons with labor power between the ages of eighteen and sixty should be given work to do;

This article was published in the Changsha *Dagongbao* on May 1, 1922. Our source is *Mao Zedong wenji,* Vol. 1, pp. 8–9, which reproduces the text as it appeared in the newspaper. (This version is superior to that in the *Mao Zedong ji. Bujuan,* Vol. 9, pp. 117–19, from which a few characters are missing because they were illegible in the photocopy available to the Japanese editors.)

thus the workers have the right to demand work. In the event that the workers, although they have labor power, are forced to remain "idle" because society has no jobs for which to buy their labor, society should pay them their regular wages, on the grounds that the fault does not lie with the workers. This is the right to work.

Whatever the workers produce should belong entirely to the workers themselves. This is the right to the full fruits of one's labor.

Of course, the right to the full fruits of one's labor will come only after Communism is put into effect. This is something with which no capitalist, no matter how astute, could concern himself. But it should not be entirely overlooked, for it is truly a great tide that already exists in the world. If the right to existence and the right to work do not, in fact, go against the interests of the capitalists, they certainly deserve everyone's attention.

While everyone is paying attention to the right to existence, let them take note of how many people are starving to death in Hunan right now. While everyone is paying attention to the right to work, let them take note of how many people are unemployed in Hunan right now.

The observance of "May Day" is to commemorate the movement for the eight-hour working day. The purpose of this movement is to reduce working hours so that people may pursue recreation and education. It is a demand of those who "are able to exist" and "have employment," who should naturally go further and demand an eight-hour working day. As for those who are unable to exist and are unemployed, the question is how to enable them to exist and gain employment. In Hunan today, I wish everyone to pay the utmost attention to this. What a pity that the Provincial Constitution, for all its pomp and ceremony, does not even touch upon these matters! They call it by the high-sounding name of rule by the whole people, but in fact it has abandoned at least 99 percent of the workers! Nevertheless, these problems already exist, and they must be resolved. No matter how much everyone ignores them, there will surely come a day when these problems will command everyone's attention! "The beacon of Yin is not remote,"[1] and Russia's capitalist class and nobility provide an example. For them it's already too late for regrets!

---

1. This line from the *Book of Poetry* III, III, I (Legge, Vol. IV, p. 410) is quoted in the *Mencius* IV, I, III, 5 (Legge, Vol. II, p. 293), where it is placed in context by par. 4, which precedes it. The passage reads: "A ruler who carries the oppression of his people to the highest pitch, will himself be slain, and his kingdom will perish. . . . This is what is intended in the words of the Book of Poetry,

'The beacon of Yin is not remote,
It is in the time of the (last) sovereign of Hsia.' "

The last sovereign of the Xia dynasty was the tyrant Jie, and the ruler of Yin was the tyrant Zhou, who in Mencius' view should have taken warning from the beacon constituted by the fate of Jie, but did not. The four characters translated "The beacon of Yin is not remote" have become a common expression of warning to someone who refuses to mend his ways.

To Shi Fuliang[1] and the Central Committee of the Socialist Youth League

(June 20, 1922)

Brother Guochang and all brothers in the Central Executive Committee:

1. Circulars no. 1, 3, 4, and 5 have all been received, and in compliance with Circular no. 1, we held a conference on June 17 to carry out a reorganization and to adopt Detailed Regulations of the League Executive Committee in Changsha. We have elected the following three people as members of the Executive Committee:

Secretary—Mao Zedong
Head of the Organization Department—Li Longzhi[2]
Head of the Propaganda Department—Luo Junqiang

2. The league members here consider that although Mao Zedong and Li Liuru[3] are over twenty-eight, they are needed to work for the league, and have therefore elected them as officers in accordance with Article 2 of the Supplement to the Statutes,[4] by a unanimous vote of those attending. We hereby apply to the Central Executive Committee for approval. Kindly send us your instructions.

3. The twelve articles of the Detailed Regulations of the League Executive Committee in Changsha were voted through by the conference. In accordance

---

This letter is translated from the text in *Mao Zedong shuxin xuanji*, pp. 21–22, which is followed by the indication "based on a manuscript copy." It does not appear to have been published previously.

1. Shi Fuliang (1899–1970), original name Shi Cuntong, alias Fang Guochang, was a native of Jinhua *xian*, Zhejiang Province. At the time he was secretary of the Central Committee of the Socialist Youth League of China.

2. On Li Lisan, original name Li Longzhi, see above, the note to the couplet Mao composed with him in November 1921. On his return to China after his expulsion from France, Li was active as a labor organizer at the Anyuan coal mines in Hunan, and in May 1922 he became head of the Anyuan Mine and Railroad Labor Union.

3. Li Liuru (1887–1973) was a native of Pingjiang *xian*, Hunan Province. He joined the Communist Party in 1921 and taught in Changsha at the time. In 1924 he was a teacher in the Junzhi school and the Public Law College of Hunan University.

4. The Statutes of the Socialist Youth League had been adopted at its first congress, which took place in Guangzhou May 5–15, 1922.

with the provisions of Article 13 of the Statutes, we ask the Central Executive Committee to approve them. Kindly send us your instructions.

4. The local Executive Committee has met today and expressed the view that the term of three months for the secretary of a small group of more than three people or for the members of the management committee of a small group of more than ten people stipulated in Article 6 of the Statutes would be too short to achieve results. We intend to ask for an extension of the term of office from three months to six months. Please let us know whether or not this is acceptable.

5. A resolution of the local Executive Committee makes the following proposal to the Central Executive Committee: The Central Executive Committee is requested to divide the provinces of the whole country into regions as soon as possible. (To what number region will Hunan then belong?) It is also requested that one local league organization be appointed to serve as the provisional executive committee of each region until the regular regional executive committees are established, in order to encourage the formation of more local league organizations in a short time and thereby accelerate the formation of regular regional executive committees.

6. Please send another copy of Circular no. 2. (From now on circulars or other important letters should be sent by registered mail.)

7. Two local organizations of the league have been established in Hengzhou and Changde. The mailing address in Hengzhou is Zhao Dan (secretary), School store, Hengzhou Third Normal School; the mailing address in Changde is Jiang Xiqing (secretary), Changde Second Normal School. Two other local organizations of the league in Pingxiang and Liling, and league branches in various *xian* are being organized. We plan to call the representative conference of local league organizations sometime in September.

We await your reply.

The Secretary: Mao Zedong
June 20

Petition for a Labor Law and a General Outline for Labor Legislation

by the Secretariat of Chinese Labor Organizations

(July 1922)[1]

Petition

This is the substance of our petition. We venture to note that the labor problem emerged long ago, following the Industrial Revolution in Europe, and during the more than one hundred years since then countless politicians and students of politics have racked their brains studying it day and night, yet no fundamental solution has been found. Only the advanced nations of Europe and America, after repeatedly accumulating experience, have drawn significant lessons from it. They have accordingly promulgated explicit laws and regulations for the protection of labor, and as a result the poor and miserable laborers who used to have no means to seek redress have gradually gained equal status with ordinary people, and the fortunes of these nations have been improved by a certain measure of peace and stability. Recently there has been the example of Soviet Russia, where a worker-peasant government founded entirely by the toilers seized political power, and the national constitution was also fashioned by the laborers. From this we may know the truly important role of a country's workers in founding the state. This is a natural law of evolution in the world; of that there can be no doubt. Lately, the workers in our country have a gained a considerable degree of consciousness. In the areas of our country where industry is somewhat developed, all the workers are forming one organization after another in the hope of pooling their wisdom and energies to improve their own status and alleviate their sufferings. This is altogether reasonable and proper. Moreover, some have been forced by the problems between labor and capital to unite in strike action. From

---

This document was first published in the Changsha *Dagongbao* on September 6, 7, and 8, 1922. Our source is *Mao Zedong ji. Bujuan*, Vol. 2, pp. 97–102.

1. This text is dated September in *Bujuan*, Vol. 2, p. 97, but according to the index volume of the *Bujuan* it was composed in July, though published in September. For a discussion of the resolution on the labor movement adopted at the Second Congress of the Chinese Communist Party in July 1922 and its relation to the position put forward here, see above, the Introduction to Volume II.

the point of view of justifiable self-defense, uniting for strike action is indeed a right to which workers are indisputably entitled. In our country, however, the elite[2] has habitually adopted the ugly attitude of despising manual workers. Because the workers' efforts to organize and all their legitimate actions are not adequately protected by law, the generality of power-holders in our country wantonly ride roughshod over the workers and treat with particular hostility their efforts to organize and all of their legitimate actions. For this reason, in recent years there have been frequent incidents everywhere arising from the problems of inequality between labor and capital. As those who wield power today are unaware of world trends and ignorant of the fundamentals of government, they think that the workers are easy to deceive. Their stupidity is truly phenomenal. In addition, lawmakers in the past have also been prisoners of such prejudices, thus failing to perceive this reality. This is why the working class in our country remains moaning in misery, with no place to turn for redress. How tragic! They are really unaware that the workers in our country are an integral part of the Republic of China, so according to the principle that all the people of the Republic of China are strictly equal, the workers in our country should also receive protection under the law and may not be arbitrarily discriminated against. Workers also constitute in fact an absolute majority of the people of the country, and according to the principle of the greatest happiness for the greatest number, how can the workers possibly be rejected and ignored? Besides, the foundation of the country rests entirely on the pillar of the domestic producers; the consumers have no part in it. All those who know anything at all about modern political, social, and economic history are in unanimous agreement with this principle. Moreover, in society, the workers devote themselves entirely to production, and they exert the greatest effort of all classes in the country, yet their lot is the cruelest, despite the fact that their contribution to state and society is greatest. Lawmakers in the past have devoted their attention to protecting the minority in our country—those special classes in society who consume but do not produce—yet they have mercilessly abandoned and excluded from the masses of the people the workers, who constitute the absolute majority of the nation's people and who exert the most effort and make the greatest contribution yet suffer the cruelest lot. How can this be deemed just as regards the proper rights and duties of the citizenry? Consequently, on the basis of the various arguments given above, and taking into account all aspects of the question, there is a definite need today to enact labor laws, and these laws must definitely be included in the fundamental basic law. Thus in the future a group that has grasped political power will not lightly venture to invent pretexts, or use special security laws and other tricks to oppress the workers. In the current process of formulating a constitution, this is indeed the most urgent task. But today there are those who argue that our country's laws

2. *Shiren*, literally the scholars, here stands for the strata of society linked to the scholar-officials in general.

have never discriminated against workers, so why cry before you're hurt? Don't you know, they say, that strikes and disturbances are clearly defined as crimes under criminal law (interim new criminal code, article no. 224) and that Mr. Yuan's[3] security laws have not yet been repealed (the Beijing Government's Directive on Security and Police, no. 28, March 1913). Thus to claim that our country's laws have never discriminated against the workers is simply to deceive oneself as well as others. The root cause of all this is that a fundamental basic law has yet to be enacted on the national level, and the Provisional Constitution does not offer explicit protection to labor, so that strikes and disturbances run afoul of the security and police laws.

Although twice the national parliament decided, at special sessions in Guangzhou, to abolish these laws, the question of the limitations on their authority to change the laws arose at the time, so [the abolition] has yet to be put into effect nationwide. This is sufficient to prove that today's labor law should be covered without delay by the fundamental basic law. Just recently the national parliament has reconvened, and the people of the country hope that it will hasten to formulate the constitution. Moreover, Mr. Li Qingfang, member of the Standing Committee of the Lower House,[4] has already proposed a draft labor-protection law, and Mr. Wu Ziyu has also proposed to attach labor-protection legislation to the fundamental basic law. Although each has a different argument, and it would not be easy to work out a compromise version, the fact that our country's elite[5] is gradually tending away from looking down upon labor and toward respecting labor is nonetheless cause for some satisfaction. All of us have been involved in the labor movement for a long time and, having witnessed year after year the tragic and violent abuses suffered by the workers in our country, we understand deeply the miseries that having no legal protection imposes on the workers in our country. We have, moreover, experienced those power-holders' clever manipulation of words and laws, and therefore feel even more stongly the importance of incorporating labor-protection legislation into the constitution. This appeal is made on behalf of the workers of the entire country and for the sake of future lawmaking in our country. We hereby present the nineteen articles of an Outline of Labor Legislation, and in accordance with the law, we petition your honorable assembly to adopt and enact it and incorporate it into the constitution. We furthermore request that, to alleviate the distress of the workers, an official resolution be passed to repeal article 224 of the interim new criminal code that makes strikes and disturbances a crime, as well as the Beijing Government's Directive on Security and Police, no. 28, of March 1913. What a blessing this would be for the workers of the country! For this reason we hereby petition, in accordance

---

3. Yuan Shikai, who was president when the directive mentioned here was adopted.

4. *Zhongyiyuan*, literally the mass (or people's) deliberative assembly, frequently translated House of Representatives.

5. *Shifu*, short for *shidafu*, the scholar-officials.

with the law, that your honorable assembly present this proposal to its entire membership for resolution and implementation. Presented to the speaker of the Lower House.

The nineteen articles of the Labor Legislation Outline are respectfully submitted below for your perusal.

Labor Legislation Outline

1. Recognize the workers' right of assembly and association.
2. Recognize the right of workers to form unions and to strike.
3. Recognize the right of labor groups to sign collective contracts.
4. Recognize the right of the workers to form an international alliance.
5. The workday is not to exceed eight hours for day workers and six hours for night workers; there must be forty-two consecutive hours of rest each week.
6. Young workers under the age of eighteen, male and female, and those performing strenuous tasks are not to work for more than six hours at a time.
7. Prohibit exceeding the legal limit on work hours. Under special circumstances, work hours may be increased with permission of the union.
8. The workday for agricultural workers may exceed eight hours, but wages for excess work hours are to be calculated on the basis of the eight-hour system.
9. There must be legal guarantees on prices for agricultural products produced by ordinary peasants who do not exploit the labor of others. Such prices are to be proposed by peasant representatives and regulated by law.
10. Work on strenuous jobs and on jobs that present health hazards, and work by workers under the age of eighteen, male or female, may absolutely not exceed the legal time limit. All female workers, and male workers under the age of eighteen, are strictly forbidden from working the night shift.
11. Female manual workers are to have eight weeks of leave both before and after childbirth. Female workers on other kinds of jobs are to have six weeks of leave both before and after childbirth. In all cases they are to receive their normal pay.
12. It is prohibited to hire child laborers, either male or female, under the age of sixteen.
13. In order to guarantee workers a reasonable minimum wage, the state must enact such protective laws. Representatives of the All-China General Labor Union[6] must be allowed to be present when such legislation is adopted. Wages in

---

6. The creation of such an organization had been proposed at the First All-China Labor Congress, held in Guangzhou in May 1922. Though it was not actually established until the Second Labor Congress of 1925, the authors of this draft may have assumed that it would shortly come into being. They may also have postulated that the Secretariat of Chinese Labor Organizations, set up in 1921 at the same time as the Chinese Communist Party and on behalf of which they signed this petition, constituted the embryo of such a national union.

both public and private enterprises and institutions must not fall below these legally guaranteed minimum limits.

14. Workers in all fields protected by their industrial or professional organizations have the right to elect representatives to participate in government enterprises and institutions, and also to elect representatives to participate in private enterprises or institutions managed by government enterprises and institutions.

15. The state has the right to set up labor inspection bureaus in all foreign enterprises, public and private.

16. The state guarantees the workers full rights to participate in the labor inspection bureaus set up by the state.

17. Workers must participate in the regulation of all insurance matters to provide protection from loss or risk for all workers employed in government, public, and private enterprises and institutions. Insurance premiums are to be paid entirely by the employers or the state; the insured is to bear no part of the cost.

18. All workers and employees have the right to one month of vacation during every year of work and two weeks of vacation during every six months of work, all with full pay.

19. The state is to guarantee by law that all workers, male and female, have the opportunity to receive remedial education.

Petitioners:

Deng Zhongxia,[7] Head Office of the Secretariat of Chinese Labor Organizations
Ruan Dashi, Shanghai Office of the Secretariat of Chinese Labor Organizations
Lin Xiangpu, Wuhan Office of the Secretariat of Chinese Labor Organizations
Mao Yunzi,[8] Hunan Office of the Secretariat of Chinese Labor Organizations
Tan Pingshan,[9] Guangdong Office of the Secretariat of Chinese Labor Organizations
Wang Jingmei, Shandong Office of the Secretariat of Chinese Labor Organizations

---

7. Deng Zhongxia (1894–1933), *zi* Zhongxie, original name Deng Kang, was a native of Yizhang, Hunan. He enrolled in the Chinese Department of Beijing University in 1917 and was active in many student societies before and during the May Fourth movement. At this time, he was a close friend of Mao Zedong; see, in particular, his introductory note to the "Statutes of the Problem Study Society," in Volume I of this edition, p. 407. He joined the Beijing Communist "small group" in 1920, and became head of the Secretariat of Chinese Labor Organizations when it was set up in 1922. His *Zhongguo zhigong yundong jianshi (1919–1926)* (Brief History of the Chinese Labor Movement, 1919–1926) remained the standard work on the subject until 1949. He was executed by the Guomindang in 1933.

8. In signing this document, Mao used a variant of his *zi*, Runzhi, pronounced as indicated.

9. On Tan Pingshan see below, the relevant note to the telegram of the All-China Peasant Association dated April 9, 1927.

Sponsors:

Tong Qizeng	Du Kaiyuan	Zhang Bingwen	Zhao Jintang
Yue Yuntao	Sun Jingqing	Li Zhaopu	Liu Wei
Xiao Xiang	Liao Xixian	Pu Boying	Lü Fu
Luo Jihan	Yao Tongyu	Zhou Jiying	Wan Jun
Peng Xuejun	Sun Zhong	Deng Yuyi	Hu Egong
Tang Songnian	Zhang Guojun		

Charter of the Changsha Masons' and Carpenters' Union

(September 5, 1922)

Article 1

This union is organized by the masons and carpenters of Changsha, and is named the Changsha Masons' and Carpenters' Union.

Article 2

The purpose of this union is to improve the life and uphold the rights of the workers.

Article 3

Any mason or carpenter in Changsha can become a member of this union upon recommendation by one or more union members and approval of the union committee.

Article 4

Members of this union shall pay an initial fee of twenty cents at the time of admission and sixty cash each month thereafter as monthly membership dues.

Article 5

The union intends to bring forward the following matters: (1) a school for remedial education, (2) a consumer cooperative, (3) health insurance, (4) mutual assistance for the unemployed, (5) other necessary items.

Article 6

The basic unit of this union is the ten-person group. Every ten members of the union form a group and elect one person as their representative for a term of one

---

This document appeared in the Changsha *Dagongbao* on September 6 and 7, 1922. Our source is *Mao Zedong ji. Bujuan*, Vol. 2, pp. 91–93.

year. For the sake of unity, within each area one or two people shall be elected from among the Representatives-of-ten to be responsible for maintaining contact and communications.

Article 7

The General Meeting of Representatives-of-ten shall elect thirty-seven members to form a union committee to serve a term of one year.

Article 8

The committee shall be divided into the following five sections: (1) General Administration Section, with one chief and four deputy chiefs to manage all general affairs of the union; (2) Documents and Correspondence Section, with one section chief and four clerks to handle all official documents and communications; (3) Accounting Section, with one section chief and four accountants to manage all financial matters; (4) General Business Section, with one section chief and four general business staff members to handle general business; and (5) Social Activities Section, with one section chief and sixteen social activities staff members to manage all matters involving social relations. Important union matters are to be decided upon after deliberation by all committee members; ordinary matters may be decided upon after deliberation by the various section chiefs. The various tasks of the committee shall be fixed by mutual consent amongst the committee members themselves.

Article 9

The union shall employ a secretary to carry out all resolutions adopted by the general meeting or the union committee.

Article 10

The General Meeting of Representatives-of-ten is the highest body of this union. When the General Meeting of Representatives-of-ten stands adjourned, the committee becomes the highest body.

Article 11

The General Meeting of Representatives-of-ten shall be held once a year. When necessary, the committee may convene special sessions.

Article 12

Congresses of the whole membership may be held on an irregular basis, to be convened by the committee when the necessity arises.

Article 13

If one-tenth or more of the Representatives-of-ten express lack of confidence in a certain committee member, the committee will be asked to convene a plenary meeting of the Representatives-of-ten at which, by majority approval, said committee member will be dismissed and his successor elected.

Article 14

The committee has the authority to dismiss a Representative-of-ten, provided that a majority of the members of his group agrees.

Article 15

The committee shall declare the dismissal of any member of the union guilty of any one of the following acts:

1. Violation of the charter of this union or any resolutions of the committee
2. Obstructing the functioning of this union
3. Failure to pay monthly dues for more than three months unless ill or unemployed.

Article 16

Those who withdraw from union membership will not be refunded any union fees paid.

Article 17

Only the General Meeting of Representatives-of-ten has the right to revise this charter.

Article 18

The charter shall take effect on the day of approval by the General Meeting of Representatives-of-ten.

The names of the committee members are as follows: Huang Zhixin, Zhu Hansheng, Bao Haiyun, Ren Shude, Dong Xianbo, Shu Yulin, Ou Yuexuan, Ren Shujie, Li Guisheng, Chen Zilin, Luo Zipei, Mo Zilin, Luo Yougui, Peng Yingqi, Wang Degui, Sheng Shaoyuan, Zhu Shusheng, Chen Chunhe, Chen Shusheng, Liang Xingcun, Qiu [X]sheng, Liu Jiheng, Liu Chunsheng, Yuan Dongsheng, Zhang Yousheng, Cai Guoqing, Yuan Fuqing, Huang Qing[X], Yang Futao, Guo Bingsheng, Wu Jujie, Luo Xianzheng, Huang Shaomei, Zhu Youfu, Wang Zifu, Liao Chunting, Huang Songquan, Huang Meixian, Ren Shumin, Dai Lancheng.

Telegram from Labor Groups to the Upper and Lower Houses of Parliament

(September 6, 1922)

To be forwarded to all publishing houses, labor unions, and other organizations nationwide courtesy of the Beijing *Morning News*, *Workers' Weekly*, Shanghai *China Times*, *Republican Daily*, Hankou *Jiangsheng ribao*, Changsha *Dagongbao*, and *People's Rule Daily*: Our organizations have sent the following telegram to the parliament in Beijing:

To the members of the upper and lower houses of the Parliament of the Republic of China: The world economy changes more rapidly every day, as the consciousness of the working class deepens day by day. The establishment of a worker-peasant state in Soviet Russia is a model for all other countries in the world! We, the laboring people, created civilization with our own hands, but we ourselves have yet to benefit from it. Although the Provisional Constitution of the Republic of China explicitly stipulates that there shall be no class distinctions among the people, the workers, who make up the overwhelming majority of the whole population, not only fail to be protected by law, but instead often suffer its oppression. In all the world of men, is there any injustice graver[1] than this? How fortunate that the movement to establish a labor law now reverberates throughout the land! What courageous and upright person does not rejoice in it? As representatives of the people, you gentlemen surely know that authority in a republic rests with the whole people. To talk of lawmaking without taking into consideration the working class, which constitutes the overwhelming majority [of the population]—would this not amount to abandoning the entire people? Our organizations, in accordance with the four cardinal principles of labor—(1) attainment of political freedom, (2) improvement in living standards, (3) participation in industrial management, and (4) attainment of training and education—thoroughly subscribe to the nineteen articles of the Outline for Labor Legislation put forward by the General Secretariat of Chinese Labor Organizations. We implore you, gentlemen, to uphold justice and fulfill your sacred duty by quickly passing the proposed labor law so that we, the workers, will no longer be a lawless people or have to resort to unlawful activities. What great good fortune [this would create]! Otherwise, you gentlemen will be irrevocably cutting yourselves off from the people, in

---

This telegram was published in the Changsha *Dagongbao* on September 10, 1922. We have translated it from the text as printed in *Mao Zedong ji. Bujuan*, Vol. 9, pp. 121–22.

1. Reading the missing character here as *shen* (extremely).

which case we laborers throughout the land will have no choice but to exercise our solemn authority and unite as one to battle for our freedom, for survival, and for the rights to which we are entitled. And we will certainly not recognize any of you as representing the will of the people in drawing up the constitution! Joint statement of the Hunan Branch of the Secretariat of Chinese Labor Organizations, the Guangzhou-Hankou Railroad Workers' Club of Xinhe, and the Guangzhou-Hankou Railroad Workers' Club of Yuezhou. We implore each and every one of you to uphold strongly the cause of justice and firmly to support our plea. We await your response most anxiously.

Attached is the Outline of Labor Legislation.

Submitted jointly by the Hunan Branch of the Secretariat of Chinese Labor Organizations, the Guangzhou-Hankou Railroad Workers' Club of Xinhe, the Guangzhou-Hankou Railroad Workers' Club of Yuezhou, and the Anyuan Railroad and Mineworkers' Club.

September 6

Guangzhou-Hankou Railroad Workers' Strike Declaration

(September 8, 1922)

Dear fellow countrymen! Workers! Farmers! Students! Brothers and Sisters!

Just look at how we proletarians are treated by society! Look at how the capitalists oppress us! In all of this vast society, where is there a place for us to have our say? But at this point, tightly encircled by dark forces that have brought us to this life-and-death crisis, we cannot but utter an urgent and solemn cry! Compatriots! We have previously declared how despotic and sinister the two villains of the Guangzhou-Hankou Railway, Zhang Enrong (supervisor) and Miao Fengmin (foreman), have been in mistreating the workers. Last year, seeking personal profit, they incited the workers to strike, making utter fools of us and plunging us into deep suffering. Afterwards, they conspired further to force us to join their organization and become weapons in their bid for power. When they failed, their humiliation turned to anger, and they made every effort to sabotage our club. How angry and hurt this made us feel! In addition, Miao even used the strike as an excuse to defraud us of our hard-earned wages. When a worker was injured on the job, Miao not only refused to let him leave for medical care, but actually docked his pay. Zhang, for his part, made use of the railways to traffic in opium, and beat up, insulted, and then fired a worker who refused to cover up for him. He also confiscated the rice that workers brought to work, and accused them of stealing coal. It would be hard indeed to describe the countless cases of his mistreating the workers. Compatriots, time and again we have asked the bureau chief to dismiss such scabs as he, but for more than ten days now, no concrete measures have been taken. The result of an interview with him in person is that he denied our demands and told us to take the case to court. Clearly he is shielding his own men so as to shirk his own responsibility. Three days ago we sent three separate telegrams to the Ministry of Transportation, setting a three-day time limit within which to settle the matter satisfactorily, or else a general strike would be held until the case is publicly judged by our fellow countrymen. The same intention was set out in a final warning submitted to the bureau chief. Now the three days are up and there is absolutely no hope for a

This declaration was published in the Changsha *Dagongbao* on September 10, 1922. Our source is *Mao Zedong ji. Bujuan*, Vol. 2, pp. 95–96.

satisfactory settlement. It is they who, by protecting their own men who have violated the law and sabotaged the public interest, have forced us to this last resort, which so greatly affects the nation! Compatriots! Zhang and Miao are villains who devour us workers. It is only natural that we swear not to coexist with them. Aside from this, as the cost of living rises, our lives become more and more difficult each day. Therefore, it is also quite urgent and highly reasonable for us to demand that our wages be raised to improve our living standard. Fellow countrymen and fellow workers! For the sake of "ending oppression," "maintaining our organization," "improving our lives," and "promoting human dignity," we have no choice but to struggle against the scabs and to resort to this final measure (a strike)! Compatriots from all walks of life! We strive only for our own immediate interests, and this has nothing to do with outside issues. Please, in the spirit of justice and truth, lend us concrete assistance! Dear fellow workers! Proletarian brothers and sisters! We are fighting for survival, for human dignity, and we vow never to give up until our goals are won! Fellow workers! Be brave! Be resolute! "Fighting for our very lives" depends entirely upon our ability to "unite" and "struggle"! Fellow workers throughout the country! "All workers are one." Let us unite and fight together against those who oppress us!

Declaration of the Guangzhou-Hankou Railway Workers.

To Mr. Zhu from the
Guangzhou-Hankou Railroad Workers

(September 10, 1922)

For the perusal of the honorable Mr. Zhu:

The current strike is a last resort on the part of the workers, who have simply suffered too much. Details of such matters as vicious personnel abusing their power and mistreating the workers have been put forward to Mr. Wang, the Railway Bureau chief, and to the foreign general manager. For more than two weeks now, the workers have been willing to bear their suffering in silence, but Bureau Chief Wang has been intentionally stalling, Zhang and Miao[1] have yet to leave, and the workers' demands have not been met, which is why all railway workers are enraged and have been forced to take this action. We cannot thank you enough for your willingness to support us. This railroad has always been of crucial importance, and since it is under systematic management, there exist as a matter of course the authorities responsible for it. What would be most advantageous is for you, Sir, speedily to enter into negotiations with Xujiapeng's bureau chief, Mr. Wang, and the foreign general manager. The very day that the eight demands are accepted, the trains will start running again and no one will disobey the order. We might add that the workers are extremely well organized. This strike was initiated by the Federation of Railroad Workers' Clubs of the entire railroad, which has full responsibility for conducting negotiations. We hereby draw this to your particular attention, at the same time as we respectfully wish you well and express our deepest appreciation for your meritorious efforts.

This appeal was published in the Changsha *Dagongbao* on September 12, 1922. We have translated it from *Mao Zedong ji. Bujuan*, Vol. 9, p. 123.

1. Zhang Enrong, the supervisor, and Miao Fengming, the foreman. See previous document, September 8, 1922.

Express Communiqué from All the Guangzhou-Hankou Railroad Workers to Labor Groups Throughout the Country

(September 12, 1922)

Extremely Urgent

Dear fellow workers of the labor groups of the whole country:

After the Guangzhou-Hankou railroad workers all went out on strike, a small number of workers from Tianjin, because of their ties as fellow provincials, willingly allowed themselves to be used by the bureau chief as his running dogs. Sabotaging the actions of the organization, they asked the bureau chief to send troops as usual to protect them. As a result, the striking workers had no other recourse but to lie down all together on the railway tracks to obstruct them. The troops, however, under the direction of the bureau chief, went so far as[1] to massacre the workers ruthlessly. When the family members of the workers went to their rescue, the troops used the same measures against them. The wailing of the children and the crying of the women was unbearable. There were countless wounded, and several dozen people jumped into the water. Seven or eight people were mortally wounded, and more than ten people were arrested. Six fellow workers from Yuezhou are already dead. Anyone with a human heart is saddened and angered! Since the workers have suffered this cruel massacre and are crying out and writhing under such extreme oppression, they can only continue firmly with the strike, swearing to die rather than to yield. We most earnestly entreat fellow workers of all the labor groups to lend us concrete assistance, and we adamantly demand: (1) withdrawal of the troops that are suppressing the workers; (2) removal and punishment of Bureau Chief Wang; (3) comfort and compensation for the wounded workers and their families; (4) complete acceptance of the conditions put forward by the workers. Fellow workers of all the labor groups! Such dark, tyrannical, and cruel oppression is visited only on our

---

This document appeared in the Changsha *Dagongbao* on September 14, 1922. Our source is *Mao Zedong ji. Bujuan*, Vol. 9, p. 125.

1. The second character of this expression is missing from our source; the sense could be "actually," "had the effrontery," or "went so far as." We have opted for the last of these, which lies in the middle of the possible range of meanings.

laboring class. How angry should we be? How bitterly must we hate? How forcefully should we rise up? Take revenge! Fellow workers of the whole country! Arise and struggle against the enemy!

All the Workers of the Federation
of Guangzhou-Hankou Railroad
Workers' Clubs[2]

2. This federation had been formed on September 6. See the account of the strike in Li Jui, *Early Mao* , pp. 229–39.

Strike Declaration by the Masons and Carpenters of Changsha

(October 6, 1922)[1]

We, the masons and carpenters, wish to inform you that for the sake of earning our livelihood, we demand a modest pay increase. Since June 1, we have been paid thirty-four cents for grade A work, and twenty-six cents for grade B work. Then recently there suddenly emerged an association of a few people, which held a meeting in opposition to this, and requested the administrative offices of the [xian] government to make a public proclamation about changes in the pay rate. But the fact is that workers like us engaged in painful toil exchange a day of our lives and of our energy for only a few coppers to feed our families. We really do not sit idle and live on undeserved income, as is the case with other illegitimate occupations. Just look at the merchants, who may simply raise the price in a matter of a few days. Why isn't there anyone to oppose that? Why do we, workers who only earn the little money from a whole day's "sweat" and "toil," have to go through such an ordeal of being trampled on?

Right now we do not have any means to deal with this. All we know is that the price of a day's bitter toil must be this much, or it just won't do. Although we cannot enjoy other rights, we deserve freedom in our occupation and our work. We are resolved to die rather than be deprived by anyone of this right. Now the only measure we adopt is to insist on the payment of thirty-four and twenty-six cents per day. All of us have joined together and decided not to work any more. We hereby make the above proclamation to this effect.

Announced by all masons and carpenters of Hunan on the sixteenth day of the eighth month.

This document was published in the Changsha *Dagongbao* on October 6, 1922. Our source is *Mao Zedong ji. Bujuan*, Vol. 2, p. 89.

1. The text of this document published in the *Bujuan*, Vol. 2, is dated at the end, "the sixteenth day of the eighth month," but as pointed out in the index to the *Bujuan*, this refers in fact to the lunar calendar and corresponded in 1922 to October 6.

Letter of Support for the Strike of the Masons and Carpenters of Changsha from the Hunan Branch of the Secretariat of Labor Organizations

(October 13, 1922)

Yesterday was the eighth day of the masons' and carpenters' strike. The staff members of their union held a discussion meeting to take advantage of the strike period to make preparations for setting up a night school for construction workers. Now various people are making all kinds of preparations toward the goal of imparting general knowledge to the completely illiterate masons and carpenters. The school is about to open. Yesterday also someone was sent to the union from no. 26 Xinghanmen to ask that the workers return to work soon because the house at that address had long been in need of repairs, which could not be further delayed. To words like "cannot wait any longer . . . ," the union replied yesterday with messages in letters from many different places. There is a lot of support from places too numerous to list here. We publish below a letter from the Secretariat of Labor Organizations. It reads as follows:[1]

Fellow construction workers, greetings!

Your current strike has been going on for several days. Gentlemen! We believe that you are absolutely justified, and it is truly outrageous that to date the capitalists have not yet completely agreed to your demands. Now all labor groups are standing up to support you, and this Secretariat will do everything it can to back you. It is our sincere hope that you will be well organized, maintain order, and hold out to the end in order to achieve ultimate victory. We are sending this especially to encourage you to make further efforts.

This letter, with accompanying commentary, appeared in the Changsha *Dagongbao* on October 14, 1922. It is reproduced in *Mao Zedong ji. Bujuan*, Vol. 9, p. 133, and we have translated it from that source.

1. The message that follows from the Labor Secretariat has been attributed to Mao, who was, as already noted, head of the Hunan office of this organization. The introductory paragraph was added by the *Dagongbao*.

Record of Conversation between the Masons and Carpenters and Mr. Wu, Head of the Political Affairs Department, Together with a Letter to the Provincial Governor

(October 24, 1922)

The overall circumstances of the petition by the masons and carpenters to the *xian* Magistrate's Office has already been reported in yesterday's paper . . . .[1] At ten o'clock yesterday morning, workers from the two trades assembled in front of the Education Council Plaza . . . .[2] Mr. Wu, director of the Administration Office, invited the representatives into the director's office where the various public groups were meeting in the guest hall. After a period of three hours and several urgent telephone calls from the workers at the council, it was said that they had not yet reached an agreement. So the workers had no choice but to go to the *xian* office to present their petition. The representatives beseeched Director Wu to respond quickly. After repeated attempts at mediation on Director Wu's part, the meeting finally came to a close at eight o'clock in the evening, when Director Wu asked those in the two trades to prepare a formal document requesting freedom to exercise one's trade for approval by the government. In addition, a record was drafted on the spot by the representatives and reviewed by Director Wu. The public notice of Changsha *xian* was declared null and void, and the workers were granted freedom to exercise their trades. While the representatives took the record to report [to those at the Education Council], a formal document was drawn up requesting the provincial governor's approval. By this time it was already nine o'clock. Presented below are the record of the face-to-face conversation between the representatives and Director Wu and the formal document presented to the provincial government office:[3]

Record of Conversation

The workers of the masons' and carpenters' trades demand an increase in their [daily] wage to thirty-four cents, and do not recognize the public notice regarding settlement of their strike issued by the Changsha *xian* magistrate on the fourteenth day of the eighth month of the lunar calendar. According to the

---

This document was published in the Changsha *Dagongbao* on October 25, 1922. Our source is *Mao Zedong ji. Bujuan*, Vol. 9, pp. 137–38.

1. Passage omitted in the *Mao Zedong ji.*
2. Passage omitted in the *Mao Zedong ji.*
3. Once again, this introductory paragraph was supplied by the *Dagongbao*; the record of the conversations and the letter to the governor are by Mao.

workers' representatives, this is a matter of free contractual relations between labor and employer, which should be negotiated freely and voluntarily by the two sides without any acts of coercion. (This last phrase was added by Director Wu.) There is no need, then, for the government office to intervene. On behalf of the provincial governor, the director of this office agrees that this matter be settled according to the above-mentioned principles and will notify the workers of this agreement.

The above text was recorded in the presence of Director Wu Jinghong, at the Office of Administration of the provincial government.

Letter to the Provincial Governor

We hereby submit this document requesting your unequivocal approval of the freedom to exercise one's trade, in order to set everyone's mind at ease. For the purposes of demanding a wage increase to thirty-four cents, and refusing to recognize the public notice issued on the fourteenth day of the eighth month of the lunar calendar by the Changsha *xian* magistrate, we have had to strike for the past twenty days and more. In accordance with Article 17 of the Provincial Constitution, yesterday all the workers marched to the Changsha *xian* government office to proclaim our sufferings and to request that the public notice issued earlier be rescinded, so as to make it possible for us to live. Even as the two sides were arguing with each other, a telegram arrived from the provincial governor, which makes it possible for the dispute to be settled satisfactorily today. It is our belief that the freedom to exercise one's trade is embodied in the constitution, and that the dispute over wages is actually a matter of free contractual relations between workers and employers, which should be voluntarily agreed to by the two sides concerned. Unless there is use of coercive force, there is no need for official intervention. The General Command Headquarters recently sent letters to various agencies, schools, and residences, recognizing the thirty-four-cent wage and urging the workers to return to work. The Changsha *xian* magistrate alone has refused to make a decision; this is a violation of the Provincial Constitution and is meant to suppress the workers. We are profoundly grateful that the provincial governor has so generously supported us, and that when Mr. Wu, the director of the Admistrative Office, met with the workers' representatives today, he agreed, on behalf of the governor, that the matter be handled in accordance with the workers' proposal. All the workers are now gathered on the grounds in front of the provincial Education Council and are unanimously appealing to the governor for a settlement that will put everyone's mind at rest. All wage increases are a matter of free contractual relations between laborers and employers, and there is no need for official intervention. We formally present this request that the provincial governor speedily and explicitly grant his approval, to be conveyed and brought back by the workers' representatives. Please also order Mr. Zhou, the Changsha *xian* magistrate, to rescind the public notice of the fourteenth day of the eighth month of the lunar calendar, so as to assure the workers' livelihood and set the people's minds at rest. This will indeed benefit the public. We hereby present this report to Governor Zhao of Hunan Province.

Masons and Carpenters of the
provincial capital of Hunan.

Ren Shude, Qiu Shousong, Du Zhongkun, Huang Shaomei, Li Haishan, Mao Runzhi, Zhu Youfu, Luo Zipei, and all of the more than 6,400 workers.

The True Circumstances of the Negotiations between the Representatives of Various Labor Organizations and Provincial Governor Zhao, Director Wu of the Administrative Bureau, Director Shi of the Police Bureau, and Magistrate Zhou of Changsha Xian

(December 14, 1922)

Dear Mr. Editor:

Our humble federation hereby submits to your distinguished paper a document of the utmost importance to working people. We respectfully request that it be printed in the news or contributions column, and will be extremely grateful if you can do so. Respectful good wishes for your editorial work.

> Submitted on the fourteenth [of December]
> by the All-Hunan Federation of Labor Organizations

The circumstances in the negotiations of representatives of the various labor organizations with the government on a variety of important issues. There has been some coverage of this matter in the various newspapers, but too much has been left out, and much does not tally with the actual circumstances of the negotiations. Nor do all the members of every labor union understand the results of these negotiations. Therefore we are revealing here the true circumstances of the negotiations with the Police Bureau, with Changsha *xian*, and with the Administrative Bureau, as well as with the governor's office.

Recently, disputes between labor and capital have been constantly increasing in number. With the steady development of the workers' organizations, the estrangement between the workers and the government has also grown increas-

---

This record was submitted on December 14, 1922, to the editor of the Changsha *Dagongbao*, and that paper published it on December 15, 16, and 17. Our source is *Mao Zedong ji. Bujuan*, Vol. 9, pp. 151–56.

ingly severe. Very often, the governmental offices have handled labor-capital disputes unfairly, two cases that have suddenly arisen lately being the taking down of the signboard of the Rickshaw-Pullers' Union by the police station of the Western District and the renewed attempt of Changsha *xian* to ban the new barber shops.[1] Also, at a time when the strike of the Writing-Brush Makers' Union had not yet been resolved, factional strife arose within the Mechanics' Union between students and on-the-job trainees, while in the Tailors' Union conflict broke out between the old annually appointed manager and his fellow members. Moreover, rumors have been rampant lately, to the effect that the government will again ignore the constitution and oppress labor. With the rumors increasing every day, the anger and fear in labor circles has also been growing day by day. For all of these reasons, eleven labor organizations, including the All-Hunan Federation of Labor Organizations, the General Union of Guangzhou-Wuhan Railway Workers, the Masons' and Carpenters' Union, the Barbers' Union, the Typesetters' Union, the Union of Lithographic Workers, the Writing-Brush Makers' Union, the Tailors' Union, the Mechanics' Union, the Rickshaw-Pullers' Union, and the Boot and Shoe Craftsmen's Union have found it necessary to approach the government offices directly at different levels. Over twenty representatives from various labor organizations met specially with Director Shi of the Police Bureau at twelve noon on the eleventh of this month and negotiated for about two hours. At three that afternoon, they all met with Magistrate Zhou for about two and a half hours. At twelve noon on the twelfth, they met with Director Wu of the Administrative Bureau for about three and a half hours. At twelve noon on the thirteenth they met with Provincial Governor Zhao and negotiated for about one and a half hours.[2] The matters discussed in these negotiations fell under the following ten headings: (1) the request that the government make clear its attitude toward labor circles; (2) the question of the freedom of association and assembly; (3) clarification of the attitude of labor circles; (4) that labor circles and the government should put their heads together on a regular basis to avoid misunderstandings; (5) a proposal to organize a

---

1. For an explanation of these two disputes, see below, the paragraphs on issues nos. 6 and 7.

2. For an account of these meetings with Zhao Hengti and others, see Li Rui, *Early Mao*, pp. 259–72. Zhao Hengti (1880–1971), *zi* Yiwu, *hao* Yanwu, was a native of Hengshan, Hunan. After studying at the Japanese Officers' Academy in Tokyo, he served in the early years of the Republic under Governor Tan Yankai in Hunan. When the northern warlord, Zhang Jingyao, who had ruled the province from 1918 to mid-1920, fell from power after a campaign in which Mao had been deeply involved (see the extensive materials in Volume I of this edition), Zhao himself became governor, despite the desire of his former superior Tan Yankai to return to the post. Zhao was an active promoter of the federalist movement, and by granting a provincial constitution and establishing a new government on January 1, 1922, made Hunan the spearhead of the movement for decentralization in China. Mao, who had supported Hunanese autonomy in 1919–1920, had now adopted a different political stance, and the two soon came into conflict.

labor-capital arbitration board; (6) the problem of rickshaw pullers; (7) the problem of barbers; (8) the problem of writing-brush makers; (9) the problem of mechanics; (10) the problem of tailors.

Concerning issue no. 1 (the request that the government make clear its position with regard to labor circles), Governor Zhao, Director Wu, Director Shi, and Magistrate Zhou all asserted that the government had adopted the principle of protecting all workers and had no intention of oppressing them. The fact that recently strikes had broken out frequently in various places, but the government had not interfered in any way, was evidence of this. Governor Zhao and Director Wu also said that even though the government had heard many reports about such things as a general strike, it had treated these as rumors, and had not taken any repressive measures. Governor Zhao also made mention of the affair of Huang and Pang, saying that in reality Huang and Pang had been executed because they were buying firearms, colluding with bandits, and agitating for a strike at the mint at the end of the year when any stoppage of work was simply out of the question, as the copper money to be coined in the mint was required for the soldiers' pay and rations. Thus this matter concerned Huang and Pang personally and was not directed against labor circles.[3] The representatives expressed their satisfaction with the attitude adopted by the government toward labor. They declared, however, that it was in fact not true that Huang and Pang had been buying firearms, colluding with bandits, or agitating for a strike at the mint. They added that all those who came to inform the governor had undoubtedly said these things were true, and that probably this was the very first time the governor had heard it said that such reports were not true. From the standpoint of the workers, to have one or two men killed and one or two unions banned was assuredly a loss, but that could in no way make them desist from their necessary activities. The government, on the other hand, by being denounced throughout the whole nation, truly suffered an immeasurable loss in reputation and legality. This alone sufficed to demonstrate that the estrangement between the workers and the government was not a good thing.

---

3. Huang Ai and Pang Renquan were anarchists whom Mao sought to convert to Marxism. Regarding their early activities in the Hunan labor movement, see above, the note to "My Hopes for the Labor Association" of November 21, 1921. In January 1922 when workers at the Huashi Cotton Mill called a full-scale strike, Zhao Hengti was determined to put an end to their year-long strike actions for improved working conditions. There were violent clashes between his soldiers and strikers, resulting in deaths and massive damage to machinery. The Hunan Labor Association protested in support of the workers on one side, and the management of Huashi Company appealed to Zhao to put an end to the trouble on the other. On January 16, Zhao invited labor leaders Huang and Pang to the mill for negotiations. They were taken into custody by Zhao's soldiers and shot in public the next morning. At the same time, the Hunan Labor Association was dissolved and its publication suppressed. For further details see Li Rui, *Early Mao*, pp. 192–99, and Angus W. McDonald, Jr., *The Urban Origins of Rural Revolution* (Berkeley: University of California Press, 1978), pp. 154–65. (Hereafter McDonald, *Urban Origins*.)

Concerning issue no. 2 (the problem of association and assembly), the representatives pointed out that the government offices often refused to grant permission, always insisting that an association must first be registered before it could be formed. They did not know that the rights of the people to form associations freely (provided they did not contravene the criminal law) and to assemble peaceably (provided they were not carrying arms) as provided by Article 12 of the Provincial Constitution, was not to be restricted by any special decree. Furthermore, there was no stipulation that an association could be formed only after receiving permission from a government office. If permission were to be required before forming an association, then government offices would be allowed great latitude in granting or denying permission, and Article 11[4] of the Provincial Constitution would be basically abrogated. The same was also true of assembly. Recently, secret agents have often appeared at meetings to create obstacles and disturbances, or armed police have even been sent to compel their dissolution. They had no idea either that the Provincial Constitution grants the people, when not carrying arms, complete freedom to assemble peaceably, and that this right can under no circumstance be arbitrarily interfered with. Governor Zhao, Director Wu, Director Shi, and Magistrate Zhou all confirmed that the constitution was, as a matter of course, perfectly valid, and that the government would naturally not interfere if the people abided by the law. At the Administrative Bureau, the representatives also stated that the law was concerned only with behavior, not with intent. In the past, the government has often interfered with assemblies, associations, speech, and the press using the excuse that the ideas behind some particular assembly, association, speech, or publication might lead to a violation of the statutes of the criminal law. This is not compatible with the fundamental meaning of the law. If the government can interfere on grounds of intent (including presumed intent) before the people have even taken any action, then anything at all could be interfered with on the grounds that it "might possibly" lead to a violation of the criminal law. The representatives cited the example of England, where the Communist Party (which has representatives in Parliament) is tolerated and not interfered with, except when the Communist Party engages in actions that violate the law (i.e., in revolution). Director Wu replied that in the field of law there were originally two factions, the motivationists and the behaviorists. It was true that the law now based itself on the behavior principle, but if a certain motivation was definitely likely to lead to some violation of the law, then it is necessary to intervene. The representatives insisted that no interference was called for where there was no behavior that directly violated the law. They also cited, in support of their argument, the fact that England and France do not prohibit people from carrying weapons, and intervene only when shooting and killing occur.

---

4. This appears to be a misprint for Article 12; Article 11 of the Provisional Constitution dealt with freedom of speech, not with association and assembly.

Concerning issue no. 3 (clarification of the attitude of labor circles), the representatives said that what the workers wished for was socialism, because socialism was really beneficial to them. But because this was difficult to achieve in China at present, in current politics they naturally accepted the principle of democracy.[5] In public statements issued by the government offices, however, it was often said that the workers widely advocated anarchism. This is entirely untrue. The workers have no faith at all in anarchism because it is extremely disadvantageous for them. As for the attitude of the workers toward the present government, if the government will only treat the workers with good will, the workers will assuredly never harbor evil intentions toward the government. Recently, in order to alleviate their own suffering, the workers have frequently engaged in various campaigns, which are referred to as the labor movement. Their demands, however, have never gone beyond three things: a raise in pay, a reduction of working hours, and an improvement in the way they are treated. The workers are absolutely not being used by any of the present political parties or factions. Any labor union that is being used by a political faction is a trade union in name only. No true industrial or professional labor union would ever allow itself to be used by them. Whenever there is a strike, however, the government, without investigating matters, immediately assumes that the workers are being used by some political faction. Such suspicions are truly erroneous. Henceforth, we request the government to distinguish between fictitious labor unions that are the instruments of others and genuine trade unions that are devoted exclusively to alleviating the sufferings of the workers themselves, and not to confuse the two, in order to avoid handling them improperly and thereby arousing bad feeling toward the government in labor circles. Governor Zhao, Directors Wu and Shi, and Magistrate Zhou all affirmed that this attitude adopted by the workers was quite proper. Directors Wu and Shi said that socialism was a progressive ideology and could certainly be realized in the future, but it could not be realized at present. Magistrate Zhou proposed that labor and capital should not fight each other, but rather seek to accomodate each other in order to avoid great social losses. Governor Zhao also said that socialism might be realized in the future, only it would be hard to put it into practice today. At the moment, the main effort should be devoted to the development of industry, so he advised the workers to put up with a little misery. In response to Magistrate Zhou's views, the representatives maintained that the government in fact bore a responsibility to get the capitalists and shop owners to make many more concessions, so that the workers would not come into conflict with them.

Concerning issue no. 4 (that workers and government put their heads together), the representatives said that if workers and government did not put their heads together, all kinds of misunderstandings could result. With the government

---

5. *Minzhizhuyi*, literally "people's-rule-ism," yet another of the older terms for democracy.

way up on high and the workers down below, it was easy for the people in the middle to play tricks and fabricate all kinds of rumors. The story propagated recently that the government would repress strikes in a big way and last year's case of Huang and Pang were examples of this. Furthermore, if the workers did not put their heads together with the government, it would be easy for the capitalists and shop owners to put their heads together with the government. If lower-level officials in the government listened only to one side, neglected to enquire into matters, and handled them carelessly, the damage done to the workers would not be the only result; the government would also have to alter its previous verdict, and as a result its prestige would suffer greatly. There had been many instances of the kind in the last few months, and more recently there had been the incident of the rickshaw pullers. It was hoped that from now on, government and workers would put their heads together from time to time, and that when an important case came up, it would not be decided until this had been done. Zhao, Wu, Shi, and Zhou all approved of this suggestion. Director Wu also said that he very much wanted to put his head together with the workers more often so as to examine and learn about the living conditions of the workers, provided only that the labor union representatives truly represented the majority. Governor Zhao said that henceforth, in the new government, the Provincial Council[6] would be invested with full responsibility, the governor being no more than a figurehead, and there could be more contacts with this organ.[7]

Concerning issue no. 5 (an arbitration board for labor-capital disputes), the representatives said that the number of disputes between labor and capital had been growing with each passing day, and that they often felt such problems were dealt with improperly by the ordinary administrative or judicial organs. Because labor-capital problems could not be treated properly without expert knowledge, it was specifically suggested to the government that, following the example of Guangdong Province, a labor-capital arbitration board be set up. Director Shi and Magistrate Zhou expressed very strong approval for this suggestion. Magistrate Zhou also offered to act as mediator in all labor disputes before the board was set up. Both Director Wu and Governor Zhao advised that the Provincial Assembly be petitioned to enact the legislation, and said that the government could then have the court set up. Governor Zhao was also willing to suggest it to the assembly.

Concerning issue no. 6 (the problem of the Rickshaw-Pullers' Union), the representatives who had been to negotiate with the Police Bureau said that the Changsha Union of Rickshaw Pullers, which had been organized in accordance

---

6. *Shengwuyuan*, literally "Provincial Affairs Council."

7. This argument of Zhao's was somewhat disingenuous. Under the terms of Section V of the Provincial Constitution, Articles 46–64, the governor was in no sense a figurehead; apart from the very wide powers attached to his own office, he was also chairman of the Provincial Council.

with Article 12 of the Provincial Constitution and had a membership of about 1,800, was extremely well organized. And yet, the police station of the Western District had suddenly taken down the union signboard under a warrant containing the words "unauthorized establishment." What was more, they had used abusive language. With a violent and threatening attitude, Zhou, a clerk in the police station, even banged the tables and chairs and spoke abusively, without the least respect for the dignity of the workers. There is a rumor, which has yet to be verified, to the effect that the rickshaw owners colluded with staff members of the station in fraudulent practices.[8] All the trade unions are extremely indignant, saying that if the signboard of one union can be taken down, the signboards of all other unions may be taken down as well. They regard this as extremely dangerous and totally in contravention of Article 12 of the Provincial Constitution. Director Wu listened to what the representatives had to say. He was extremely shocked and denied that he had ever issued such an order. He accepted then and there the registration of the Rickshaw-Pullers' Union and said that as soon as the written document arrived, it would be immediately approved. He also urged the workers to pay no attention to the meeting called by Wu Hesheng, saying that sham trade unions would naturally perish. The representatives responded favorably.

Concerning issue no. 7 (the problem of barbers), the representatives, both at the Changsha *xian* [office] and at the Administrative Bureau, pointed out the various abuses involved in this case and also noted that the original verdict violated the provision in the Provincial Constitution regarding freedom to do business, adding that the corruption in the districts[9] really must be cleaned up, and that dividing the receipts on a basis of 40 percent and 60 percent[10] was fairest to both sides. Magistrate Zhou agreed to suspend the execution of the original verdict, after which the matter could be finally settled once the provincial government had modified the original verdict. He also assented to the re-

---

8. The organization in question was, of course, a modern-style union, which had placed itself in opposition to the guild—dominated by the rickshaw owners—that had formerly controlled the trade. The owners had long enjoyed a mutually profitable relationship with the police.

9. The Chinese term *matou* has the basic meaning of "wharf" or "pier," but it can also signify "market," and it is used here in a sense derived from this. The barbers of Changsha were divided into districts or trading areas called *matou*, each under the control of a master barber. In June 1921, a group of young rebels had set up seven new shops of their own outside this framework. The conflict had dragged on for over a year. Then, in August 1922, the authorities of Changsha *xian* had endorsed the point of view of the guild masters and arrested five of the rebels. (This was the "banning of the new barber shops" referred to in the list of disputes at the beginning of the present text.) On the barbers' strike and its background, see McDonald, *Urban Origins*, pp. 186–87, and *Hunan jinbainian dashi jishu* (An Account of Important Events in Hunan during the Past Hundred Years), 2nd ed. (Changsha: Hunan Renmin Chubanshe, 1979), pp. 505–6. (Hereafter *Jinbainian*.)

10. I.e., 40 percent for the workers and 60 percent for the owners. (Previously it had been 30 percent and 70 percent.)

lease from prison on bail of the worker Luo Meixiang. Director Wu actually denied that there was any new order instructing Changsha *xian* to execute the original verdict, saying, "I have no knowledge of this." (This shows that the extent of corrupt practices in this case was extremely great.) He subsequently agreed to handle the case according to the resolution of the Provincial Assembly. If agreement was not reached on a resolution, labor circles could petition for a change in the original unjustifiable verdict, and the case could then be finally resolved.

Concerning issue no. 8 (the problem of the strike of the writing-brush makers), negotiations took place at the Changsha *xian* [office]. The representatives explained the wretchedness of the lives of their fellow workers in the writing-brush making industry, and said that the owners of the enterprises, wanting to put the workers in a desperate situation, had been delaying matters and refused to resolve the issue. Magistrate Zhou thereupon agreed to act as mediator and set the twelfth as the date for the representatives of both sides, employers and employees, to meet at the Changsha *xian* office to come to a settlement.

Concerning issue no. 9 (the problem of the Mechanics' Union), negotiations were held at the Administrative Bureau. Director Wu, having heard first a one-sided account from the students, asked if this were true. The representatives then recounted how, since its founding, the Mechanics' Society had been made use of by others in various ways, while the real workers could have no say, and how recently the genuine fellow workers had started a thorough reform, had met to carry out new elections, and had resolved to change the name to the Mechanics' Union. Director Wu agreed that the matter should be settled in accordance with the real situation and he could by no means accept the one-sided account of the other party.

Concerning issue no. 10 (the Tailors' Union), the negotiations were held at the Changsha *xian* [office]. The representatives explained that if the former annually appointed manager refused to hand over the property records, this was simply a case of the minority opposing the majority. Magistrate Zhou agreed to mediate, and a date was fixed for the morning of the twelfth, when both sides would meet at the Changsha *xian* office for a settlement.

> Representatives of the All-Hunan Federation of Labor
> Organizations[11]—Mao Runzhi and Yang Runxi
>
> Representatives of the General Union of Guangzhou-
> Wuhan Railway Workers—Guo Liang and Xu Zhongyun

---

11. The All-Hunan Federation of Labor Organizations (*Hunan quansheng gongtuan lianhehui*) had been established in early November 1922 by Mao Zedong and other Marxist intellectuals. At a meeting on November 5, 1922, Mao was elected head or general secretary (*zheng zongganshi*) of the federation, a post he occupied until he left the province in April 1923. Building in part on the foundation laid by the Labor Association of Huang Ai and Pang Renquan, who had been executed in January 1922, the new Federation drew together unions representing a number of trades and industries. Many of these are listed below; see also the relevant section of the text of July 1, 1923, "Hunan under the Provincial Constitution."

Representatives of the Masons' and Carpenters' Union—Ren Shude and Chou Shousong

Representatives of the Barbers' Union—Wang Zishou, Yang Qiusheng, and Ma Ziqiang

Representatives of the Tailors' Union—Tang Bi, Zhang Hanfan, and Zheng Fusheng

Representatives of the Writing-Brush Makers' Union—Zheng Yingkui and Zhang Bingshen

Representatives of the Typesetters' Union—Xiao Ru and Liu Maonan

Representatives of the Union of Lithographic Workers—Tan Yingzhu and Zhang Haiping

Representatives of the Rickshaw-Pullers' Union—Huang Jie and Luo Rongxi

Representatives of the Mechanics' Union—Wang Lusheng and Xiao Kaizhen

Representative of the Boot and Shoe Craftsmen's Union—Li Binggan

Letter from the Typesetters' Union to Reporter Dun of the **Dagongbao**

(December 14, 1922)

Mr. Dun:

Naturally we are very thankful for your great kindness in donning your long gown to exhort us workers. But would we not be even more grateful to you, sir, if you were to take off your long gown and stand on the side of us workers to give us your sincere advice? We ourselves recognize that we are not college students, that we hold no doctorates, that we do not belong to the upper classes. We are, very simply, each and every one of us, workers. So of course we should be subject to the "generous instruction" of others. But we also recognize that in this world there is not only one group of people that is to be lectured to. Speaking of the present, students, workers, and the people are the ones who are lectured to; those doing the lecturing are naturally the ones in the society of long gowns. Among students, workers, and the people there are none who are not ignorant and unschooled. So it is entirely appropriate that those others don long gowns and bring out their intellectual chauvinism and their academic chauvinism with which to teach other people lessons. Their class is the intellectual class; the tools of their trade are scholarship and learning. The way they make their living is by knowing how to write articles and lecture people. It is also entirely appropriate that we and they each defend our respective interests and give full play to our respective abilities. However, as for those who lecture people, we very much hope that they will first take a look at the second chapter of Tolstoy's *Confession*. We ourselves are not qualified to lecture people, but we wish to invite Old Man Tolstoy to imitate them in giving sincere advice.

We recognize that we ourselves are ignorant and unschooled and need to be instructed by others, and very much hope that others are able to teach us. Harsh words are good medicine and honeyed words are poison; how dare we not respectfully accept them? But what we wish to make clear is the following:

1. Our hope is that those giving us instruction can do so by standing on our side; that they can come down to our level and be our friends, instead of acting

---

This letter, and Dun's reply, appeared together in the Changsha *Dagongbao* on December 14, 1922. Thus the date shown above is that of publication, rather than that of composition. We have translated these two items from *Mao Zedong ji. Bujuan*, Vol. 2, pp. 103–7.

as our teachers or superiors. Instead of always coming out with such phrases as "you workers," or "lacking common sense," or "being disorderly," or "becoming more and more depraved," or "we give you workers sincere counsel," or "encouraging bad habits among the workers," it would be so much better to say, "all of us." Gentlemen, can you truly help us and give us sincere counsel? In that case, we are very eager to shake your hand. Please extend us your hand right now, and don't keep saying "you people, you people," as if "we" were some sort of "officials" and "you people" were no more than "insignificant wretches."

2. Our hope is that those giving us instruction would investigate the facts clearly and not make any sinister insinuations. Even less should they denigrate the human dignity of others. For example, if we say that your newspaper receives certain amounts of money from a certain individual every month, will you admit it? Let me ask you further: when you refer to "not again (the word 'again' was deleted by our workers when they set the type) being manipulated by others or becoming the victims of others' ideological experiments," have you, sir, actually seen anything that would justify your saying this? We beg you to give us a response as soon as possible. How we wish that journalists would stick to the facts a little more when they speak! You will surely say that you wish us not to act this way. If you are really making sinister insinuations, we will, of course, disagree with you. It is excusable if you say you do hope we act this way, but we will not grant that you are well-meaning. To denigrate the human dignity of us workers could not be your sincere desire, and such wishes should not reside in the heart of the same Mr. Dun who has expressed sympathy for us workers. In addition you say that "because of this victory, from now on the workers are bound to become gradually more aggressive; they will grow daily in number and variety. Despite the presence of people in charge of maintaining order, I'm afraid it cannot be done." What evidence have you seen to justify such a prediction? We are afraid that once certain words are written down, it may be difficult to retract them—do you really have a crystal ball? These words, like the ones you uttered before, are not what you should have said. Moreover, isn't what you say about "failure to maintain order" rather deliberately exaggerated and unnatural?

3. It is our hope that those instructing us will come down to our level and actually do some teaching. It is quite right that what we workers need is knowledge. We workers also very much wish that educated people would come forward and become our true friends! Sir, you say that we are being manipulated by others and are the victims of others, and that you "pity" us. Then you, Sir, should be our true guide. We very much wish that you would take off your long gown, resign your position as high and mighty editor, and help us run the labor movement. At the very least, you should be a true labor educator and never again stand on the sidelines saying things like, "I thus give further sincere counsel to those of you engaged in the labor movement." Sir, we only acknowledge as good friends those who can sacrifice their position and endure hunger and hardship to work to advance the interests of the great mass of us workers! Since you say that

we are wrong, that our teachers are wrong, and that we are being manipulated and victimized by others, we are going to sack our teachers immediately. With 110 percent sincerity, we welcome you, Sir, our peerless sympathizer! Would you kindly honor us with your visit? Hurry, please, and take off your long gown!

4. If only those who give us instruction would look at things closely from our point of view. How could we gain the opportunity to study and get some exercise? Newspaper production workers at a newspaper have to work both during the day and at night, and you are very much in favor of their working the night shift. Let us leave aside for now the issue of night work. We ask you, though, where can they get the time to go to remedial schools [for adults] to study? Do you mean to say that they have some kind of power to be in two places at once? Before you open your mouth, please look into how many such schools there are and how many workers there are, in the city of Changsha. We admit now that unless our work hours are reduced, we will not have the opportunity to study. Unless we ourselves unite and establish our own adult education schools, we will not have a place to study. We want to reduce our work hours, but the employers ignore us. We want to unite, but others undermine us, so we have no alternative but to have a movement. We want to support our interest in study, but others say we should not do so. We want to invite people to guide us and become our true friends and teachers and again, others say we are "being manipulated by others" and "the victims of others' ideological experiments." Fine. So then we invite those who were doing all the talking about these things, but again they want to don their long gowns, and cannot come after all. Sir, please come help us work out a better way of acquiring knowledge so that we may be spared having to go on forever receiving the instruction of others!

As for working the night shift, you feel that as far as the principles of health are concerned, there is no problem. Indeed, newspaper editors work at night; officials, politicians, and members of parliament all work at night. Why are they all so nice and plump? We work not only at night, but also during the day. We cannot sleep until late afternoon. We do not have any meat to eat. The health of laborers is often impaired by poor nutrition and overwork. The only remedy for the poor is sleep and rest. Don't you know that? You even want us manual laborers to do physical exercises after we are exhausted from work! Sports? Do you really want to see us dead? The two issues you have raised, the night shift and the [labor] movement, cannot be explained to you in a word or two. We are not going to say any more at this point, but allow us to give you a bit of counsel for a change. You really have been reading too much! We would like to invite you to come and have a taste of physical labor with us.

Sir, we very much want to thank you. We also want to express our great love and respect for you, as you are not totally indifferent to us. You are much better than many of the big-shot journalists at many of the big-shot newspapers in Changsha, who haven't had a word to say about our problems! But when we have something to say, we feel compelled to say it to you, just as when you have something to say, you must say it to us. Wherever we have used offensive words, we ask you, please, to pardon the workers' ignorance. That is our weakness!

[Dun's reply]

I'm extremely happy that the workers can conduct a proper written debate with me. However, I mean to be giving the workers sincere counsel in good faith, but they consider it lecturing to them. What I express as hope for the workers, they regard as sinister insinuations. I can't say anything! For example, there are two sentences in the article: do not be manipulated by others; do not be the victims of others' ideological experiments. (I might add here that the version I submitted to the typesetters did not contain the word "again," which was not deleted by the typesetters.) I said this because in this world there are often those who use labor movements for experimental purposes. My hope is that the workers will watch out for such people in the future, and not fall unwittingly into their trap. I did not say that the workers had already been manipulated by others or fallen victim to their experiments. This cannot be construed as being mean-spirited. Finally, I also want to offer a few words of sincere advice. Now that the workers' wages are being increased and their work hours are being reduced, if they want to seek long-term independence and true happiness, it would still be a good idea for them to find some time every day to do some studying and physical exercise! (Dun)

—————————1923—————————

Telegram to Mr. Xiao Hengshan[1] from the All-Hunan Federation of Labor Organizations

(February 20, 1923)

To Mr. Xiao Hengshan at Wuchang:

The troops under your command have murdered thirty-two railway workers,[2] an oppressive act so savage as to make the rivers freeze over. Sir, you are like a sly

---

This telegram has been translated from *Mao Zedong ji. Bujuan*, Vol. 9, p. 161, where the source is given as *Beifang diqu gongren yundong ziliao xuanbian (1921–1923)* (Beijing: 1981). There is no indication that the text was published prior to 1981. We have no direct evidence that Mao participated in writing this document, or the three texts on the February 7th massacre which follow, but he is uniformly characterized as the leader and moving spirit of the All-Hunan Federation of Labor Organizations at this time. (See Li Jui, *Early Mao*, p. 262, and Li Yongtai, *Mao and the Great Revolution*, p. 144.) Thus, whether or not Mao actually drafted them, we feel that these four brief documents have their place here.

1. Xiao Yaonan (1875–1926), *zi* Hengshan, a trusted subordinate of Wu Peifu, had been appointed military governor of Hubei in August 1921 in the context of the campaign by the Zhili faction to oppose Zhao Hengti's attempts at extending his influence into the neighboring province. Wu Peifu (1874–1939), *zi* Ziyu, was a native of Shandong. After graduating from the Baoding Military Academy, he rose through the ranks of the military, under Yuan Shikai and Cao Kun. In 1918 Wu led troops into Hunan and recovered most of the province for the Beijing government. When Premier Duan Qirui refused to appoint him governor of Hunan, Wu followed an increasingly independent course. In 1920 he joined Cao Kun in the so-called Zhili-Anhui war, which led to the overthrow of Duan Qirui and great power for Wu, who was appointed inspector general of Hubei and Hunan. After defeating Zhang Zuolin in the first Zhili-Fengtian war in 1922, Wu Peifu became the dominant military figure in North China.

2. In the spring of 1922, an agreement had been concluded between the Communist leadership of the Secretariat of Chinese Labor Organizations, which was then actively engaged in setting up unions of railroad workers, and Wu Peifu. It provided for the appointment of six "secret inspectors," who were given free passes for travel throughout the rail network. Wu Peifu had been described by the Second Congress of the Chinese Communist Party as a "comparatively progressive militarist," and his program called for the "protection of labor" (*baohu laodong*). From Wu's point of view, the Communists could be useful in undercutting the influence of his pro-Japanese rivals of the Communications clique on the railroads, from which he derived revenues to maintain the Zhili army and finance his plans to unify China. In the autumn of 1922, during the first rail strikes, Wu Peifu had required the management to adopt a conciliatory attitude. In January 1923, however, when workers on the Beijing-Hankou line announced their intention of forming a General Union of the Beijing-Hankou Railway, which would be an amalgamation of

fox, relying on the might of the tiger Wu Ziyu[3] to hold sway over the Yangzi and the Han, and make mincemeat of the common people. How valiant the Beijing-Wuhan Railway workers who made persistent efforts and won a decisive victory! It is commonly held that "labor is sacred." You, Sir, must hold that "warlords are sacred." Judging by recent events in Wuhan, the warlords are sacred indeed. We've heard it said, however, that there are so many laborers in this world that they cannot be exterminated, but we've heard no such thing about warlords. Just think of those around you, Sir! Other than the hundred or so division commanders, brigade and regiment commanders, garrison captains, and police chiefs such as the unspeakably evil Du Xijun and He Xifan, who is there who is not one of our working class comrades? The soldiers using bullets to kill laborers today could turn around and use their weapons against the warlords tomorrow, if the workers were to use their own tears as a guide. You would call them rebels, but don't you know that rebels are everywhere, that 390 million of our 400 million people are rebels? Instead of making efforts to win over the people, you devote your energies to harming them; instead of considering self-reflection, you think only about killing. Anger and resentment is rising against you, and you may be forced into a precarious position when all the people, even the old and infirm,[4] rise up to make trouble for you. As vast as are the heavens and earth, you will be unable to find a foothold anywhere. These are our sincere words of advice to you; make your own choices as you see fit.

Respectfully submitted,

All-Hunan Federation of Labor Organizations
The twentieth

---

the various local rail workers' clubs, Wu Peifu decided that things had gone too far. He announced the prohibition of the inaugural meeting, which was to be held in Zhengzhou, and when the meeting was held nonetheless, on February 1, he sent troops to break it up. As a result, a full-scale strike of railroad workers was called on February 4. The workers demanded punishment of the troops involved in the action, dismissal of some railroad managers, and pay increases. On February 7, 1923, Cao Kun in Beijing, Wu Peifu in Luoyang, and Xiao Yaonan in Wuchang sent troops to attack the strikers. Thirty to thirty-five workers were killed and many more seriously wounded. The incident, which became known as the "February 7 Massacre," was an important turning point in the political situation, as well as in the history of the labor movement.

3. Wu Peifu.

4. The metaphor used here, literally "like a withered tree," is taken from the biography of Zou Yang, as it appears in Vol. 83 of the *Records of the Historian*.

Telegram to Mr. Wu Ziyu[1] from the All-Hunan Federation of Labor Organizations

(February 20, 1923)

To Mr. Wu Ziyu at Luoyang:

More than three hundred Beijing-Wuhan Railroad workers[2] have been massacred in cold blood for demanding freedom of assembly and association. This is an incident such as has never been heard of in any modern civilized country. A nation maintains an army to protect the people, but now they are destroying our people. From Changxindian in the North to Wuhan in the South, blood-thirsty shouts are everywhere, and the cries of those wronged shake the heavens, while you, Sir, sit calmly issuing orders in Luoyang. Only after the dam at Jinkou had been dug up,[3] and disorder had arisen in Chongqing,[4] did you undertake the campaign. This can hardly be considered courageous. We are told that there were popular uprisings in ancient times; now it is workers' uprisings. When the workers rose up in Russia, the line of Nicholas, which had held power and influence for hundreds of years, became overnight as weak and brittle as dry weeds and rotten wood. In countries like Germany, France, and Italy, once rebellion breaks out, their warlords, politicians, and capitalists will all be like Nicholas. Our countrymen still feel kindly toward you because you strongly resisted the Anhui and Fengtian cliques.[5] Now,

---

We have taken the text of this telegram, like that of the previous document, from *Mao Zedong ji. Bujuan*, Vol. 9, p. 163, where the same 1981 documentary collection is cited as the source.

1. Wu Peifu.

2. This telegram reports that "over three hundred workers" were killed, whereas that to Xiao Hengshan says that only thirty-two were killed. As indicated in the note to the previous text, most accounts give a figure of thirty to thirty-five. *Hunan jinbainian*, p. 515, refers, however, to a total of "several hundred" killed and wounded.

3. In the campaign against the Hunan army commanded by Zhao Hengti in 1921, Wu Peifu ordered the Jinkou dam opened so that his enemies would be drowned and their provisions flooded. At the same time, tens of thousands of farmers and their crops were destroyed.

4. In October 1921, Wu Peifu had driven back an attack by Sichuanese troops in western Hubei.

5. See the note to the previous text summarizing Wu Peifu's career.

however, you suddenly say that no one may harm you, as you are the High Inspecting Commissioner or Deputy Commissioner for Hebei, Shandong, Henan, Hunan, and Hubei. So the people will beat the drums and attack, in reaction to this notion of yours.

Respectfully submitted,
All-Hunan Federation of Labor Organizations

An Open Telegram from the All-Hunan Federation of Labor Organizations in Support of Fellow Workers of the Beijing-Wuhan Railroad

(February 1923)

To all labor unions, chambers of commerce, peasants' associations, educational societies, and student associations, and to all newspapers and organizations throughout the nation:

When the workers of the Beijing-Wuhan Railroad called a conference to found a general trade union and were dispersed by armed force, they called a joint strike. But the unspeakably evil warlords Cao Kun, Wu Peifu, Xiao Yaonan, Zhang Fulai, and others sent a large contingent of soldiers to force the workers back to work, as a result of which over three hundred workers were killed and countless others were wounded. They also executed Shi Yang,[1] Wu Ruming, and Lin Xiangqian,[2] all leaders of the working people, and closed down all the labor unions of the Beijing-Wuhan Railway and the All-Hubei Association of Labor Unions. Freedom of assembly and of association is stipulated in the Constitution. These unions have been in existence for years and made remarkable achievements. The conference to found a general labor union was a perfectly legal action to which the workers are properly entitled. When Cao and Wu dispersed them by force, this already constituted a violation of the Constitution and a trampling on human rights. As if that were not enough, they further incited the troops to wanton killing to force the workers back to work. This tyrannical use of

---

This document was first published in the Changsha *Dagongbao* on February 28, 1923. We have taken it from the text as reproduced in the *Mao Zedong ji. Bujuan*, Vol. 9, pp. 159–60.

1. Shi Yang, a lawyer, was active in the labor movement in Hankou and on the Guangzhou-Wuhan railway during the early 1920s and served in particular as legal adviser to the unions. He was arrested and executed on February 7, 1923.

2. Lin Xiangqian (1892–1923) was a mechanic from Fujian Province who worked as a railwayman on the Beijing-Wuhan line. In 1922 he joined the Communist Party and also became secretary of the Jiang'an Railway Union and later chairman of the Jiang'an branch of the Beijing-Wuhan Railway Trade Union. On February 7, 1923, he was decapitated on the platform at Jiang'an Station after he had refused to give the order to return to work.

armed force and utter disregard for human life makes them criminals for ten thousand generations and a common foe of all mankind. As fellow members of the labor world, related to our fellow workers of the Beijing-Wuhan Railway by ties of flesh and blood, we and all the masses are full of rage at the wanton slaughter committed by these extremely vicious warlords. In response to the demands of the broad masses of the people, we hereby proclaim the founding of the Committee in Support of the Beijing-Wuhan Railroad, which shall henceforth lead the tens of thousands of Hunan working people against the warlords who have illegally and in cold blood murdered our fellow workers of the Beijing-Wuhan Railroad, and vow to avenge this monumental crime and destroy these common foes of all mankind. We are sending this open telegram in the hope that you will join us in expressing our common indignation and in beating the drums to launch an attack with us. Otherwise the warlords will step up their evil deeds, and we fear that our 400 million countrymen will all fall prey to them. We anxiously await your reply.

Respectfully,

The Committee of Hunan Labor Unions in Support of the Beijing-Wuhan Railroad

The Second Open Telegram of the All-Hunan Federation of Labor Organizations in Support of Fellow Workers of the Beijing-Wuhan Railroad

(February 1923)

To all newspapers and labor organizations, and to elders, brothers, and sisters in all walks of life throughout the nation:

The extraordinarily vicious warlords Wu Peifu, Xiao Yaonan, and Cao Kun, wantonly abusing their power, have disbanded all the labor unions of the Beijing-Wuhan Railroad. They have directed the military police at Changxindian, Zhengzhou, and Jiang'an stations to massacre over three hundred workers, to execute the workers' leaders Wu Ruming and Shi Yang, and to cut in twain Lin Xiangqian, chairman of the Beijing-Wuhan Railroad Labor Union. They have closed down the All-Hubei Federation of Labor Organizations. Since these events, every compatriot who has seen these traitors to the people, who have violated and betrayed the Constitution[al guarantees of] freedom of assembly and association, bristles with anger and regrets that he cannot devour their flesh and make a bed of their skins. For this reason, this federation directed all labor organizations throughout Hunan Province to support their fellow workers of the Beijing-Wuhan Railroad in taking various measures to overthrow the warlords. It dispatched the first open telegram calling for sympathy from people in all walks of life; it sponsored and organized the "All-Hunan Committee of Labor Organizations to Support the Beijing-Wuhan Railroad," which has provided all kinds of relief; and it sent telegrams denouncing the two arch-criminals Wu Peifu and Xiao Yaonan. In addition, the association is now sending this second open telegram to express the hope that all groups and organizations throughout the nation will respect the Constitution, uphold human rights, purge China of these warlords, and join together in a single will and common spirit that will not rest until the people's right to free assembly and association is won, all banned labor

---

This document, like the previous one, was published in the Changsha *Dagongbao* on February 28, 1923. We have translated it from the *Mao Zedong ji. Bujuan*, Vol. 9, p. 161.

unions are restored, the military police who caused disasters are punished, and our bereaved and wounded fellow workers of the Beijing-Wuhan Railroad are fully comforted and compensated. We anxiously await your reply.

Respectfully,

The All-Hunan Federation of
Labor Organizations

Letter to Shi Cuntong

(March 7, 1923)

Brother Guangliang:[1]

I have received your letter of the 24th. As for holding the national examinations[2] in Hunan, the local Educational Conference[3] has passed a resolution to do so. My only suggestion is that the date would best be postponed until early June (or the end of May)—that is, after the School Conference.[4] This is an important matter. It is hoped that you will give it your consideration.

Your younger brother, Ziren[5]
March 7

P.S. We urgently need four hundred copies of [your] history of labor.[6] Please have them sent promptly.

This letter has been translated from the manuscript in Mao's calligraphy reproduced on the cover of the present volume. Our source is a copy on display at the Mao Museum in Shaoshan, photographed by the editor in 1986. The letter does not appear to have been published heretofore.

1. Shi Guangliang is yet another name for Shi Cuntong, the secretary of the Central Committee of the Socialist Youth League of China. (On Shi, see above, the note to Mao's letter to him dated June 20, 1922.)

2. "National examinations" is a code word for the forthcoming Second Congress of the Communist Youth League.

3. "Educational Conference" is code for the Changsha Executive Committee of the Socialist Youth League.

4. "School Congress" is code for the Third Congress of the Chinese Communist Party, which was held June 12–20, 1923, in Guangzhou. (See below, the "Resolution on the Peasant Question" adopted at this congress, and the note thereto.) Mao originally wrote another character before *xiao* (school); it appears from the manuscript copy that he crossed this out, rather than modifying it. In any case, the meaning is clear. It had been decided that the Second Congress of the Socialist Youth League should be held in Hunan, but in the late spring the political situation there became very tense as a result of the boycott of Japanese goods launched to protest against the continuing Japanese occupation of Dairen. On June 1, Japanese marines disembarked from a gunboat on the Xiang River and killed and wounded a number of citizens of Changsha. In the aftermath of these events, the Second Congress of the Socialist Youth League was moved to Nanjing, where it met in August 1923.

5. Ziren was one of Mao's pen names. It means literally "son of Ren," and he had adopted it to express his admiration for Liang Qichao, whose *hao* was Rengong.

6. The reference is to Shi Cuntong, *Laodong yundong shi* (History of the Labor Movement), published in April 1922 by the Labor Secretariat.

On the Publication of New Age

(April 10, 1923)

This publication has been founded by fellow members of the Hunan Self-Study University. It is also the house organ for publishing the results of their research.

This publication is different from the usual school journal, which is a kind of literary department store. This journal, on the contrary, has a definite point of view, a definite orientation. We fellow students and faculty are confident that we all have a spirit of independence and self-reliance, that we all have a will that refuses to bend before adversity. It is only because we are painfully aware of the wrongs of the social system and the inadequacy of the educational institutions that we have joined together to organize this band of academic outcasts, to study hard the most useful disciplines, and to carry out preparations for social reform. Even though the Self-Study University has only just begun its work, our ideals are still in the experimental stage, and we cannot predict what the future results will be, we are confident that this initial objective is most correct. By proceeding in accord with this spirit and this resolve, our hopes for success will be very fair, and this publication will become a standard for experimentation.

Consequently, the mission of this publication at its birth is extremely important. In the future, this journal must contribute basic research and concrete proposals on such problems as how to reform the state, how to clean up politics, how to strike down imperialism, how to overthrow the politics of the militarists, how to reform the educational system, and how literature, the arts, and other scholarly fields are to be revolutionized and reconstructed. If, in this way, we can inspire those with similar convictions and similar resolve to throw themselves into both action and research directed toward the reform of society, our hopes will have been more than fulfilled.

This introductory editorial appeared in the first issue of *Xin shidai*, the organ of the Hunan Self-Study University, which was published on April 10, 1923. We have translated it from *Mao Zedong ji*, Vol. 1, p. 87.

The Foreign Powers, the Warlords, and the Revolution

(April 10, 1923)

In the last analysis, can the unification of China be realized or not? Leaving aside what we hear from ignorant and presumptuous people such as Zhang Shaozeng[1], everyone understands that it is impossible in the near future. There is no way in which the various influential factions within the country can be made to unite at present. Union is, of course, not the same as just mixing them together, so for the present such things as "meetings of the provinces," "consultative conferences on national affairs," or even sending delegates to consult the leaders of the various factions are nothing but empty talk. If we analyze the influential factions within the country, there are only three: the revolutionary democratic faction, the non-revolutionary democratic faction, and the reactionary faction. The main body of the revolutionary democratic faction is, of course, the Guomindang; the rising Communist faction is cooperating with it.[2] Formerly, the nonrevolutionary dem-

---

This article appeared in the first issue of *Xin shidai* in 1923. We have translated it from the text as reproduced in *Mao Zedong ji. Bujuan*, Vol. 2, pp. 109–11.

1. Zhang Shaozeng (1880–1928), a graduate of the Japanese Military Academy who had served in various military and political offices before and after the Revolution of 1911, was premier of the government in Beijing at the time Mao wrote this article. In the autumn of 1921, he had suggested the calling of a National Conference to discuss and settle the affairs of the country.

2. This is the first reference in Mao's known writings to Guomindang-Communist cooperation. As discussed above in the Introduction to this volume, the Chinese Communist Party had adopted in 1921 an extremely sectarian line excluding all relations with other parties. Under pressure from the Comintern, the Chinese Communist Party had endorsed a "democratic united front" with the Guomindang at its Second Congress in June 1922. In August 1922, at the Hangzhou Plenum, the Comintern representative confronted his Chinese comrades with an explicit written order from Moscow to take the further step of joining the Guomindang as individuals, thereby establishing the so-called "bloc within." Mao had not attended either the Second Congress or the Hangzhou meeting, but (as shown by the materials translated above) he was directly involved in the events leading up to the February 7, 1923, massacre of railroad workers. This development convinced many skeptics that the young Chinese Communist Party was too weak to face the warlords in isolation, and therefore needed to secure the suppport of the Guomindang. It is not known whether Mao had already joined the Guomindang by the time he wrote this article, but he had done so by June 25, 1923, when he signed the letter of that date translated below.

ocratic faction consisted of the Progressive Party.[3] The Progressive Party having been disbanded, its only direct descendant for the moment is the Research clique.[4] The faction of the rising intellectual class, [led by] Hu Shi,[5] Huang Yanpei,[6] and others, and the faction of the rising commercial class, [led by] Nie Yuntai,[7] Mu Ouchu,[8] and others also belong to this faction. The reactionary faction is the most extensive and comprises the Zhili,[9] the Fengtian,[10] and the Anhui[11]

---

3. The Jinbudang or Progressive Party was, in fact, a rather conservative party founded by Liang Qichao with the support of Yuan Shikai in May 1913. Mao's perception may have been colored by the fact that Li Dazhao, one of the two founding fathers of the Chinese Communist Party, had worked within it for a time in 1916. Li Dazhao (1889–1927), *zi* Shouchang, a native of Hebei, had studied in Japan. In 1918, he became head of the Beijing University library, and in this capacity provided employment for Mao as a library assistant during Mao's first visit to Beijing in the winter of 1918–1919. As early as 1918, Li had published an article, "The Victory of Bolshevism," and he went on to play a leading role both in establishing the Chinese Communist Party and in forging the alliance between it and the Guomindang.

4. A faction made up largely of politicians and journalists, which obtained a modest share of the seats in the warlord-dominated parliament elected in 1918. Li Dazhao had also joined the Research clique when it was founded in 1916, though he broke with it at the end of that year.

5. Regarding Hu Shi, see above, the "Report on the Affairs of the New People's Study Society," December, 1920.

6. Huang Yanpei (1878–1965), subsequently a leading figure in the "third force" between the Communists and the Nationalists of the 1930s and 1940s, was a partisan of American-style vocational education.

7. Nie Yuntai (1880–1953), known as C. C. Nien, was a grandson of the prominent nineteenth-century statesman Zeng Guofan. A successful industrialist, he played a leading role in the Shanghai business community, becoming president of the Chamber of Commerce in 1920.

8. Mu Xiangyue (1876–1942), *zi* Ouchu, Western name H. Y. Moh, was a native of Shanghai. After taking a B.S. in agriculture and an M.S. in the economics of the textile industry in America, he founded the United Association of Chinese Cotton Mills in 1915. In 1920 he organized the Chinese Cotton Goods Exchange in Shanghai, of which he was president until 1926.

9. The Zhili clique, one of the three major warlord groupings, had its main power base in the area around Beijing, though it controlled a number of other provinces. It was headed at this time by Cao Kun (1862–1938), *zi* Zhongshan, a native of Tianjin and a graduate of the Tianjin Military Academy. Two months later, in June 1923, Cao carried out a coup d'état with the object of seizing the presidency for himself. For Mao's reaction to this event, see below, the article dated July 11, 1923, "The Beijing Coup d'État and the Merchants."

10. The Fengtian clique, another major warlord grouping, headed by Zhang Zuolin, was based in the northeast. The area it controlled had been much reduced as a result of the First Zhili-Fengtian War of 1922. On Zhang, see below, the relevant note to the article of July 1, 1923, "Hunan under the Provincial Constitution."

11. The Anhui clique, the third major warlord grouping, headed by Duan Qirui, had seen its power base reduced as a result of the Anhui-Zhili war of 1920 to only a few coastal provinces, including in 1923 Shandong to the immediate south of the capital. On Duan, see above, the relevant note to Mao's letter of December 1, 1920, to Xiao Xudong and others.

cliques. (Although for the moment, the Fengtian and Anhui cliques are cooperating with the Guomindang, this cannot last long, for they are after all the most reactionary.) Of these three factions, the first two will wish to cooperate henceforth for a certain period. Because the reactionary forces confronting them are extremely great, the Research clique, as well as the intellectual and commercial factions, will temporarily abandon their nonrevolutionary views and cooperate with the revolutionary Guomindang, just as the Communist Party has temporarily abandoned its most radical views in order to cooperate with the relatively radical Guomindang. So in the future, the political situation in China will take the following form: on the one hand, the most advanced Communist faction and the moderate Research clique, intellectual faction, and commercial faction will all cooperate with the Guomindang to form a great democratic faction in order to overthrow their common enemies; on the other hand, there will be the reactionary warlord faction. The outcome of this political situation in China will be the victory of the democratic faction over the warlord faction, but in the immediate future and for a certain period, China will necessarily continue to be the realm of the warlords. Politics will become even darker, the financial situation will become even more chaotic, the armies will further proliferate, industry and education will become yet more stagnant, the methods for the oppression of the people will become even more terrible. To put it bluntly, the mask of democracy will be further ripped off, completely reactionary feudal politics will be imposed, and this kind of situation may last for a period of eight or ten years.

How do we know that it will necessarily be like this? Just look at how reactionary the political system of international capitalist imperialism is! Right now they are coordinating their steps to invade China. Formerly their moves were not coordinated. After some discussion at the Washington Conference,[12] they have become coordinated. Although their coordination will eventually break down, at present and in the near future, in order to make up for the loss they suffered from the last World War and to store up energy for the next, they will definitely want to take measures aimed at coordination. The fact that the United States Open Door policy could be accepted by England, France, and Japan, which possess spheres of influence in China, is clear proof of this. In itself, the division of China is not advantageous to international capitalist imperialist aggression; a China united by the democratic factions would, however, be even more disadvantageous to international capitalist imperialism than a China thrown into confusion by the struggle between the democratic and warlord factions. For them, the most advantageous situation would be the complete subjection of China to reactionary politics. This is the principal reason why China is at present, and will remain in the near future, the domain of the reactionary warlords. The

---

12. The naval conference of 1921–1922, which brought together eight Western powers and Japan, and also dealt with the position of the powers in China and their relations with the Chinese.

White Wolf[13] and the "Old Foreigners" were able to band together several tens of thousands of followers in the Henan area and to harass several provinces. More than 90 percent of the people are uneducated. Except for the little industry and commerce along the coast and along the railroads, the whole [country] lives the life of an agricultural economy. Except for a few feeble organizations of industrialists, businessmen, teachers, clerks, and students along the rivers, the coast, and the railroads (corresponding to their economic circumstances), popular organizations are almost entirely self-sufficient clan, village, or handicraft organizations. In places such as Mongolia, Xinjiang, Qinghai, Tibet, Shaanxi, Gansu, Sichuan, Guizhou, and Guangxi there is not, to this day, so much as an inch of railroad. There is not in the whole country a political party that can claim a genuine membership of 300 thousand. In the whole country, there is not a single newspaper with sales of 200–300 thousand. There is no periodical with total sales of 20–30 thousand. And yet China as a whole has a population of 400 million and an area of more than 30 million square *li*. Now, under such social and economic conditions, who would be able to rule if not the warlords? This is the second reason why now, and in the near future, China will necessarily continue to be in the realm of the warlords.

On the basis of internal and external political and economic conditions, we may conclude that China, at present and in the immediate future, will necessarily remain under the reactionary domination of the warlords. This period will be the period when the foreign powers and the warlords collude in order to carry out evil deeds, a period when extremely reactionary and confused politics will necessarily prevail. But if politics becomes more reactionary and more confused, the result will necessarily be to call forth revolutionary ideas among the citizens of the whole country,[14] and the organizational capacity of the citizens will likewise increase day by day. On the one hand, it will in the end prove impossible for the north to unite the various southwestern provinces;[15] although there will unavoidably be a few small warlords, [the southwest] will remain to the end a refuge of the revolutionary elements. During this period, the democratic factions will daily become more numerous and their organization will daily become stronger. The result will be the victory of the democratic faction over the warlord faction, so that only during this

---

13. A notorious outlaw of the period.

14. The idea that extremes engender one another, and in particular that oppression leads to revolt, or to revolution, is extremely characteristic of Mao's philosophy. See, for example, in Volume I, pp. 378–89, his article of 1919, "The Great Union of the Popular Masses," which declares in the concluding paragraph: "Our Chinese people possesses great inherent capacities! The more profound the oppression, the more powerful its reaction . . ."

15. The Guangxi clique, in particular, was frequently at war with the central government, first in Beijing and then after 1927 in Nanjing, during the 1920s and 1930s.

period can an independent and democratic government be fully established in China.

We know only that the present is an era of confusion, and certainly not an era of peace and unification, in which politics can only grow more reactionary and confused. But this [situation] is the source of peace and unification, it is the mother of revolution, it is the magic potion of democracy and independence. Everyone must be aware of this.

Admissions Notice of the
Hunan Self-Study University

(April 10, 1923)

(I) This university of ours was not set up by some other group of "educational administrators." Rather, it is set up by a group of students with an interest in learning, who feel that the current educational system is not good, and who want to combine the advantages of the traditional academies and of the modern schools, and change from passive learning to self-motivated learning. Our school has just opened its doors and is indeed very simple and crude. Whether or not the students who come here do well depends entirely on whether or not they themselves are truly able to work hard. It is, however, our strong hope that many young people with noble aspirations will come here to be our fellow students. We do not study without a purpose, and that purpose is to transform existing society. In pursuing our studies, we seek the learning necessary to realize this goal. We do not want among our fellow students a "young master" or a "young lady," nor do we want anyone who is apathetic or muddle-headed. Therefore, we have adopted a rather cautious attitude in admitting new students. For each student who enters the school, we need to know about the following points:

1. Which schools has he attended in the past? What has he done in the past? What is his family's financial situation, and his own?
2. What subjects does he want to study? Why does he want to study these subjects?
3. What courses has he studied in the past?
4. How many semesters does he want to study? What does he want to do in future?
5. His views regarding a philosophy of life.
6. His criticisms of society.

All those who wish to apply will need to write a letter answering the above six questions in detail and mail it to the secretary-general of the student union of the school, who will pass it on to the president for review. The final decision will be made later, after a personal interview.

This document was published in the first issue of *Xin shidai* in 1923. We have translated it from the text as reproduced in *Mao Zedong ji. Bujuan*, Vol. 2, pp. 85–86.

(II)[1] Those admitted to the school need to pay the monthly food expenses, sundry fees, and student union fees.

(III) After a new student is admitted, he has the obligation to submit articles to the school's monthly publication.

(IV) After a new student is admitted, he has the obligation to obey the school compact.

(V) Because our funds are limited, the school is currently adopting the principle of wholly independent study. Those who feel that they do not have the capacity to study independently need not apply.

---

1. In the available Chinese text of this document, the four points beginning here are numbered from 1 to 4. The form of the numbers is, however, the same as that used for the lead paragraph, and logically the points seem to follow on from that. On the assumption that there has been a typographical error, we have re-numbered this and the succeeding paragraphs.

Resolution on the Peasant Question

(Resolution of the Third National Congress of the Chinese Communist Party[1])

(June 1923)

Ever since the various imperialists started using military force to impose the importing of foreign goods, the rate of price increases for household necessities has far exceeded that for agricultural produce. The former sideline industries of the peasants (such as handweaving) have also been totally destroyed. Moreover, since the 1911 Revolution, the life of the peasants has been made increasingly difficult by the continual wars among the warlords for spheres of influence, and the bandits everywhere, plus the exorbitant taxes levied by corrupt officials (such as advance cash levies on the land tax, extra fees, etc.) and the savage oppression carried out by local ruffians and bad gentry. Because of all these various kinds of oppression, a spirit of rebellion has naturally arisen among the peasants. The widespread peasant antirent and antitax riots are clear evidence of this. Therefore, our Party's Third Congress resolves that it is necessary to gather together small peasants, sharecroppers, and farm laborers to resist the imperialists who control China, to overthrow the warlords and corrupt officials, and to resist the local ruffians and bad gentry, so as to protect the interests of the peasants and to promote the national revolutionary movement.

Our translation is based on *Zhonggong zhongyang wenjian xuanji,* Vol. 1, 1921–1925, p. 151. This text reproduces that of the brochure containing the resolutions and manifestos of the Third Congress published in July 1923.

1. The Third Congress, held in Guangzhou June 12–20, 1923, formally adopted the policy of a united front with the Guomindang in the shape of a "bloc within." Mao, who had argued at the congress in favor of this line, was elected to the new Central Executive Committee, of which he was appointed secretary, and also became a member of the five-man Central Bureau, the Party's organ for dealing with day-to-day affairs. During the discussion of the peasant question at the congress, he declared: "The Chinese Communist Party should not see only the Guomindang in the small area near Guangzhou, it should attach importance to the broad masses of the peasantry throughout the country." For further details about Mao's role at the Third Congress, and the Chinese Communist Party's views regarding the peasantry beginning in 1922, see above, the Introduction to Volume II.

Letter to Sun Yatsen

(June 25, 1923)

[The letter] proposes that the Guomindang "set up, in Shanghai or Guangzhou, a strong and powerful executive committee, with the mission of combining our efforts to promote the activity of party members, and develop propaganda on a broad scale. . . . We cannot simply follow along imitating the orientation of the feudal warlords, who use armed force to seize political power and occupy spheres of influence. To do this will give people the impression that we and the warlords belong to the same family. To use the old methods and the old armies to build a new China is not only illogical, but is absolutely impossible to carry out in practice. The old armies have ten times as many soldiers as we do. We can only use new devices, adopt a new orientation, and create a new force. In our dealings with the citizens, we must unite with the merchants, the students, the peasants, and the workers, and moreover draw them to rally around the flag of our party. The new army, built from among the people, will use new methods and a new spirit of friendship to defend the republic." In the letter, the hope was expressed that Sun Yatsen would not inconsiderately place his faith in the warlords of the various southern provinces. "The crimes [of the southern warlords] are in no way less than those of the northern warlords. . . . We request you, sir, to leave Guangzhou, to proceed to the center of public opinion, Shanghai, and when you get there to call together a national assembly (such as the one you discuss in 'The Three-power Constitution,' but not limited simply to mass demonstrations). In this way, a centralized army that solves the problems of the whole country can be built, a centralized national-revolutionary army can be built. If we act in this way, we will not lose our leading position in the national-revolutionary movement."

This letter was signed jointly by Mao Zedong, Chen Duxiu, Li Dazhao, Cai Hesen, and Tan Pingshan in their capacity as members of the Guomindang. The full text does not appear to have been published. Our version corresponds to the excerpts, linked by summaries in indirect discourse, to be found in the *Nianpu*, Vol. 1, p. 115.

Hunan under the Provincial Constitution

(July 1, 1923)

I'm afraid that very few people who are not Hunanese know anything about what Hunan is really like under the Provincial Constitution. A detailed description of its politics, economics, culture, and education, as well as of the labor movement that has recently arisen there, would require more than just a short essay. A brief general outline follows.

A. Politics

1. The Provincial Constitution. Proposals for provincial constitutions began in Hunan, and up to now only Hunan has a provincial constitution, for a very simple reason. Situated in the middle between North and South China and having been trampled on three times by the Beiyang factions' military forces under Tang Xiangming, Fu Liangzuo, and Zhang Jingyao, the people have a deep hatred of the military forces of the northern factions. When the Hunan Army of Tan Yankai and Zhao Hengti pursued Zhang Jingyao, it just so happened that the northern Zhili and Anhui factions were beginning to split up, so the proposal for provincial self-rule and a provincial constitution was entirely a reaction against the Beiyang military forces. Without the protective talisman of a provincial constitution, Hunan could easily be invaded, a situation that the people did not like and the warlords liked even less. The result has been that, taking advantage of the popular will, the warlords have used the Provincial Constitution for their own protection and preservation. Thus the Provincial Constitution, in this geographically precarious Hunan, amounts to no more than an insurance policy for a weak and petty warlord (Zhao Hengti). In other provinces, strong warlords such as Wu Peifu definitely do not want provincial constitutions. Zhang Zuolin[1] wants only self-rule, without a provincial constitution. A warlord who is weak, but

---

This article was originally published in *Qianfeng*, No. 1, July 1, 1923. Our translation has been made from the text as reproduced in *Mao Zedong ji. Bujuan*, Vol. 2, pp. 113–22.

1. Zhang Zuolin (1873–1928), *zi* Yuting, was born in Fengtian (now Liaoning). He began his military career as a local army leader in Fengtian and commander in charge of the Mukden (Shenyang) garrison under Yuan Shikai. He consolidated his personal control of South Manchuria after Yuan Shikai's death in 1917, becoming military and civil leader of the area. He ruled Manchuria as a virtually autonomous state from 1919 until his assassination in 1928.

because he is situated in a remote area does not greatly fear invasion from outside, and still thinks that he can occasionally get supplies for his troops from neighboring provinces, as in the case of Tang Jiyao, will also not want a provincial constitution. Thus it is only here in Hunan that a provincial constitution could appear. However, it can hardly be long-lived, because although at the moment it so happens that there are external worries, it is ultimately a rope that binds and restrains the warlord, as in the case of the provision in the Hunan Constitution that military expenses be reduced to one-third of annual income. The current budget is already such that it cannot be kept within the stipulations of the Provincial Constitution. Furthermore, the contention between the Tan Yankai and Zhao Hengti factions is sure to force one of them to bring in outside troops to seize control of the situation. The life span of the Provincial Constitution is definitely limited. Realization of a federation of self-ruled provinces is even less of a possibility under any circumstances.

2. Political Factions. Tan Yankai, Zhao Hengti, and Lin Zhiyu[2] make up three separate factions. The People's Well-Being Society [*Minkang she*] of the Tan faction, the People's Renewal Society [*Minxin she*] of the Zhao faction, and the Hunan Society [*Xiang she*] of the Lin faction are their political parties. The Lin faction has no real military strength and is simply a bunch of the lowest type of politicians whose self-serving goals have brought them together. They wait to move in or retreat according to the rise and fall of the Tan and Zhao factions, and of the three factions they are the worst. The political life of the Zhao faction, which is now in power, is actually founded upon the threats and blessings of Wu Peifu in the balancing act between north and south (this is also the basis of the Provisional Constitution). Thus, although they are less powerful militarily than the Tan faction, they can maintain their position over a period of time. The Tan faction has already been out of power for three years, but they still have a lot of strength and have recently joined the Guomindang in the hopes that Sun Yatsen will help them regain political power.[3] Their struggle with the Zhao faction is unusually intense. In addition, the Political Studies clique[4] has attached itself to the Zhao faction in order to further its interests.

---

2. Regarding Tan Yankai, see the note to Mao Zedong's "Letter Refuting Unjust Accusations" of December 3, 1920. On Zhao Hengti, see the note to the record of Mao's negotiations with him on December 14, 1922. Lin Zhiyu, a politician, became civil governor (*shengzhang*) when Zhao Hengti first wrested control of Hunan from Tan Yankai in November 1921. In September 1922, Zhao assumed this title as well, but the Lin faction retained some influence in the Provincial Assembly.

3. Tan Yankai had, in fact, met with Sun Yatsen in August 1922 in Shanghai and given Sun a substantial sum of money to help him rebuild his forces. In return, he received Sun Yatsen's support in his confrontation with Zhao Hengti, who was backed by Wu Peifu.

4. The Political Studies clique was formed in 1916 by members from both the Progressive Party and the Guomindang. It was a highly conservative clique, and its members were known for their opportunism.

3. The Government. The new government that was formed according to the Provincial Constitution in January of this year is divided into seven departments: Internal Affairs, External Relations, Finance, Business, Education, Judiciary, and Military Affairs. The heads of the seven departments are under the head of the Provincial Council, with strict cabinet responsibility, and the provincial governor acts as president. The provincial governor is Zhao Hengti; the head of the Provincial Council is Li Jiannong; the head of the Department of Internal Affairs is Wu Jinghong; the head of the Department of External Relations is Yang Xuancheng; the head of the Department of Finance is Yuan Huaxuan; the head of the Department of Business is Tang Chengxu; the head of the Department of Education is Li Jiannong; the head of the Department of the Judiciary is Xu Zhongchong; and the head of the Department of Military Affairs is Li Shiwen. This is the organization of the government.

4. The Assembly. The government is selected from the assembly, so the assembly has considerable authority. Membership in the assembly is entirely bought with money. Some of the members are bureaucrats, some are lavish gentry, and some are politicians. In terms of party affiliation, two-thirds belong to the Zhao faction and one-third belongs to the Tan and Lin factions. The new Hunan Provincial Assembly as presently constituted has thoroughly manifested its despicable venality, its tyranny, and its stupidity, and public opinion hates it bitterly.

5. The Armed Forces. At present the army is made up of two divisions and five brigades, the organization and deployment of which are generally as follows. Division commander of the First Division is Zhu Hegeng, with commander of the First Brigade He Yaozu and regiment commanders Zheng Honghai and Xie Yudao stationed at Changde and Yiyang. The Second Division, commanded by Tang Shengzhi, with regiment commanders Liu Xing and Li Pinhe, is stationed at Changde. The calvary regiment of He Jian is stationed at Taoyuan. The artillery regiment of Huang Yaozu is stationed at Changde. The regiment of Wang Lei also belongs to the First Division and is stationed at Chenzhou. The Second Division, commanded by Lu Diping, with Liu Xing as commander of the Third Brigade and regiment commanders Ye Qi and Yuan Zhi, is stationed at Nanxian and Xiangtan. The Fourth Brigade, commanded by Tang Rongyang, with regiment commanders Tang Shengming and Tang Zhenduo, is stationed at Lixian and Shimen. The calvary regiment of Tang Xibian is stationed at Xiangtan, and the artillery regiment of Dai Yue is stationed at Changsha. The First Mixed Brigade [*Hunchenglu*], commanded by Ye Kaixin, with regiment commanders Jiang Chu'ou, Liu Zhongwei, Zou Pengzhen, and Zhu Yaohua, is stationed in the area of Changsha, Liling, and Xiangyin. The artillery battalion of Yin Fuling is stationed at Changsha. Director of defense for the town of Hengyang and commander of the mixed brigade, Xie Guoguang, with regiment commanders Tan Daoyuan, Cheng Guangyao, and Liu Xuegan, is stationed in the three *xian* of Hengyang, Guiyang, and Yongzhou. Director of defense for the

town of Baoqing and commander of a mixed brigade, Wu Jianxue, with regimental commanders Wu Jiaquan and Zhang Xiangdi, is stationed in Baoqing and Wugang. Director of defense for the town of Yuanling and commander of the Ninth and Tenth Brigades is Cai Juyou. Liu Xuyi, brigade commander of the Ninth Brigade, and regimental commanders He Longgan and Tan Runshen are stationed in western Hunan in Qianyang and Hongjiang. The Tenth Brigade under the command of Tian Zhenfan, with regimental commanders Peng Shouheng and Yang Yufen, is stationed in Chenzhou and Qianyang in western Hunan. In addition, there are also the more than ten defense patrol battalions under Chen Quzhen in Baojing, Qianxian, Zhendan, and Suiqing in western Hunan, one regiment of the Hubei Army under Xia Douyin stationed in Liuyang, and one battalion of militia under Wang Deqing stationed at Yongzhou. The total troop strength of the Hunan armed forces numbers about 40,000. Of these, the three groups of He Yaozu, Tang Shengzhi, and Ye Kaixin belong to the Zhao Hengti faction, and the mixed brigade of Ye Kaixin, which is nearly division size, is considered to be the main column of the Zhao faction. The regiment of the Hubei Army under Xia Douyin is neutral. The others all belong to the Tan Yankai faction. Because Hunan is a poor province it has no military factories, so it cannot support a large army. Since they do not have a great many troops it is not difficult to supply the troops adequately, and they should at least be able to meet expenses for a period of time without any serious trouble arising. This is rather different from the situation in provinces such as Sichuan and Yunnan that support overly large armies and sometimes are forced to get food from outside. Thus, Hunan desires only that others do not invade her and has no need to invade others. The economic aspect of the so-called Monroe Doctrine of provincial self-rule was built on these facts, and has endured for two or three years, right up to the present.

6. Finances. The annual income of Hunan is a total of 14 million *yuan* (including that of places under state control), and the national taxes that should be turned over to the central government are withheld for provincial uses. This too is an economic impetus for self-rule. As for the stipulation in the Provincial Constitution that military expenses be one-third, educational expenses be one-third, and administrative expenses one-third, this is the new budget that has not yet been implemented, nor can it ever be implemented. The financial system is already in a state of extreme chaos. The only income the government receives directly, and can use for its daily expenses, is in the form of a small amount of taxes from the provincial capital and the income from two or three organs such as the Transportation Monopoly Bureau and the Currency Mint. Most of the receipts from the land tax of the other *xian* and from all the regular and miscellaneous taxes are appropriated by the military. Thus the finances cannot be straightened out. The debts for military expenses and even for educational and administrative expenses accumulated from the past are so large that there is no way they can be paid off. If old debts cannot be cleared, it becomes even less

possible to straighten out finances. The Zhao government's schemes to borrow funds from abroad were also undermined in a number of ways by the Tan Yankai clique and fell through several times. Hunan has already been without incidents for four years, so in these four years the financial resources of the province as a whole have still not had to support a large army and have been helped by the army tax on individual opium smokers, making it possible to get by peacefully and without incident. Today, having been at peace for a while, the sum of unpaid back wages for the army has gradually mounted, and looting has become a severe problem. Unable to secure loans or to cut the army by a single man, the Zhao government's financial base is already very weak. Should the Tan clique find an excuse to mount an attack, Zhao would surely either have to surrender to Wu Peifu or be overthrown.

B. Economics

1. Industry. All of Hunan Province is in the stage of handicraft industries. Except for the provincially owned First Silk Factory, the officially managed Shuikoushan lead mines, and the commercially managed Xikuangshan (in Xinhua [*xian*]) lead mines,[5] we can point to no other moderately large industries. There are not a few commercially managed small mines and there are a lot of small-scale lead and antimony smelting factories, but they involve very little capital. Since the end of the European war the price of lead and antimony ore has been very low, so business has been very depressed. The First Silk Factory, with government capital of two million *yuan*, is leased to and operated by private merchants and does a business of less than 200 thousand *yuan*, but its business situation is still good with the price of its 100 *yuan* stock at 115 per share. The Hunan and Guanghua electric light companies provide electric lighting in the provincial capital, and the two companies are in intense competition, but neither company has grown (Hunan is doing better than Guanghua), and their stocks have fallen to 60 *yuan* or 40 *yuan*. The currency mint is managed by the government with the goal of extracting a surplus profit on the casting of inferior quality 20 cent copper coinage. On a monthly minting of 2.1 million strings of cash, it can make a profit of 150 thousand to 160 thousand *yuan*. In the marketplace, the value of the copper cent is 210 for one *yuan* of silver. This hurts the people very badly. Except for the small-scale foreign-owned ore smelting at Shuikoushan, there are no foreign businesses in Hunan Province.

2. Commerce. All are small-capital businesses concentrated in the three cities

---

5. For Mao's earlier involvement with struggles over the Shuikoushan lead and zinc mines, see the "Petition Opposing Zhang Jingyao's Secret Agreement to Sell the Mines," dated December 27, 1919, in Volume I, pp. 460–62. Regarding the Xikuangshan mines, which were the richest source of antimony in the world, see McDonald, *Urban Origins*, pp. 68–75.

of Changsha, Xiangtan, and Changde. Of the foreign businesses, British commercial establishments are the largest, with the Japanese second, followed by the Americans and Germans. All four countries have set up consulates in Changsha.

3. Agriculture. In Hunan there is much mountainous land and little land in the plains. Apart from the few relatively large agricultural exploitations along the shores of Lake Dongting, the rest is all small-scale exploitations by peasant proprietors or sharecroppers. The life of the sharecroppers is even more painful than that of the agricultural laborers, because the laborers have relatively small families to look after while the sharecroppers have relatively large families. The rent to the landlords is normally half the crop; a high rate is 70 percent to the landlord, and 30 percent to the tenant, while the highest rate is 80 percent to the landlord and 20 percent to the tenant. As a result, it would be absolutely impossible for sharecroppers to live on income from cultivating the land alone, and they all supplement this by raising pigs, cultivating side crops, etc. For a number of years, Hunan suffered from the depradations of the militarists, and this caused considerable shortages. The economy has been slightly improved in the past two or three years. As regards the province's rice production, the area along the lake has a surplus for export in normal years, and elsewhere there is just enough to feed the inhabitants. So the saying "When the crop ripens in Hunan, there is abundance throughout the land" no longer corresponds to reality. Every year at the beginning of winter the Yuezhou customs house[6] is opened, and at the beginning of spring it is closed, and the government collects one *yuan* in taxes on every picul of rice to supplement its budget.

C. General Culture and Education

1. General Culture. The thinking of the small peasants has changed little. Their political demands are simply for honest officials and a good emperor. Among women, 30 to 40 percent still have bound feet, but men no longer wear pigtails, even in remote places. In education, the new studies system has in large measure already been adopted. It is only the school administrators who have basically made no great changes. Most representative of this are the members of the Provincial Assembly, who use the new bourgeois political system but whose speech and actions fully betray the fact that all the old forms of patriarchal society have not changed in the least. Protestant and Roman Catholic churches exist throughout the entire province, having invaded even the small hamlets in remote areas. American missionary enterprises are especially aggressive, centering around their youth groups while also engaging in educational and charitable enterprises. Because they have no commercial power in Hunan, the Americans

---

6. Yuezhou was an important point on the recently opened Wuhan-Changsha Railroad.

put all their energies into charitable enterprises such as raising funds for religion, education, and hospitals. The average student who goes to study in the United States consequently develops a rather strong pro-American attitude. In the provincial capital there are nine daily newspapers, of which only the *Dagongbao* has a higher circulation of 2,300 to 2,400. The others have a circulation of between 100 and 500, and most of their content is of very low quality.

2. Education. By education we mean schools, which in Hunan are run by people of many different factions, as listed below.

Higher Agricultural School [*Danong*]⁷ faction—An amalgam of graduates from the former Qing dynasty School of Higher Education [*Gaodeng xuetang*], the Seek Truth Academy [*Qiushi shuyuan*], and the Seek Loyalty Academy [*Qiuzhong shuyuan*]. Because many in it have returned from studying in the West, it is also called the Western faction. The director of the Department of Education, Li Jiannong⁸, is its leader, and most of its disciples are intellectually conservative. The higher agricultural schools are their headquarters; they are rather widely scattered throughout educational circles.

Superior [*Youji*] faction—From the Superior Normal School. Their thinking is decadent. Quite influential in educational circles.

Higher Normal [*Gaoshi*] faction—From Hunan Provincial Higher Normal School. Their thinking is relatively modern.

Beijing Higher Normal [*Beigao*] faction—From Beijing Higher Normal School. Of all the factions, this group is the most modern in its thinking. Their organization is the Youth Education Society [*Qingnian jiaoyushe*].

Higher Industrial [*Gaogong*] faction—From the Higher Industrial School of the former Qing dynasty and from the present Industrial Technical School. Entrenched in the technical schools, with influence in the assembly and government. The most reactionary and vicious.

South City [*Chengnan*] faction—From the Qing dynasty South City Academy and the Central Road [*Zhonglu*] Normal School. As decadent in their thinking as the Superior faction. Entrenched in the Education Council [*Jiaoyuhui*].

---

7. None of the three schools subsequently enumerated were, strictly speaking, agricultural schools. The meaning appears to be that these institutions provided a traditional-style education suitable for the sons of landlords; perhaps a more accurate translation of *Danong xuexiao* would be "schools for big agriculturalists."

8. Li Jiannong (1880–1963), a native of Hunan, studied in Japan and England. He was a historian and journalist, and was appointed head of the Hunan Political Council, and concurrently head of the Department of Education by Zhao Hengti in December 1922. He is best known in the West as the author of Li Chien-nung [Li Jiannong], *The Political History of China, 1840–1928* (Stanford: Stanford University Press, 1956), hereafter Li Chien-nung, *The Political History of China.*

Common People's University [*Pingda*] faction—A small group of people such as Yi Jiayue, Luo Dunwei, and Zhang Ziping[9] from the Research clique and the Creation Society who organized the Common People's University [*Pingmin daxue*]. Their thinking can be regarded as the most outstanding of all the factions.

First Normal [*Yishi*] faction—From First Normal School. Influential in elementary education. Part conservative, part new in their thinking.

Eastern Seas [*Dongyang*] faction—Those who have studied in Japan. Their base is the Category A Industrial School [*Jiazhong gongye xuexiao*]. As reactionary and vicious as the Higher Industrial faction.

Gentlemen [*Junzi*] faction—This faction is represented by men such as Chen Peilin, Zhu Jianfan, Hu Zijing, and Peng Guojun. They are among the earliest of those who studied in the Japanese Short-term Normal School. Their base is in the following four schools: the Chuyi School, the Mingde School, the Xiuye School, and the Zhounan School. Conservative in their thinking but fairly upright, they are called the gentlemen.

Of these factions, the Superior faction is of the older generation, and although the members of the Higher Agricultural faction are older, their union is new. These two factions should be called the two tyrants of the educational world at present. Although the Higher Normal and Superior factions originally constituted a fraternal partnership, they have very sharp diffences because of their separate spheres of influence. The Higher Industrial and the Eastern Seas factions have recently fallen from power, but they have considerable potential power. The South City faction is a bunch of thieving rats and dogs who rely on Zhao Hengti for their existence. The Gentlemen faction, under the former Qing dynasty, and up until 1919, was known as the education monopoly and was the best-known and most influential, but as other groups have sprung up from 1920 on, its influence has declined. The Beijing Higher, Common People's University, and First Normal factions are known as the New Faction, and they have joined forces in a united front against the power of the Old Faction. In Hunan, there are more private schools than public schools. Most of the factions have their home base in private schools and look upon the public schools as colonial territories. Education expenses, including the expenses of sending students to study abroad, approach two million. Private schools routinely receive subsidies. The larger subsidies amount to more than 10 thousand and even the smaller subsidies are several thousand or so. This is the reason for the development of private schools.

---

9. Zhang Ziping (1893–1947), a writer who studied in Japan, was one of the organizers of the Creation Society.

D. The Labor Movement

The Hunan labor movement and the labor movements in other places in the country arose at the same time, and the workers' activities have attracted much attention in society. We have compiled the following data on the various labor groups and strikes.

1. Labor Groups with the New-style Organization

Name	Date Organized	Number of Members	Location	Other
All-Hunan Federation of Labor Organizations	November 1911		Changsha	
Anyuan Road Mine Workers' Club	May 1922	11,000	Pingxiang	Well-organized and fairly strong
Shuikoushan Mine Workers' Club	October 1922	3,000	Shuikoushan	Well-organized and fairly strong
General Union of Guangzhou-Wuhan Railway Workers	November 1922		Changsha	Coalition of the Xujiazhou, Yuezhou, Changsha, and Zhuping unions
Guangzhou-Hankou Line Yuezhou Union	May 1922	300	Yuezhou	
Guangzhou-Hankou Line Changsha Union	August 1922	600	Changsha	
Mint Workers' Club	January 1923	1,500	Changsha	Well-organized and fairly strong
First Silk Factory Staff and Workers' Club	March 1923	1,500	Changsha	Includes staff, so less well organized, but fairly strong
Masons' and Carpenters' Union	September 1922	2,000	Changsha	Relatively weak
Garment Workers' Union	September 1922	1,500	Changsha	Not well-organized and weak; dispute with owners still not resolved
Typesetters' Union	October 1922	350	Changsha	Well-organized and fairly strong

Lithographers' Union	October 1922	300	Changsha	Not well organized or strong
Electrical Workers' Club	February 1923	100	Changsha	Still not well-organized
Lead Smelting Factory Workers' Club	February 1923	300	Changsha	Well-organized and fairly strong
Rickshaw-Pullers' Union	October 1922	1,850	Changsha	Well-organized and fairly strong
Mechanics' Union	November 1922		Changsha	Set up in opposition to the Hunan Mechanics' Union
Barbers' Union	October 1922	500	Changsha	Waged a two-year struggle with the master barbers; has some vitality
Scribes' Union	October 1922	300	Changsha	Weak
Boot and Shoe Craftsmen's Union	November 1922	1,100	Changsha	Not well organized, weak

The twenty-three workers' organizations listed above have a total membership of about 30 thousand.

2. Old-Style Workers' Groups

Labor Association	There are two labor associations, one that was disbanded by Zhao Hengti and now has operations offices in Shanghai, and the other one organized by the capitalist owners of the First Silk Factory with the objective of supplanting the old labor association.
The Mechanics' Association	A group of students specializing in industry that includes a small number of workers and apprentices, led by Bin Bucheng.[10]
The Industrial General Union	A group of handicraft shop owners in the provincial capital, recognized by the government as a legal organization.

---

10. Bin Bucheng was a Changsha merchant and powerful bureaucrat. He was made a member of the Board of Directors of the Huashi [Cotton Mill] Company in April 1921. He later became head of the provincial mint, and in January 1923 some 1,600 workers at the mint organized themselves into a Currency Workers' Club, demanding that work conditions be improved and that Bin Bucheng be dismissed. He was then appointed head of the Provincial Mining Bureau by Zhao Hengti in November 1923. Bin became more opposed to union strike action over time, and it was he who quickly closed down the Shuikoushan Trade Union.

| China Labor Union | Organized by the hoodlum Chen Jia'nai with its general association in the provincial capital and branches in every *xian*. |
| Worker Comrades' Association | Set up by some workers of Bin Bucheng's faction in the Currency Mint in opposition to the Currency Workers Club. |

Of the five workers' groups listed above—except for the Worker Comrades' Association, which has over 400 members, and the Mechanics' Association, with a membership of 200 to 300—the Labor Association, the Industrial General Union, and the China Labor Union have no workers. Before it was closed down, the old Labor Association had 2,000 to 3,000 members organized in the old style and included all different trades, but as soon as it was closed down its members dispersed.

3. Strike Figures

Strikers and Number of Strikes	Number of Strikers	Strike Demands	Number of Days	Victory or Defeat
Anyuan Mine and Zhuzhou-Pingxiang Railroad; once	11,000	Right to organize and higher wages	5 days	Total victory
Guangzhou-Hankou Railroad; twice	800	First time, higher wages and driving out Zhang and Miao. Second time, in support of Beijing-Hankou Railroad	First time, 19 days. Second time, 1 day.	First time, largely victorious. Second time, defeat.
Changsha masons and carpenters; once	4,000	Higher wages	24 days	Total victory
Shuikoushan; once	3,000	Higher wages	23 days	Total victory
Changsha garment workers; once	800	Higher wages	10 days	A small victory
Changsha silk factory; once	1,500	Higher wages	20 days	Partial victory

Changsha barbers; once	500	Freedom of assembly and association, higher wages, and equal share of proceeds with employers	20 days	Largely victorious
Changsha scribes; once	300	Higher wages	35 days	Partial victory

Thus there were a total of ten strikes. Nine were victorious or semivictorious, and one failed. The total number of persons participating in the strikes amounted to 22,250. The strike objectives had mostly to do with wages, but a few of them involved a struggle for the freedom [to organize]. All of the strikes took place between August and December of last year.

The Beijing Coup d'État *and the Merchants*

(July 11, 1923)

The present coup d'état has startled the merchants, who have persistently ignored politics, and made them suddenly look up and pay attention to politics. This is most welcome news! On June 14, the Shanghai General Federation of Merchant Street Associations[1] put out a declaration calling for the convening of a national assembly to deal with national affairs. The Shanghai General Chamber of Commerce,[2] in accordance with a resolution passed by its membership at a general meeting on June 23, has issued a declaration to the whole nation which reads in part:

> We venture to proclaim with sincerity to the Chinese and to the foreigners that from the fourteenth of this month, the people of our nation do not recognize any of the various actions, whether in domestic or in foreign affairs, that have been taken by Cao Kun,[3] Gao Lingwei,[4] et al., since their usurpation of political power as being the actions of qualified representatives of the state. In addition to sending telegrams to all top provincial military and civilian officials asking them to maintain peace and order and the status quo within the areas under their jurisdiction, we shall seek, together with the people of the whole nation, to devise an appropriate solution to the problems of reconstruction and of planning a better future.

This article was originally published in the Communist Party organ *Xiangdao zhoubao* (henceforth *Xiangdao*), No. 31–32, July 11, 1923. Our translation is based on the text as reproduced in *Mao Zedong ji*, Vol. 1, pp. 87–90.

1. The Shanghai General Federation of Merchant Street Associations was inaugurated on October 26, 1919. It was formed as an umbrella organization for the numerous city street unions that emerged during the shopkeepers' strikes of the May Fourth Movement. The federation became the voice of the small merchant enterprises, mostly shopkeepers who owned their own premises.

2. The Shanghai General Chamber of Commerce was established in 1902 as an organization to represent the commercial interests of important businesses, bankers, merchants, and industrialists against the foreign threat. In the early 1920s the group remained dominated by the old elite comprador merchants and the powerful Ningbo group. Its membership was limited by high annual subscription fees, and a powerful directorship of wealthy merchants controlled decision making.

3. Cao Kun, leader of the Zhili clique and military governor of the northern provinces, led a coup that ousted Li Yuanhong and imposed himself as leader of the Beijing government on June 13, 1923. He officially assumed office as president on October 10, 1923.

4. Gao Lingwei, member of the Zhili clique and associate of Cao Kun, was appointed acting prime minister of the new Beijing government.

At the same time, the General Chamber of Commerce resolved not to recognize the parliament, which "cannot represent the people's will," and moreover to organize a committee for people's rule as an organ for dealing actively with national affairs. This action of the Shanghai General Federation of Merchant Street Associations and the Shanghai Chamber of Commerce may be considered as the first instance of merchant involvement in politics, and as a manifestation of the fact that the merchants, who for three years had remained silent, now speak in awesome tones.

The present political problem in China is quite simply the problem of the national revolution. To use the might of the people to overthrow the warlords and also to overthrow foreign imperialism, which colludes with the warlords in their evil acts—such is the historic mission of the Chinese people. This revolution is the task of all the people. Among the Chinese people as a whole, the merchants, workers, peasants, students, and teachers should all alike come forward to take on responsibility for a portion of the work of revolution. But because of historical necessity and the trend of current realities, the task that the merchants should shoulder in the national revolution is more urgent and more important than the work that the rest of the Chinese people should take upon themselves. We know that the politics of semicolonial China is a politics of the dual oppression of the warlords and foreign powers, which have banded together to fetter the people of the whole country. Under the politics of this kind of dual oppression, the people of the whole country naturally all suffer profoundly together. Nonetheless, the merchants are the ones who feel these sufferings most keenly, most urgently. Everyone knows that the *lijin*[5] and customs duties are two life-and-death matters for the merchants. The urgent demand of the merchants that the *lijin* be reduced and that customs duties be raised is the expression of their most immediate interests. But abolishing the *lijin* and raising the customs duties is not something that can be easily done, for abolishing the *lijin* would hurt the interests of the warlords, while raising customs duties would also hurt the interests of the imperialists. If the *lijin* were abolished completely, the warlords would get thinner day by day, and the merchants fatter. Then the merchants would only have to rise up and "give a shout" in order to overthrow the warlords. But the clever warlords will certainly not do anything so stupid as to lift a stone in this way to crush their own feet. And if the customs duty on foreign goods were raised considerably, or if we even went so far as to abolish the treaty tariffs and replace them by protective tariffs fixed by China itself, thus unshackling the Chinese merchants, the domestic industry and commerce would develop more rapidly, and foreign goods would no longer be able to gain a foothold in China. The cunning foreign imperialists are even less likely to do something this stupid. Consequently, abolishing the *lijin* and increasing customs duties are quite simply

---

5. The transportation tax on goods moved within the country, commonly transcribed *likin* in English-language sources of the period.

matters of life and death both to the foreign imperialists and to our own warlords. This absolutely cannot be achieved through some comical order by Li Yuanhong,[6] as though at the sounding of a reveille. If we also consider how just recently Cao Rui[7] and Jin Yunpeng[8] sabotaged the Shanghai textile merchants' demand that the state provide public loans for the textile industry, and how the foreign diplomatic corps wrecked the demand for a national ban on the export of cotton,[9] we see further and sufficient proof that the position of the foreign powers and warlords on the one hand, and of the merchants on the other, are incompatible. All of this bitterness has been personally tasted by those dignified merchants like Mr. Mu Ouzhai[10] who attended the general conference of the Shanghai General Chamber of Commerce on the 23rd of last month!

Hitherto the merchants have always "dearly loved peace," and have never imagined that political reform required a revolution, and could not be achieved with just a few telegrams on "reducing troops, drawing up a constitution, and managing finances." Still less did they imagine that they themselves would have to participate actively in the revolution, and that only by calling for the organization of all the people and creating a broad mass movement could a revolutionary force be created. They even believed that political reform did not require a political party, going so far as to criticize the revolutionary efforts of the Guomindang as superfluous. If we compare this childish and timid mentality of the merchants in the past with the present situation, how can we stifle a laugh? In the past there were also some merchants with a superstitious faith in America. They firmly believed that America was a good friend who helped China; they did not realize that America is actually the most murderous of hangmen. If we consider such actual recent examples as how America schemed to help Cao Kun, who was opposed by the merchants and by all the people of China, to usurp political power, and how it exerted every effort to obstruct the demand of the merchants for a ban on exporting cotton, and so on, it becomes apparent how

---

6. Li Yuanhong, former military governor of Hubei and member of the Guomindang, was vice president of the first republican government in 1912. He was president of the Beijing government at the time of the 1923 coup.

7. Cao Rui, Cao Kun's younger brother, was civil governor of Zhili province from 1917 until June 1922.

8. Jin Yunpeng, former army official of the Zhili clique, was prime minister in Beijing in 1920–1921.

9. In late 1922 the Association of Chinese Spinning Mill Owners requested an embargo on cotton exports, which was then approved by official decree by the Beijing government. The petition was made in response to a worldwide rise in the price of raw cotton which inconvenienced Chinese mill owners and led to a buying up of Chinese cotton by Japanese mill owners. Protests from the Japanese, with the support of the foreign diplomatic corps, led the Chinese government in May 1923 to abrogate its earlier decree.

10. Ouzhai appears to be a variant of the zi, Ouchu, of Mu Xiangyue, president of the Shanghai Cotton Exchange. On Mu, see, above, the relevant note to the article of April 10, 1923, "The Foreign Powers, the Warlords, and the Revolution."

wrong it is to have a superstitious faith in America. Judging from the actions of the Shanghai merchants in response to the coup d'état, we know that they have already changed their attitudes, cast away their pacifism, adopted revolutionary methods, and drummed up the courage to shoulder responsiblity for national affairs; they have progressed remarkably fast! From their anger at the American schemes of aggression against China, as evidenced in the telegram of the Shanghai General Chamber of Commerce and the Banking Association opposing the U.S. Chamber of Commerce and Overseas Chinese Association for "taking advantage of the struggle of our people in the movement for democracy, to make proposals to our national government, singing loudly a tune that surreptitiously implies joint control of China and falsely suggesting that the Chinese Chamber of Commerce and banking circles have already agreed," we can see that they have been at least partially cleansed of their bad name as "Chinese merchants who fawn on foreigners."

The Shanghai merchants have arisen and begun to act. We hope that merchants outside Shanghai will all rise up together and act in unison. The present crisis is one of extreme urgency, as though the fire were already singeing our eyebrows, and does not permit us idly to fall asleep once more. At present, we must unite the people of the whole country to carry out the revolutionary movement. It is not a time that allows the merchants to continue to split into factions. It must be understood that the foreign powers and the warlords are the common enemy of all the merchants, as well as of the whole nation. Moreover, the advantages obtained after the success of the revolution will be common advantages. It is absolutely essential that we unite and struggle together to overthrow the common enemy in order to secure the common interest. We hope that the merchants of both Tianjin and Beijing will not be deceived by Cao Rui and a group of "bureaucratic capitalists," that the merchants of Hankou will not be manipulated by Wu Peifu, but that they will rise up together and take united revolutionary action with the merchants of Shanghai. The broader the unity of the merchants, the greater will be their influence, the greater their strength to lead the people of the entire nation, and the more rapid the success of the revolution!

In conclusion, we must still address the following warnings to merchants throughout China. First, the great enterprise of revolution is no easy matter, above all in the circumstances of China, a country where the revolution is subjected to twofold repression by the foreign powers and the warlords. Only if we call upon the merchants, the workers, the peasants, the students, and the teachers of the whole country, as well as all the other members of our nation who suffer under a common oppression, and establish a closely knit united front, can this revolution succeed. We must put into practice the proclamation of the General Chamber of Commerce calling for "solving [this problem] together with the people of the entire nation." We must not repeat the previous mistake that the United Association of Merchants and Teachers made of rejecting the participation of the workers. Secondly, since the merchants have already courageously taken the first step toward revolution, they must quickly take the second step, firmly support solving national affairs by convening a national assembly, strictly coordinate their advance, push forward vigorously, and not stop until the objective is won. We must never stop moving forward on meeting slight resistance, still less go off onto the wrong road of compromise with the foreign powers and warlords. We must all have faith that the one and only way to save oneself and the nation is the national revolution. Many revolutionary causes throughout history may serve as references and guides. Circumstances call upon us to perform a historic task. We can no longer shirk our duty! To open a new era and create a new nation by revolutionary methods—such is the historic mission of the Chinese people. We must never forget it!

The "Provincial Constitution Sutra" and Zhao Hengti

(August 15, 1923)

" . . . [S]ince the western Hunan problem arose,[1] Mr. Zhao's position has been shaken and he has had to rely on the Provincial Constitution to defend himself. Thus a few days ago, he ordered his henchmen, such as Fang Kegang and Li Jimin,[2] to bribe public bodies to send telegrams, and to create a mass movement . . . in order to protect Mr. Zhao, under [the slogan of] upholding the Provincial Constitution. . . . A street demonstration was fixed for 8:00 A.M. on the fifth. . . . These people sent letters mostly to worker organizations, figuring that workers are simpleminded, and that a thousand or more would surely show up. To their amazement, they waited that day until 10:00, but not a single organization arrived, and even the few individuals who did come included nobody but their close friends. They were terribly nervous and upset, so they sent people out in all directions to such places as the China Labor Union, which is no more than a pack of thugs,[3] and even to the Temple for Nurturing Perfection [*Yangji yuan*] and the Buddha Transformation Lecture Hall [*Fohua jiangyanyuan*]. By giving each person fifty cents and some breakfast to eat, they hired over a hundred people to come out and march on the street at 12:00. Before the march they held a meeting at the slide projection theater of the Education Association, attended by a party of 120 to 130 monks and beggars. The meeting began:

1) The monk Chipei, who presided, announced the guiding principles of the meeting. His remarks can be summed up as follows: that the Provincial Constitu-

---

This article originally appeared in *Xiangdao* No. 36, August 15, 1923. Our translation is based on the text as reproduced in *Mao Zedong ji*, Vol. 1, pp. 91–92.

1. In June 1923 the commander of the Ninth and Tenth Brigades in western Hunan, Cai Juyou, declared western Hunan independent of Changsha. Cai organized his forces into an army of opposition to Governor Zhao Hengti, which then joined forces with Tan Yankai's army. A number of Zhao's generals were unwilling to fight Cai Juyou, and Zhao was faced with the problem of losing control of western Hunan.

2. At about this time, Zhao Hengti appointed his follower Li Jimin principal of First Normal School in the hope of putting an end to radicalism and anti-Zhao activities there. Although troops were sent to the school repeatedly, organized resistance to Li's appointment continued until early 1924.

3. On the China Labor Union (*Zhonghua gonghui*), see the section on the labor movement in the text dated July 1, 1923, "Hunan under the Provincial Constitution."

tion [*Sheng xianfa*] might better be called the Provincial Constitution Sutra [*Sheng xianjing*], as in the Buddhist sutras. . . . The monks and beggars in the audience flailed their arms wildly.

2) After the meeting, they set out: In front were two large banners, one reading, 'Association for Upholding the Provincial Constitution,' and the other 'Petitionary Assembly of the People of the Province.'

The first group of marchers—twenty or thirty people in long gowns and mandarin jackets, truly the dignified representatives of the people of the province.

The second group of marchers—five or six people from the China Labor Union.

The third group of marchers—forty or fifty bald-headed, loose-robed individuals from the Buddha Transformation Lecture Troupe.

The fourth group of marchers—about forty from the Temple of Nurturing Perfection.

A mixture of all kinds and types . . . their performance was truly a hilarious farce . . . ." (See the *Republican Daily*)

We have always opposed a federation of self-governing provinces, because it would not be a federation of self-governing provinces but rather a federation of military governors in their separatist regimes. We have always opposed the provincial constitutions concocted by the warlords and corrupt politicians, which falsely usurp the name, because they cannot serve as safeguards for the people, but are, on the contrary, safeguards for the powers and interests seized by the warlords and corrupt politicians. Hunan is the best proof of this. Zhao Hengti has now become the stately and magnificent "Guardian of the Constitution," but for the last two years— since the Provincial Constitution came into existence—he has cruelly massacred the workers (such as Huang and Pang),[4] closed down newspapers (*Dagongbao*, *Zizhi xinbao* [Self-rule News], and *Xin Xiang bao* [New Hunan Reporter]), and robbed the people of the freedom of correspondence (his postal censors have never been withdrawn even for a single day). He has taken away the freedom of assembly and of association (by closing down the Rickshaw-Pullers' Union, the Rice Millers' Union, and the Society for Supporting the Conduct of Foreign Affairs,[5] and repeatedly

---

4. On the execution of Huang Ai and Pang Renquan, see the note to the text of December 14, 1922, entitled "The True Circumstances of the Negotiations . . . with Governor Zhao."

5. The Hunan Society for Supporting the Conduct of Foreign Affairs [*Hunan waijiao houyuan hui*] had been established on April 4, 1923, to promote the boycott of Japanese goods referred to above, in the note to Mao's letter of March 7, 1923. It played a leading role in this movement, and its inspectors were active on the docks on June 1, when Japanese marines fired into the crowd, killing two people and seriously wounding nine others. Zhao Hengti, bent on conciliating Japan, proclaimed martial law, and ordered the dissolution of the Society on April 9. On these events, see McDonald, *Urban Origins*, pp. 201–205.

forbidding students' and workers' meetings). He has shielded opium traffic and opium production by his troops, bought elections (by sending his henchmen to fabricate the vote count for the Provisional Constitution, using money to create his own Provincial Assembly, and buying the provincial governorship).[6] He has exacted contributions from merchants (the head of the Changsha General Chamber of Commerce has been forced to flee several times), he has levied from the peasants advance payments of land taxes (some *xian* have been forced to make advance payments down to the year 1928), and he has violated the legally established budget ratios, reducing educational expenses and raising military expenses. He has colluded with Wu Peifu and Xiao Yaonan. In every single case, he has donned the mask of the Provincial Constitution, but has acted in fact as the enemy of the people! His present calling up of troops and mobilization of the masses also began with a fight with Cai Juyou[7] over the opium tax (the so-called special tax). Zhao Hengti, this outrageously and unpardonably wicked creature, still stands there boasting and beating the drum in the phoney name of "protecting the constitution," all unconcerned that he is causing the Hunanese people to die of shame!

---

6. When Zhao Hengti first succeeded Tan Yankai as military commander-in-chief (*zong siling*) of Hunan in November 1921, the office of civil governor (*shengzhang*) was assumed by Lin Zhiyu. Following a heavily manipulated electoral process, which lasted from June to September 1922, Zhao Hengti was declared the "popularly elected" civil governor, and thereafter, until he was driven out of the province in March 1926, he held both titles.

7. One of the reasons Cai Juyou declared the area under his control independent of Changsha in June 1923 was a disagreement with Zhao Hengti over his opium income.

The British and Liang Ruhao

(August 29, 1923)

The Weihaiwei[1] negotiations are now pressing toward a signing. Why is it that, except for the people of Shandong, no one in the entire nation has said anything about it? Do you mean to say that the Chinese people are so busy with the movement for the return of Lüshun and Dalian[2] that they have forgotten the movement for the return of Weihaiwei? Or is it that our countrymen know only that they should hate Japan and not that they should hate Great Britain? Do they know only that Japanese imperialism has invaded China, and not that the British imperialist invasion of China has been much worse than that of Japanese imperialism?

Those in charge of the Weihaiwei negotiations are Commissioner Liang Ruhao and Assistant Commissioner Chen Shaotang. Chen Shaotang announced the crimes of Liang Ruhao at the Association of Fellow Shandongese in Beijing saying, "Intent on flirting with the foreigners, Commissioner Liang has offered the British a scheme for retaining Liugong Island.[3] The return of Weihaiwei has

---

This article appeared in *Xiangdao* No. 38, August 29, 1923. We have translated it from *Mao Zedong ji*, Vol. 1, pp. 93–95.

1. The Chinese naval base of Weihaiwei, located on the tip of the Shandong peninsula, was ceded to Great Britain in July 1898 during the foreign scramble for influence in China. The lease provided that Britain should retain possession "for so long a period as Port Arthur shall remain in the occupation of Russia." For the text of the convention, see Pamela Atwell, *British Mandarins and Chinese Reformers* (Hong Kong: Oxford University Press, 1985), pp. 215–16. On February 1, 1922, at the Washington Conference, Great Britain proposed that Weihaiwei should be returned to China, and in May 1922 Liang Ruhao was appointed Chinese rendition commissioner. Two years later, criticism of Liang had become so intense that he resigned this office, and responsibility for the negotiations was assumed directly by the Foreign Ministry. Just as a draft rendition agreement was about to be signed, Feng Yuxiang overthrew the Beijing government, and the matter was held in abeyance until the late 1920s. Rendition finally took place in October 1930.

2. Lüshun (most commonly known as Port Arthur) and Dalian were included in the twenty-five-year lease of territory of the Liaodong peninsula in Fengtian to the Russians in March 1898. (It was to balance this Russian stronghold that Britain had originally sought a lease of Weihaiwei.) Russian rights and interests in the area were transferred to Japan in May 1905 at the Russo-Japanese Peace Conference following the Russo-Japanese War.

3. Liugong Island, the largest of several small islands just off the coast of Weihaiwei, was part of the leasehold and was important because of its naval facilities. The draft agreement of 1924 did indeed contain a provision for its continuing use by the British Navy.

a very important relationship to military matters. With no qualms about selling out his country, Mr. Liang has turned the unconditional return of Weihaiwei into a continuing lease, which is then turned into a lease in perpetuity, in return for which he must certainly be expecting a personal reward. . . . Fearing that I would wreck his dark scheme for selling out the country, he first had someone else contact me with offers of a bribe, stressing that in the future all my personal expenses could be reimbursed, and that after the treaty was concluded I could also have a share in all kinds of benefits. From my repeated refusals and my subsequent demand that all be made public, realizing that I could not be moved by bribes, Mr. Liang then resorted to threats. Whenever he got very excited and couldn't make me back down, Mr. Liang would invariably pound the desk and shout at me, 'I have full authority over this matter,' at which point he would direct his aides to escort me out the door. Unable to control my anger I contemplated suicide a number of times. One day I grabbed an inkstone and was about to bash in my own head with it, frightfully startling a certain Englishman who was there and who urged me to stop. Mr. Liang was totally unmoved. . . . "

The Jinan People's Congress, on August 23, has already pointed out the major points in which the Weihaiwei draft treaty as decided upon by Liang Ruhao and the British, comprising two parts, A and B, with 23 articles, gives away sovereignty and is an insult to the nation.

1. The return is turned into a continuing lease. The draft treaty permits the British to continue to have a lease for ten years, and after that ten years they have the right to continue the lease on a temporary basis. Furthermore, Weihaiwei City itself, which has never before been leased to Britain,[4] is to be carved out and leased as special district.

2. Sovereign territory and territorial waters are given away. The draft treaty stipulates that: (1) Local Chinese authorities are to give the British lessees a document of "permanent lease"; (2) The future procedure for permanent leasing by the foreigners of Chinese territory is to include no service charge; (3) Territories retained by the British for official use cannot be taken or used by China, and China must recognize properties that Britain leases out. What does it mean to give away sovereign territory? The draft treaty stipulates that: (1) The sea anchorage of Liugong Island can be used by China only when not being used by the British navy; (2) The British navy can send troops ashore on Liugong Island for training exercises and target practice; (3) The British navy may use the Liugong Island anchorage as part of training maneuvers on the high seas. According to these stipulations, both the army and naval forces of Britain occupying Liugong Island and its waters are permitted to come and go freely on our sovereign territory and territorial waters.

3. National sovereignty is given away. The draft treaty stipulates that the

---

4. The lease of 1898 provided that the Chinese authorities should continue to exercise authority over the old walled city of Weihaiwei.

territory between Liugong Island and Weihaiwei will be carved out as a special district that will be neither under the jurisdiction of Shandong Province, nor really under the jurisdiction of the central government. Although our government will in name appoint officials, the police will be under the command of the British and finances will be managed by the Customs Commissioner (an Englishman), while the city will be under the control of a Chinese-British committee organized jointly by China and Great Britain. The administrative officials appointed by China will have empty, meaningless titles and will be responsible only for the repayment of debts to Britain and for arranging for public expenditures. Weihaiwei will thus become a second Hong Kong and national sovereignty will have been given away completely.

To my compatriots who superstitiously believe in the Washington Conference: What has the Washington Conference given us? To my compatriots who believe that Britain is better than Japan: In what way is Britain any better than Japan? The return of Weihaiwei is about to turn Weihaiwei into a second Hong Kong. When the leases on the British concession at Hankou and the British concession at Tianjin[5] come due, we shall be forced to continue the leases. The demand that the Guangzhou-Jiulong and Guangzhou-Hankou railroads be connected will open the upper reaches of the Yangzi River and the provinces of the southwest to economic invasion by the Hong Kong government. It is proposed that the Conference on Tariffs be limited to studying the problem of *lijin* only (London teletype of August 26). Most recently, all the masks have been peeled off even further with the proposal for joint control of the railroads. To my compatriots who superstitiously believe in the Washington Conference and who believe that Britain is better than Japan: Please tell me what has the Washington Conference given us? In what way is Britain any better than Japan?

Our fellow countrymen must quickly rise up and oppose the naked invasion of China by the British pirates!

Our fellow countrymen must quickly rise up and oppose the traitor Liang Ruhao!

---

5. Hankou and Tianjin were both treaty ports at which Great Britain had concessions. These were returned to China in 1927, in the course of the Northern Expedition.

The Cigarette Tax

(August 29, 1923)

We often say: "The Chinese government is the countinghouse of our foreign masters." Perhaps there are some people who don't believe this. Do we not also say repeatedly: "The false show of friendship by foreigners (especially the British and Americans) is merely a pretense of 'amity' in order that they may squeeze out more of the fat and blood of the Chinese people"? Perhaps there are some who don't believe this either. Ever since the ban on exporting cotton was abrogated because of opposition by our foreign masters,[1] it has been impossible not to give some credence [to this view]. Now that our foreign masters have again put pressure on the government to withdraw the cigarette tax in Zhejiang and other provinces, it has become even more impossible not to give some credence to it. A dispatch from Beijing in *Shenbao*, dated August 28, says: "The Cabinet discussion of opposition from the British and American ministers to raising the local cigarette taxes resulted in telegrams being sent to all the said provinces ordering them to stop collecting the tax." Just what is the levying of a cigarette tax? Let's look at the telegram of June 31 [*sic*] from the Hangzhou General Chamber of Commerce to the Beijing government:

> We humbly submit that levying taxes on luxury goods is a general practice of all nations. Cigarettes have become very popular in recent years, and in Zhejiang Province alone annual sales have surpassed ten million, an enormously high rate of consumption that is shocking to hear. The poisonous effects are no less than those of opium. When the local authorities had considered this, they issued a special order for the establishment of a bureau to levy a tax that would turn the consumption of a useless item into the properly useful construction of roads. We now hear that the foreign merchants, using their treaty rights as a pretext, have repeatedly intervened with the government, ignoring the fact that this kind of a special tax is imposed solely on the cigarette smoker and has nothing to do with the tobacco merchant. This is strictly a tax borne by the people of Zhejiang, yet the foreign merchants again make an effort to intervene! Furthermore, we must not allow the foreigners to interfere with our sovereignty over domestic administrative matters. We must stand on principle and forcefully fight back, rejecting all pretexts. This will be very advantageous indeed for our sovereignty.

This article, like the previous one, appeared in *Xiangdao* No. 38, August 29, 1923, and is translated from *Mao Zedong ji*, Vol. 1, pp. 97–98.

1. For details, see the note to the text of July 11, 1923.

In the past, basing themselves on the treaties regulating taxes, the British and Americans have not allowed China the freedom to levy taxes on luxury items imported from abroad. Regardless of the fact that this is "strictly a tax borne by the people of Zhejiang" involving "sovereignty over domestic administrative matters," simply because it concerns foreign goods, in the end, the tax cannot be levied.

Of the cigarettes produced by the British and American Tobacco Company,[2] a small portion is imported from Britain, America, and Japan. A large portion is manufactured by British and American tobacco merchants using Chinese tobacco and hired Chinese labor in factories set up in Shanghai, Hankou, and elswhere in China. When the production leaves the factory, a very light tax is paid, in accordance with the "treaties," and the cigarettes are shipped in wholesale batches to the various provinces. Thereafter, China is denied the "freedom" to impose taxes. In Zhejiang Province alone the sale of cigarettes amounts to "over ten million a year." There is no reliable total figure for the annual sale of cigarettes in the country as a whole, but if we estimate on the basis of the example of the single province of Zhejiang, it must be over 200 million *yuan*. This is really "startling to hear"! I ask my 400 million fellow countrymen to think it over—what really is the point of the foreigners' "amity"?

The "Cabinet meetings" of the Chinese government are really both clever and straightforward. Every fart of our foreign masters is a lovely "perfume." If our foreign masters want to take away our cotton, the cabinet meeting orders that the ban on the export of cotton be lifted. If our foreign masters want to send us cigarettes, the cabinet meeting "sends telegrams to all the said provinces ordering them to stop collecting the tax." Again I ask my 400 million fellow countrymen to think about it: Is it really true or not that "the Chinese government is the countinghouse of our foreign masters"?

---

2. The British and American Tobacco Company (commonly known as the B.A.T.), founded in London in 1902, was well known in China. In 1920 the company owned factories in Shanghai, Hankou, and Mukden, with branches in Changsha and Wuhan, and employed around 25,000 Chinese residents.

Reply to the Central Executive Committee of the Youth League, Drafted on Behalf of the Central Committee of the Chinese Communist Party

(September 6, 1923)

To the Central Executive Committee of the Youth League:

We have received both your letters.

It has been resolved that your esteemed committee shall be represented at meetings by the chairman and secretary of the committee. Please notify one of these two persons when meetings are to be held.

As for publications, the publications department has already been instructed to present to your esteemed committee two copies of each issue of *Xiangdao*, and one copy of each issue of *Qianfeng* and *Xin qingnian*. For other titles such as *Gongren zhoukan*, please have your committee arrange direct exchanges of publications.

September 6 Zhongying (C.P.)[1]

This letter was first published in *Wenwu tiandi*, No. 6, 1981. Our translation is based on this text, as reproduced in *Mao Zedong ji. Bujuan*, Vol. 2, p. 123.

1. For reasons of discretion, this letter was signed with two Chinese characters pronounced as shown, which are intended to suggest *Zhongyang*, or Central [Committee], followed by the Roman letters C.P. for Communist Party.

Letter to Lin Boqu and Peng Sumin

(September 28, 1923)

Comrades Boqu[1] and Sumin,[2]

I arrived in Changsha on the sixteenth. Since then the political situation has suddenly changed again. Zhao[3] entered the province from Pingjiang on the twenty-third, putting up placards everywhere to announce that the provincial government had been resumed. A part of the Northern Army[4] has already reached Yuezhou, but the future is as yet hard to predict. The only [clear point is] that Tan's[5] Army is now in a stronger position; to the south of Changsha it is drawn up along the Xiang River, and to the north it is occupying half of Liling. Hence the Northern Army is simply holding Yuezhou, without any attempt to forge ahead, as Zhang Fulai did the year before last.[6] In these circumstances, Tan

---

This letter has been translated from the text in *Mao Zedong shuxin xuanji*, pp. 23–25, which is followed by the indication "based on a manuscript copy." It does not appear to have been published previously.

1. Lin Boqu (1886–1960) was a native of Linfeng *xian*, Hunan Province. He joined Sun Yatsen's Chinese Revolutionary Party, the predecessor of the Guomindang, in 1914, and the Chinese Communist Party in 1921. He became deputy director of the General Affairs Department of the Guomindang Central Headquarters in 1923 and took part in the reorganization of the Guomindang.

2. Peng Sumin (1885–1924) was a native of Qingjiang *xian*, Jiangxi Province. He was director of the General Affairs Department of the Guomindang Central Headquarters at the time.

3. Zhao refers to Zhao Hengti (1880–1971). See above, the text of December 14, 1922, recounting Mao's negotiations with him. At this time he was commander-in-chief of the Xiang Army appointed by the Beijing government.

4. In the summer of 1923, war broke out within the Xiang Army between Tan Yankai and Zhao Hengti for control over Hunan. "The Northern Army" refers here to the forces of Wu Peifu, which were supporting Zhao Hengti.

5. Tan refers to Tan Yankai. (See the note to the text of December 3, 1920, on the incident of tearing down the flag, and also Mao's account of his faction in "Hunan under the Provincial Constitution" of July 1, 1923.) At the time Mao wrote this letter, Tan Yankai was engaged in an expedition against Zhao Hengti, which was ultimately unsuccessful because Wu Peifu came to Zhao's assistance. At the First National Congress of the Guomindang, he became a member of the Central Executive Committee and of the Central Political Council.

6. In August 1921, Wu Peifu and Zhao Hengti were waging a war for the territory of Hubei Province. Zhang Fulai, the frontline commander-in-chief of Wu Peifu's army, led his troops to defeat the Xiang Army, capturing Yuezhou in Hunan. Wu and Zhao then made a truce and negotiated peace in pursuit of their own respective interests. Wu stopped advancing southward after he gained favorable conditions that allowed him to garrison Yuezhou and hence easily check Zhao Hengti.

and Zhao would have to negotiate peace, and Zhao would be unable to hold his ground.

Concerning the matter of developing our party[7] in Hunan, which should still be actively carried on even during a period of military activity, I discussed yesterday with Comrade Xia Xi[8] (Xia Xi is very able and influential in the students' circles) a method for doing this in three steps. The first step would be to organize the Changsha branch; the second step would be to form the Changde, Hengzhou, and other possible subbranches; the third step, then, would be to form the Hunan general branch. As regards the Changsha branch, we have now decided to rent a house and set up a preparatory organ (secret) within the next few days to attract many people who believe in the Three People's Principles and have a capacity for action to join the party. Afterward, we will hold an inaugural meeting to elect a candidate for branch leader and apply to the Central Headquarters[9] for his appointment. The only extremely difficult problem is shortage of funds. Since the office is to be set up, it needs at least about a hundred *yuan* per month. We are now gathering together enthusiastic comrades to find a way to solicit contributions for our use. When I was in Shanghai, I asked the Central Headquarters to confer on me the title of preparatory agent (Xia Xi is the preparatory director) to facilitate making contacts in different quarters. Please send me the letter of appointment at an early date!

A letter from Comrades Sumin and Suzhong[10] and four copies of *Correspondence* have arrived. I shall act in accordance with your directions. *Correspondence* may have a better sale soon. Please send me in good time two copies of each issue of the *Bulletin of the Central Headquarters*, and also send me a complete set of all previous issues.

Your younger brother Zedong
September 28

---

7. The reference is to the Guomindang. As discussed in the Introduction to this volume, the Third National Congress of the Communist Party of China had adopted, in June 1923, a resolution in favor of cooperation with the Guomindang, including the provision that Communist Party members should join it as individuals. As evidenced by the letter of June 25, 1923, translated above, Mao Zedong had already done so by that time. In September 1923, Mao was working in his capacity as a member of the Guomindang for the development of the Guomindang party organization in Hunan. The first efforts to reestablish the Guomindang in the province after a lapse of nearly a decade had been made in April 1923 by Liu Shaoqi and Xia Xi (mentioned below). (See McDonald, *Urban Origins*, pp. 136–37.)

8. Regarding Xia Xi, see above, the note to the "Report on the Activities of the New People's Study Society" of December 1920. In early 1924, Xia was again sent to Hunan by the Guomindang to reorganize the party branch there.

9. Here Central Headquarters (*benbu*) refers to the highest leading bodies of the Guomindang at the time.

10. Suzhong refers to Xu Suzhong, who was the secretary of the Director General's Office of the Guomindang in 1923.

This letter will be brought to Hankou to mail by someone I trust. Because the censorship is extremely severe, please address me as Mao Shishan[11] instead of Mao Zedong when you write.

---

11. Shishan ("Stone Mountain") is the pseudonym under which Mao had written the long article of July 1, 1923, "Hunan under the Provincial Constitution."

Poem to the Tune of *"Congratulate the Groom"* [1]

(December 1923)[2]

A wave of the hand, and the moment of parting has come.[3]
Harder to bear is facing each other dolefully,
Bitter feelings voiced once more.
Wrath looks out of your eyes and brows,
On the verge of tears, you hold them back.
We know our misunderstanding sprang from that last letter.
Let it roll away like clouds and mist,
For who in this world is as close as you and I?
Can Heaven fathom our human maladies?
    I wonder.

This poem was first published in *Renmin ribao*, September 9, 1978. We have translated it from *Shici duilian*, pp. 10–13.

1. The title of this poem is what is called a "tune title" (*cipai*), conventionally attached to this type of classical poetry, and has nothing to do with the theme or expressions in the particular poem. Mao wrote it for his first wife, Yang Kaihui, as he left Changsha for Shanghai at the end of 1923, en route to the First National Congress of the Guomindang in Guangzhou. Nothing is known about the nature of the quarrel evoked in the poem. Yang Kaihui (1901–1930), *zi* Mingjun, a native of Hunan, was the daughter of Mao's ethics teacher at First Normal School, Yang Changji. (On Yang see, in Volume I, pp. 487–89, the obituary notice signed by Mao, and the many other references to him scattered throughout the volume.) Mao had married her in late 1920, after her father's death. Their eldest son, Mao Anying, had been born in October 1922, and the second son, Mao Anqing, in November 1923. Yang Kaihui joined Mao in Shanghai in June 1924, but from this time on, much of their time was spent apart. Yang Kaihui had joined the Chinese Communist Party in 1921, and in Hunan she engaged in revolutionary activities even after the break of 1927 between the Guomindang and the Communists, when she was living secretly in Changsha. In October 1930, following the unsuccessful onslaught of the Red Army against the city in the summer, she was captured by the authorities, and subsequently executed when she refused to renounce her marriage with Mao. Mao dedicated a moving poem to her memory in 1957, and in 1976–1978 her image served as a powerful symbol for mobilizing opinion against Jiang Qing.

2. In the Chinese text the poem is dated simply 1923, but all sources agree that it was written at the end of December. We therefore give that date.

3. Like most of Mao's poems, this one contains many classical allusions. The first line is taken from "Bidding Farewell to a Friend" (*Song youren*) by the celebrated Tang dynasty poet Li Bai, with the alteration of only one character.

This morning frost lies heavy on the road to East Gate,[4]
The waning moon lights up the pond[5] and half the sky—
How cold, how desolate!
One wail of the steam whistle has shattered my heart,
Now I shall roam alone to the uttermost ends of the earth.
Let us strive to sever those threads of grief and anger,
Let it be as though the sheer cliffs of Mount Kunlun collapsed,
And as though a typhoon swept through the whole universe.
Let us be once again two birds flying side by side,
Soaring high as the clouds.

---

4. East Gate is commonly used in classical Chinese poetry to denote a place to see someone off on a journey. In addition, the train station in Changsha was located outside the East Gate of the city.

5. The term Mao uses here for "pond," *hengtang*, originally referred to a causeway built in the state of Wu during the Three Kingdoms period. It is commonly used in classical poetry to mean the place where a woman lives, or a place where lovers part. It so happens as well that Mao and Yang Kaihui lived at the time on a pond at the eastern edge of Changsha.

——————————————————————1924——————————————————

Minutes of the [First] National Congress of the Chinese Guomindang

(Session 2, January 20, 1924, 2:00 P.M.)[1]

. . .

No. 106 Zhu Jixun: A nation must definitely have a government. Right now China has no government because Cao Kun's kind of government is not recognized by us. Therefore, China needs a regularly constituted government at this time. Just now, in discussing the organization of a government, the word "national"[2] was placed in front of government. I have grave doubts about this. For example, Britain has the British government and America has the U.S. government, and there is no reference to the British such-and-such government or the U.S. such-and-such government. Therefore, I suggest that when we organize our government, we call it the Government of the Republic of China, and not the National Government. We had better not put anything in front of government. Otherwise, it would be preferable to call it the "founding"[3] government; this would be grander and more appropriate.

No. 108 Jiang Weifan: In organizing a government, we must base ourselves in the first instance on the people's mentality. At present what the people all want is a good and properly constituted government. Therefore, when we organize the government we can inject the party's spirit into it, but as for its title, we should define it as a properly constituted government, and not use words such as "founding" or "national."

Our source for this text is the minutes of the First Congress, published in Guangzhou in 1924 under the title *Zhongguo Guomindang quanguo daibiao dahui huiyilu*, and reprinted in 1971 by the Center for Chinese Research Materials, Washington, D.C.

1. In this and other extracts from the proceedings of the First Guomindang Congress of 1924 and the Second Guomindang Congress of 1926, Mao's own remarks are sometimes limited to a few brief words. In certain cases, these are of substantive interest; in other instances, as in the present text, he merely makes a procedural point. All these contributions are, however, part of the record of his political career, and we have therefore included them here, adding enough of the context to make Mao's position comprehensible.

2. *Guomin*, as in Guomindang.

3. *Jianguo*, as in Sun Yatsen's *Jianguo dagang* (Fundamentals of National Reconstruction).

Chairman:[4] Now our time is running out. Please do not go beyond the two points of the motion when you discuss it.

No. 67 Ju Zheng:[5] This motion should be reviewed.

No. 39 Mao Zedong: This motion is entitled "The necessity of organizing a national government." It does not specify how to organize a government, or when. May I suggest to the chairman that we vote on the original heading?

No. 70 Hu Wencan: May I ask the chairman to put the heading of the resolution, "The necessity of organizing a national government," to the vote right now?

Chairman: This motion was a resolution. Now that we have concluded our discussions, we shall put it to vote. Those who are in favor of the motion, "The necessity of organizing a national government," please raise your hand. All are in favor, and it is so resolved.

---

4. Sun Yatsen.
5. Ju Zheng (1876–1951), *zi* Juesheng, *hao* Meichuan, was a native of Hubei Province. He studied in Japan, and there joined the Tongmenghui. In 1912 he was director of the Guomindang Liaison Bureau in Shanghai, and in 1919 he was appointed head of the party's Department of General Affairs and a member of the Military Committee. At the First Congress in January 1924 he was elected to the party's Central Executive Committee and to the Standing Committee. He opposed Sun Yatsen's policy of cooperation with the Communist Party, and because of this withdrew for a time from active participation in party affairs.

Minutes of the [First] National Congress of the Chinese Guomindang

(Session 11, January 25, 1924, 10:00 A.M.)

. . .

No. 133 Dai Jitao:[1] I would like to call your attention to the so-called procedures, by which I mean those that have already been decided by the Central Executive Committee. The most important point of the entire report is the last paragraph at the end of the conclusion of the review.[2] Please pay attention to the whole text.

No. 39 Mao Zedong: May I suggest that the chairman[3] put the entire text of the conclusion of the review to a vote?

Chairman: Are there any objections to our voting on the entire text of the conclusion of the review? (All said, "No.")

Chairman: Let all those who are in favor of the entire text of the conclusions to the reviews raise their hands. (Majority.) It is so resolved.

This text has been translated from the same source as that dated January 20, 1924.

1. Dai Jitao (1891–1949), *zi* Chuanxian, *hao* Tianchou, was a native of Sichuan. He studied law in Japan and while there founded the Chinese Students' Association. On his return to China he joined the Tongmenghui and was active in opposition to the Qing. He became Sun Yatsen's personal secretary in September 1912 and held that position until Sun's death in 1925. Dai disapproved of the Guomindang-Communist alliance and was at first unwilling to attend the January 1924 Congress. He was nonetheless elected to the Central Executive Committee and the Central Political Council, and also became head of the party's Propaganda Department. In May 1924 he was named director of the Huangpu (Whampoa) Military Academy, but only held this post for a few months. After Sun's death he was outspokenly anti-Communist.

2. The matter under discussion at this time was the report of the Review Committee on Propaganda regarding the problem of publication and propaganda. The conclusion to this report presumably contained concrete policy recommendations. The debate before Dai Jitao and Mao intervened had turned on whether or not *duifu* should be replaced by the slightly less forceful term of *yingfu* to convey the idea of "responding" to Chinese and foreign criticisms of the Guomindang. It was no doubt impatience with such linguistic hairsplitting that provoked Mao's proposal that the congress come to the point, and vote.

3. This session was chaired by Hu Hanmin. On Hu, see below, the note to the session of January 28.

Minutes of the [First] National Congress of the Chinese Guomindang

(Session 12, January 28, 10:00 A.M.)

. . .

No. 105 Fang Ruilin: . . . I advocate adding, after Chapter 1, article 2 [of the statutes], an article reading: "Members of this party may not join any other party."

Chairman: Does anyone second Mr. Fang's proposal? (There are more than ten seconders.)

Member of the Presidium Li Shouchang:[1] [Mounts the platform and says in essence] I want to state on behalf of the Third International and of the Communist Party that if all of our comrades join this party, it is to obey the principles of this party, observe the statutes of the party, and participate in the revolutionary cause of the Guomindang. It is absolutely not with a view to turning the Guomindang into the Communist Party, but in order that members of the Third International and of the Communist Party, in their individual capacity, may join the Guomindang and work effectively for the cause of national revolution. We wish, moreover, to be guided in all things by comrades of the older generation.

. . .

Member of the Presidium Hu Hanmin:[2] [Mounts the platform and says in essence] I have been listening to your debates, and in reality, there is not that much disagreement. The focal point of the discussion lies in the fear that our party's doctrine or ethos, or its statutes, may be violated. These concerns merely

---

This text has been translated from the same source as that dated January 20, 1924.

　　1. Li Dazhao.

　　2. Hu Hanmin (1879–1936), *zi* Zhantang, *hao* Bukui Shizhu, was a native of Guangdong. He studied briefly in Japan and was an early member of the Tongmenghui. In 1911 he was appointed governor of Guangdong, and in 1917 he was named minister of communications in the new government headed by Sun Yatsen, later moving to Shanghai where he was active in disseminating Sun's ideas. At the First Congress in January 1924, Hu was appointed head of the Shanghai Executive Bureau of the Guomindang, of which Mao was named as an alternate member.

need to be dealt with in terms of discipline, and it will be all right. There are already special chapters on these matters, so it seems that we do not need to add articles to the statutes specifying which kinds of behavior should be banned. We only need to explain clearly the importace of discipline.

No. 39 Mao Zedong: Please put this to a vote.

Chairman: Now let's put it to the vote that there should be no specific regulations in the statutes that do not allow party members to join other parties. We only need to stress the importance of discipline and that will suffice. Those who are in favor, please raise your hand. (Majority.) It is so resolved.

Minutes of the [First] National Congress of the Chinese Guomindang

(Session 14, January 29, 1924, 10:00 A.M.)

. . .

Chairman:[1] Now we will discuss the first motion, "Our party should set up a research department." May I ask the person who made this motion to give his explanations, please?

No. 41 Tan Xihong: [Mounts the platform and says in essence] Our party has always emphasized putting things into practice, but on the other hand, it should emphasize research. That is why I proposed this motion. (1) Motive: Before our party determines its tactics and its attitude toward various important national and international political, economic, and social issues, we should carry out thorough studies. The party should assign comrades with special skills in various fields of knowledge to organize the research department and study each issue individually. (2) Duties: No action should be taken on those problems that it has been agreed should be studied until they have been studied by the research department. Only in the case of those problems that have already been studied should it be left to the executive bureaus to decide whether action should be taken. (3) Organization: For the time being, the research department will be divided into three branches: political, economic, and social. One person will be made responsible for each branch, under whom an indefinite number of researchers will be placed. There will also be a head of the research department, who will be responsible for all the affairs of the department. The locations of the department and its branches should be determined by the locations of the researchers. Since I think this motion is closely related to the party's future, I ask you all to discuss it.

Chairman: Are there any views?

No. 4 Shen Dingyi:[2] I agree to a large extent with the motion. The first three points in the motion may be kept, but the fourth point should be removed,

---

This text has been translated from the same source as that dated Janaury 20, 1924.

1. Lin Sen.
2. Shen Dingyi (1892–1928) was a progressive publicist in Shanghai in the early 1920s, a founding member of the Chinese Communist Party, and an instructor at Shanghai University. In August 1923 he participated in the mission sent by Sun Yatsen to the Soviet

because it should be dealt with by the Central Executive Committee. If we take it away from the Central Executive Committee, I am afraid things cannot be done systematically. I think the content of research should be determined by the research department, but the means of implementation should be determined by the Central Executive Committee.

No. 39 Mao Zedong: I am against this motion because its basic idea is to separate application from research. This, however, is something that our party, as a revolutionary party, cannot do. In my opinion, we can accept the spirit of this motion, but the article as it stands should not be adopted.

No. 27 Zhang Qiubai: I am rather in favor of this motion. The nature of this motion is similar to that of a special committee. Whenever there is a need in a particular locality, a special committee should be established. But it should be under the jurisdiction of the Central Executive Committee. It may only offer ideas to the Central Executive Committee for it to take action on them. Though the specific means may be regulated separately, the main ideas should not be violated. It will be a great shame if we kill this motion right away.

No. 41 Tan Xihong: I would like to clarify two points: (1) This motion does not separate research from application, and was never intended to do so. (2) As for the way to organize, I have also said that it is not fixed because I don't quite understand the organization of the Central Executive Committee yet.

No. 93 Yuan Dashi: I am opposed to this motion because it will seriously interfere with application. When problems arise, they should be handed over to the Propaganda Department to be dealt with.

No. 41 Tan Xihong: There should be no hindrance at all to application. For only if no action is taken without detailed studies can we avoid hasty and ill-considered actions.

No. 124 Xia Xi:[3] I do not think this motion should be passed. Because the Central Executive Committee is our party's highest organ, there should be no other separate organizations in addition to it trying to organize application and research.

No. 41 Tan Xihong: I do not mean at all that some people will be only engaged in research and not in application. There are some among our party members

---

Union to study Soviet military institutions and obtain Soviet aid. At the First Congress in January 1924 he was one of seven Communists, including Mao, to be elected as alternate members of the Central Executive Committee. He later joined the right wing of the Guomindang.

3. Xia Xi was one of the nine-member Hunan delegation that attended this First Congress of the Guomindang in January 1924. In March 1924 he was appointed senior Guomindang official in Hunan. At the Second Guomindang Congress in January 1926 he was elected an alternative member of the Central Executive Committee.

who are especially skilled in research. Either the Director General or the Central Executive Committee may appoint these people to do research. Meanwhile, they can all carry out application at the same time. There is actually no division into two.

No. 128 Chen Yougeng: I am in favor of this motion because research and application do not hinder each other, but rather complement each other. Before any application, the methods to be adopted have to be studied, especially in the case of specialized problems. As for ordinary problems, they do not need to be studied before application. I suggest that a research department be set up and whenever important issues are brought to our attention, they can be handed over to the research department for study.

No. 132 Fu Rulin:[4] I am in favor of this motion because in our present society people are idol worshippers and follow blindly. They do not really understand the potential pitfalls. Therefore all things should be studied clearly. It is not right that we hand over any problems that may arise to the Propaganda Department.

No. 133 Dai Jitao: We have had much discussion over this motion. I do not think that this motion needs to be passed by the Plenary Session. It should be dealt with rather by the Central Executive Committee, because it involves so many factors such as personnel, finances, organizations, and so on, which cannot be voted on by the Congress. Moreover, the party has decided to set up a university, a printing office, a party newspaper, and so on in Shanghai, and the research staff will have to be placed under one of these three organs. Therefore, I feel we do not have to set up a separate research department. As long as the Central Executive Committee is capable of dealing with it, everything will be all right.

Chairman: Any more discussion? (Everyone said no.)

Chairman: If there is no more discussion on this, I will put it to the vote. As a result of the discussions, there are four positions: (1) Those who are opposed to the motion; (2) Those who are in favor; (3) Those who think the matter should be dealt with by the Central Executive Committee; and (4) Those who are in basic agreement with the original motion, except for leaving out item four concerning the location of the research department. First I would like to put Delegate Dai's suggestion to the vote: "This should not be voted on by the Congress, but rather be handed over to the Central Executive Committee to be dealt with." Those who are in favor, please raise your hand. (Majority.) Passed.

. . .

---

4. Fu Rulin (1895–1985), *zi* Mubo, was born in Heilongjiang Province. He was a graduate of Beijing University and an early member of the Guomindang. At the First Congress he was elected an alternate member of the Central Executive Committee.

No. 50 Huang Jilu:[5] The system of proportional representation can eliminate the corrupt practices of the present electoral system. For in essence, under the present electoral system the majority oppresses the minority. Under the system of proportional representation, each can develop in accordance with his own strength, and there will be no points of conflict. . . .

. . .

I am not proposing a motion. This is something I bring up for inclusion in the political platform. Please put it to a vote.

Chairman: Once it has been decided, it can be left to the Central Executive Committee to adopt and implement. I now invite Delegate Wang Heng to speak.

No. 155 Wang Heng: [Mounts the platform and speaks as summarized below] I am in favor of this suggestion. I think the current elections should absolutely adopt the proportional representation system so that all the pitfalls that have been incurred by the domestic, provincial, and national elections may be eliminated. This is indeed a splendid opportunity. Elections are the first step toward a peaceful movement. In order to win the right to speak in Parliament, there ought to be competition in elections. But the opportunities for competition should not strengthen the stronger and weaken the weaker, thus forming a pyramid. Therefore I am basically in favor of this suggestion. There is one more thing: This suggestion is in total harmony with our party's principle of people's livelihood. Please pay special attention to this and let it be passed.

No. 133 Dai Jitao: I think this suggestion is of grave significance because it is closely related to our party's political platform. Moreover, the contents of this suggestion are quite complicated. If we put the conclusions of today's brief discussion to the vote, it will be quite inappropriate. I suggest that we place this suggestion on the agenda of next year's congress as one of the motions definitely to be discussed.

No. 71 Liu Luyin: The system of proportional representation is one of the principles and aims of people's rights. The methods vary. As to which methods to follow, we need to study the matter carefully. It is not an issue we have to face right now. I dare not go along with Mr. Dai's idea to table it until next year. I suggest that we put to the vote the principle of a proportional representation system in this session. As for the methods, we may leave them for the Central Executive Committee to study and work out in the long run.

---

5. Huang Jilu (1899–1985) was a native of Sichuan Province. He joined the Western Hills faction in September 1925, and was elected to the rival Guomindang Central Executive Committee convened by the rightists in Shanghai in March 1926.

No. 39 Mao Zedong: The current proportional representation system is the result of proposals put forward by the minority parties. Our party, being a revolutionary party, should adopt measures conducive to the revolution, but reject those detrimental to revolution. The proportional representation system is detrimental to the revolutionary party because once a minority gets elected they will have the power to sabotage the revolutionary cause. This is to offer an opportunity to the minority factions. I am absolutely opposed to this motion. We should neither discuss it nor put it to a vote.

No. 85 Xuan Zhonghua: The proportional representation system is actually a trick of the bourgeoisie. I am against Mr. Huang's proposal.

No. 50 Huang Jilu: I have to clarify that the proportional representation system does not represent the bourgeoisie, nor is it detrimental to the revolutionary cause. It is actually representative of the politics of the whole people. Since you two gentlemen have thus spoken, I can't help but say something in defense of the proportional representation system.

No. 85 Xuan Zhonghua: I oppose this motion because our party advocates that the party should build the nation and rule the state. The proportional representation system is fundamentally incompatible with this.

No. 39 Mao Zedong: Although the Socialist Party is in favor of the system of proportional representation, this is only the case before it succeeds; once it succeeds, it will no longer hold the same opinion. This system is extremely harmful to the revolution, for once freedom is given to the opposition party it will put the cause of revolution in great danger.

No. 133 Dai Jitao: Since I have foreseen that this proposal could not be put to the vote quickly, I have suggested that it should be tabled for next year's congress. Please pay attention to this.

Chairman: Please also note that the Director General has divided the application of the [Three People's] Principles into three periods: the period of military government, the period of political tutelage, and the period of constitutional government.

No. 70 Liu Luyin: The proportional representation system is not conducive to capitalism but, rather, to socialism. As for the argument that it is detrimental to our party, this is not a problem either, because there are three periods: the period of military government, the period of political tutelage, and the constitutional period. It is only a matter of time. Please do not confuse these matters.

No. 176 Wang Leping: I have two points to make regarding this suggestion: (1) This suggestion affects the political platform. Since the platform has been passed in the declaration and cannot be revised during this congress, it can only be tabled until next year's congress; and (2) It has been laid down in our party's platform that we would have general elections. I once had a question about this and inquired of the Declaration Review Committee. According to them, it was only a formality. Because our party is in the periods of military administration and political tutelage, such an election method, of course, is not applicable. Later the Director General added a program to regulate various examination systems to complement the shortcomings of the election system. From this we can see that, at the present time, only the system of election through examinations is appropriate. All other election methods are not applicable.

No. 97 Hu Qian: There should be room to study various election systems. The proportional representation system suggested by Delegate Huang just now might be advantageous in Europe and the United States, but whether it will work within the Chinese Revolutionary Party needs to be studied. Moreover, our party advocates the five-power Constitution with an emphasis on the examination system. The spirit of this suggestion and that of the five-power Constitution advocated by the Director General are in fundamental conflict. Therefore, I am basically against this suggestion.

No. 13 Liu Bolun: I second Delegate Dai's motion that this suggestion be tabled until next year's congress. For the platform has already been passed in the declaration. If this suggestion gets established, the platform will need to be revised, and this will definitely affect all the other motions that have been passed. But only the Director General has the right to ask that a proposal already passed be reviewed, and it cannot be revised at the same congress. Please understand this.

Chairman: Is there any more discussion? (All said no.)

Chairman: I now proclaim the end of the discussion regarding this suggestion. There are three options: (1) Opposed, (2) In favor, and (3) To be tabled. Let us first vote on Delegate Dai's motion, "To table this suggestion until next year's congress, to be one of the motions that must be discussed at that time." Those who are in favor of this, please raise your hand. (Majority.) It is thus resolved.

Fourth Meeting of the Central Party Bureau of the Chinese Guomindang

(February 9, 1924)

The minutes of the third meeting were read out.

Items for discussion:

1. Proposal for supplementing the expense funds of the major city, *xian*, and district party offices. (Put forward by Mao Zedong.)[1]

Justification: Expense funds should certainly not be used only for party offices at the two high levels of center and provinces (which are hollow offices). Without supplementary funding, the city and *xian* party offices and the district party offices (the real party offices) will definitely find it hard to manage, and will have difficulty in developing. For the monthly dues collected from party members suffice, at most, to meet the expenses of the district branch offices (the living costs and the cost of the activities of the district branch committee). They cannot provide for the district party offices, much less for the city or *xian* party offices. And yet it is the city and *xian* offices, as well as the district offices, that are the most decisive organs by which our party directs the activities of party members. If these two levels of the party are not strong, the entire party will inevitably lose its strength. Only if the expense supplements were generally too large, or if supplements were given to party offices in unimportant remote areas, would they be senseless. Expense supplements should be given selectively to city and *xian* party offices and district party offices that are doing real work in the mass movements among workers, peasants, students, merchants, etc. Expense supplements are needed more urgently by these party offices than by provincial party offices. (If provincial party offices are not at the same time the city party offices where they are located, then there is even less reason for large expense allocations for their use alone.)

This text appeared in *Zhongguo Guomindang zhoukan* No. 9, February 24, 1924. We have translated it from *Mao Zedong ji. Bujuan*, Vol. 2, pp. 125–26.

1. Mao had also attended the first three meetings of this organ, on January 31, February 1, and February 6. He left for Shanghai in mid-February to join the Shanghai Bureau of the Guomindang.

Resolved: Send to the Budget Committee for review.

2. Proposal that before the end of this year, all provincial party offices should at the same time administer the city party offices where they are located, and the central and the local executive offices should concurrently administer the special district party offices where they are located. (Put forward by Mao Zedong.)

Resolved: According to the regulations on organization, this proposal cannot be passed.

3. Proposal that when the Central Executive Committee and the local executive offices are effectively organized, attention should be paid to real needs. (Put forward by Mao Zedong.)

Justification: The Central Executive Committee and the four executive offices in Beijing, Shanghai, Ha'erbin, and Hankou are to have a total staff of more than sixty at the organizational and administrative level and above. Within half a year after the congress, a staff this large should definitely not be established. The reasons are as follows. (1) Local party work has only just begun, so the work of the Central [Executive Committee] and of the executive offices cannot be that great. (2) All our energies should be concentrated on developing lower-level party offices, and the human resources of the party should not all be concentrated in the higher party organs. (3) This many useful people can certainly not be found immediately, and it would make no sense to fill a quota indiscriminately. Consequently, when the time comes actually to organize the Central [Executive Committee] and the local executive offices, attention should be paid their actual needs. Open an office only where an office is really needed, and hire someone only when that person is needed.

Resolved: Send to the Central Executive Committee for consideration.

4. Proposal that by the end of this year a plan should be established for local organizing according to the importance and urgency of each place. (Put forward by Mao Zedong.)

Justification: Local organizing should not be spread around broadly; we should select a few important places, establish a plan, and concentrate our human and financial resources for the current year to focus solely and firmly on these places. If we grasp this key thread, then by the time of the Second Congress we will be able to see some real results. The places on which we should focus our energies this year should be divided into two levels of priority. On the first level are up to eight or nine of those places that are most important and that have the potential for development today, such as Shanghai, Beijing, Guangzhou, Hankou, Ha'erbin, and so on. Seventy percent of our strength (our human and financial resources) should be devoted to such places. On the second level are those eleven or twelve places of secondary importance and in which there is today an opportunity to get involved, such as Taiyuan, Hangzhou, Nanchang, and so on. We should devote 30 percent of our force to such places. Aside from these, during the current year, we can ignore all those places where the opportunities are nil, to avoid dispersing our energies to no good result.

Resolved: Send to the Central Executive Committee for consideration.

(Proposals that follow, put forward by others, are omitted here.)

Memo from the Organization Department of the [Shanghai] Executive Bureau [of the Guomindang] to Comrade Shouyuan

(March 31, 1924)

Comrade Shouyuan:[1]

We have seen the report of the Fifth Subdistrict of the Third District, and from it we have learned that Mao Yongxun[2] and Tan Liming[3] of the executive committee [of this subdistrict] are also members of the Central Committee. According to the statutes, it is not permitted [for Central Committee members] to occupy posts concurrently in subdistrict offices. Please hold another election.[4]

The source for this memo is a manuscript document held in the Guomindang archives in Taibei, as copied by Professor Yeh Wen-hsin of the University of California at Berkeley, in the course of her research on the Shanghai Executive Bureau. Professor Yeh has kindly made the Chinese text available to us, and has also provided the information regarding the Third District which appears in the first footnote. In the document itself, authorship is attributed simply to the Organization Department of the Shanghai Bureau, but Professor Yeh has no doubt that the original is in Mao Zedong's hand. That would, in any case, be a reasonable supposition, since Mao was, as indicated in the Introduction to this volume, the secretary of the Organization Department.

1. We have been unable to identify this individual, who was obviously an official of the district or of the subdistrict concerned. The Third District, one of a number which existed at this time in Shanghai, corresponded to the French Concession. A high proportion of the members there were Guomindang veterans not in sympathy with the transformation of their party inaugurated at the First Congress. Of all the subdistricts the fifth was regarded as the worst, and had already been criticized by the Executive Bureau for failure to submit a roster of members as required by the party statutes.

2. Mao Zuquan (1883-1952), *zi* Yongxun, a native of Jiangsu, was elected a member of Parliament in April 1913. At the First Congress of the Guomindang he was elected an alternate member of the Central Executive Committee, and at the first meeting of the Shanghai Executive Bureau on February 25, 1924, he had been appointed head of the Investigation Department. He was thus a close colleague of Mao Zedong.

3. Tan Zhen (1885-1947), *zi* Liming, a native of Hunan, was a founding member of the Tongmenghui. In 1913, he was elected to Parliament. From 1918 to 1924, he worked to establish a political base for the Guomindang in Guangdong, and at the First Congress in January 1924, he was elected a full member of the Central Executive Committee.

4. It is of interest to note that, at the Second Congress in January 1926, Mao successfully proposed that this provision of the statutes be modified to allow Central Committee members to serve simultaneously on lower-level party organs, with the authorization of the Central Committee. See below, the extracts from the record of the Second Congress, and the note regarding this point.

Letter to the Committee for Common People's Education

(May 26, 1924)

Comrades of the Committee for Common People's Education:

Because my mental ailment has been daily growing worse, and because of the burden of work in the Organization Department and the Secretariat, it is truly difficult for me to acquit myself of my duties as a member of the Standing Committee of the Commitee for Common People's Education.[1] I beg you to accept my resignation, and to appoint another person in my place. I have asked Comrade Liu Bolun to deputize for me at the meeting of the Standing Committee to be held today.

Mao Zedong

The source for this letter is a copy of the Chinese text made in the late 1960s by a scholar who prefers to remain anonymous. The original in Mao's hand was located at that time in the Guomindang archives.

1. By "mental ailment" [*naobing*] (a term which he also used in the letter of February 14, 1926, translated below), Mao presumably meant simply that he was under great strain. He did indeed have a crushing workload. At the first meeting of the Shanghai Executive Bureau of the Guomindang, which took place on February 25, 1924, the day before he wrote this letter, Mao had been appointed secretary of the bureau's Organization Department and acting head of the documents section of the Secretariat, in which capacity he had kept the minutes of the meeting. In addition to these new responsibilities in the Guomindang, he had been, since the Third Congress of the Chinese Communist Party in 1923, secretary of the Central Bureau and head of the Organization Department of that party. Mao Zedong had been involved in education for the masses since his school days. (See the materials of 1917 regarding a workers' night school translated in Volume I of this edition, pp. 143–56.) In 1922 he had organized a movement for common people's education (*pingmin jiaoyu*, also translated as mass education or popular education) in Hunan, which served as cover for making contact with labor circles in Anyuan and elsewhere. (On this, see Li Jui, *Early Mao*, pp. 185–88.) The committee from which he resigned on this occasion was one set up by the Shanghai Executive Bureau of the Guomindang at its second meeting on March 6, 1924.

The Struggle Against the Right Wing of the Guomindang

(Central[1] Circular no. 15)

(July 21, 1924)

To all the comrades of each district committee and local committee, and comrade leaders of each independent group:

It is very important, and at the same time extremely difficult, to work within the Guomindang. All of us in different localities must be constantly alert and keep making efforts!

Since the convening of the Enlarged Meeting of the Central Executive Committee of our Party,[2] overt and covert attacks on us and attempts to push us out have been mounting daily on the part of a majority of Guomindang members. The aim is to expel us radical elements, so that the great powers and warlords will mitigate their pressure on the Guomindang. At present only a very few Guomindang leaders, such as Sun Yatsen and Liao Zhongkai,[3] have not yet made

---

Our translation is based on *Zhonggong zhongyang wenjian xuanji*, Vol. 1, 1921–1925, pp. 282–84, where the text is followed by the indication "based on the original document in the Central Party Archives."

1. "Central" (*zhongyang*) refers here to the Central Bureau, speaking in the name of the Central Executive Committee.

2. The reference is to the First Enlarged Session of the Central Executive Committee of the Chinese Communist Party, which took place in Shanghai on May 10–15, 1924. On this occasion, much of the discussion was devoted to the role of Communists within the Guomindang. Broadly speaking, the policies decided on called for supporting and strengthening the left wing of the Guomindang and for carrying out propaganda against imperialism and the warlords, against landlord oppression of the peasants, and in favor of democratic rights. See above, the Introduction, for further details about this gathering.

3. Liao Zhongkai (1878–1925), originally Liao Enxu, was born in San Francisco and received his early education in the United States. In 1902 he went to Japan to study political economy. There he met Sun Yatsen and joined the Tongmenghui. He returned to China with Sun in March 1916. By 1921 he was the Guomindang's leading financial expert and chief fund-raiser for the party's military campaigns. He was a close ally of Sun Yatsen, and with him was a chief architect of the Guomindang-Communist alliance. At the First Congress of the reorganized Guomindang in January 1924, he was elected to the Central Executive Commitee, and shortly thereafter he was appointed Guomindang repre-

up their mind to separate from us, but they also certainly do not wish to offend the right-wing elements. They have decided to call a plenary session of the Central Executive Committee in the fall to resolve their relationship with us. For the sake of uniting the revolutionary forces, we must absolutely not allow any separatist words or actions to emerge on our side, and we must try our best to be tolerant and cooperate with them. Nevertheless, considering the Guomindang's revolutionary mission, we cannot tolerate nonrevolutionary rightist policies without correcting them. What we should do is as follows:

(1) Every organization or local party section of the Guomindang that is under our direction should express its dissatisfaction with the rightists to the Central Executive Committee of the Guomindang. The major mistakes committed by the right are:

(a) not wanting to oppose the imperialist great powers;

(b) opposing the Sino-Russian Agreement[4] and, moreover, opposing Soviet Russia, which is said to be the enemy of the Guomindang;

(c) repressing the munitions factory workers who try to organize labor unions and obstructing students of Holy Trinity from leaving the school;[5]

(d) conniving with the Merchants' Corps in Jiangmen and Fushan in trampling on the workers and peasants;

(e) rejecting the Communists.

(2) Our comrades should launch discussions in the party meetings at all levels of the Guomindang on the difference between the political views of the left and the right.

---

sentative at the Huangpu (Whampoa) Military Academy. In July 1925, when the national government was established in Guangdong, Liao became a member of the Government Council and of the Military Council. Many Guomindang conservatives resented the concentration of so much power in his hands, and saw this as a sign of the victory of the left wing, of which Liao was regarded as a leader. As a result, he was assassinated on August 20, 1925.

4. On May 31, 1924, the Soviet Union signed a treaty with the Beijing government that normalized diplomatic relations between the two states and recognized Chinese sovereignty over Outer Mongolia. The Soviet Union renounced in principle its extraterritorial privileges and concessions in China. A separate agreement provided for the "provisional administration" of the Chinese Eastern Railway (pending its eventual redemption by China) by a joint Sino-Russian board, with a chief manager of Soviet nationality.

5. The Holy Trinity College, located in Guangzhou, was established and administered by the Anglican Church. Beginning in April 1924, its students rose up in protest against the "enslaving education" and "imperialist oppression and indoctrination" perpetrated by their British "masters." The college authorities retaliated by declaring an early recess, forbidding the organization of a student association, and expelling student leaders. The students, in turn, launched a movement of strikes and then withdrawal from missionary schools, which in the ensuing months spread to other parts of the country and to schools run by American and French missionaries as well.

(3) From now on, we must not recommend for party membership of the Guomindang anyone who does not manifest a left-wing orientation.

(4) We must strive to win or maintain in our own hands "the real power of leading all organizations of workers, peasants, students, and citizens," in order to consolidate our strength within the left wing of the Guomindang, and vigorously oppose an invasion of these organizations by right-wing forces.

(5) It is urgent in all regions to establish the "People's Association for Foreign Affairs," which will on the one hand serve as the heart of the anti-imperialist alliance, and on the other hand prepare the ground for the crystallization of the Guomindang left or a possible new Guomindang in the future.[6] This organization must accept only individual members, who must fill in application forms at the time of joining; people must on no account be allowed to join in groups. There is no need at present to be eager for an increase in the number of new members, but we ought to pay attention to clearly defined quality. Here the most important criterion must be disapproval of the views of the Guomindang rightists. This association is an independent body in the social movement. It must not be mixed up with Guomindang organizations, still less be controlled by the Guomindang. Only in those places where the Guomindang is not an open party, and its local organizations are entirely created by us, can we work openly under the name of this association. We must, however, absolutely not allow anyone with right-wing ideas to remain within it.

All district committees, local committees, and leaders of independent groups are asked, after receiving this circular, to discuss it and carry it out effectively in the light of local conditions, and report in detail to the Central Executive Committee on the circumstances of discussion and implementation. This circular must be kept strictly secret from outsiders.

Chairman: T. S. Chen
Secretary: T. T. Mao[7]

---

6. In the report of the Shanghai office of the Chinese Communist Party to the Enlarged Plenum of May 1924, it was stated that "Citizens' Associations for Foreign Affairs" (*Shimin waijiao xiehui*) were already in existence in the city. Here, in the discussion of the problem on the national level, the term employed is *Guomin duiwai xiehui*. It is not known what role Mao may have played in creating such organizations for mobilizing the masses in Shanghai, or whether the "People's Associations" he advocated in 1924 owed anything to the precedent of the "Society for Supporting the Conduct of Foreign Policy" active in Hunan in 1923. (See above, the relevant note to the text of August 15, 1923.)

7. The names appear in Roman script on the Chinese original. The initials correspond to the given names of the signatories in the transcription they commonly used at the time: Tse-tung Mao and Tu-siu Chen. Mao, as noted above, had been elected secretary of the Central Bureau at the Third Congress in June 1923. Chen Duxiu was the chairman.

On the Question of Opposing the War between the Warlords of Jiangsu and Zhejiang

(Central Circular no. 17)

(September 10, 1924)

The war being waged between Jiangsu and Zhejiang[1] is clearly one manifestation of the struggle between warlords for territory and of the manipulation of Chinese politics by international imperialism. Any words and deeds in favor of whatever side of the war serve to boost the arrogance of the oppressive forces at the expense of the interests of the people. Our proper task during the present war is simply to expose the true nature and context of the war to the people, letting the people know that there is no way to achieve peace in China under this twofold oppression. Every time, the chaotic wars among warlords only increased the suffering and enslavement of the populace. People cannot pin their hopes, to the slightest extent, on any wars between warlords, and the only chance of saving China is the national revolution. We should make the most of this war as concrete teaching material, and work even harder to make propaganda in favor of the national revolution and to arouse the popular masses to organize the veritable force of the national revolution! The Central Bureau has decided to issue a declaration on the current political situation in this connection, making known our Party's position on the present war! The declaration is already being printed and will be sent to all localities within the next few days. Our Party organizations at different levels should give orders immediately after receiving this circular that all Party members must go into action; they must on no account let matters drift, and relinquish this incomparable opportunity of conducting propaganda!

Our translation is based on *Zhonggong zhongyang wenjian xuanji*, Vol. 1, 1921–1925, pp. 285–86, where the text is followed by the indication "based on the original document in the Central Party Archives."

1. This war had broken out on September 1, 1924. The military governor of Jiangsu, Qi Xieyuan (1897–1946), *zi* Fuwan, was a native of Hebei, and a member of the Zhili faction. Lu Yongxiang, the military governor of Zhejiang, was supported both by Zhang Zuolin of the Fengtian faction and by Sun Yatsen in Guangzhou. The immediate object of their clash was control of Shanghai and Songjiang, over which Lu claimed authority though they were part of Jiangsu Province. For details of this complicated struggle, which involved most of the leading warlords in China and ended in the defeat and exile of Lu Yongxiang, see Li Chien-nung, *Political History of China*, pp. 468–70.

As for our approach in this work, all activities must be in line with the instructions given in this circular and in the declaration. If there are Party organs at any level or individuals speaking or acting independently, they would be regarded without exception as violators of Party discipline.

Chairman: T. S. Chen
Secretary: T. T. Mao

Strengthening Party Work and Our Position on Sun Yatsen's Attendance at the Northern Peace Conference

(Central Circular no. 21)

(November 1, 1924)

To leading comrades of each prefectural committee, district committee, and small group:

The resolution of the last Enlarged Plenum and several previous documents issued by the Central Bureau have repeatedly stressed the point that inner-party organizational work is the central task of the Party, with which all internal and external developments are closely related. Recently Party work has become heavier day by day, but inner-party organization has made no outstanding progress. Some local committees have not reported [to the Central Bureau] for a long time. Some others have sent reports, but they are either completely unsystematic or just too brief, and therefore give no clear idea of the progress of the work. If such a careless attitude continues, it will have very bad effects. Notice is hereby given once again to every comrade in a responsible position that in the days to come he must be sure to pay particular attention to putting this matter right, and at the very least accomplish the following tasks:

1. Group and local meetings must be held as usual without interruption.
2. At the meetings, concrete political questions should be constantly raised for discussion in order to educate each comrade on the basis of our stand stated in the official organ of our Party.
3. Responsible Party headquarters or group leaders should design work, assign jobs to all comrades, and train each of them to be a truly capable Party member.
4. Directives from the Central Bureau should be immediately laid before a

---

Our translation is based on *Zhonggong zhongyang wenjian xuanji*, Vol. 1, 1921–1925, pp. 299–300, where the text is followed by the indication "based on the original document in the Central Party Archives."

meeting for discussion whenever they arrive, and should be put into effect as far as possible. Any obstacles that may be encountered during implementation, and the result, must be reported to the Central [Bureau].

5. Committee or group leaders should report to the Central [Bureau] at least once a week on the work done during that week.

6. The report ought not to be unduly sketchy, but should give a systematic explanation of the details of every item of your work.

Chairman: T. S. Chen
Secretary: T. T. Mao

P.S. (Nov. 6) After sending out this circular, the Central Bureau has slightly changed its policy. Now we have no fundamental objection to Sun Yatsen's participation in the Northern Peace Conference,[1] but would seriously admonish him to speak at the conference in conformity with the Party Program and the Political Program of the Guomindang, as well as the Manifesto on the Northern Expedition, and to expose the plot of the imperialists and warlords to act in collusion at the conference for invading and ruling China.

---

1. On November 2, 1924, Cao Kun, who in the previous year had forced Li Yuanhong to resign as president and taken his place, was himself compelled to abandon the presidency and placed under house arrest by Feng Yuxiang. Feng, Duan Qirui, and Zhang Zuolin met in Tianjin on November 19 and organized a new government with Duan Qirui as provisional chief executive. Together, they sent Sun Yatsen an invitation to come to the north to discuss plans for national peace. The Guomindang was at first divided: the left-wing and Communist members objected, fearing that Sun might make too many concessions; the right-wing and conservative members favored a compromise with the northern warlords in order to further the party's political power. Sun Yatsen left Guangdong on November 13, 1924, and arrived in Beijing on December 31, 1924, via Shanghai, Japan, and Tianjin.

Changsha
(To the Tune of "Spring in Qin Garden")[1]

(Autumn)

I stand alone in the autumn cold,
Where the River Xiang flows northward,
At Orange Island's head.[2]
I see a myriad peaks all red,
Dyed through and through by serried woods;
On the wide stream's limpid blue-green waters,
A hundred boats battle the current.
Eagles strike at the endless void,
Fish hover in the shallow bottoms,
All creatures strive for freedom under the frosty sky.

Baffled by this immensity,
I ask the vast expanse of earth,
Who, then, controls the rise and fall of fortunes?

Hand-in-hand with all my companions, I roamed this place in the past.
Now I call to mind those glorious years and days of old.
School friends just in the prime of youth,[3]
We were then at life's full flowering;

This poem was first published in the January 1957 issue of *Shikan.* We have translated it from *Shici duilian*, pp. 14–17.

1. On the convention of "tune title"*(cipai),* see above, the note to Mao's 1923 poem for his wife, Yang Kaihui. Qin Garden refers to the garden of Princess Qin Shui of the Western Han dynasty.

2. Orange Island is a narrow strip of land to the west of Changsha, in the middle of Hunan's largest river, the Xiang. Mao and his youthful companions frequented the place to enjoy the scenery and to swim in the river.

3. This is very likely an allusion to the third of Du Fu's famous "Eight Autumn Meditations" *(Qiuxing bashou).* Mao uses the same four characters as Du Fu to refer to his youthful schoolmates: *tongxue shaonian.* The lines in question from Du Fu have a cynical tone to them —he writes toward the end of his life of his former companions having done well for themselves, in contrast to his own "failure" with regard to worldly concerns. A. C. Graham's translation, in *Poems of the Late T'ang* (Harmondsworth: Penguin, 1965, p. 53) reads: "Of the school friends of my childhood, most did well. /By the Five Tombs in light cloaks they ride their sleek horses." William Hung's translation in *Tu Fu: China's Greatest Poet* (Cambridge, Mass.: Harvard University Press, 1952, p. 235) reads: "Most of my schoolmates are now in prominence; I can imagine their fine raiment and fast horses in the neighborhood of Ch'ang-an."

With the scholar's idealistic fervor,
Upright and fearless, we spoke out unrestrainedly.[4]
Pointing the finger at our land,
Impassioned exhortations we wrote,
Counting as dung and dust the high and mighty of the day.
Do you still remember,
How we thrashed about[5] in midstream currents,
Making a wake that stayed the speeding boats?

---

4. Here Mao alludes to the *Zhuangzi*, the chapter called "Tian Zifang." Burton Watson's translation of the passage in question (*The Complete Works of Chuang Tzu,* New York: Columbia University Press, 1968, p. 231) reads: "Po-hun Wu-jen said, 'The Perfect Man may stare at the blue heavens above, dive into the Yellow Springs below, ramble to the end of the eight directions, yet his spirit and bearing undergo no change. . . .' " Mao uses here the term *huijin,* rendered by Watson as "ramble," which also means to command in a lordly manner. We have translated this as "unrestrainedly," since commentaries on both the *Zhuangzi* and Mao's poem indicate this sense.

5. Mao's own note to this line explains that "thrashing about in the water" here means to swim. The note also refers to a poem of that time, of which he remembered only two lines when he came to write the note to this one. These two lines have been translated in Volume I as a couplet written circa 1917, "In Praise of Swimming."

Editorial for the First Issue of the Daily Bulletin of the Congress of Guangdong Provincial Party Organizations

(October 20, 1925)

While our party's Guangdong Provincial Congress is in session, we are putting out a daily bulletin, so there should be an introductory editorial.

From the Tongmenghui to the Chinese Guomindang, our party has a history of twenty years, and in January of last year, there was the reorganization. There have been fourteen years since the success, and then the failure, of the 1911 Revolution, and at present our party is leading the people of the whole country in a revolution against imperialism and the warlords. Now the Guangdong Provincial Congress is being called together amidst the clamor of imperialist massacres throughout the country, strong repression of the patriotic movement by the warlords, and the roar of cannons in the East River area. All these things are not the accidental result of subjective individual actions or of a single crisis. They are all the necessary consequences of the circumstances that we observe, and are set in motion by historical realities. In the course of last year's January congress, we grasped a correct revolutionary strategy. During the ensuing two years, in the high tide of the nationwide movement against the imperialists and the warlords, we have succeeded, by applying our correct revolutionary strategy, in obtaining propaganda, organization, and the experience of offense and defense in encountering the enemy. What will we obtain from this Guangdong Provincial Congress?

Our great leader, Mr. Sun Yatsen, in response to the objective circumstances in which China is suffering from the manifold oppression of the foreign powers, the warlords, the compradors, and the landlords, laid down for us the revolutionary Three People's Principles. Although our great leader has died, the revolutionary Three People's Principles have not died. The sole task of our Guangdong comrades is how to realize the revolutionary Three People's Principles in Guangdong.

Our late leader, Mr. Sun Yatsen, saw clearly that our principal enemy is imperialism, and laid down [the principle of] revolutionary nationalism. He also

---

This editorial first appeared in the Guomindang's *Guangdong sheng dangbu daibiao dahui huichang rikan* for October 20, 1925. We have translated it as reproduced in *Mao Zedong wenji*, Vol. 1, pp. 15–17.

saw clearly that an important instrument for the exploitation of the Chinese people by imperialism was constituted by the warlords, the big merchants and compradors, and the landlords, and he also laid down the revolutionary [principles] of people's rights[1] and people's livelihood. Revolutionary nationalism calls on us to resist imperialism and to bring about the liberation of the Chinese nation. The revolutionary principle of people's rights calls on us to resist the warlords so that the people of China may establish themselves in the position of rulers. The revolutionary principle of people's livelihood calls on us to resist the big merchants and compradors, and especially the landlord class, which is the fundamental source of all those reactionary feudal-patriarchal forces, so that the great majority of poor people in China may enjoy prosperity. In all the very great movements against imperialism (the Shamian strike,[2] the Guangzhou-Hong Kong strike[3]), against the warlords (overthrowing Chen and Lin,[4] overthrowing Yang and Liu[5]), against the big merchants and compradors (putting down the Merchants' Corps[6]), against the landlords (the bitter battles of the peasants with the landlords in Haifeng, Guangning, Shunde, Bao'an, and other *xian*), the comrades from Guangdong have always been the leaders of the people. In these movements of resistance, 200,000 organized workers, 500,000 organized peasants, and tens of thousands of trained fighters in military units, as well as many patriotic merchants and students have all rallied to the banner of our party in order to establish a revolutionary base for our party in the south! On this base, we have established the national government, which is directing the revolutionary movement in the whole country. In every movement, though many comrades from other provinces have participated, the Guangdong comrades have truly constituted the greatest force.

---

1. *Minquan*, Sun's term for democracy.

2. Regarding the strike of June 1924 against the British concession of Shamian (commonly spelled Shameen in Western sources) in Guangzhou, see below, the relevant note to Mao's Report on Propaganda of January 8, 1926.

3. Regarding the great Guangzhou–Hong Kong strike, which began in June 1925 and lasted sixteen months, see below, the note to the Manifesto dated October 26, 1925.

4. Chen Jiongming and Lin Hu. As indicated above, in a note to the report of the New People's Study Society of May 1921, Chen Jiongming had been governor of Guangdong in 1920-1922, in the Guangzhou régime headed by Sun Yatsen, but he then broke with Sun, and his forces were driven out of Guangzhou in 1923. He established himself in eastern Guangdong, but was defeated by Chiang Kaishek in the First Eastern Campaign of February-April 1925. At this time, the Second Eastern Campaign against him was still in progress, but his defeat had been sealed by the capture of his bastion of Huizhou on October 14. Lin Hu (1887-1960), a native of Guangxi, had served under Chen Jiongming in 1922. In May 1924, he was appointed commissioner in Guangdong by the Beijing government.

5. On Yang Ximin and Liu Zhenhuan, see below, the relevant note to the circular of December 4, 1925.

6. Regarding the conflict with the Merchants' Corps in 1924, see below, the relevant note to the manifesto of October 26, 1925.

Guangdong is a region in close proximity to British imperialism; it is a region in which Chen, Lin, Deng Benyin,[7] and other such warlords in reduced circumstances are hatching their crafty schemes; it is a region where Chen Lianbo[8] and other big merchants and compradors have gathered; and it is a region where the landlords, in collusion with imperialism and the warlords, are severely oppressing the peasants. It is the responsibility of the Guangdong Provincial Congress to decide how we should review our previous work, determine the methods to be applied in future, create a powerful supreme leading organ for the whole province, and use it to develop the organization of people of all circles, especially the organization of those broad peasant masses who constitute 80 percent of the population of Guangdong, or twenty-some millions, in order to guarantee and expand our victory and realize the Three People's Principles completely in Guangdong.

Down with British imperialism!

Down with Chen Jiongming, liquidate all counterrevolutionaries!

Down with the compradors who endanger Guangdong!

Down with the landlords, who collude with imperialism and the warlords to massacre the peasants!

Long live the revolutionary Three People's Principles!

---

7. Deng Benyin (?–1926) was a supporter of Chen Jiongming based in Southern Guangdong. For another reference to him, see below, the propaganda guidelines for the war against the Fengtian clique of November 27, 1925.

8. For another reference to Chen Lianbo, President of the Guangzhou Chamber of Commerce, in the context of Mao's analysis of the comprador class, see below, "Analysis of All the Classes in Chinese Society" of December 1, 1925.

Manifesto of the First Guangdong Provincial Congress of the Chinese Guomindang

(October 26, 1925)[1]

In Guangdong, the first starting point of the revolution, representatives of all the *xian* and towns have now assembled together to hold their first congress. At the same time, they have set up the supreme organ of all the party councils in the province, the Guangdong Provincial Party Council. In the course of this congress of ours, apart from loyally accepting the former Director General's testament and engaging energetically in struggle, we are most sincerely making our views known to the popular masses of the whole world. From the time of its reorganization,[2] this party, having established and applied its political program, has never failed to devote all its energies to pursuing the interests of the popular masses. At the same time, it has joined in the cooperative efforts to assure equal treatment for our nation, in the sincere belief that the national revolution in a semicolony cannot be separated from the world revolution, and struggle all by itself. Therefore, when the 1911 Revolution, led by our party, did not achieve complete success, it was necessary to wait until now to continue our efforts. For at that time, various isolated forces were struggling on their own, and as yet there was no worldwide revolutionary situation in which people got together for joint action. Now, however, the forces in the world are manifestly divided into two kinds, namely the revolutionary forces and the counterrevolutionary forces. In the East the movements of national revolution of the oppressed nations are growing daily, and in the West the movements of social revolution of the oppressed classes are also arising vigorously. This is a mani-

---

This manifesto appeared in the Guangzhou *Minguo ribao* for October 27, 1925, and our translation has been made from that source.

1. According to *Nianpu*, Vol. 1, p. 26, and other sources, this is the date on which the present manifesto, drafted by Mao and others, was adopted by the congress. (In the index volume of the *Bujuan*, it is dated October 20, 1925, but this is undoubtedly an error, resulting from the fact that the editors had not seen a copy of the text.) Our translation has been made from the version published in the Guangzhou *Minguo ribao* of October 27, 1925.

2. I.e., beginning with the First Congress of January 1924.

festation of the fact that the revolutionary forces of the whole world are already mustered. Moreover, all the imperialist countries of Europe, America, and Japan, apart from severely exploiting and oppressing the worker and peasant classes of their own countries, are also colluding with the militarists, politicians, compradors, and landlords of the colonial and semicolonial countries to exploit and oppress the middle and lower strata of the popular masses there. This is a manifestation of the fact that the counterrevolutionary forces of the whole world are also already mustered. Thus, the inevitable struggle between these two great forces has progressively been drawing nearer and intensifying. Looking at the situation from today's perspective, the serious prospect of a great decisive struggle in the whole world may materialize at any moment. Such being the position in China, the revolutionary demands of the middle and lower strata of the popular masses are, on the one hand, naturally becoming more pressing with every passing day. On the other hand, the British, the Americans, the French, the Japanese, and all the imperialists must also unite with the great and small warlords within the country, the Anfu clique, the Research clique, the Federalist clique, and all the other cliques of politicians, the compradors from various places such as Hong Kong and Shanghai, and the local bullies and bad gentry of the whole country to form a counterrevolutionary movement. From the big massacre by the Merchants' Corps during the October 10 holiday last year[3] to the cruel massacres during the May 30th Incident,[4] revolution and counterrevolution have already become two opposing camps locked in struggle. Moreover, Guangdong is the place where we confront British imperialism directly. It is the place where the comprador class of Chen Lianbo[5] and others is concentrated and the place where militarists in straitened circumstances, such as Chen Jiongming,[6] craftily spin their outrageous schemes. For more than a decade, and especially during the past few years, our party has stood in the forefront of the revolutionary forces and has waged a fierce struggle against the counterrevolutionary forces led by British imperialism. Moreover, since Chen and Lin[7] were driven out and Liu and Yang were put

---

3. The reference is to the conflict between the Merchants' Corps, organized by the Guangzhou merchants to oppose the financial and political demands of Sun Yatsen's government, and the armed forces under Sun's command, which came to a head on October 15, 1924. For a longer note, see below, the text of December 5, 1925, "Zou Lu and the Revolution."

4. See below, Mao's discussion of the May 30th Incident of 1925 in his article "To the Left or to the Right" of December 13, 1925, and the accompanying note.

5. Chen Lianbo was the president of the Guangzhou Chamber of Commerce. For another reference to him, see below, "Analysis of all the Classes in Chinese Society," of December 1, 1925.

6. On Chen Jiongming, sometime ally of Sun Yatsen who had repeatedly rebelled against him, see above, the relevant note to the preceding text.

7. Chen and Lin are, once again, Chen Jiongming and Lin Hu. (See above, the editorial of October 20, 1925, and the relevant note.)

down,[8] and since the butchery in Shakee,[9] and the Hong Kong strike, the revolutionary forces have been even more concentrated, and British imperialism, in a panic, has led all the counterrevolutionary forces, united them, and attacked us once again. Then there was the death of Comrade Liao Zhongkai,[10] the rebellion of Zheng and Mo,[11] and the three-cornered uprising of Chen Jiongming, Deng Benyin, and Xiong Kewu in the east, the south, and the north.[12] Now we have already liquidated Zheng and Mo, dispersed Xiong's troops, and attacked Huizhou.[13] In the future, it will not be difficult, within a relatively short time, to sweep away Chen and Deng and exercise a controlling influence over the Hong Kong government, so as to obtain the victory of the strike. From all this, we can be confident that the development of the revolutionary forces definitely has the power to progress with lightning speed. Now, however, war has broken out between Jiangsu and Zhejiang, and this is not merely a local question between Jiangsu and Zhejiang. It is obviously a struggle between the Fengtian and the Zhili cliques, in alliance with English and Japanese imperialism, to seize the opportunity to exploit the Chinese people.[14] These two warlord cliques, regardless of who wins or loses, are both harmful to China. As far as we the people of

---

8. Liu Zhenhuan, commander of the Guangxi forces, and Yang Ximin, commander of the Yunnanese forces in the 1923 war against Chen Jiongming, had been forced to flee to Hong Kong in June 1925. See below, the announcement of December 4, 1925, and the relevant note thereto.

9. The "Shakee [Shaji] Massacre" of June 23, 1925, in which more than fifty Chinese were killed and over a hundred wounded, led to a sixteen-month boycott of trade with Hong Kong and made Great Britain the principal villain in the eyes of Nationalists and Communists alike. For a brief account, see the *Cambridge History of China*, Vol. 12, pp. 551–53.

10. Regarding Liao Zhongkai and his assassination on August 20, 1925, see above, the note to Central Circular no. 15 of July 21, 1924.

11. The reference is to Zheng Runqi and Mo Xiong (1891–1980), *zi* Zhi'ang, subordinate commanders of the Guangdong forces of the national government. In September 1925, they were suspected of being in collusion with Chen Jiongming, and their troops were attacked and defeated by Chiang Kaishek's forces. See also, below, the announcement of December 4, 1925, which accuses Zheng and Mo of complicity in the assassination of Liao Zhongkai.

12. It was a renewed attack on the Guomindang national government in Guangzhou in October 1925 by Chen Jiongming from the east, the Sichuanese general Xiong Kewu from the northwest, and Guangdong troops under Deng Benyin from the southwest that had triggered the Second Eastern Expedition against Chen mentioned above. On the campaigns against them during the ensuing three months by Chiang Kaishek and his subordinates, see *Cambridge History of China*, Vol. 12, pp. 555–56.

13. The main bastion of Chen Jiongming's forces.

14. For Mao's own analysis of the Jiangsu-Zhejiang war of the previous year (1924) and its relation to the conflict between the Zhili and Fengtian cliques, see below, "Propaganda Guidelines of the Chinese Guomindang in the War against the Fengtian Clique," dated November 27, 1925.

Guangdong are concerned, let these counterrevolutionary militarists, compradors, village bullies and bad gentry, and shameless politicians one and all join the counterrevolutionary front led by the British and Japanese imperialists. All we oppressed popular masses and revolutionary elements will take our stand on the side of the revolutionary front under the leadership of the Guomindang, unite all the forces in the revolutionary front, and attack the counterrevolutionary forces. Such is our sole task, and we will certainly be able to obtain final victory. Let the people of the whole country arise, and in this chaotic struggle on the territory of the whole country, in which the imperialists and warlords are striving to exploit the Chinese people, we must stand entirely on the opposite side. Let us organize our own forces, unite under the leadership of the Guomindang, and go on the offensive against all our enemies. Let the revolutionary popular masses of Guangdong strive with all their might to be the reliable rear of the revolutionary popular masses of the whole country. Unite all revolutionary forces! Down with all counterrevolutionary forces! Long live revolutionary solidarity! Long live the Chinese Guomindang! Long live the liberation of the Chinese nation!

Speech at the Closing Ceremony
of the Guangdong Provincial Congress
of the Chinese Guomindang

(October 27, 1925)[1]

This is the closing day of the Congress of Representatives of the Guangdong Council of the Chinese Guomindang, and I, your younger brother, have the opportunity to offer some suggestions to all you comrades. That is an excellent thing. There is no need for me to praise the past work of all you comrades, nor do I think I should praise it. Consequently, for now I will only raise one question for discussion with all the comrades. Because in the case of any question whatsoever, it is only if it can be fully discussed within the party that it can be uniformly propagated outside the party, and at the same time the Second National Congress will soon be opening, and so it becomes even more necessary to raise and discuss this question. What is this question I wish to raise for discussion? It is the question of the middle elements. At the First Congress, our party decided on various policies, and the results of their application during the past two years have already demonstrated that the policies of the First Congress were correct. As regards the policy toward the peasants, our party decided to support the middle and lower strata of the peasantry in their efforts to get organized, and to help them eliminate their misery by such means as rent reduction. But because of this, another question arose. As soon as the movement for rent reduction was launched, it was necessary to oppose the village bullies and bad gentry, and criticisms then surfaced. Some comrades held that the present period is the period of unity against the foreigners, and we should all unanimously oppose imperialism. The landlords are our Chinese compatriots, and we must not advocate attacking one another. Comrades of this type seem to

---

This speech appeared in the Guangzhou *Minguo ribao* for October 28, 1925, and our translation has been made from that source.

1. On October 5, 1925, Wang Jingwei, who had been concurrently chairman of the national government and head of the Propaganda Department of the Guomindang Central Executive Committee, proposed to the Standing Committee of the Guomindang Central Bureau that, because he was fully occupied by his work in the government, Mao Zedong should be appointed acting head of the Propaganda Department. This is Mao's address to the closing session of the congress in that capacity.

want to constitute something like an intermediate faction within the party. In my oppinion, this problem is extremely important. Formerly, Comrade Liao Zhongkai had a slogan, "Let the revolutionary factions unite!" Since Comrade Liao was slaughtered, Comrade Wang Jingwei has put forward another slogan, "Those who wish to make revolution should move toward the left!"[2] Those comrades who want to create an intermediate faction hold that right is no good and left is no good either; only the way of the invariable mean[3] is good. But all of you comrades must ask yourselves whether this thinking is correct or not. Are their views harmful or beneficial to the party and to the interests of the majority of the popular masses? Can such an intermediate faction be created, exist, and develop within the party and within China? According to my observations, this intermediate faction will not be able to exist. I/shall now put forward three proofs. First of all, before the European war there were intermediate factions in all the European countries, and moreover rather big and powerful intermediate factions, such as the Social Democratic Party in Germany, the Labor Party in England, and the Socialist Party in France. They all took up an intermediate position, but after the European war the world was divided into two big camps. One is the great camp of counterrevolution, led by the big bourgeoisie; the other is the great camp of revolution, led by the proletariat. Once these two are engaged in close combat, the basis of the intermediate faction is shaken, and so the intermediate faction undergoes further splits. One part subordinates itself completely to the counterrevolutiuonary forces of the bourgeoisie, and another part joins the revolutionary forces of the proletariat. Such is the situation in Europe. Secondly, in China, since the 1911 Revolution, there have been some instances of strong intermediate factions. At that time, the faction of the left was the Guomindang, and the faction of the right was Yuan Shikai.[4] The intermediate faction was the Progressive Party, which later became the Research clique and then joined with a number of backward members of the Guomindang to split off and form the Political Studies clique.[5] It even regards itself as an intermediate

---

2. Wang Jingwei (1883–1944), zi Jixin, original name Zhaoming, was born in Guangdong. In 1905, while a student in Japan, he joined the Tongmenghui, and from that time forward he was closely associated with Sun Yatsen. In 1910, he led an attempt to assassinate the prince regent, which made him a national hero when he was released from prison after the 1911 Revolution. He accompanied Sun Yatsen on his journey to Beijing at the end of 1924, and it was he who drafted the testament that Sun signed on his deathbed. In July 1925 he was elected chairman of the national government formed in Guangzhou. Though he ended his life as the premier of the Japanese puppet government in Nanjing, he was regarded at this time, as the slogan quoted by Mao indicates, as a leading figure in the Guomindang left.

3. Zhongyong zhi dao, the Confucian "Doctrine of the Mean."

4. The Chinese text actually has you [right] for the faction represented by the Guomindang, and zuo [left] for Yuan Shikai. This must be a printer's error.

5. See above, Mao's article of April 10, 1923, "The Foreign Powers, the Warlords, and the Revolution," in which he evokes these various centrist factions, and the notes thereto.

faction. These people oppose the Guomindang on the one hand and the oppression of the warlords and the foreigners on the other, but if we watch what this lot finally becomes, it turns into the running dog of the imperialists and the warlords. They turn completely into the public enemy of the popular masses; they turn completely into a counterrevolutionary faction. Thirdly, let us look once more at the situation in Guangdong. It is evident that Guangdong is split at present into two great factions: the counterrevolutionary forces, led by Hong Kong and British imperialism, and the revolutionary forces, led by the left and the Guomindang. A lot of people want to stand between the two, but just consider whether they can do this or not. If they stand in the middle, the counterrevolutionary faction of the right will try to drag them over, and the leftists—that is to say the revolutionary faction—will want to shoot at them. Consequently, no one in Guangdong dares to stand in the middle at present. We have demonstrated by the foregoing facts that the centrist faction cannot stand in the middle. Because only leftist theory and tactics constitute the theory and tactics of our party. Mr. Sun's theory and tactics, the theory and tactics of the First Congress, are like this. If there are people who want to create centrist theory and tactics, and who want to attempt to revise the revolutionary theory and tactics of Mr. Sun, they have turned against the party and will definitely stand on the side of counterrevolution. [They have turned against] the interests of the majority of the popular masses of the whole country.[6] They have turned against Mr. Sun. Although at present they do not want to be frankly counterrevolutionary, or to stand frankly on the side of imperialism, they will assuredly become counterrevolutionaries in the future and go over to the side of the imperialists. So I, your younger brother, would like to leave all you comrades with these two sentences. One is that spoken by Liao Zhongkai, "Let revolutionaries unite!" The other is that spoken by Wang Jingwei, "Those who wish to make revolution should go toward the left!" [At the end of the speech, all the party members present shouted the slogans: "Down with imperialism!" "Down with the warlords!" "Down with the counterrevolutionaries!" "Liquidate corrupt officials and evil armed forces!" "Eliminate the village bullies, bad gentry, big landlords, and compradors who oppress the classes of the peasants and the workers!" "Long live the unity of the revolutionaries!" "Long live the great union of the workers and the peasants!" "Long live the great union of all classes!" "Long live the Congress of Party Members of Guangdong Province!" "Long live the Chinese Guomindang!" "Long live the liberation of the Chinese nation!"][7]

---

6. There is evidently a misprint in this clause, which has no verb; the sense appears to be as indicated by the words in square brackets.

7. The passage which we have placed in square brackets was, of course, added by the newspaper at the end of Mao's remarks.

A Filled-out Form for the Survey Conducted by the Reorganization Committee of the Young China Association

(November 21, 1925)

Name	Mao Zedong (Runzhi)	
Native Place	Hunan Province, Xiangtan *xian*	
Mailing Address	Most recent	Guomindang Central Executive Committee, Guangzhou
	Permanent	Cultural Book Society, Changsha
Type of theory espoused regarding China, caught today between domestic anxieties and foreign troubles	I believe in Communism and advocate the social revolution of the proletariat. The present domestic and foreign oppression cannot, however, be overthrown by the forces of one class alone. I advocate making use of the national revolution in which the proletariat, the petty bourgeoisie, and the left wing of the middle bourgeoisie cooperate to carry out the Three People's Principles of the Chinese Guomindang in order to overthrow imperialism, overthrow the warlords, and overthrow the comprador and landlord classes (that is to say, the Chinese big bourgeoisie and the right wing of the middle bourgeoisie, who have close ties to imperialism and the warlords), and to realize the joint rule of the proletariat, the petty bourgeoisie, and the left wing of the middle bourgeoisie, that is, the rule of the revolutionary popular masses.	
Attitude toward the reform of this society's work	There clearly are points of mutual conflict among the views held by the society's members, and furthermore there are a number of members who are not committed to the society in spirit, who think that the Young China Association is not necessary at this time, and who advocate that it be disbanded.	

Mao's reply was included in the results of this survey as reported in 1926 by the Reorganization Committee of the Young China Association. We have taken as our source the version reproduced in *Mao Zedong ji. Bujuan*, Vol. 2, pp. 127–28.

Brief history of activities since joining the association	Studies	Have studied the social sciences with an emphasis at present on the problem of the Chinese peasantry.
	Work	Taught for one year; worked for two years in the labor movement, half a year in the peasant movement, and one year in the Guomindang organization.
Date filled out	November 21, 1925	
Remarks	This arrived today from Changsha.	

Propaganda Guidelines of the Chinese Guomindang in the War Against the Fengtian Clique

(November 27, 1925)

Because of the importance of the war against the Fengtian clique, a war which is by nature one episode in the national revolutionary movement against British and Japanese imperialism, the Propaganda Department of the Central Executive Committee of the Chinese Guomindang [instructs] party offices in every locality and at every level immediately to direct all comrades to engage in widespread propaganda so that the people of the whole country may understand the causes and objectives of this war. We have specially prepared an outline for this propaganda, which begins with an analysis of various aspects of the war against the Fengtian clique, then puts forward the main themes of propaganda, and finally lists nine slogans. Proposed by Department Head Mao Zedong,[1] this was passed at a meeting of the Central Executive Committee on November 27. The complete text follows.[2]

A. Analysis of Various Aspects of the War Against the Fengtian Clique

1. The Imperialists. Last year's war between the Fengtian and Zhili cliques resulted from the attempt by the British and American imperialists to use the Zhili clique to unify China and drive out the influence of the Japanese imperialists. Hostilities broke out in the form of the Jiangsu-Zhejiang war, in which the American imperialists were seeking to gain a monopoly on the loans to Jiangsu for radio telegrams and prevent Japan from providing the loans. At the time, therefore, the United States and the pro-American faction put every effort

---

These guidelines appeared in the Guomindang organ *Zhengzhi zhoubao*, No. 1, December 5, 1925. Our source is the version reproduced in *Mao Zedong ji*, Vol. 1, pp. 101–7.

1. As indicated above in a note to his speech of October 27, 1925, Mao's title was, in fact, that of acting head.

2. This note preceded the text of the guidelines when it was first published in *Zhengzhi zhoubao*. Since Mao was editor in chief of this magazine, the note may also be attributed to him. In some versions, the Propaganda Guidelines are dated December 3, 1925, because that is when they were first publicly released.

into helping Qi Xieyuan, while Japan and the pro-Japanese faction worked hard to support Lu Yongxiang.[3] The present war against the Fengtian clique is a direct continuation of this, with Japanese imperialism standing behind the Fengtian clique and American imperialism standing behind the Zhili clique. As for the British imperialists, having discovered following the Fengtian-Zhili war last year just how useless the Zhili clique was, they had no choice during the nationwide May 30th movement against the British but to make every effort to compromise with Japan and use large bribes to induce Zhang Zuolin to suppress the anti-British movement in Shanghai. Afterwards, it is rumored that Britain gave a huge sum of money to help the Fengtian clique expand the Fengtian armaments factories with the intent to use the Fengtian clique to unify China. At this point, since the increase in troops in Shanghai under Yang Yuting, governor of Jiangsu, and the conference on customs duties held in Beijing[4] were to the advantage of Zhang Zuolin, it was inevitable that the Zhili clique would soon be in trouble. In the present war, it is still difficult to judge with certainty whether the crafty British imperialists are helping the Fengtian clique or whether they are helping the Zhili clique. Most likely, in its plan to resist the United States, Japan would prefer to draw Britian into joint control over Zhang Zuolin. But if and when they discover that the situation does not favor Zhang Zuolin, and that their old servant Wu Peifu might be victorious, it is entirely conceivable that, in order to consolidate their sphere of influence in the Yangzi River basin, they would discard their new favorite and associate again with their old friend. Thus the attitude of British imperialism is to see which side has the greater chance of success and then to help that side.

2. The Warlords. In the confrontation between the Zhili and Fengtian cliques, the territory held by the Zhili side includes the seven provinces of Hunan, Hubei, Jiangxi, Anhui, Jiangsu, Zhejiang, and Fujian. Sichuan under Yuan Zuming and Guizhou, which is under Yuan Zuming's control, also belong nominally to the Zhili clique. But each of these provinces has its own individual internal factions, and a split between Wu Peifu and Sun Chuanfang is inevitable. While the war against the Fengtian clique was raging, Sun and Wu naturally had to ally with each other in the fight, but now that the fighting has stopped the signs of division are already appearing, and when Zhang Zuolin and the Fengtian clique are defeated there can be no doubt that they must split. As for the Fengtian clique, it

---

3. Regarding Qi and Lu, see the note to the text of September 10, 1924, "On the Question of Opposing the War between the Warlords of Jiangsu and Zhejiang." Although, as indicated there, Qi Xieyuan, supported by Wu Peifu, had been victorious in this area, the Zhili clique suffered a grave defeat in the wider war for control of China, because of the split between Wu Peifu and Feng Yuxiang.

4. The Special Conference on the Chinese Customs Tariff was convened in Beijing on October 26, 1925. It was adjourned in July 1926 following the collapse of the Beijing régime.

has always had two factions, the old and the young.[5] Ever since the defeat of the Zhili faction last year, the internal struggle over the distribution of power has become more and more severe. They are financially bankrupt, and the Fengtian currency has fallen by more than 50 percent. The earlier seizure of Zhili, Shandong, Jiangsu, and Anhui was an attempt to solve the financial problem. At present, Jiangsu and Anhui have already been lost, and because of the threat of the National People's Army,[6] they will not be able to hold Shandong and the Zhili section of the Beijing-Hankou railroad. Their financial resources south of the Great Wall are exhausted. The several hundred thousand underfed troops assembled in the vicinity of Shanhaiguan would be useful for a short war, but they could not hold out for long. No matter which of these two warlord cliques wins out, Fengtian or Zhili, it will be bad for China, for behind both of them stand vicious imperialisms. During the nationwide anti-Fengtian movement, the Zhili clique must, of course, be considered one participant in the common cause of resisting our present powerful enemy. After the fall of the Fengtian clique, the power of the people will liquidate the Zhili clique; this is a tactical necessity.

3. Political Tendencies. In the present war against the Fengtian clique, the political factions whose attitudes should be watched are the Anfu clique, the Research clique,[7] the Federalist clique,[8] the New Foreign Affairs clique, and also the comprador class in the Shanghai-Nantong area. At present the military power of the Anfu clique may already be said to be nonexistent. Moreover, its political power has long been split between the pro-Zhili and the pro-Fengtian factions. It

---

5. The "old" faction was that around Zhang Zuolin himself; the "young" faction was that loyal to his son Zhang Xueliang and to the effective commander of the latter's forces, Guo Songling.

6. The Guominjun, or National People's Army, had been organized by Feng Yuxiang and other generals after they had defeated Wu Peifu and driven him out of Beijing in October 1924. Feng Yuxiang (1882–1948), *zi* Huanzhang, had risen through the ranks to become an influential military figure by 1914. In that year, he joined the Methodist church and was henceforth commonly known as the Christian general. In 1918, he instituted methods of training and indoctrination involving a combination of Christian and traditional Chinese values, centering on the individual's moral obligations to society. During the years 1918–1922, he was associated with Wu Peifu, but in 1923 Feng turned against Wu and supported Cao Kun's coup d'état against him. In the fall of 1924, after Feng Yuxiang's troops occupied Beijing, he became commander-in-chief of the newly formed Guominjun. In April 1925, in return for Russian instructors and military aid, Feng agreed to permit Guomindang political work in his army, but at the same time intensified his own program of indoctrination.

7. On the Anhui or Anfu clique, and the Research clique, see the notes to the text of April 10, 1923.

8. The partisans of the *liansheng zizhi yundong*, or "movement for a federation of self-governing provinces" (abbreviated here to *lianzhi*), were mainly representatives of the bourgeoisie, seeking emancipation from bureaucratic rule. See Marie-Claire Bergère, in *Cambridge History of China*, Vol. 12, pp. 778–80.

is only because of the loss of influence of the pro-Zhili faction that the pro-Fengtian faction has taken power in Beijing. Thus the Beijing government has become entirely the creature of Zhang Zuolin. When Cao Kun and Wu Peifu came to power, the Research clique subordinated itself to Cao and Wu, and although Cao and Wu were defeated it is still controlled by Wu Peifu. With the present resurgence of the Zhili clique, Jiang Fangzhen and others of the Research clique and some of the piggish parliamentarians[9] belonging to this clique have gathered in large numbers in Hankou to take advantage of the situation. The Federalist clique, composed of minor political factions such as the Mutual Benefit Society of the Political Studies clique and politicians such as Zhang Binglin[10] of the so-called Guomindang Comrades' Club, have also now gathered under the banner of Wu Peifu to plot their actions. The so-called New Foreign Affairs clique of Gu Weijun[11] has always been a traitorous group of brokers between the Zhili clique and the British and American imperialists. This clique is now intimately associated with the Research clique and the comprador class of the Shanghai-Nantong area, all of whom have joined together under the banner of the Zhili clique and are working hard on their movement to sell out the country. During the anti-Zhili war last year, the comprador class of the Shanghai-Nantong area, at the direction of the American imperialists, sided with the Zhili clique. With the present resurgence of the Zhili clique, at the suggestion of their masters (the American imperialists), they immediately rallied to the Zhili call and went so far as to become a major pillar of Zhili power. Except for the Anfu clique, which represents the interests of Japanese imperialism and of the bureaucrats and is on the side of the Fengtian clique, all the rest of the above political factions—the Federalist clique and the Research clique, which represent the interests of the bureaucrats and of the landlord class; the New Foreign Affairs clique, which represents British and American (especially American) interests; and the Shanghai-Nantong comprador class—are on the side of the Zhili clique.

4. The National People's Army. The National People's Army has no ties to British, American, or Japanese imperialism and is thus sympathetic to the anti-

---

9. Literally, "little pig parliamentarians" (*Zhuzai yiyuan*). The reference is to those of the remaining members of the 1913 Parliament who had joined in electing Cao Kun to the presidency in 1923. They were known under this derogatory epithet because they had sold their votes for 5,000 *yuan* each.

10. On Zhang Binglin, see above, the relevant note to Mao's letter of December 1, 1920, to Xiao Xudong and others.

11. Gu Weijun (1888–1985), *zi* Shaochuan, better known in the West as V. K. Wellington Koo, studied at Columbia University, where he received a Ph.D. in 1912. After serving as minister in Washington and London, and as China's representative to the League of Nations, he became foreign minister in early 1922. Gu held this post for most of the time from 1922 until July 1924 and served as acting premier from July to October 1924, when he was forced to resign following Feng Yuxiang's overthrow of the Beijing government. At the time that Mao wrote this article, Gu was living in the foreign concession in Tianjin.

imperialist movement; this is its most important characteristic. For the present, out of tactical necessity, it has not yet broken with Zhang Zuolin or has even reached a temporary compromise, but this is only a temporary situation. Following the anti-Fengtian war, our party wishes to take a great stride forward toward the success of the national revolution, and one of the important keys to this is truly the victory of the National People's Army in the north.

5. The National Government. Our party's base in Guangdong is now already fully secure. The detachments of Xiong Kewu[12] in the Beijiang[13] area were disposed of some time ago. The forces of Chen Jiongming[14] in the Dongjiang area, too, have already been eliminated, and troops have been dispatched to pursue and mop up those small detachments that have fled into the Fujian border area. The troops of Deng Benyin[15] in the southern region will also be disposed of any day now. The unification of the entire region may be said to be completed. The plot of British imperialism, in collusion with Chen Jiongming, et al., to extinguish the revolutionary power of our party has already failed completely. The Hong Kong merchants and the Hong Kong government already realize that they have no further resource for standing up against the problem of the Guangzhou–Hong Kong strike. Right now they are looking for a way out, and a victorious solution can shortly be achieved. At present, the main efforts of our party in Guangdong are focused on strengthening and expanding the military might of the revolutionary army, on cleaning up and reorganizing the financial, judicial, and educational system of the people's government, and on expanding the mass movement of workers, peasants, merchants, and students. In sum, the party is actively preparing its forces in the shortest possible time so that, when the situation in the north and south develops to the right stage, it can send troops to the north and lead the people of the entire nation toward a thorough solution of national issues. Our party has issued, in the name of the Central Executive Committee, an announcement on the current situation which elucidates the ob-

---

12. Xiong Kewu (1884–1970), *zi* Jinfan, a native of Sichuan, had studied at the military academy in Japan and there joined the Tongmenghui. He participated in Cai E's campaign of 1916 against Yuan Shikai, and in 1918–1920 he was military governor of Sichuan. In January 1924, he was one of the few active military commanders elected to the Central Executive Committee of the Guomindang. In the following year, he sought to move his Sichuan army to Guangzhou. Because he had established links with Chen Jiongming, this action was regarded by Chiang Kaishek as participating in a joint attack against the Guomindang forces, and when he reached Guangzhou he was placed under arrest and detained for two years.

13. Beijiang (North River) and Dongjiang (East River) are two important rivers of Guangdong that give their names to the adjoining areas of the province.

14. On Chen Jiongming, see the note to Mao's editorial of October 20 1925. By the end of November 1925, his forces had, as indicated here, been virtually destroyed, and Chen sought refuge in Hong Kong.

15. An officer of the Guangdong Army who had collaborated with Chen Jiongming.

jectives of the war against the Fengtian clique. Also, in the name of the National Government Council,[16] telegrams are being sent to the major leaders of both the Zhili and the Fengtian cliques, urging them to coordinate their actions to overthrow Zhang Zuolin, and after Zhang's power in Fengtian is broken to join in setting up a government and policies that are in accordance with the objectives of the popular masses. This will serve as a test of whether they accept or reject our party's proposal to uphold the interests of the masses.

6. The Popular Masses. In the consciousness of the popular masses, the present anti-Fengtian movement is a movement that opposes the warlords of the Fengtian clique, who support British and Japanse imperialism and suppress the patriotic movement. Thus the main body of this present anti-Fengtian movement should be the revolutionary popular masses of the entire nation. The initiative taken by the Zhili clique represents merely one branch of the forward units and cannot be considered the main body of the movement. This time the people's anger against the warlords of the Fengtian clique is greater than ever before. The concept of the popular masses of the whole nation according to which opposing the Fengtian clique means opposing British and Japanese imperialism, and victory over the Fengtian clique means victory over the British and Japanese, is the same as the concept held by the popular masses of Guangdong according to which the punitive expedition against Chen Jiongming meant striking a blow at British imperialism, and the victory of the Eastern Expedition was a victory for the strikes. Thus, this war against the Fengtian clique, from the perspective of the consciousness of the popular masses, is different from all the several "Zhili-Anfu" and "Fengtian-Zhili" wars.

B. Our Propaganda and Preparations

Responsible comrades in the party organizations at all levels in all localities must, in an organized and planned way, seek every opportunity and bend every effort to explain to comrades, and to propagate among the popular masses, the following points:

1. The plots of the various imperialists in the present war.
2. The grave danger that a victory for the warlords of the Fengtian clique, who are running dogs of the British and Japanese imperialists, would pose to the popular masses.
3. The popular masses can make use of the Zhili clique's opposition to the Fengtian clique for the time being, but the Zhili clique must not be allowed to

---

16. The National Government Council (*Guomin zhengfu weiyuanhui*), established in Guangzhou on July 1, 1925, and chaired by Wang Jingwei, was the most inclusive organ of the national government; it was, of course, subordinated to the leading party bodies.

replace Zhang Zuolin and the Fengtian clique at the helm of government, because if the Zhili clique simply replaced Zhang and the Fengtian clique it would be extremely dangerous for the people. The people should not forget the previous experience when the Zhili clique took over the state. In the areas of all provinces along the Yangzi River where the atmosphere of welcoming Wu Peifu and Sun Chuanfang is very prevalent among the merchant class, this point is especially worth emphasizing in our propaganda.

4. All counterrevolutionary groups, including the Anfu clique, the Research clique, the Federalists, the New Foreign Affairs clique, and the comprador class, have interests that are absolutely incompatible with those of the people, and we must exhaust every effort to reveal and reject totally all of their self-serving schemes.

5. Among the various forces that are opposing the Fengtian clique, the difference between the Feng Yuxiang faction and the Wu Peifu–Sun Chuanfang faction is that Feng has no ties with the imperialists and supports the national revolution, whereas Wu and Sun take instructions from the imperialists and are hostile to the national revolution. Thus, for the people the distinction between who is a friend and who is an enemy depends entirely on whether or not someone has connections with imperialism. If anyone, no matter who or when, establishes links with imperialism, the people will not recognize him as a friend.

6. The true leader of the people is the Chinese Guomindang. The true government of the people is the national government in Guangzhou. The true army of the people is the Guangdong National Revolutionary Army. Because the Guomindang, the national government, and the National Revolutionary Army are the spearhead of anti-imperialism, they are the defenders of the interests of the people, the bearers of comfort and relief to the suffering of the people. (Point out the facts of the Guangdong opposition to imperialism and the present unification and active reconstruction of Guangdong.)

7. The whole of the oppressed popular masses of China is the master of all the problems of China. It is the people who should be the commander-in-chief of this present war against the Fengtian clique. The people must immediately get organized and take charge of this anti-Fengtian movement.

8. The four proposals of Guomindang propaganda regarding the current situation are: (1) Establish a unified nationwide national government; (2) This national government must, as soon as possible, convoke a National Assembly Preparatory Congress; (3) This national government must, in the shortest possible time, convene a National Assembly Preparatory Congress to achieve a fundamental solution to the unequal treaties; (4) This national government must guarantee to the people freedom of speech, association, and assembly. This is the only way to bring an end to the present war. If these four items are not fulfilled, then an end to warfare would still leave the situation under the joint control of the warlords and imperialists, and this would be just as dangerous for the people as what they suffered previously.

9. To put into practice the Guomindang's proposals, we must speedily prepare for a national assembly that is truly representative of the people. Among all the organizations of the people, we should prepare for a renewed general propaganda campaign on the "necessity for a national assembly to resolve national matters," continuing last year's campaign. When necessary, all provincial and special city party councils should mobilize all members in their districts to carry out intensive propaganda campaigns for a national assembly, to arouse the attention of the popular masses.

C. Slogans

1. Down with Zhang Zuolin and Duan Qirui.
2. Down with British, American, and Japanese imperialism.
3. Down with all scheming political factions.
4. Let the people rise up and take charge of the anti-Fengtian movement.
5. Let a National Assembly that represents the people bring an end to the war against the Fengtian clique.
6. Establish a national government to unify the whole country.
7. Abolish the unequal treaties.
8. Freedom of association, assembly, speech, and strikes.
9. Let all revolutionary elements quickly join the Guomindang.

The Central Executive Committee of the Chinese Guomindang Sternly Repudiates the Illegal Meeting of Beijing Party Members

(November 27, 1925)

Telegram to All Party Offices at All Levels

For the information of all comrades in party offices at all levels of the Chinese Guomindang:

The telegram (of November 6) recently received from Beijing members of the Central Executive Committee, Lin Sen,[1] et al., proposing that the Fourth Plenum of the Central Executive Committee be convened in the Western Hills in Beijing, has already been sternly repudiated in a telegram of reply from the Central Executive Committee. From the standpoint of legality, since the Third Plenum of the Central Executive Committee passed a resolution that national party congresses and plenums of the Central Executive Committee must meet in Guangzhou, no one, no matter who, may violate the resolution. From the standpoint of the concrete situation, a plenum of the Central Executive Committee is public in nature, and if it were held in Beijing, externally it would be subject to pressure from the warlords, while internally reactionary elements would use the warlords to cause obstructions from within. It was precisely for this reason that, in April of this year, the Third Plenum of the Central Executive Committee had to halt its meeting less than halfway through and go south to reconvene in Guangzhou. He who does not forget the past is master of the future. How can the Fourth Plenum of the Central Executive Committee make the same mistake again and allow the warlords and the reactionary elements to continue pursuing their scheme of destroying the revolution? The Second National Congress, origi-

---

This telegram appeared in *Zhengzhi zhoubao*, No. 1, December 5, 1925. Our source is the version reproduced in *Mao Zedong ji*, Vol. 1, pp. 99–100.

1. Lin Sen (1868-1943), *zi* Zichao, was a native of Fujian. In 1912–1913, he was chairman of the Senate in Beijing, but fled abroad when Yuan Shikai dissolved parliament. In 1917 he participated in the rump parliament convened in Guangzhou, which established a revolutionary government headed by Sun Yatsen. Though he had played a leading role in the First Guomindang Congress of January 1924, he became increasingly hostile to collaboration with the Communists. He was, with Zou Lu, one of the two main architects of the Western Hills meeting of 1925, and subsequently headed the dissident Central Executive Committee chosen in April 1926, in Shanghai.

nally slated to open on August 15 in Guangzhou, was postponed several times as a result of the Guangzhou–Hong Kong strike, the transportation stoppage, the cleaning out of reactionaries in Guangzhou, and the continuous warfare. But now the entire province of Guangdong has been unified, and Guangzhou is as stable as a rock, so even though transportation may seem inconvenient it presents no obstacle to holding a meeting. Thus the Central Executive Committee has already decided to convene the Fourth Plenum of the Central Executive Committee on December 11 in Guangzhou, and to hold the Second National Party Congress beginning January 1, 1926. A telegram has already been sent to Comrades Lin Sen, et al., advising them to respect this resolution, to consider carefully the actual situation, and to come speedily to Guangzhou to attend the meetings, and not stick to a different position that can only lead to divisiveness. Apart from Comrade Hu Hanmin who is presently in Moscow and Comrades Li Liejun and Bai Wenwei who are working outside Beijing, all of whom have already sent telegrams indicating their agreement, we all respect the resolution of the Third Plenum of the Central Executive Committee and the recent proposal of the Central Executive Committee, and are exerting all our efforts to respect and implement them. This announcement is respectfully offered for your consideration. Members of the Central Executive Committee, Wang Zhaoming, Tan Yankai, Tan Pingshan, Lin Zuhan, Li Dazhao, Yu Youren, Yu Shude, Wang Faqin, Ding Weifen, Enkebatu; alternate members of the Central Executive Committee, Mao Zedong, Qu Qiubai, Han Linfu, Yu Fangzhou, and Zhang Guotao. Sincerely (November 27).

Analysis of All the Classes in Chinese Society [1]

(December 1, 1925)

Who are our enemies? Who are our friends? He who cannot distinguish between enemies and friends is certainly not a revolutionary, yet to distinguish between them is not easy.[2] If the Chinese revolution, although it has been going on for thirty years, has[3] achieved so little, *this is not because its goal was wrong, but entirely because its strategy has been wrong. The strategic error* has consisted precisely in[4] the failure to unite with real friends in order to attack real enemies. *The reason for this failure is the inability to distinguish clearly enemies from friends.* A revolutionary party is the guide of the masses. *No army has ever been known to achieve victory when its chiefs have led it in a false direction*, and no revolutionary movement has ever been known to succeed when the revolutionary party has led it in a false direction. *We are all members of the revolutionary party, all leaders of the masses, all guides of the masses. We cannot but ask ourselves, however: Do we have this capacity? Will we not end up by leading the masses onto an erroneous road? Will we definitely achieve success?* To ensure that we will "not lead the masses astray" and will "definitely achieve success," *we must pay careful attention to the very important question of strategy. In order to determine this strategy,* we must first distinguish clearly friends from enemies.[5] *The Manifesto of the*

This text, previously dated March 1926 in the official canon of Mao's *Selected Works*, is now known to have first appeared in the December 1, 1925, issue of *Geming*, the semi-monthly organ of the Guomindang's National Revolutionary Army (see *Nianpu*, Vol. 1, p. 143). Our source is this earliest version, as reproduced in *Dangde wenxian*, No. 1, 1989, pp. 40–45. This text differs in one significant respect, noted below, from that which appears in *Mao Zedong ji*, Vol. 1, pp. 161–74.

1. This is the first item in our edition which also appears in the *Selected Works of Mao Zedong*, as published in Beijing in Chinese and English. All such texts are here presented in such a way as to show the variants between what Mao originally wrote, and the revised versions, produced under Mao's personal supervision, in the 1950s. An explanation of the typographical and other devices by which this is done can be found above, in the Note on Sources and Conventions.

2. He who cannot distinguish between enemies and friends is certainly not a revolutionary, yet to distinguish between them is not easy → This is a question of the first importance for the revolution.

3. If the Chinese revolution, although it has been going on for thirty years, has → If all China's previous revolutionary struggles have

4. Has consisted precisely in → The basic reason was

5. We must first distinguish clearly friends from enemies → We must pay attention to uniting with our real friends in order to attack our real enemies.

First National Congress of the Guomindang proclaimed this strategy and traced the boundary between our enemies and our friends. But this declaration was very concise. If we want to understand this important strategy and to distinguish our real enemies from our real friends, we must make a general analysis of the economic status, *the class character, and the numerical strength* of the various classes of Chinese society, as well as of their respective attitudes toward the revolution.

In any country, whether of heaven's creation or the earth's design, there are always three categories of people: upper, middle, and lower. If we analyze things in more detail, there are five categories: the big bourgeoisie, the middle bourgeoisie, the petty bourgeoisie, the semiproletariat, and the proletariat. As regards the countryside, the big landlords are the big bourgeoisie, the small landlords are the middle bourgeoisie, the owner-peasants are the petty bourgeoisie, the semiowner tenant peasants are the semiproletariat, and the farm laborers are the proletariat. In the cities, the big bankers, big merchants, and big industrialists are the big bourgeoisie; the moneychangers, middle merchants, and owners of small factories are the middle bourgeoisie; the shopkeepers and master craftsmen are the petty bourgeoisie; the shop assistants, street vendors, and handicraft workers are the semiproletariat; and the industrial workers and coolies are the proletariat. Each of these five categories of people has a different economic position and a different class nature. Consequently, they manifest different attitudes toward the present revolution, namely opposing the revolution, partially opposing the revolution, observing neutrality toward the revolution, participating in the revolution, and serving as the main force of the revolution.

The attitudes of the various classes in China toward the national revolution are virtually identical with those of the various classes in the capitalist countries of Western Europe toward social revolution. This may seem strange, but in fact it is not strange at all. This is because the goals and techniques of the present revolution are the same everywhere, the goal being to overthrow international capitalist imperialism, and the method being to unite the oppressed peoples and classes for the fight. This is the most important characteristic that distinguishes today's revolution from all other revolutions in history.

Let us take a look at what the various classes in Chinese society are like.

First, the big bourgeoisie.[6] In economically backward and semicolonial China, the big bourgeoisie[7] is wholly a vassal of the international bourgeoisie, depending entirely on imperialism for its survival and development. *For exam-*

---

6. The big bourgeoisie → The landlord class and the comprador class
7. The big bourgeoisie → The landlord class and the comprador class

ple, the comprador class—the bankers (Lu Zongyu,[8] Chen Lianbo,[9] etc.); the businessmen (e.g., Tang Shaoyi,[10] He Dong,[11] etc.); the industrialists (e.g., Zhang Jian,[12] Sheng Enxi,[13] etc.); those who have close relationships with foreign capital.

The big landlords (e.g., Zhang Zuolin,[14] Chen Gongshou,[15] etc.)

The bureaucrats (e.g., Sun Baoqi,[16] Yan Huiqing,[17] etc.)

---

8. Lu Zongyu (1876–1941), a native of Zhejiang, obtained the degree of *juren* in 1905. In 1913 he was elected senator in the first Beijing Parliament. He served as minister to Japan from December 1913 through 1915 and was thus involved in the negotiations regarding the Twenty-one Demands. A friend of Cao Rulin, he became associated with the Bank of Communications, which obtained many loans from Japan in support of the Beijing warlords. This background made him one of the "three traitors" (together with Cao Rulin and Zhang Zongxiang) against whom the May Fourth student demonstrations were directed.

9. Chen Lianbo was the chief comprador of the Hong Kong and Shanghai Banking Corporation in Guangzhou and president of the Guangzhou Chamber of Commerce.

10. Tang Shaoyi (1860–1938), *zi* Shaochuan, was a native of Guangdong. He gained the favor of Yuan Shikai in 1884 and retained close links with Yuan throughout his career in the imperial bureaucracy. When Yuan Shikai became president in 1912, he appointed Tang as premier, but the two men soon drifted apart. In 1917, Tang joined Sun Yatsen's military government in Guangzhou as minister of finance; after the collapse of peace negotiations between the north and the south in October 1919, he lived in retirement in his native Xiangshan. The nature of his business activities is not clear.

11. He Dong (1862–1956), *zi* Xiaosheng, Western name Sir Robert Ho-tong, was a native of Hong Kong. From 1882 onward, he was associated in various capacities with Jardine, Matheson & Co. He Dong became Hong Kong's largest property owner and one of its wealthiest citizens, and was associated with many companies including the Hong Kong and Shanghai Banking Corporation and other shipping, insurance, investment, and manufacturing concerns. He was knighted in 1915 because of his loyal services to Britain during the First World War. In 1922 he acquired a controlling interest in the *Gongshang ribao* (Industry and Commerce Daily), which Mao stigmatized in his report of January 8, 1926, on Propaganda to the Second Guomindang Congress (see below) as an organ of the comprador class and an enemy of the revolution.

12. On the industrialist and reformer Zhang Jian, see the note to the text of July 14, 1919, "What Kind of Talk Is This?" in Volume I, p. 355.

13. Enxi may be a typographical error for Enyi (the characters here transcribed "xi" and "yi" are not dissimilar), and the reference may be to Sheng Enyi (a son of the noted comprador Sheng Xuanhuai) who as general manager of the Anyuan coal mines had called in the troops in September 1925 to put down a strike. (See Li Jui, *Early Mao*, p. 212.)

14. On Zhang Zuolin, the dominant figure in northeast China until his assassination in 1928, see above, the note to the text of July 1, 1923, "Hunan under the Provisional Constitution."

15. A great landowner from Foshan in Guangdong, who was vice president of the Guangdong Chamber of Commerce.

16. Sun Baoqi (1867–1931), *zi* Muhan, was a native of Hangzhou. After occupying many important bureaucratic and diplomatic posts under the empire, he served as foreign minister of the Beijing government from 1913 to 1915. As premier in 1924, he established diplomatic relations with the Soviet Union. In 1925, he became president of the Hanyeping iron and steel complex and of the China Merchants' Steam Navigation Company.

17. Yan Huiqing (1877–1950), *zi* Junren, Western name W. W. Yen, was a native of Shanghai. He served as minister of agriculture and commerce in the cabinet of his father-in-law, Sun Baoqi, in 1924, and was himself briefly premier in September 1924 and in 1926.

The warlords (e.g., Zhang Zuolin, Cao Kun,[18] *etc.)*

The class of the reactionary intellectuals is an appendage of the above four kinds of people. The high-ranking staff of banking, industrial, and commercial enterprises of comprador character, plutocrats and high-ranking government officials, politicians, part of the students who have studied abroad in Japan and in the West, part of the teachers and students from universities and specialized schools, eminent lawyers, and so on all belong to this category. The goals of this class[19] and those of the national revolution are absolutely incompatible. From beginning to end, they[20] side with imperialism and are an extreme counterrevolutionary group.[21] *This class probably numbers no more than a million, or one in four hundred in a population of four hundred million people. It is a deadly enemy within the national-revolutionary movement.*

Second, the middle bourgeoisie.

The banking, industrial, and commercial class who own Chinese capital. (Because in economically backward China, the development of national banks, industry, and commerce by national capital is still limited to the level of the middle class. Here "bank" refers to the small banks or moneylenders; "industry" refers to small-scale manufacture; "commerce" refers to the business of trading in national goods. No part of large-scale banking, industry, and commerce is unrelated to foreign capital. They can only be counted as part of the comprador class.)

Small landlords. Many of the higher intellectuals—the employees of Chinese commercial banking, industry, and commerce, the majority of the students who study in Japan and in the West, the majority of university and special school professors and students, and small lawyers all belong to this category. This class aspires to attain the position of the big bourgeoisie, but it suffers from the blows of foreign capital and the oppression of the warlords, and cannot develop. This class[22] has *adopted* a contradictory attitude toward the national revolution. When it suffers from the blows of foreign capital and the oppression of the warlords, it feels the need for revolution and favors the revolutionary movement against imperialism and the warlords. But *at present*, when the proletariat at home takes

---

18. On Cao Kun, leader of the Zhili clique of warlords, see the note to the text of July 11, 1923, "The Beijing Coup d'État and the Merchants."

19. The goals of this class → These classes represent the most backward and most reactionary relations of production in China and hinder the development of her productive forces. Their goals . . .

20. From beginning to end, they side . . . → The big landlord and big comprador classes in particular always side . . .

21. Counterrevolutionary group → Counterrevolutionary group. Their political representatives are the *Étatistes* and the right wing of the Guomindang.

22. This class . . . → This class represents the capitalist relations of production in China in town and country. The middle bourgeoisie, by which is meant chiefly the national bourgeoisie . . .

a militant part in the revolution and the international proletariat abroad lends active support, it senses a threat to its own development *and existence* as a class that aspires to move up into the class of the big bourgeoisie, and becomes skeptical about the revolution. *This class is the so-called national bourgeoisie,* and politically they stand for *Étatisme*—that is, the realization of a state under the rule of a single class, the national bourgeoisie. A self-styled "true disciple" of Dai Jitao put forward the following opinion in the Beijing *Morning Post*: "Raise your left hand to knock down imperialism! Raise your right hand to knock down the Communist Party!" This *vividly* illustrates the contradictory and fearful attitude of this class. They are against interpreting the Principle of People's Livelihood according to the theory of class struggle, and oppose the Guomindang's alliance with Russia and the admission of Communists. But the attempt of this class to establish a state under the rule of the national bourgeoisie is completely impracticable, because the present world situation is one in which the two great forces of revolution and counterrevolution are engaged in the final struggle. Two huge banners have been raised by these two great forces. On the one hand is the red banner of revolution, held aloft by the Third International and rallying all *the oppressed nations and* the oppressed classes of the world; on the other is the white banner of counterrevolution, held aloft by the League of Nations and rallying all the counterrevolutionary elements of the world. The intermediate classes, *such as the so-called Second International in the West and those so-called* Étatistes *in China,* will beyond doubt disintegrate rapidly, some sections turning left and joining the ranks of the revolutionaries, others turning right and joining the ranks of the counterrevolutionaries. There is no room for them to remain "independent." Therefore, the Chinese middle bourgeoisie's idea of an "independent" revolution, in which its own class *interests* would constitute the main theme, is a mere illusion. *To be sure, they are now still in a semi-counterrevolutionary position and are not yet our direct enemy. Nevertheless, when they sense a daily increasing threat from the worker and peasant classes, namely when they are forced to make a few more concessions to the interests of the worker and peasant classes (such as the movement for reducing rent in the countryside, and the strike movement in the cities), they or a part of them (the right wing of the middle bourgeoisie) will definitely take a stand on the side of imperialism, will definitely become completely counterrevolutionary, and will definitely become our direct enemy. In fact, there is a group of which it is impossible to distinguish clearly whether or not its members belong to the comprador class. As regards commerce, many merchants certainly distinguish very clearly between foreign goods and domestic goods, but there are also shops that display both domestic and foreign goods. As for the intellectual class, those from small landlord backgrounds who have gone to study in capitalist countries of the Eastern Sea* [i.e., Japan] *definitely show very clearly that, alongside their indigenous characteristics, they have also acquired foreign characteristics. Even those children of small landlord backgrounds who study at specialized schools and universities inside China, and who are steeped in the influence of these half indigenous and half foreign returned students, inevitably take on this half indigenous and half foreign nature. People of this kind do not have an unmixed national-bourgeois nature; one might call them the "seminational bourgeoisie."*

They constitute the right wing of the middle bourgeoisie, and as soon as the national-revolutionary struggle becomes intense, these people will certainly rally the ranks of imperialism and the warlords and make splendid partners of the comprador class. The left wing of the middle bourgeoisie is composed of those who absolutely refuse to follow imperialism. At times, this group has a certain amount of revolutionary character (for example, during the high tide of boycotting foreign goods). But it is extremely difficult to get rid of their "pacifist" attitudes, which are quite empty of meaning but to which they have been attached for a long time, and they are often seized with terror when faced with "Red" tendencies. Hence their intermittent collaboration with the revolution cannot last. Therefore, the Chinese middle bourgeoisie, whether it be its right wing or its left wing, contains many dangerous elements, and one absolutely cannot expect it to strike out resolutely on the path of revolution and to participate loyally in the revolutionary cause along with the other classes, except for a few who find themselves in special circumstances of history and environment. The middle bourgeoisie numbers at most one out of one hundred people within the country (1 percent), that is, four million people.

Third, the petty bourgeoisie. For example,
>   the owner peasants,
>   the small merchants,
>   the master handicraftsmen,
>   the lower levels of the intellectual class—petty functionaries, office clerks, middle school students, primary and secondary school teachers, and small lawyers—

all belong to this category. Both because of its size and because of its class character, this class deserves very close attention.[23] *Among those making up the petty bourgeoisie, the owner-peasants alone number from 100 million to 120 million. The small merchants, the master handicraftsmen, and the intellectual class probably number from 20 to 30 million, making a total of 130 million.* Although this class has[24] the same petty bourgeois economic status, they fall *in fact* into three different sections. The first section consists of those who have some surplus money or grain; that is, those who by manual or mental labor earn more each year than they consume for their own support, *thereby creating the so-called initial accumulation of capital.* Such people very much want to "get

---

23. Close attention. → Close attention. The owner-peasants and the master handicraftsmen are both engaged in small-scale production.

24. This class has → These various strata among the petty bourgeoisie have

rich"; while they have no illusions about amassing great fortunes, they invariably desire to climb up into the middle bourgeoisie. Their mouths water copiously when they see the respect in which those small moneybags are held, and they pray to Marshal Zhao *(the god of wealth)* most assiduously. People of this sort are *extremely* timid, afraid of government officials, and also a little afraid of the revolution. Since they are fairly close to the middle bourgeoisie in economic status, they have a lot of faith in its propaganda and are suspicious of the revolution. This section is, *however*, a minority among the petty bourgeoisie, *probably making up no more than 10 percent of the total number of petty bourgeois (or approximately 15 million), and constitutes* the right wing of the petty bourgeoisie. The second section consists of those who are just self-supporting.[25] *What they earn and what they consume each year even out, no more, no less.* This section of people is very different from the people in the first section; they also want to get rich, but Marshal Zhao never lets them get rich. Their sufferings in recent years from the oppression and exploitation of the imperialists, the warlords, and the big and middle bourgeoisie[26] have given them the feeling that the world is no longer what it was. They perceive that if they now work only as hard as before, they cannot earn enough to live on. To be able to support themselves they have to work longer hours (that is to say, get up earlier[27]), and devote more attention to their work. They become rather abusive, denouncing the foreigners as "foreign devils," the warlords as "robber commanders," and the local bullies and bad gentry as "the heartless rich." As for the movement against the imperialists and the warlords, they simply suspect that it may not succeed, on the ground that "the foreigners and the commanders seem so powerful," refuse to join it recklessly, and take a neutral position, but they never oppose the revolution. This section is very numerous, about one-half of the petty bourgeoisie *(50 percent), or about 75 million.* The third section consists of those who have a deficit[28] *every year.* Many in this section, who originally belonged to better-off families, are undergoing a gradual change from a position of being barely able to eke out a living to having a deficit. When they come to settle their accounts at the end of each year, they are shocked, exclaiming, "What? Another deficit!" Such people, because they have known better days in the past and are now going downhill with every passing year, their debts mounting and their life becoming more and more miserable, "shudder at the thought of the future." They suffer mental distress greater than that of anyone else[29] because there is such a contrast between their past and their present. Such people are rather important for the

---

25. Are just self-supporting → Are, in the main, economically self-supporting
26. The big and middle bourgeoisie → The feudal landlords and the big comprador bourgeoisie
27. Get up earlier → Get up earlier, leave off later
28. Have a deficit → Are in more and more reduced circumstances
29. Mental distress greater than that of anyone else → Great mental distress

revolutionary movement *and can contribute substantial strength to the advancement of the revolution. They make up 40 percent of the petty bourgeoisie, or 60 million*—a not inconsiderable mass, which constitutes the left wing of the petty bourgeoisie. In normal times the three sections of the petty bourgeoisie discussed above differ in their attitude to the revolution. In times of war, however, that is to say, when the tide of the revolution runs high and the dawn of victory is in sight, not only will the left wing of the petty bourgeoisie join the revolution, but the middle section too may join. Even right-wingers, swept forward by the great revolutionary tide of the proletariat and of the left wing of the petty bourgeoisie, will have no alternative but to go along with the revolution. We can see from the experience of the May 30th movement and the peasant movement in various places *during the past two years* that this conclusion is correct.

Fourth, the semiproletariat. What is here called the semiproletariat consists of six categories:[30]

1. the semiowner peasants,[31]
2. *the sharecroppers,*
3. the poor peasants,
4. the handicraftsmen,
5. the shop assistants, and
6. the street vendors.

Among the Chinese peasants, the semiowner peasants number about 50 million and the sharecroppers and poor peasants number about 60 million each, with the three categories totaling 170 million. They are an extremely large mass in the rural areas. The so-called peasant problem is in large part their problem. Although these three categories of peasants[32] belong to the semiproletariat, they may be further divided into three smaller categories, upper, middle, and lower, according to their economic condition. The semiowner peasants are worse off than the owner-peasants, because every year they are short of about half the food they need and have to make up this deficiency by cultivating others' land, working,[33] or engaging in petty trading. In late spring and early summer, when the crop is still in the blade and the old stock is consumed, they borrow money from others at exorbitant rates of interest and buy grain at high prices. Their plight is naturally harder than that of the owner peasants, who need no help from others,

---

30. Six categories → Five categories (Category 2, "share-croppers," is omitted.)

31. The semiowner peasants → The overwhelming majority of the semiowners

32. These three categories of peasants → The semiowner peasants, the poor peasants, and the small handicraftsmen are engaged in production on a still smaller scale. The overwhelming majority both of the semiowner peasants and of the poor peasants

33. Working → Selling part of their labor power

but they are better off than the sharecroppers.[34] For the sharecroppers[35] own no land, and receive only half[36] the harvest for their year's toil, while the semiowner peasants, though receiving only half or less than half the harvest on land rented form others, can keep the entire crop from the land they own. The semiowner peasants are therefore more revolutionary than the owner-peasants, but less revolutionary than the sharecroppers.[37] The *sharecroppers and* poor peasants are all tenant peasants in the countryside who are exploited by the landlords, but there is a substantial difference in their economic status.[38] The sharecroppers[39] *have no land,* but have relatively adequate farm implements and a reasonable amount of circulating capital.[40] Peasants of this type may retain half the product of their year's toil. To make up the deficiency, they cultivate side crops, catch fish or shrimps, raise poultry or pigs, and thus eke out[41] a living, hoping in the midst of hardship and destitution to tide over the year. Thus, their life is harder than that of the semiowner peasants, but they are better off than the poor peasants.[42] They are more revolutionary than the semiowner peasants, but less revolutionary than the poor peasants. As for the poor peasants,[43] they have neither adequate farm implements nor circulating capital nor enough manure; their fields yield meager crops, and they have little left after paying the rent.[44] In hard times, they piteously beg help from relatives and friends, borrowing a few *dou* or *sheng* of grain to last them a few days, and their debts are many and diverse like loads on the backs of oxen. They are the most wretched among the peasants and are extremely receptive to revolutionary propaganda. The handicraftsmen are called semiproletarians because they have their own tools,[45] and belong to a kind of liberal profession. Their[46] economic status is somewhat similar to that of the sharecroppers in agriculture.[47] Because of heavy family burdens and the disparity between their earnings and the cost of living, the constant pinch of poverty, and the dread of unemployment, their situation is broadly similar to that of the

---

34. The sharecroppers → The poor peasants
35. The sharecroppers → The poor peasants
36. Half → Half or less than half
37. The sharecroppers → The poor peasants
38. There is a substantial difference in their economic status. → They must be divided into two categories.
39. The sharecroppers → One category
40. Circulating capital → Funds
41. And thus eke out → Or sell part of their labor power, and thus eke out
42. The poor peasants → The other category of poor peasants
43. The poor peasants → The so-called other category of poor peasants
44. Have little left after paying rent. → Have little left after paying rent, and have an even greater need to sell part of their labor power.
45. Because they have their own tools → Because, though they own some simple means of production
46. Their → They are often forced to sell part of their labor power, and their
47. The sharecroppers → The poor peasants in the rural areas

sharecroppers.[48] The shop assistants are employees of small and middle businessmen,[49] supporting their households on meager pay and getting a raise in pay perhaps only once in several years while prices rise every year. If by chance you get into intimate conversation with them, they invariably pour out their endless grievances. Roughly the same in status as the handicraftsmen,[50] they are extremely receptive to revolutionary propaganda. The street vendors, whether they carry their wares around on a pole or set up stalls along the street, have tiny funds and very small earnings and do not make enough to feed and clothe themselves. Their status is roughly the same as that of the poor peasants, and like the poor peasants they need a revolution to change the existing state of affairs. *The handicraftsmen number about 6 percent (that is, 24 million) of the total population. There are about 5 million shop assistants and about 1 million street vendors. Together with the semiowner peasants, sharecroppers, and tenant peasants,*[51] the total for the semiproletariat as a whole is 200 million, which makes up half of the entire population.

Fifth, the proletariat. *Its categories and its numbers are as follows:*
the industrial proletariat [52]—about 2 million,
the coolies in the cities—about 3 million,
the rural proletariat—about 20 million.
Altogether they number about 45 million.[53] Because China is economically backward, there are not many *industrial* workers (the industrial proletariat[54]). These 2 million industrial workers are primarily in five industries—railways, mining, maritime transport, textiles, and shipbuilding—but the majority[55] are in[56] enterprises owned by foreign capitalists. Therefore, though not very numerous, the industrial proletariat has become the leading force in the revolutionary movement.[57] We can see the important position of the industrial proletariat in the

---

48. The sharecroppers → The poor peasants
49. Small and middle businessmen → Shops and stores
50. The handicraftsmen → The poor peasants and the small handicraftsmen
51. Mao here uses "tenant peasant" (*diannong*) rather than "poor peasant" (*pinnong*), but he is obviously referring to the same social group, since the implied total of 170 million semiowner peasants, sharecroppers, and poor (or tenant) peasants corresponds to that in the first sentence of this section, following the initial list of six categories.
52. The industrial proletariat → The modern industrial proletariat
53. The difference between the 25 million for the above three categories, and the total of 45 million given here, is accounted for by the 20 million *youmin* or lumpenproletarians included by Mao in the proletariat, and discussed separately in the second half of this paragraph.
54. The industrial proletariat → The modern industrial proletariat
55. The majority → A great number of them
56. Are in → Are enslaved in
57. Has become the leading force in the revolutionary movement. → Represents China's new productive forces, is the most progressive class in modern China, and has become the leading force in the revolutionary movement.

national revolution[58] from the strength it has displayed in the strikes of the last four years, such as the seamen's strikes,[59] the railway strikes,[60] the strikes in the Kailuan and Jiaozuo coal mines,[61] as well as[62] the general strikes in Shanghai and Hong Kong after the May 30th Incident. The first reason why the industrial workers hold this position is their concentration. No other section of the people is so *organized and* concentrated" as they are. The second reason is their low economic status. They have been deprived of tools,[63] have nothing left but their two hands, have no hope of ever becoming rich and, moreover, are subjected to the most ruthless treatment by the imperialists, the warlords, and the comprador class.[64] This is why they are particularly good fighters. The coolies in the cities are also a force very much worth reckoning with. They are mostly dockers and rickshaw pullers, and among them, too, are sewage carters and street cleaners. Possessing nothing but their hands, they are similar in economic status to the industrial workers, but are less organized and concentrated,[65] and play a less important role in the productive forces. There is as yet little modern capitalist farming in China. By agricultural proletariat is meant farm laborers hired by the year, the month, or the day. Having neither land, farm implements, nor circulating capital,[66] this kind of farm laborers can live only by selling their labor power. Of all the workers they work the longest hours, for the lowest wages, under the worst conditions, and with the least security of employment. This kind of people are the most hard-pressed in the villages, and their position in the peasant movement is as important as that of the poor peasants. The lumpenproletariat[67] is made up of peasants who have lost their land and handicraftsmen who cannot get work. *They number over 20 million and are the source of [manpower for] fighting among soldiers and bandit misfortunes within our country. The largest*

---

58. The national revolution → The Chinese revolution

59. The reference is to the Hong Kong seamen's strike of January–March 1923, which ended in a victory for the workers.

60. The reference is to the Guangzhou-Hankou railroad workers' strike of September 1922 and the Beijing-Wuhan railroad workers' strike of February 1923; see above, the declaration of September 8, 1922, regarding the former, and the two telegrams of February 20, 1923, regarding the latter.

61. The strike in the Kailuan (Kaiping and Luanzhou) collieries in Hebei took place in October 1922. The strike at Jiaozuo in Henan lasted from July 1 to August 9, 1925.

62. As well as → The Shamian strike, as well as

63. Tools → All means of production

64. The comprador class → Bourgeoisie

65. Less organized and concentrated → Less concentrated than the industrial workers

66. Circulating capital → Funds

67. Lumpenproletariat → Apart from all these, there is the fairly large lumpenproletariat. (In general, *youmin* is translated "vagrants" in this edition, because Mao uses the term almost exclusively of vagabond or floating elements in the countryside. Here, however, where it also includes urban lumpenproletarians, we have used the more Marxist term.)

number of the lumpenproletariat are bandits; the second largest are soldiers, followed in order by robbers, thieves, and prostitutes. Among the whole population, they are those who lead the most precarious existence. In every part of the country they have their secret societies, which serve as[68] their mutual-aid organs in the political and economic struggle, such as the Triad Society in Fujian and Guangdong; the Elder Brother Society in Hunan, Hubei, Guizhou, and Sichuan; the Big Sword Society in Anhui, Henan, Shandong, and other provinces; the Rational Life Society in Zhili and the three northeastern provinces; and the Green and Red Gangs in Shanghai and elsewhere. China's greatest and most difficult problem is how to handle these people. *China has two problems: one is poverty and the other is unemployment. Therefore if the problem of unemployment is solved, half of China's problem is solved.* This group of people can fight very bravely; if we can find a way to lead them,[69] they can become a revolutionary force.

What has been said above can be summed up in the following table:[70]

Class	Population	Attitude toward Revolution
Big bourgeoisie	1,000,000	Extremely reactionary
Middle bourgeoisie	4,000,000	Right wing is very nearly counterrevolutionary; left wing can join the revolution at times, but will compromise with the enemy; as a whole, semicounterrevolutionary
Petty bourgeoisie		
Well-off elements (right wing)	15,000,000	In normal times, close to the semicounter-revolutionary attitude of the middle bourgeoisie; in time of war, can go along with the revolution
Self-sufficient elements (center)	75,000,000	In normal times, neutral; in times of war, joins the revolution

---

68. Serve as → Were originally

69. If we can find a way to lead them → But they are apt to be destructive; if we can find a way to lead them

70. The whole of this table has been deleted in the *Selected Works* version.

Nonself-sufficient elements (left wing)	60,000,000	Welcome it
TOTAL	150,000,000[71]	
Semiproletariat		
Semiowner peasants	50,000,000	Participate
Sharecroppers	60,000,000	Actively participate
Poor peasants	60,000,000	Struggle bravely
Handicraftsmen	24,000,000	Same as sharecroppers
Shop assistants	5,000,000	Same as sharecroppers
Street vendors	1,000,000	Same as poor peasants
TOTAL	200,000,000	
Proletariat		
Industrial proletariat	2,000,000	Main force
Urban coolies	3,000,000	Main force, second to the industrial proletariat
Agricultural proletariat	20,000,000	Struggle bravely
Lumpenproletariat	20,000,000	Can be led to become a revolutionary force
TOTAL	45,000,000	

Who is our enemy? Who is our friend? We can now answer these questions. All[72] those in league with imperialism—the warlords, the bureaucrats, the comprador class, the big landlords, and the reactionary intellectual class, *that is, the so-called big bourgeoisie in China*—are our enemies, *our true enemies.* All the petty bourgeoisie, the semiproletariat, and the proletariat[73] are our friends, *our true friends.* As for the vacillating middle bourgeoisie, its right wing must be considered our enemy; *even if it is not yet our enemy, it will soon become so.* Its left wing may be considered as our friend—but *not as our true friend,* and we

71. In the previously available version of this article, reproduced by the *Mao Zedong ji* from the text printed in *Zhongguo Nongmin* No. 2, 1926, the table is garbled here. Neither the indication *gong* (total), nor the figure of 150 million appears.

72. All → To sum up what has been said above, it can be seen that all

73. All the petty bourgeoisie, the semiproletariat, and the proletariat → The industrial proletariat is the leading force in our revolution. All the semiproletariat and the petty bourgeoisie

must be constantly on our guard against it. We must not allow it to create confusion within our ranks! *How many are our true friends? There are 395 million of them. How many are our true enemies? There are 1 million of them. How many are there of these people in the middle who may be either our friends or our enemies? There are 4 million of them. Even if we consider these 4 million as enemies, this only adds up to a bloc of barely 5 million, and a sneeze from 395 million would certainly suffice to blow them down.*

Three hundred and ninety-five million, unite!

Announcement of the Chinese Guomindang to All Party Members Throughout the Country and Overseas Explaining the Tactics of the Revolution

(December 4, 1925)

For the consideration of party branches at all levels, and of all comrades through-out the country and overseas: Ever since the time when the former Director General was still alive, we observe that revolution has had a long but unsuccessful history. When it was resolutely decided to reorganize our party, already at that time there were a band of good-for-nothing rightist party members who wanted to avoid genuine revolution, for they knew that reorganization and renovation were not advantageous for thieving idlers, monopolists, and those who seek office in order to enrich themselves. They obstructed it in every possible way, and after the First National Congress decided on revolutionary tactics, people of that ilk, knowing that obstruction could not in the end prevail, openly rebelled. Feng Ziyou, Ma Su, and others colluded with Duan Qirui and Zhang Zuolin, and formed a group urging them on.[1] After Yang Ximin and Liu

---

This text does not bear Mao's name, but according to a handwritten copy from the Guomindang archives it was drafted by him in his capacity as acting head of the Propaganda Department on November 27, 1925. It was approved by the Central Executive Committee of the Guomindang on December 4 and published on December 5, 1925, in the first issue of *Zhengzhi zhoubao*. It also appeared on the same day in the Guangzhou *Minguo ribao*. The latter version omits the reference to tactics in the title and emphasizes three brief passages by setting them in large characters. It also contains minor typographical errors. Our translation follows the text as printed in *Zhengzhi zhoubao*.

1. Feng Ziyou (1882–1958), *zi* Jianhua, was born in Yokohama of parents from Guangdong. In Japan he organized the Youth Society, joined the Tongmenghui, and was an anti-Qing activist. In 1914 Sun Yatsen sent him to the United States to take charge of affairs there, and on his return to China in 1917 he was elected to the Beijing Senate as a representative of overseas Chinese. Although present at the First Guomindang Congress in January 1924, he was excluded from higher party councils because of his strong opposition to Sun Yatsen's policy of cooperation with the Chinese Communist Party. After Sun's death he played a leading role in setting up the Guomindang Comrades' Club, the group alluded to here, which was on friendly terms with the militarists and politicians in Beijing. Ma Su was also an early associate of Sun Yatsen, who had been his personal representative in Washington at one time. He, too, had opposed Sun's policy of collaboration with the Communists and had joined in setting up the Comrades' Club.

Zhenhuan had colluded with British imperialism to cause trouble in the rear,[2] Liang Hongkai, Zheng Runqi, Mo Xiong, Zhu Zhuowen, and others acted even more ruthlessly in savagely assassinating our brave Comrade Liao Zhongkai.[3] Thus they sought to overturn the Guangzhou revolutionary base at a single stroke. At this juncture, when the existence or ruin, the disappearance or survival of our party are at stake, we cannot but take the sternest measures against those party members who have betrayed the party, in order to preserve our party's revolutionary position. Fortunately, we can rely on the prestige of the former Director General's revolutionary spirit,[4] and on the resolute and courageous efforts of all the comrades. In June of this year, we swept away Yang and Liu, and in September we eliminated[5] all the traitors of the Liao affair. Thus the Guangzhou base was returned from danger to security, and the cause of revolution, after a detour, returned to its old course. Thus our unity was tempered, and further advances could be expected. We did not provide for the fact that those people, with their unspeakably evil hearts, would once again collude with Xiong Kewu in an attempt to take Guangzhou from north of the river, attacking from three directions, together with Chen Jiongming and Deng Benyin, under the

---

2. Yang Ximin, commander in chief of the Yunanese forces, and Liu Zhenhuan, who commanded a small army from Guangxi, had participated in the struggle to retake Guangzhou from Chen Jiongming in 1923, after which they never left the Guangzhou area. In order to conciliate them, Sun Yatsen had given them high positions within the Guomindang, but they were uninterested in revolution. Their monopolization of revenues and collection of opium and smuggling taxes made them extremely unpopular. They occupied a key position in Guangzhou at the time of the May 30th Incident, because most of the other Guomindang forces were in eastern Guangdong, pursuing the campaign against Chen Jiongming. They sought an understanding with the British and refused to allow antiforeign demonstrations in the city, thus causing "trouble in the rear." Troops from the Eastern Expedition thereupon returned to fight them, and in a battle lasting from June 6 to June 12 both generals were defeated and forced to flee to Hong Kong.

3. Regarding the assassination of Liao Zhongkai, see above, the note to Central Circular no. 15 of July 21, 1924. For Zheng Runqi and Mo Xiong, see above, the note to the Manifesto of the First Guangdong Provincial Congress of the Guomindang, dated October 26, 1925. Liang Hongkai (1887–1956), *zi* Jingyun, was a native of Guangdong. An early member of the Tongmenghui, he became commander of the first Guangdong army in 1924. In 1925, he was imprisoned for three years, on suspicion of complicity in Liao Zhongkai's murder. Zhu Chao (?–1936), *zi* Zhuowen, a native of Guangdong, was a veteran follower of Sun Yatsen who had participated in the establishment of the Gemingdang (Revolutionary Party) in 1913. In the early 1920s, he was involved in aviation in Guangdong. The circumstances surrounding Liao's death have never been fully elucidated, but apart from Liang, the four persons mentioned here are not commonly regarded as among the main culprits.

4. Here, and wherever they appear subsequently in this text, the three characters *xian zongli* (the former Director General) are preceded by a blank space—the equivalent of elevating each mention of Sun to the top of the next line as a sign of respect.

5. The term translated "eliminate," *suqing*, is the same one Mao used in the 1950s to designate the Movement to Eliminate Counterrevolutionaries.

command of British imperialism, in the hope of destroying our revolutionary forces.[6] Once again, thanks to our comrades' united efforts, within two months these obstinate enemies approaching from three sides were eliminated and the forces of revolution were strengthened. At this time, a small number of comrades in Beijing once again announced the convening of the Fourth Plenum of the Central Executive Committee.[7] Now it would appear that, in accordance with the decision reiterated at the Third Plenum of the Central Committee on May 21 and May 23, the Fourth Plenum of the Central Committee can only be held in Guangzhou. For it has long been decided that the Second National Congress should meet in Guangzhou, and also that a Fourth Plenum of the Central Committee should be held to prepare resolutions for the Congress. On October 30, the Central Committee decided that the Fourth Plenum should be convened three weeks before the national Congress. This being the case, and **Guangzhou being our party's revolutionary base, whereas Beijing is a place where warlords and counterrevolutionaries gather and exert great pressure, and given that the Congress is public in nature, how can we reject Guangzhou and go to Beijing?**[8] Manifestly, a band of party members who oppose the party has seized a fraudulent occasion and is egging on a minority of Central Committee members whose revolutionary convictions are wavering, with a view to actions that are not in the interest of our party. One of them is Zou Lu. Now we observe that in our party, from its reorganization to the present, reactionary party members from Feng Ziyou to Zou Lu have consistently attacked our party and its government; they have uttered accusations such as "Communism," "uniting with Russia," "accepting Communist elements," **"supporting Communism" and so on. This is a tactic used by the imperialists and the warlords to sow dissension within the alliance of all the classes for the national revolution. Since our comrades have no affinity with the imperialists and the warlords, they should not aid their propaganda,**[9] thereby causing confusion in the national consciousness. Moreover, facts are facts, and these rumors cannot survive for long. For uniting with Russia, and accepting Communists, are important tactics of our party in pursuing the goal of victory in the revolution. The late Director General was the first to decide on them, and after they were adopted at the First National Congress, they had an objective basis and a profound justification. Now, today's revolution is an episode in the final decisive struggle between the

---

6. For another reference to the "three-cornered uprising" of Chen, Deng, and Xiong, see the "Manifesto of the First Guangdong Provincial Congress" of October 26, 1925.

7. Regarding this announcement, in a telegram of November 6, 1925, from Lin Sen and others, see also, above, "The Central Executive Committee of the Chinese Guomindang Sternly Repudiates the Illegal Meeting of Beijing Party Members," dated November 27, 1925.

8. The passage in bold is emphasized in the *Minguo ribao* text by setting it in double-sized characters.

9. This passage is also set in big type in the *Minguo ribao* version of the Chinese text.

two great forces of revolution and counterrevolution in the world. It is different in nature from all other revolutions in history. Consequently, the progress of the revolution is naturally different as regards its tactics. Today imperialism has long since banded together to exercise pressure on our party. If our party's revolutionary strategy does not take as its starting point union with Soviet Russia; if it does not secure the great masses of the worker and peasant classes as its foundation; if it does not accept the Communists, who advocate the interests of the peasants and workers; then the revolutionary forces will sink into isolation, and the revolution will not be able to succeed. The reason our party could not achieve victory in the 1911 Revolution is that at the time, the counterrevolutionary forces were united on an international basis, whereas the revolutionary forces of our party as yet belonged to no international union. Moreover, within our country, a great mass basis had not yet been called into being, and we were reduced to isolation and therefore were obliged to accept compromises, which ultimately led to defeat. Things having reached the point where they are today, how can we follow along in the same old track? Those imperialists and militarists are truly terrified lest we adopt revolutionary tactics, and they seek on every hand to sow dissension and to sabotage us, with the aim of making our party lose all its friends and allies inside and outside the country, and of placing us once more in our previous isolated situation. Thus the cause of revolution could never triumph, and those people would finally realize their dream of ruling China forever. Their scheme is truly as venemous as this. A small group of our comrades, making inadequate observations, has always been fooled by these divisive policies. Most of the disruption within the party over the years originates with this. We must recognize that in today's situation, he who is not for the revolution is for counterrevolution. There is absolutely no neutral ground in the middle. But if you want revolution, you must unite with all revolutionary factions internationally and within the country. Only if you unite as one can you fight the decisive battle against counterrevolution without being defeated. Otherwise, there is no way you can avoid defeat. Not only will you be defeated, but you yourself might fall into the danger of sinking into counterrevolution. The cases of all those party members who have betrayed the party, from Feng Ziyou to Zou Lu, are proof of this. The matter of this meeting in Beijing has already been the subject of a severe warning from this committee,[10] and it has moreover been decided that the Second Congress will meet on January 1 of next year. On December 11 of this year, the Fourth Plenum of the Central Committee will meet in Guangzhou. We have already telegraphed to all members of the committee in Beijing and Shanghai urging them to come south on that day to participate in the meeting. The majority of the committee members are of the same mind, so originally there was no problem at all. Recently, however, rumors have been rife inside and outside the

---

10. The reference is no doubt to the telegram of the Central Executive Committee dated November 27, 1925, already cited above.

party, many of them arising from failure to understand our party's policy. Consequently, we are sending this circular telegram to comrades everywhere throughout the country, regarding the process of struggle with counterrevolution since reorganization and the revolutionary principles adopted by the former Director General. **We hope that every comrade will support the Director General's views and will not be misled by heterodox doctrines.**[11] The future of the revolution depends unequivocally on this. The present announcement is sent to make this known to you.

> The Central Executive Committee of the
> Chinese Guomindang
> December 4 of the fourteenth year of the
> Republic of China

---

11. Emphasized in the *Minguo ribao* version.

Reasons for Publishing the Political Weekly

(December 5, 1925)

Why are we publishing the *Political Weekly*? For the revolution. Why do we want revolution? In order to achieve the liberation of the Chinese nation, in order to bring about people's rule, in order that the people may attain economic prosperity.

For the sake of the revolution, we have offended all our enemies—imperialism throughout the world, warlords big and small throughout the country, the comprador class, local bullies, and bad gentry wherever they are, and all the reactionary political factions, such as the Anfu clique, the Research clique, the Federalists, and the *Étatistes*.[1] These enemies have intensified their oppression against us as our revolutionary strength has developed, and have mustered all their forces in the attempt to destroy us. They have navies, armies, and police, both foreign and domestic. They have vast international propaganda organs (such as Reuters). They have the newspapers and schools of the whole country. Although they have frequent clashes among themselves because of their differing interests, when it comes to their attitude toward us, not one of them cherishes good intentions.

Since putting down Yang [Ximin] and Liu [Zhenhuan],[2] and eliminating Zheng [Runqi] and Mo [Xiong],[3] our work here in Guangdong has clearly entered a new era. We have established peace and tranquillity in the city of Guangzhou such as has been unknown in the past fourteen years. The people have really obtained freedom of assembly, freedom of association, freedom of speech, and the freedom to strike. The armies of the Eastern Expedition did not conscript laborers, and gambling has been eliminated in the market of Guangzhou. The entire province has been militarily and politically unified. The

---

This editorial appeared in *Zhengzhi zhoubao*, No. 1, December 5, 1925. Our source is *Mao Zedong ji*, Vol. 1, pp. 109–11.

1. *Guojiazhuyi pai*. Although this term could be loosely translated as "nationalists," we follow the usage of rendering it as "*Étatiste*" because it focuses on the state (*guojia*) rather than on the people constituting the nation, as do *guomin* and *minzu*.

2. On Yang Ximin and Liu Zhenhuan, see above, the note to the text of December 4, 1925.

3. As indicated above, in a note to the Manifesto of October 26, 1925, Zheng Runqi and Mo Xiong were subordinate commanders of the Guomindang forces in Guangdong.

financial administration is also being gradually centralized. The harsh taxes crushing the people have already been partly eliminated, and steps for eliminating the rest have also been decided on. The judicial, educational, and communications organs of the people's government have all established reforming policies. The counterrevolutionary remnants in the North River, East River, and southern regions have been successively cleaned out. We are supporting the strikes and large-scale blockade of Hong Kong in order to uphold the patriotic workers' movement. We in no way hide our shortcomings, and we do not say that Guangdong has already been reformed—the reform of Guangdong has indeed only begun. There are still a number of local bandits who are disrupting the peace. There are still a number of local bullies, bad gentry, corrupt bureaucrats, and greedy officials who are oppressing the people. Within the inner offices of the civil administration, the judiciary, and the education and communications departments, there are still accumulated evils that have not yet been completely eliminated. We do not deny that these shortcomings exist. We do say that we already have a revolutionary power; that we already have the opportunity to wipe out the local bandits; that we already have a force to do battle with the local bullies, bad gentry, and corrupt and greedy officials; and that the administrative, financial, education, and communications organs of the people's government are already in a position to begin the task of renovation. In short, we already have a revolutionary base. All of our actions are based on the revolutionary policies of Mr. Sun Yatsen, and are open for all to see and hear. But the British imperialists in Hong Kong, all the counterrevolutionary remnants such as Chen Jiongming and Deng Benyin, and the countless local bullies, bad gentry, and corrupt and greedy officials cannot but tremble together before us. In the excess of their hatred and rage, there are no limits to the extremes of curses and slander that they will use to wound us. The propaganda organs of the counterrevolutionaries in Beijing, Tianjin, Shanghai, and Hankou are screaming in fear with their evil mouths and poisonous tongues, and they, too, will go to any extremity of curses and slander to wound us. The people of the whole country, especially those of whatever milieu living everywhere in the north and along the Yangzi River, are deceived by this and are completely cut off from the truth about Guangdong. Even among comrades, doubts inevitably arise, while those who do not have doubts are also without the facts on which to base a concrete argument. Expressions such as "internal turmoil" and "Communist" are spread about everywhere. It seems as though Guangdong has truly turned into a hell.

We can no longer let things go on like this. We must begin a counterattack against them. "To counterattack counterrevolutionary propaganda, so as to demolish counterrevolutionary propaganda," such is the task of the *Political Weekly*.

Our method of counterattack against the enemy by no means involves the extensive use of polemics; it consists simply in faithfully reporting the facts about our revolutionary work. The enemy says, "Guangdong is Communist." We say, "Please look at the facts." The enemy says, "Guangdong is in turmoil." We say, "Please look at the facts." The enemy says, "The Guangzhou government is colluding with Soviet Russia, has abandoned our sovereignty and shamed the nation." We say, "Please look at the facts." The enemy says, "Under the rule of the Guangzhou government the people, caught between deep water and hot fire, cannot make a living." We say, "Please look at the facts."

The style of the *Political Weekly* will be 90 percent narration of the actual facts and only 10 percent arguments against the propaganda of the counter-revolutionaries. Revolutionary people of the whole country, accept our honest reporting on the work of the revolution, and arise!

The 3–3–3–1 System

(December 5, 1925)

"What is Communism? All property is confiscated. Private accumulation is not allowed, and poor and rich are alike impoverished. To give it an appealing name, it's called emphasizing agriculture. In reality, 3–3–3–1 will not work. Three parts for the landlord, three parts for the state. Three parts for oneself, and one for the use of the [peasant] association." This is a notice in four character per line verse posted inside and outside the city of Huizhou by Yang Kunru.[1] A friend newly arrived from Beijing who is considered clear-headed asked me, "Is there really such a thing as this 3–3–3–1 system?" I was very surprised to hear this. Before replying to him, I thought to myself: Can it be that even he has doubts about whether or not Guangdong is carrying out some "3–3–3–1" system? In a rather cool tone of voice I then answered him, "There is, but only in the notices of Yang Kunru." He said, "Isn't the Hong Kong *Morning Post* a Guomindang newspaper? It's in their headlines." This was the first I had heard that the Hong Kong *Morning Post* was also taking up such fresh new arguments as these. Originally, before the rebellion of Yang and Liu,[2] the Hong Kong *Morning Post* did indeed have connections with the Guomindang. After the rebellion of Yang and Liu and the Guangzhou–Hong Kong strike,[3] it was bought up by Liu Zhenhuan and turned into an organ of our foreign masters in Hong Kong and of the so-called commander-in-chief, Chen Jiongming. Taking advantage of the fact that communications were cut off between Guangdong and Hong Kong, that rag the Hong Kong *Morning Post*, located on that barren island of Hong Kong, poured out a bunch of "facts." The 3–3–3–1 system was but one of this bunch of "facts," but I had not expected that it would travel all the way to Beijing to delight the eyes of our friends in Beijing. It was because of this that I thought: In the present world, nothing, whether animate (like man) or inanimate (like news-

---

This text appeared in *Zhengzhi zhoubao*, No. 1, December 5, 1925. We have followed this version, rather than that in the *Mao Zedong ji*, Vol. 1, pp. 113–14, which contains some errors.

1. Yang Kunru, warlord of Huizhou (Guangdong) and a subordinate of Chen Jiongming.
2. On the action against the corrupt warlords Yang Ximin and Liu Zhenhuan, and their flight to Hong Kong, see note 2 to the announcement of December 4, 1925.
3. The strike of Chinese workers in Guangzhou, in support of their comrades in Hong Kong, was set off by the celebrated Shakee Massacre of June 23, 1925, and lasted sixteen months.

papers), should be regarded in too cut-and-dried a fashion. Because now that there is a divorce between "revolutionaries" and "counterrevolutionaries" those animate and inanimate things that belong to one household today may belong to another household tomorrow. When the Hong Kong *Morning Post* belonged to the Guomindang, it served as the organ of the Guomindang. But after it was bought out by the Hong Kong foreign masters, Mr. Liu Zhenhuan, and that so-called commander-in-chief, Chen Jiongming, it could only be considered to have become their organ. This is just like the fact that when people like Feng Ziyou and Ma Su[4] were in the Guomindang they were Guomindang members, but when they sold out to Duan Qirui, even though they still said they were Guomindang members and hung out a signboard reading "Guomindang Club," they could only be considered Duan Qirui's men. I do not especially hate the Hong Kong *Morning Post*, nor Messrs. Feng, Ma, and the others, but I must take advantage of this example to show to some of our friends both at home and abroad that they should not let themselves be cheated by the people they meet or the things they read. As for the literary excellence of Yang Kunru's notice, it is only the line "In reality will not work" that must be considered a failure. Is this not a case of the single mouse dropping that spoils the whole pot of soup? But that was the secretary's fault.

---

4. On Feng and Ma, see above, the relevant note to the document of December 4, 1925.

Yang Kunru's Public Notice[1] and Liu Zhilu's[2] Telegram

(December 5, 1925)

We've already been instructed by Yang Kunru's public notice, and there is also a telegram which is a little different from the above, from Liu Zhilu et al. to a number of people: "Chief Executive Duan[3] and all ministers and vice-ministers in Beijing, Fengtian Inspector General Zhang Zuolin,[4] Hunan Governor Zhao, Wuhan Inspector General Xiao,[5] Jiangxi Commander Fang,[6] Fujian Commander Zhou,[7] Mr. Cen Xilin,[8] Mr. Wu Ziyu,[9] Mr. Kang Nanhai,[10] and Mr. Liang Rengong."[11] In discussing "their seventh crime," the telegram states: "The society of our country has always been known for emphasizing agriculture. Landlord and tenant have always shared equally in the proceeds, in a spirit of mutual assistance and natural harmony. Today, seduced by the theory of equal land distribution, chaos is brought to the orderly system of mutual benefit." This would seem to conflict with the statement of Yang Kunru. According to Yang Kunru, "Three parts for the landlord, three for the state, three for oneself, and

---

This text appeared in *Zhengzhi zhoubao*, No. 1, December 5, 1925. Our source is *Mao Zedong ji*, Vol. 1, p. 115.

1. See the previous text.

2. Liu Zhilu, a military man born in Guangdong, had thrown in his lot with Chen Jiongming. When Chen was defeated in 1925, he went north, and rallied to Wu Peifu.

3. Duan Qirui had become provisional chief executive of the Beijing government on November 24, 1924, following the defeat of Wu Peifu and the removal of Cao Kun from the presidency.

4. Zhang Zuolin had been appointed inspector general of the Three Eastern Provinces by Duan Qirui in September 1918.

5. Xiao Yaonan.

6. Fang Benren.

7. Zhou Yinren.

8. Cen Chunxuan (1861–1933), *zi* Yunjie, is here called Xilin after his native district in Guangxi. A former high imperial official and rival of Yuan Shikai, he had become a member of the directorate of Sun Yatsen's military government in Guangzhou in 1918 and succeeded Sun as its head. On the collapse of this régime in 1920, he retired from public life.

9. Wu Peifu.

10. Kang Youwei.

11. Liang Qichao.

one for public use." Everyone gets a little something, so this might be called "mutual benefit." Liu Zhilu speaks, however, of "equal land distribution," meaning that the Guangzhou government has instructed the peasants to seize the land from the landlords and distribute it equally, after which the landlords would receive no rents, so that the "order based on mutual benefit is disrupted." One says that the landlord receives three parts, the other says he receives nothing. I wonder which of these two versions our friends in Beijing and elsewhere really believe.

If They Share the Aim of Exterminating the Communists, Even Enemies Are Our Friends

(December 5, 1925)

The telegram of Liu Zhilu et al., after listing the eight crimes of the national government, adds a sigh, "Alas," and continues, "In short, bring out the troops who will quell the disturbance, punish their crimes, and save the people. If they share the common aim of exterminating the Communists, even enemies are our friends. The upright army is the stronger; victory need not wait until battle is joined. He who receives [the support of] heaven will prosper; it is not hard to distinguish between benevolence and violence." All of those listed in Liu's telegram, such as Chief Executive Duan Qirui, all ministers and vice ministers, the inspectors general, provincial governors, and commanders Zhang, Xiao, Zhao, Fang, and Zhou,[1] and even Messrs. Cen, Wu, Kang, and Liang,[2] of course share the aim of exterminating the Communists. But do not Governor Clementi[3] of Hong Kong and Prime Minister Baldwin[4] in London share this aim as well? These high positions are not on the list. Furthermore, Governor Clementi has helped out with a good deal of money and military supplies, and he has also protected Commander-in-Chief Chen by setting up a general headquarters in Hong Kong. His anti-Communist resolve shines like the sun, but his exalted office has been omitted from the list. I really do not understand what this means! The statement at the end of the telegram, "the upright army is the stronger," must be classed as even more mixed up. Actually, he has written a hymn to the merits and virtues of the national government.

This text appeared in *Zhengzhi zhoubao*, No. 1, December 5, 1925. Our source is *Mao Zedong ji*, Vol. 1, p. 117.

1. I.e., Zhang Zuolin, Zhao Hengti, Fang Benren, and Zhou Yinren.
2. I.e., Cen Xilin, Wu Peifu, Kang Youwei, and Liang Qichao.
3. Sir Cecil Clementi was governor of Hong Kong from November 1925 to February 1930.
4. Stanley Baldwin organized his second cabinet and became prime minister in November 1924, and remained in office until May 1929.

The Sound of Hymns of Praise from All Nations

(December 5, 1925)

There exists a Chaozhou and Mei *xian* Association of Gentry, Students, and Merchants, which has sent a response to the telegram of Liu Zhilu, reading in part: "The diabolical Communist Party has already brought disaster to Guangdong Province; at home it is capable of plunging China into irreversible total calamity, while abroad it threatens to bring about the extinction of the human race throughout the world. Our Mr. Liu is the first in the realm who has answered the call of duty in the face of this threat. Wherever they march with their banners, people will welcome them with wine and food. The rotten deadwood will be pulled out, and the great and meritorious task will be accomplished.[1] Bolshevization[2] will be rooted out, and the foundation of the state will be honored and secure. Sooner or later the tripod of the Yunnan uprising and the oath at Machang[3] will be completed. As a result, mankind will be safeguarded throughout the entire world, and the disaster threatening the globe will be turned back; the event will be commemorated for a thousand autumns, and the sound of hymns of praise will be heard from all nations." Everywhere "the whole world," "the entire globe" are kept in mind. How sweeping is their vision! If Liu Zhilu really rooted out "Bolshevization," the "sound of hymns of praise" would most certainly be heard. We don't know about *all* nations, but at least it would come from the following four nations: Britain, America, France, and Japan.

This text appeared in *Zhengzhi zhoubao*, No. 1, December 5, 1925. Our source is *Mao Zedong ji*, Vol. 1, p. 119.

1. The two-character expression we have translated "will be accomplished" is *lijiu*. There follows a parenthetical note by "the writer," i.e., Mao, reading "The character *li* is wrong." Presumably he thought some more common compound for "to succeed," such as *chengjiu*, should have been used.

2. Literally, "making red" (*chihua*), a common expression at the time for "Communize," "Bolshevize," or "Sovietize."

3. The uprising in Yunnan refers to the campaign against Yuan Shikai's attempt at making himself emperor, launched in 1916 by Cai E, Li Liejun, and Tang Jiyao. It was from Machang, south of Tianjin, that Duan Qirui in 1917 led his forces, supported by Cao Kun and others, to frustrate Zhang Xun's action in putting the last Manchu emperor back on the throne. The authors of the text Mao is quoting appear to suggest that the Communist attempt to conquer the world is akin to these two efforts at imperial restoration and will likewise be defeated.

Long Live the Grand Alliance of the Anti-Communist Chinese People's Army

(December 5, 1925)

This is one of the slogans that appears in the anti-Communist literature put out by Chen Jiongming in the East River area. It certainly is a resounding slogan. The only problem is that the "Anti-Communist Chinese People's Army" seems to have a bit of difficulty in achieving a "Grand Alliance." Troops like those of Fengtian's Inspector General Zhang and of Hankou's Mr. Wu Ziyu[1] may indeed be considered as "Anti-Communist Chinese People's Armies," but where is the "Grand Alliance"?

This text appeared in *Zhengzhi zhoubao*, No. 1, December 5, 1925. Our source is *Mao Zedong ji*, Vol. 1, p. 121.
   1. Once again, the reference is to Zhang Zuolin and Wu Peifu.

The *"Communist Program"* and
"Not Really Communist"

(December 5, 1925)

In general, the counterrevolutionary parties refer to the national revolution as the Communist revolution, the Guomindang as the Communist Party, the national government as the Communist government, and the National Revolutionary Army as the Communist army. All of this is nothing but following the suggestions of the imperialists by concocting a few simple epithets and spreading them around with the intention of smashing the united front of cooperation among various classes in the national revolution. But such creations as these can only be rather abstract. They cannot be too concrete, for if they are too concrete, it will be easy for their authors to expose their nakedness so that people will not believe them. And yet, on this occasion, staking everything on a single throw, and having already exhausted every conceivable method, Chen Jiongming in the East River area recently fabricated a so-called "Communist Program" to scare the people. Among their propaganda leaflets there is one of which the title reads "An Exhortation to the people of Guangdong to help the Guangdong Army Subdue the Red Party." In the text, it is stated: "Alas! Elders and bretheren, do you know of the Communist Program drafted by Jiang Zhongzheng?[1] From my insignificant position, I am concerned lest the people in their ignorance imagine that the Communists will share out only the property of the wealthy, and will not bother ordinary poor people. They even think that the Communists will benefit the poor

---

This text appeared in *Zhengzhi zhoubao*, No. 1, December 5, 1925. Our source is *Mao Zedong ji*, vol. 1, p. 123–24.

1. Jiang Jieshi (1887–1975), here called by his school name Zhongzheng, is (with Sun Yatsen) one of two persons referred to in these volumes by the Cantonese form of his name, in the spelling long used in the West, Chiang Kaishek. A native of Zhejiang, Chiang Kaishek received military training in Japan, where he joined the Tongmenghui in 1908. Though he was in frequent contact with Sun Yatsen from 1910 onward, the turning point in their relationship occurred in 1922 when he rallied to Sun after Chen Jiongming had turned against him. In 1923, Chiang became chief of staff in Sun's headquarters in Guangzhou and was chosen by Sun to head a special mission to Moscow to obtain arms. In April 1924, he became commandant of the Huangpu Military Academy. In early 1925, Chiang led the victorious Eastern Expedition against Chen Jiongming, and in the summer of 1925 he became commander of the First Army of the newly established National Revolutionary Army. By the time Mao wrote this article, Chiang was, with Wang Jingwei, one of the two top Guomindang leaders in Guangzhou.

people. Don't they know that this is a big lie? I would summarize their program generally as follows: There is the so-called 3–3–3–1 system, which pertains to productive lands. There is the so-called 4–4–2 system, which refers to houses and buildings. As for factories and commercial establishments with a moderate amount of capital, everything will be confiscated." But recently the Hong Kong *Industrial and Commercial Daily* reported: "When the representatives of the Guangzhou Chamber of Commerce arrived in Hong Kong, the representatives of the Hong Kong Chamber of Commerce invited the representatives of the Guangzhou Chamber of Commerce to the Chinese Merchants' Club for a second conference to discuss solving the strikes and restoring communications. Chinese gentry and merchants sat around a long table with the representatives of the Guangzhou Chamber of Commerce. The representative of the Guangzhou Chamber of Commerce, Jian Qinshi, began by saying that the Guangzhou government was not really carrying out Communism." If someone should ask Chen Jiongming about this statement of Jian Qinshi, I expect that Chen Jiongming would have to reply: "Jian Qinshi is himself lying. Others have communized his property and he still says that it hasn't been communized."

Zou Lu[1] and the Revolution

(December 5, 1925)

Zou Lu says, "We comrades of the Guomindang should be conscious of the fact that we certainly cannot negate all the old comrades just because some people say that they are not revolutionary. If our comrades had not fallen down repeatedly and got up again, how could there be a republic? If it had not been for all the campaigns to punish Yuan Shikai and to protect the constitution, to punish the rebels and carry out the Northern Expedition, history would not be what it is today. As for the exploit of which the Communists are so proud, the burning of the Merchants' Corps, they had to rely on Yang and Liu.[2] To defeat Yang and Liu they had to rely on Xu Chongzhi[3]

This text appeared in *Zhengzhi zhoubao* No. 1, December 5, 1925. Our source is *Mao Zedong ji*, Vol. 1, p. 125.

1. Zou Lu (1885-1954), *zi* Haibin, was a native of Guangdong who played an active role in Sun Yatsen's efforts to establish a territorial base in Guangdong in the years from 1917 to 1923. In January 1924, at the First Congress of the Guomindang, he was elected to the Standing Committee of the Central Executive Committee. He was strongly opposed to radicalism and to cooperation with the Communist Party. Zou Lu was one of the instigators of the Western Hills Conference of November 1925, and at the Second Guomindang Congress in January 1926 it was resolved that he be removed from the party. He retired from political life in 1928, and in 1932 became chancellor of National Sun Yatsen University in Guangzhou, which he had founded in 1924.

2. The Merchants' Corps, or Merchants' Association Volunteer Corps, had been organized in May 1924 by the Guangzhou merchants as an instrument to resist the financial demands and military pressure of Sun Yatsen's government. When, in the summer and autumn of 1924, they bought large numbers of rifles, Sun decided to take action. Despite strong support for the merchants by the British consul, who threatened military intervention if force were used against them, the Merchants' Corps was surrounded and disarmed on October 15, 1924, by armies including a contingent of Huangpu cadets. At the same time, a large part of Guangzhou's commercial quarter was destroyed by fire. Yang Ximin and Liu Zhenhuan, who had links with foreign interests, were not in sympathy with this move and played no part in it.

3. Xu Chongzhi (1887-1965), *zi* Ruwei, a native of Guangdong, was a graduate of the Japanese Military Academy. He joined the Guomindang in 1912, and from then on was closely associated with Sun Yatsen. In 1924, he became head of the Military Affairs Department of the Guomindang, and in May 1925, he played a decisive role in suppressing the revolt of Yang Ximin and Liu Zhenhua (see note to text of December 4, 1925, for details). In July 1925, he became minister of war in the new national government. Following the assassination of Liao Zhongkai, he became a member of a three-man body to deal with the emergency, together with Wang Jingwei and Chiang Kaishek. Soon, however, he

and Liang Hongkai.[4] And in the present campaign against Xu and Liang, who is there, once again, but the old comrades?"[5] Very good, Mr. Zou! Then we invite you to make revolution! Indeed there is not a single person who dares undertake to negate the old revolutionary comrades! We must realize it is not enough just to have "the republic" and "history." Revolution is still what we need today, and what we will need in the future. I think it would be better to use fewer examples of those old comrades like Yang and Liu and old comrades like Xu and Liang.

---

displayed a lack of firmness in dealing with Chen Jiongming, and on September 21, he was expelled from Guangzhou on Chiang Kaishek's orders. Suggestions of complicity in Liao's assassination appear to be unfounded. The Soviet military adviser Cherepanov, who writes at some length of these events, is harshly critical of Xu's rightist and compromising tendencies, but does not even hint at any involvement in Liao's death. See A.I Cherepanov, *Zapiski voennogo sovetnika v Kitae* (Notes of a Military Adviser in China), Moscow: Izdateol'stvo "Nauka," 1964, pp. 242-250, and the corresponding passage in the abridged translation of this and the second volume of Cherepanov's memoirs, A.I. Cherepanov, *As Military Adviser in China*, Moscow: Progress Publishers, 1982, pp. 157-62.

4. On Liang, see above, the relevant note to the announcement of December 4, 1925.

5. This is an accurate quotation from Zou's article "Gao Fu Mu" (To Fu Mu), written in 1925, replying to criticisms, in the Guangzhou *Minguo ribao*, of Guangdong University (later Sun Yatsen University), which he had founded in 1924. For the full text, see *Zou Lu quanji* (Complete Works of Zou Lu), Volume 9, pp. 69-75.

Revolutionary Party Members Rally Together *en Masse against the Meeting of the Rightists in Beijing*

(December 13, 1925)

"Revolutionaries, unite!"

The dispute about the meeting place of the Fourth Plenum of the Guomindang Central Executive Committee is in reality a dispute on whether to continue the revolution or to abandon it. For even if we leave aside the issue that the Resolution of the Third Plenum and the legal procedures for convening meetings by the Central Secretariat have been violated, and consider only the fact that Beijing, which is under Duan Qirui's rule, is preferred for the meeting to Guangzhou, where the revolution has reached its high tide, we would ask: what is the significance of this? The Central Executive Committee of the Guomindang has sternly condemned this affair in a telegram to Beijing, and more than ten members of the Central Committee, including Wang Jingwei and Tan Zu'an, have sent an open telegram[1] summing up the main points of the condemnation to the party headquarters at all levels throughout the country. Also, the Central Committee has made a full and clear announcement to enumerate the counterrevolutionary activities of the right wing party members in the last two years, so as to warn other party members not to by confused by them. All of these materials were printed in last week's issue of this periodical. Since then the Central Committee of the Guomindang has already received some twenty messages from various regions opposing the Beijing meeting, and the same voice of opposition will no doubt spread all over the country. For in China today, there is absolutely no other way out but to make revolution. Any party member who has a strong sense of being a revolutionary will certainly never chime in with the right, forsake his glorious revolutionary standing, and thus help boost the arrogance of the imperialists and warlords. We expect that party members everywhere will not only refuse to follow [the right], but will also achieve greater unity in consequence. "Revolutionaries, unite!" is a slogan initiated by Comrade Liao Zhongkai, and "Whoever

---

This text appeared in *Zhengzhi zhoubao*, No. 2, December 13, 1925. Our source is *Mao Zedong ji. Bujuan*, Vol. 2, pp. 129–30.

1. The text of this telegram, dated November 27, 1925, of which Mao was a signatory, appears above.

wants to be revolutionary goes to the left!" by Comrade Wang Jingwei. Today these two slogans will certainly spread widely among the revolutionary comrades and the revolutionary masses of all parts of the country. From a wave of protest spreading to the following places against the rightists' meeting in Beijing, we can foresee an inevitable and nationwide popularization of the slogans.[2]

---

2. When this piece was originally published in *Zhengzhi zhoubao,* it was followed by the texts of the "twenty messages from various regions" referred to above by Mao. The first of these emanated from the Beijing Executive Bureau of the Guomindang; the other nineteen were mostly from the Shanghai and Guangzhou areas. Since these materials were not written by Mao, they are not included in the Tokyo edition of his writings, and we have likewise omitted them here.

Students Are Selected by the Chinese Guomindang to Go to Sun Yatsen University in Moscow

(December 13, 1925)

Mr. Sun Yatsen's revolutionary spirit has been respected and admired not only by the Chinese people, but also by all the oppressed popular masses of the whole world. Only the ruling classes who oppress the people in various countries, namely the imperialists and warlords, detest him. When Soviet Russia was just undergoing her revolution, and the imperialist countries colluded with the white Russian counterrevolutionaries such as Denikin, Wrangel, and Kolchak to invade and attack Russia from all sides, the desperate situation there was similar to that of Guangdong two months ago. At that time, Mr. Sun telegraphed Lenin a message of encouragement. According to Borodin,[1] the Russian representative who spoke at the reception banquet of the American Alliance on November 22, Lenin and other leaders were deeply grateful to Mr. Sun Yatsen for his telegram, which they received at that crucial moment and in which he encouraged their struggle. So when Mr. Sun sought shelter in Shanghai from Chen Jiongming's betrayal, Soviet Russia dispatched her representative, Joffe,[2] to Shanghai to greet Mr. Sun, though at the time Sun's force was quite weak. The message Joffe transmitted was that Soviet Russia hoped to cooperate with Sun in overthrowing imperialism. That was the origin of the great alliance of China and Russia, and so on. Indeed today, the only formidable enemy of the oppressed popular masses

---

This text appeared in *Zhengzhi zhoubao*, No. 2, December 13, 1925. Our source is *Mao Zedong ji. Bujuan,* Vol. 2, pp. 131–37.

1. Mikhail Markovitch Borodin (Grusenberg) (1884-1951), a member of the Bolshevik faction of the Russian Social Democratic Labor Party from 1903, participated in the First and Second Congresses of the Communist International. In May 1923, he was appointed Soviet advisor to Sun Yatsen and the Guomindang and representative of the Communist International at Guangzhou, where he arrived in October 1923. He played an important role in the reorganization of the Guomindang and in cooperation between the Guomindang and the Chinese Communist Party from then until his departure from China in mid-1927. He was arrested in Moscow in 1949, and died in a labor camp in 1951.

2. Adolf Abrahamovich Joffe (1883-1927) was sent to China in 1922 by the Soviet government as plenipotentiary representative to the Beijing régime. His negotiations with the warlord government having been unsuccessful, he went to Shanghai in 1923 to meet with Sun Yatsen and issued a joint declaration with Sun.

of the whole world is imperialism. And to overthrow imperialism, the revolutionary forces of all countries must unite as one so that they can avert defeat during the decisive battles. This is why China needs Soviet Russia, and Soviet Russia needs China too. A group of high-level intellectuals in Beijing, Shanghai, and several other places are in an uproar against the alliance with Russia. This attitude is caused by their blindness to the present international situation in which struggle is engaged between the two sides of revolution and counterrevolution, and by their blindness to the significance of the revolutionary tactics of the Guomindang as well. The foundation of Sun Yatsen University in Moscow shows the Russian people's respect and admiration for Mr. Sun's revolutionary spirit. The university aims at enrolling those revolutionary young people from China who believe in Mr. Sun's doctrine to undertake thorough research, thus training them to become qualified leaders of the Chinese national revolution. A letter from Moscow says that Mr. Sun's two monumental works, *The Three People's Principles* and *Fundamentals of National Reconstruction*, have been translated into Russian by Russian scholars. Sun Yatsen University is being actively prepared, and according to its current progress it will certainly achieve very gratifying successes in the future. Famed Dr. Joffe, the former Russian representative to China, chairs its board of directors. The directors are Radek,[3] the university president; Bukharin,[4] the editor in chief of *Pravda*; Madame Krupskaya;[5] M. Tomsky, the president of the Trade Union Executive, and other distinguished personages. As donations from many organizations and individuals in both China and Russia have been very numerous, the university has fairly sufficient funds. According to President Radek, the goal of the university is to foster talented leaders for society. The major courses, he says, are Trends in Modern Economic Thought, Modern World History, the History and Significance of the Russian Revolution and, in particular, a special course concerning the Chinese national revolutionary movement. In general, the teaching method in each of these courses will emphasize research; students will be encouraged to carry out independent study of political, economic, and other social problems, and to produce creative work. Moreover, their results of all kinds will be published in major newspapers and magazines. As for the number of students at Sun Yatsen University, we are told that the first year enrollment is 500, of which 150 are from the Guangdong area. Now the Central Political Council of the Guomindang has already selected 147 people from 1,030 candidates. Only those who got excellent marks in both written and oral examinations passed the test. Their names are listed below:

Liang Fuwen, Liang Ganqiao, Zhong Shutang, Huang Yongwei, Zhu Guozhen, Ou Jiuxian, Zou Shitian, Lin Yaohuan, Liu [X]zhu, Bai Yu, Guo

---

3. Karl Radek was replaced as head of Sun Yatsen University by Pavel Mif in 1927.
4. Nikolai Ivanovich Bukharin.
5. Lenin's widow.

Mingsheng, Zhu Rui, Xie Zhenhua, Long Qiguang, Chen Fu, Chen Biguang, Lin Aimin, Deng Gongwu, Miao Zhenheng, Zhong Jiben, Tang Xuehai, Liang Shaoqiang, Liu Ma'ou, Huang Gantang, Zheng Zhongmin, Lin Xia, Lin Xiewen, Ye Enpu, Zhou Xueliu, Liao Huaji, Shao Yechang, Wu Zhongliang, Huang Fa, Li Lin, Fang Tao, Nie Ganyu, Feng Degong, Zeng Renliang, Chen Zhengye, Xu Kang, Shen Yuanming, Feng Shengnan, Chen Zaoxin, Yang Huabo, Zhang Minquan, Zhai Rongji, Lin Shushan, Lin Daowen, Li Wenda, Zhen Zhaoquan, Dong Liangshi, Zheng Qi, Dong Zhengxing, Li Wenguan, Huang Dajun, Dong Yu, Han Liangjian, Zheng Jiemin, Yang Jiateng, Liang Zhenyang, Tang Juncui, Zhi Wenyi, Ma Weiyu, Liu Muqiang, Xu Ying, Li Huifang, Ruan Chi, Zhang Renquan, Huang Zhongli, Cen Yanzao, Zhang Shuan, Zeng Shang, Huang Yimin, Xiao Hao, Ye Junhao, Liu Dayuan, Li Yanliang, Huang Yonghong, Huang Ju, Huang Wenjie, Zhang Xing, Liu Fuxin, Fang Tan, Luo Ying, Wang Zhihong, Wu Lu, Zhang Yinlan, Lu Najie, Deng Hanzhong, Zheng Renbo, Ao Kai, Zhong Kunyu, Feng Jiefen, Wei Bihui, Liu Manshu, Huang Dingxin, Zhou Ai, Zhao Yu, Chen Daoshou, Lu Kuiwen, Huang Yibai, Xiao Aixian, Kang Ze, Luo Derong, Wu Su, Wang Guangyue, Wan Xuru, Zhang Yuanliang, Li Guanying, Zheng Guochen, Peng Wenchang, Wang Jueyuan, Chen Shengfu, Zhang Yuanyou, Deng Dunhou, Xu Junhu, Yu Guan, Yu Chufan, Li Kun, Peng Taogao, Yang Zhenxi, Yang Zhenzao, Hu Mingxun, Zhou Yongnan, Gao Yunshang, Cai Riqiu, Duan Shiyuan, Chen Haizhou, Pan Xinwei, Duan Ping, Wang Zuocai, Wu Guoqian, Wu Junshi, Chen Zhilu, Huang Changguang, Wen Shu, Lai Fanggeng, Chen Xianshang, Zhang Sinan, Liu Wukun

Here we have in all 140 names; another 7 remain to be identified. The statistics regarding the sex, native place, age, and other attributes of the students as tabulated by the Central Political Council[6] are as follows:

1. Sex: male, 139; female, 8
2. Birth place: Guangdong, 71; Hunan, 28; Jiangxi, 10; Yunnan, 7; Sichuan, 7; Jiangxi,[7] 5; Hubei, 5; Zhejiang, 3; Guizhou, 3; Fujian, 2; Jiangsu, 1; Shandong, 1; Shanxi, 1; unknown, 3
3. Age: under twenty, 36; under twenty-five, 86; under thirty, 20; unknown, 5
4. Marital status: married, 45; single, 96; unknown, 6
5. Occupation: academic circles, 55; educational circles, 7[8]; journalistic circles, 2; agricultural sector, 1; others, 7; unknown, 10

---

6. Taking *Zhengzhi shiyuanhui* to be a misprint for *Zhengzhi weiyuanhui*.

7. It is not clear why there are two figures for Jiangxi. The editors of the Tokyo edition have queried the name of the province here, but it is hard to think what the correct characters could otherwise be.

8. This is probably a misprint for 72, which would make the figures for occupation add up, like all the others above, to 147. It would also be consistent with what is known of the social composition of this group.

All these students are preparing for going abroad in separate batches, and the first group will leave in a few days directly for Haishenwai [Vladivostok] by boat. Each person should bring 250 *yuan* as traveling expenses, of which 100 *yuan* are subsidized by the Guomindang, and 150 *yuan* must be secured by the individual. During the last few days, send-off parties have been given on all sides, by bodies including the New Student Society, the Guangdong Provincial Party Headquarters of the Chinese Guomindang, and others. The national government also invited the students to get together once. At that meeting, Wang Jingwei delivered a speech of encouragement and agreed with the students on the following three points: (1) The government should report once a week, or once every two weeks, on the political situation in Guangzhou to all Chinese students studying in Russia; they also hoped that the students would report back constantly on the situation in their vicinity; (2) The Chinese students at Sun Yatsen University must unite and pledge to fight steadfastly for Sun Yatsenism; (3) As for the various aspects of preparations for going to Russia, several students should be elected to take responsiblity for maintaining liaison with the government, so that they could keep everyone else informed of the government's response. Borodin, the Russian representative, also made a long speech at the meeting, explaining the goals of Sun Yatsen University. In his opinion science, when it is controlled by the imperialists, is an instrument for oppressing the small and weak nations. But if it is in the hands of these nations, it can be used as the instrument of their emancipation. Universities in the United States, as well as in England, Germany, and other imperialist countries, are the propaganda agencies of imperialism. In contrast, the purpose of Sun Yatsen University is to help ordinary students understand Mr. Sun Yatsen's ideology in order to carry the Chinese national revolution to completion. A transcript of the complete text of his speech follows:

It is a great honor and my pleasure to be with you today at this grand gathering. You are going to Russia soon to study at Sun Yatsen University. I am not sure whether we shall meet again in Moscow or only in China after your return. Since the Russian revolution, this is not the first time that Chinese have gone to Russia. A lot of Chinese went there eight years ago when the revolution had just broken out. Many of them, because they supported the Russian revolution, joined the revolutionary army, in which quite a few laid down their lives. You will see the graves of these Chinese martyrs in Russia and so realize that many Chinese comrades have devoted themselves to the Russian revolution. Their strength was actually very effective in the Red Army, and the story was reported in the newspapers. Moreover, there was also a report saying that a number of local Soviet governments could not have been set up without the Chinese. The time when the Russian revolution achieved success, and when the University of [the Toilers of] the East was set up in Moscow, was a time when the nations of the East were pursuing their own liberation by means of revolutionary movements. Meanwhile the war in Europe was not yet over. They claimed it was being waged for national self-determination, but the outcome was extremely disappointing. Many nations, when they saw that everything the imperialist great powers had said was nothing but trickery, were not merely disappointed but also gradually became awakened. In particular, the nations of the East came to realize that the Paris Peace Conference could not be relied on, and consequently turned away from the Wilsonist way and moved into the Russian Bolshevist camp. Such people detested Paris and turned away from it, going instead to Moscow. But what was the real situation then in Paris and Moscow? Let us make a comparison. There were coal, bread, and beef in Paris at that time, while in Moscow there were none of these. In the one place, one could enjoy favorable material conditions of existence, while in the other place one had nothing to keep out the cold, and all that was available to stave off the oppressive hunger was merely black bread and watery soup. And yet so many came from Egypt, China, Persia, Korea, and other nations to attend the newly established University [of the Toilers] of the East. As it was perfectly possible for them to go to study in the countries of Europe or America, where comfortable housing and plentiful food were available, why were they determined to go to Moscow, a city in the grip of hunger? The only reason was that they wanted to go to Moscow to study revolutionary doctrine and acquire revolutionary experience, with which they could return and save their own nations and peoples. So in order to satisfy their mental hunger, they were willing to undergo physical hunger. Since then, the situation in Russia has changed step by step, and the counterrevolutionaries have also gradually been eliminated. The obstacles having been removed, development has progressed favorably. The problem of the standard of living has also been resolved in consequence. Today our daily life is much better. We have coal and bread, and the supply of beef and of cakes is even ampler than that in Paris. Nevertheless, such material progress will definitely not lead us to think only of food and clothing, and to lose our revolutionary consciousness. In any big organization, there are normally some unworthy members. Only we are different; the majority of our party members have preserved their revolutionary spirit and work hard for the revolution. Now, in addition to the University [of the Toilers] of the East, there is also Sun Yatsen University. What are its goals? How is it organized? As time is limited, we cannot give you a detailed report on this now. Everything will become clear to you when you reach Moscow. Today I will simply give you a broad outline. The countries of Europe and America generally welcome foreign students. Science, they say, knows no national or political boundaries, and belongs to everyone. Is that true or not? These are nothing but the imperialists' hollow words. We believe that science is an instrument that can be used for both good and evil purposes. The imperialists use it for oppressing the small and weak nations, but in the hands of these nations it can be used as the instrument of their own emancipation. We are persuaded that educational institutions of whatever kind are the propaganda organs of certain classes or social groups. Columbia University in the United States is funded by the banker Morgan, and will therefore surely not allow any propaganda against the interests of financial capital. Similarly, the University of Chicago is supported by the Standard Oil Company, and will by no means tolerate any advocacy of views opposed to the trust system. Many American universities have links with the capitalists. As for colleges in Germany or England, how can they be different? Since the imperialists make of the schools the organs of their imperialist propaganda, we must have our own educational institutions as propaganda organs for the national revolution. Every school is a means to a certain end. What, then, is the goal of Sun Yatsen University? It is to help the students in general to understand the ideology of Mr. Sun Yatsen and to continue his work, in order to complete China's national revolution. In the future, the graduates of this university will be able to replace those who received their education in the imperialist universities, and shoulder the responsibility for transforming Chinese society. Today many returned students have no idea at all of the way to change China. But one day, when you come back from Russia, you will resolve China's problems by using revolutionary methods. Indeed, these problems can only be solved by revolutionary means. Hence, everything depends entirely on your study of revolutionary doctrine and revolutionary experience, motivated by your zeal as members of the revolutionary party. In the future, when you return home, you can use this knowledge to attain our goal of liberating China. Such a great task must inevitably encounter difficulties, but it is worth making sacrifices to surmount these difficulties. For the goal we cherish, namely the success of the Chinese national revolution, is most lofty. All of you are going to fight for China's national revolution. China's destiny is in your hands. All of you are leaders of the Chinese national liberation movement. I wish you success!

To the Left or to the Right?

(December 13, 1925)

For half a year now, one group of people has been arguing that the left is no good, and that the right is no good either, and have put forward as an alternative a kind of centrist view. Rejecting both the right-wing faction and the left-wing faction, they tell the world that it is they themselves who occupy the central position. This kind of thing does not appear much in Guangdong but is quite common in the Jiangsu-Zhejiang area. Because in Guangdong, the left is Guangzhou and the right is Hong Kong. Those who take a stand beneath the Guangzhou banner invariably are opposed to Hong Kong, and those who stand beneath the Hong Kong banner are invariably opposed to Guangzhou. The counterrevolutionary faction, led by Chen Jiongming and made up of military men, politicians, compradors, local bullies, and bad gentry, stands under the Hong Kong banner, while the workers, peasants, soldiers, students, merchants, and revolutionary popular masses of all kinds, led by the left wing of the Guomindang, stand beneath the Guangzhou banner. Thus the two sides bombard each other with their cannons. There can be no centrist faction in the midst of this bombardment. If there is, it has to cover up its head and face and hide under the banner of one of the factions, speak softly and tread lightly. Anyone who wanted to stand between Guangzhou and Hong Kong would have to proclaim that "Hong Kong is no good, and Guangzhou is no good either," in which case the cannons both of Hong Kong and of Guangzhou would certainly be aimed directly at him. At present there are as yet no big guns bombarding each other in the Jiangsu-Zhejiang area, so the argument that "both sides are no good" is very popular there. On May 30 of this year,[1] the cannons of one side boomed out in the Nanjing area. Fortunately the other side did not have any cannons, only some

---

This text appeared in *Zhengzhi zhoubao*, No. 2, December 13, 1925. Our source is *Mao Zedong ji*, Vol. 1, pp. 127–29.

1. On May 30, 1925, British police of the International Settlement fired on unarmed Chinese demonstrators on Nanjing Road in Shanghai. Ten demonstrators were killed and more than 50 injured. The background to the incident was a series of labor conflicts over low wages and poor working conditions. On May 15, 1925, a clash broke out between Chinese workers and supervisors at a Japanese cotton mill, in which one worker was killed and others wounded. Widespread protests followed, and a massive demonstration was organized for May 30. On May 31, following the incident, a general strike and a boycott of foreign goods was declared, resulting in a complete shutdown of Shanghai business. Sympathy strikes occurred in some 24 other Chinese cities.

fists that couldn't return the salvo. Since a chaotic situation of direct confrontation had not yet come about (the brief labor strike didn't amount to anything), it was still possible to promote openly the argument that "both sides are no good" and to "remain upright between the two, preserving freedom in the realm." But let us assume a hypothetical situation in which those popular masses on Nanjing Road had not only their fists but also cannons; that they were under the leadership of Wang Jingwei and Chiang Kaishek; that they demolished that police station with one blow and then went on to occupy the Municipal Council, capturing all those "red-headed types"; that they had then immediately sealed off the mouth of the Wusong River and set up cannons at Nantang, Beitang, and at Shizilin (as was done at Humen), and over the gun emplacements had raised the banner "Bombard Imperialism."[2] At this point, Shanghai would have unfortunately fallen into the same "chaotic situation" as Guangzhou, would have set up a defense headquarters, would have asked men like Mr. Wang Maogong[3] to take command, and would have patrolled the streets every day in their military vehicles. Newspapers like the *China Times*[4] would certainly be closed, and possibly even the *Awakened Lion Weekly*[5] could not have avoided the same fate. Freedom of speech would be allowed only to those in the majority, while those in the minority would have their free speech taken away from them, exactly the opposite of the situation prevailing previously. At this point, the centrist faction, just as in the case of Guangzhou, would not be able to make propaganda openly. Then what? Of course, there is still Beijing. But Beijing cannot be counted on for long, for it all depends on the stability of the position of the chief executive, Duan Qirui. As long as Duan's position is secure, there's no problem. Not only can the Guomindang Comrades Club hang its signboard on high, the Fourth Plenary Session of the Central Executive Committee can also hold its meetings there. It would be freer than Zhangjiakou. But even as I say this, I am still today a little confused. Why is it that the Fourth Plenary Session of the Central Executive Committee couldn't be held in Zhangjiakou? Isn't it under the direct control of the Duan Qirui government? If Chief Executive Duan Qirui wasn't there—just a minute—even if Chief Executive Duan was there, it would be hard to

---

2. Humen, literally "Tiger's Mouth," known in the West as "Bocca Tigris" or "The Bogue," was the main passage leading into the Pearl River south of Guangzhou. The forts on the shore there had played an important role in confrontations between the Chinese and the British from the time of the Opium War. The Wusong River joins the Huangpu River in Shanghai, and flows together with it into the Yangzi. Nantang, Beitang, and Shizilin are strategic points on the shore immediately north of the city.

3. Wang Maogong (1891–1961), Guomindang military man.

4. The *Shishi xinbao* (commonly translated China Times) was founded in 1908. At this time it was an organ of the Research Clique. Mao, in his Report on Propaganda of January 1926 translated below, accuses it of "supporting the interests of the bureaucrats and big landlords."

5. The *Xingshi zhoubao*, or Awakened Lion, was the organ of the *Étatistes*. For Mao's opinion of this paper, too, see his Report on Propaganda of January 1926.

avoid something unexpected happening. Haven't we heard that two men were grabbed, forced into a car and driven into the city, beaten up, and then made to write confessions? Ai! When even under the direction of Chief Executive Duan such terrible things as this occur, it's really hard to say what will happen in this world! Even more distressing is the fact that, according to a telegram from the Beijing executive office, a revolutionary movement took place on November 28 in which the townspeople surrounded and attacked the executive office in an attempt to drive Duan Qirui out. The telegram also states that the first of the three articles making up the resolution on the National Assembly provided for organizing a national government. (Most unfortunate! It would naturally be modelled on that of Guangzhou.) Also, according to a Reuters telegram: "In the demonstration in Beijing on the 28th, the students carried the Guangzhou flag, the workers carried the red flag, and there was no national flag in sight. The marchers distributed propaganda leaflets calling for such things as the overthrow of Duan Qirui, the punishment of Zhu Shen,[6] the execution of traitors, the dissolution of the Customs Conference, a national people's army, a popular mass revolution, and a real National Assembly." In the *Shishi Xinbao*, the headline preceding the telegram from Duan Qirui read, "Shocking Demonstration"! What should we do? There has been another "shocking demonstration" here. If in the future some "National Government" should really be organized, and if the "Guangzhou flag" is flown high above the rooftops of that government, wouldn't this stir up yet another "chaotic situation" like that of Guangzhou? And furthermore, this "chaotic situation" might spread throughout the nation as place after place follows suit, as the majority of the people rise up for "freedom" and insist on "no freedom" for the minority. Gentlemen standing in the middle! Tell us, please, what is to be done? [Will you] go left? Or [will you] go right?

---

6. Zhu Shen (1879-1943) was an important Anfu clique politician who ended his life as a member of the Japanese puppet government in Beiping in 1938-1943.

That's What Bolshevization Has Always Been

(December 13, 1925)

Morning Post dispatch, dateline Beijing, November 23: "The diplomatic corps has received detailed reports from Guangdong that although the ideology of Chiang Kaishek manifests Bolshevization, he cares for the people, while on the other hand, when the troops of the anti-Communist forces of Chen, Lin, Hong,[1] and others reach a locality, they are guilty of many Communist activities." Bolshevization has always meant caring for the people. If Bolshevization meant appropriating for personal use, how could it have spread throughout all of China!

This text appeared in *Zhengzhi zhoubao*, No. 2, December 13, 1925. Our source is *Mao Zedong ji*, Vol. 1, p. 131.

1. Lin Hu and Hong Zhaolin were both subordinates of Chen Jiongming. On Lin, see above, the note to Mao's editorial of October 20, 1925. Hong Zhaolin, a native of Hunan, was a powerful commander, widely regarded as corrupt. He had, in fact, been assassinated on December 7, 1925.

The Causes of the Reactionary Attitude of the Shanghai Minguo Ribao and the Handling of This Matter by the Central Executive Committee of the Guomindang

(December 20, 1925)

Since November 20, the day the newspaper published the text of the circular telegram of the Beijing meeting of rightists, the Shanghai *Minguo ribao*, directed by Ye Chucang[1] and other Guomindang rightists, has publicly proclaimed the fact that it has become an organ of the reactionaries. It has proclaimed the fact that it has broken away from the revolutionary Guomindang, compromised with the imperialists and warlords, and become one of their propaganda organs. We are not in the least surprised by the reactionary attitude of the Shanghai *Minguo ribao*, because it was formerly a newspaper of Ye Chucang and other individuals. Only after last year's First National Congress was it taken over by the party, yet from the very beginning it could not be an organ for Guomindang opinion. It often refused to publish, or made cuts in, what it regarded as "extreme" anti-imperialist and antiwarlord writings; it hid the evil of the imperialists and warlords and praised them in every possible way; it proved unable to propagate to the slightest extent the revolutionary policies of the Guomindang and of the national government. During the war in Jiangsu and Zhejiang last year, this newspaper completely abandoned its Guomindang identity and became a mouthpiece of Lu Yongxiang and the Anfu clique. When the Nanyang Tobacco Company made several thousand of its workers unemployed[2] and turned them into homeless

---

This text appared in *Zhengzhi zhoubao*, No. 3, December 20, 1925. Our source is *Mao Zedong ji. Bujuan*, Vol. 2, pp. 139–40.

1. Ye Chucang (1883–1946), *zi* Xiaofeng, was a native of Jiangsu Province. Ye, an early member of the Tongmenghui, was a cofounder in 1915 of the *Minguo ribao* (Republican Daily), which served as the mouthpiece of Sun Yatsen and the Guomindang cause. In January 1924, at the First Congress of the reorganized Guomindang, he was elected a member of the Central Executive Committee and director of the Department of Youth and Women in the party's Shanghai Executive Bureau. In November 1925 he attended the Western Hills Conference of Guomindang conservatives, but by 1926 he was already back in Guangzhou as secretary general of the Central Political Council.

2. A large-scale strike of workers at the Nanyang Tobacco Company in September 1924 resulted in many workers being laid off. The strike was supported by the Communist Party, but curbed by the moderate-led workers' club and by the Federation of Labor Organizations. The *Minguo ribao* attacked the strikers.

wanderers, this paper gave enormous publicity to the arguments of the capitalists in justification of their oppression of the workers, while reports from the workers' side were either simply rejected or only carried after cuts had been made. In the May Thirtieth Movement this year, the Shanghai *Minguo ribao*'s anti-imperialist propaganda fell far short of that in the official newspaper of the Research clique.[3] During the past few months, this paper has refused to publish many important news items about matters in Guangdong such as the anti-imperialist movement, the struggle against the warlords, and the elimination of counterrevolutionaries. In contrast, stories of Sun Chuanfang's[4] military actions filled its pages. All these were presages of this newspaper's turn toward reaction, with which every revolutionary party member has long been extremely dissatisfied. So there is really nothing new; the paper has simply taken the occasion of the Beijing meeting of rightists to declare 'formally' its reactionary stand. Since it did this on November 20, the paper has daily made many propaganda attacks on the left. This is naturally its duty, because without attacking the left it cannot qualify as the official newspaper of the right, nor can it seek merit in the eyes of the Municipal Council in Shanghai and of Duan Qirui in Beijing and get them to recognize its counterrevolutionary position, or attain its reactionary goals. We consider the reactionary attitude of the Shanghai *Minguo ribao* fully logical. It demonstrates the strength of the Guomindang Left and the development of the movement against imperialism and the warlords in China. It also demonstrates, finally, that a close combat between Chinese revolutionaries and counterrevolutionaries has already been engaged, and that the success of China's national revolution will come very soon. In China today, all the people and the newspapers in the center must change their stand soon. Either they must go to the left and join the revolutionary camp, or they must go to the right and join the counterrevolutionary camp; it is simply no longer possible to go on wearing that gray mask of neutrality. Having grasped this point, we can understand why the Shanghai *Minguo ribao* has become reactionary; why recently papers such as the *Chenbao* and *Xingshi zhoubao* have been attacking the Guomindang and the Communist Party much more fiercely than before, and why the leaders of the Guomindang right were obliged to meet in Beijing at the present time to counter the Central Executive Committee and the national government in Guangzhou led

---

3. The "official" newpapers of the Research clique were the *Chenbao* and the *Shishi xinbao*. See below, Mao's Report on Propaganda of January 1926.

4. Sun Chuanfang (1884–1935), *zi* Xingyuan, was associated with the Zhili clique of warlords. In March 1923 he became military governor of Fujian, and in September 1924 military governor of Zhejiang. He then embarked on military exploits to increase his power. By 1925 he was the strongest warlord of the Zhili clique, and in October he appointed himself commander in chief of the allied armies of Jiangsu, Zhejiang, Jiangxi, Anhui, and Fujian. In December he declared that provinces under his control would not be subject to orders from Beijing. His power collapsed in 1927. For his role in the Jiangsu-Zhejiang War, see above, the note to the circular of September 10, 1924.

by the Left. As for what action should be taken against the Shanghai *Minguo ribao*, the Central Executive Committee of the Guomindang has already resolved to send someone to the newspaper for an investigation and appropriate action. At the same time, the Central Executive Committee has sent a circular telegram to the party headquarters at all levels and in all localities, denouncing the reactionary and absurd conduct of the paper. The text of the telegram is reproduced below:

> Send to 8 Cuihua Lane, Beijing, and at the same time for transmittal to the party headquarters of Zhili, Shandong, Henan, Shanxi, Shaanxi, Chaha'er, Suiyuan, Rehe, Harbin; to the party headquarters of Jiangsu Province, Yongji Lane, Wangzhi Road, Shanghai; Zhejiang Province, Hangzhou; Hunan Province, Changsha; Jiangxi Province, Nanchang; Hubei Province, Wuchang; Sichuan Province, Chongqing; Fujian Province, Xiamen; Guangxi Province, Nanning; Guangdong Province, Guangzhou; and please pass on to the party headquarters at lower levels; to all newspaper offices in Beijing, Tianjin, Shanghai, and Hankou; to overseas party headquarters in different places. Would every comrade please note: the Shanghai *Minguo ribao* has recently been taken over by reactionary elements; the views it publishes are fallacious and are fundamentally contrary to the principles of the party. Emissaries have been sent to investigate and deal with the matter. You are hereby informed of this. From the Central Executive Committee of the Chinese Guomindang.

The Beijing Right-Wing Meeting and Imperialism

(December 20, 1925)

The imperialists bitterly hate the left-wing Guangzhou Central Executive Committee of the Guomindang for its overall leadership of the nationwide anti-imperialist movement, which has caused all the imperialists to tremble in fear; the right-wing meeting in Beijing resolved to suspend the authority of the Guangzhou Central Executive Committee. The imperialists bitterly hate the Guomindang Political Council for its ability to concentrate its powers on directing the Guangzhou-Hong Kong strikes and on cleaning out their various useful tools—Yang Ximin, Liu Zhenhuan, Liang Hongkai, Zheng Runqi, Mo Xiong, Wei Bangping,[1] Chen Jiongming, Lin Hu,[2] Hong Zhaolin, Deng Benyin,[3] Xiong Kewu;[4] the right-wing meeting in Beijing resolved to abolish the Political Council. The imperialists bitterly hate the left-wing leader of the Guomindang, Wang Jingwei,[5] for being able to lead the national revolution in the life-and-death war against imperialism; the right-wing meeting in Beijing resolved to expel Wang Jingwei from the party. The imperialists bitterly hate the assistance that Soviet Russia has given the Guomindang and the Russian advisors hired by the national government, which have augmented the strength of the attack on imperialism; the meeting of the right wing in Beijing resolved to dismiss the Russian advisor, Borodin. The imperialists bitterly hate the fact that the Guomindang has admitted Communist Party elements, which add one more major anti-imperialist army; the right-wing meeting in Beijing resolved to expel Li Dazhao, Tan Pingshan, and others from the party. This shows us just what kind of jobs the right-wing meeting in Beijing has been doing for the imperialists.

This text appeared in *Zhengzhi zhoubao*, No. 3, December 20, 1925. Our source is *Mao Zedong ji*, Vol. 1, p. 135.

1. Wei Bangping (1880-1935) was a Guangdong army commander and high-ranking subordinate to Xu Chongzhi.

2. Regarding Lin Hu, see above, the relevant note to the editorial of October 20, 1925.

3. Deng Benyin, military commander and supporter of Chen Jiongming, had just been defeated in southern Guangdong.

4. On Xiong Kewu, see the note to the "Propaganda Guidelines in the War Against the Fengtian Clique" of November 27, 1925.

5. On Wang Jingwei, see the note to Mao's speech of October 25, 1925.

The Last Tool of Imperialism

(December 20, 1925)

The right-wing meeting in Beijing has done a number of jobs for the imperialists that they needed done, as recounted above.[1] This is, however, one of the very last of the methods available to the imperialists for dealing with the Chinese anti-imperialist movement. The plot of the tools of imperialism, Yang Ximin and Liu Zhenhuan, to realize the objectives of the present right-wing meeting in Beijing by overthrowing the Guangzhou government had failed. The plot of the tools of imperialism, such as Liang Hongkai, Zheng Runqi, Wei Bangping, Mo Xiong, and Zhu Zhuowen, to realize the objectives of the present right-wing meeting following the murder of Liao Zhongkai had also failed. The plot of the tool of imperialism, Xiong Kewu, to realize the objectives of the present right-wing meeting in Beijing by conquering Guangzhou from the North River area had also failed. The plot of the tool of imperialism, Duan Qirui, to realize the objectives of the present right-wing meeting in Beijing by sending warships from Humen to attack Guangzhou had also failed. The tools of imperialism Chen Jiongming and Deng Benyin had also failed to realize the objectives of the present right-wing meeting in Beijing by striking at Guangzhou from both the east and the south. The work of all these tools of imperialism had been unsuccessful. The right wing of the Guomindang was very upset and flustered, so they convened this meeting in Beijing. They have changed their methods from "rifle and cannon bombardment" to "resolutions." But how effective has this method been? It's really hard to say. Naturally, the various resolutions of the right-wing meeting can only be considered an infantile charade. However, this method of "rebellion from within" is indeed a step forward from "rebellion from without." After using up all of its tools, imperialism discovered this last tool, which has suddenly given it a little consolation in the midst of all its failures. Even if within the right wing there are a few who still give lip service to opposing imperialism, even if there is still one part of the right wing that is not sincerely committed to being used by imperialism, even if they refuse in any way to admit that they are the tools of imperialism, they are nevertheless, in reality, providing a great deal of assistance to imperialism and acting as the tools of imperialism, because the work they are doing addresses the needs of imperialism.

This text appeared in *Zhengzhi zhoubao*, No. 3, December 20, 1925. Our source is *Mao Zedong ji*, Vol. 1, pp. 137–38.

1. I.e., in the preceding article, "The Beijing Right-Wing Meeting and Imperialism."

The Greatest Talent of the Right Wing

(December 20, 1925)

An editorial that appeared on December 3 in the right-wing organ, the Shanghai *Republican Daily*, states, "The warlords fear the revolutionary party, but since when does the revolutionary party fear the warlords?" This is the reason they use to oppose the following telegram from Wang Jingwei and others: "The plenary sessions of the Central Executive Committee are open meetings. If held in Beijing, the meetings would be subject to external pressure from the warlords and to internal obstruction by reactionary elements making use of the warlords." Thus the *Republican Daily* thinks that by holding its plenary session in Beijing the Central Executive Committee would be able to demonstrate courage and show that it did not fear the warlords. Why is the *Republican Daily* wrong? It is wrong in that it does not understand that there is a distinction between the open activities and the secret activities of a revolutionary party. When acting within the enemy's sphere of influence, a truly revolutionary party organizes and meets in total secrecy, while its proposals and propaganda are public. When within the enemy's sphere of influence, if the party wants to hold a public meeting on party organization, it must first obtain dispensation from the enemy. There must be at least a few things that are in the enemy's interest before he will give his tacit approval, much less his protection. But what kind of a party would this be? This would simply be a friend of the enemy, and not a revolutionary party that wants to overthrow the enemy. Duan Qirui gave permission for the right wing to hold open meetings in Beijing, but would he permit Wang Jingwei, Tan Yankai, and others like them to hold open meetings in Beijing? This paper also states that Director General Sun Yatsen went to Beijing last year and was not afraid of Duan Qirui. They ignore the fact that there were two factors that made it possible for Director General Sun to go to Beijing last year. One factor was that, having just taken office, Duan Qirui's political position was not yet secure, and he had not yet decided on the policy of suppressing the Guomindang; and the other factor was that power over the police was still in the hands of Feng Yuxiang, who was sympathetic to the Guomindang. If it had not been for these two factors, Mr. Sun would not have been able to go openly to Beijing. If Mr. Sun were still alive, Duan Qirui would definitely not allow him to engage openly in

---

This text appeared in *Zhengzhi zhoubao*, No. 3, December 20, 1925. Our source is *Mao Zedong ji*, Vol. 1, pp. 139–40.

the revolutionary movement in Beijing today, and he would certainly have to go into hiding or flee somewhere else. In Beijing and in all places throughout China that are under the control of the reactionary warlords, there are Guomindang organizations. There are organs of all levels of the party everywhere, party members and cadre comrades all hold frequent meetings, and they all have various courageous tasks in the advancing struggle, in the attempt to destroy the power of the enemy. But this is all in secret. Within these organizations and tasks, it is only the left wing that is there, continually struggling. The right-wing members of the party are all afraid to get near the front. The strong points of the right wing are that they can open their mouths and spout a few slogans like "Down with imperialism" or "Down with the warlords," and that they can also recite the resolutions of the party strictly from memory. As for taking any real measures to engage in real activities, they get frightened out of their wits if they even hear about them. The right wing is all mouths, without hands and feet. They only have the guts to hold meetings in front of Duan Qirui. They don't have the guts to come to meetings in Guangzhou because the revolutionary atmosphere of Guangzhou would scare them to death. They have resolved that their so-called Second National Congress will be held in March of next year in either Shanghai or Beijing. As I see it, if their congress really is able to convene (no matter how many attend), they may not necessarily dare to hold it in Beijing, because the dragon throne of Chief Executive Duan is already not very stable. They will probably meet in Shanghai.[1] To hold the National Party Congress of the Guomindang openly, right in the old lair of the imperialists, right in front of all the foreign consuls and the City Council and that red-headed guy from the police station of the big foreigners, that would really be a show of "courage." To be able to hold meetings openly, right in front of the warlords and imperialists, this is the greatest talent of the right wing. Left wingers could never match this!

---

1. Mao's conjecture was correct. The Guomindang Party Congress which the Western Hills Faction proposed to hold, in opposition to that of January 1926 in Guangzhou, finally convened in April 1926 in Shanghai and elected Lin Sen as chairman of a rival Central Executive Committee. The "Shanghai" Guomindang existed until the reunification of the party following the reconciliation between Chiang Kaishek and the Wuhan or "Left" Guomindang in September 1927.

—1926—

An Analysis of the Various Classes among the Chinese Peasantry and Their Attitudes toward the Revolution

(January 1926)

No matter where you go in the countryside, provided that you are a careful observer, you will see the following eight different types of people:

Big landlords
Small landlords
Owner-peasants
Semi-owner peasants
Sharecroppers
Poor peasants
Farm laborers and rural artisans
Vagrants

These eight types of people form eight separate classes, each having different economic positions and living conditions. This in turn influences their psychology, so that their attitudes toward the revolution also differ.

A large portion of China's big landlords come from among the descendents of the former Qing dynasty bureaucracy and aristocracy and from the present-day bureaucrats and warlords. A small portion are rich urban merchants who have bought land. There are very few who have raised themselves to the status of big landlords by their industrious cultivation of the land. Their interests are founded upon the severe exploitation of the five types of peasants: the owner-peasants, the semi-owner peasants, the sharecroppers, the poor peasants, and the farm laborers. Their methods of exploitation may be divided into five types, the first of which is high rents, from 50 to 80 percent.[1] In the exploitation of the semi-owner peasants, the sharecroppers, and the poor peasants, this form of exploitation is very prevalent and extremely cruel. The second method is usury, for

---

This document was first published in the organ of the Guomindang Peasant Department, *Zhongguo nongmin*, Vol. 1, No. 1, 1926. Our translation is based on this text, as reproduced in *Mao Zedong ji*, Vol. 1, pp. 153–59.

1. These are, of course, rents in kind, amounting to a percentage of the harvest.

which the monthly interest ranges from 3 to 7 percent, and the yearly interest from 36 to 84 percent. This is also a form of exploitation of the semi-owner peasants, the sharecroppers, and the poor peasants, and one which is sometimes even more grievous than rent. It frequently happens that the burden of debt and interest leads to total bankruptcy within a few years. The third method is the heavy levies, in which some kind of pressure is used to force the owner-peasants and semi-owner peasants to contribute so much per *mu* to the expenses of the local defense forces. These defense forces (also called the militia) are the armed forces of the landlord class, the necessary device for suppressing peasant uprisings and maintaining the system of exploitation of the landlord class. The fourth method is the exploitation of the farm laborers, that is, the appropriation of their surplus labor. But China still has little capitalist agriculture, and most of the big landlords do not manage the land themselves. Consequently, this form of exploitation is practiced more by the small landlords than by big landlords. The fifth method is practiced in collusion with the warlords and corrupt officials, and consists in paying the land taxes this year in advance on behalf of the peasant, and then next year imposing heavy interest payments on the peasant who owed the tax. The suffering inflicted on the peasants by the combination of these five kinds of exploitation is truly indescribable. Hence China's big landlords are the deadly enemies of the Chinese peasantry, the true rulers of the countryside, the real foundation of imperialism and the warlords, the only secure bulwark of feudal and patriarchal society, the ultimate cause for the emergence of all counterrevolutionary forces. If we count as big landlords those who control 500 *mu* or more, they probably constitute (together with their families) about 0.1 percent of the peasantry, or approximately 320,000 persons in a total peasant population of 320 million for the whole country (calculated as 80 percent of the total population).

The small landlords are more numerous than the big landlords, numbering at least two million in the country as a whole. Most of them are owner-peasants who have raised themselves to this status by hard work, though some of them are urban merchants who have bought land, and others are the descendants of officials who have seen better days, or present-day petty officials. Their methods of exploitation are three: high rents, usury, and the exploitation of surplus labor. People of this kind suffer to a substantial extent from the oppression of the warlords and big landlords, and as a result have considerable spirit of resistance, but they are also afraid of "Communism," and therefore have a contradictory attitude toward the present revolution. Most of the higher intellectuals in China, such as the teachers and students of the universities and specialized schools, and those who study abroad both in the East and in the West, are the sons of small landlords, and it is they who advocate what is called *Étatisme*. These small landlords are China's middle bourgeoisie. Their aspiration is to achieve the status of the big bourgeoisie and to establish a state ruled by one class. They suffer, however, from the blows of foreign capital and the oppression of the warlords and cannot develop, so they need revolution. But because the present revolutionary movement in China involves the militant participation of the proletariat at home and is actively supported by the international proletariat abroad, they sense a threat to their existence and development as a class that aspires to achieve the status of the big bourgeoisie and to establish an *Étatiste* state, and therefore have doubts about the revolution. A self-styled true disciple of Dai Jitao put forward the following opinion in the Beijing *Morning Post*: "Raise your left hand to knock down imperialism; raise your right hand to knock down the Communist Party." This vividly illustrates the contradictory and fearful attitude of this class. They are against interpreting the Principle of People's Livelihood according to the theory of class struggle, and they oppose the Guomindang's alliance with Russia and its admission of Communist elements. These people constitute the right wing of the Chinese middle bourgeoisie and have a strong tendency to move toward a counterrevolutionary position. But within the middle bourgeoisie there is a left wing, which, at the proper time, can be led toward the path of revolution. For instance, when the enthusiasm for the peasant association movement is running high, the left wing elements among the small landlords can be led to help in the work of the peasants' associations. But by nature they are very much inclined to compromise, and their blood ties ultimately make them closer to the right wing of the small landlords and to the big landlords than to the peasants' associations. With the exception of a few who are in special circumstances, because of history or environment, we definitely cannot expect them to set out courageously on the path of revolution, or faithfully to serve the revolutionary cause together with other classes.

The owner-peasants belong to the petty bourgeoisie. They are also of three types. The first type of owner-peasant consists of those who have surplus money and grain. That is, after their own needs have been met, the product of their labor leaves them each year with a surplus that can be used for what is called the initial accumulation of capital. Such people are very much concerned with "getting rich." Although they have no vain hopes of enriching themselves greatly, they all want to climb up to the position of being small landlords. Their mouths water copiously when they see the respect in which those small moneybags are held, and they pray to Marshall Zhao most assiduously. Such people are extremely timid; they are afraid of officials, and also a bit afraid of revolution. Because their economic position is rather close to that of the middle-bourgeois small landlords, they are rather inclined to believe in the propaganda, "Beware the extremists!" and "Beware the Communists!" of "Venerable so-and-so," "Honorable so-and-so," or "Bearded so-and-so" among the small landlords in the countryside. Of course, these warnings also flow from the lips of those "Great Men" and "Venerable Masters" among the big landlords. This group of people with surplus money and food constitutes the right wing of the petty bourgeoisie, and they adopt a skeptical attitude toward the present revolution before they have

properly understood it. But such people form only a minority of the owner-peasants, probably less than 10 percent of the total. Some say that the number of
owner-peasants in China is greater than the total of tenant farmers and farm
laborers. But if we exclude the semi-owner peasants, then they are definitely
only a minority of the peasantry, probably 100 million to 120 million. About 10
percent, or 12 million, of the owner-peasants are well-to-do. The second type of
owner-peasants are those who are just able to meet their own needs. What they
earn and what they consume each year even out, no more, no less. These owner-
peasants are very different from the first type of owner-peasants. They, too, want
to get rich, but Marshall Zhao does not permit them to do so. As a result of their
recent oppression and exploitation by the imperialists, the warlords, and the
landlord class, they feel that the world today is not what it used to be. They feel
that if they work only as hard as before, they will not be able to stay alive. They
must work longer hours, get up earlier and work later every day, and double their
attention to their work, just to make ends meet. They are somewhat abusive; they
curse the foreigners as "devils," the warlords as "money-grabbing commanders,"
the local bullies and evil gentry as "the heartless rich." As for the movement
against the imperialists and the warlords, they simply suspect that it may not
succeed, on the ground that "the foreigners and the commanders seem so powerful," refuse to join it recklessly, and take a neutral position, but they absolutely
do not oppose the revolution. This group of people is numerous, constituting
probably half the owner-peasants, or approximately 60 million. The third type of
owner-peasant has a deficit every year. Quite a few of this group of owner-peasants came originally from so-called well-to-do families who gradually fell to the
point that they could only just manage, and then gradually went into debt. At the
end of every year when the accounts are settled, they are startled and exclaim,
"Ai! Another deficit." Because such people have lived well in the past but have
then fallen behind year by year, with their debts continually mounting and their
lives more and more miserable, they "think of the future and shiver even if it is
not cold." Mentally, such people suffer more than than all the others because
they see the contrast between the past and the present. Such people are of
considerable importance in the revolutionary movement and can contribute substantial strength to the advancement of the revolution. They number roughly 40
percent of the owner-peasants, i.e., 48 million—a not inconsiderable number,
which constitutes the left wing of the petty bourgeoisie. In normal times, the
above three types of owner-peasants differ in their attitudes toward the present
Chinese revolution. In time of war, however, when the tide of revolution is at the
flood and the dawn of victory is in sight, not only do the left-wing owner-peasants
immediately join the revolution, but the middle-of-the-road owner-peasants may
also join the revolution, and even the right-wing owner-peasants, caught up in
the revolutionary tide of the sharecroppers and the left-wing owner-peasants,
have no alternative but to go along with the revolution. Thus, it is possible that
the whole of the petty-bourgeois owner-peasants may side with the revolution.

The three categories of semi-owner peasants, sharecroppers, and poor peasants probably account for between 150 million and 170 million of the Chinese peasantry. Looked at separately, the semi-owner peasants probably number 50 million, the sharecroppers and poor peasants 60 million each. This is an extremely large mass of people in the countryside. The so-called peasant problem is in large part their problem. Although all three of these types of peasants belong to the semi-proletariat, they differ greatly in their economic conditions. The life of the semi-owner peasants is harder than that of the owner-peasants because every year they are short of half the food they need and must rent land from others or work as laborers or engage in petty trading to make up the difference. Between spring and summer, when the new crops are not yet ripe and last year's grain is exhausted, they borrow at high rates of interest and buy[2] grain at high prices from others. Naturally their lot is much harder than that of the owner-peasants, who seek nothing from others. Nevertheless, they are better off than the sharecroppers, because the sharecroppers have no land and receive only half the harvest from the land they cultivate. Although the semi-owner peasants receive only half, or even less than half, of what they grow on the land they rent from others, still they get the whole crop from their own land. Hence, the semi-owner peasants are more revolutionary than the owner-peasants, but less so than the sharecroppers.

The sharecropper and the poor peasant are both tenants in the countryside, subject to the exploitation of the landlords, but there is a certain difference in their economic positions. The sharecroppers have no land, but they have relatively adequate farm implements and a reasonable amount of liquid capital. These peasants receive half the product of their annual labor. They make up what they lack by planting side crops, catching fish and shrimp, and raising poultry and pigs. In this way, they eke out a living. Surrounded by difficulties and privations, they are continually preoccupied with how they will get through the year. Thus their life is harder than that of the semi-owner peasants, but better than that of the poor peasants. They are more revolutionary than the owner-peasants, but they do not match the poor peasants.

The poor peasants do not have sufficient farm implements nor do they have any liquid capital. They are short of fertilizer and reap only a meager harvest from the fields. After paying the rent, very little is left. In times of drought and famine, they piteously beg from friends and relatives, and borrow a few measures of grain to tide them over for four or five days. Their debts pile up like the burden on the backs of oxen. They are the most miserable among the peasants and are most receptive to revolutionary propaganda.

---

2. The text here reads *tiao*, "sell," but this must be a misprint for *di*, "buy." (The two characters are very similar.)

The farm laborers are the agricultural proletariat. There are three categories, hired by the year, the month, or the day. Not only do such farm laborers have neither land nor farm implements, they also have not a penny of liquid capital. Hence they can subsist only by their labor. In terms of their long hours of work, their low wages, the mean way they are treated, and the insecurity of their employment, they are worse off than other workers. This group of people, of all those in the countryside, suffers most bitterly, and should be accorded the utmost attention by those working in the peasant movement. The position of the rural handicraft workers is higher than that of farm laborers, because they have their own tools and belong to a kind of free profession. But because of heavy family burdens and the disparity between their earnings and the cost of living, and because they frequently suffer from the burdens of poverty and the fear of losing their jobs, their situation is not much different from that of the farm laborers.

The vagrants consist of peasants who have lost their land, and handicraft workers who have lost all opportunity of employment as a result of oppression and exploitation by the imperialists, the warlords, and landlord class, or as a result of natural catastrophes such as flood and drought. They can be divided into soldiers, bandits, thieves, beggars, and prostitutes. These five categories of people have different names, and the status accorded them by society is also somewhat different, but they are one in that each of them is a "human being" having five senses and four limbs. They each have their different ways of making a living: the soldier "fights," the bandit "robs," the thief "steals," the beggar "begs," and the prostitute "seduces." But to the extent that they all seek to make a living and get food to eat, they are all one. They lead the most precarious existence of any human being. They have secret organizations everywhere, which serve as their organs for mutual aid in the political and economic struggle; for example, there is the Triad Society [Sanhehui] in Fujian and Guangdong; the Elder Brother Society [Gelaohui] in Hunan, Hubei, Guizhou, and Sichuan; the Big Sword Society [Dadaohui] in the provinces of Anhui, Henan, and Shandong; the Society of Observance of Principle [Zailihui] in Zhili and the three [North]eastern provinces; and the Green Gang [Qingbang] of Shanghai and elsewhere. To deal with these people is the greatest and the most difficult problem facing China. China has two problems: poverty and unemployment. Hence if the problem of unemployment can be solved, half of China's problems will be solved. The number of vagrants in China is fearfully large, probably more than 20 million. These people are capable of fighting very bravely, and if a method can be found for leading them, they can become a revolutionary force.

Our work of organizing the peasantry involves gathering together into a single organization five categories of peasants: owner-peasants, semi-owner peasants, sharecroppers, poor peasants, and farm laborers and handicraftsmen. Toward the landlord class, we adopt in principle the method of struggle, demanding from them economic and political concessions. In special circumstances, when we encounter the most reactionary and vicious local bullies and evil gentry who exploit the people savagely, as in Haifeng and Guangning,[3] they must be overthrown completely. As for the vagrants, we should exhort them to side with the peasant's associations and to join the great revolutionary movement, in order to find a solution to the problem of unemployment. We must never force them to go over to the side of the enemy and become a force in the service of the counterrevolutionaries.

---

3. It was in Haifeng that the very first peasant movements in China were launched as early as 1922. Their principal architect was Peng Pai (1896-1929), a landlord's son from the area. After studying in Japan, Peng returned to Haifeng in 1921, joined the Socialist Youth League, and began organizing the peasants in the following year. The most authoritative work regarding his experience is that of F. Galbiati, *P'eng P'ai and the Hai-Lu-feng Soviet* (Stanford: Stanford University Press, 1985). On Peng's efforts to organize the peasants of Guangning, a *xian* northwest of Guangzhou, see Galbiati, pp. 181-82.

Report on Propaganda

(January 8, 1926)

Written Propaganda

I. Newspapers

A. Papers run by the party:

1. The Shanghai *Minguo ribao* (Republican Daily). Formerly under the private ownership of Ye Chucang and others, it came under party management following the First National Party Congress, at which point tens of thousands of *yuan* were spent to enlarge it, with later monthly expenses amounting to 2,500 to 3,000 *yuan*. But from the beginning it could never be considered a true party paper, since it contains a great deal of false and specious views and reporting. Since the Western Hills Conference it has become an organ of the reactionaries.

2. The Guangzhou *Minguo ribao* (Republican Daily). Formerly run by the Guangzhou municipal party office, in October of 1924 it came under the management of the Central Propaganda Department.[1] Its distribution has increased from something over 1,000 copies to more than 11,000 copies.

3. The Guangzhou *Guomin xinwen* (National News). Formerly an organ of the reactionaries, following the Liao affair[2] it became a party paper under the management of the Central Propaganda Department, and when the Guangdong provincial party office was established it reverted to the provincial party office. At present more than 7,500 copies are issued daily.

4. The Xiangjiang[3] *Chenbao* (Morning Post). For a period of time it was run by the party; then it defected to the party of the enemy, and has since ceased publication.

5. The Hong Kong *Xinwenbao* (News). Since August of 1924, when it severed relations with Chen Jiongming, it has been under the guidance of our party. At the beginning of the strikes it was closed down by the Hong Kong government. Before being closed down, its circulation had reached more than 8,000, most of which were sold abroad, with Hong Kong sales next.

This report was first published in *Zhengzhi zhoubao*, Nos. 6–7, April 10, 1926. Our translation is based on the version reproduced in *Mao Zedong ji*, Vol. 1, pp. 141–51.

1. I.e., the Propaganda Department of the Central Executive Committee of the Guomindang, as acting head of which Mao delivered this report.

2. I.e., the assassination of Liao Zhongkai on August 20, 1925. See the note to the text of July 21, 1925, "The Struggle against the Right Wing of the Guomindang."

3. Possibly a misprint for Xianggang (Hong Kong).

6. The Beijing *Minbao* (People's Paper). Not long after it began publication it was shut down by Zhang Zuolin.

B. Daily newspapers run by individual comrades or in the name of associations or organizations: Having as yet no complete survey, we have no statistics.

C. There are many daily newspapers run by overseas Chinese party offices abroad, but having as yet no complete survey, we have no statistics.

II. Weeklies

A. Party run:

1. The *Zhongguo Guomindang zhoukan* (Guomindang of China Weekly). Published by the Central Executive Committee following the First National Party Congress and discontinued soon afterwards.
2. The eight weekly supplements of the Guangzhou *Minguo ribao* (Republican Daily), in the fields of literature, science, studies on the thought of Sun Yatsen, economics, the common people, agriculture, women, and films. Soon ceased publication.
3. The *Dangsheng zhoukan* (Party Voice Weekly). Under the direction of the Central Propaganda Department. In the beginning it belonged to the *Republican Daily*. It later became independent but soon ceased publication.
4. The *Pinglun zhi pinglun* (Review of Reviews). Following the First National Party Congress, it was under the direction of the Propaganda Department of the Shanghai Executive Bureau and distributed by the Shanghai *Republican Daily*. Soon ceased publication.
5. The several weekly supplements of the Shanghai *Republican Daily*, on science, the common people, etc., all of which lasted only a short time.
6. The *Zhejiang zhoubao* (Zhejiang Weekly). Published by the Zhejiang provincial party office. Soon ceased publication.
7. The *Xinmin zhoubao* (New People's Weekly). Published by the Hunan provincial party office, following the First National Party Congress. Soon ceased publication.
8. *Zhongguo guomin* (People of China). Published by the Shanghai Federation of District Party Offices, following the Western Hills Conference. Mainly devoted to opposing the Western Hills Conference and the arguments of the right wing. Now published every three days.
9. The *Wuhan pinglun* (Wuhan Review). Sponsored by the Hubei provincial party office, it has continued publication without interruption.
10. The *Zhengzhi zhoubao* (Political Weekly). Began publication in December 1925, under the sponsorship of the Central Propaganda Department, in 40,000 copies per issue, with the objective of destroying the counterrevolutionary propaganda of the North and of the Yangzi River areas.

B. Various Guangdong military and military academy weeklies and semi-monthlies, such as:

1. *Huangpu chao* (Huangpu Tides) of the Huangpu Military Academy.
2. The *Geming banyuekan* (Revolutionary Semimonthly) of the Second Army.
3. The *Junsheng* (Army Voice) of the Fourth Army.
4. *Rendao* (Humanism) of the Army to Attack Hubei (Gong'ejun), etc.

C. Periodicals published by comrades in the name of associations. There are many in this category, such as:

1. The periodicals of student groups found everywhere, such as *Zhongguo xuesheng* (The Chinese Student), etc.
2. Periodicals of worker groups, such as *Gongren zhi lu* (The Worker's Road), etc.
3. Periodicals of peasant groups, few in number, some in Guangdong.
4. Periodicals of army groups, such as, in the Guangdong area, *Zhongguo junren* (The Chinese Soldier), *Gemingjun* (Revolutionary Army), *Qingnian junren lianhehui zhoukan* (Young Soldiers' Association Weekly); and in Yantai, *Xin haijun* (The New Navy), etc.
5. Periodicals of women's groups, of which there are four or five nationwide.
6. Periodicals published by other groups.

III. Monthlies

The year before last, there were two: *Xin jianshe* (New Reconstruction) and *Xin minguo* (New Republic), which appeared for only a short time. At present there is only *Zhongguo nongmin* (The Chinese Peasant), published by the Central Peasant Department, which has just begun publication.

IV. News Agencies

1. The Central News Agency (Zhongyang Tongxunshe), directly under the management of the Central Propaganda Department, has been quite successful and has been in operation for two years now.
2. Several other news agencies have relations with us.

V. Books

1. Central: The Central Propaganda Department has published about 30 (of which 12 are about Mr. Sun's *Three People's Principles*, his *Fundamentals of National Reconstruction*, and so on; 11 are on the collected talks of comrades such as Wang Jingwei;[4] and about 5 are compilations from the

---

4. Since Wang Jingwei had been head of the Propaganda Department until October 1925, when Mao succeeded him, it was natural that Wang's talks should be featured in the department's publications.

Central Propaganda Department), in a total of 393,959 copies. They have mainly been distributed only in Guangdong.

2. Local: Not clear, no statistics.

VI. Propaganda Leaflets

1. Central: The Central Propaganda Department has in all 83 propaganda leaflets, distribution limited solely to Guangdong.
2. Local: Not clear, no figures.

VII. Posters

1. Central: In Guangzhou city, the Central Propaganda Department and the Guangzhou Bureau of Public Security have cooperated in putting out two kinds of posters, one to be tacked up on telephone poles and one to be written on walls. The topics are all taken from the Manifesto of the First National Party Congress and from the testament of Mr. Sun.
2. The armies: The political departments of the First, Second, Third, and Fourth armies, the navy, and the Huangpu Military Academy, and the officers' schools attached to the Second and Third armies have put out many posters that have been widely effective.
3. Popular mass groups: In Guangdong, peasant associations and labor unions have printed a great many.

Pictorial Propaganda

I. The Importance of Pictorial Propaganda

1. More than 90 percent of the Chinese people are illiterate. Only a small portion of the popular masses throughout China can understand the written propaganda of our party, so pictorial propaganda is particularly important.

II. Achievements to Date

1. Central organs: Began only in April of last year. Rather little has been done, and again mostly in Guangdong, in the following three projects.
   a. Four small satirical cartoons have been submitted weekly to the Guangzhou *Republican Daily* (with some lapses).
   b. One piece of pictorial propaganda has been put out once a week (at times one every two or three weeks).
   c. Small photographs of Mr. Sun Yatsen and Mr. Liao Zhongkai have been printed.
2. The various armies: The political departments of the armies have done quite a bit of pictorial propaganda, and especially when engaged in battles, they have put up a lot of pictorial propaganda in the places reached in their campaigns, which has had a great deal of influence on the popular masses.
3. The various popular mass organizations: The Guangdong Workers' Asso-

ciation and Peasant Association have done a lot of pictorial propaganda that is really able to arouse the workers, peasants, and popular masses. There has also been a little in Beijing and in Shanghai.

Oral Propaganda

I. Oral propaganda occupies an important position in propaganda, both as to quantity and effectiveness.

II. Oral propaganda frequently takes the form of speeches on various kinds of topics delivered at meetings of peasants, workers, soldiers, and students.

III. The speeches given when there are political changes going on or at demonstrations and marches are a form of oral propaganda that addresses the issue of the moment. The Central Propaganda Department has numerous times organized propaganda teams. All provinces and cities have organized propaganda on a large scale and have done a great deal during and since the May Thirtieth Movement.

IV. The reports on political party work presented by the responsible cadres at meetings of party members are educational for comrades within the party. At the memorials for the Director General,[5] this is usually done by the central departments of the party.

Propaganda on Fourteen Important Events of the Past Two Years

I. Our party reorganization: Publication of the manifesto and political program clearly revealed our opposition to imperialism and to its hangers-on. The results were:

1. It made the popular masses understand our party and our party's objectives, and changed the attitudes of those who formerly were skeptical of our party. It was extremely effective for propaganda outside [the party].
2. The unification of objectives and methods within the party has gradually weeded out those individuals and small groups harboring their own objectives and methods. This has been highly effective as regards education within the party.

II. The incident of resuming control of the Guangdong customs:[6] Our anti-imperialist propaganda made plain the hostility of imperialism to our party, and

---

5. I.e., Sun Yatsen.

6. In December 1923 Sun Yatsen, having returned to power in Guangzhou, demanded a share of the customs revenues collected there by the Maritime Customs Service, which was under the control of the government in Beijing and of the diplomatic corps. When this was refused to him, he threatened to seize the Guangzhou customs house and to appoint his own officials. The foreign powers responded by a naval demonstration of 23 gunboats in neighboring waters, and in the face of this threat, and of opposition from the Guangzhou merchants, Sun was obliged to back down. These events contributed considerably to his reputation as an anti-imperialist fighter.

our party's opposition to the imperialists. From the standpoint of propaganda, this had great impact.

III. The anti-imperialism of the Shamian strike.[7]

IV. The Merchants' Corps incident:[8] Made the popular masses recognize the crimes of the comprador class. But our party's propaganda regarding this incident was not very forceful, while the propaganda of the counterrevolutionaries attacking our party was formidable.

V. The Sino-Russian agreement:[9] From this the Chinese came to understand that in international affairs there is a distinction between imperialist and anti-imperialist nations. Anti-imperialist alliances have sprung up in Beijing and in other places. The popular masses have begun to accept the slogan, "Oppose Imperialism," and our party has put out a statement on this issue.

VI. The war against the Zhili clique:[10] From this time forward, the popular masses lost their faith in the powerful warlords. Mr. Sun issued a manifesto regarding the Northern Expedition.

VII. The trip of the Director General to the North:[11] A statement on the trip to the North was issued, which raised the two slogans, "Convene a National People's Assembly" and "Abolish the Unequal Treaties."

VIII. The movement to promote the formation of a National People's Assembly: Directed at Duan Qirui, this has caused the popular masses to lose faith completely in Duan's "Reconstruction Conference,"[12] and at the same time has made the people understand more fully the political proposals of our party. In the course of this movement, the two slogans "Convene a National People's Assem-

---

7. The British and French concessions were located on the island of Shamian (commonly written Shameen in Western sources) in the middle of Guangzhou. In June 1924, after an attempt by a Vietnamese revolutionary to assassinate the governor-general of Indo-China, who was visiting there, the foreign authorities imposed a system of passes on Chinese employees working on the island. After a strike and blockade of Shamian lasting nearly two months, these regulations were rescinded by the consuls.

8. Regarding this incident, in the autumn of 1924, see the note to the text of December 5, 1925, "Zou Lu and the Revolution."

9. On the Sino-Soviet agreement of May 31, 1924, see the note to the text dated July 21, 1924, "The Struggle against the Right Wing of the Guomindang."

10. The reference is to the defeat of Wu Peifu in the fall of 1924 by the armies of Feng Yuxiang, acting in concert with Zhang Zuolin, and with the tacit support of Sun Yatsen, which led to the removal of Cao Kun from the presidency.

11. On Sun Yatsen's trip to the North in November-December 1924, see the text of November 1, 1924, "Strengthening Party Work and our Position on Sun Yatsen's Attendance at the Northern Peace Conference," and the note thereto.

12. The Shanhou huiyi (literally, "conference so things will be better afterwards," commonly translated Reconstruction Conference) was convened by Duan Qirui in February 1925 in his capacity as provisional chief executive of the Beijing government.

bly" and "Abolish the Unequal Treaties" have become widely accepted among the popular masses.

IX. The movement to mourn the Director General: Caused the popular masses to understand Mr. Sun, our party, and our party's objectives. This movement was very widespread, reaching even the impoverished countryside and remote hamlets. As a result, the two slogans "Convene a National People's Assembly" and "Abolish the Unequal Treaties" became even more fully accepted by the people. At this time, our party issued a statement breaking off relations with Duan Qirui.

X. The May Thirtieth Movement:[13] Unprecedented anti-imperialism. In the course of this movement, we spelled out the content of abolishing the unequal treaties: such things as recovering the concessions, recovering the customs service, recovering judicial authority, withdrawal of foreign naval and land forces stationed in China, etc. Because of this, the popular masses have come to understand what the unequal treaties are. Because of the severe oppression of the warlords of the Fengtian clique, this movement failed. But there was one positive achievement: The workers of Shanghai and Hong Kong stood up. This time, our propaganda was extremely effective. The peasant masses in the countryside became universally aware that our party had a manifesto supporting the people and opposing imperialism.

XI. The assassination of Liao Zhongkai: The popular masses recognized the violence used by imperialism and its underlings. Our party used the mourning ceremonies to put out quite a lot of written and pictorial propaganda.

XII. The war against the Fengtian clique:[14] Made the masses of the people clearly recognize the relationship between the imperialists and their tools, the Chinese warlords, and how quickly the Chinese warlords would crumble. In this war, the popular masses had a feeling of the imminence of the victory of the revolution. During the movement against Duan Qirui, slogans were raised everywhere directly attacking local warlords. For example, the people of Beijing had their "Drive out Duan Qirui," the people of Wuhan had their "Drive out Wu Peifu," and the people of Changsha had their "Down with Zhao Hengti." Once the former peaceful attitude of avoiding direct conflict changed, the revolutionary atmosphere became charged as never before.

XIII. The movement against religion: In the last two years, organizations and propaganda against Christianity have spread throughout the entire nation, so that the popular masses now recognize the invasion of imperialist religion.

XIV. Political education in times of peace and political propaganda in times of

---

13. On the events of May 30 and their aftermath, see the note to the text of December 13, 1925, "To the Left or to the Right."

14. See "Propaganda Guidelines of the Chinese Guomindang in the War against the Fengtian Clique," dated November 27, 1925, and the notes thereto.

war among the armed forces: The political education carried out by our party at the Huangpu Military Academy and in the National Revolutionary Army has created an anti-imperialist military force. Propaganda for an alliance between the army and the people during the several campaigns in Guangdong has made the army care for the people, and has made the people support the army. This fact, too, may be considered a very great success by our party.

Enemy Propaganda

Part of our propaganda must be directly aimed at the enemy's propaganda, so let us now take a look at the counterrevolutionary propaganda put out by the enemy over the past two years.

I. The imperialists: Because our party's anti-imperialist propaganda has been especially aggressive in the past two years, the slanderous attacks against our party in imperialist propaganda have also been especially strong. Thus they have raised the two slogans "Oppose Communism" and "Red Imperialism" to rally their tools in China—the bureaucrats, warlords, comprador class, local bullies, and evil gentry—to attack our party. The various foreign papers and the foreign news agencies in Hong Kong, Shanghai, Tianjin, Beijing, Fengtian, and Hankou may be said to have stopped at nothing in their rumor mongering, lies, provocations, and insults.

II. The various warlords: All the various domestic cliques of warlords, big and small, have consistently defended and greatly expanded upon the slogans put out by the imperialists, "Oppose Communism" and "Red Imperialism."

III. The comprador class: Their counterrevolutionary propaganda work has been the same as the above, but they have worked harder at propaganda than any other counterrevolutionary faction. The Hong Kong *Gongshang ribao* (Industry and Commerce Daily) and the Shanghai *Xinwen bao* (News) may be taken as representative.

IV. The Research clique: Representing the interests of the bureaucrats and large landlords, their counterrevolutionary propaganda has been the same as above, as represented by the *Shishi xinbao* (China Times) and the *Chenbao* (Morning Post).

V. The Anfu clique: Representing Japanese imperialism, their counterrevolutionary propaganda has been the same as above. The *Xin shenbao* (New Times) is their organ.

VI. The Federalists: Defending the interests of the bureaucrats and landlords, their counterrevolutionary propaganda has been the same as above, and the *Zhonghua xinbao* (China News) is their organ.

VII. The *Étatistes*: Copying something of the style of the Western *Étatistes*, they defend the interests of the small landlords and Chinese industrial and commercial bourgeoisie. Very stridently "anti-Communist" and "anti-Soviet Russia," they are represented by the *Xingshi zhoubao* (Awakened Lion Weekly).

VIII. The right wing of the Guomindang: Following the Western Hills Conference, the right wing of our party has also taken up the two slogans "Oppose Communism" and "Oppose Soviet Russia," and has started fighting along with the counterrevolutionary factions, adopting a hostile attitude towards our party. The Shanghai *Republican Daily* represents them.

During the past two years, in the mutual opposition between revolutionary propaganda and counterrevolutionary propaganda, revolutionary propaganda has truly taken the offensive. This offensive stance was particularly evident in the May Thirtieth Movement. From the beginning, counterrevolutionary propaganda has been on the defensive, and it was only when it could not parry the blows that it picked up the two shields of "Oppose Communism" and "Red Imperialism." This phenomenon of direct confrontation between offense and defense has resulted in the increasing unity and aggressiveness of the Chinese revolutionary forces and the increasing tottering and crumbling of the counterrevolutionary forces.

Shortcomings

The following shortcomings have been discovered in our propaganda work of the past two years.

I. Our party newspapers are less than perfect.

II. The direction of propaganda regarding important events has not been quick and alert, and much of it has been done without putting our full effort into it.

III. We have totally lacked a system of leadership, and the upper and lower echelons of the party propaganda offices have completely lost touch with each other. This has created a battle situation of every man for himself, and a number of those in positions of responsibility in the propaganda offices have given up on their duties.

IV. The tasks of investigation and correction have been totally neglected.

V. There has been absolutely no collection of propaganda materials, and supplying of them to lower-level party offices.

VI. There has been hardly any planned education within the party.

VII. We have concentrated too much on city people and neglected the peas-antry.[15]

We have concentrated too much on the written word and neglected pictorial [propaganda].

The above are all among the greatest shortcomings in our party's propaganda work up until now. Henceforth, they should be corrected one by one.

---

15. Mao's report as originally published in *Zhongguo nongmin* has *tongmin* instead of *nongmin* (peasant) here. This seems so obviously a typographical error that the editors of the *Mao Zedong ji* (Vol. 1, p. 151) have simply substituted *nong* for *tong* (meaning through, or the whole), without even indicating the fact. When this text was reproduced in *Mao Zedong xinwen gongzuo wenxuan* (Selected Writings by Mao Zedong on Journalistic Work, [Beijing: Xinhua shudian, 1983], p. 12), the character *tong* was retained. Ques-tioned about this, responsible officials of the Department for Research on Party Literature, which edited this volume, said that they were not sure whether it should be *nongmin* (peasant) or *xiangmin* (country dwellers). They had no doubt, however, that it should have been one or the other of these. Finally, both the "Resolution on Propaganda" and the "Resolution regarding the Report on Propaganda," which appear below, underscore the importance of not neglecting the peasants and the countryside.

Reasons for the Breakaway of the Guomindang Right and Its Implications for the Future of the Revolution

(January 10, 1926)

Some people say that, if a rightist faction has now once again split off from the Guomindang, this is a result of the impetuosity of leftist elements in the party and is a misfortune for the Chinese Guomindang and the Chinese national revolution. This opinion is incorrect. Such a split should occur today in the party of national revolution in semicolonial China. This is an inevitable phenomenon, and although not a cause for rejoicing, it is, on the other hand, assuredly not something unfortunate. If you want to know why this is the case, it suffices to look at the political situation of modern times and the history of the Guomindang from the Revive China Society to the present time, and then you will understand completely. The democratic revolution in Europe, North America, and Japan, from the late eighteenth to the mid-nineteenth century, in which the bourgeoisie opposed the feudal aristocracy, is totally different in nature from the national revolution in the colonies and semicolonies in the late nineteenth and early twentieth century, in which the petty bourgeoisie, the semiproletariat and the proletariat cooperate against imperialism and its tools, the bureaucrats, warlords, compradors, and the landlord class. Moreover, the nature of the Revolution of 1911 is also different from that of the current revolution. The bourgeois revolutions of the previous era in England, France, Germany, America, and Japan were carried out by a single class, the bourgeoisie. Their target was the feudal aristocracy within each country, and their goal was to establish nationalist[1] states, that is to say states ruled by the bourgeoisie alone. Their slogans of so-called liberty, equality, and fraternity were only put forward at that

---

This article was first published in *Zhengzhi zhoubao*, No. 4, January 10, 1926. Our source is *Mao Zedong ji. Bujuan*, Vol. 2, pp. 143–49.

1. Mao uses here the term *guojiazhuyi*, which literally means "statism" or "*Étatisme*." Because of the central role of the state in nationalist ideology, especially in continental Europe, this word is not unrelated to nationalism, but on the whole we have preferred to translate it as "*Étatisme*" to avoid confusion with terms such as *guomin geming* and *minzu geming*, which do mean precisely "national revolution" in the sense of the revolution of the political or biological nation. In the present context, however, we have translated loosely as nationalist to avoid the clumsy combination "*Étatiste* state" or "statist state."

time as tactics for winning over and deceiving the petty bourgeoisie, the semiproletariat, and the proletariat. Their ultimate outcome was to develop colonies and semicolonies throughout the world and to create international capitalist imperialism. In contrast, the contemporary revolution in colonies and semicolonies is a revolution jointly carried out by three classes: the petty bourgeoisie, the semiproletariat and the proletariat. The big bourgeoisie, as an appendage to imperialism, is a counterrevolutionary force. The middle class wavers between revolution and counterrevolution. Only the alliance of the three classes of the petty bourgeoisie, the semiproletariat, and the proletariat is truly revolutionary. The target of this revolution is international imperialism, and its objective is to establish a state jointly ruled by the revolutionary popular masses. The principles of People's Rights and People's Livelihood for which it calls in no sense represent the tactics employed by a single class for winning over and deceiving the others for its own purposes; they constitute rather the joint political and economic demands of all the revolutionary classes. These principles have been laid down in the program of the political party of the revolutionary classes by their representative (Mr. Sun Yatsen). The result of the revolution will be the achievement of a country ruled jointly by all the revolutionary popular masses, and its final outcome will be to eliminate imperialism throughout the world and to build a genuinely equal and free global union (that is, the equality of the human race and worldwide great harmony[2] advocated by Mr. Sun). Now let us look at the differences between the Revolution of 1911 and the present one. The Revolution of 1911 ought to have been in essence a revolution against international imperialism, but because most party members at the time were not clear about this, and rightist leaders such as Huang Xing, Zhang Binglin, and Song Jiaoren[3] recognized only the Manchu aristocracy within the country as the enemy, the slogan of the revolution became simply "Away with the Manchus."

---

2. *Datong.*

3. Although the three men cited here had indeed been, prior to 1911, anti-Manchu nationalists, they are in other respects a somewhat ill-assorted group. Zhang was above all an enemy of the foreign dynasty and, as indicated above in a note to Mao's letter of December 1, 1920, to Xiao Xudong and others, had in recent years been evolving in an increasingly conservative direction. Song Jiaoren (1882–1913), *zi* Tunchu, *hao* Yufu, a founding member of the Tongmenghui in 1905, was a firm partisan of Western-style parliamentary democracy. He was the principal architect of the electoral victory of the Guomindang over the partisans of Yuan Shikai, and it was because of this that Yuan had him killed. Huang Xing (1874–1916), *zi* Jinwu, *hao* Keqiang, had participated with Sun Yatsen in the creation of the Tongmenghui in 1905, and led the Guangzhou uprising of April 1911. Minister of war in Sun's government in 1912, he subsequently showed reluctance to oppose Yuan Shikai with force and went into exile in the United States. Mao's judgement of him here stands in sharp contrast with the veneration for Huang he had displayed in 1917. See, in Volume I, pp. 111–12, the "Letter to Miyazaki Tōten" of March 1917.

Also, because at the time there were no organized masses of workers and peasants, both the organizational form and substance of the Guomindang were extremely rudimentary, and its fighting ranks extremely isolated and weak. There was then in our country no Chinese Communist Party to represent the interests of the proletariat. In addition, the international situation then was that a few big powers dominated the whole world. There was only the counter-revolutionary alliance of the classes of the oppressors, and no revolutionary alliance of the oppressed classes. There were only bourgeois states, and no proletarian states. For all these reasons, the Chinese revolution in those days was without international support. Compared with 1911, the situation has completely changed today. The target of the revolution has already been shifted to international capitalist imperialism. The party's organization has gradually been tightened and developed because worker and peasant elements have joined it, and at the same time the worker and peasant classes have taken shape as a social force. There is now a Communist Party. On the international scene there has also suddenly appeared a proletarian state, Soviet Russia, and a revolutionary alliance of the oppressed classes, the Third International, both of which provide powerful backing for the Chinese revolution. For these reasons, among all those who joined the revolution in 1911, only a few whose revolutionary will is strong continue to advocate revolution. The great majority have either given up the revolutionary cause because of their fear of the current revolution, or gone over to the counterrevolutionary ranks and oppose the Guomindang as it is today. This is why, with the development of the revolution and the progress of the Guomindang, old and new rightists have broken away from the party one after another, just as bamboo shoots lose their skins. To achieve a comprehensive understanding of the reasons for this split, we must also consider the class nature of the members of our party since the Revive China Society.[4] As we know, Hong Xiuquan,[5] who led the rural proletariat in a peasant revolution against the Qing aristocracy and the landlord class, was the source of Mr. Sun Yatsen's earliest revolutionary thought. In terms of organization, the Revive China Society was nothing but a secret society recruiting from among the vagrants.[6] The organization of the Tongmenghui was composed in part of overseas Chinese workers, in part of secret societies within the country; another component was made up of students from small landlord families who studied abroad, and students in China from both small landlord and owner-peasant backgrounds. In sum, the composition of the Tongmenghui consisted of a gathering together of

---

4. The Xingzhonghui or Revive China Society was founded by Huang Xing in 1903 and incorporated into the Tongmenghui in 1905.

5. Hong Xiuquan (1814-1864), a native of Guangdong, was the principal leader of the Taiping Heavenly Kingdom.

6. *Youmin.* As already noted in various contexts, this term, though it can refer to the urban lumpenproletariat, evokes in the first instance *rural* vagabonds or floating elements.

four classes: the proletariat (the secret societies), the semiproletariat (the over-seas Chinese workers), the petty bourgeoisie (part of the home students), and the middle class (students who had gone abroad and another part of the home students). At this time, confrontation took shape between the Society to Protect the Emperor of Kang Youwei and his faction, which led China's big landlord class, and the Tongmenghui of Sun Yatsen and his faction, which led the proletariat, the semiproletariat, the petty bourgeoisie, and the middle class in China. When the Revolution of 1911 achieved its initial successes, the faction representing the small landlords in the Revolutionary Alliance disapproved of putting into effect Mr. Sun's equalization of land ownership and control of capital. As a result, the revolutionary Tongmenghui was dissolved, and reorganized as the nonrevolutionary "Guomindang."[7] Moreover, it came to include many political groups representing the interests of the small landlord class, so that the small landlord class controlled the absolute majority in the party. Although this party then still stood opposed to the Progressive Party, which represented the big landlord class, it had virtually no revolutionary character. (The Progressive Party had its origin in the provincial assemblies at the end of the Qing dynasty, which were organs of the big landlords in each province, just as today's provincial assemblies in various provinces are organs of the big landlords.) Mr. Sun was extremely indignant at this and decided to reorganize the party as the Chinese Revolutionary Party. He resolutely used the word "revolution" in naming the party, not hesitating to break with the leaders of the small landlord class such as Huang Xing in order to maintain the authentic revolutionary tradition. After Huang Xing and his faction among the leaders of the small landlords refused to join the Chinese Revolutionary Party because of their fear of revolution and broke with Mr. Sun, they established a separate organization, the Society for the Study of European Affairs. This society soon expanded, attracting a large number of both big and small landlords, and formed the Political Study Society. It suffices to note the fact that there is virtually no one in the Political Study Society who is not from the landlord class to understand why they had to break with Mr. Sun; why they had to abandon revolution; why they gradually began to flirt with the Research clique, which was the product of a metamorphosis of the Progressive Party and represented the big landlord class; and why in recent years they have finally organized the Federalist clique (a political party that the landlord class in various southern provinces has been trying in vain to organize for the past four years) to support Zhao Hengti, Chen Jiongming, Tang Jiyao, and Xiong Kewu,[8] the men who have seized political power in all the provinces of Southwestern China and used the armed forces controlled by the provincial and *xian* assemblies and by the militia offices as their instrument to visit extreme

---

7. The text here is corrupt, but this appears to be the meaning.
8. On Xiong Kewu, see the note to "Propaganda Guidelines in the War against the Fengtian Clique" of November 27, 1925.

oppression on the owner-peasants, tenants, and farm laborers in the countryside, as well as on the workers, students, and small merchants in the towns; and why they stand wholly on the side of counterrevolution. When the Chinese Revolutionary Party was transformed into the Chinese Guomindang, yet another batch of middle class nonrevolutionary elements joined it; at the same time, some elements representing the comprador class sneaked into the party and occupied a commanding position within it, so that Mr. Sun and the minority of revolutionaries were not able to make revolution, even though they held leading posts. So in January of last year, [Sun Yatsen] resolutely called the First National Congress of the Party, which clearly laid it down that the party should uphold the interests of the working class and the peasantry, expand the Guomindang organization drawing from these classes, and allow Communists to enter the party. At the banquet given by Mr. Sun in January of last year to the delegates to the congress at the Changdi Asia Restaurant in Guangzhou, Mao Zuquan raised an objection to the proposal for admitting Communists to the party. Mr. Sun thereupon stood up and delivered a long speech in which he said:

> For the past twenty years, party members have persistently obstructed me in making revolution, and have persistently cast aside the principle of the People's Livelihood. I have a great many followers, but they always think they can make their own decisions. Those who truly follow me in making revolution, like Mr. Wang Jingwei, are no more than twenty. Now today you even want to restrict me in accepting revolutionary youth!

All those who attended the First National Congress heard Mr. Sun's words. However, the new policy offended, above all, those party leaders who represented the comprador class. Feng Ziyou and Ma Su among others were the first to collude with the imperialists and warlords and dropped out of the Guomindang, forming a separate organization, the Comrades' Club. The work of the Guomindang Left in Guangdong during the past two years has offended the imperialists and the comprador class by supporting workers' solidarity and strikes; it has offended the landlord class by backing peasants' solidarity and rent reduction; it has offended Wei Bangping,[9] Chen Jiongming, and Xiong Kewu, tools of the imperialists who represent the compradors and the landlord class, by its severe measures to fight counterrevolutionaries in order to preserve the revolutionary bases. This once again provoked the emergence of a group of new rightists, who have already held a meeting in Beijing and are scheming to withdraw from the Guomindang led by the left and to organize another Guomindang standing on the right. But it was reported that during the meeting those who represented small landlords as well as the national bourgeoisie of

---

9. On Wei Bangping, see the note to the text of December 20, 1925, "The Beijing Right-Wing Meeting and Imperialism."

industrialists and merchants held opinions different from those of the representatives of the comprador class, and left Beijing for the south even before the meeting closed. We consider this phenomenon, too, as inevitable. The moment of hand-to-hand combat in China has already arrived. On the one side, a counterrevolutionary united front has been organized with imperialism as its leader and commander, comprising the comprador class, the big landlords, the bureaucrats, the warlords, and other big capitalist classes. On the other side, a revolutionary united front has been organized, with the revolutionary Guomindang as its leader and commander, a united front of the petty bourgeoisie (owner-peasants, small merchants, master artisans), the semiproletariat (semi-owner peasants, tenant peasants, handicraft workers, shop assistants, peddlers), and the proletariat (industrial workers, coolies, farm laborers, and vagrants). The middle class (small landlords, small bankers and old-style private bank owners, merchants dealing in Chinese goods, and factory owners supported by national capital) standing between the two sides originally wanted to reach the status of the big bourgeosie. But, as they cannot develop under the oppression of imperialism, the comprador class, the big landlords, the bureaucrats, and the warlords, they need revolution. However, the present revolution, marked by the brave and vigorous participation of the Chinese proletariat, as well as the active support of the international proletariat, unavoidably terrifies these people, who are also suspicious of a revolution jointly made by several classes. Even today the middle class in China (except for its left wing, i.e. a small number of middle-class people who, because of peculiarities resulting from history and circumstances, can cooperate with other classes in the revolution) is still dreaming of a Western-style democratic revolution like that of the previous era; they are still dreaming of bringing about *Étatisme*; they are still dreaming of an "independent" revolution led by a single class, namely the middle class, without external help and taking advantage of the workers and peasants; they still imagine that, after the success of the revolution, they will be able to develop themselves into a strong bourgeoisie and to set up a state autocratically ruled by a single class. Their starting point for revolution is totally different from that of the other classes. They want revolution in order to get rich, while other classes want revolution to relieve suffering; they want revolution in order to make themselves into a new class of oppressors, while other classes want revolution to achieve their own liberation and to ensure that in the future they will be forever free from class oppression. These middle-class "independent" revolutionaries (most are of small-landlord origin) are still doing business under the emblem of Mr. Sun's legitimacy, saying that Mr. Sun's "ideology" and "doctrinal heritage" represents their views. This is absolutely untrue. Mr. Sun's ideology and doctrinal heritage definitely aimed at "relieving suffering," not "getting rich"; it definitely aimed at liberating mankind from class oppression, not at preparing the way for a new class of oppressors. No matter how one may distort Mr. Sun's ideology and doctrinal heritage, this aspect of its significance can absolutely never change.

Situated as they are between the revolutionaries and the counterrevolutionaries, these people imagine that they can make a revolution independently, but in reality there can be no such thing. They are suspicious and envious of the rise of the working class and the peasantry, as well as of help from the political parties of both the Chinese and international proletariat. Given the situation of China, as a semicolony in the twentieth century exposed to powerful pressures, both internal and external, thus to cast aside the masses and to cast aside those who offer assistance is assuredly not the way to carry out a successful revolution. In terms of population, of China's 400 million people the compradors, big landlords, bureaucrats, warlords, and suchlike, who constitute the big bourgeoisie, number at most 1 in every 400 (1/400), or 1 million; the small landlords, businessmen dealing in Chinese goods, and so on, who compose the middle class, number about 1 in 100 (1 percent), or 4 million. The balance all belong to other classes: owner-peasants, small businessmen, master artisans, and such, who form the petty bourgeoisie, make up about 150 million; semi-owner peasants, tenants, handicraftsmen, shop assistants, peddlers, and so on, who comprise the semi-proletariat, are the most numerous, about 200 million; industrial workers, urban coolies, agricultural laborers, vagrants, and others, who are wholly proletarian, account for about 45 million. According to this analysis, how many of these revolutionary popular masses who want to fight to relieve suffering and seek their own liberation are there in China? There are 395 million of them, making up 98.75 percent of the population. How numerous are their enemies? There are 1 million of them, or 0.25 percent. How many are there of the middle elements? There are 4 million, amounting to 1 percent. Under these circumstances, we can conclude without the slightest hesitation that the breaking away of the Guomindang rightists who represent the middle class from the Guomindang is in no way capable of halting the development of the party, nor can it obstruct China's national revolution. Their split was founded in their own class nature and in the specific political situation of the present period, which obliged them to break away, rather than in any so-called impetuosity of the left. What is called the impetuosity of the left (left refers to the left faction of the Guomindang and not at all to the Communist Party; the Communist Party members within the Guomindang are the Communist faction and not the Guomindang left faction) is nothing but the revolutionary work done by it, including crushing Yang and Liu, putting down Zheng and Mo,[10] and clearing the East River, Southern Route, and North River areas, thereby inflicting heavy blows on Chen Jiongming, Deng Benyin, and Xiong Kewu; and firmly upholding the Guangzhou-Hong Kong strike, thus hitting a heavy blow at British imperialism. Once again, all this is founded in the class nature of the revolutionary faction and the peculiarities of the current situation, which were such that they could not but fight, could not but

---

10. The persons mentioned are, in order, Yang Ximin, Liu Zhenhuan, Zheng Runqi, and Mo Xiong.

make revolution, because fighting and revolution were their only way out. This has nothing to do with so-called impetuosity. In such a pressing situation as this, there is no hope of relaxation; on the contrary, the tension will continue to mount. We can foresee that in the conditions which will prevail in the near future, the middle elements will have only two roads from which to choose: either toward the right to join the counterrevolutionaries, or toward the left to join the revolutionaries. (This latter possibility exists in the case of their left wing.) There is absolutely no third way. At present, if these people remain within the Guomindang, they will indeed be what Mr. Wang Jingwei has called the "fake revolutionary faction," and will be not only useless but harmful. Because of their split and their reaction against and attacks on the revolutionaries (the left), the revolutionaries will achieve an even a greater solidarity. This is why, wherever we go nowadays, the slogan we hear is almost always: "Revolutionaries of the whole country, unite!"

Opposition to the Right-Wing Conference
Spreads throughout the Whole Country

(January 10, 1926)

The right wing of the Guomindang, including Lin Sen, Zou Lu, Xie Chi, Zhang Ji, Ju Zheng, Tan Zhen, Shi Ying, Ye Chucang, Shen Dingyi, Fu Rulin, Mao Zuquan, Shao Yuanchong, and others[1] withdrew from the battlefront of the national revolution just at the moment when the nationwide anti-imperialist movement was reaching its peak and left-wing comrades were engaged in a desperate struggle. Slowly, over a period of time, they have changed from a revolutionary position to a nonrevolutionary position and then from a nonrevolutionary position to a counterrevolutionary position. It is for this reason that they called the so-called Western Hills Conference. This Western Hills Conference has adopted an attitude that is absolutely identical with that of imperialism. It has adopted a stance of attacking the left wing of the Guomindang and the national government in Guangzhou. When the news was announced, the whole nation was thrown into in an uproar. The people of the entire nation love the national government of the left wing of the Guomindang because it is truly capable of opposing imperialism. How, then, can those who call themselves members of the Guomindang scheme, on the contrary, to attack and destroy it? So the left-wing members of the party and the organizations of the revolutionary popular masses have joined together to oppose them, sending a flood of letters and telegrams every single day since early December, as reported in the previous issue of this magazine. We shall set out below, for all to examine, letters and telegrams attacking the right wing received from various places in mid-December.

This text first appeared in *Zhengzhi zhoubao*, No. 4, January 10, 1926. Our source is *Mao Zedong ji. Bujuan*, Vol. 2, pp. 141–42.

1. The men listed here were, as Mao indicates, leading figures in the Western Hills faction. On Zou Lu, see the note to Mao's article dated December 5, 1925, "Zou Lu and the Revolution." On Lin Sen, see the relevant note to "The Central Executive Committee Sternly Repudiates the Illegal Meeting," November 27, 1925. Xie Chi (1876–1939), *zi* Huisheng, a native of Sichuan, and Zhang Ji (1882–1947), *zi* Puquan, a native of Zhili, were both Guomindang veterans who had been among the first, in June 1924, to impeach the Communists and demand their expulsion from the party. On Ye Chucang, see the note to "The Causes of the Reactionary Attitude of the Shanghai *Minguo ribao*," December 20, 1925. On Ju Zheng, see above, the note to the session of the First National Congress on January 20, 1924. He played a major role in the Western Hills Conference, and was elected to the rival Central Executive Committee in April 1926. The others mentioned by Mao were of lesser importance.

Of the several hundred thousand party members nationwide, not more than a few thousand are real rightists, while the vast majority belong to the revolutionary left wing. The organizations of the peasant, worker, merchant, and student popular masses throughout the country are all under the leadership of the left wing. Within this single month, an antirightist atmosphere has spread throughout the entire land. At present, the Second National Congress has already met and has taken a very stern position vis-á-vis the right wing. Those who were there on New Year's Day, when the congress reviewed the troops on the parade grounds and the cry "Down with the right wing!" shook heaven and earth, could see the direction in which things were moving. Last time we noted antirightist writings through No. 20, so we here note them from No. 21 on.[2]

2. "Last time" refers to Mao's comment on December 13, 1925, "Revolutionary Party Members rally *en Masse* . . . , which introduced "antirightist writings" Nos. 1 through 20. As indicated in a note to that text, these materials, which are not by Mao, were omitted from the Tokyo edition of Mao's works, and have not been translated here. the same applied to documents Nos. 21 to 49, which followed this piece in *Zhengzhi zhoubao*.

The Great Guangzhou Demonstration of December 20 Opposing Duan Qirui

(January 10, 1926)

Most recently the popular masses of Beijing and Shanghai have risen up to oppose Duan [Qirui] and Zhang [Zuolin]. Guo Songling turned his dagger in the same direction,[1] and the popular masses of all the major provinces and regions, recognizing that this *coup d'état* was a manifestation of the national revolution throughout the whole country, have joined together in a response throughout the country. For this war shows us, on the one hand, that the nationwide high tide of opposition to the Fengtian clique has already forced the warlords of the Fengtian clique to split up and crumble, making it easy for the movement to oppose the Fengtian clique and overthrow Duan Qirui to succeed; it also shows, on the other hand, that the popular masses have not engaged in positive armed actions, so as to turn the Zhili-Fengtian war into a bloodless success of the people over the warlords. The result was that the people could not grasp political power and regain their position as masters of the state. Taking stock of this, the popular masses in various places are rising up to engage in violent demonstrations. Following the sudden outbreak in Beijing, a furious tide of revolution immediately arose in Shanghai, Zhengzhou, Wuchang, and Changsha that has shaken the entire land. As the revolution was consolidating its foundations in the high tide of the nationwide movement against the Fengtian clique, Guangdong, the vanguard of the Chinese revolution, responded and immediately followed up by leading the people of the whole country in carrying out a great revolutionary movement to unite the entire country. Because of this, the various large people's groups, such as the All-China General Labor Union, the Guangzhou-Hong Kong Strike Committee, the Workers' Congress, the Guangdong Peasant Association, the Young Soldiers' Association, the Revolutionary Youth Association, the Guangzhou Students' Association, the New Student Society, the Hong Kong Student Association, and the Guangzhou Chamber of Commerce, together asked

---

This article first appeared in *Zhengzhi zhoubao*, No. 4, January 10, 1926. We have taken it from that source because there are a number of missing characters in the text as reproduced in the *Mao Zedong ji. Bujuan*, Vol. 2, pp. 151-56.

1. In November 1925, in the context of a war between Feng Yuxiang and Zhang Zuolin, Fengtian general Guo Songling (1887-1925) entered into a secret agreement with Feng Yuxiang to turn against Zhang. In the event, however, Guo was defeated, captured, and executed in December 1925. Feng Yuxiang also suffered heavy casualties, and his position was seriously weakened.

the Central Executive Committee of the Guomindang to hold a march against Duan Qirui and also to supervise speeding up the national government's preparations to raise troops for the Northern Expedition, since it is necessary to overthrow the traitorous government of Duan Qirui, which brings calamity to the people, to establish a united national government in the whole country, to abolish all the unequal treaties, and bring the national revolution to a successful conclusion within a short period of time. All the groups held several preparatory meetings, decided on December 20 as the date for the march, and issued propaganda guidelines as follows:

Propaganda Guidelines for Supporting the Beijing and Shanghai Demonstration Movement Opposing Duan Qirui

1. The ease with which Wu Peifu, who is well known for his military prowess, was defeated last year; the fact that the great momentum that Zhang Zuolin gained from his defeat of Wu Peifu did not last long and dissolved as soon as he ran into Sun Chuanfang, crumbling before battle with the National People's Army even began —all this demonstrates that the Chinese warlords are already in the process of toppling very rapidly.

2. Because, after May 30, the anti-imperialist movement was crushed by the warlord Zhang Zuolin and has not been able to wage a war to the death against imperialism, the popular masses want to throw out Zhang Zuolin and make it possible for the anti-imperialist movement to be victorious. Thanks to the daily increasing power of the popular masses and to the struggle against the rapidly declining warlord Zhang Zuolin, the fall and defeat of Zhang Zuolin is inevitable. The reason why Sun Chuanfang, with a small number of troops, was able to chase the Fengtian army of well over 100,000 troops out of Jiangsu and Anhui is that Sun Chuanfang at that moment took the position of being an instrument of the popular mass forces. Under pressure from the forces of the masses, the Fengtian army could not avoid the emergence of internal splits, and this is the reason for the occurrence of the incident in which Guo Songling led his troops against the Fengtian clique.

3. Last year, following the overthrow of Cao and Wu,[2] despite the advocacy and leadership of Mr. Sun Yatsen, it was unfortunately impossible to unite the force of the popular masses, so the opportunity for the people to seize political power was lost and the forces of the warlords solidified once more. Consequently, they regained the reins of government and continued to serve imperialism in its exploitation and oppression of the people. The then head of the Fengtian clique, Zhang Zuolin, had already fallen, and since the people did not

---

2. The reference is to the defeat of President Cao Kun and his military backer Wu Peifu by Feng Yuxiang in November 1924. See, above, the note to the circular of November 1, 1924.

rise up and take over political control in his stead, political power fell into the hands of the warlords. This fall of Zhang Zuolin was brought about by the unwitting instruments of the people, Sun Chuanfang of the Zhili clique and Guo Songling of the Fengtian clique, and did not depend directly on the forces of the people themselves or the forces of their conscious instruments. If, at present, the people do not quickly arise and pursue the matter, and take political power into their own hands, the warlords will inevitably continue to rule over China, prolonging the oppression and suffering of the Chinese people. This is because, no matter who the warlord that takes over may be, he will hasten to fawn on the imperialists and to oppress the people in exactly the same old way. This is in the very nature of warlords.

4. The recent insurrection of the popular masses in Beijing shows that the people are no longer willing to be oppressed by imperialism and by the warlords, and are planning to seize political power. The masses of the people everywhere should respond to the popular mass movement in Beijing and demand that political power be returned to the people and that the Duan Qirui government be overthrown and that a people's government be organized to guarantee the freedoms of the people, to convene a national assembly, and to abolish the unequal treaties.

5. Whether or not these demands of the people can be achieved depends on the attitude of the National People's Army, because since the loss of power of Zhang Zuolin and the Fengtian clique, the people have turned their attention entirely to the National People's Army.[3] But the attitude of the National People's Army depends entirely upon whether or not the power of the popular masses is solidified. If the people can mount a large-scale movement and show that they are serious about the National People's Army, then the National People's Army will certainly be able to decide quickly what kind of an attitude to take toward the exercise of political power by the people.

6. Guangdong is the revolutionary base of the Chinese people. Guangdong occupies an extremely important position in the Chinese revolutionary movement. The strength and solidity of Guangdong and its development influence the development of the movement nationwide. Within a short period of time, Guangdong has already been able to eliminate counterrevolutionary forces throughout the province, and Hong Kong has already capitulated and is willing to send representatives to settle the strike. If the people of Guangdong are able to continue to support the striking workers throughout the negotiations, then a settlement by the striking workers will certainly be able to guarantee the next future great movement of the striking workers. All the provinces bordering on Guangdong have one after the other manifested a friendly and non-hostile

---

3. On the National People's Army of Feng Yuxiang and others, see the "Propaganda Guidelines in the War Against the Fengtian Clique," November 27, 1925, and the notes thereto.

attitude toward Guangdong. The Guangdong government has already obtained the support of the people, and now if it does even more in such matters as financial unification, reorganization of the administration, getting rid of bandits, and maintaining order, it will definitely be able to gain even greater support from the people. Since the Guangdong revolutionary base has already been consolidated, the Guomindang can extend its movement to the rest of China by developing the Guomindang organization in the whole country, and expanding the military forces of the Northern Expedition. The people of Guangdong and the people of the entire nation should assist the Guomindang with the various plans to consolidate the revolutionary base and to develop the nationwide revolutionary movement.

7. The people's seizure of political power, the success of the national revolution, relies on the nationwide revolutionary forces joining together with the left wing of the Guomindang. One of the major reasons for the failure last year of the movement called for by Mr. Sun Yatsen was indeed the disruption by reactionary elements within the party. This bunch of reactionary elements are now once again making preparations, in Beijing, to sabotage the Guomindang organizations by shaking the leadership of the revolutionary movement and by putting obstacles in the way of the popular mass movement against Duan Qirui in Beijing. If the Guomindang is not able to eliminate this bunch of reactionary elements, the leadership of the revolution will not be consolidated, the revolutionary politics of the Guomindang will be affected, and the nationwide movement will inevitably be badly hurt.

8. Slogans: (1) Arm the Chinese revolutionary masses. (2) Down with the betrayers of the nation, the Duan Qirui government. (3) Down with all counter-revolutionary forces. (4) Establish a unified national government for the whole country. (5) Support the revolutionary Guomindang. (6) Convene a national assembly, retrieve the sovereignty of the people, abolish all unequal treaties. (7) Restore patriotic groups everywhere. (8) Support the Guangdong-Hong Kong strike. (9) Consolidate the Guangdong revolutionary base, make preparations to mobilize troops for the Northern Expedition, and carry out the unification of the revolution. (10) Let the revolutionary popular masses seize political power. (11) Resume control over customs duties. (12) Kick out representatives of all nations to the Customs Conference. (13) Free the jailed anti-imperialist fighters.

At 11 o'clock in the morning on December 20, a crowd of 100,000 people gathered at the Eastern Parade Ground[4] in Guangzhou. The largest number of them were workers, followed by soldiers, and then people from all walks of life. Flags and banners flew over the square. Wherever you looked, there was the blue sky, white sun, and broad red field of the national flags, the blue sky and white sun of the party flag, and the red banners of the labor unions. In the square, three

---

4. The Eastern Parade Ground [Dongjiaochang] was located just to the east of the old city of Guangzhou.

platforms had been set up. On the central platform were the peasants, workers, and merchants, led by Li Sen of the All-China General Labor Union and He Youti of the Provincial Peasant Association. On the platform on the right was the military, led by Zhou Yijun, and on the platform on the left were the students, led by Shen Bantong of the Revolutionary Youth Association and Li Zhaokui of the Guangzhou Student Alliance. Suspended all around the platforms were banners such as "Down With All Counterrevolutionary Forces," "Regain Sovereignty Over Customs Duties," "Restore Patriotic Groups Everywhere," "Down With the Duan Qirui Government." The meeting began at 12:30 noon, and amidst loud shouts of support passed the following resolutions:

1. Resolution Concerning the Northern Movement Against Duan Qirui

In a very short period of time, the deeply entrenched Guangdong warlords have already been rooted out by the Guangdong revolution and the government representing the popular masses. Zhang Zuolin with his several hundred thousand crack troops, and with the support of the powerful imperialists behind him, was totally defeated without even a fight. This indeed proves that the warlords are crumbling at an ever-increasing rate and that their dying gasps for breath cannot last long. Since the May Thirtieth Movement, the anti-imperialist movement of the popular masses has been rising higher and higher, and even though the warlords may trample over us and we may suffer from sabotage by the counterrevolutionary forces, the movement does not stop growing. Recently, in Beijing, in Shanghai, and elsewhere, the popular masses have again risen up in insurrection. In order to expand their revolutionary forces, in order to confront the imperialists directly, the popular masses are already anxious to seize political power, to guarantee all the people's freedoms, to coordinate the revolutionary front, and to bring the anti-imperialist movement under a unified command. Since the people of Guangdong have already grasped political power, by uprooting the counterrevolutionary forces within the province of Guangdong, they should join with the popular masses of the entire nation and together strike down the Duan Qirui government and all counterrevolutionary forces, and set up a unified national government all over the country that will guarantee the people's freedoms and fight the imperialists.

2. Resolution Regarding Feng Yuxiang and the Attitude of the National People's Army

Just at this time, when the ruling warlords are losing their power and the people are making forceful efforts to seize political power, the National People's Army is in a pivotal position, so this great meeting resolves to send telegrams to Feng Yuxiang and to the National People's Army asking them to clarify their attitudes. Will they decide to be a military force of the people to help the people gain political power, or will they decide to retrace the disastrous path of Zhang Zuolin's Fengtian clique and help the government of Duan Qirui so that the warlord forces will be solidified again?

3. Resolution Regarding Guo Songling

Since Guo Songling, under pressure from the forces of the people, has already turned against Zhang Zuolin, thus causing the forces of the popular masses to take a great stride forward in their development, he should further decide boldly that he himself is willing to be a self-conscious instrument of the people, in order to promote the realization of the people's demands. Otherwise, if he turns his back on the popular masses in hopes of replacing Zhang Zuolin as leader of the Fengtian forces, his own destruction will come even more quickly than did that of Zhang Zuolin.[5]

4. Resolution on Supporting the Striking Workers and on Negotiating with Hong Kong

The 200,000 striking workers in Guangdong and Hong Kong now fighting for the freedom of the Chinese nation,[6] braving hunger and cold, have held out for six long months, a sacrifice and determination unprecedented in the history of the Chinese revolution. This strike has not only dealt a great blow to the Hong Kong imperialists, it has also retrieved the respect and honor of China that was lost eighty-five years ago, and it has also helped the revolutionary government to complete the task of sweeping out the counterrevolutionary forces and of consolidating the revolutionary base in Guangdong. Today, in settling the strike between Hong Kong and the striking workers, the people of our entire province of Guangdong should continue to support the demands of the workers until victory is achieved. Our 200,000 compatriots must not be allowed to suffer alone in their sacrifices in the difficult struggle for the revolution and the nation.

5. Resolution Regarding Lin Sen and Zou Lu

Earlier, having accepted the responsibility of leading the foreign affairs delegation entrusted to them by the people of Guangdong, Lin Sen, Zou Lu, and others went north to fight imperialism and look into the traitorous activities of Duan Qirui's traitorous government. Since going north, Li Sen and Zou Lu have not only betrayed the people's trust, they have not struck a single blow at the imperialists and have not censored the traitorous actions of the Duan Qirui

---

5. As indicated above, in the first note to this text, Guo Songling had been captured and executed in December 1925, so this resolution, when adopted, was already out of date.

6. *Zhongguo minzu.*

government. They have, moreover, linked up with the rebel elements of the Guomindang and attempted to put out propaganda for the discredited Guomindang opposing the Guangdong government that is supported by the people of Guangdong. In recent days they have aligned themselves even more closely with the Duan Qirui government in a scheme to destroy the movement of the popular masses of Beijing to overthrow Duan's government. This mass meeting resolves to send out telegrams denouncing their criminal actions of selling out the country, selling out the province, and selling out the party.

After the resolutions were passed, slogans were loudly proclaimed, and all those assembled went out and marched as one body, every hand waving a small flag as far as the eye could see. Leaving the Eastern Parade Ground via Hui'ai East Road, they passed the West Gate, continued along South Taiping Road, and dispersed on arrival at Xiguayuan.[7] Along the way, forty to fifty different propaganda leaflets were distributed, in a total of 100,000 copies.

---

7. The route described here went straight across the heart of the old city from east to west, turned south at the West Gate, and ended about half way from Hui'ai Road (now Zhongshan Road, or Sun Yatsen Road) to the Pearl River. Xihaokou, the name here rendered as "West Gate," signifies literally "the western opening in the moat," which had earlier surrounded the city walls. The gate itself had recently been pulled down, together with the walls, to permit the building of boulevards. Xiguayuan means "Watermelon Garden," and watermelons had in fact been raised there in Qing times. By the 1920's, the area was empty and abandoned, and thus offered space for mass gatherings. It was there that two years later, on December 12, 1927, Zhang Tailei proclaimed the establishment of the short-lived "Canton Commune."

Resolution Concerning Party Newspapers

Resolution of The Second National Congress of the Chinese Guomindang

(January 16, 1926)

What was deemed the most important point by the Second Congress of the Chinese Guomindang is the promulgation of the revolutionary principles of our party—the Three People's Principles in their entirety—with the hope that they will be fully realized following the success of the national revolution. If only one or two but not all of the Three People's Principles are carried out, the national revolution cannot be considered successful. But the congress was fully aware that the two principles of people's rights and people's livelihood cannot be realized until nationalism has been solidly established and firmly edified. This is our Director General's will, which this congress has pledged to accept.

During the period of time between the adjournment of the Second Congress and the convocation of the Third Congress, our party should, as quickly as possible, arouse and call upon all the revolutionary factions to facilitate the realization of nationalism. This is the most urgent task of our party and the first and foremost goal that the party newspapers should strive to achieve.

As pointed out at the First Congress, the significance of nationalism is for China to break out of her hypocolonial status and to enjoy equality with all the other nations in the world. A hypocolony was defined by the Director General to be a nation that is under the rule of many imperialists.[1] So the status of a hypocolony is worse than that of a colony, which is controlled by only one imperialist power. He also said that nationalism sought to achieve unifica-

---

This text was first published in the records of the Second Congress, *Zhongguo Guomindang dierci quanguo daibiao dahui huiyi jilu* ([Guangzhou]: Zhongguo guomindang zhixing weiyuanhui, April 1926), pp. 137–40. Our translation is based on that version, which is also reproduced in *Mao Zedong ji. Bujuan*, Vol. 9, pp. 175–80.

1. For Sun's definition of the term *cizhimindi*, see the second lecture on Nationalism in his *Sanmin zhuyi*. The Chinese expression might also be rendered as "subcolony," but the standard translation has long been "hypocolony." See Sun Yat-sen, *San Min Chu I. The Three Principles of the People*, translated by Frank W. Price (Shanghai: China Committee, Institute of Pacific Relations, 1927), p. 39.

tion for China and furthermore, to bring her under a central government that is based on the five-power constitution.

The Second Congress demanded that the party newspapers frequently remind the masses of the two important points of nationalism: (1) to break away from the oppression imposed by the imperialists and achieve independence; and (2) to form a unified government in China based on the five-power constitution. In order to form a unified government in China, we must do away with imperialism.

Our party newspapers should point out that it is a dangerous fantasy to try to achieve unification based on our party's five-power constitution or any other laws before China breaks out of her hypocolonial status. All the failures of our party in the past serve to illustrate this.

Our party's newspapers should furthermore point out that it is also impossible under the yoke of unequal treaties to seek economic progress to meet China's needs. The more remarkable the economic development of the trading ports, the tighter the grip of the foreign financiers on the nation's wealth; the result will be the continued impoverishment of the interior of our country and the gradual transformation of our country's industrial and banking enterprises into the vassals of foreign economies. The party newspapers must frequently point this out. Members of our party who work in various capacities in schools or are involved in socioeconomic surveys, and who totally agree with the explanations of nationalism given by the First Congress, should participate in the editorial work of the party newspapers so that they can fully utilize their knowledge and communication skills to prove that our party's stand on industrial development is correct, beyond the shadow of a doubt.

In a systematically planned fashion, our party newspapers should also point out to students, workers, peasants, and merchants how they can satisfy their demands after the unequal treaties are abolished, and how once the peasants' welfare is served, national consumer markets will definitely expand. As consumer markets expand, the need for laborers will grow, resulting in wage increases and improved living conditions. Improvement of the peasants' and workers' economic conditions will lead to the expansion of the services of the intelligentsia—teachers, engineers, and managers. During this time, commerce will naturally grow rapidly. The party newspapers should point out that all these improvements and progress cannot be gained until the unequal treaties are abolished, control over customs is recovered, and China is unified. Therefore, all students, workers, peasants, and merchants must take part in the national revolutionary movement led by the Chinese Guomindang.

There are numerous plans to save China. But the party newspapers should point out that among them, all those that do not call for the abolition of unequal treaties and recovery of the foreign concessions and of control over customs are dangerous propaganda and constitute obstacles to the unification and liberation of China. This is an attitude to which party members should especially hold fast. Commentary in the party newspapers should be constructive, not uniformly destructive. It should be easy for the masses to understand, and not destined exclusively for perusal by a small minority.

The Second Congress also instructed the party newspapers to propagate the following slogans and policies:

1. Guangdong is the base for the movement of the Chinese national revolution.

2. Because of its loyalty to the late Director General's teachings, and under the rule of the Guomindang guided by the First Congress, Guangdong has made great progress administratively, militarily, financially, and economically. The people of Guangdong have also begun to have deeper faith in the principles and deeds of the Guomindang.

3. All those who are opposed to the national government and who seek to topple its regime, to damage its reputation, or to organize other small groups in conspiracy against it are counterrevolutionaries, either conscious or unconscious.

4. The Guomindang is currently engaged in the work of unifying national politics in Guangdong. The Guomindang's success in Guangdong will facilitate the realization of the national revolution. All obstacles to Guangdong's success should be swept away without consideration for sentiments and without fear of any dangers.

5. Party members should hold the interests of the national revolution higher than their own interests and also as compared to the interests of their families, relatives, or other organizations.

6. The Guomindang is not a mutual-aid organization, but rather a revolutionary party that strives for a free and unified China. To abandon the task of national revolution or to forget this great responsibility would be to betray the wishes of the Director General and of the citizens. We will never allow this to happen within the Guomindang.

7. Our party's discipline is a weapon to defeat imperialism and warlordism and to win unification for China. Those who violate party discipline are tantamount to soldiers in retreat from the battlefield.

8. Talking revolution but failing to obey directives from above in the organization and failing to carry out orders received both constitute violations of discipline. Only by doing one's best to proclaim revolutionary ideas and engage in revolutionary work can the national revolution be facilitated.

9. It is inevitable that some party members, sacrificing themselves and out of love for their compatriots, will need to deal severely with some minority elements. If we cannot gain unification for the 400 million people by peaceful means, violence is necessary. By violence is meant organization and discipline. Each party member is ruled by the party, and his personal welfare is contained within that of the party. Therefore, a party member's welfare should be sacrificed for the welfare of the party.

10. Only a Guomindang that is well organized and well disciplined can establish a national government after our domestic and foreign enemies are defeated. We shall follow the example of our late Director General, who fought for China and sacrificed for the revolution over a period of forty years.

11. The party only needs to ask each member: Can you participate in the movement to abolish unequal treaties with all your might? Can you make every effort to defeat the warlords? Can you strive towards the founding of the national government of the Guomindang so as to unify China? If the answer is yes, then that person is a Guomindang party member.

That our party's newspapers have failed to reveal and explain many domestic events is indeed a big shortcoming. The training of members and the cultivation of leaders in the party cannot be accomplished through abstract principles. We must make use of existing facts to explain things to the party members and to analyze their political significance, so as to enrich the members' revolutionary experience and foster their revolutionary morale. Our party constantly fights for the masses of the whole nation, with current events as our study topics. The party newspapers are teachers for all party members. In explaining current events, they should point out the causes and their influence on the nationalist revolution. Take the incident of a coolie being beaten by an imperialist as an example. This has enormous significance, and our party newspapers should feature it in a prominent position, using it to illustrate the necessity of the national revolution. The plight of the factory and mine workers should be described in detail. The reason for the miserable conditions of the workers is the backwardness of Chinese industries, and the reason for that is the bondage of the unequal treaties. The warlords often create a sensation among the masses by making use of the slogans of fighting in the interests of the country and of the people. The party newspapers should point out the facts and attack the contradictions between their words and their deeds. Whenever there are writings in Chinese newspapers and books disseminating the culture of the imperialists and praising their supposed friendliness to China, our party newspapers must miss no opportunity to refute them. The party newspapers should point out not only the political and economic aggression of the imperialists, but especially their cultural aggression, which undermines the ideology of the national revolution, causes splits in the ranks of the intellectuals, and dopes the minds of the revolutionary masses in general. Our party newspapers should be especially wary of this danger. Concerning this point the party newspapers should propagate the following slogans:

1. The freedom and unity of China must be based on an ideology that has been produced in Chinese conditions. In particular, it can only be achieved through an awareness born of the demand of the masses for survival. Imperialist academic learning cannot save China.

2. Academic thought and and academic research is worthless dross unless it is in the service of the demands of the masses for social and economic liberation and for survival.

3. The slogan for the intelligentsia should be "Go among the masses." China's liberation can be found only among the masses.

4. Anyone who divorces himself from the masses has lost his social basis. All of his activities will, without exception, be ineffectual.

5. The imperialists have spent millions of *yuan* to gain control over our thoughts. We should fight dauntlessly to defeat their crafty plot.

6. The imperialists have spent millions of *yuan* to propagate Christianity. This is a very powerful tool they are using to undermine our nationalism.

The party newspapers should pay special attention to promulgating the above points, and they should instruct the intelligentsia to make efforts to introduce nationalism to the masses of the entire nation. They must never allow themselves to be used as willing tools for the propagation of imperialist culture.

The Second Congress puts special emphasis on the work of the party newspapers, and therefore directs the Central Executive Committee and all provincial executive committees to insist on our party's propaganda policies in all dailies and weeklies, allowing for no vacillation or hesitation. The Central Executive Committee and the provincial executive committees are to appoint the editorial staff of the dailies and weeklies, and to oversee everything they write. Since the central and the provincial committees bear total responsibility for the party's policies, they may remove or change editorial staff and shut down any propaganda organs according to circumstances.

The Central Party Bureau will establish investigators, and will supply reports and discussion pieces to all the party newspapers. The Propaganda Department of the Central Executive Committee should periodically notify the party organs of the party's resolutions on various events and issues.

Resolution on Propaganda Adopted by the Second National Congress of the Chinese Guomindang

(January 16, 1926)

With the purpose of carrying out our party's policy of awakening the masses and realizing as quickly as possible the behest of our late Director General, the Second National Congress regards propaganda work as our most urgent task at this moment. Our plan for propaganda work is as follows:

1. Unify the actual propaganda work of the Central Executive Committee and all provincial executive committees.

2. To unify propaganda, it is necessary for the Central Propaganda Department and all provincial propaganda departments to devote themselves to explaining current policy. All of the party's articles, magazines, newspapers, leaflets, notices, directives aimed at guiding the masses, and slogans drawn up for the demonstration movement should be centered around current policy.

3. The policy that this party urgently needs to carry out right now is clearly laid down in the will of the late Director General. Detailed resolutions concerning the methods of implementing this policy have already been adopted during the First and Second National Congresses. The Central Propaganda Department and all provincial propaganda departments must thoroughly introduce the will of the late Director General to the masses of peasants, workers, businessmen, and intellectuals, and help them understand its significance as well as the tremendous benefits to be gained by the masses all over the country once it is implemented. The Central Propaganda Department and its subordinates in all the provinces should base their propaganda work on the slogan, "The fulfillment of the Director General's will means the success of China's liberation."

4. If a political party merely propagates theory and doctrine that are favorable to the masses, it will assuredly be incapable of bringing the masses and the political party to adopt a unified attitude in action. Consequently, abstract propaganda cannot create a mass party; only when a party's work for the people is concretely manifested can a mass party be created. Although sometimes the policies propagated by our party, such as the reduction of rent, the abolition of exorbitant taxes, the elimination of warlords, the increase in wages, the establish-

---

Like the previous document, this resolution appeared in the records of the Second Congress, pp. 135–36. Our translation is based on this text, which is reproduced in *Mao Zedong ji. Bujuan*, Vol. 2, pp. 159–62.

ment of educational funds, the reform of business, and the development of industry, may not all be realizable overnight, we must convince the masses that our party can actually bring them some concrete benefits.

5. If we continue to present all the things that the party should do for the masses as the path toward China's national liberation, this will surely be recognized by the masses. This is the only way to bring into being a party of the masses that can truly lead the popular masses to carry through the national revolution.

6. Therefore, the Central Committee of the party and all provincial party committees must carry out their propaganda work on the basis of the concrete interests of the masses, whether in schools and villages or in factories and shops in the city. To this end, the slogan for our propaganda work is "Accomplish the national revolution bequeathed to us by the late Director General in accordance with the needs of the masses." Apart from this, there is simply no shortcut to the liberation of China.

7. Although each individual member of the masses has his particular needs based on his social status, there is no doubt that all of them cherish the same desire to accomplish the national revolution. The liberation and unification of China are what most people want. For this reason, the majority of the masses forms the foundation for the national revolution. All propaganda departments must clearly point this out. The Guomindang advocates a wage increase, but without hindering the development of industry in our country. Not only is the development of industry not hindered, but it is rather strongly enhanced. The same reasoning applies in the case of the strike movements launched by European and American workers during the nineteenth century, which rather than jeopardizing the development of industry, actually pushed it forward. To help the peasants by reducing rent and abolishing various exorbitant taxes is also a necessary policy for the Guomindang. Because the more the oppression of the peasants is relieved, the quicker the national revolution will be accomplished. At present, among those who are still exploiting the peasants, some are feudal landlords and some are counterrevolutionaries under the aegis of imperialism. If we want to turn the national revolution into a success, we must uphold the interests of the peasants. The Propaganda Department should formally issue a directive declaring that only those who endorse the liberation movement of the Chinese peasants are faithful revolutionary members of the party; if not, they are counterrevolutionaries. By doing so, the Propaganda Department may enable the Guomindang, which has the mission of accomplishing national revolution, to establish a solid foundation and translate the unfulfilled wish of the Director General into reality within the shortest time possible.

8. The success of a party depends on its center of gravity. The center of gravity of China's Guomindang lies hidden among the vast majority of the exploited peasant masses. It is necessary for the Propaganda Department to remind every party member of this point, and moreover constantly to instruct party members to take the party's center of gravity very seriously.

9. Attention must be paid to extending the party's propaganda to all parts of the country. No affairs, major or minor, whether occurring in villages, *xian*, provinces, commercial cities, or towns, should escape the party's attention. The Central Propaganda Department and all provincial propaganda departments are our party's agents for deciding on tactics for dealing with such issues. Each time an incident occurs, therefore, all the departments should first of all present to the party and the people all over the country an accurate report, explaining the cause of the incident and its impact upon the national revolution, and then offer suggestions on how to make use of the incident to further the party's policies.

10. In the army, it is the department of military supplies that provides uniforms and armaments to all units. The Propaganda Department in the party performs a similiar function to that of the department of military supplies in the army. It provides party members as well as the masses with knowledge of politics and the strategy for action, enabling them to struggle hard through the arduous process of national revolution and to uphold the party's stand amidst conflicting views and emotions. The Propaganda Department should instruct each party member on how to conquer the evil forces of the imperialists and counterrevolutionaries. More importantly, it should transform party members who are impulsive, pessimistic, or lacking in self-confidence into a sound and solid force for revolution.

11. The Propaganda Department should be the liveliest and the most quick-witted unit in the party. All party members who are able to write books and pamphlets, edit articles and commentaries, or draft declarations and slogans should take part in the work of the Propaganda Department. Authors or journalists who are not able to do so personally should devote part of their time and energy to the Propaganda Department's work. From this perspective, the Propaganda Department is a general unit in the party, which assembles, employs, and directs the mental labor force inside the party to carry out the policy of the party.

12. Communication between the Propaganda Department and party members, as well as the masses, is extremely important. If the documents and directives issued by the Propaganda Department cannot be applied by the party members, or if they can be applied but do not meet the needs of the masses, then there is no point in doing any propaganda whatsoever and the Propaganda Department becomes utterly useless. Prompt delivery of propaganda materials can be guaranteed only by rapid transportation and a perfect organizational system within the Propaganda Department. The Central Propaganda Department should maintain, based on a predetermined schedule, close contact with all provincial propaganda departments, the various departments in the party, and various public organizations by means of correspondence, telegrams, and special courier.

13. All propaganda departments within the territory under our party's control should devote themselves wholeheartedly to general propaganda work and win the support and sympathy of the popular masses for the government of this party.

Statements Made at the Second National Congress of the Chinese Guomindang

(January 18 and 19, 1926)

Day 12, Session No. 23
Date: January 18, the fifteenth year of the Republic
Time: 10 A.M.–12:30 P.M.
Number of participants: 180
Chairman: Wang Jingwei
Secretary-General: Wu Yuzhang[1]

. . .

Chairman: Now let's look at the points in the general statutes that need revision and discuss them article by article.

Chairman: Are there any objections to Article 15?[2] (Passed with no objections.)

Chairman: Are there any objections to Article 24?[3]

The debates at the congress were first published in the stenographic record already cited. The extracts we have translated correspond broadly to those which appear in *Mao Zedong ji. Bujuan*, Vol. 2, pp. 163–71, but we have added, in the footnotes, some additional material regarding the issues under discussion without which it is hard to make sense of the statements by Mao and the other delegates.

1. Wu Yuzhang (1878–1966), also known as Yongshan, a native of Sichuan, was an early member of the Tongmenghui. He served as secretary to Sun Yatsen at the First Congress in January 1924. At this time he was head of the Sichuan branch of the Guomindang, and he was elected to the Central Executive Committee of the party at the Second Congress.

2. Article 15 of the statutes provided that party bureaus of special areas, like provincial party bureaus, were subject to the control and supervision of the central party organs.

3. Article 24 of the statutes, as adopted at the First Congress in 1924, provided simply that the Director General should have the final power of decision regarding resolutions of the Central Executive Committee. The draft of the revised version of the statutes under discussion on this occasion added, after Article 24, a supplementary note stating that the whole of Chapter IV, Articles 19 through 24, relating to the powers of the Director General, was left intact as a permanent memorial for Sun. This note further stipulated that the ceremonies honoring Sun should take three forms: his picture should be hung in all meeting places, his testament should be read at the beginning of every meeting, and a commemoration should be held once a week. Mao's motion refers to the third of these provisions. The addition he suggested appears word for word in the final text of the statutes as adopted by the Second Congress.

Comrade Mao Zedong made a motion: Below the words "The commemoration should be held once a week," a proviso should be added, "Under special circumstances, with the permission of the provincial party headquarters, the commemoration may be held every two weeks."

No. 32 Comrade Yu Shude: The commemoration should be held once a week. If there is practical difficulty, it should be flexible. To add a proviso is right.

No. 140 Comrade Liu Songfen: It is better with the proviso.

No. 139 Comrade Fang Weixia: I also agree that it is better to add the proviso.

Chairman: Are there any objections to the proviso? (Passed.)

. . .

Chairman: Are there any objections to Article 73?[4]

. . .

No. 16 Comrade Mao Zedong: This time there are many members of the Central Executive Committee and Central Supervisory Committee. I think that these members should be allowed to serve concurrently as members of the executive and supervisory committees of the provincial party organs as well. In reality, they may and they should be both.

. . .

Day 12, Number 24
Date: January 18
Time: 2:30–5:30 P.M.
Number of participants: 165
Chairman: Wang Jingwei

. . .

I. Comrade Gan Naiguang[5] reported on the resolution on the Merchants' Movement.

---

4. The general statutes, as passed at the First Congress, contained a prohibition against concurrent membership in party organs at more than one level. Mao himself, acting in the name of the Shanghai Executive Bureau, had been obliged on at least one occasion to apply this provision. (See above, the text dated March 31, 1924.) Article 73 of the revised statutes, as adopted by the Second Congress, reads as follows: "Members of executive committees and supervisory committees at all levels must not serve concurrently as members of the executive committees of other party bureaus, but members of the Central Executive Committee, and of the Central Supervisory Committee, with the approval of the committee in question, may serve concurrently on the executive committee or the supervisory committee of another party bureau." Once again, Mao's proposed change was adopted.

5. Gan Naiguang (1897–1956), *zi* Ziming, a native of Guangxi, joined the Guomindang in 1924, initially working as Liao Zhongkai's secretary. In 1925 he worked at the Huangpu Military Academy and also managed the *Minguo ribao* (Republican Daily). He was elected to the Central Executive Committee and to the party secretariat at the Second Congress. In May 1926, he became director of the Peasant Department.

II. Comrade Mao Zedong reported on the resolution of the review committee on propaganda.[6]

Chairman: Those in favor, please raise your hands. (Passed by a majority.)

III. Comrade Jiang Zhongzheng [Chiang Kaishek] put forward a motion on improving the economic conditions of the soldiers.

. . .

IV. **Chairman:** Copies of the resolution on the Merchants' Movement have been distributed to everyone. It is now open to the floor.

No. 98 Comrade Hou Shaoqiu: Chapter 2, item 6. I don't think we should mix the party up with a merchants' organization.

No. 16 Comrade Mao Zedong: I suggest that the constitution of the Merchants' Association not be included among the resolutions. It might best be handed over to the Central Executive Committee for discussion and decision.

Comrade Gan Naiguang: It is indeed difficult to discuss the constitution here. We had better submit it to the Second Central Executive Committee and let it decide at its discretion. Let us now confine ourselves to discussing the eight resolutions.

No. 58 Comrade Chen Gongbo:[7] The congress should only decide on the principles, not the content of the constitution. It should be submitted to the Central Executive Committeee for discussion. (Over ten people seconded.)

Chairman: All those who approve of the eight principles of the Merchants' Movement resolutions but consider that their constitution should be submitted to the Second Central Executive Committee for review, please vote by raising your hands. (Passed by a majority.)

---

6. Mao, who had delivered the report of the Propaganda Department on January 8, had been appointed on January 9 a member of the committee to review his own report. For the text of the resolution which he submitted on this occasion, and which was adopted by the congress, see below, the "Resolution on the Propaganda Report."

7. Chen Gongbo (1892–1946), from Guangdong province, a graduate of Beijing University, was one of the earliest members of the Chinese Communist Party and attended the First Congress in July 1921 as Guangdong representative. He withdrew from the party in 1922, went to the United States, and took an M.A. at Columbia University. He joined the Guomindang in 1925; at the Second Congress he was elected to the Central Executive Committee.

V. Resolution regarding the Report on Central Party Affairs.

. . .

Chairman: May we ask the review committee for the Resolution regarding the Report on Party Affairs to report on their review procedures?

No. 201 Comrade Zhan Dabei[8] reported. (The text of the draft is appended.)

Chairman: Are there any objections to the resolution? Please discuss.

No. 46 Comrade Huang Guowei: As regards paragraph IIC of the resolutions, "To upgrade the status of the provincial party headquarters and the overseas general branch and to increase their responsibilities," all the special municipal party headquarters should also be upgraded and expanded with clear regulations.

Chairman: Any seconders? The number of people seconding is insufficient, the proposal cannot be carried.

No. 16 Comrade Mao Zedong: In paragraph VI,[9] the phrase "All political statements expressed" should be changed to "Regarding statements expressing or amending our party's resolutions and political policies." Also, to the phrase "the establishment of study associations" should be added the words "any and all." "Must get the party's permission beforehand" should be changed to "must get permission from the highest party organization of that locality." "Or get the party's recognition retroactively" should be deleted.

No. 37 Comrade Zhou Shouyu: Above "party organization" should be added, "the highest."

No. 10 Comrade Fan Hongjie: I suggest that it be changed to "All statements expressing political views."

---

8. Zhan Dabei (1888–1927), *zi* Zhicun, a native of Hubei, was an early member of the Tongmenghui and a strong supporter of Sun Yatsen. At the Second Congress, he was elected an alternate member of the Central Executive Committee. He returned to Hubei to work as finance commissioner in the provincial government, and was executed as a Communist partisan in 1927.

9. Paragraph VI of the resolution, as adopted by the congress, reads as follows: "Revolutionary life is only collective, and not individual. All actions of the individual must receive the guidance and instruction of the party. Henceforth, all party members must pay attention to this. No statements regarding politics or party affairs may be in conflict with our party's policies or resolutions. The establishment of any and all study associations requires permission from the highest party organization of that locality."

Comrade Yu Shude: I do not feel that these changes are adequate. Since party members really express political opinions every single day, if every statement needed party endorsement, it would be an unbearable nuisance. In reality, it is impossible. After "All political statements" should be added, "must not be in conflict with our party's policies or resolutions."

No. 59 Comrade Gao Yuhan:[10] The scope of the word "statements" is vast. A thousand or a few hundred words may also be a statement. I think we should limit it to published writings. For instance, things such as Comrade Dai Jitao's pamphlet published several months ago need the party's endorsement. If all bits and pieces of expression need the party's endorsement, it will be too much of a nuisance and is really not feasible. Therefore, I suggest that we change "statements" to "writings."

No. 16 Comrade Mao Zedong: I don't think what No. 59 said was entirely appropriate either. For instance, Lin Sen's recent speech in Beijing, though brief, has had great impact. Therefore, we cannot limit it to small pamphlets, either.

. . .

Chairman: Now we have three suggestions for amendments. First of all, let's put Comrade Yu Shude's amendment to vote: "All statements concerning politics and party affairs may not be in conflict with our party's policies and resolutions. The establishment of any and all study associations requires permission from the highest party organization of that locality." All those who agree, please raise your hand. (Passed by a majority.)

Chairman: Do we need to discuss this resolution further?

. . .

No. 16 Comrade Mao Zedong: In paragraph IIE,[11] "In all important areas" should be changed to "at appropriate locations." (More than ten people seconded.)

Chairman: Any objections? (Passed with no objections.)

No. 163 Comrade Zhang Wenqing: In paragraph VIII, "So it is accepted that the late Director General allowed Communist Party members to join our party to

---

10. Gao Yuhan was a former Communist Party member who had been opposed to collaboration with the Guomindang. In 1924 he went to study in Germany, and on his return in 1925 joined the Guomindang. In mid-1926 he became chief political officer of the 12th division of the Northern Expedition Army.

11. This sentence, as adopted by the congress, reads as follows: "In all important areas there must be established a communications office responsible for communications, transmitting orders, and distributing propaganda."

strive together," should be changed to "We shall abide by the late Director General's proposal that Communist Party members be allowed to join our party."[12]

No. 63 Comrade Zhang Tinggan: It should be changed to "The late Director General held the view that Communist Party members should be allowed to join our party to work together. In the future, if there are any party members who do not understand our late Director General's will as it refers to the acceptance of Communist Party members, and if disputes arise within the Party, we need to discuss these matters openly together."

No. 81 Comrade Xu Zhuoran: Such wording still sounds biased. I don't think it's appropriate. Let's all discuss this.

No. 16 Comrade Mao Zedong: I still propose that we keep the original proposal as it is; there is no need to change it.

No. 55 Comrade Yuan Tongchou: I think this problem should be solved once and for all. If the proposal endorses this kind of attitude, I'm afraid that it might create more misunderstandings and disputes. The Western Hills Conference this time called for anti-Communism. Actually we think that they were counterrevolutionary. It is not an issue of pro- or anti-Communism. There is no doubt about it. But we, the students of Huangpu Military Academy, also have had similar disputes. We also admit that we can debate in class, but we have to join hands to attack imperialism. We cannot say that they are counterrevolutionaries. Paragraph VIII of this resolution stipulates that, if we have disputes, we may discuss them openly under the guidance of the party organization. But this is only a temporary solution. If we want to end such disputes, we should not shy away from a permanent solution. According to my years of experience of administering the Huangpu Military Academy, I am fully aware that these disputes are not disputes over ideology. Because the Three People's Principles also include Communism. The goals of both sides are the same. Nor is it a problem of whether the party members work hard or not. Actually, there are misunderstandings between them. Some always think that many Communist comrades do not want to engage

---

12. Paragraph VIII, as adopted by the congress, reads as follows: "The efforts of the revolution are concentrated on the principle of promoting the success of the national revolution, and nothing else, so it is accepted that the late Director General allowed Communist Party members to join our party to strive together. From now on, all disputes about such matters may take the form of open discussions under the guidance and supervision of the party bureaus, so that all misunderstandings may be resolved in a rational and satisfactory manner. No emotional attacks may, however, be permitted, as such behavior could place in jeopardy the basic policies underlying the concentration of our revolutionary forces."

in party activities out in the open, and have never acknowledged their membership in the Communist Party. Because of this suspicion, many disputes have arisen between the two sides. Therefore, I think that to solve the problem at its root, what is most important is to let both sides get to know each other. As I consider this, I think there are several things that the comrades who are Communist Party members should be expected to do: (1) When Communist Party members join the Guomindang, they should declare their membership in the Communist Party. (2) Communist Party members should do things openly within the Guomindang. (3) When Guomindang members join the Communist Party, they need the permission of the party organization in that locality. If these three requirements can be met, the disputes will be resolved naturally. As for myself, I have never belonged to the Communist Party nor have I joined any other anti-Communist groups. I am not prejudiced against either side. I absolutely respect the Communist Party comrades. Now I'm sincerely asking the congress to solve this problem. Because if we don't solve this problem once for all, later when disputes arise, it will not be good. (Over ten people seconded.)

Comrade Zhang Guotao:[13] The three points brought up by Comrade Yuan Tongchou are all excellent, but probably they cannot be carried out in reality. Let's take the first point. If the whole country were like Guangdong, there would be no problem. Because it really cannot be done outside of Guangdong. If we request all those Communist Party members who join the Guomindang to let the highest Guomindang organization know, this poses no problem. But there are many party organizations. The regional branches are also party organizations. There are many Guomindang party members who do not understand this. If we let the lower-level party organizations know, there will be danger. Even if there is no danger in Guangdong, there will surely be danger elsewhere. Now I will take up the second point. Political parties should be granted the freedom to operate openly. But under the current warlord oppression, the Communist Party cannot help but operate in secret. If you act openly, you will be arrested immediately by police and spies. A number of Communist Party comrades have already been oppressed in the North, and this constitutes a precedent. So it is impossible to act openly. That is why the Director General resolved during the Second Central Executive Committee meeting that the Communist Party members may join our party, and as long as they obey the party's discipline, nothing

---

13. Regarding the early career of Zhang Guotao (1897–1979), see the note to "A Fund-Raising Notice for the Shanghai Work-Study Mutual Aid Society," dated March 5, 1920, in Volume I, p. 500. Although, at the Third Congress of the Chinese Communist Party in June 1923, Zhang had expressed reservations about entering into too intimate an alliance with the Nationalists, he had been elected an alternate member of the Guomindang Central Executive Committee at the First Congress in 1924, and was at this time playing a very active role in the "bloc within."

else will be required of them. If the regulations require the Communist Party members to act openly, this implies distrust and scrutiny. This was not the Director General's will either. (The Chairman announced that time was up, but proposed that the session not be adjourned until this problem was solved. The participants agreed.) As for the third point, all Guomindang members wishing to join the Communist Party need to get their local party organization's permission. This is also very proper. But we should be aware of the history of the world's political parties. Each member has his freedom to join a party or to leave it. There have been Communist Party members who have left the Communist Party to join the Guomindang, and the Communist Party comrades were not upset about it. As for the Guomindang members who joined the Communist Party, the total number is no more than 3 percent of the Communist Party membership. This number is very, very small. We should ask him whether he is for revolution or not, but not whether he is a Communist or not. The only exception is when a Communist Party member, after he leaves the Party, becomes a counterrevolutionary; then, of course, we will oppose him. If a good Communist Party member becomes a good Guomindang member, he is still a good revolutionary, standing on the same side of revolution with us. This is very good. We are not against him. It should be like this according to the principles of the political party. But when some people are in both the Communist Party and the Guomindang, we will not be in the least upset. I still remember what Comrade He Huihan said to me several years ago. He said that a good Communist Party member must be a good nationalist revolutionary. A good nationalist revolutionary must not be opposed to the well-being of the peasants and workers. This is very accurate. Since Comrade Yuan has brought this up today, I am very glad. I also want to put in my honest opinion.

Comrade Mao Zedong: Indeed we need to discuss the problem brought up by Comrade Yuan. What Comrade Zhang has said is also well founded, and is worthy of our attention. Furthermore, we are not afraid of these three conditions. As far as the first point is concerned, if someone is afraid to admit that he is a Communist, he is not a real Communist. But the Communist Party in China is still a secret organization. In contrast to the Russian Communist Party, which is in power and can operate openly, it is very different. As long as the Chinese Communist Party cannot obtain legal status, it cannot help but operate secretly. If one admits that he is a Communist in places such as Shanghai, he will be immediately shot. Concerning the second point, it is similar to the first. As long as we are in the realm of our sister party, the Chinese Guomindang, it is all right to declare ourselves openly. But if we were to go public anywhere else, we would soon be dissolved and wiped out. Consequently, a part of the strength of the national revolution would be hit hard, and this would be disadvantageous to the future of the national revolution. Concerning the third point, no matter which party, the party members should be given absolute freedom to join or leave. There really shouldn't be any restrictions.

. . .

Day 13, Number 25
Date: January 19, the fifteenth year of the Republic of China
Time: 10:30 A.M. - 1:10 P.M.
Number of participants: 188
Chairman: Tan Pingshan
Secretary-General: Wu Yuzhang

. . .

I. Chairman Wang Jingwei reported that the presidium brought up our party's propaganda outline for the current situation in the north after the closing of the congress

. . .

II. Financial resolutions

. . .

III. Resolutions on Discipline

Comrade Lu Youyu reported the results of the investigation by the Review Committee. (See Appendix)

No. 32 Comrade Yu Shude: In principle, I agree with this resolution, but we need to pay attention to the wording, because I'm afraid that some have already announced that they have left the Comrades' Club, but we do not yet know. There are many Chinese newspapers. Though I am not able to prove otherwise, I cannot help wondering about this.

No. 59 Comrade Gao Yuhan: I think those who have declared that they have left the Comrades' Club must both make a statement in a newspaper and notify the Central Party Headquarters.

No. 201 Comrade Zhan Dabei: In my opinion, we can only get an accurate understanding of the resolution from the party's point of view, not from a political standpoint.

No. 16[14] **Comrade Mao Zedong:** I also agree that we should not mix this resolution up with the Western Hills Conference. Rather, we should deal with the problems within the scope of party affairs after the Western Hills Conference.

No. 21 Comrade Dong Yongwei: In my view, as regards punishment for Ju Zheng and the like, we should try to think about the future of party affairs in various places, and whether or not there will be difficulties; only thus can we form an appropriate opinion. Therefore I propose that Ju Zheng and Shi Qingyang be expelled from the party permanently. As for Dai Jitao, we should not add any more punishment for him.

Chairman: Now we can change the mode of discussion. Let's discuss this resolution item by item. Let's solve the Ju Zheng case first.

No. 215 Comrade Zhu Jianfan: I think there is no need to discuss it anymore. We can put it to the vote right away, because there is no one among us who would go along with this reactionary element who has collaborated with the warlords and has damaged party affairs.

Chairman: Those who wish that Ju Zheng be expelled from the party permanently, please raise your hand. (Passed by a majority.)

Chairman: About the second item. Shi Qingyang has framed comrades. Although the Sichuan representative, Wu Yuzhang, declared that there is no proof yet, there are many comrades who can testify that he has colluded with warlords. Please discuss whether he should be expelled from the party or not.

No. 215 Comrade Zhu Jianfan asked that the Congress put the original resolution to a vote.

Chairman: Those who are in favor of expelling Shi Qingyang from the party, please raise your hand. (Passed by a majority.)

Chairman: Item 3 concerns Tan Zhen, Shi Ying, and Mao Zuquan.[15] The resolution suggests that they be given a warning and be given one month to declare

---

14. Mao's delegate number is given here as 15, but this must be a typographical error since throughout the stenographic record of the congress he appears as No. 16.

15. On the early careers of Tan Zhen and Mao Zuquan, see above, the notes to the memo of March 31, 1924. Of the two, Tan was the more influential. He had stayed in Beijing after Sun Yatsen's funeral in March 1925, and organized the Comrades' Club (*Tongzhi jubu*) referred to in these debates. He was also a founding member of the Western Hills faction, and participated in its meeting of November 1925. Subsequently he continued to be identified with this faction and with its opposition to cooperation with the

that they have left the Comrades' Club, and to notify the Central Party Headquarters in writing. Otherwise, they will be expelled. What do you think?

No. 16 Comrade Mao Zedong: I propose that it be changed to two months. The first reason is that one month is not enough for mail to travel back and forth, because of the inconvenience of transportation. The second reason is that we will thus show them once again how careful we are in dealing with this resolution. The third reason is that we still hope they will return to the path of revolution. (Over ten people seconded.)

Chairman: Let's put Comrade Mao's amendment to the vote. (Passed.)

. . .

Communists. It is, of course, impossible to say whether Mao's hope that these old comrades would return to the revolutionary path resulted from his previous association with them, or whether he simply thought that a show of forebearance would be politically expedient.

Resolution on the Propaganda Report

Resolution Adopted by the Second National Congress of the Chinese Guomindang

(January 18, 1926)

1. Since the First National Congress promulgated the manifesto or platform of our party, which clearly defined the goals and methods of the national revolution, there has been a great change in what we see and hear both inside and outside the party. Outside the party, the popular masses have gradually realized that the goal of the national revolution led by our party is to overthrow the international imperialists and all their accomplices, and to fight for the interests of the popular masses. Consequently, the popular masses have changed their previous suspicious attitude toward our party to an attitude of support for our party. Within the party, all party members have been brought together within the framework of a common goal and common method to march in the same direction and work in good order. Gradually, those who tried to smuggle in individual goals and methods incompatible with these common goals and methods have been weeded out, and this has served a very great educational function. In the domain of propaganda, however, we have not succeeded, in the course of the past two years, in implanting profoundly the party's goals and methods among the masses of workers, peasants, and small merchants who make up the vast majority of our country's population. As regards education, we have been even less capable of establishing a concrete plan for educating party members and revolutionizing the whole membership of the party. These are shortcomings. The congress holds that henceforth these defects in the propaganda work of the party must absolutely be corrected.

2. During the past two years, amidst all the crucial events that have taken place in the country as a whole, our party has truly been capable of taking an offensive stance in its propaganda and of explaining the significance of these events for the popular masses. Whether it be the affair of the [attempted] recovery of the Guangdong Customs, the strike in Shamian, the incident of the Merchants' Corps, the Sino-Russia Agreement, the anti-Zhili war, the movement to

This resolution was first published in *Zhengzhi zhoubao*, Nos. 6–7, April 10, 1926. Our translation is based on this text as reproduced in *Mao Zedong ji. Bujuan*, Vol. 2, pp. 157–58.

convene a national assembly, the movement to mourn the Director General, the May Thirtieth Movement, the Guangzhou-Hong Kong strike, the case of Liao,[1] the purge of counterrevolutionaries by the national government, or the recent war against the Fengtian clique, the party has always been capable of seizing the occasion, launching a widespread propaganda campaign, exposing the offenses of the imperialists and of their tools—the warlords, the bureaucrats, and the comprador class—and pointing the way out to the popular masses. In addition, even greater achievements have been recorded in political education within the National Revolutionary Army and in propaganda about the unity between the army and the people in time of war. The congress holds that, in the course of the various events which will continue to unfold in the country, the party should take full advantage of every occasion to expose the plots and misdeeds of all the reactionary forces on the one hand and, on the other hand, to make known our party's principles and policies, and promote the constantly increasing revolutionization of the oppressed popular masses of the whole country. Now, if we wish to implant the doctrine and policy of the party deeply among the popular masses, there is no way to achieve this save by striving to carry out our propaganda with regard to those events, large or small, local or nationwide, in which the interests of the popular masses are at stake. As for political propaganda in the army, it is of the utmost importance, and should be expanded as much as possible in the future.

3. During the past two years, imperialism has put forth two slogans, "Oppose Communism" and "Red Imperialism," and has called upon its tools in China—the bureaucrats, the warlords, the comprador class, and the village bullies and bad gentry, as well as various ridiculous political factions, such as the Anfu clique, the Research clique, the Federalists, and the *Étatistes*, etc.—to make every effort to spread their destructive and slanderous propaganda. Their purpose is to break up our party's revolutionary united front both at home and abroad. It is imperative to unmask in the eyes of the popular masses the slanderous and erroneous nature of such counterrevolutionary propaganda, and at the same time to instruct the masses and make them understand that the revolutionary united front both at home and abroad must be expanded and consolidated if they desire the success of the revolution.

4. As for the deficiencies in the leadership system for our propaganda work, the inadequacies of our party newspapers, the laxity of our investigations, the one-sided distribution of our propaganda materials, the weakness of our propaganda in the rural areas, and the lack of a plan for the education within the party, which have been the main deficiencies for the past two years, in future they should all be properly corrected on the basis of the new propaganda plan.[2]

---

1. I.e., the assassination of Liao Zhongkai on August 20, 1925.
2. See the resolutions on propaganda and on party newspapers, dated January 16, 1926.

Resolution Concerning the Peasant Movement

Resolution of the Second National Congress of the Chinese Guomindang

(January 19, 1926)[1]

1. China now has not yet gone beyond the agricultural economy and peasant production, and the peasants account for as much as 90 percent of the total productive output. If we wish to carry out the Director General's Three People's Principles, the first thing is to liberate the peasants. Since peasants in fact make up over 80 percent of the population of our country, then among the 400 million people of the country, peasants actually number over 300 million. Therefore, China's national revolution is, to put it plainly, a peasant revolution. If we wish to consolidate the foundation of the national revolution, we must, once again, first liberate the peasants. It follows from the arguments presented above that the Chinese Guomindang should always and everywhere consider the peasant movement as its foundation. Both political and economic movements should have the peasant movement as their foundation. The party's policies should focus first and foremost on the interests of the peasants themselves, and the actions of the government should also be designed to liberate them in accordance with their interests, for the liberation of the peasants represents the completion of the major part of the national revolution and the basis for our party to realize the Three People's Principles.

2. Since the peasant movement came into existence in Guangdong no more than seven months ago, our party has [created] peasant associations in thirty-seven *xian*, membership has increased to 620,000 people, and [there is] an organized peasant army of 30,000 men. Peasants participated mightily in our party's

---

This resolution was published in *Zhengzhi zhoubao*, Nos. 6–7, April 10, 1926. Our translation is based on this text as reproduced in *Mao Zedong ji. Bujuan*, Vol. 2, pp. 173–76.

1. When the report on the peasant movement was first laid before the congress on the morning of January 18, 1926, one speaker characterized it as "not bad," but too narrowly focussed on Guangdong. It was therefore decided that the report should be resubmitted the following morning, after being revised by an enlarged review committee. Mao Zedong, who had not been involved in drafting the original report, was appointed to this review committee on the afternoon of January 18. It was Chen Gongbo who presented the revised report, translated here, on the morning of January 19, but Mao undoubtedly played a role in drafting it.

expeditions against Yang and Liu in the past and in its unification of Guangdong this time. All this proves that our party is essential for the peasants to make progress and for them to seek their own emancipation, and also shows the strength they can contribute on joining the national revolution. Besides Guangdong, peasant movements have also emerged in Guangxi of the Pearl River Basin, in Hunan, Hubei, and Anhui of the Yangzi River Basin, and in Shandong, Henan, and special districts such as Zhili, Rehe, and Chaha'er of the Yellow River Basin. Thus far, they are less well organized, and have not shown marked effectiveness. In order to involve the peasants all over the country in the political struggle, our party must try its best to focus attention on the two regions of central and northern China. Otherwise, it certainly cannot promote the organization of the peasants of the whole country to strive for the national revolution within the shortest period of time. Therefore, our party must make special efforts to establish a unified plan for a national peasant movement, and must also set aside funds for carrying out such a plan.

For the reasons stated above, the congress adopts three resolutions on the peasant movement, dealing respectively with the political, economic, and educational aspects.

1. The political aspect:

   a. Guide peasants to become organized popular masses and take part in the national revolution.
   b. Eliminate warlords, the comprador class, corrupt officials, bad gentry and local bullies, and others who harm the interests of the peasants.
   c. Dissolve armed organizations that oppress the peasants.
   d. Clearly stipulate the principle of peasants' self-preparation and self-defense.
   e. At all times, our party and government should stand on the side of the peasants and fight for their interests.
   f. Formulate laws for the protection of peasants.
   g. Put into force standard weights and measures.

2. The economic aspect:

   a. Strictly forbid making usurious loans to peasants.
   b. Stipulate the highest land rent and the lowest grain price.
   c. Reduce farm laborers' working hours and increase their pay.
   d. Abolish exorbitant taxes, fees, and extra levies; stop collecting money and grain in advance; and eliminate payments in money and grain for those who have no land.
   e. Forbid the agricultural contract system.
   f. Rapidly set up agricultural banks and promote the cause of peasants' cooperation.

    g. Speedily engage in plowing and arranging land, rebuild irrigation works, and improve agriculture.

    h. Investigate official famine relief to unemployed peasants.

    i. Abolish unscrupulous merchants' monopoly prices.

    j. Improve the treatment of young farm laborers and women farm laborers.

3. The educational aspect:

    a. Strictly implement compulsory education and adult education in the countryside.

    b. Use local public funds to run various kinds of adult education schools for peasants.

    c. Encourage the peasants as forcefully as possible to set up various schools themselves.

To relieve the sufferings of peasants, to enable them to become organized popular masses, and to facilitate the success of the revolution, our party must make careful and thorough plans for its internal organization. Considering the course of the peasant movement during the past year, the congress holds that it has made fairly good progress, but that further efforts should be made in the future. The congress sets forth the following special regulations for the planning of internal work:

1. Party headquarters of all provinces should establish peasant departments, and should also maintain close links with the Peasant Department of the Central Committee and implement the plans of the Central Party Headquarters for a unified movement.

2. Under the guidance of the Central Party Headquarters, select appropriate locations in the two regions of Central and North China for setting up Peasant Movement Training Institutes, with a view to expanding China's peasant movement.

3. Specifically allocate and increase funds for the peasant movement.

4. The propaganda departments of all city- and provincial-level party headquarters should keep close contact with their own peasant departments and with the Peasant Department of the Central Committee in particular, so as to enable this type of movement to become a unified movement of our party as a whole.

Letter to the Standing Committee of the Secretariat

(February 14, 1926)

Comrades of the Standing Committee of the Central Secretariat:[1]

Because my mental ailment has increased in severity, I am obliged to request a two-week leave in order to go to Shaozhou to recuperate.[2] I have handed over all the affairs of the Propaganda Department to Comrade Shen Yanbing[3] for him to deal with. I hereby inform you respectfully of this, and I shall be grateful if you will take note of it.

Mao Zedong

For the source of this text, see above, the note to the letter of May 26, 1924.

1. The reference is, of course, to the Secretariat of the Central Executive Committee of the Guomindang. Similarly, the Propaganda Department referred to below is that of the Guomindang, of which Mao had been appointed acting head on October 5, 1925.

2. Once again, as in the letter of May 1924, "mental ailment" should presumably be taken to mean extreme strain and fatigue. Following his original appointment as acting head of the Guomindang Propaganda Department on October 5, 1925, Mao had contributed some twenty articles to the *Political Weekly* and had played an extremely active role at the Second Congress of the Guomindang, presenting the report on propaganda and drafting several resolutions on related topics. (All of these materials are translated above.) Mao's leave of absence was for exactly two weeks; on February 28 he addressed the opening session of the Guomindang Political Training Group. (For a summary of his remarks on that occasion, see *Nianpu*, 1, p. 157.) According to the recollections of Shen Yanbing (on Shen see the following note), though Mao used the excuse of illness in requesting this leave, his real object was to go on a secret trip to the Hunan-Guangdong border area to inspect the peasant movement there. See *Nianpu*, 1, p. 156.

3. Shen Dehong (1896–1981), *zi* Yanbing, a native of Zhejiang, is best known under his pen name of Mao Dun. After studying at Beijing University from 1913 to 1916, he went to Shanghai, where he worked as editor and translator for the Commercial Press. Contrary to some published accounts, he became a member of Chen Duxiu's Communist group in Shanghai as early as the summer of 1920. On December 31, 1925, his long association with the Commercial Press came to an end, and he embarked the next day for Guangzhou to attend the Second Guomindang Congress. At the third meeting of the Standing Committee of the Central Executive Committee on February 8, 1926, he was appointed secretary of the Propaganda Department in response to a proposal by Mao Zedong, who had himself been reappointed acting head of that department at the second Standing Committee meeting on February 5. He also became editor of the *Political Weekly* when it resumed publication on March 6, 1926, with issue No. 5. (Mao Zedong had ceased work on it after the appearance of No. 4, on January 10, 1926, because he was taken up with his other activities.)

Resolutions Presented to the Twelfth Meeting of the Standing Committee of the Guomindang Central Executive Committee

(March 16, 1926)[1]

. . .

2. Draft resolution put forward by the Propaganda Department regarding the problem of the Sun Yatsenism [*Sun Wenzhuyi*] Study Society in Beijing, Shanghai, and other places.

Explanation: The news columns of the Beijing *Jingbao* for February 12 contain two items regarding the recent situation of the Beijing Sun Yatsenism Study Society. In brief, the contents are that the Sun Yatsenism Study Society is an organization based on prior consultation among comrades in various places. Consequently, after it was first established in Guangzhou, in less than two months it was also established in more than ten places one after the other, including Shanghai, Beijing, Zhejiang, Nanjing, Wuhu, Wuhan, Jiujiang, Chongqing, Chengdu, Chaozhou, Shantou, and Xi'an. Since the Western Hills Conference[2] decided to remove Communists from membership in the party and dissolve party organs at various levels controlled by the Communists, they have ordered the reregistration of all party members. The Beijing Sun Yatsenism Study Society, in order to support the real Guomindang and the movement to purge the party, have published manifestos and so on, especially in the recent past. It is also reported that the Executive Committee of this society has recently

---

Our source for this document is *Zhongguo Guomindang diyi, er ci quanguo daibiao dahui huiyi shiliao*, Vol. 1, pp. 504–07.

1. Mao, who was not a member of the Standing Committee of the Central Executive Committee, attended this meeting as a nonvoting delegate in his capacity as acting head of the Propaganda Department of the Guomindang. Proposals Nos. 2, 3, 4, and 5 are described as having been made by the Propaganda Department. Proposal No. 7, which bears Mao's name, was presumably put forward on his personal initiative. Proposals Nos. 1 and 6, which do not involve Mao, are omitted here.

2. Regarding the meeting of right-wing Guomindang leaders opposed to collaboration with the Communists in the Western Hills near Beijing, see above, the texts of November and December 1925, and in particular "The Beijing Right-Wing Meeting and Imperialism" and "The Greatest Talent of the Right Wing" of December 20, 1925, and the notes thereto.

decided that the Sun Yatsenism Study Society should have publications appearing at fixed intervals everywhere. Already there are the Guangzhou *Guomin geming*, the Shanghai *Geming daobao*, the Zhejiang *Sun Wenzhuyi xunkan*, the Nanjing *Guomin xunkan*, and so on, and it has been decided that publications of a similar type should be issued, and so on. Also, according to the reports in the *Jingbao*, the Beijing Sun Yatsenism Study Society has been organized exclusively by a small number of reactionaries belonging to the Western Hills Faction. Consequently, the Propaganda Department considers that the Central Committee should send a circular to party offices at all levels, proclaiming that this society is a reactionary body. In order to prevent such confusion resulting from the use of similar names, the Central Committee should also write to the Sun Yatsenism Study Societies in Guangzhou, Chaozhou, Shantou, and other such places declaring that relations are being broken off with them, and a declaration should also be sent to the Beijing Municipal Party Office.

Decision: To deal with the matter using the methods proposed by the Propaganda Department.

3. Draft resolution proposed by the Propaganda Department regarding the request from the Guangzhou Sun Yatsenism Study Society for financial aid, and the revision of the statutes.

Explanation: The said society's earlier request for financial assistance from the Central Committee was handed over to the Propaganda Department to investigate and report back. Now, on the basis of a further communication from the society in question, together with its statutes, the Propaganda Department considers that the financial assistance could be accorded, to the amount of 300 *yuan* a month, as requested by the society. There are, however, two points that should be changed in the society's statutes. (1) From the organizational standpoint, the said society has not yet clearly defined its relations with the party offices, and some such provision as "will be subject to the guidance and supervision of the Central Executive Committee of the Guomindang" should be added. (2) If it is a body that engages in action, the said society has a certain similarity to an organization of our party and could easily fall into the danger of independent or individual action vis-à-vis the organization; if it is a research body, it should accept the guidance of the Propaganda Department.

Decision: Adopted. A letter should also be written to the Sun Yatsenism Society asking them to amend their statutes and to send the new version.

4. The Propaganda Department proposes a resolution to the effect that, since the Shanghai *Geming daobao* is an organ of the bogus central organ,[3] we should ask

---

3. I.e., of the rival Central Executive Committee, which had just been set up in Shanghai by Lin Sen and other anti-Communist leaders.

the center to send a circular to party organs at all levels forbidding them to circulate it.

Decision: Adopted.

5. The Propaganda Department proposes a resolution to the effect that, within the Committee on Compilation of the Chinese Guomindang, a Committee for Compiling Textbooks be established, and that Comrade Wu Yanyin be invited to become the chairman.

Decision: To appoint Comrade Wu Yanyin a member of the Committee on Compilation of the Chinese Guomindang, with exclusive responsibility for compiling textbooks. There is, on the other hand, no need to establish a Committee for Compiling Textbooks.

. . .

7. Comrade Mao Zedong proposes a resolution calling on the Center to praise and encourage Comrades Li Zongren, Huang Shaoxiong, and Bai Chongxi from Guangxi.[4]

---

4. These three generals had recently joined the Guomindang and permitted the party to operate in the regions of Guangxi they controlled. Their forces became the Seventh Corps of the National Revolutionary Army.

Some Points for Attention in Commemorating the Paris Commune

(March 18, 1926)

Today, for the first time, the Chinese popular masses are commemorating the Paris Commune.[1] It is now already fifty-five years since the event known as the Paris Commune took place, so why is it only now that we know we should commemorate it and are carrying out this commemoration? Because previously the Chinese revolution was the undertaking of a minority, and only now that the tide of revolution is rising ever higher has the revolutionary movement been broadened from a minority of people to the majority of the people. Now a majority of the popular masses of peasants and workers are already participating in it, and it is moreover led by Guomindang members of the left. There is the state of the workers' dictatorship, Soviet Russia, to serve as a model. For all of these reasons, the Chinese popular masses have only now become aware of today's date for commemoration and are only now able to carry out today's commemoration.

As regards the unfolding of the Paris Commune, the newspapers have all carried reports during the last few days, and the book called *New Perspectives on Society*[2] contains a brief account. I think all the comrades have read this, so there is no need for me to speak about it at length. Now I will limit myself to a few remarks on the deep significance of commemorating the Paris Commune.

The Paris Commune was the first revolutionary movement in which, on March 18, 1871, the working class of Paris rose up. That was during the Tenth Year of the Tongzhi reign of the former Qing dynasty, exactly fifty-five years ago today. We must ask ourselves why such a movement did not break out a hundred years ago, but did occur fifty-five years ago. We know that, whenever any kind of movement breaks out, it does not occur without reason or cause; the objective conditions must exist. We note that the Paris Commune was thirty years after the Opium War in China, and during these thirty years the "Treaty of Nanjing," the "Treaty of Tianjin,"

This speech by Mao was published in the organ of the Guomindang Political Training Group, *Zhongguo Guomindang zhengzhi jiangxiban xunkan*, No. 2, March 31, 1926. We have translated it from this text as reproduced in *Mao Zedong wenji*, Vol. I, pp. 33–36.

1. This is the text of a lecture in commemoration of the 55th anniversary of the Paris Commune given by Mao to the Guomindang Political Training Group. (This unit had been established on February 28, 1926; Mao had delivered the address at the opening ceremony.)

2. *Xin shehui guan*, a translation of a work by one Guofanlunke (as yet unidentified), had been published in Chinese in June 1925.

the "Treaty of Beijing," and so on were concluded.[3] This suffices to demonstrate that the European countries already had the capacity to progress forcefully toward the East, that from capitalism they had already progressed to imperialism, that within those countries a mighty working class had already been formed. Only thus could such a powerful working-class revolutionary movement appear. This is the first point to which we should pay attention.

Marx says that international wars, in which the capitalists strive with one another for their own interests, are meaningless. Only class wars within a country can liberate humanity. The Great War in Europe, which broke out in the third year of the Chinese Republic, brought about the loss of many lives and the wasteful expenditure of incalculable sums, but what was the result? The revolution of the Russian workers, who rose up in the sixth year of the Chinese Republic, overthrew the state of the capitalists, successfully established the dictatorship of the toilers, and opened a new, bright road in the world. Is its value not inestimable? The Russian October Revolution and the Paris Commune are acts in which the working class, by its own strength, has pursued the true equality and liberty of humanity. Their significance is similar; they differ only as regards victory and defeat. We can say, therefore, that the Paris Commune saw the opening of a bright flower, while the Russian Revolution represents the happy fruit—the Russian Revolution is the continuation of the Paris Commune. At present, all the propaganda of the capitalists says: "Foreign wars are advantageous, civil wars are not." We must go further and say: "The international wars in which the capitalists contend for their own interests are meaningless; only international wars in which capitalism is overthrown are significant. Internal wars in which the warlords contend for power and advantage are valueless; only civil wars in which the oppressed classes rise up and overthrow the classes of the oppressors are of value." All the *Étatistes* keep preaching their slogan "sacrifice for the fatherland is most glorious." These are the words by which the capitalists trick people, and we must on no account allow them to make fools of us! This is the second point to which we must pay attention.

At present, there are a considerable number of people within the country who doubt or oppose class struggle. This is because they do not understand the history of human development. Marx says: "The history of humanity is a history of class struggle." This is a fact, and cannot be denied. The progress of the human race from primitive society to patriarchal society, feudal society, and finally to the present-day state has in all cases taken place through an evolution marked by class struggle between the ruling class and the class of those who are ruled. The Paris Commune was the first political and economic revolution in

---

3. The Treaty of Nanking of 1842, following the Opium Wars, opened the first five "treaty ports" to the Europeans. The Treaty of Tianjin of 1858, confirmed and extended by the Convention of Beijing of 1860, laid the foundations for the system of extraterritoriality and foreign concessions which lasted until 1949.

which the working class arose to overthrow the ruling class. In the past, in reading Chinese history, we did not pay attention to the reality of class struggle. In fact, how can we say that the four thousand years of Chinese history are not a history of class struggle? For example, in the time of the second Qin emperor, those who arose and made revolution, Chen Sheng and Wu Guang, were peasants. Han Gaozu[4] was a vagabond [*liumang*]; that was also a revolution in which the proletariat overthrew the aristocracy. In a peasant society, however, after the success of the revolution, they in turn acted as emperors, and themselves became aristocrats. The Taiping King, Hong Xiuquan, called on a broad group of unemployed peasants to rise up and make revolution, and this had great significance as a social revolution. Director General Sun also had great admiration for him. Everyone knows that the Qing dynasty overthrew him, but they don't know that the main military force which really overthrew him represented the landlord class. The one who contributed the greatest effort toward the overthrow of the Taiping Heavenly Kingdom was Zeng Guofan. At that time, he was the leader of the landlord class. Zeng Guofan originally rose by training the *tuanlian*.[5] The *tuanlian* were the military force of the landlords for oppressing the peasants. When they saw Hong Xiuquan leading a peasant revolution that was not in their interests, they put forth the greatest efforts to overthrow him. Thus, the affair of the Taiping Heavenly Kingdom was not a war between the Manchus and the Hans, but was actually a class war between the peasants and the landlords.[6] This is the third point to which we should pay attention.

The Paris Commune existed for only seventy-two days. How did it come to fail in such a short time? There are two main causes: (1) There was no united, centralized, and disciplined party to lead it—if we want the revolution to succeed, we must concentrate our forces and unify our actions, so we must rely on a unified and disciplined party to give the orders. At the time of the Paris Commune, because there was no unified political party, opinions within [the Commune] were divided, and forces were scattered. This gave an opportunity to the enemy and was the primary cause of defeat. (2) The attitude toward the enemy was too conciliatory and too merciful—to be merciful toward the enemy is to be cruel to our comrades. The success of the Russian October Revolution of 1917, the overthrow of Yang and Liu,[7] and the liquidation of the counterrevolutionary

---

4. The founding emperor of the Han dynasty, Liu Bang.

5. The *tuanlian* (literally "grouping and drilling") were the officially sanctioned local militia in the mid-nineteenth century.

6. A decade earlier, Mao's attitude toward both Zeng Guofan and the Taipings had been very different. See Volume I of this edition, *passim*, and especially p. 131, the letter of August 1917 in which Mao stated that Zeng's handling of the campaign in which he disposed of Hong Xiuquan was "perfectly flawless."

7. On the action against Yang Ximin and Liu Zhenhuan in June 1925, see above, the relevant note to the "Announcement to All [Guomindang] Party Members" of December 4, 1925.

faction by the national government in the fourteenth year of the Republic all resulted entirely from adopting absolutely stern measures toward the enemy without the slightest hint of compromise. Because if we do not adopt severe measures against the enemy, the enemy will employ cruel measures against us. The Paris Commune did not deal severely with the enemy and moreover allowed the enemy to seize control of the financial organs and to concentrate their armies, so they were exterminated by the enemy in the end. All comrades should take cognizance of this and take warning from the past to avoid errors in the future. Never should they forget this sentence: "If we do not inflict a mortal blow on the enemy, the enemy will inflict a mortal blow on us." If we want to make revolution, we must learn the methods of revolution from this [example]. This is the fourth point to which we should pay attention in commemorating the Paris Commune.

At present, the imperialists seek to disperse the union of the revolutionary forces, and they energetically make propaganda about the "red terror." They say the Russian Revolution killed thousands and tens of thousands of people. In reality, it is only the "white terror" of the imperialists that is a real terror! Just look how, after the defeat of the Paris Commune, the number of people massacred by the capitalists totaled not less than 100,000, while the number killed by the Russian Revolution was not more than a few thousand. The "red terror" is in fact far from equaling the "white terror." The bloody events of May 30 and the Shakee massacre are an even greater proof regarding the "white terror." So we must shout loudly: "Oppose the white terror! Oppose the butchery of the proletariat by the imperialists!"

Politics and Mass Movements Are Closely Linked

(March 30, 1926)[1]

. . .

3. Comrade Mao Zedong proposed that Comrade Gao Yuhan be appointed head of political training at the Peasant Movement Training Institute.

(Decision) Approved.

. . .

4. Comrade Mao Zedong reported on the matter of selecting students from Guangxi. Previously it was resolved that thirty students should be selected from the training institute for propaganda workers run by the party in Wuzhou. Yesterday, however, we became aware that, according to Comrades Li Xielei and Yang Wenzhao, students at the training institute for propaganda workers are drawn on an equal basis from various *xian* in Guangxi, but the peasant movement in Guangxi should begin in the *xian* near Wuzhou. It is requested that the previous resolution be modified somewhat.

(Decision) The thirty students should still be selected under the responsibility of the Wuzhou municipal party bureau, but should not be restricted to those from the training institute for propaganda workers. The only requirement is that all of them must be young comrades who are residents of various *xian* near Wuzhou and who are working resolutely in the peasant movement.[2]

The minutes of the Guomindang Peasant Department from which this text is taken were published in *Zhongguo nongmin*, No. 5, 1926. Our translation has been made from that source.

1. This text comprises Mao's contributions at the Second Meeting of the Peasant Movement Committee under the Guomindang Peasant Department, held on the date indicated. The numbers preceding each paragraph are those attributed to them in the minutes.

2. These students were being selected to attend the forthcoming sixth session of the Peasant Movement Training Institute, of which Mao would be the principal.

. . .

14. Comrade Mao Zedong proposed a resolution as follows: The movements of the popular masses are closely linked to politics. At present, the peasant movements in the various provinces should pay the utmost attention to the areas that the revolutionary armies will traverse during the Northern Expedition, such as Jiangxi, Hubei, Zhili, Shandong, and Henan.[3]

---

3. The significance of this fragment lies in the fact that it shows how Mao foresaw, and perhaps contributed to, the upsurge of peasant activism that accompanied the subsequent progress of the Northern Expedition.

Resolution Presented to the Seventeenth Meeting of the Standing Committee of the Guomindang Central Executive Committee

(April 2, 1926)[1]

. . .

4. Draft resolution put forward by the Propaganda Department regarding the fact that the Jiling Book Company has been falsely making use of the late Director General's name in issuing a little pamphlet called *On Socialism*, and whether or not this should be forbidden.

Explanation: The Propaganda Department of the Central Committee has recently discovered that there is a so-called Jiling Book Company, of no fixed address and with no person responsible for publication, which has put out a little booklet entitled *On Socialism*, passing it off as a posthumous work by Director General Sun. Stealing a few sentences from the Director General's lectures on "People's Livelihood,"[2] they have cut them into fragments and then cobbled these bits together into a poorly written and unsystematic work. It seems that at present our party is using the Director General's testament and all of the works he has left us as an invisible Director General. The party's policies and actions are rigorously controlled by this testament and these works. Consequently, whenever any publication impinges on the Director General's actions and words, it must first be checked by the Central Propaganda Department before it can be issued, and is therefore subject to very tight procedures. By issuing such a publication as this, the book society in question is manifestly engaging in sordid

---

Our source for this document is *Zhongguo Guomindang diyi, er ci quanguo daibiao dahui huiyi shiliao*, Vol. 1, pp. 516–19.

1. This was a special enlarged meeting, including not only members of the Standing Committee, but all department heads, as well as members of the Central Supervisory Committee. Mao Zedong, in his capacity as acting head of the Propaganda Department, was therefore a full participant with voting rights, and not merely in attendance as on March 16, 1926. He put forward, on the other hand, only one resolution instead of five as on the previous occasion. Proposals 1 to 3, 5, and 6, in which he was not involved, are omitted here.

2. I.e., from part III of the *Three People's Principles*.

dealings with a view to profit. If it is not sternly suppressed, this tendency will grow. Those aiming only for profit, and the counterrevolutionaries, will lead the masses to draw wrong conclusions, fabricate texts and pass them off as the posthumous works of the Director General, and create confusion in society. The result will be a great impediment to the future progress of our party, and we must therefore forbid this publication.

Decision: (1) Find out the origin of this book from the stores that sell it; (2) Ask Comrades Wang Jingwei, Chiang Kaishek, and He Xiangning[3] to find out whether or not it came from the Director General's hand and decide what to do.

---

3. He Xiangning (1879–1972), born in Hong Kong, was the widow of Liao Zhongkai, who had been assassinated in August 1925. She had been the first woman to join the Tongmenghui in 1905, and one of three women to participate in the First Congress of the Guomindang in 1924. After her husband's death she continued to play an important role in the party, and was elected a full member of the Central Executive Committee at the Second Congress in January 1926.

Report on the Work of the Propaganda Department from February 1 to May 15[1]

(May 19, 1926)

Since the close of the Second National Congress, that is, since the beginning of February, our assignment of duties to staff members and all of our plans have proceeded in accordance with the Resolution on Propaganda adopted at the Second Congress. Here I shall report succinctly on the circumstances of the work of our department from February 1 to May 15 of this year, as follows:

I. *Launching a Party Newspaper*

A. The party newspaper in Shanghai. Since the Shanghai *Minguo ribao* went over to supporting the Western Hills faction and thereupon ceased to be recognized by the Central Committee as a party newspaper,[2] the only party newspaper directly under the control of our department has been the Guangzhou *Minguo ribao*. Because there was no party paper in Shanghai, in early April our department sent a responsible party person from the Shanghai Special Municipal Party Office to take control of the property of the *Zhonghua xinbao*. Originally, the name *Zhonghua xinbao* was to be taken over as well, but because they refused to relinquish it, the paper will be published under the name *Guomin ribao*. The date for beginning publication has been announced by the Shanghai Special Municipal Party Office as May 16. The cost of taking over the assets of the *Zhonghua xinbao* and launching the new paper comes to a total of 7,400 big foreign dollars.[3] The regular monthly expenses will be 4,000 big foreign dollars. Decisions on expenditures, and the appointment of staff members, are in the hands of the

---

Our source for this document is a manuscript copy from the Guomindang archives, obtained through the courtesy of Eugene Wu, Director of the Harvard-Yenching Library.

1. This report was delivered at the Second Plenum of the Second Guomindang Central Executive Committee. As indicated in the Introduction to this volume, it was decided in the course of the proceedings that members of "other parties" (i.e. of the Communist Party) should no longer be allowed to serve as department heads, and Mao was therefore forced to resign a few days after presenting this report. His resignation as acting head of the Propaganda Department was accepted on May 28.

2. On these developments, see above, Mao's Report on Propaganda of January 8, 1926, to the Second Guomindang Congress.

3. The expression *da yang*, here translated "big foreign dollars," referred to silver coins, or banknotes, issued in China in units of one dollar. "Small foreign dollars" (*xiao yang*) consisted of silver coins for fractions of a dollar, commonly 20 cents, and the corresponding notes. As will appear from Mao's calculations later in this text, they were not in fact worth their face value in terms of the whole-dollar coins or notes.

Standing Committee of the Central Executive Committee; the Propaganda Department is responsible for implementation.

B. The party newspaper in Hankou. There has never been a party paper in Hankou. At the First Plenum of the Central Committee it was decided that a party newspaper should be launched in Hankou and that the Hubei Provincial Party Committee should be responsible for establishing it and running it. Because the running costs were fixed at 840 big foreign dollars a month, it was possible to produce only a small paper. It appeared on March 24 and is titled the *Chuguang ribao*.[4]

C. The party paper in Hunan. Since the number of party members in Hunan has progressed to 20,000, a small-scale party organ is required both for political and party work and for propaganda among the masses. The Hunan Party Bureau requests the Central Committee to provide a monthly amount of 600 big foreign dollars from the unused expenses for the Hong Kong party organ. The name of the paper would be the *Hunan minbao*.

As for the Hong Kong party paper, it was impossible to launch it before the strike was settled.

The Beijing party paper was originally the *Guomin xinbao*, managed by the comrades. It was changed into an official party paper under the direction of the Central Committee. At present, however, with Beijing under the reactionary forces, open revolutionary propaganda can, of course, survive only with great difficulty. Consequently, it has ceased publication.

In addition, there is also the *Zhengzhi zhoubao*, which was set up in accordance with a decision of the Political Council. Expenses were also to be covered entirely by the Political Council, with our department performing no more than a supervisory function.[5] So far twelve issues have appeared, printed in Guangzhou and Shanghai. At present, 30,000 copies of each issue are printed, of which 10,000 each are distributed in the North, the Center, and the South. This is a type of special propaganda periodical.

II. *Programs for Making Propaganda*

Since February, our plans for making propaganda have included three programs:

1. Program for propaganda regarding the Second National Congress (in the name of the Central Committee)

---

4. The character "chu" is the ancient name for Hubei; thus the name translates as *Light of Hubei Daily*.

5. Regarding the *Zhengzhi zhoubao* (Political Weekly), which began publication on December 5, 1925, under Mao's editorship, see above, the editorial from the first issue and the numerous other articles by Mao that appeared in it between December 5, 1925, and January 10, 1926.

2. Program for propaganda commemorating the anniversary of the Director General's demise (in the name of the Central Committee)

3. Program for propaganda regarding the commemoration of May Fourth (in the name of our department)[6]

III. *Establishing a Review Conference*

For carrying out the work of review, the Central Propaganda Department should have three people whose job it is to review materials published inside and outside the party. Hitherto, however, review has consisted in little but clipping newspapers. Beginning this year, in order to inaugurate reform, a review conference has been established and its detailed rules and regulations fixed. In accordance with these rules and regulations, each review worker is to carry a small notebook in which to record every day the results of his review work and put them forward for discussion at the review conference. As regards erroneous views contained in publications appearing inside and outside the party, the review conference should correct and refute each one. This program should be dealt with separately by the secretariat of our department. It has been going on for three months, and the achievements are not very great. The reason lies in the instability of review writers, and in the difficulty of finding suitable people to specialize in this work.

IV. *Management of the Shanghai Communications Bureau and the Shipment of Propaganda Materials to the North and the Center*

During the past two years, a situation has arisen in which it is extremely difficult for propaganda materials to be sent from the Central Committee to the various party bureaus in the North and in the Center. The Propaganda Department therefore proposed to the Central Committee the establishment in Shanghai of a Communications Bureau to facilitate relations between the Center and the various localities. The Central Committee decided that this should be established, and because there are large quantities of propaganda materials to be shipped, the Propaganda Department was made responsible for the operation of this bureau in November of last year. Following the Second National Congress, our department continued to operate it until the beginning of this month, when the running of it was handed over to the Secretariat. As for the propaganda materials of our department, for the previous two years they have been disseminated almost exclusively in the area around Guangdong. It is only since the Communications Bureau was established that propaganda materials in large

---

6. Although the significance of the events of May 4, 1919, had been widely recognized at the time, and the date was occasionally noted during the ensuing years, such celebrations were scattered and unsystematic. The organized commemoration of the anniversary began in 1924 or 1925, no doubt because of the growing political role played by the May Fourth generation, in the context of the First United Front. Mao's role in fostering this trend is worthy of note.

quantities have been sent to the North and to the various provinces along the Yangzi. During the three and a half months from February to the present, propaganda materials (including books, pamphlets, pictorials, and posters) of 41 varieties, totaling 221,284 copies, have all been sent from the Shanghai Communications Bureau. In addition, documents directly distributed by our department to Guangdong, Guangxi, and Fujian during the past three and a half months for purposes of propaganda have included 15 different kinds, amounting in all to 57,562 copies.

V. *The Establishment of the Propaganda Committee*

Propaganda is an important task of our party. In the past, the organization of our department comprised only a head of the department, responsible for leadership and planning. Within the department, the staff carried out their work on the basis of a division of labor. But as the scope of propaganda continually expanded, it could easily prove inadequate for the department head (or acting head) alone to give consideration to planning. Consequently, we have specially proposed to the Central Committee the organization, under the Propaganda Department, of a Propaganda Committee responsible for discussing plans for nationwide propaganda. By a decision of the Standing Committee of the Central Committee, ten people, including Wang Jingwei, Gu Mengyu, Chen Gongbo, Gan Naiguang, Hu Hanmin, Lin Zuhan, Peng Zemin, Chen Qiyuan, Shao Lizi, and Mao Zedong were appointed members. It held its first meeting on May 13.

VI. *The Relations between Our Department and the Propaganda Departments of the Various Provinces*

During the past two years, there have been no direct relations between our department and the propaganda departments of the various provincial party organizations. It might be said that the sphere of our department's control did not extend beyond the Guangdong area. Following the Second National Congress, our department has done its utmost to change this situation and has repeatedly sent notices to the propaganda departments of the various provinces to the effect that they must develop close relations with our department. Down to the present, however, we have not been completely successful in this. Statistics follow regarding the reports that have been received by our department from the propaganda departments of the various provinces during the past three months.

1. A total of seven reports from the Jiangsu Provincial Propaganda Committee
2. One report from the Hankou Municipal Propaganda Department
3. One report from the Wuzhou Municipal Propaganda Department
4. One from the Guangdong Provincial Propaganda Department
5. A total of three items from the Hunan Provincial Propaganda Department

6. A total of four items from the Guangxi Provincial Propaganda Department
7. A total of two items from the Zhejiang Provincial Propaganda Department
8. One item from the Kaifeng Municipal Propaganda Department
9. A total of two items from the Shanghai Municipal Propaganda Department
10. One item from the Shanxi Provincial Propaganda Department
11. One item from the Shandong Provincial Propaganda Department
12. A total of three items from the Guangzhou Municipal Propaganda Department

VII. *Establishing an Organ for Storing Propaganda Materials*

For the past two years, our department has had no organ for storing propaganda materials. Things have gone so far that many materials have not been collected at the time and subsequently cannot be collected. This is truly regrettable. Beginning in February of this year, a reference room has been created under the Propaganda Department. Statistics regarding the materials collected there in the course of three months are as follows:

1. Daily newspapers published in China (124 titles)
2. Papers in Chinese published abroad (21 titles)
3. Western-language newspapers (5 titles)
4. Weeklies and other small periodicals (122 titles)
5. Pictorials (13 titles)
6. Wall newspapers (2 titles)
7. Chinese-language magazines (15 titles)
8. Western-language magazines (2 titles)
9. Books in Chinese (289 titles, 581 volumes)
10. Books in English (3 titles)
11. Three pictures (12 sheets)

VIII. *Taking Over and Running the Guomin Tongxunshe*

In Shanghai, apart from taking over the *Zhonghua xinbao* and turning it into a party organ, we also took over the Guomin tongxinshe[7] and made of it the party's press organ. In Shanghai, the Guomin tongxinshe is the number two big press agency, second only to the Guowen tongxunshe (Chinese Press Agency). The Shanghai Special Municipal Party Bureau has requested that we take over this agency, and our department is also of the opinion that at times the efficacy of one press agency may be greater than that of several newspapers. There are, moreover, special requirements in Shanghai. Therefore we request the Standing Committee of the Central Committee to decide on taking over [this

---

7. The name of this agency appears in the available text both as Guomin tongxunshe and as Guomin tongxinshe. There is no real difference in meaning between the two terms, both of which signify "National Press Agency."

agency] and to make available, beginning in May, a monthly amount of 800 big foreign dollars for running expenses.

IX. *Plan for Subsidies to Newspapers and for Expanding Propaganda in Various Places*

Throughout all provinces of the whole country, apart from a few remote places, there are organizations of our party. In many provinces the number of party members is gradually increasing, and in such localities there should be an open propaganda organ for our party. Available human and financial resources prohibit, however, the establishment of newspapers everywhere. If we adopt the method of subsidizing [other] newspapers, considerable results can be achieved at relatively low cost. For example, if we make the calculation for the twenty most important places in the country, assuming that there is one newspaper in each locality and each paper receives a subsidy of 200 dollars, the total monthly expenditure on subsidies will be 4,000 dollars. Thus, for the amount expended on only one party newspaper, the result covers the whole country. The minimal condition for newspapers to receive such subsidies is that, on the negative side, they at least refrain from attacking our party and the national government. Our real goal is to induce them to provide appropriate support for our party and the national government. The present plan having been put forward, the Central Committee decided that it should be put into operation and instructed the Political Council to take note of it. At present, already receiving a subsidy from our department is the Jiujiang *Jiangsheng ribao*, introduced by the Provincial Party Bureau in Nanchang; the *Hangzhou chenbao*, introduced by the Zhejiang Provincial Party Bureau, is now requesting a subsidy.

X. *Plans for Compiling and Printing a Series on the National Movement*

In the course of the past two years, the success of our department in compiling propaganda materials has not been very great. The reason is that the method of engaging a specified group of people to gather the facts is not so good as deciding on the topics and soliciting manuscripts accordingly. The Propaganda Department therefore has the intention, and has proposed, to change the method of compilation, and in accordance with present circumstances, to compile and publish *Collected Writings on the National Movement*. Because Shanghai is the place where intellectual circles are concentrated, we have decided to establish in Shanghai a locale for soliciting manuscripts. The ten principles for gathering materials for *Collected Writings on the National Movement* have been adopted by the Standing Committee. In accordance with a decision of the Central [Executive Committee], Comrade Shen Yanbing[8] has been appointed as editor in chief, residing in Shanghai. His responsibility will be to collect manuscripts for the series and to send them to the Central Propaganda Department. When they have

---

8. On Shen Yanbing (Mao Dun), see above, the notes to Mao's letter of February 14, 1926.

been edited and put into final form there, they will be sent back to Shanghai for printing and distribution (for sale). When they have been printed, half of them will be sent to the Central Propaganda Department for free distribution to party members. Royalties for manuscripts and salaries for the editorial office will amount to 800 big foreign dollars a month. We plan to put out ten titles a month on the average, so sixty titles can appear in the first half year. Now we reproduce below the method for compiling the *Collected Writings on the National Movement,* as adopted by the Standing Committee, and the table of contents, as determined by the Propaganda Committee.

Methods of the Central Propaganda Department for Compiling Collected Writings on the National Movement

1. With a view to propaganda outside the party, education and training within the party, and making known the international political and economic situation, the Central Propaganda Department considers that it is necessary to compile, within a short time, a series of small volumes. It has been decided that the name of this series should be *Collected Writings on the National Movement.*

2. This series will be divided, according to the nature of the topics, into five categories: (a) international politics and economics; (b) world revolutionary movements (including peasant movements); (c) principles and tactics of our party; (d) studies of the Soviet Union, and (e) domestic politics and economics and the various movements of the popular masses.

3. The method for compiling this series is that the Propaganda Department will first determine the title and subject of each volume to be included and then allot these topics to specialists to write about. After they have been authorized by the Committee on Propaganda of the Central Propaganda Department, they will then be printed.

4. Specially commissioned manuscripts will be paid for at the rate of 4 *yuan* (or 5 small foreign dollars) per thousand words.[9] Each title will comprise a maximum of 12,000 and a minimum of 8,000 words.

5. Apart from being supplied to party bureaus at all levels, this series will also be put on sale throughout the country at a minimal price.

6. At least six volumes and a maximum of twelve volumes of this series will be published every month. Twelve volumes will constitute a subdivision [of the series]. Every subdivision should contain one or two books from each of the five categories enumerated in section 2 above.

7. For the sake of convenience in collecting materials and specially commissioning manuscripts, as well as printing and distribution, a "Shanghai Branch

---

9. Here *yuan* stands for "big foreign dollars." As will be seen from the present example, one dollar in the fractional silver coinage known as "small foreign dollars" was worth only 80 cents at this time.

Office for Coordinating the Compilation of the Series" should be set up under the direct supervision of the Central Propaganda Department.

8. In the Shanghai Office there should be a manager in charge of editorial work, with a monthly salary of 100 big foreign dollars, and two secretaries, with monthly salaries of 30 big foreign dollars. Paper and other miscellaneous supplies come to 40 big foreign dollars, making in all 200 big foreign dollars per month (including everything—the salaries of the personnel, rent for the premises, and miscellaneous expenses).

9. The operating expenses of the office and the honoraria for manuscripts should be paid from the current funds of the Central Propaganda Department. Each month, a maximum of 600 big foreign dollars will be spent on honoraria (12 titles of 10,000 words each). Together with the expenses of the office, amounting to 200 dollars a month, this makes a total of 800 big foreign dollars a month.

10. Ten thousand copies of each title will be printed at a cost of approximately 100 big foreign dollars. Thus the twelve titles published each month will cost in all 1,200 big foreign dollars. The books can be sold outside [the party] for 5 cents. Thus, if 5,000 copies of each title are sold, we can get back the cost of printing. For each title printed, apart from giving copies to the various party offices, any remaining sums from sales after the cost of printing has been recovered can be used for printing the [*Political*] *Weekly*.

End [of the Report].

Table of Contents of Collected Writings on the National Movement

Subdivision I (Twelve titles, each of a maximum of 12,000 words and a minimum of 8,000 words)

1. *A Brief History of the Chinese Guomindang*, by Wang Jingwei (already exists)
2. Survey of Chinese history during the past century (to be written)
      In this book, attention should be paid to failures in diplomacy and to the development of national thought. It is not appropriate to record nothing but politics so that it reads like a family chronicle.
3. Political issues in nineteenth-century Europe (to be written)
4. The Industrial Revolution (to be written)
5. From primitive communal society to feudal society (to be written)
      There is one book that can serve as a reference here. It was written by a Russian who explained history from a purely materialist point of view. It was originally written as a survey of world history. We could divide it into three volumes and give each a title so that they may be read either together or separately. Or we could add a subtitle: *Survey of World History, Part I.*

6. A brief history of the women's liberation movement (to be written)

> *Women and Socialism*, by the German author Bebel, can serve as a blueprint.[10]

7. A history of the imperialist invasion of China (to be written)
8. "Revolution" (to be translated)

> This is a piece of fiction by the American writer Jack London. Extremely famous.[11]

9. A brief history of the Russian social revolution (to be written)
10. The significance of the great German revolution (to be written)
11. Worldwide peasant movements (I) (to be translated)

> The overall title here is one, but the material is actually divided by country.

12. A complete account of the February 7th Movement (to be written)

Subdivision II

1. The mission of the Chinese Guomindang (to be written)
2. The first decade after the World War (to be written)
3. *Socialism in Relation to Religion and Art* (translation)[12]
4. The First and Second Congresses of the Chinese Guomindang (to be written)
5. From the free citizens of the Middle Ages to the Industrial Revolution (*Survey of World History, Part 2*) (to be written)
6. Turkey's National Revolution (to be written)
7. *The Soviet System* (translation)[13]
8. *The Foreign Relations of Soviet Russia* (translation), by Chicherin, the Russian foreign minister[14]
9. Worldwide peasant movements (II) (to be written)
10. The occupation of the Ruhr and the Dawes Plan (to be written)

---

10. The reference is to *Die Frau und der Sozialismus*, by the Social Democratic leader August Bebel. Published in 1883, this work achieved such popularity that it was reprinted fifty times before the outbreak of the First World War.

11. "Revolution," here called a piece of fiction (*xiaoshuo*), was in fact an essay written in March 1905, and first published in the *Contemporary Review*, No. 93, 1908. In it, Jack London proclaimed the unanimous support of the 7 million American workers for the February 1905 revolution in Russia, and the unity of the revolutionary forces throughout the world.

12. We have not been able to identify this work, of which a Chinese translation apparently already existed.

13. This work, presumably by a Soviet author, has not been identified.

14. Georgii Vasil'evich Chicherin (1872–1936) was Soviet foreign minister from May 1918 until his resignation in June 1930. It is impossible to be certain which of his many articles and speeches Mao proposed to have translated, but the reference may well have been to his report of March 3, 1925, to the Third Session of the Central Executive Committee of the Soviet Union. For the text, which provides an overview of Moscow's relations with all the major countries, including China, see G. V. Chicherin, *Stati i rechi*, pp. 342–69.

11. The revolutionary movement of the blacks (to be written)
12. Before and after the May 30th Massacre (to be written)

Subdivision III

1. *The Ideology of Sun Yatsen*
2. *Marx's Historical Method* (translation)[15]
3. From the beginning of the labor movement to the Russian social revolution (*Survey of World History, Part III*)
4. The international situation after the Washington Conference (to be written)
5. The literature of revolution (to be written)
6. Analysis of the European Security Pact (to be written)
7. *The Concentration of Capital and the Decline of the Middle Class* (translation)[16]
8. Worldwide peasant movements (III)
9. Education in Soviet Russia (to be written)
10. The Red Army (to be written)
11. The Jewish national liberation movement (to be written)
12. The Moroccan War (to be written)

Subdivision IV

1. Nationalism and *Étatisme*[17] (to be written)
2. The Locarno Conference (to be written)
3. The Paris Commune (to be written)
4. The May 1st holiday of the toilers (to be written)
5. *Marx on National Revolutions in the East* (translation). This contains three extremely important articles.[18]
6. The arts in Soviet Russia (to be written)
7. Worldwide peasant movements (IV) (to be written)
8. The Egyptian national liberation movement (to be written)
9. The Syrian War (to be written)
10. The coming great international war (to be written)

This would be a comparative study on the relative strength of the armed forces and the readiness for a new kind of combat of the various

---

15. It has not been possible to identify this work, which may have been either an anthology of Marx's own writings on this theme, or a study by another author.

16. It has not been possible to identify this work, or its author.

17. The Chinese terms are *minzuzhuyi* and *guojiazhuyi*.

18. It is not possible to say which three of Marx's numerous writings on this theme were included in this volume. It may be assumed that his famous article "Revolution in China and in Europe" was one of them. For the full text of this, see Dona Torr (ed.), *Marx on China 1853–1860: Articles from the* New York Daily Tribune.

imperialist countries and the Soviet Union. To be based on an essay by the head of the Russian Military Soviet, Frunze.[19]

11. A History of the defeat of the Hungarian social revolution of 1919 (to be written)
12. The Balkans under reactionary power (to be written)

Subdivision V

1. The Chinese national revolution and the world revolution (to be written)
2. The Shakee Massacre and the Guangzhou-Hong Kong strike (to be written)
3. March 8th, International Women's Day (to be written)
4. War and peace under capitalism (to be written)
5. The Fascists (to be written)
6. The Mexican Revolution (to be written)
7. The Persian problem (to be written)
8. The Mosul oil mines (to be written)
9. International clashes of interest between Great Britain and the United States (to be written)
10. The worldwide women's movement after the Great War (to be written)
11. Recent revolutionary movements in the colonies (to be written)
12. The Disarmament Conference (to be written)

Apart from those on the history of the Guomindang, the remainder of the sixty titles listed above are still to be written or translated. We must now distribute these sixty topics to various people to write about them. There should be about ten people, each of whom will write on six topics, turning in two [manuscripts] a month. Thus, we will be able to publish twelve volumes a month.

P.S. Among the above sixty titles, there is theory and political affairs. In the future there will be history, as well as political reports, and these will gradually go into a subdivision VI, or even a subdivision VII. So after these sixty volumes have been completed, people will still be given the task of writing.

The decisions of the Propaganda Committee of the Propaganda Department regarding the above table of contents, after assessing it, are as follows:

---

19. Mikhail Vasil'evich Frunze (1885–1925), after playing a major role as a commander in the civil war of 1918–1920, took the lead in organizing the Soviet Red Army, and laying down its military doctrine. The essay referred to here is most likely one written in 1921, entitled "On the reorganization of the French Army" (in M. V. Frunze, *Sobraniye sochinenii,* Vol. 1, pp. 228–55). This text lays emphasis on France's progress in military technology, and the implications of these changes for the Soviet Union.

1. The following four topics should be added:
   The Versailles Treaty
   The League of Nations
   The Peasant Movement in China
   The Labor Movement in China

2. The *Brief History of the Chinese Guomindang* and *The Ideology of Sun Yatsen* will be the responsibility of members of the Central Committee. The editors are not to solicit additional manuscripts [on these topics].

3. In principle, each volume will contain a maximum of 12,000 words. Those [topics] that cannot be dealt with in 12,000 words, such as the brief history of China during the past hundred years or the history of the imperialist invasion of China, should be divided into parts I, II, III, and so on.

4. Subdivisions I, II, and so on will not be published separately, nor need the works appear in the order laid down in the original table of contents. We should select those works on the list that are most necessary at present and put them out first, identifying them as No. 1, No. 2, and so on in the *Collected Writings on the National Movement*.

5. A digest of some of the pamphlets compiled, such as the *Brief History of the Chinese Guomindang*, *The History of the Imperialist Invasion of China*, and *The Ideology of Sun Yatsen*, should be translated into English and sent to the overseas Chinese.

XI. *Financial Situation*

1. Shanghai *Guomin ribao*—4,000 big foreign dollars a month. (Payment beginning in May.)

2. Guangzhou *Minguo ribao*—3,000 small foreign dollars a month. (Continuing last year's payments.)

3. Hankou *Chuguang ribao*—800 big foreign dollars a month. (Payment beginning in February.)

4. *Hunan minbao*—600 big foreign dollars a month. (Payment beginning in April.)

5. Shanghai Guomin tongxunshe—800 big foreign dollars a month. (Payment beginning in May.)

6. Honoraria and editorial expenses for *Collected Writings on the National Movement*—800 big foreign dollars a month. (Payment beginning in May.)

7. Printing costs for *Collected Writings on the National Movement*—1,200 big foreign dollars a month. (Payment beginning probably in June; payments will continue only for four months, after which there will be circulating capital.)

8. Expenses for books and periodicals for the reference room of our department—200 big foreign dollars a month. (To be paid as usual after May;

before May, this figure was slightly higher, and was settled separately.)

9. Printing of books for our department—3,000 small foreign dollars a month. (The accounts for the period before May have already been settled separately; this is the figure to be paid from May onwards.)

10. Expenses of the Central Press Agency—660 small foreign dollars a month. (Continuing last year's payments.)

11. Subsidy to the *Jiangsheng ribao* in Jiujiang—100 big foreign dollars a month. (Payment beginning in March.)

The total of the above figures is 8,500 big foreign dollars and 6,660 small foreign dollars.

The First Plenum of the Central Committee following the [Second] Congress decided to allocate 10,800 big foreign dollars to special propaganda expenses (i.e., for the expenses of running party newspapers along the Hong Kong-Shanghai and Hankou-Beijing railroad lines) and 7,000 small foreign dollars for running expenses (including the printing and purchase of books, editorial expenses, the expenses of the Guangzhou *Minguo ribao*, and so on). In reality, we have not spent this much; every month, we have economized 2,300 big foreign dollars and 340 small foreign dollars. If you add to this the fact that the expenses of 1,200 big foreign dollars for printing the *Collected Writings on the National Movement* indicated under point 7, above, have not yet begun to be paid out and will be paid out only after six months, we are currently able to save 3,500 big foreign dollars and 340 small foreign dollars a month.

XII. *Other Items*

The Guangzhou *Minguo ribao* and Zhongyang tongxunshe continue as before, without major changes, so it is pointless to give details.

I now report the statistics regarding documents received, sent out, and dealt with by our department during the past three and a half months, which are as follows:

1. Circulars[20] sent out: 6
2. Documents received: 899
3. Documents sent out: 527

The rapporteur is the acting head of the Propaganda Department, Mao Zedong. May 19, 15th Year of the Chinese Republic.

---

20. *Tonggao*, formal party notices or circulars. The "documents" (*wenjian*) referred to in points 2 and 3 are miscellaneous pieces of paper of all descriptions.

Address to the Ninth Congress of the Agricultural Association of China

(August 14, 1926)[1]

Gentlemen! As you meet in Guangdong, it is most important not to forget the more than 800,000 peasants.[2] Peasants are the foundation of agriculture and the foundation of China! All you gentlemen, as you visit here today, would be well advised to go to the countryside, to go amongst the people, to go directly to guide the peasants, to arouse them from their bad conservative natures, and to effect the fundamental salvation of agriculture. Present here are many graduates of agricultural schools, and not a few who have returned from abroad, but they have all encountered the obstruction of the peasants. In fact, the obstruction they encounter results from their own earlier failure to go and lead the peasants, and so they still haven't achieved much good to this day!

At present, the rural economy is extremely backward and crude, and the lives of the peasants are extremely difficult. For this reason, the problem of the peasants in Guangdong is a problem for all you gentlemen meeting here. The hope for a satisfactory resolution of this problem lies with all of us!

The text of Mao's address was published in *Zhonghua nongxuehui bao* (English title on the cover: "The Journal of Agricultural Association of China"), No. 52, November 1926, pp. 99-100. We have translated it from that source.

1. This congress was held at the Institute of Agriculture of Sun Yatsen University, near Guangzhou. Mao had been invited to attend in his capacity as head of the Peasant Movement Training Institute and made this address on behalf of that institute.

2. This figure almost certainly refers to the number of peasant association members in Guangdong Province, which Mao put at over 600,000 in the Resolution Concerning the Peasant Movement of January 19, 1926, translated above, and which had grown further in the intervening half year. On the other hand, it seems odd that Mao should have called for arousing the peasants from their "bad conservative natures" if he was talking about those who had already become revolutionary activists. Perhaps he was urging his listeners to go out and organize those who had not joined.

The National Revolution and the Peasant Movement

(*Introduction to* Collected Writings on the Peasant Problem)[1]

(September 1, 1926)

The peasant problem is the central problem of the national revolution. If the peasants do not rise up and join and support the national revolution, the national revolution cannot succeed. If we do not speedily create a peasant movement, the peasant problem cannot be solved. If the peasant problem is not properly solved in the context of the present revolutionary movement, the peasants will not support this revolution. Right down to the present day, there are still a number of people, even within the revolutionary party, who do not understand these points. They do not understand that the greatest adversary of revolution in an economically backward semicolony is the feudal-patriarchal class (the landlord class) in the villages. In an economically backward semicolony, the imperialists outside the country, and the ruling class within, rely entirely on the unstinting support that the landlord class gives them in their attempt to carry out the oppression and exploitation of the objects of their oppression and exploitation in that territory, who are primarily the peasants. Otherwise, they would be unable to carry out

This article was published in *Nongmin yundong* (an organ of the Peasant Department of the Guomindang Central Executive Committee), No. 8, September 21, 1926. We have translated it from that version, which is conveniently reprinted in *Mao Zedong ji,* Vol. 1, pp. 175–79.

1. The earliest available text of this essay, published in *Nongmin yundong*, is followed by an editorial note reading as follows: "This is the introduction written by Comrade Mao to *Nongmin wenti congkan* (Collected Writings on the Peasant Problem). We regard this as very relevant to the national revolution, and it is specially included here for the reference of the average comrade working with the peasant movement. As for the content of this series, readers wishing to examine it are invited to purchase copies from the Guoguang Shuju. We add this further introductory comment to the writer's explanatory note." This four-volume series of materials compiled by the Peasant Movement Training Institute was originally for use only within the Institute, and for distribution to peasant movement activists. Information regarding some of the items included is given by Mao in the concluding section of the present article. Regarding the reprinting of this series in the spring of 1927 for a wider public, see below, the letter by Mao published on March 14, 1927, and the notes thereto.

their oppression and exploitation. Consequently, in an economically backward semicolony, the feudal class in the countryside constitutes the only solid basis for the ruling class at home and for imperialism abroad. Unless this basis is shaken, it will be absolutely impossible to shake the superstructure built upon it. The Chinese warlords are merely the chieftains of this rural feudal class. To say that you want to overthrow the warlords but do not want to overthrow the feudal class in the countryside, is quite simply to be unable to distinguish between the trivial and the important, the essential and the secondary. A clear example of this is to be found in Guangdong. Any *xian* in which the local bullies, bad gentry, greedy bureaucrats, and corrupt officials are relatively restrained is most assuredly a *xian* in which the peasant movement has already been established, and in which the peasant masses have joined the peasant associations. In other words, a *xian* in which the power of Chen Jiongming[2] has been diminished is assuredly a *xian* in which the peasants have arisen. We cannot deny the fact that one year ago Guangdong belonged to Chen Jiongming, and not at all to the revolutionary government. For the past year, and down to the present day, the realm of Guangdong has been evenly divided between the revolutionary government and Chen Jiongming, even though Chen Jiongming himself has not been within the borders of Guangdong. The peasants must now gradually continue to rise up in every *xian* of Guangdong; only this will really demonstrate that the power of Chen Jiongming is being gradually reduced in every *xian* of Guangdong. Chen Jiongming's native district of Haifeng *xian* has historically been aswarm with local bullies, bad gentry, greedy bureaucrats, and corrupt officials, but ever since it has had a peasant association of 50,000 families, with 250,000 members, it has been cleaner than any other *xian* in Guangdong.[3] The *xian* magistrate dares not do evil, the tax collectors dare not extort money above the assessment, there are no bandits in the whole *xian*, and the savage oppression of the people by local bullies and evil gentry has virtually stopped altogether. Thus we can see that the form of the Chinese revolution can only be as follows: it does not constitute a base for the imperialists and the warlords, where local bullies, bad gentry, greedy bureaucrats, and corrupt officials keep the peasants down, but rather a base for the revolutionary forces, where the peasants have arisen to keep down the local bullies, bad gentry, greedy bureaucrats, and corrupt officials. The Chinese revolution has only this form and no other. Every place in China must become like Haifeng, for only then can the revolution be considered to have achieved victory. Otherwise, no matter what happens, it cannot be considered a victory. Only when every place throughout China becomes like Haifeng can it be said that the basis of imperialism and the warlords has truly been toppled; otherwise, this will not be the case. Thus we see that what is called the national revolutionary

---

2. Regarding Chen Jiongming, see the note to Mao's editorial of October 20, 1925.

3. Peng Pai had, in fact, begun organizing the peasants of Haifeng as early as 1922. See above, the note to the text of January 1, 1926.

movement is, for the most part, the peasant movement. Thus we see that all those who look down on or even suppress the peasant movement really sympathize with the local bullies, bad gentry, greedy bureaucrats, and corrupt officials, that they really do not want to overthrow the warlords and do not want to oppose imperialism.

There are those who say that the rampant savagery exercized by the comprador class in the cities is altogether comparable to the rampant savagery of the landlord class in the countryside, and that the two should be put on the same plane. It is true that there is rampant savagery, but it is not true to say that it is of the same order. In the whole country, the areas where the comprador class is concentrated include only a certain number of places such as Hong Kong, Guangzhou, Shanghai, Hankou, Tianjin, and Dalian, on the sea coast and the rivers. This is not comparable to the domain of the landlord class, which extends to every province, every *xian*, and every village throughout China. In political terms, the various warlords, big and small, throughout the country are all the chieftains chosen by the landlord class (not including the bankrupt small landlords). This gang of feudal landlord chieftains, that is to say, the feudal warlords, use the comprador class in the cities to dally with the imperialists; both in name and in fact, the warlords are the hosts, and the comprador class are their retainers. Financially, 90 percent of the yearly expenses of several hundred million *yuan* of the warlord governments are extracted directly or indirectly from the peasants, who live under the domination of the landlord class. Comparatively speaking, occurrences such as the granting of a conditional loan to the Beijing government by comprador class elements, such as the Bankers' Association,[4] are in the last analysis very rare. Hence, although we are all aware that the workers, students, and middle and small merchants in the cities should rise and strike fiercely at the comprador class and directly resist imperialism, and although we know that the progressive working class in particular is the leader of all the revolutionary classes, yet if the peasants do not rise and fight in the villages to overthrow the privileges of the feudal-patriarchal landlord class, the power of the warlords and of imperialism can never be hurled down root and branch.

For this reason, in addition to the numerous tasks of our comrades in organizing the workers, the students, and the middle and small merchants, a large number of comrades must immediately summon up their resolve, and go to undertake that grandiose task of organizing the peasants. They must resolve immediately to begin studying the peasant problem. They must resolve immediately to ask the party to order them to go into that countryside with which they may or may not be familiar, in the blazing heat of the summer sun and in

---

4. The reference is presumably to the Chinese Bankers' Association, founded in 1920, which on occasion did indeed impose conditions on the government for the purchase of its bonds.

the bitter cold of the winter snow storms, to grasp the hand of the peasants and ask them about their suffering, to ask them what they want. From their suffering and their needs, they must lead the peasants in organizing; lead them in the struggle against the local bullies and bad gentry; lead them in cooperation with the workers and students and the middle and small merchants in the cities, to establish a united front; lead them to participate in the anti-imperialist, anti-warlord national revolutionary movement. We estimate that if one tenth of the more than 300 million peasant masses in the whole country were to join peasant associations, there would be more than 30 million organized peasants. Especially in the provinces of Hunan, Guangdong, and Jiangxi in the south, of Zhili, Shandong, and Henan in the north, and of Hubei and Anhui in central China, which are of particular importance politically, great efforts must be put into the job of organizing. If the peasants of these several important provinces rise up, it will be easy for the peasants in the rest of the provinces to rise up with them. We must reach this point before the base of the imperialists and the warlords can truly be shaken, before the national revolution can truly be victorious.

Speaking of studying the peasant problem, I feel that there is a very great shortage of materials. Collections of this sort of materials can, of course, only become increasingly abundant as the peasant movement develops. At present, except for Guangdong, the peasant movement has everywhere only just begun, so materials are exceedingly scarce. Here we have collected the few available materials and are printing them in this series so that comrades in the peasant revolution in different places can use them for reference.[5] One part of these is made up of investigations into the situation in the peasant villages of various provinces as carried out by more than 300 students from the Sixth Session of the Peasant Movement Training Institute.[6] These have been discussed in the peasant problem study meetings organized by the students in these respective provinces, and have been examined quite closely before being printed. Most of the students had never before investigated in detail the situation of the peasants and therefore their writings provide only a general overview. However, before this there wasn't even a general overview, and now even this little bit we feel is precious. We should start from this brief overview, and before long, from real investigations of the real work done in different places, we should derive a detailed, concrete nationwide survey. As for materials on the question of agricultural production, this volume includes only five items (nos. 22

---

5. The only edition available to us is that in four volumes published in Shanghai in May 1927 by the Wusan shudian, under the title *Nongmin congkan*. Information given below in the notes about items cited by Mao is based on that source.

6. The Peasant Movement Training Institute in Guangdong was established by the Peasant Department of the Guomindang Central Executive Committee on June 30, 1924, as a training ground for peasant organizers. Mao was in charge of the sixth session, from May 3 to September 11, 1926.

to 26).[7] There is no great shortage of materials on this question, but because there was not enough time to collect and edit them before going to press, they will be published separately at a later date. The peasant problem includes basically two areas of problems, namely, the problems of man-made oppression from the imperialists and warlords, etc., and the problems of oppression from natural events such as flood, drought, and other natural disasters, and from disease, pestilence, poor technology, declining production, etc. The former area of problems is of course the most urgent problem at present, and the attention of comrades is naturally focused here. But the latter area of problems is also extremely severe, and we must actively pay attention to them. Finding a solution to the latter problems requires nationwide revolutionary political power and the scientific method. This is not something that can be accomplished overnight, but that day is indeed fast approaching, and we need to make preparations in anticipation. The five items of materials on Guangdong included here constitute the best section of this volume.[8] They give us a method for our work in the peasant movement. There are a number of people who do not understand how to work in the peasant movement, and they are invited to examine this section with particular care. It also helps us understand the basic nature of the peasant movement in China and makes us realize that the peasant movement in China is a movement of class struggle that combines political and economic struggle. Its peculiarities are manifested especially in the political aspect. In this respect, it is somewhat different in nature from the workers' movement in the cities. At present, the political objectives of the urban working class are merely to seek complete freedom of assembly and of association; this class does not yet seek to destroy immediately the political position of the bourgeoisie. As for the peasants in the countryside, on the other hand, as soon as they rise up, they run into the political

---

7. In the May 1927 edition of *Collected Writings on the Peasant Problem* available to us, the items included are not numbered, either in the text or in the table of contents that appears at the beginning of the first volume. If one counts the main headings in the table of contents, the following sections appear to correspond to the "five items" referred to by Mao: 24, China's main agricultural products; 25, An overview of foreign trade in China's agricultural products; 26, National administrative, experimental, and educational organs with reference to agriculture; 27, The progress of agriculture in various countries and its causes; 28, The problem of China's agricultural production. (These materials appear on pp. 12-134 of Volume IV.) It will be seen that the item numbers are 24-28, rathei than 22-26. The discrepancy no doubt results from the fact that additional materials were included in the compilation between September 1926 and the spring of 1927. The edition available to us contains, in particular, the resolutions of the First Hunan Provincial Peasant Congress of December 1926, though these have been added at the end of Volume IV.

8. The five items relating to Guangdong include, in addition to the resolutions of the Provincial Peasants' Congress and the three reports on Haifeng, Guangning, and Puning mentioned below by Mao, a "General account of the Guangdong peasant movement." They occupy a total of over 300 pages out of the 800 in the four volumes, including the whole of Volume III.

power of those local bullies, bad gentry, and landlords who have been crushing the peasants for several thousand years. (This political power of the landlords is the true foundation of the political power of the warlords.) If they do not overthrow this political power that is crushing them, there can be no place for the peasants. This is a very important peculiarity of the peasant movement in China today. Looking at the process of the peasant movements in different places over the past five years, and reading in this volume the resolutions of the Guangdong Peasant Congress, the report on the Haifeng peasant movement, and the full record from beginning to end of the two peasant rebellions against the landlords in Guangning and in Puning, we can't escape the feeling that the material relating to the foreign nations collected here—though there is a little (items 15 to 18)—is too scanty.[9] There is an abundance of material on the peasant movements and on agricultural economics of various foreign nations, especially Russia. Unfortunately, no one has translated them in detail. In this work, only the article on the Russian peasants and the revolution may be considered to be relatively detailed, making it also very possible for us to use it to make a comparison with the situation in China.

September 1, 1926

---

9. In the edition available to us, sections 17, on the Japanese peasant movement, 18, on the Italian peasant movement, and 19 on the German peasant movement total only 34 pages. There are, however, nearly 100 pages on Soviet Russia, distributed over three sections. Of these, section 11 on the Russian peasants and the revolution is, as Mao says, "relatively detailed," and accounts for 49 pages.

Basic Program of the National Union of
People's Organizations

(October 27, 1926)[1]

Explanation by committee member Xu Qian, who was in attendance

Remarks in brief: At yesterday's plenary session,[2] the present member and others were charged with drafting the current document. Having met in consultation, the present member and others came to the unanimous conclusion that the basic program of the national union is the practical application of the political program of the party. This sort of union is, indeed, the propaganda organ for realizing the political program of the party; therefore, absolutely no clauses whatsoever may be added to its basic program apart from the political program of the party. It is requested that this point be called to everyone's attention. The various points in the current document have been compiled by taking from the party's most recent political program the points having a national scope. Aside from a small degree of consolidation in a few places, in principle there has been no change. The entire text will now be read aloud, along with elucidation of points of discrepancy: (1) In item 3, "assembly" has been written incorrectly as "gathering."[3] (2) In item 4, "state-run" should read "within the nation."[4] (3) Item 9, "modify the land tax" should be combined with item 25, "standardize the land tax to eliminate exorbitant rates," to form a single item. (4) The phrase "Carry

---

Our source for this document is a manuscript copy from the Guomindang archives, obtained through the courtesy of Eugene Wu, Director of the Harvard-Yenching Library.

1. The Chinese text is dated "15th year of the Republic."
2. The reference is to the October 26 meeting of the Joint Session of Guomindang Central Executive Committee Members and of Representatives from Party Councils in the Various Provinces and Districts [*Guomindang zhongyang zhixingweiyuan he ge sheng qu dangbu daibiao lianxi huiyi*]. This gathering had been convened on October 15 to work out new policies in the light of the rapid and victorious advance of the Northern Expedition. Mao was, with Xu Qian, one of the seven people appointed to draft this document. Although the resulting text was called, following a discussion reported below, the program of the "National Union of People's Organizations," it was, in effect, the political program for the Guomindang adopted by the National Joint Session, and is so characterized in the *Nianpu*, Vol. 1, p. 171. The "people" were involved only to the extent that the party was seen as representing them, or perhaps because mass organizations were to be created subsequently.
3. I.e., *jihe* appears instead of *jihui*.
4. I.e., it should read *guonei* instead of *guoli*.

out village self-rule" in item 11 should be listed as item 12, and the phrase "Take practical and planned measures to annihilate bandits" should be listed as item 13. When the reading was finished, it was once again earnestly declared that the most important point of this document is to cause this kind of union to accept the political program of the party and promote its implementation, to achieve the aims of the national revolution. Discussion is requested.

The chairman opens the meeting to discussion (complete text as follows):

The Political Program of the National Union:

1. Achieve national political and economic unification.
2. Eliminate all warlord systems such as the provincial military governor and the commissioner, and establish a democratic government.
3. Guarantee to the people complete freedom of **gathering** (*sic*),[5] freedom of association, freedom of speech, freedom of publication, and so on.
4. All **state-run** (*sic*)[6] national minorities have the right to self-determination.
5. Separate military and civilian authority.
6. Unify national finances.
7. [Establish] tariff autonomy; strive to carry out a protective tariff policy.
8. Eliminate all *lijin* taxes[7] and institute new [forms of] taxation. I.e., eliminate all exorbitant taxes and levies.
9. Reform the land taxation.
10. Establish a uniform currency and uniform standards of weights and measures.
11. Establish a national bank. Develop agricultural, industrial, and commercial enterprise through minimal interest rates. Carry out village self-rule. Take practical and planned measures to annihilate bandits.
12. Build railroads.
13. Construct roads.
14. Regulate rivers and watercourses.
15. Build new ports.
16. Make improvements in irrigation works.
17. Reform the educational system.
18. Designate educational funds.
19. Enforce and make universal compulsory education, and promote vocational education.
20. Promote a literacy campaign among the populace.
21. The government should assist the development of new industries.

---

5. Here and below, what is in boldface represents a character in the original with a dot beside it—indicating the errors pointed out above. In this case, the original reads *jihe* ("gathering") where it should read *jihui* ("assembly").

6. As indicated above, "state-run" (*guoli*) should read "within the nation" (*guonei*).

7. For an earlier discussion by Mao of the road tax on goods called *lijin* (commonly transcribed "likin" in Western sources), and its impact on commerce, see above, his article "The Beijing Coup d'État and the Merchants" of July 11, 1923.

22. Eliminate special privileges for foreign industries in China.
23. The government should ensure transportation safety and protect commercial travel.
24. Reduce by 25 percent the land rental fee for tenant farmers.
25. Standardize the land tax to eliminate exorbitant rates.
26. In times of famine, land rent should be waived.
27. Prohibit the practice of usury. Maximum interest rate is not to exceed an annual rate of 20 percent.
28. The government should help organize and develop the enterprise of reclamation and cultivation of wasteland.
29. The government should adopt measures for famine relief and famine prevention.
30. Monetary and grain taxes are not to be levied in advance.
31. The peasants have the freedom to establish peasant associations.
32. Establish a labor law to guarantee workers the freedom to organize and the freedom to strike and outlaw excessive exploitation by employers. Pay special attention to the protection of women workers and child workers.
33. Abolish the system of contract labor.
34. Restrict work hours to no more than 54 hours per week.
35. Raise and improve the living standards of soldiers.
36. Take measures to have overseas Chinese receive fair treatment in their place of residence.

(Discussion)

1. Gan Naiguang, Yu Shude, Chen Qiyuan, and other comrades suggested that the title "National Union" be changed to "National Union of People's Organizations." (Seconded by more than 10 people.)
2. Comrade Mao Zedong suggested that it be changed to "National Union of Citizens." (Seconded by more than 5 people.)
3. Comrade Ding Jimei suggested that it be changed to "National People's Union." (Seconded by more than 5 people.)

Resolution: Amended as per Comrade Gan's suggestion and passed.

4. Comrades Chen [X], Deng Yingchao,[8] and others suggested that two items under "Treatment of Women" be added. (No objections.)

---

8. Deng Yingchao (1904–1992), alternative name Wenshu, also known as Yihao, was a native of Guangxi. While a student at the First Girls' Normal School in Tianjin, she participated in the May Fourth movement, and joined the Awakening Society, of which Zhou Enlai was one of the organizers. She and Zhou were married in 1925. Deng Yingchao joined the Socialist Youth League in 1924, and the Communist Party, as well as the Guomindang, in 1925. At the Second Congress of the Guomindang in January 1926, she was elected an alternate member of the Central Executive Committee.

5. Comrade Sun Ke[9] suggested that after item 4, an item be added reading "Abolish unequal treaties and conclude new treaties that respect China's sovereignty." (No objections.)

6. Comrade Yu Shude suggested that item 6 be incorporated into item 1 and changed to read "Unify finances and bring about national political and economic unification." (Voted down.)

7. Comrade Xu Qian suggested that item 6 be kept as it stands. (No objections.)

8. Comrade Sun Ke suggested that before item 5 another item be added reading "Strictly punish bribery and corruption, strive to carry out clean government." (No objections.)

9. Comrade Chen Xihao suggested that an item be added reading "Overseas Chinese returning to China and establishing enterprises must be given special protection." (No objections.)

---

9. Sun Ke (1891-1973), *zi* Zhesheng, also known as Sun Fo, a native of Guangdong, was the son of Sun Yatsen. Because of that fact, he occupied various important political and administrative posts under the Guomindang in the mid-1920s.

Remarks at the Joint Session of [Members of] the Guomindang Central [Executive] Committee and of Representatives of Provincial and Local Councils During Discussion of the Question of Levying Monetary and Grain Taxes in Advance

(October 27, 1926)

Record of the Joint Session of the Chinese Guomindang Central [Executive] Committee and of Provincial [Representatives]
Day 11, Session No. 11

Date: October 27, 15th year [of the Republic]
Time: 9:50 A.M.
Presidium: Tan Yankai, Zhang Renjie, Xu Qian, Song Qingling, Wu Yuzhang

Participants:

Twenty-six Central Committee members

Peng Zemin	Wu Yuzhang	Dai Jitao
Zhang Renjie	Mao Zedong	Zhou Tigang
Tan Yankai	Chen Jiayou	Song Ziwen
Gan Naiguang	Xie Jin	Ding Chaowu
Ding Weifen	Chu Minyi	Guo Chuntao
Li Jishen	Sun Ke	Deng Yingchao
Yang Pao'an	Xu Suhun	Yu Shude
Chen Guofu	Deng Zeru	Huang Shi
Song Qingling	Xu Qian	

Fifty-one representatives from various localities

Lin Songyao	Zhen Xiangquan	Gao Jingyu
Hou Shaoqiu	Zhu Qiqing	Zhang Shushi

Our source for this document is a manuscript copy from the Guomindang archives, obtained through the courtesy of Eugene Wu, Director of the Harvard-Yenching Library.

Lin Boqi	Wang Jiheng	He Yanheng
Chen Xihao	Deng Wenhui	Fan Yusui
Liang Liudu	Li Yuejian	Miao Peicheng
Wang Zizhuang	Wang Fu	Han Juemin
Guang Mingfu	Zhou Songfu	Wu Wenxian
Liu Yihua	Gao Shuying	Chen Renyi
Jian Qinshi	Yu Zhuoli	Dong Haiping
Yang Yaokun	Chen Fumu	He Chuqiang
Yun Lin	Wang Buwen	Ding Jimei
Ou Hanying	Chen Hanzi	Jiang Hao
Xuan Zhonghua	Luo Gonghua	Li Yuyao
Zhou Yili	Liu Jiliang	Zhang Suwu
Ta Gegong	Dong Fangcheng	Qu Banghou
Huang Fusheng	Wang Jianhai	Zeng Xianhao
Lai Guohang	Liao Xiwu	Chen Qiyuan

In all, 77 people.

Chairman: Tan Yankai

Recording Secretaries: Zhang Guangzu, Ge Jianshi

11. Comrade Song Ziwen asked: Item 79 contains the stipulation that "monetary and grain taxes are not to be levied in advance," but according to a resolution adopted by the Political Council a month ago, a clear order has already been given to levy in advance one year's worth of money and grain in Guangdong. Whether or not this poses a problem is something the congress[1] should be requested to discuss and explain.

A. Comrade Sun Ke said: The resolution of the Joint Session cannot be abolished, yet the resolution to levy in advance one year's worth of money and grain in Guangdong is also something already decided by the Political Council. I propose that this session resolve that levies in advance will not be permitted in the future, but that what happened in the past may be overlooked.

B. Comrade Jiang Hao proposed: Let us not add any more words [to the resolutions].

C. Comrade Mao Zedong said: The fact that we ourselves have made a decision, and yet we are unable to carry it out, constitutes a very great conflict. Our party's most important policy is the policy towards the peasants. To levy monetary and grain taxes in advance is sure to arouse suspicion on the part of the

---

1. The use of the term *dahui* (congress) reflects the somewhat ambiguous status of this "Joint Session" of central and local party leaders, which was not in fact a congress but had assumed some of the prerogatives of a congress. This issue is discussed at some length below in the text of October 28 on the nature of the Joint Session.

peasants towards our party. It would be more feasible to obtain [revenue] from the wealthy minority through the issuance of bonds.

D. Comrade Song Ziwen said: Guangdong has already issued 15 million *yuan* worth of bonds, so whether or not it can issue more is a question. Levying monetary and grain taxes in advance is surely a bad policy, but during the military period the peasants must necessarily endure a certain amount of hardship. Therefore I agree with Comrade Sun Zhesheng's[2] suggestion.

E. Comrade Chen Qiyuan said: The prohibition against levying monetary and grain taxes in advance is something decided at this meeting; [what happened] in the past naturally poses no problem.

F. Comrade Li Yuyao suggested: What is already being carried out need not be further questioned. From now on [the policy] should be conscientiously carried out.

G.[3] At present, on the one hand we want money, and on the other we want the popular masses; thus there may be a clash. Let me now first ask Comrade Song what the figures are for a year's advance levy of monetary and grain taxes.

H. Comrade Song Ziwen answers: The quota for a year is four million, and what is actually collected is something over three million. In addition, it must be stated that the next three or four months are the most crucial. If a new method is used, I am afraid it would be too slow to save the critical situation. Therefore, since this instance of levying monetary and grain taxes in advance will have occurred before the resolution was taken, would it not be possible to invoke past laws [to justify it]?

I. Comrade Zhou Yili suggested: For such a small gain of only three million *yuan*, instead of using the label levying monetary and grain taxes in advance, it would be better to use the method of issuing bonds.

J. Comrade Zeng Xianhao supported the use of bonds.

K. Comrade Song Ziwen said: It would be best if these one or two [instances] could be accepted; otherwise we will be unable to establish a footing in Guangdong. Soliciting money from the big landlords is of course a good way to do things, but it takes too long and we cannot wait.

L. Comrade Chen Qiyuan said: One is a question of ideals, the other is a question of the reality, and it is not easy to decide at this moment. Let us have the Presidium designate several people to discuss the matter at length with Department Chief Song and report back to the plenary session tomorrow. (Seconded by more than five people.)

Decision: With regard to the matter of levying monetary and grain taxes in advance, the Presidium designates seven people, namely Chen Qiyuan, Gan Naiguang, Sun Ke, Mao Zedong, Zeng Xianhao, Jiang Hao, and Li Yuyao, to confer with Comrade Sung Ziwen and report the results tomorrow (meeting to be held this afternoon at four o'clock at the Central Party Bureau).

---

2. As indicated in a note to the previous text, Zhesheng was the *zi* of Sun Ke, also known as Sun Fo, the son of Sun Yatsen, whose remarks appear in paragraph A, above.

3. The name of the speaker who made this comment is not given in the available text.

[From the minutes of the next day, October 28]

The chairman declares the meeting in session according to the agenda for the day.

1. Discussion on the report of the committee on levying monetary and grain taxes in advance.

The chairman called for discussion of the committee's report (basically the same as the written report, appended here).

Brief remarks: At the request of yesterday's plenary session, a meeting was held at 4 P.M. to discuss the matter of levying monetary and grain taxes in advance in Guangdong. Present were the following seven people: Song Ziwen, Chen Qiyuan, Mao Zedong, Gan Naiguang, Zeng Xuanhao, Jiang Hao, and Li Yuyao. Comrade Song Ziwen began with a report on the difficult financial situation, in which only by raising three or four million within the next three months can we get by. The order to levy monetary and grain taxes in advance was issued much earlier, based on a resolution of the Political Council. To revoke the previous order and instead issue bonds would involve procedures much too cumbersome and would truly be too slow to save the critical situation. Moreover, bonds have already been issued twice and cannot be issued again. The burden on the city of Guangzhou is already rather heavy and cannot be increased. Comrade Mao advocated that within the Western calendar year, monetary and grain taxes not be levied in advance, and that the Finance Department's order not be revoked either, but that the time limit be simply extended for two months to begin on the first day of the first month of next year, to conform to the idea that taxes not be levied again within the year.[4] Comrade Zeng and others advocated that short-term bonds be issued based on next year's monetary and grain revenue and sold to merchants and peasants or sold diligently by the party bureau. Comrade Li Yuyao advocated levying monetary and grain taxes in advance in the name of issuing bonds. Comrade Gan said that if the program of peasant political power were to oppose the levying of monetary and grain taxes in advance, the future would be gravely endangered. Moreover, the bad gentry of the Chen[5] faction and the militia and local bandits could make use of precisely this to incite the peasants to rise up in opposition, which would be very bad. The discussion lasted for a long while, but no appropriate method for getting money was devised. The conclusion was to follow the principle of prohibiting the levying of two years' worth of monetary and grain taxes within one year, excepting the money and grain that has already been collected this year, and not beginning to collect next year's taxes until the first day of the first month of next year.

---

4. The text here reads simply *mingnian yiyue yiri* (the first day of the first month of next year). This would involve extending the time limit by two months only if "the first month" is understood to refer to the Chinese New Year, in mid-February of the Western calendar.

5. Chen Jiongming.

However, Department Chief Song reported that the financial situation for the two [remaining] months of this year is extremely difficult, and collection in advance is a necessity. He requested that the plenary meeting discuss the question of whether there is in fact some good way to remedy the situation.

(Discussion)

1. Comrade Song Ziwen said: This matter is of great importance and the need for money is also urgent. Perhaps it would be too difficult for the plenary meeting in great haste to come up with a good way out. The matter of levying monetary and grain taxes in advance was decided by the Political Bureau several weeks before the present meeting began, and an order was issued to handle it. The present member proposes that the plenary session be requested to hand back the matter to the Political Council for an appropriate solution.

2. Comrade Xu Qian said: The plenary meeting's resolution against levying monetary and grain taxes in advance refers to not taxing in advance from now on. As for the fact that before this meeting the national government already issued an order to levy in advance, it seems that this meeting's resolution can be deemed irrelevant to it and not to interfere with it. As for the discussion of the committee members and Comrade Song, and their suggestion to begin collecting from the first day of the first month of next year, this amounts to levying monetary and grain taxes in advance. Rather than revoking our own resolution without dissenting opinions, it would be better not to question what has already happened in the past and concentrate on taking strict preventive measures for the future.

3. Comrade Jiang Hao said: The popular masses do not interpret laws in the same way we do but are concerned only with the facts. If we pass a resolution against levying monetary and grain taxes in advance, and at the same time there is an order to levy monetary and grain taxes in advance, will not the people be even more suspicious of our policies?

4. Comrade Mao Zedong said: According to what Department Chief Song said yesterday, what may be obtained from levying monetary and grain taxes in advance is a mere two or three million *yuan*. For such a meager sum, is it worth having the tens of millions of peasants, or the majority of the people, doubt that our resolutions can be carried out? This member holds to his previous proposal that three million in substantial bonds be issued and [money] be collected from wealthy merchants.

5. Comrade Song Ziwen said: Bonds have already been issued [once] and would probably be too slow [a way] to save the situation. This member proposes that this matter be handed back to the Political Council for an appropriate solution.

The chairman declares: To be handled according to Comrade Song's proposal. (No dissenting opinions.)

(Note:) There was much discussion of this matter, basically the same as the above written account, so it is omitted here.

Statements During a Discussion of the Nature of the Joint Session of [Members of] the Guomindang Central Executive Committee and of Representatives of Provincial [and Local] Councils[1]

(October 28, 1926)

Record of the Joint Session of the Chinese Guomindang Central [Executive Committee] and of Provincial [Representatives]

Day 12, Session No. 12
Date: October 28, Fifteenth Year [of the Republic of China]
Time: 9:50 A.M.
Presidium: Tan Yankai, Zhang Renjie, Xu Qian, Wu Yuzhang

Participants:

Twenty-two Central Committee members:

Ding Chaowu	Wu Yuzhang	Yu Shuda
Zhou Tigang	Chen Jiayou	Jing Hengyi
Zhang Renjie	Chu Minyi	Yun Daiying
Peng Zemin	Song Ziwen	Gan Naiguang
Xu Qian	Zhu Jixun	Yang Pao'an
Deng Yingchao	Huang Shi	Sun Ke
Guo Chuntao	Xu Suhun	Li Jishen

Fifty delegates from various localities:

Zhu Jixun	Dong Haiping	He Yanheng
Hou Shaoqiu	Zhang Shushi	Lin Songyao

Our source for this document is a manuscript copy from the Guomindang archives, obtained through the courtesy of Eugene Wu, Director of the Harvard-Yenching Library.

1. On the nature of this gathering, see above, the note to the "Basic Program of the National Union of People's Organizations" of October 27, 1926. It is not clear why Mao is not listed among the Central Committee members, although he was present and spoke. There may have been a copyist's error, or he may have arrived late.

Zhen Xiangquan	Ding Jimei	Xuan Zhonghua
Wang Fu	Chen Renyi	Han Juemin
Deng Wenhui	Wang Jiheng	Liu Jiliang
Luo Gonghua	Chen Xihao	Gao Shuying
Fan Yusui	Wang Zizhuang	Miao Peicheng
Liao Xiwu	Yu Zhuoli	Guang Mingfu
Zhou Songfu	He Chuqiang	Yun Lin
Liang Liudu	Li Yuyao	Zhou Yili
Liu Yihua	Zhang Suwu	Jiang Hao
Yang Yaokun	Chen Hanzi	Wang Jianhai
Lin Boqi	Huang Fusheng	Lai Guohang
Ding Weifen	Li Yuejian	Wang Buwen
Ta Gegong	Qu Banghou	Jian Qinshi
Ou Hanying	Wu Wenxian	Dong Fangcheng
Gao Jingyu	Chen Qiyuan	

In all, 72 people.

Chairman: Wu Yuzhang

Recording secretaries: Ge Jianshi, Zhang Guangzu

The chairman respectfully reads the Director General's testament[2]—everyone stands in silence.

The chairman announces: The Association of Overseas Comrades from Chaozhou has sent a telegram requesting that Chairman Wang[3] abandon his leave (the text of the telegram is as follows):

> For the inspection of the Joint Session, in care of the Overseas Office of the Central Party Office: Chairman Wang, the linchpin of the party and the government, went on leave for reasons of illness, and there is on file a request made previously by our humble association that he abandon his leave. Now we are delighted to hear that the gentleman[4] has done so. At the present moment,

---

2. The words *zongli* (Director General) are preceded by a space—the equivalent of raising them to the top of the next line as a sign of respect.

3. Wang Jingwei, the former chairman of the national government in Guangzhou and of the Guomindang Central Executive Committee, had resigned from both these offices in April 1926 in the context of Chiang Kaishek's campaign against the left in the aftermath of the March 20 coup. In May, he had traveled to France "for a rest," and he was still there at this time. One of the themes of the Joint Session was the promotion of a "Welcome Wang" movement, but despite this encouragement Wang Jingwei did not return to China until April 1927, on the eve of Chiang Kaishek's final break with the Communists.

4. Once again, the character *shi* is preceded by a space to indicate respect.

with the victory of the Northern Expedition and rapidly changing circumstances, the central organs[5] are eagerly awaiting his return to take charge. We therefore appeal to you once again to transmit to him the request to abandon his leave immediately and come forward to assume responsibility in the present difficult. circumstances, for the great good fortune of the party and the state. The Association of Overseas Comrades from Chaozhou bows respectfully to you. [Seal].

. . .[6]

Report by Comrade Ding Weifen: The present Joint Session has been specially convened. In the last analysis and in terms of our party's general statutes, are its status and powers equivalent to those of a national congress? This delegate ventures to make a concise statement to the effect that they are absolutely not equivalent, that [this joint session] is subordinated to the national congress, and its status is equivalent to that of the Central Executive Committee. This meeting is, in fact, an enlarged session of the Central Executive Committee, and its status is therefore similar to that of the Central Executive Committee. Its powers are naturally similar to, and cannot exceed those, of that body. This proves that the Joint Session has no power to change or overturn the decisions of the Central Executive Committee. If any such errors were to take place, they would be in violation of the general statutes, and whatever violates the general statutes is null and void. This delegate, having perceived this point, has especially made this report and requests all delegates, especially the presidium, to take note of it.

Comrade Zhang Shushi says: The intent of Comrade Ding's statement is hard to grasp. Is it to overturn the decisions of this Joint Session? I ask him to reply.

Comrade Ding Weifen replies: In a word, the Joint Session has no power to overturn the decisions of the Central Executive Committee.

Comrade Zhang Shushi says: With reference to what Comrade Ding has just said, which article of the general statutes is he referring to? Would he please read it.

Comrade Ding Weifen replies: It is article 28 of the general statutes, "the

---

5. I.e., the central organs of the Guomindang and of the national government, both of which Wang had formerly headed.

6. A passage in the minutes relating to minor changes in the record of the previous day's proceedings is here omitted.

system." (He reads the text of this article.)[7] Moreover, in the light of this article, can the status and powers of our Joint Session really be placed above those of the Central Executive Committee and on the same level as those of a national congress?

Comrade Jiang Hao says: The present session has already been going on for twelve days, and today is the last day. Hitherto, Comrade Ding has never made any such remarks. Today, he suddenly raises this question. This is truly strange. Is it because in yesterday's discussion of the resolution on levying monetary and grain taxes in advance our session discussed overturning a resolution of the Central Executive Committee? If that is the case, he is quite simply bent on overturning completely the decision of the Joint Session.

Comrade Fan Yusui says: The Joint Session can overturn the decisions of the Central Executive Committee. Its powers are naturally superior to those of the Central Executive Committee. Otherwise, the action of the Central Executive Committee in summoning this Joint Session would have been meaningless and superfluous.

Comrade Tan Yankai says: The status and powers of this gathering have already been solemnly proclaimed by the Presidium at the opening session. There is no need to discuss the matter further.

Comrade Zhu Jixun says: Amending the political program is the official prerogative of the national congress. For our session to amend the statutes today seems inappropriate. After the resolution is adopted, it should be proclaimed that because circumstances have suddenly arisen which do not permit the convening of a national congress, the Joint Session will remit the resolution to the Third National Congress for confirmation.

Comrade Xu Qian says: In the future, the political program as revised by the present session will have to be reported to the Third National Congress. If there is anything inappropriate, it can be changed by the Third National Congress.

---

7. Article 28 of the general statutes [*zongzhang*] of the Guomindang, as adopted at the First Congress, stipulates: The functions and powers of the National Congress shall be as follows:

A. To receive and adopt the reports of the Central Executive Committee and of the various central departments
B. To revise the political program and the statutes of our party
C. To decide on the policies and tactics to be adopted by our party in dealing with current problems
D. To elect full and alternate members of the Central Executive Committee and of the Central Supervisory Committee

The statutes were revised at the Second Congress, but no changes were made in this article.

Comrade Zhang Shushi says: If there is evidence for what Comrade Ding has said, let it be put forward so it can be discussed.

Comrade Li Yuyao says: At the first discussion meeting, Comrade Ding was the chairman, and already on that occasion he explained with the utmost clarity that the Joint Session was an enlarged meeting of the Central [Executive Committee]. Today, when we are about to close the meeting, he suddenly says, what is the status and what are the powers [of the Joint Session]. What, in the last analysis, is his intention? It truly leaves people confused.

Comrade Chen Qiyuan says: The position of the Joint Session is between that of a congress and of the Central Executive Committee. Naturally, it is not equivalent either to a congress or to the Central Executive Committee. I don't know whether the political program we have adopted will be promulgated or not. If it can be promulgated, then as for which is the higher organ, [our Joint Session] is naturally a bit broader than the Central Executive Committee.

Comrade Jiang Hao says: What Comrade Ding says about status and powers simply poses no problem. At present, the military situation at the front is urgent. If I may speak frankly, we in the rear should do whatever must be done and dispense with empty talk.

Comrade Mao Zedong says: At the opening session, Chairman Tan spoke very clearly about the nature of the Joint Session.[8] Today, Comrade Ding has suddenly raised doubts. This is truly a strange affair. As Comrades Xu Qian and Zhu Jixun have just said, the resolutions of the Joint Session will, in any case, be submitted to the Third National Congress for approval. Now, whether the resolutions of our Joint Session have, in fact, any force or not is a very important question. This delegate holds that whether the powers of the Joint Session exceed those of the Central [Executive Committee] or not is a legal question. Since the Joint Session has been convened by the Central, if there is any error the Central itself should be censored by the Third Congress. The foreign newspapers say that this Joint Session of ours is an extraordinary meeting to deal with extraordinary

---

8. On this occasion, Tan Yankai had declared that, in the light of the victories already obtained by the Northern Expedition: "[W]e must have new methods for responding to the situation. Consequently, after discussion by the Standing Committee of the Central Committee and the Political Council, it was held that a national congress should be convened to decide on a new orientation [*fangzhen*], but for the time being it was not convenient to do so. If a plenum of the Central Committee were convened, there would not be many people present, so all provinces would be invited to send people to participate, and they would all meet and hold a discussion. . . . At this meeting, all participants have the right to vote on resolutions." (See *Nianpu*, Vol. 1, p. 172.)

circumstances. If you say the Joint Session has no standing, what about the fact that Central summoned this meeting? The action taken today in revising the resolutions of the First and Second Congresses displays powers that in fact go beyond those of a national congress. In my view, all the resolutions of the Joint Session are completely valid and can no longer be modified.

Comrade Xu Qian says: The convocation of the Joint Session was decided by the Central [Executive Committee]. Comrade Ding participated in earlier discussions by the Political Council and the Standing Committee, and has moreover participated in the Joint Session for twelve days already. Why did Comrade Ding not express his doubts at the time, but put them forward only today at the closing session? The Joint Session has no responsibility whatsoever to the Third National Congress. In accordance with article 28 of the general statutes, it is the Central Executive Committee which bears full responsibility toward the Third National Congress. Whether in future the Third National Congress accepts, modifies, or rejects the resolutions of the Joint Session is entirely a matter for which the Central Executive Committee is responsible and need not be discussed any further.

Comrade Han Juemin says: The Central [Executive Committee] has collected a number of unresolved matters and proceded to convene the Joint Session. After this Joint Session has resolved them, it is necessary to hand all these matters over to the Third National Congress for adoption. On this occasion, delegates from various localities have travelled thousands of *li* to Guangdong, at considerable expense to Central, and spent more than ten days discussing these unresolved matters, and yet in the end, the effectiveness of all this has been equal to zero. Has it not all been a dream?

Comrade Ding Jimei says: If the question of whether or not the resolutions of this Joint Session are, in the last analysis, valid or not is not resolved, will this meeting not have been in vain?

Comrade Chen Xihao says: I ask Comrade Ding whether, in the end, he is prepared to put forward a single fact by way of evidence, so we can have a really good discussion.

The chairman declares: The discussion is at an end. I would add that, since the validity of the resolutions of the Joint Session has now been called into question by Comrade Ding's questions about the status and validity of the Joint Session, there must be a way to resolve [this issue]. This delegate proposes a form of words along the lines: "The resolutions of the Joint Session must now be fully applied. Only the Third National Congress will have the right to amend them." What do all of you think about using the method of a resolution to guarantee the resolutions of this Joint Session?

Decision: A resolution as proposed by the chairman is adopted.

The chairman reports: The Presidium proposes that since the present Joint Session has already been extended for two days, if there are any resolutions that have not been dealt with today, they should be handed over by this Joint Session to the Central Executive Committee for deliberation, and there will be no further prolongation of this meeting. (There are no dissenting opinions.)

Resolution on the Problem of Mintuan[1]

(October 28, 1926)

. . .

III. Gan Naiguang and others put forward a draft resolution regarding the problem of the *mintuan* (the original text was as follows):

Organizations such as the militia, the civil defense bureau, and the security bureau, which have existed in the past, are all, in reality, the military forces of the village bullies, bad gentry, and lawless landlords.[2] Such forces have often been used by the imperialists, the warlords, and the reactionaries to sabotage the peasant movement and shake the foundations of our party and of the national government. The danger [they pose] to the future of the party and the government is truly acute. For the sake of warding off this danger, the session resolves as follows:

1. The heads of the militia, the civil defense bureau, or the security bureau must be elected at meetings of the township population. Bad gentry are forbidden to deal with this matter themselves.
2. The soldiers of the militia, the civil defense bureau, or the security bureau must be made up of peasants with an occupation in the township in question.
3. People will be sent from the party office to carry out political training in the militia, the civil defense bureau, or the security bureau.
4. The sole task of the militia, the civil defense bureau, or the security bureau will be defense against bandits and against conflicts among bandit troops; apart from this, they will have no right to kill anyone arbitrarily.

Our source for this document is a manuscript copy from the Guomindang archives, obtained through the courtesy of Eugene Wu, Director of the Harvard-Yenching Library.

1. On October 25, the joint session had rejected a resolution put forward by delegates from Hunan and elsewhere calling for the dissolution of the *mintuan* or landlord-controlled militia. Mao, who had supported that proposal, was one of thirty sponsors of the present resolution, which was passed on October 28.

2. As indicated in the text, *mintuan* (literally "civil corps," commonly translated "militia"), *tuanfangju* ("civil defense bureau"), and *baoweiju* ("security bureau") were different names employed for local armed forces at the disposal of the landlords to enforce their demands on the peasants.

5. The militia, the civil defense bureau, or the security bureau are not allowed to receive and act on civil and criminal complaints.
6. Apart from what is approved by the meeting of the people of the township for the expenses of the militia, the civil defense bureau, or the security bureau, pretexts must not be devised to take other amounts without authority.
7. The expenditures of the militia, the civil defense bureau, or the security bureau must be determined in accordance with an openly published budget.
8. In localities where there is already a peasant self-defense army, no militia, civil defense bureau, or security bureau may be created anew.
9. Any militia, civil defense bureau, or security bureau that molests or kills the peasants must be dissolved and put down by the government.

The chairman calls for discussion.

(Discussion)

1. Comrade Zhang Shushi proposes: The principle having been established, the original resolution can be adopted.

(There are no dissenting opinions.)

The chairman declares: Since there are no dissenting opinions, we will deal with the matter in accordance with Comrade Zhang's proposal.

Plan for the Current Peasant Movement

Resolution of the Central Bureau

(November 15, 1926)

Since the establishment of the Central Commission on the Peasant Movement by resolution of the Enlarged Meeting of the Central Executive Committee last year,[1] its organization has developed slowly and has not yet been perfected because of various difficulties. Only after Comrade Mao assumed the position of secretary of the Central Commission on the Peasant Movement in November was it formally decided that seven people—Ruan, Peng, Yi, Lu, Xiao, and C.Y.—will together form the Central Commission on the Peasant Movement, with one of the members always present in the bureau to take care of things.[2] An office has also been set up in Hankou to facilitate guidance of the peasant movement in Hunan, Hubei, Henan, Jiangxi, and Sichuan, and a plan for the current peasant movement has been drawn up, as follows:

1. An order of priority for the development of the peasant movement in various areas should be established on the basis of the following criteria:

    a. Areas where there is relatively more freedom of assembly and freedom to form associations

---

Our source for this document is *Mao Zedong ji. Bujuan*, Vol. 2, pp. 187–89. The Japanese editors have taken the text from a documentary collection published in 1981: *Zhonggong zhongyang zhengzhi baogao xuanji (1921–1926)*. The resolution also appears in *Zhonggong zhongyang wenjian xuanji*, Vol. 2 (1926), pp. 461–63, where it has been reproduced from a mimeographed document in the Party Archives. This latter version does not include the introductory note which appears at the beginning of our translation, but is otherwise the same.

1. The reference is to the Second Enlarged Session of the Central Executive Committee of the Chinese Communist Party in October 1925. In addition to the Commission on the Peasant Movement mentioned here, commissions on the workers' movement and on military affairs were also established on this occasion, but particular emphasis was placed on agrarian problems. An "Address to the Peasants" was adopted in which for the first time the Party called explicitly for a policy of "land to the tiller." See above, the Introduction to Volume II. A partial English translation of the "Address to the Peasantry" can be found in Saich, *Rise to Power*, Document B.13, pp. 163–66.

2. This list in fact includes only five names. The sixth person, designated by the initials C.Y., was the secretary of the Communist Youth League, whoever he might be. The seventh was presumably Mao himself, as secretary of the commission.

    b. Areas that occupy an important political position

    c. Areas along railways and rivers that are easily accessible

    d. Areas where peasants suffer particular economic deprivation and where uprisings have already occurred or are easy to instigate

2. Under current circumstances, the principle of concentration should be adopted in developing the peasant movement. In the country as a whole, in addition to Guangdong, development should be concentrated in the four provinces of Hunan, Hubei, Jiangxi, and Henan. Next, substantial efforts should be made in the seven provinces of Shaanxi, Sichuan, Guangxi, Fujian, Anhui, Jiangsu, and Zhejiang.

3. The principle of concentration should also be adopted within each province. For example:

Hunan—We should concentrate on the areas within the prefectures of Changsha, Yuezhou, Changde, Hengzhou, and Baoqing.

Hubei—We should concentrate on the *xian* along the [Yangzi] River and the railways, particularly the three *xian* of Wuchang, Hanyang, and Xiakou.

Jiangxi—We should concentrate on the band of territory that extends from Ji'an through Nanchang to Jiujiang.

Henan—We should concentrate on the areas along the three railway arteries of Beijing-Hankou, Shaanxi-Haizhou,[3] and Daokou-Qinghua.[4]

Shaanxi—Concentrate on the Central Shaanxi plain, that is, the *xian* along the Wei River.

Sichuan—Treat Chongqing and Chengdu as the two centers; their neighboring *xian* should also be emphasized.

Guangxi—Concentrate on the band of territory that extends from Baise through Nanning to Wuzhou. At the moment, we should pay special attention to linking Enlong, Fengyi, Enyang, Baise, and other *xian* under the power of Fan Shisheng to Donglan *xian*, where [the peasant movement] is already developed.

Yunnan—Treat Kunming as the center, and concentrate on the areas along the Yunnan-Guangzhou Railway.

Fujian—Treat Yongding as the center, and concentrate on the *xian* in southern Fujian.

Zhejiang—Concentrate on the areas within the jurisdictions of Ningpo and Shaoxing.

---

3. This railroad ran across Henan from west to east, through Luoyang, Zhengzhou, and Kaifeng, to the Yellow Sea. Mao refers to it by its abbreviated name of Longhai, in which "Long" stands for Shaanxi Province, and "hai" for the eastern terminus at Haizhou (now called Lianyungang) in northern Jiangsu. In 1926 portions of the line had not yet been completed, but the name Longhai was already in use.

4. This rather short rail line ran across the northern tip of Henan between Daokou in the east (now called Huaxian) and Qinghua (now called Boai) in the west.

Jiangsu—Concentrate on *xian* such as Chongming, Jiangyin, Danyang, Wuxi, Taixing, Tongshan, and Suining.

Shandong—Concentrate on the areas along the Jiaozhou-Jinan[5] and and Tianjin-Pukou[6] railways.

Anhui—Concentrate on northern Anhui; treat Shou *xian* and Hefei as the center.

Zhili [Hebei]—Concentrate on the areas along the Beijing-Hankou, Beijing-Suiyuan,[7] Beijing-Fengtian,[8] and Tianjin-Pukou railways.

Zhili and the special capital district should be divided into two areas for the peasant movement. Within the Guomindang system, the peasant movement in Zhili is under the jurisdiction of the Guomindang party organization of Zhili Province, with Tianjin as the center. The peasant movement in the capital district should be under the jurisdiction of the special municipal party organization of Beijing, with the immediate suburbs of Beijing as the center.

4. Peasants in the immediate suburbs of provincial capitals and other key cities must be specially organized into "peasant associations of the immediate suburbs." The Guomindang party organizations or special municipal party organizations in such cities must set up peasant departments to guide the peasant movement in the immediate suburbs.

5. [We] must cooperate closely with the left wing of the Guomindang in [organizing] the peasant movement in all areas and also encourage the Peasant Department of the Guomindang Central Committee to establish an office in Wuhan.

6. Set up a peasant movement training institute in Wuchang.

---

5. This line ran from Qingdao and Jiaozhou (now Jiaoxian) in the east to the provincial capital of Jinan in the west.

6. Until the building of the bridge over the Yangzi in the 1950s, Pukou, on the north bank of the river opposite Nanjing, was the southern terminus of the railway line from Tianjin.

7. The reference is to the line leading westward to Zhangjiakou, and thence to Baotou in Suiyuan Province (now the Inner Mongolian Autonomous Region).

8. The line leading to the three Northeastern Provinces.

The Bitter Sufferings of the Peasants in Jiangsu and Zhejiang, and Their Movements of Resistance

(November 25, 1926)

In China, the two provinces of Jiangsu and Zhejiang are especially advanced in industry and commerce, and for this reason it is easy for people to recognize the importance of workers and merchants there. But few recognize the importance of the peasants of these two provinces, and most people believe that since these two provinces are peaceful and prosperous the peasants do not suffer much. In fact, such a view is totally superficial and shows no understanding whatsoever of the actual conditions in the peasant villages of Jiangsu and Zhejiang. We carried out an investigation into the actual conditions in the peasant villages in Jiangsu and Zhejiang and discovered that the real situation is completely the opposite of what had been conjectured. The following description of the concrete facts in various *xian* constitutes only a very small portion of the materials we have recently gathered, but it is sufficient to prove that the peasantry of Jiangsu and Zhejiang is certainly not as stable and prosperous and free from suffering as most people imagine.

Chongming

An island at the mouth of the Yangzi River, of which the entire territory belongs to Chongming *xian*. It has been formed by the accumulated sedimentation of the sand and silt carried by the Yangzi River. Every four years, flooding brings new sand deposits, thus a great many of its fields are tidal lands, and a great many of its peasants are tenants. Take one place, Shangsha, as an example. Here the exploitation of the tenant farmers by the landlords is exceptionally severe. For every 1,000 *bu*[1] of fields a guarantee deposit of 50 *yuan* must be paid. These fields are entirely of newly deposited sand. The peasant takes care of the fields

---

This article was originally published in *Xiangdao*, No. 179, November 25, 1926. (The date on the title page of this issue is October 25, 1926, but this is a typographical error.) Our translation has been made from this source, as reproduced in *Mao Zedong ji,* Vol. 1, pp. 181–85.

1. A unit of area six *chi* or Chinese feet square. Since the Chinese foot corresponds to 14.1 English inches, or .3581 meters, this amounts to 2.15 x 2.15 meters, or an area of approximately 4.6 square meters. A field of 1,000 *bu* would therefore contain 4,600 square meters, or slightly under one-half a hectare.

for the landlord and gradually makes them mature for farming. After they become mature, the landlord owns the field and the peasant has the right to farm it. The peasant has to provide all of the manpower, fertilizer, farm tools, and seed for the planting each year. Each year after the autumn harvest, for each 1,000 *bu* of fields the rent in grain is 500 *jin* or more. When the landlord visits a peasant's home, the peasant must treat him to good food and wine—otherwise his rent is likely to go up. The scales for weighing the harvest rent are probably all set at over 20 *liang*.[2] If the peasant objects in the slightest, he is immediately sent to the *xian* magistrate. If the peasant has a debt of five *yuan* one year he must repay it with ten or twenty *yuan* the next year, and he must pay it no matter what. Thus every year there are peasants who go bankrupt. In 1922 there was a peasant revolt in this area, although there was no Red or extremist party at all to incite the peasants to action. They rose up themselves in great numbers, demolished the police station, and cut off the ear of a landlord named Tao. They also staged a demonstration at the *xian* magistrate's office demanding a reduction in rents. But they failed in the end because they were not solidly united and the leader was arrested. This year Jiangsu Province suffered widespread drought and the fields yielded a reduced harvest. In the area of Shangsha, for each 1,000 *bu* of fields, the peasants harvested only 300 or 400 *jin* of grain, but the landlords insisted on demanding rents on the old basis of 500 *jin*. The landlords used a "resolution of the Tenancy Maintenance Association" to cheat the peasants (the Tenancy Maintenance Association was organized by the landlords in 1922 to cheat the peasants), whereupon the peasants, in their increasing hatred for the landlords, again rose up in revolt.

Jiangyin

If you take a steamship up the river from Wuxi,[3] you arrive at place called Gushan market town, which lies between the *xian* Jiangyin, Changshu, and Wuxi. In these three *xian* there are many big landlords who oppress the tenant farmers very severely. In the autumn of last year, a native of Gushan who had studied in Japan, Zhou Shuiping (a graduate of Wuxi Normal School), returned to his native village. He could not bear the sight [of such oppression], and urged the tenant farmers to form an organization called the "Tenant Families Cooperative Self-Help Society." Zhou went from village to village, speaking with tears in his eyes of the sufferings of the peasants. The peasants of Gushan followed him in great numbers, and in all the border areas adjoining Jiangyin, Changshu, and Wuxi *xian* the peasants were aroused. They rose like clouds to oppose the rich but heartless bad gentry and big landlords, demanding in unison a reduction in rents. But before the peasants had united completely, the bad gentry and land-

2. I.e., at 20 *liang* (or ounces) per *jin* (or catty), instead of the standard proportion of 16.
3. Jiangyin is a village north of Wuxi.

lords had long since united, and the gentry and landlords of the three *xian* of Jiangyin, Changshu, and Wuxi acted simultaneously. Letters and telegrams rained down on Sun Chuanfang, and since he has never been known not to heed the voices of the bad gentry and the landlords, Sun dissolved the Tenant Families Cooperative Self-Help Society in November of last year, had Zhou Shuiping arrested, and had Zhou executed in January of this year. Thus the movement to reduce rents was put down for a time. But when Zhou Shuiping's casket was returned to Gushan and laid out in his house, the peasants came every day in great flocks to kowtow before his coffin, saying: "Mr. Zhou died for us. We will avenge him!" This year there was a big drought and the harvest was poor; the peasants once again thought of rising up to demand rent reduction. This shows that they do not in the least fear death, and that they know the only way to reduce the exploitation of the greedy and cruel landlords is through collective struggle. Again, in the eastern part of Jiangyin county there is a place called Shazhou where there was also an incident of peasant opposition to the landlords. Here it is the cruel practice of the landlords to collect the rent in advance; the people of Jiangsu call this "paying before planting," and it is a great financial hardship for the peasants. The peasants there are in the midst of a struggle to have rents paid only after the harvest.

Danyang

Here we'll tell the story of two incidents that took place in Lüchengzhen of Danyang *xian* (this Lüchengzhen is in eastern Danyang, near the Shanghai-Nanjing railroad). The first action was against a pawnshop that cheated the peasants. It took place this year in the summer. One day a pawnshop in Lüchengzhen was robbed by bandits, the remnants of a contingent of Ma Yüren's troops who came down from Mao Mountain in the western part of the *xian*. They didn't take much. The pawnshop owner made a big fuss in reporting the loss, saying that all of the pawned clothing had been stolen. In fact, secretly by night, he had hidden the clothing somewhere else. The owners of this pawned clothing were peasants from various villages near the town. Hearing what was happening, they intercepted him en route and got back a portion of their goods, but were unable to recover what had already been moved into hiding. The peasants who had pawned their things rose up and organized an "Association of Pawnshop Customers," which presented a bill to the pawnshop in Lüchengzhen. Consequently, the pawnshop had to make restitution for that part of the value lost, i.e., each person was compensated for the pawn value of his goods, a total compensation of 900 *yuan*. This incident proves that when the peasants unite they can achieve victory. If at this time they had not united they would have let this weasel of a pawnshop merchant cheat them out of everything they had pawned. The other action was against the bad gentry and rich peasants forcing the peasants to pay for pumped irrigation water. This incident took place in the summer and autumn of this year and has not been resolved to this day. On the rivers of all the rural *xian* of Jiangsu, a kind of mechanical water scoop called a "water scooping machine" is in widespread use today. It replaces the old method of pumping water using a hand or foot operated water mill. The peasants from several of the villages in the vicinity of Lüchengzhen thought that they would like to use a machine to pump the water. The bad gentry and rich peasants in the area, to take advantage of this for their own profit, stepped in and acted first by organizing a "Mechanized Water Scooping Company" in which they put together 1,400 *yuan* to buy one of the machines and set it up in the river. In the company's name they posted a notice requiring from the peasants an annual fee according to acreage. Those who did not pay would not be allowed any pumped water. The peasants calculated that the money paid in one year on the fields of these villages would be enough to buy one of these machines. Pooling their money and buying a machine themselves, they could put out the money once and continue to use it year after year, whereas if they used the company machine they would have to put out the same amount of money every year. Thus there was strong opposition to the company of the bad gentry and rich peasants. There were in the area several elementary school teachers who came to the aid of the peasants and helped them organize what they called a "Peasant Advancement Society." Within this organization they formed a "Mechanical Water Scooping Cooperative," which also used the method of collecting money according to acreage. They raised the 1,400 *yuan* themselves and bought a water scooping machine. At this point there were two water scooping machines in the river, one the company's and the other the cooperative's. The company's machine just sat there and nobody paid any attention to it. The bad gentry were very angry. Making up all kinds of lies, they reported to Sun Chuanfang. As a result, troops were sent to the villages and they carried out a big search for the extremist party. Four people were arrested, a warrant was put out for three more, and it was announced that anyone who did not use the company machine would be severely punished. When the troops arrived, all the adult males of the village were hiding in the fields, leaving only the elderly and infirm, the women and children, to face the soldiers.

These peasants, guilty of a serious crime, made a present of more than 1,000 *yuan* to the commander of the troops, just to escape being arrested, and this does not include the other things that were plundered. This case remains unresolved to this day. Fortunately, things are not going so well for Sun Chuanfang at present, and perhaps the bad gentry of Lüchengzhen are feeling just a little that they can't have everything their way, but we'll have to wait and see.

Wuxi

In the town of Xuxiang, 15 *li* from Wuxi, there was also a small disturbance not long ago. A big merchant-landlord from this area by the name of Rong Desheng wanted to built a road through the village. He wanted to tear down houses and buy up at a cheap price the fields through which the road would pass. This would have meant a direct financial loss for the peasants, so they organized a peasants' club to oppose Rong Desheng, with the result that Rong Desheng gave in and agreed to pay 200 *yuan* per *mu*, 10 cents per tree of newly planted mulberry groves, and not to tear down any of the houses.

Qingpu

Last month there was an incident in Qingpu *xian*, which runs along the road from Shanghai to Hangzhou, in which the peasants opposed paying high prices for wasteland. In this *xian* the peasants have always paid a fixed price of three *yuan* per *mu* for wasteland. Then, the evil gentry, in collusion with the *xian* magistrate, Li Zhenyi, organized a company that obtained wasteland for three *yuan* per *mu* and sold it to the peasants at twelve *yuan* per *mu*. To oppose this, the peasants organized a Reclamation Association, which really frightened the bad gentry and officials. This struggle is still going on.

Taixing

In a place in eastern Wangjiazhuang, because of a poor harvest resulting from the drought, the peasants requested rent reductions and rose up in an intense struggle against the landlords. Not only were the landlords unwilling to reduce the rents, they have even put pressure on the peasants. One of the peasants who was extremely angry planned to kill one of the evilest of the landlords. The landlord reported it to the *xian* offices, and thirty peasants were arrested.

Tai *xian*

This past summer in Sensenzhuang of Tai *xian*, the peasants asked for rent reductions because of the drought and started a movement. The landlords suppressed it and arrested several of the leaders.

Xuzhou

Among the peasants of Jiangsu, those in the area of Xuhai, north of the Yangzi River, can be said to suffer the greatest hardship. There are Red Spear Societies and United Village Societies everywhere,[4] and all kinds of struggles going on in

---

4. The Red Spears [*hongqianghui*] were a peasant self-defense force which combined some of the religious beliefs of the secret societies with a strongly developed military organization. They had emerged in the early 1920s, and became prominent in North China in 1925. The United Village Societies [*lianzhuanghui*] were an older and looser type of association which coexisted with the Red Spears at this time.

the villages, more than in other places, too many to be described. In northern and eastern Tongshan *xian* the topography is low-lying and last year the crops were completely destroyed by flooding. Fortunately, the second crop had already been planted and the peasants still hoped to "turn a bad year into a good one." Then this autumn, uninterrupted heavy rains finally drowned the young sprouts, which rotted from wilt-rust. For their half year of backbreaking labor, the peasants were left empty-handed. At this time the land is still covered with sheets of water. It is too late to replant the second crop, and the sounds of grumbling and resentment are everywhere, all expressing a condition of tragic misery. In addition to natural disasters, there are also the exorbitant taxes of the warlords and greedy officials, plus the heavy rents and high interest charged by the landlords—layer upon layer of crushing exploitation. For this reason, many peasants are running away and becoming bandits. This is why the Xuzhou area has become notorious as a bandit district.

Cixi

Cixi is in Zhejiang, west of Ningbo. In recent months, in the area north of the mountains of this *xian*, a big uprising has broken out. The peasants of this area north of the mountains have always been extremely intrepid and frequently engage in armed combat. On top of this, the bureaucrats and police have been unreasonably oppressive in recent years, and the bad gentry and landlords have redoubled their oppression, so the pent-up anger of the peasants was already profound. As luck would have it, the weather this year was abnormal, and neither the rice nor the cotton crops were good, but the landlords refused to make any reduction whatever in their cast-iron rents. The peasant insurrection against famine thereupon exploded. As soon as the peasant revolt broke out, the lumpen-proletarians as a whole bravely joined in. On the morning of September 13, more than 2,000 people gathered in front of the police station to report the famine and clashed with the police. They burned down the police station and seized the weapons of the police. They then turned toward the homes of the local gentry and landlords to "eat up big families." After eating, in their anger at the viciousness of the local gentry and landlords, they totally demolished all their screens, paintings, and sculptured ancient doors and windows. They did this every day; they paid little heed to others' exhortations, but just went on venting their anger in this way.

The day after, the local gentry fled to the city to report the uprising. One group of soldiers and police after another came down to the countryside to put down the peasants in a big way. Most of the peasant leaders had already fled and scattered. There was already widespread propaganda about "lawlessness" and "crimes," which started to frighten the peasants, and the uprising was quelled. The reason that this uprising failed was that the popular masses were totally unorganized and had no leadership. Thus it became a primitive revolt and ended in failure.

Speech at the Welcome Meeting Held by the Provincial Peasants' and Workers' Congresses

(December 20, 1926)

In the afternoon of the day before yesterday (December 20), the Peasants' and the Workers' Congresses held a joint meeting in the magic lantern theater to welcome Mr. Mao Runzhi and Mr. Bu Lici, the representative of the Peasant International.[1] Over three hundred people attended the meeting, and the audience was very enthusiastic. The upstairs hall was practically filled to capacity. The meeting began at 2 P.M. with the ringing of a bell. Chairman Liu Jingtao first made introductory remarks. He said, "This afternoon we are here to welcome two guests. The first one is Mr. Mao Runzhi. Born in Xiangtan, Hunan Province, Mr. Mao is a leader of the Chinese revolution, and he has paid particular attention to the peasant movement. He has come back to Hunan at this time specially to investigate the peasant movement. At the beginning of our congress, we sent a telegram to Mr. Mao asking him to come back to give his guidance to the congress. We are very pleased to have Mr. Mao back here at this time. Our second guest is Mr. Bu Lici, the representative from the Peasant International. Mr. Bu Lici has been sent by the Peasant International to

---

This summary of Mao's speech was published at the time in the *Daily Bulletin* of the Workers' and Peasants' Congresses. Our translation is based on the reprint of the entire collection of this periodical under the original title: *Hunan quansheng diyici gongnong daibiao dahui rikan* (Daily Bulletin of the First Workers' Peasants' Congresses of Hunan Province) (Changsha: Hunan renmin chubanshe, 1979), pp. 338–40. Mao's remarks are also reproduced in *Mao Zedong ji. Bujuan*, Vol. 2, pp. 205–06.

1. We have not been able to identify the person whose name is given as Bu Lici. The Peasant International, an emanation of the Comintern, which held its First Conference in October 1923, was nearing the end of its active life at this time, though a second and final conference would take place in the autumn of 1927. In his speech, delivered after the five-minute break which followed Mao's talk, the representative of the Peasant International began by stressing that in Europe the peasantry had not been revolutionary prior to the First World War. Although the 12 million deaths in the war had brought about a major change in this respect, cooperation between peasants and workers had nevertheless proved difficult to achieve. This, suggested Bu Lici, had been an important reason for the defeat of the German and Bulgarian revolutions. In the light of these remarks, it is conceivable that the emissary was a German or an East European, and since the Chinese do not always distinguish clearly between voiced and unvoiced consonants, Bu Lici might be a transcription for something like Politzer, but no such person is known to have participated in the activities of the Peasant International. Simply on phonetic grounds, a name which fits the Chinese rendering reasonably well is that of Bouysse, a French peasant who was a delegate to the First Conference, but we have found no evidence that he ever visited China.

China to observe the peasant movement. We have invited him to give a report today. His report will consist of three parts: the first is about the peasants' conditions in Russia; the second is about the policies of the Soviet government towards the peasants; and the third is his opinions on the peasant movement in China. Now Mr. Mao has arrived, let's welcome Mr. Mao to speak to us." (Applause)

The speech of Mr. Mao is quite long, and will be published later after having been edited. Here are the main ideas:

I have been away from Hunan for only one year, but the situation this year is quite different from what it was last year. At that time, it would have been impossible to hold a mass meeting like this. At that time, the government was that of warlord Zhao Hengti; this year the government is one that can more or less work in cooperation with the people. Last year, the peasant movement was in its embryonic stage; this year it already has 1.2 million organized peasants. All this is the result of the efforts on the part of all you comrades. The topic of my speech today is the union of workers, peasants, merchants, and students. The national revolution is the joint revolution of all classes, but there is a central problem of the national revolution, which is the peasant problem. Everything depends on the solution to this problem. The demand of the workers in the national revolution is for adequate raw materials and abundant manufactured goods. Only the peasants can solve this problem. The problems of the merchants in the national revolution are of two types: one concerns the industrialists, and the other the businessmen. The market for manufactured goods is in the villages, and it is the peasants who buy manufactured goods. The raw materials for the merchants' commodities are sent from the countryside. The market for their commodities is also in the countryside. If they want good sales for their products, the merchants must have the peasant problem solved, so that peasants have extra money with which to buy their goods. As for students in the national revolution, some of them are involved in the peasant and labor movements. Some of them are studying industry, and some of them are studying commerce, and the reason they haven't gone to work in industry and commerce lies in the fact that the peasant problem has not yet been solved. That is why many Chinese students are involved in the revolutionary movement, while students in other countries oppose revolution. Most Chinese students live a very hard life, and after they graduate they have no place to use what they've learned, so they have no choice but to make revolution. Chinese students are quite important, but they are not the only important ones. It's like a three-storied building. On the top floor are the imperialists, the warlords, and local bullies and bad gentry. On the bottom floor are the classes of workers and peasants. In the middle are the students. Some of them go up and link up with the imperialists, some go down and link up with the workers and peasants, and then there are some who go neither up nor down. A phenomenon among Chinese students is that the revolutionary ones are a minority and so are the counterrevolutionary ones, while those who do not participate in the revolution are the majority. At present, the time for us to overthrow the landlords has not yet come. We must make some concessions to them. In the national revolution, now is the time to knock down the imperialists, the warlords, and the local bullies and bad gentry, to reduce land rents, to reduce interest, and to increase the wages of farm laborers. All of this is part of the peasant problem. If the peasant problem is solved, the problems of the workers, merchants, students, educators, and others will likewise be solved.

> By this time, it was already 4 P.M., and the chairman announced a five-minute break . . . (balance omitted).

———————————1927———————————

Report to the Central Committee on Observations Regarding the Peasant Movement in Hunan

(February 16, 1927)

Having arrived from Changsha in Wuchang on February 11, I hereby report as follows on various matters.

1. On December 17, I arrived in Changsha from Hankou to participate in the Provincial Congress of Peasants' Representatives. At the Committee for Drafting Resolutions of the Congress we discussed various resolutions. All the resolutions adopted on this occasion may be considered fairly realistic. The congress closed on December 30. In accordance with a decision [X] of the district committee, all comrades who were representatives to the congress held a brief training session at which I presented three reports on the peasant question and on methods of investigation.

2. Starting on January 4, I went to the countryside to carry out an investigation, which lasted until February 5. Altogether the investigation continued for thirty-two days and covered the five *xian* of Xiangtan, Xiangxiang, Hengshan, Liling, and Changsha. In the countryside and in the *xian* seats, experienced peasants were invited to meet with peasant movement comrades in an investigation meeting. The materials obtained are not inconsiderable. What we saw and heard in the rural areas of these *xian* is almost totally different from what we have seen and heard in Hankou and in Changsha. I shall first set forth several large errors in our previous policy for dealing with the peasant movement. After the investigation of the three *xian* of Xiangtan, Xiangxiang, and Hengshan, I returned to the district committee and gave a detailed report to the responsible comrades. I also presented reports both at the party school and at the [Youth] League school. Following the investigations in the two *xian* of Liling and Changsha, I gave several reports to the district committee. The former errors of the party in the peasant movement have already been corrected in part. The important points are as follows: (1) The fact that "the peasant movement is fine" has served to correct the unanimous view on the part of the government, the

Our source for this document is the reproduction in *Mao Zedong ji. Bujuan*, Vol. 2, pp. 255–57, of the text as displayed at the Museum of the History of the Chinese Revolution.

Guomindang, and all sectors of society that "the peasant movement is terrible." (2) The fact that "the poor peasants are the vanguard of the revolution" has been used to correct the opinion universally held in all circles about a "movement of riffraff," a "movement of lazy peasants."[1] (3) The fact that no kind of united front existed at all in the past was used to correct the argument that peasant associations are wrecking the united front. The problem from now on is not to accuse anyone of wrecking the united front, but jointly to shoulder responsibility for **setting up**[2] a united front. (4) The peasant movement falls into three periods: first, the period of organization; second, the period of revolution; and third, the period of proposing a united front. Every place, no matter where, must go through the second period before it can make the transition to the third period. It is absolutely impossible to leap from the first period to the third period without going through the second period of violently overthrowing the power and prestige of the feudal landlords. (5) Most of the *xian* of central and southern Hunan have experienced a stormy period of rural revolution (the second period). The countryside has fallen into a state of anarchy, and a system of democratic rural self-rule must immediately be created to change anarchy into a situation with a government that has taken concrete measures to establish a rural united front in order to avoid the danger of the peasant villages becoming isolated. Only then will such problems as weapons, public food supplies, education, construction, and [X][X] be settled in the countryside. Presently, no political problem in Hunan is more pressing than this point of carrying village self-rule through to completion. There can be no question of provincial people's assemblies or *xian* people's assemblies until after village self-rule has been completed. (6) During the second period (the period of the revolutionary uprising in the countryside), all actions of the peasants against the feudal landlord class are correct. Even if there are some excesses, they are still correct, because unless they learn to go too far [X][X], they will certainly not be able to overthrow the power of the feudal class built up over several thousand years, and will certainly not be able to complete the democratic revolution quickly. To right a wrong it is necessary to exceed the proper limits; the wrong cannot be righted without doing so.[3] It is for this reason that the peasant associations must not under any circumstances ask the government or the militia to arrest so-called "riffraff." They can only raise the slogan of "peasant associations rectify discipline" and go themselves to rectify those "few undesirable elements" in lower-level peasant associations. Otherwise, it is impossible to avoid undermining the resolve of the peasants and increasing the prestige of the landlords. (7) The problem of hoarding grain is a

---

1. These are the same terms used in Mao's longer report on the Hunan peasant movement, translated below.

2. Emphasized by the use of dots next to the characters in the original.

3. This entire sentence in Chinese is identical with that in Mao's longer report on the Hunan peasant movement. See the following text.

problem for all levels of society. Actually, most of the poor peasants want to hoard grain, and only a small minority of the rich peasants want it to be released. The peasant association can only play a role of persuasion, of persuading the poor peasants to make concessions to the rich peasants. It cannot represent the rich peasants and go out and attack the poor peasants. If hoarding is so severe, this is entirely because of anarchy in the countryside, which makes it impossible to guarantee public food supplies. This is the responsibility of government. It is not wholly the responsibility of the peasant associations. If we want grain to circulate, the only way is quickly to set up new organs of village self-rule that will take responsibility for guaranteeing the public food supply. (8) The various conflicts in the countryside, such as the conflicts between peasants and workers, between peasants and merchants, between peasants and students, between peasants and the party, between poor and rich peasants, between the peasants and the government, must all be resolved under the banner of the Guomindang;[4] we must absolutely not raise immediately the banner of the Communist Party[5] to resolve them. Thus among the peasants we must develop the Guomindang everywhere, letting it take the lead in mediating and directing these matters that are very difficult to mediate and direct. In the past, there has been too great a gap between the degree of the Guomindang's development and the degree of development of the peasant movement. We must develop the organization of the Guomindang in a big way among the peasantry, especially among the poor peasants. (9) The peasant problem is solely a problem of the poor peasants, but there are two poor peasant problems, the problem of capital and the problem of the land. Both these problems are no longer problems of propaganda but are problems requiring immediate action. (10) In many of the *xian* of Hunan, the peasants have already completed the democratic revolution in the countryside. The revolutionary feelings of the poor peasants are accordingly very high, and given the present circumstances, they are absolutely resolved to proceed rapidly to yet another revolution! This being true, the broad masses of poor peasants, in their tens of millions (according to the investigation in Changsha, 70 percent are poor peasants, 20 percent are middle peasants, and 10 percent are rich peasants), want to go forward to another revolution. My investigation indicates that no force can resist them for long. Today the masses are going to the left, and in many places our party, not to mention the Guomindang, shows that it has not reached the same level of revolutionary feeling as the masses. This is something that very much demands our attention. (11) For this reason, it should be said that in order (a) to deal with the current situation and (b) to prepare for the revolution which is soon to come, our party must be greatly developed. For the small Hunan

---

4. Here (and throughout this passage) the Guomindang is designated in the Chinese text by the letters "K.M.T.," standing for Kuomintang. This was common usage in CCP documents of the time.

5. The text here has the letters CP.

party to be effective it must expand to 20,000 members within six months (it now has only 6,000) and must establish a local [organization] in every *xian* where the peasant associations have more than 20,000 members. (12) The Hong Society[6] is a force [to be reckoned with]. We must win over such forces and never adopt the method of attacking them. (13) The situation is extremely favorable for women and children to rise up in the countryside. The women in particular are a great force and must not be neglected. Above, I have outlined the essential features of the thirteen items listed. Beginning tomorrow, within three or four days I shall write a detailed report on the situation and send it to you for your inspection, corrections, and further guidance.

---

6. A secret society, descended from the Heaven and Earth Society (*Tiandihui*), widespread in the Yangtze valley. The term may stand here for secret societies in general.

Report on the Peasant Movement in Hunan

(February 1927)[1]

I. Rural Revolution

1. The Importance of the Peasant Problem

During my recent visit, I made a first-hand investigation of the five *xian* of Xiangtan, Xiangxiang, Hengshan, Liling, and Changsha. In the thirty-two days from January 4 to February 5, I called together fact-finding conferences in villages and *xian* towns, which were attended by experienced peasants and by comrades in the peasant movement, and I listened attentively to their reports and collected a great deal of material. Many of the arguments of the peasant movement were the exact opposite of what I had heard from the gentry class in Hankou and Changsha. I saw and heard many strange things of which I had hitherto been unaware. I believe that the same is also true of every province in all of China.[2] *Consequently*, all criticisms directed against the peasant movement

---

The full text of this report was first published in *Zhanshi*, a weekly put out by the Hunan District Committee of the Chinese Communist Party, Nos. 35–36, 38, and 39, between March 5 and April 3, 1927 (see *Nianpu*, Vol. 1, p. 284). Our translation is based on the text in *Mao Zedong ji*, Vol. 1, pp. 207–49, which is taken from the 1944 and 1947 editions of Mao's *Selected Works*.

1. Although this text is dated March 1927 in the *Selected Works*, and was first published in March, it was almost certainly written in February. As indicated below, the investigation on which it is based took place between January 4 and February 5, 1927. On February 16, Mao produced the report to the Chinese Communist Party Central Committee translated above, which ends with the statement that he will be writing a longer report during the next few days. The version of Parts I and II of this report published in *Xiangdao* No. 191, March 12, 1927, carries the parenthetical indication after the title: "Correspondence of February 18 from Changsha." That date is perhaps as likely as any, but since it is not otherwise confirmed, we give simply the month.

The variants between what Mao originally wrote in 1927, and the text as he revised it for publication in 1951, are indicated below by the devices explained in the "Note on Sources and Conventions" which appears at the beginning of this volume. One exception should, however, be noted. In the new version, the main headings, "I. Rural Revolution," and "II. The Revolutionary Vanguard," have been eliminated. To indicate this by setting these headings in italics would lead to confusion with the next level of subheadings, which appear in italic bold throughout the volume. We have, however, put in Roman the second half of subheading II2, which has been dropped in the *Selected Works*. Other changes in the headings are indicated in the notes. None of the headings in the revised version are numbered, except for the "fourteen great achievements" with which the report ends.

2. Every province in all of China → Many other places

must be speedily set right, and the *various* erroneous measures adopted by the revolutionary authorities concerning the peasant movement must be speedily changed. Only thus can the future of the revolution be benefited. For the present upsurge of the peasant movement is a colossal event. In a very short time, several hundred million peasants in China's central, southern, and northern provinces will rise like a fierce wind or tempest, a force so swift and violent that no power, however great, will be able to suppress it. They will break through all the trammels that bind them and rush forward along the road to liberation. They will, *in the end*, send all the imperialists, warlords, corrupt officials, local bullies, and bad gentry to their graves. All revolutionary parties and all revolutionary comrades will stand before them to be tested, to be accepted or rejected as they decide. To march at their head and lead them? To stand behind them, gesticulating and criticizing them? Or to stand opposite them and oppose them? Every Chinese is free to choose among the three, but by the force of circumstances you are *fated* to make the choice quickly. *Here I have written up my investigations and opinions in several sections, for the reference of revolutionary comrades.*

2. Get Organized

The peasant movement in Hunan, so far as it concerns the *xian* in the central and southern parts of the province, where the movement is already developed, can be roughly divided into two periods. The first, from January to September of last year, was one of organization. Within this period, January to June was a time of secret [activity], and July to September, when the revolutionary army was driving out Zhao, an open time. During this period, the membership of the peasant associations did not exceed 300,000 to 400,000, and the masses directly under their command[3] numbered little more than a million; there was as yet hardly any struggle in the rural areas, and consequently there was very little criticism of the associations in other circles. Because its members served as guides, scouts, and porters, even some of the officers[4] had a good word to say for the peasant associations. The second period, from last October to January of this year, was one of revolution. The membership of the associations jumped to 2 million and the masses directly under their command[5] increased to 10 million. (The peasants generally enter only one name for the whole family on joining a peasant association; therefore a membership of 2 million means a mass following of 10 million.) Almost half the peasants in Hunan are now organized. In *xian* like Xiangtan, Xiangxiang, Liuyang, Changsha, Liling, Ningxiang, Pingjiang, Xiangyin, Hengshan, Hengyang, Laiyang, Chenxian, and Anhua, nearly all the peasants have gone into the peasant associations or have come under their command.[6] It

---

3. Command → Leadership
4. The officers → The officers of the Expeditionary Army
5. Command → Leadership
6. Command → Leadership

was on the strength of their extensive organization that the peasants went into action and within four months brought about a great revolution in the countryside, a revolution without parallel in history.

3. Down with the Local Bullies and Bad Gentry! All Power to the Peasant Associations!

Now that the peasants have got themselves organized, they are beginning to take action. The main targets of their attack are the local bullies, the bad gentry, and the lawless landlords, but in passing they also hit out against patriarchal ideas and institutions of all kinds, against the corrupt officials in the cities, and against bad practices and customs in the rural areas. In force and momentum the attack is quite simply tempestuous; those who submit to it survive, and those who resist perish. As a result, the privileges the feudal landlords have enjoyed for thousands of years are being shattered to pieces. Their dignity and prestige are being completely swept away. With the collapse of the power of the gentry,[7] the peasant associations have now become the sole organs of authority, and "All power to the peasant associations" has become a reality. Even trifling matters such as quarrels between husband and wife must be brought before the peasant association for settlement. Nothing can be settled in the absence of peasant association representatives. *Whatever nonsense the people from the peasant association talk at meetings, that, too, is sacred.*[8] The association actually dictates everything in the countryside, all rural affairs, and quite literally, "whatever it says, goes." People outside the associations can only speak well of them and cannot say anything against them. The local bullies, bad gentry, and lawless landlords have completely lost their right to speak, and none of them dares even mutter dissent. Faced by the intimidating force of the peasant associations, the top local bullies and bad gentry have fled to Shanghai, those of the second rank to Hankou, those of the third to Changsha, and those of the fourth to the *xian* towns, while the fifth rank and the still lesser fry surrender to the peasant associations in the villages.

"Here's ten *yuan.* Please let me join the peasant association," one of the lesser bad gentry will say.

"Ha! Who wants your filthy money?" is the peasants' reply.

Many middle and small landlords, rich peasants, and even some middle peasants, who were formerly opposed to the peasant associations, are now seeking admission. Visiting various places, I often came across such people who pleaded with me, "Mr. Committeeman from the provincial capital, please be my guarantor!"

Under the Qing dynasty, the household census compiled by the local authorities consisted of a regular register and "the other" register, the former for honest

---

7. The gentry (*shenshi*) → The landlords

8. Literally, "If a member of a peasant association lets a fart ... ," this being a common Chinese metaphor (much used by Mao) for talking nonsense.

people and the latter for burglars, bandits, and similar undesirables. In some places the peasants now use this to scare those who were formerly against the associations. They say, "Put their names down in the other register!"

Afraid of being entered in the other register, such people try various devices to gain admission into the peasant associations. Their minds are entirely set on this, and they do not feel safe until their names are entered in the peasant association register. More often than not the peasant associations turn them down flat, and so they are always on tenterhooks; with the doors of the association barred to them, they are like tramps without a home or, in rural parlance, "mere trash." In short, what was generally sneered at four months ago as the "peasants' gang" has now become something most honorable. Those who formerly prostrated themselves before the gentry[9] now all prostrate themselves before the power of the peasants. Everyone, no matter who, admits that the world has changed since last October.

4. It's Terrible and It's Fine

The peasants' revolt in the countryside disturbed the gentry's sweet dreams. When the news from the countryside reached the cities, the urban gentry were immediately in an uproar. When I first arrived in Changsha, I met all sorts of people and picked up a good deal of gossip. From the middle strata of society upwards to the Guomindang right-wingers, there was not a single person who did not sum it all up in the phrase, "It's terrible!" Even very revolutionary people, influenced by the views of the "It's terrible!" school which dominated the climate in the city, became downhearted when they tried to picture the situation in the countryside in their mind's eye and were unable to deny the word "terrible." Even very progressive people could only say, "This kind of thing is inevitable in a revolution, but still it's terrible." In short, no one at all could completely reject this word "terrible." But as I have already said, the fact is that the broad peasant masses have risen to fulfill their historical mission, and that the democratic forces in the countryside have risen to overthrow the forces of feudalism in the countryside.[10] This overthrowing of the feudal forces is the real objective of the national revolution. What Mr. Sun Yatsen wanted, but failed, to accomplish in the forty years he devoted to the national revolution, the peasants have accomplished in a few months. *The patriarchal-feudal class of local bullies, bad gentry, and lawless landlords has formed the basis of autocratic government for thousands of years, and is the cornerstone of imperialism, warlordism, and corrupt officialdom.* [To overthrow them] is a marvelous feat never before achieved, not just in forty but in thousands of years. It is fine. It is not "terrible"

---

9. Before the gentry → Before the power of the gentry

10. The *Selected Works* text moves to this point the sentence beginning "The patriarchal-feudal class of local bullies," which appears in italics three lines below.

at all. It is anything but "terrible." *To give credit where credit is due, if we allot ten points to the accomplishments of the democratic revolution, then the achievements of the city dwellers and the military rate only three points, while the remaining seven points should go to the achievements of the peasants in their rural revolution.* "It's terrible!" is obviously a theory for combating the rise of the peasants in the interests of the landlords; it is obviously a theory of the landlord class for preserving the old feudal order and obstructing the establishment of the new democratic order; it is obviously a counterrevolutionary theory. No revolutionary comrade should echo this nonsense. If your revolutionary viewpoint is firmly established, and if you go to the villages and have a look around, you will undoubtedly feel a joy you have never known before. Countless thousands of slaves—the peasants—are there overthrowing their cannibalistic enemies. What the peasants are doing is absolutely right; what they are doing is "fine!" "It's fine!" is the theory of the peasants and of other revolutionaries. Every revolutionary comrade should know that the national revolution requires a great change in the countryside. The Revolution of 1911 did not bring about this change, hence its failure. Now a change is taking place, and this is an important factor for the completion of the revolution. Every revolutionary comrade must support this change or he will be a counterrevolutionary.[11]

5. The Question of "Going too Far"[12]

Then there is another section of people who say, "Although peasant associations are necessary, their actions at present are undeniably going too far." This is the opinion of the middle-of-the-roaders. But what is the actual situation? True, the peasants are in a sense "unruly" in the countryside. Supreme in authority, the peasant association allows the landlord no say and sweeps away the landlord's prestige. This amounts to striking the landlord down into the dust and trampling on him there. *They coined the phrase: "If he has land, he must be a bully, and all gentry are evil."*[13] *In some of the places even those who own 50 mu of fields are called local bullies, and those who wear long gowns are called bad gentry.* The peasants threaten, "We will put you in the other register!" They fine the local bullies and bad gentry, they demand contributions from them, and they smash their sedan-chairs. In the case of local bullies and bad gentry who are against the peasant association, a mass of people swarm into their houses, slaughtering their pigs and consuming their grain. They may even loll on the ivory-inlaid beds belonging to the young ladies in the households of the local bullies and bad

---

11. Will be a counterrevolutionary → Will be taking the stand of counterrevolution
12. "Going too far" → The so-called "going too far"
13. This is a free rendering of a play on the four Chinese characters (*tuhao lieshen*) translated as "local bullies" and "bad gentry"; the original reads, *"Youtu bi hao, wushen bulie."*

gentry. At the slightest provocation they make arrests, crown the arrested with tall paper hats, and parade them through the villages, saying, "You dirty landlords, now you know who we are!" Doing whatever they like and turning everything upside down, they have even created a kind of terror in the countryside. This is what ordinary people[14] call "going too far," or "going beyond the proper limits in righting a wrong," or "really too much." Such talk may seem plausible, but in fact it is wrong. First, the local bullies, bad gentry, and lawless landlords have themselves driven the peasants to this. For ages they have used their power to tyrannize over the peasants and trample them underfoot; that is why the peasants have reacted so strongly. The most violent revolts and the most serious disorders have invariably occurred in places where the local bullies, bad gentry, and lawless landlords perpetrated the worst outrages. The peasants are clearsighted. Who is bad and who is not, who is the worst and who is not quite so vicious, who deserves severe punishment and who deserves to be let off lightly—the peasants keep clear accounts, and very seldom has the punishment exceeded the crime. *Therefore, Mr. Tang Mengxiao*[15] *also said "The peasants are arresting local bullies and bad gentry; nine of ten arrested deserve it."* Secondly, a revolution is not like inviting people to dinner, or writing an essay, or painting a picture, or doing embroidery; it cannot be so refined, so leisurely and gentle, so "benign, upright, courteous, temperate and complaisant."[16] A revolution is an uprising, an act of violence whereby one class overthrows the power of another. A rural revolution is a revolution in which the peasantry overthrows the power of the feudal landlord class. If the peasants do not use extremely great force, they cannot possibly overthrow the deeply rooted power of the landlords, which has lasted for thousands of years. The rural areas must experience a great, fervent revolutionary upsurge, which alone can rouse the

---

14. Ordinary people → Some people

15. Tang Shengzhi (1889–1970), *zi* Mengxiao, was a native of Dongan *xian*, Hunan, and a graduate of Baoding Military Academy. Early in his career, in 1918, he aligned himself with Zhao Hengti, under whom he served as a regimental commander beginning in 1918. Following Zhao's assumption of the governorship, he was promoted to divisional commander. During the 1923 war between Zhao Hengti and Tan Yankai, he remained loyal to Zhao. In March 1926, however, he was able to force Zhao to resign in his favor. In July 1926, Chiang Kaishek appointed him commander in chief of front-line operations in the Northern Expedition, with six Hunan divisions under him. In the spring of 1927, he took the side of the Guomindang Left against Chiang Kaishek and was thus regarded by Mao, at the time of writing, as a revolutionary military man. Indeed, on March 30, he was appointed a member of the Interim Executive Committee of the All-China Federation of Peasant Associations (see the text of April 9, 1927, which appears below). By late summer, however, he had turned against the Communists, and in November, 1927, he retired to Japan.

16. These are the qualities that enabled Confucius, according to his disciple Zigong, to obtain information about the government of the countries he visited. See the *Analects*, I, X, 2 (Legge, Vol. I, p. 142).

peasant masses in their thousands and tens of thousands to form this great force. All the excessive actions[17] mentioned above [result from] the power[18] of the peasants, mobilized by the great, fervent revolutionary upsurge in the countryside. It was highly necessary for such things to be done in the second period of the peasant movement, the period of revolutionary action. Such actions were extremely necessary during the second period of the peasant movement (the period of revolution). In this period, it was necessary to establish the absolute dominance of the peasants. It was necessary to forbid criticism[19] of the peasant associations. It was necessary to overthrow completely the authority of the gentry, to knock them down and even stamp them underfoot. All excessive[20] actions had revolutionary significance during the second period. To put it bluntly, it is necessary to bring about a brief reign of terror in every rural area; otherwise we could never suppress the activities of the counterrevolutionaries in the countryside or overthrow the authority of the gentry. To right a wrong it is necessary to exceed the proper limits; the wrong cannot be righted without doing so. The argument of this group seems on the surface to differ from that of the group discussed earlier, but essentially they proceed from the same standpoint and likewise voice a landlord theory that upholds the interests of the privileged classes. Since this theory impedes the rise of the peasant movement and so disrupts the revolution, we must firmly oppose it.

II. The Revolutionary Vanguard

1. The Movement of the Riffraff[21]

The right wing of the Guomindang says, "The peasant movement is a movement of the riffraff, a movement of the lazy peasants." This argument has gained much currency in Changsha. When I was in the countryside, I heard the gentry say, "It is all right to set up peasant associations, but the people now running them are no good. They ought to be replaced!" This argument comes to the same thing as what the right-wingers are saying. Both admit that it is all right to have a peasant movement (since the peasant movement has already come into being, no one dare say otherwise), but they regard the people running it as no good. Their hatred is directed particularly against those in charge of the associations at the lower levels, whom they call "riffraff." *Those people in the countryside who used to go around in worn-out leather shoes, carry broken umbrellas, wear green gowns, and gamble*—in short, all those who were formerly despised and kicked into the gutter by the gentry, who had no social standing, and who were

---

17. Excessive → Which have been labeled as "excessive"
18. Power → Have been created by the power
19. Criticism → Malicious criticism
20. Excessive → Which were labeled as "excessive"
21. The movement of the riffraff → The so-called "movement of the riffraff"

completely deprived of[22] the right to speak, have now dared to lift their heads. Not only have they raised their heads, they have also taken power into their hands. They are now running the township peasant associations (the lowest level of peasant associations), and have turned them into a formidable force. They raise their rough, blackened hands and lay them on the heads of the gentry. They tether the bad gentry with ropes, crown them with tall paper hats, and parade them through the villages. (In Xiangtan and Xiangxiang they call this "parading through the township" and in Liling "parading through the fields.") Every day the coarse, harsh sounds of their denunciations pierce the ears of these gentry. They are giving orders and running everything. They, who used to rank below everyone else, now rank above everybody else—that is what people mean by "turning things upside down."

2. *Vanguard of the Revolution or* Outstanding Contributors to the Revolution

When there are two different ways of looking at a certain thing, or a certain kind of people, two opposite assessments emerge. "It's terrible!" and "It's fine!" are one example and "riffraff" and "vanguard of the revolution" are another. We said above that the peasants had accomplished a revolutionary task for many years left unaccomplished and had done the principal[23] work in the national revolution. But has this great revolutionary task, this principal[24] work in the revolution, been performed by all the peasants? No. There are three kinds of peasants: the rich, the middle, and the poor peasants. These three categories live in different circumstances and so have different ideas about the revolution. In the first period, what appealed to the rich peasants (*those who have surplus money and grain are called rich peasants*) was the talk about the Northern Expeditionary Army's sustaining a crushing defeat in Jiangxi, about Chiang Kaishek's being wounded in the leg and flying back to Guangdong, and about Wu Peifu's recapturing Yuezhou. The peasant associations would certainly not last and the Three People's Principles could never prevail, because they had never been heard of before. Thus an official of the township peasant association (generally one of the riffraff[25] type) would walk into the house of a rich peasant, register in hand, and say, "Will you please join the peasant association?" How did the rich peasants reply? "Peasant association? I have lived here for decades, tilling my land. I never saw such a thing before, yet I've managed to live all right," says a rich peasant with a tolerably decent attitude. "I advise you to give it up!" A really vicious rich peasant says, "Peasant association! Nonsense! Association for

---

22. Completely deprived of → Had no
23. Principal → Important
24. Principal → Important
25. Riffraff → The so-called "riffraff"

getting your head chopped off! Don't get people into trouble!" Yet, surprisingly enough, the peasant associations have now been established for several months and have even dared to stand up to the gentry. The gentry of the neighborhood who refused to hand over their opium pipes were arrested by the associations and paraded through the villages. In the *xian* towns, moreover, some big landlords were put to death (such as Yan Rongqiu of Xiangtan and Yang Zhize of Ningxiang). On the anniversary of the October Revolution, at the time of the anti-British rally and of the great celebrations of the victory of the Northern Expedition, tens of thousands[26] of peasants, holding high their banners, big and small, along with their carrying poles and hoes, demonstrated in massive, streaming columns. The rich peasants[27] began to get perplexed and alarmed *in their hearts*. During the great victory celebrations of the Northern Expedition, they learned that Jiujiang had also been taken, that Chiang Kaishek had not been wounded in the leg, and that Wu Peifu had been defeated after all. What is more, they saw "Long live the Three People's Principles!" "Long live the peasant associations!" "Long live the peasants!" and so on and so forth clearly written on the red and green proclamations (slogans).

"What?" wondered the rich peasants, greatly perplexed and alarmed, " 'Long live the peasants!' Are these people now to be regarded as emperors?"[28] So the peasant associations are putting on grand airs. People from the associations say to the rich peasants:

"We'll enter you in the other register!"

"In another month, the admission fee will be ten *yuan* a head!"

Only under the impact and intimidation of all this are the rich peasants tardily joining the associations, some paying fifty cents or one *yuan* for admission (the regular fee being a mere ten coppers), some securing admission only after asking other people to put in a good word for them. But there are quite a number of diehards who have not joined to this day. When the rich peasants join the associations, they generally enter the name of some sixty- or seventy-year-old member of the family, for they are in constant dread of conscription. After joining, the rich peasants are not keen on doing any work for the association. They remain inactive throughout. How about the middle peasants? *(Those who do not have any surplus money and rice, are not in debt, and are able to assure themselves of clothing, food, and shelter every year are called the middle peasants.)* The attitude of the middle peasants is a vacillating one. They think that the revolution will not bring much good to them. They have rice cooking in their pots and no creditors knocking on their doors at midnight. They, too, judging a thing by whether it ever existed before, knit their brows and think to themselves, "Can the

---

26. Tens of thousands . . . → Tens of thousands . . . in every township
27. The rich peasants → It was only then that the rich peasants
28. The most common expression in Chinese for "Long live!" is *wansui*, literally "ten thousand years," which was used of the emperor.

peasant association really last?" "Can the Three People's Principles prevail?" Their conclusion is, "Afraid not!" They imagine it all depends on the will of Heaven and think, "A peasant association? Who knows if Heaven wills it or not?" In the first period, people from the association would call on a middle peasant, register in hand, and say, "Will you please join the peasant association?" The middle peasant replied, "There's no hurry!" It was not until the second period, when the peasant associations were already exercising great power, that the middle peasants came in. *Even though* they[29] are *somewhat* better in the peasant associations than the rich peasants, they are never very enthusiastic,[30] *and retain their vacillating attitude.* The only kind of people[31] in the countryside who have always put up the bitterest fight are the poor peasants. From the period of underground work *straight through* to the period of open activity, it is they who have fought.[32] *As for organization, it is they who are organizing things there, and as for revolution, it is they who are making revolution there. They alone* are the deadly enemies of the local tyrants and evil gentry, and they strike them without the slightest hesitation. *They alone are capable of carrying out the work of destruction.* They say to the rich *and middle* peasants:

"We joined the peasant association long ago, why are you still hesitating?"

The rich and the middle peasants answer mockingly:

"What is there to keep you from joining? You people have neither a tile over your heads nor a speck of land under your feet!"

It is true that the poor peasants are not afraid of losing anything. *They are the disinherited or semidisinherited in rural life.* Some of them really have "neither a tile over their heads nor a speck of land under their feet." What, indeed, is there to keep them from joining the associations? According to the survey of Changsha *xian*, the poor peasants[33] comprise 70 percent, the middle peasants 20 percent, and the rich peasants[34] 10 percent. The 70 percent, the poor peasants, may be subdivided into two categories, the utterly destitute and the less destitute. The "utterly destitute" are the completely dispossessed, that is, people who have neither land nor capital, are without any means of livelihood, and are forced to leave home and become mercenaries or hired laborers and wandering beggars, *or*

---

29. They → Their behavior
30. They are never very enthusiastic → They are not as yet very enthusiastic; they still want to wait and see. It is essential for the peasant associations to get the middle peasants to join and to do a good deal more explanatory work among them.
31. The only kind of people → The main force
32. Have fought → Have fought militantly. They are the most responsive to Communist Party leadership.
33. The poor peasants → Of the population in the rural areas, the poor peasants
34. The rich peasants → The landlords and the rich peasants

commit crimes and become robbers and thieves. They make up 20 out of the 70 [percent]. The less destitute are the partially dispossessed, that is, people with just a little land or a little capital who eat up more than they earn and live in toil and distress the year round, such as the handicraftsmen, the tenant-peasants (not including the rich tenant-peasants), and the semitenant-peasants. These make up 50 out of the 70 [percent]. (*The number of poor peasants in other* xian *may be smaller than in Changsha, but there should not be a big discrepancy*). This great mass[35] of poor peasants constitute the backbone of the peasant associations, the vanguard in overthrowing the feudal forces, and the foremost heroes who have performed the great revolutionary task which for long years was left undone. Without the poor peasant class (the riffraff, as the gentry call them), it would never have been possible to bring about the present revolutionary situation in the countryside, or to overthrow the local bullies and bad gentry and to complete the democratic revolution. The poor peasants (especially the portion who are utterly destitute), being the most revolutionary group, have gained the leadership of the peasant associations. In both the first and second periods almost all the chairmen and committee members in the peasant associations at the lowest level (*i.e., the township associations*) were poor peasants (of the officials in the township associations in Hengshan County the class[36] of the utterly destitute comprise 50 percent, the class of the less destitute 40 percent, and poverty-stricken intellectuals 10 percent). This leadership by the poor peasants is extremely necessary. Without the poor peasants there would be no revolution. To deny their role is to deny the revolution. To attack them is to attack the revolution. From beginning to end, the general direction they have given to the revolution has never been wrong. They have discredited the local bullies and bad gentry. They have knocked down the local bullies and bad gentry, big and small, and trampled them underfoot. Many of their "excessive"[37] deeds in the period of revolutionary action were in fact the very things the revolution required. Some xian governments, xian headquarters of the Guomindang, and xian peasant associations in Hunan have already made a number of mistakes; some have even sent soldiers to arrest officials of the lower-level associations at the landlords' request. A good many chairmen and committee members of township associations in Hengshan and Xiangxiang xian have been thrown in jail. This mistake is very serious and *unintentionally* feeds the arrogance of the reactionaries. To judge whether or not it is a mistake, you have only to see how joyful the lawless landlords become and how reactionary sentiments grow whenever the chairmen or committee members of local peasant associations are arrested. We must combat the counterrevolutionary slogan of a "movement of riffraff" and a "movement of lazy peasants," but *at the same time* we should be especially careful not to help the local bullies

---

35. Mass → Mass, altogether 70 percent of the rural population
36. The class → The stratum (here and in the following phrase)
37. "Excessive" → So-called "excessive"

and bad gentry (*however unintentionally*) in their attacks on the leadership[38] of the poor peasant class. In fact, though a few of the poor peasant leaders undoubtedly did "gamble, play cards, and not earn their living by hard work,"[39] most of them have changed by now. They themselves are energetically prohibiting gambling and suppressing banditry. Where the peasant association is powerful, gambling has stopped altogether and the peril of banditry has vanished. In some places it is literally true that people do not take articles left by the wayside and that doors are not bolted at night. According to the Hengshan survey, 85 percent of the poor peasant leaders have made great progress and have proved themselves capable and hard-working. Only 15 percent retain some bad habits. The most one can call them is "an unhealthy minority," and we must not echo the local bullies and bad gentry in undiscriminatingly condemning them as "riffraff." As to dealing with the "unhealthy minority," we can proceed only under the peasant associations' own slogan of "strengthen discipline," by conducting propaganda among their masses, by training the "unhealthy minority," and by improving the discipline of the associations; in no circumstances should soldiers be arbitrarily sent to make such arrests as would weaken the faith[40] [in] the poor peasants and feed the arrogance of the local bullies and bad gentry. This point requires careful attention.

III. Peasants and the Peasant Associations[41]

Most critics of the peasant associations allege that they have done a great many bad things. I have already pointed out in the preceding two sections that the peasants' attack on the local bullies and bad gentry is entirely revolutionary behavior and in no way blameworthy. But the peasants have done a great many things, and[42] we must closely examine all their activities to see whether or not what they have done is really all bad, as is being said from without. I have summed up their activities of the last few months; in all, the peasants under the command[43] of the peasant associations have the following fourteen great achievements to their credit.

1. Organizing the Peasants under Peasant Associations[44]

This is the first great thing the peasants have achieved. In *xian* such as Xiangtan, Xiangxiang, and Hengshan, nearly all the peasants are organized and there is

---

38. Leadership → Erroneous actions
39. Did "gamble, play cards, and not earn their living by hard work" → Did have shortcomings
40. Weaken the faith in → Damage the prestige of
41. Peasants and the peasant associations → Fourteen great achievements
42. Here the *Selected Works* text inserts: "in order to answer people's criticisms."
43. The command → the leadership
44. Under the peasant associations → In the peasant associations

hardly a remote corner where they are not on the move; these are the best places. In some *xian* like Yiyang and Huarong, the bulk of the peasants have arisen,[45] with only a small section not yet arisen; these places are in the second grade. In other *xian*, like Chengbu and Lingling, while a small section has arisen, the bulk of the peasants have still not arisen; these places are in the third grade. Western Hunan, which is under the control of Yuan Zuming, has not yet been reached by the associations' propaganda, and the peasants of many of its *xian* have completely failed to rise; these form a fourth grade. Roughly speaking, the *xian* in central Hunan, with Changsha as the center, are the most advanced, those in southern Hunan come second, and western Hunan is only just beginning to organize. According to the figures compiled by the provincial peasants' association last November, organizations with a total membership of 1,367,727 have been set up in thirty-seven of the province's seventy-five *xian*. Of these members, about one million were organized during the time of October and November when the power of the associations rose high, while up to September the membership had only been 300,000 to 400,000. Then came the two months of December and January, and the peasant movement continued its brisk growth. By the end of the month[46] the membership must have reached at least two million. As a family generally enters only one name when joining and has an average of five members, the mass following must have reached ten million. This astonishing and accelerating rate of expansion explains why the local bullies, bad gentry, and corrupt officials have been isolated; why society has been amazed at how different the world was before and after; and why a great revolution has been wrought in the countryside. This is the first great thing that the peasants have achieved under the command[47] of the peasant associations.

The table on the following pages gives the membership of the peasant associations in all the xian *in Hunan Province as of last November.*[48]

2. Dealing Political Blows to the Landlords

After the peasants are organized, the first thing they do is to smash the political prestige of the landlord class, and especially of the local bullies and bad gentry, that is, to pull down the power and influence of the landlords and build up the power and influence of the peasants in rural society. This is a most serious and urgent struggle; it is the central struggle in the second period, the period of revolution. If this struggle is not victorious, there can be no possibility of victory in any of the economic struggles, such as the struggle for rent and interest reduction, or for capital and land,[49] and so on. In many places in Hunan like

---

45. Here, and throughout this paragraph, Arisen (*qilai*) → Organized (*zuzhi qilai*)
46. The month → January
47. The command → The leadership
48. The whole of the following table has been omitted in the *Selected Works*.
49. For capital and land → To demand land and other means of production

COMPARATIVE TABLE OF PEASANT ASSOCIATION MEMBERSHIP BY XIAN

Name of xian	No. of qu assns	No. of xiang assns	Agr. laborers	Share croppers	Semi owner peasants	Owner peasants	Handi-craft workers	Primary school teachers	Small merchant	Women	Other	No. of Members
Xiangxiang	44	499	16,400	91,500	41,000	13,100	28,000	450				190,544
Xiangyin		67	15,857	87,590	52,635	14,793	12,514	151	634	57	400	176,000
Liuyang	21	568										139,190
Xiangtan	17	450	27,000	54,100	12,400	8,460	7,400	1,100				120,460
Hengyang	23	244	17,358	37,725	7,532	5,628	6,135	2,256			1,579	88,223
Changsha	12	640	17,527	25,948	9,131	5,381	4,915	1,425	1,463	643		66,415
Anhua	15	120										62,300
Liling	15	323	6,746	35,460	6,920	3,998	3,643	230	601	195	683	58,476
Ningxiang	18	400	5,000	20,000	10,000	4,000	8,400	600				58,000
Chenxian	14	696	19,725	26,898	2,124	2,550	5,711	118	100	16		57,262
Hengshan	13	203	3,623	16,993	2,965	2,174	3,328				1,133	30,016
Suburbs		169	9,509	10,646	3,563	2,893	1,794	332	582	156		29,475
Linwu	6	32	2,183	10,143	4,146	2,291	933	254				20,000
Youxian		29										18,400
Yiyang	7	67	1,568	5,017	6,586	1,586	784	32	126			15,680
Huarong	6	49	2,000	6,595	2,453	1,887	501	1,216				14,652
Yizhang	10	185	1,438	8,936	1,637	1,283	802	87				14,183
Laiyang	9	149	1,145	6,865	2,684	1,844	342	66				12,946
Linli	6	49	2,000	3,000	2,400	4,000	200	60				11,660

Chaling	4	124	500	7,000	2,500	1,000	200	60				11,260
Yongxing	16	107	1,200	2,800	4,020	2,200	200	30				10,450
Pingjiang	17	162	1,023	4,298	1,781	1,612	1,093	214	85		42	10,152
Xinning	9	25	1,722	6,533	858	375	184	74		4		9,746
Changde	3	59	890	2,800	2,080	3,500	310	65				9,545
Baoqing	7	136	1,438	2,367	1,481	1,744	771					9,377
Wugang	8	40	1,800	4,500	900	900	900	900				9,000
Rucheng	6	46	406	4,195	2,957	1,228	41	38				8,865
Hanshou	69	1,125	3,276	1,047	1,378	228	33	61	78		7,226	
Nanxian	6	49	1,384	4,064	907	406	69	89	45		36	7,000
Zhuping Lu			997	3,152	732	539	687	50	297	10		6,464
Xinhua	6	21	1,526	3,246	497	424	472	202				6,377
Guiyang	4	52	445	274	1,673	1,525	402	24				6,245
Qiyang	15	70										6,000
Lingxian	12	48	1,312	1,917	601	492	546	218	382			5,468
Zixing	5	79	2,148	1,123	891	341	699	122				5,324
Guidong	7	95	816	1,156	1,022	1,507	94	62	204	297	25	5,193
Xintian	8	47	456	2,927	955	488	299	25				5,150
Changning		78	486	2,378	823	536	96	12		34	178	4,549
Cili	11	48	263	1,550	601	1,806	236	40				4,496
Linxiang	7	95	624	995	847	1,195	47	31	105	152	81	4,077
Taoyuan	7	36										4,000
Yuanjiang	3	19	241	11,,74	520	1,615	243	46				3,839
Lanshan	4	51	765	1,499	604	385	41	21			35	3,350
Lixian	4	16	597	1,033	389	249	215	66				2,549

COMPARATIVE TABLE OF PEASANT ASSOCIATION MEMBERSHIP BY XIAN (continued)

Name of xian	No. of qu assns	No. of xiang assns	Social Status of Members									No. of Members
			Agr. laborers	Share croppers	Semi owner peasants	Owner peasants	Handi-craft workers	Primary school teachers	Small merchant	Women	Other	
Jiahe	3	27	295	598	588	850	89	32				2,452
Anxiang	6	13	280	760	680	440	120	18				2,298
Yongming	5	31	58	522	1,150	420	21	11				2,182
Yueyang	7	47	136	830	410	558	65	11				2,010
Xupu	2	11	540	775	331	204	108	7				1,965
Daoxian	13	39	136	540	282	403	56	18				1,435
Luxi	3	17	102	350	520	240	82	12				1,306
Suining	4	15	121	314	332	297	13	34				1,111
Ningyuan	8	13	86	480	105	159	42	20				892
Chengbu	1	8	130	195	372	101	74	13	14			889
Lingling	4	15	23	133	167	251	8	28	29		58	697
Mayang		9	130	348	36	19	4	3	21	21	48	630
Zhijiang		4		118	76	73		7				274
Total	461	6,867										1,367,727

Xiangxiang, Hengshan, and Xiangtan *xian*, this is of course no problem since the power of the landlords has been overturned and the peasants constitute the sole power. But in *xian* like Liling, there are still some places (such as the two western and southern *xian*[50] of Liling) where the power of the landlords seems weaker than that of the peasants but, because the political struggle has not been sharp, landlord power is in fact surreptitiously opposing peasant power. In such places it is still too early to say that the peasants have gained political victory; they must wage the political struggle more vigorously until the power of the landlords is completely cast down. Generally speaking, the methods used by the peasants to deal political blows to the landlords are as follows:

a. Auditing the accounts. Most of the local bullies and bad gentry are guilty of embezzling the public funds entrusted to them, and the books are not in order. This time, the peasants have used the auditing of accounts as an occasion to bring down countless local bullies and bad gentry. In many places auditing committees have been set up for the specific purpose of settling accounts with the local bullies and bad gentry, who shudder at the mere sight of such an organ. Auditing campaigns like this have been carried out extensively in all the *xian* where the peasant movement has arisen. Their significance lies not so much in recovering the funds as in exposing the crimes of the local bullies and bad gentry and knocking them down from their political as well as their social positions.

b. Imposing fines. The peasants work out fines for such offenses as irregularities revealed by the audits, past outrages against the peasants, current activities that undermine the peasant associations, violations of the ban on gambling, and refusal to surrender opium pipes. For crimes like these, the peasants resolve that such and such a local bully must pay so much, and such and such a member of the bad gentry so much, the sums ranging from tens to thousands of *yuan*. Naturally, a man who has been fined by the peasants completely loses face.

c. Levying contributions. Rich but heartless landlords are made to contribute funds for the relief of the poor, for running cooperatives and rural credit agencies, or for other purposes. Though milder than fines, these contributions are also a form of punishment. To avoid trouble, quite a few landlords voluntarily make contributions to the peasant associations.

d. Minor protests. When someone harms a peasant association by word or deed and the offense is a minor one, the peasants collect in a crowd and swarm into the offender's house to remonstrate with him not too severely. He is usually let off after writing a pledge to "cease and desist," in which he explicitly undertakes to refrain henceforth from words and deeds that would harm the reputation of the peasant association.

---

50. The two . . . *xian* → The two . . . districts

e. Major demonstrations. A big crowd is rallied to demonstrate against *the house of* a local bully or one of the bad gentry who is hostile to the association. The demonstrators eat at the offender's house, slaughtering his pigs and consuming his grain as a matter of course. Quite a few such cases have occurred. There was a case recently at Majiahe, Xiangtan *xian*, where a crowd of fifteen thousand went to *the houses of* six of the bad gentry to condemn them; the whole affair lasted four days, during which more than 130 pigs were killed and eaten. After such demonstrations, the peasants usually impose fines.

f. Parades through the villages in tall hats. This sort of thing is very common everywhere. One of the local bullies or bad gentry is crowned with a tall paper hat bearing the words "Local bully so-and-so" or "So-and-so, one of the bad gentry." He is led by a rope and escorted with big crowds in front and behind. Sometimes brass gongs are beaten and flags are waved to attract people's attention. This form of punishment, more than any other, makes the local bullies and bad gentry tremble. Anyone who has once been crowned with a tall paper hat loses face altogether and can never again hold up his head. Hence many of the rich prefer being fined to wearing the tall hat. But wear it they must, if the peasants insist. One township peasant association did things most ingeniously. It arrested a member of the bad gentry and announced that he was to be crowned that very day. The man turned blue with fear. But then *in the end* the peasants decided not to crown him that day. They argued that if he were crowned right away, he would become case-hardened and no longer afraid, and that it would be better to let him go home and crown him some other day. Not knowing when he would be crowned, the man was in daily suspense and was never at ease, whether sitting or lying down.

g. Imprisonment in the *xian* jail. This is a heavier punishment than wearing the tall paper hat. A local bully or one of the bad gentry is arrested and locked up in the *xian* jail, and the *xian* magistrate is asked to sentence him. Those who are locked up today are not the same as they used to be. Formerly it was the gentry who sent peasants to be locked up; now it is the other way around.

h. "Banishment." This applies to the most notorious criminals among the local bullies and bad gentry. The peasants have no desire to banish them, but would rather arrest or execute them. Afraid of being arrested or executed, they then run away. In *xian* where the peasant movement is well developed, almost all the important local bullies and bad gentry have fled, and this amounts to banishment. Among them, the top rank has fled to Shanghai, the second rank to Hankou, the third rank to Changsha, and the fourth rank to the *xian* towns. Of all the fugitive local bullies and bad gentry, those who have fled to Shanghai are the safest. Some of those who fled to Hankou, like the three from Huarong, were eventually captured and brought back. Those who fled to Changsha are in still greater danger of being seized at any moment by students in the provincial capital who hail from their *xian*; I myself saw two captured in Changsha. Those who have taken refuge in the *xian* towns are only of the fourth rank, but there are many eyes and ears,[51] and they can easily be discovered. The financial authorities have blamed the difficulties encountered by the Hunan Provincial Government in raising money on the fact that the peasants were banishing the well-to-do. This, too, gives an idea of the extent to which the local bullies and bad gentry are not tolerated in their home villages.

i. Shooting. This is confined to the worst local bullies and bad gentry and is carried out by the peasants jointly with other sections of the popular masses. For instance, Wang Zhize[52] of Ningxiang, Zhou Jiagan of Yueyang, and Fu Daonan and Sun Bozhu of Huarong were shot by the government authorities at the insistence of the peasants and all circles. For example, in the case of Yan Rongqiu of Xiangtan, it was the peasants and all circles who compelled the magistrate to execute him directly.[53] Liu Shao of Ningxiang was beaten to death by the peasants themselves. For example, the executions of people like Peng Zhifan of Liling, Zhuo Tianjue, and Cao Yun of Yiyang are pending, subject to review by the "Special Tribunal for Trying Local Bullies and Bad Gentry." The execution of one such big member of the bad gentry or big local bully reverberates throughout a whole *xian* and is very effective in eradicating the remaining evils of feudalism. Every *xian* has such big local bullies and bad gentry, some as many as several dozen, and others at least a few, and the only effective way of suppressing the reactionaries is to execute at least one or two[54] in each *xian* who are guilty of the most heinous crimes. When the local bullies and bad gentry were at the height of their power, they killed peasants literally without batting an eyelid. He Maiquan, for ten years head of the defense corps in the town of Xinkang, Changsha *xian*, was personally responsible for killing almost a thousand poverty-stricken peasants; this action he euphemistically described as executing bandits. In Yintian Temple, Xiangtan,[55] Tang Junyan and Luo Shulin who headed the defense corps have killed more than fifty people and buried four alive in the fourteen years since the second year of the Republic. Of the more than fifty they murdered, the first two were perfectly innocent beggars. Tang Junyan said, "Let me make a start by killing a couple of beggars." And so these two lives were snuffed out. Such being the cruelty of the local bullies and bad gentry in former days, and such being the white terror they created in the countryside, how can one say that the peasants should not now rise and shoot one or two[56] of the local bullies and bad gentry and create just a little reign of terror in order to suppress the counterrevolutionaries?

---

51. But there are many eyes and ears → But the peasantry, having many eyes and ears
52. Wang Zhize → Yang Zhize
53. Execute him directly → To agree to hand him over from prison, and the peasants themselves executed him.
54. One or two → a few
55. In Yintian Temple, Xiangtan → In the town of Yintian of my native *xian* of Xiangtan
56. One or two → A few

3. Dealing Economic Blows to the Landlords

a. Prohibition on sending grain out of the area, forcing up grain prices, and hoarding and cornering. This is one of the great events of recent months in the economic struggle of the Hunan peasants. Since last October the poor peasants have prevented the outflow of the grain of the landlords and rich peasants and have banned the forcing up of grain prices and hoarding and cornering. As a result, the poor peasants have fully achieved their objective; the ban on the outflow of grain is *indeed* watertight, grain prices have already fallen considerably, and hoarding and cornering have disappeared. *This has outraged the landlords, rich peasants, the merchants, and even the government, but this is done by the broad peasant masses who make up 70 percent. In terms of their immediate interests, they think it should be this way. The political and economic explanation of this matter I shall take up again later.*

b. Prohibition on increasing rents and deposits; agitation for reduced rents and deposits. Last July and August, when the peasant associations were still in an era of weakness, the landlords, following their long-established practice of maximum exploitation, served notice one after another on their tenants that rents and deposits would be increased. But by October, when the peasant associations had grown considerably in strength and had all come out against the raising of rents,[57] the landlords dared not breathe another word on the subject. From November onwards, as the peasants have gained ascendancy over the landlords, they have taken the further steps of agitating for reduced rents and deposits. What a pity, *all the* peasants say, that the peasant associations were not strong enough when rents were being paid last autumn, or we could have reduced them then. The peasants are carrying out extensive propaganda for rent reduction in the coming autumn, and the landlords are all asking how the reductions are to be carried out. *It is absolutely impossible for them to oppose this.* As for the reduction of deposits, this is already under way in Hengshan and other *xian.*

c. Prohibition on cancelling tenancies. In July and August of last year there were still many instances of landlords cancelling tenancies and reletting the land. *But* after October, nobody dared cancel a tenancy. Today, the cancelling of tenancies and the reletting of land are quite out of the question; all that remains as something of a problem is whether a tenancy can be cancelled if the landlord wants to cultivate the land himself. In some places even this is not allowed by the peasants. In others the cancelling of a tenancy may be permitted if the landlord wants to cultivate the land himself, but then the problem of unemployment among the tenant-peasants arises. There is as yet no uniform way of solving this problem.

d. Reduction of interest. Interest has been generally reduced in Anhua, and there have been reductions in all other *xian*, too. But wherever the peasant

---

57. Raising of rents → Raising rents and deposits

associations are powerful, the landlords, for fear that the money will be communized, have completely stopped lending, and virtually no loans are available in
the countryside. *This is a big problem in the rural areas; it will be discussed
in some detail later.* What is currently called reduction of interest is confined
to old loans. Not only is the interest on such old loans reduced, but the
creditor is actually forbidden to press for the repayment of the principal. The
poor peasant replies, "Don't blame me. The year is nearly over. I'll pay you
back next year."

4. Overthrowing the Feudal Politics[58] of the Local Bullies and Bad Gentry in the Rural Areas— Smashing the Du and the Tuan

The old organs of rural administration[59] in the *du* and *tuan*,[60] and especially at
the *du* level (namely just below the *xian* level), used to be almost exclusively in
the hands of the local bullies and bad gentry. They[61] had jurisdiction over a
population of from ten to fifty or sixty thousand people. They had their own
independent armed forces, such as the township defense corps; their own independent fiscal powers, such as the power to levy taxes;[62] and their own judiciary,
which could freely arrest, imprison, try, and punish the peasants and so on. The
bad gentry who ran these organs *of rural administration* were virtual monarchs
of the countryside. Comparatively speaking, the peasants were not so much
concerned with the president of the republic, the provincial military governor, or
the *xian* magistrate; their real "bosses" were these rural monarchs. A mere
snort,[63] and the peasants *all* knew they had to watch their step. As a consequence
of the present revolt in the countryside, the authority of the landlord class has
been struck down everywhere, and the organs of rural administration dominated
by the local bullies and bad gentry have naturally collapsed in its wake. The
heads of the *du* and the *tuan* all steer clear of the people, dare not show their
faces and hand all local matters over to the peasant associations. They put people
off with the remark, "It is none of my business!"

Whenever their conversation turns to the heads of the *du* and the *tuan*, the
peasants say angrily, "That bunch! They are finished!"

Yes, the term "finished" truly describes the state of the old organs of rural
administration wherever the storm of revolution has raged.

---

58. Feudal Politics → Feudal Rule
59. Organs of rural administration → Organs of political power in the countryside
60. Here the *Selected Works* adds a parenthetical remark: (i. e., the district and the
township)
61. They → The *du*
62. To levy taxes → To levy taxes per *mou* of land
63. Snort → Snort from these people

5. Overthrowing the Armed Forces of the Landlords and Establishing Those of the Peasants

The armed forces of the landlord class were smaller in central Hunan than in the western and southern parts of the province. An average of 600 rifles for each *xian* would make a total of 45,000 rifles for all the seventy-five *xian*; there may, in fact, be more than this number. In the southern and central parts where the peasant movement is being developed, the landlord class cannot hold its own because of the overwhelming momentum with which the peasants have risen, and its armed forces have largely capitulated to the peasant associations and taken the side of the peasants; examples of this are to be found in such *xian* as Ningxiang, Pengjiang, Liuyang, Changsha, Liling, Xiangtan, Xiangxiang, Anhua, Hengshan, and Hengyang. In some *xian* such as Baoqing and so on, a small number of the landlords' armed forces are taking a neutral stand, though still with a tendency to capitulate. Another small section are opposing the peasant associations, but the peasants are attacking them and may wipe them out before long, as, for example, in such *xian* as Yichang, Linwu, and Jiahe. At the present time, stronger measures are being taken against these forces, which may *all* be eradicated soon. The armed forces thus taken over from the reactionary landlords are all being reorganized into a "standing household militia" and are under the new organs of rural self-government, which are organs of the political power of the peasantry. This "taking over these old armed forces" is one part of building up an armed force of the peasantry. *Even though some of them are still struggling, the various* xian *in southern and central Hunan have no problems any more. There are some problems only in western Hunan.* In addition, there is a new way for establishing an armed force of the peasants, which is through the setting up of spear corps under the peasant associations. The spears have pointed, double-edged blades mounted on long shafts, and there are now 100,000 of these weapons in Xiangxiang *xian* alone. Other *xian* such as Xiangtan, Hengshan, Liling, and Changsha have 70,000 to 80,000, or 50,000 to 60,000, or 30,000 to 40,000 each. In every *xian* where there is a peasant movement, the spears are spreading rapidly. These peasants thus armed form an "irregular household militia." This multitude equipped with spears, which is larger than the old armed forces mentioned above, is a newborn "thing,"[64] the mere sight of which makes the local tyrants and evil gentry shiver. The revolutionary authorities in Hunan should see to it that this kind of thing[65] is built up on a really extensive scale among the more than 20 million peasants in the seventy-five *xian* of the province, that every peasant, whether young or in his prime, possesses a spear, and that no restrictions are imposed as though a spear were something dreadful. Anyone who is scared at the sight of the spear corps is indeed a weakling! Only

---

64. "Thing" → Armed force
65. This kind of thing → This armed power

the local bullies and bad gentry are frightened of them, but no revolutionaries should take fright.

6. *Overthrowing the Political Power of the* xian *Magistrate and His Bailiffs*

That only if the peasants rise can the *xian* government be cleaned up has already been proved in Haifeng, Guangdong Province. On this occasion in Hunan, we have obtained further ample proof. In a *xian* that is under the sway of the local bullies and bad gentry, the magistrate, whoever he may be, is always[66] a corrupt official. In a *xian* where the peasants have risen there is clean government, whoever the magistrate may be. In the *xian* I visited, the magistrates had to consult the peasant associations on everything in advance. In *xian* where the power of the peasant movement was very strong, the word of the peasant association worked miracles. If the peasant association demanded the arrest of a local bully in the morning, the magistrate dared not delay till noon; if they demanded it by noon, he dared not delay till the afternoon. When the power of the peasants was just beginning to make itself felt in the countryside, the magistrate worked in league[67] with the local bullies and bad gentry. When the peasants' power grew till it matched that of the landlords, the magistrate took the position of trying to accommodate both sides, accepting some of the peasant association's suggestions while rejecting others. The remark that "the word of the peasants[68] works miracles" applies only when the power of the landlords has been completely beaten down by that of the peasants. At present the political situation in *xian* such as Xiangxiang, Xiangtan, Liling, and Hengshan is as follows:

a. All decisions are made by a joint council consisting of the magistrate and the representatives of the revolutionary mass organizations. The council is convened by the magistrate and meets in his office. In some *xian* it is called the "joint council of public bodies and the local government," and in others the "council of *xian* affairs." Besides the magistrate himself, those attending *but not voting* are the representatives of the *xian* peasant association, trade union council, merchant association, women's association, school staff association, student association, and Guomindang party office. At such council meetings the magistrate is influenced by the views of the public organizations and "invariably does their bidding." The adoption of a democratic committee system of *xian* government does[69] not, therefore, present *the slightest* problem in Hunan. The present *xian* governments are already quite "democratic" both in form and substance. This situation has been brought about only in the last two or three months, that

---

66. Always → Almost always
67. Worked in league → Worked in league . . . against the peasants
68. The peasants → The peasant association
69. Does → Should

is, since the peasants have risen all over the countryside and overthrown the power of the local bullies and bad gentry. It has now come about that the magistrates, seeing their old props collapse and needing new props to retain their posts, have begun to curry favor with the public organizations, and the situation has changed as described above.

b. The judicial assistant has scarcely any cases to handle. The judicial system in Hunan remains one in which the *xian* magistrate is concurrently in charge of judicial affairs, with an assistant to help him in handling cases. To get rich, the magistrate and his underlings used to rely entirely on "collecting taxes and levies, procuring men and provisions for the armed forces," and "extorting money in civil and criminal lawsuits by confounding right and wrong," the last being the most regular and reliable source of income. In the last few months, with the downfall of the local bullies and bad gentry, all the legal pettifoggers have disappeared. What is more, the peasants' problems, big and small, are now all settled in the peasant associations at the various levels. Thus the *xian* judicial assistant simply has nothing to do. The one in Xiangxiang told me, "When there were no peasant associations, an average of sixty civil or criminal suits were brought to the *xian* government each day; now it receives an average of only four or five suits a day." So it is that the purses of the magistrates and their underlings perforce remain empty.

c. The armed guards, the police, and the bailiffs all keep out of the way and dare not go near the villages to practice their extortions. In the past the people in the villages were afraid of the people in the towns, but now the people in the towns are afraid of the people in the villages. In particular the vicious curs kept by the *xian* government—the police, the armed guards, and the bailiffs—are afraid of going to the villages, or if they do so, they no longer dare to practice their extortions. They tremble at the sight of the peasants' spears.

7. Overthrowing the Clan Authority of the Ancestral Temples and Clan Elders, the Religious Authority of Town and Village Gods, and the Masculine Authority of Husbands

A man in China is usually subjected to the domination of three systems of authorities: (1) the state system (political authority), ranging from the national, provincial, and *xian* government down to that of the township; (2) the clan system (clan authority), ranging from the central ancestral temple and its branch temples down to the head of the household; and (3) the supernatural system (religious authority), ranging from the King of Hell down to the town and village gods belonging to the nether world, and from the Emperor of Heaven down to all the various gods and spirits belonging to the celestial world. As for women, in addition to being dominated by these three,[70] they are also dominated by men

---

70. These three → These three systems of authority

(the authority of the husband). These four authorities—political, clan, religious, and masculine—are the embodiment of the whole feudal-patriarchal ideological system,[71] and are the four thick ropes binding the Chinese people, particularly the peasants. How the peasants have overthrown the political authority of the landlords in the countryside has been described above. The political authority of the landlords is the backbone of all the other systems of authority. With the politics[72] of the landlords overturned, the clan authority, the religious authority, and the authority of the husband all begin to totter. Where the peasant association is powerful, the clan elders and administrators of temple funds no longer dare oppress those lower in the clan hierarchy or embezzle clan funds. The worst clan elders and administrators, being local bullies, have been thrown out. No one any longer dares to practice the corporal and capital punishments[73] that used to be inflicted in the ancestral temples, such as flogging, drowning, and burying alive. The old rule barring women and poor people from the banquets in the ancestral temples has also been broken. The women of Baiguo in Hengshan *xian* gathered in force and swarmed into their ancestral temple, firmly planted their backsides on the seats, and joined in the eating and drinking, while the venerable clan bigwigs had willy-nilly to let them do as they pleased. At another place, where poor peasants had been excluded from temple banquets, a group of them flocked in and ate and drank their fill, while the local bullies and bad gentry and other long-gowned gentlemen all took to their heels in fright. Everywhere religious authority totters as the peasant movement develops. In many places the peasant associations have taken over the temples of the gods as their offices. Everywhere they advocate the appropriation of temple property for peasant schools and to defray the expenses of the associations, calling it "public revenue from superstition." In Liling *xian*, prohibiting superstitious practices and smashing idols have become quite the vogue. In its northern districts the peasants have prohibited the incense-burning processions to propitiate the god of pestilence. There were many idols in the Daoist temple on Fubo Hill in Lukou, but when extra premises were needed for the district party offices [of the Guomindang], they were all piled up in a corner, big and small together, and no peasant raised any objection. Since then, sacrifices to the gods, the performance of religious rites, and the offering of sacred lamps have rarely been practiced when a death occurs in a family. Because the initiative in this matter was taken by the chairman of the peasant association, Sun Xiaoshan, he is hated by the local Daoist priests. In the Longfeng Nunnery in the North Third District, the peasants and primary school teachers chopped up the wooden idols and actually used the wood to cook meat. More than thirty idols in the Dongfu Monastery in the

---

71. Ideological system → Ideology and system
72. Politics → Political authority
73. The corporal and capital punishments → The cruel corporal and capital punishments

Southern District were burned by the students and peasants together, and only two small images of Bao Gong were snatched up by an old peasant who said, "Don't commit a sin!" Everywhere it has always been the case that[74] only the older peasants and the women believe in the gods; all the younger peasants do not.[75] Since the latter control the associations, the overthrow of religious authority and the eradication of superstition are going on everywhere. As to the authority of the husband, this has always been weaker among the poor peasants because, out of economic necessity, their womenfolk have to do more manual labor than the women of the richer classes and therefore have more say and greater power of decision in family matters. *In sexual matters, they also have relatively more freedom. Among the poor peasants in the countryside, triangular and multilateral relationships are almost universal.* With the increasing bankruptcy of the rural economy in recent years, the basis for men's domination over women has already been weakened. With the rise of the peasant movement, the women in many places have now begun to organize rural women's associations; the opportunity has come for them to lift up their heads, and the authority of the husband is getting shakier every day. In a word, the whole feudal-patriarchal ideological system[76] is tottering with the growth of the peasants' power. But *in the past and* at the present time, the peasants are concentrating *entirely* on destroying the landlords' political authority. Wherever it has been wholly destroyed, they are beginning to press their attack in the three other spheres of the clan, the gods, and male domination. But such attacks have only just "begun," and there can be no thorough overthrow of all three until the peasants have won complete victory in the economic fight. Therefore, our present task is to lead the peasants to put their greatest efforts into the political struggle, so that the landlords' authority is entirely overthrown. The economic struggle should follow immediately, so that the economic problems[77] of the poor peasants may be fundamentally solved. As for smashing the clan system, superstitious ideas, and one-sided concepts of chastity,[78] this will follow as a natural consequence of victory in the political and economic struggles. If too much of an effort is made arbitrarily and prematurely to abolish these things, then the local bullies and bad gentry will seize the pretext to put forward such slogans[79] as "the peasant association has no piety towards ancestors," "the peasant association is blasphemous and is destroying religion," and "the peasant association stands for the communization of wives," all for the purpose of undermining the peasant movement. A case in point is the recent events at Xiangxiang, Hunan, and Yangxin, Hubei,

---

74. Everywhere it has always been the case that . . . → In places where the power of the peasants is predominant, . . .

75. All the younger peasants do not → All the younger peasants no longer do so

76. Ideological system → Ideology and system

77. The economic problems → The land problem and the other economic problems

78. One-sided concepts of chastity → Incorrect relationships between men and women

79. Such slogans → Such counterrevolutionary slogans

where the landlords exploited the opposition of some peasants to smashing idols. It is the peasants who made the idols, and when the time comes they will cast the idols aside with their own hands; there is no need for anyone else to do it for them prematurely. Our[80] propaganda policy in such matters is, "Draw the bow, but do not release the arrow, having seemed to leap."[81] The idols should be removed by the peasants themselves, the ancestral tablets should be smashed by the peasants themselves, the temples to martyred virgins and arches for chaste and filial widows and daughters-in-law should be demolished by the peasants themselves.[82]

While I was in the countryside, I did some propaganda against superstition among the peasants. I said: "If you believe in the Eight Characters, you hope for good luck; if you believe in geomancy, you hope to benefit from the location of your ancestral graves. This year within the space of a few months the local bullies, bad gentry, and corrupt officials have all fallen from power. Is it possible that until a few months ago they all had good luck and enjoyed the benefit of well-sited ancestral graves, while suddenly in the last few months their luck has turned and their ancestral graves have ceased to exert a beneficial influence?

"The local bullies and bad gentry jeer at your peasant association and say, 'How odd! Today, the world is a world of committeemen. Look, you can't even go to pass water without bumping into a committeeman!' Quite true, the towns and the villages, the peasant associations and the labor unions,[83] the Guomindang and the Communist Party, all without exception have their executive committee members—it is indeed a world of committeemen. But is this caused by the Eight Characters and the location of the ancestral graves? How strange! The Eight Characters of all the poor wretches in the countryside have suddenly turned auspicious! And their ancestral graves have suddenly started exerting beneficial influences!

"The gods? Worship them by all means. But if you had only Lord Guan and the Goddess of Mercy and no peasant association, could you have overthrown

---

80. Our → The Communist Party's

81. Mao here takes his text from the *Mencius*, VII, I, XLI, 3 (Legge, Vol. II, p. 474). Legge adds the words "with it to the mark" after "having seemed to leap," to convey his understanding of the passage. Couvreur (*Les quatre livres*, Vol. IV, p. 628) translates "Il saute en quelque sorte"; his parenthetical explanation reads: "C'est-à-dire, le sage enseigne ses disciples beaucoup plus par ses examples que par ses paroles; il les précède dans la voie, et avance comme par bonds." The moral that Mao wished to draw from the passage is clear, in any case: the master illustrates the action to be taken, driving home the message with dramatic gestures, but leaves it to the disciples to carry out the action. No doubt he also had in mind a sentence which comes immediately after the one he cited: "Those who are able, follow him."

82. By the peasants themselves → By the peasants themselves; it is wrong for anybody else to do it for them.

83. The peasant associations and the labor unions → The labor unions and the peasant associations

the local tyrants and evil gentry? The 'gods' and 'goddesses' are indeed misera-ble objects. You have worshipped them for several thousand years,[84] and they have not overthrown a single one of the local bullies or bad gentry for you! Now you want to have your rent reduced. Let me ask you, what method will you use? Will you place your faith in the gods, or in the peasant associations?"

When I spoke these words, the peasants laughed, and in the midst of their laughter, I imagined that the gods and idols all fled from sight.

8. Spreading Political Propaganda

Even if ten thousand schools of law and political science had been opened, could they have brought as much political education to the people, men and women, young and old, all the way into the poorest and remotest corners of the country-side, as the peasant associations have done in so short a time? I think they certainly could not have. Down with imperialism! Down with the warlords! Down with the corrupt officials! Down with the local bullies and bad gentry!— these political slogans have grown wings, they have found their way to the young, the middle-aged, and the old, to the women and children in countless villages, they have penetrated into their minds and flowed back from their minds into their mouths. Suppose, for example, you watch a group of children at play. If one gets angry with another, if he glares, stamps his foot, and shakes his fist, you will then immediately hear from the other the shrill cry: "Down with imperialism!"

In the Xiangtan area, when the children who pasture the cattle get into a fight, one will take the part of Tang Shengzhi and the other that of Ye Kaixin.[85] When, after a while, one is defeated and runs away with the other chasing him, it is the pursuer who is Tang Shengzhi and the pursued Ye Kaixin. As to the song "Down with the Imperialist Powers. . . ," of course almost every child in the towns can sing it, and now many village children can sing it too. Some of the peasants can also recite a little of Mr. Sun Yatsen's Testament. They pick out from it the terms "freedom," "equality," "the Three People's Principles," and "unequal trea-ties" and apply them, if rather crudely, in their life. When somebody who looks like one of the gentry encounters a peasant on the road and stands on his dignity, refusing to make way along a pathway, the peasant will say angrily, "Hey, you local bully, don't you know the Three People's Principles?"

Formerly, when the peasants from the vegetable farms on the outskirts of Changsha entered the city to sell their produce, they used to be pushed around by

---

84. Several thousand years → Several hundred years

85. As indicated above, in note 15 to the present text, Tang Shengzhi had forced Zhao Hengti to resign the governorship to him in March 1926. Zhao thereupon appealed for aid to his principal ally, Wu Peifu, who sent a strong force from Hubei under the command of Ye Kaixin (like Tang Shengzhi a Hunanese). On May 2, Ye's troops entered Changsha, and continued to press their attack southward. Tang Shengzhi responded by aligning himself with the Guomindang, was appointed commander in chief of front line operations for the Northern Expedition, and had soon fought his way back to Changsha. By early July, Tang was firmly reestablished as governor, and Ye Kaixin had retreated to Wuhan.

the police. Now they can find a weapon, which is no other than the Three People's Principles. When a policeman strikes or swears at a peasant from a vegetable farm, the peasant from the vegetable farm immediately answers back by invoking the Three People's Principles and the policeman has not a word to say. Once in Xiangtan, when a district peasant association and a township peasant association could not see eye to eye about a certain matter, the chairman of the township association declared: "Down with the district peasant association's unequal treaties!"

The spread of political propaganda throughout the rural area is entirely an achievement of the peasant associations.[86] Simple slogans, cartoons, and speeches have produced such a widespread and speedy effect among the peasants that it is as though every one of them had been to a political school. According to the reports of comrades engaged in rural work, the influence of extensive political propaganda was to be found in the three great mass movements:[87] the anti-British demonstration, the celebration of the October Revolution, and the victory celebration for the Northern Expedition. In these movements, political propaganda was conducted extensively wherever there were peasant associations, arousing the whole countryside. *Consequently,* the impact was very great. From now on, care should be taken to make use of every opportunity gradually to enrich the content and clarify the meaning of the simple slogans mentioned above!

9. Peasant Bans and Prohibitions

When the peasant associations[88] establish their authority in the countryside, the peasants begin to forbid strictly or to restrict the things they dislike. Gaming, gambling, and opium smoking are the three things that are most strictly forbidden.

Gaming: Where the peasant association is powerful, mahjong, dominoes, and card games are wholly banned.

The peasant association in the Fourteenth District of Xiangxiang burned two basketfuls of mahjong [pieces].

If you go to the countryside, you will find none of these games played; anyone who violates the ban is promptly and strictly punished.

Gambling: Former hardened gamblers are now themselves forcefully suppressing gambling; this abuse, too, has been swept away in places where the peasant association is powerful.

Opium smoking: The prohibition is extremely strict. When the peasant association orders the surrender of opium pipes, no one dares to raise the least objection. In Liling *xian,* one of the bad gentry who did not surrender his pipes was arrested and paraded through the villages.

---

86. The peasant associations → The Communist Party and the peasant associations
87. Mass movements → Mass rallies
88. The peasant associations → The peasant associations, under the leadership of the Communist Party

The peasants' campaign to "disarm the opium smokers" is no less impressive than the disarming of the troops of Wu Peifu and Sun Chuanfang by the Northern Expeditionary Army. Quite a number of venerable fathers of officers in the revolutionary army, old men who were opium addicts and inseparable from their pipes, have been disarmed by the "emperors" (as the peasants are called derisively by the bad gentry). The "emperors" have banned not only the growing and smoking of opium, but also trafficking in it. A great deal of the opium transported from Guizhou to Jiangxi via the various *xian* of Baoqing, Xiangxiang, Yuoxian, and Liling has been intercepted on the way and burned. This has affected government revenues. As a result, out of consideration for the army's need for funds in the Northern Expedition, the provincial peasant association ordered the associations at the lower levels "temporarily to postpone the ban on opium traffic." This, however, has upset and displeased the peasants.

There are many other things besides these three that the peasants have prohibited or restricted, the following being some examples:

The flower drum. An *obscene and vulgar* local opera. Its performances are forbidden in many places.

Sedan-chairs. In many *xian*, especially Xiangxiang, there have been cases of smashing sedan-chairs. *A prohibition on taking sedan-chairs has become a vogue. The only people who can take sedan-chairs are the peasant movement officials; otherwise, they will be smashed.* The peasants, detesting the people who use this conveyance, are always ready to smash the chairs, but the peasant associations forbid them to do so. Peasant movement officials tell the peasants, "If you smash the chairs, you only save the rich money and lose the carriers their jobs. And the carriers will be out of a job if they have no work to do. Will that not hurt yourselves? Seeing the point, *the peasants answer, "That's right."* They then adopt a new [policy on] sedan chairs[89]—"to increase considerably the fares charged by the chair-carriers" so as to penalize the rich.

Distilling and sugar-making. The use of grain for distilling spirits and making sugar is everywhere prohibited, and therefore the distillers and sugar refiners are constantly complaining. Distilling is not banned in Futianpu, Hengshan *xian*, but prices are fixed very low, and the wine and spirits dealers, seeing no prospect of profit, have had to stop it.

Pigs. The number of pigs a family can keep is limited, for they consume grain.

Chickens and ducks. In Xiangxiang *xian* the raising of chickens and ducks is prohibited, but the women object. In Hengshan *xian*, each family in Yangtang is

---

89. New [policy on] sedan chairs → New method

allowed to keep only three chickens, and in Futianpu five chickens. In many places the raising of ducks is completely banned, for ducks not only consume grain but also ruin the rice plants and so are worse than chickens.

Feasts. Sumptuous feasts are generally forbidden. In Shaoshan, Xiangtan *xian*, it has been decided that guests are to be served only three kinds of animal food, namely, chicken, fish, and pork. It is also forbidden to serve bamboo shoots, kelp, and lentil noodles. In Hengshan *xian* it has been resolved that eight dishes and no more may be served at a banquet, and not even one more is allowed. Only five dishes are allowed in the East Third District in Liling *xian*, and only three meat and three vegetable dishes in North Second District, while in the West Third District New Year feasts are forbidden entirely. In Xiangxiang *xian*, there is a ban on all "egg-cake feasts," which are by no means sumptuous. When Tie Jiawan in the Second District gave an "egg-cake feast" at a son's wedding, the peasants, seeing the ban violated, swarmed into the house and destroyed the "egg-cake feast." In the town of Jiamuo, Xiangxiang *xian*, the people have refrained from eating expensive foods and use only fruit when offering ancestral sacrifices.

Oxen. Oxen are treasured possessions of the peasants *in the South*. "Slaughter an ox in this life and you will be an ox in the next" has become almost a religious tenet; oxen must never be killed. Before the peasants had power, they could only appeal to religious taboos in opposing the slaughter of cattle and had no real power to ban it. *People in the towns always want to eat beef, and therefore people in the towns always want to kill cattle.* Since the rise of the peasant associations, their *real* jurisdiction has extended even to the cattle, and they have prohibited the slaughter of cattle in the towns. Of the six butcheries that formerly existed in the *xian* town of Xiangtan, five are now closed and the remaining *merchant* slaughters only enfeebled or disabled animals. The slaughter of cattle is totally prohibited throughout Hengshan *xian*. *No one in the* xian *town dares slaughter either.* A peasant whose ox *fell from a high place, broke a leg,* and is now disabled *dared not kill it.* He consulted the peasant association *and got their permission* before he dared kill it. When the chamber of commerce of Zhuzhou rashly slaughtered a cow, the peasants *one day swarmed* into town and demanded an explanation. *As a result, the chamber,* besides paying a fine, had to let off firecrackers by way of apology.

Vagrant ways. A resolution passed in Liling *xian* prohibited the drumming of New Year greetings or the chanting of praises to the local deities or the singing of lotus rhymes. Various other *xian* have *passed resolutions* prohibiting this; in other places, these practices have disappeared of themselves, and no one engages in them any more. The "beggar-bullies" or "vagabonds," who used to be extremely evil,[90] now have no alternative but to submit to the peasant associations.

---

90. Evil → Fierce

In Shaoshan, Xiangtan *xian*, the vagabonds used to make the temple of the Rain God their regular haunt and could not be persuaded by anyone,[91] but since the rise of the associations they have all stolen away. The peasant association in Huti *tuan*[92] in the same *xian* caught three such vagabonds and made them carry clay for the brick kilns. Resolutions have been passed prohibiting the wasteful customs associated with New Year calls and gifts.

Besides these, a great many other minor prohibitions have been introduced in various places, such as the Liling prohibitions on incense-burning processions to propitiate the god of pestilence, on buying preserves and fruit for ritual presents, on burning ritual paper garments during the Festival of the Dead, and on pasting up good-luck posters at the New Year. At Gushui in Xiangxiang County, there is even a prohibition on smoking water pipes. In the Second District, letting off firecrackers and ceremonial guns is forbidden, with a fine of 1.20 *yuan* for the former and 2.40 *yuan* for the latter. Religious rites for the dead are prohibited in the Seventh and Twentieth Districts. In the Eighteenth District, it is forbidden to make funeral gifts of money. Things like these, which defy enumeration, may be generally called "peasant bans and prohibitions." They are of great significance in two respects. First, they represent a revolt against bad customs,[93] such as gaming, gambling, and opium smoking. These customs arose out of the rotten political environment of the landlord class and are swept away once its authority is overthrown. Second, the prohibitions are a form of self-defense against exploitation by city merchants; such are the prohibitions on feasts and on buying preserves and fruit for ritual presents. Because manufactured goods are extremely dear and agricultural products are extremely cheap, the peasants[94] are very ruthlessly exploited by the merchants, and they must therefore engage in passive resistance.[95] The reason for all this is that the unscrupulous merchants exploited them;[96] it is not a matter of their rejecting manufactured goods[97] in order to uphold the Doctrine of Oriental Culture. The peasants' economic protection of themselves necessitates that the peasants organize consumers' cooperatives for collective sale and production.[98] Furthermore, it is also necessary for the

---

91. Could not be persuaded by anyone → Feared nobody

92. Huti *tuan* → Huti Township

93. Bad customs → Bad social customs

94. The peasants → The peasants are extremely impoverished

95. Engage in passive resistance → Encourage frugality to protect themselves. As for the ban on sending grain out of the area, it is imposed to prevent the price from rising because the poor peasants have not enough to feed themselves and have to buy grain on the market.

96. The reason for all this is that the unscrupulous merchants exploited them → The reason for all this is the peasants' poverty and the contradictions between town and country

97. Manufactured goods → Manufactured goods or trade between town and country

98. Collective sale and production → Collective purchase and consumption

government to provide help to the peasant associations in establishing credit cooperatives. If these things were done, the peasants would naturally find it unnecessary to ban the outflow of grain as a method of keeping down[99] the price; nor would they have to prohibit the inflow of manufactured goods[100] as the sole method of economic self-defense.

10. Eliminating Banditry

In my opinion, no ruler in any dynasty from Yao, Shun, Yu, and Tang[101] down to the Qing emperors and the presidents of the Republic has ever shown as much prowess in eliminating banditry as have the peasant associations today. Wherever the peasant associations are powerful, there is not even the shadow of a bandit. It is truly amazing! In many places there are no longer even those pilferers who stole vegetables *at night*. Though there are still pilferers in some places, in the *xian* I visited, even including those that were formerly bandit-ridden, there was no trace of bandits. The reasons are: First, the members of the peasant associations are spread out everywhere over the hills and dales, spear or cudgel in hand, ready to go into action in their hundreds, so that the bandits have nowhere to hide. Second, since the peasants have prohibited the outflow of rice,[102] the price of rice is *extremely* modest. It was six *yuan* a picul of rice last spring but only two *yuan* last winter. *The poor peasants can buy more grain with less money.* And the problem of food has become less serious than in the past for the people. Third, members of the secret societies have *all* joined the peasant associations, in which they can openly play[103] the hero and vent their grievances, so that there is no further need for the secret "mountain," "lodge," "shrine," and "river" forms of organization. In killing the pigs and sheep of the local tyrants and evil gentry and imposing heavy levies and fines, they have adequate outlets for their feelings against those who oppressed them. Fourth, the armies are recruiting large numbers of soldiers and many of the "unruly" have joined up. Thus the evil of banditry has been eliminated with the rise of the peasant movement. On this point, even the well-to-do approve of the peasant associations. Their comment is:

> The peasant associations? Well, to be fair, there is also something to be said for them.

In prohibiting gaming, gambling, and opium smoking, and in eliminating banditry, the peasant associations have won general approval.

---

99. Keeping down → Controlling
100. Manufactured goods → Certain manufactured goods
101. Yao, Shun, Yu, and Tang → Yu, Tang, Wen, and Wu
102. Since the peasants have prohibited the outflow of rice → Since the rise of the peasant movement
103. Openly play → Openly and legally play

11. *Abolishing Exorbitant Levies*

As the whole country has not yet been unified and the authority of the imperialists and the warlords has not been overthrown, there is as yet no way of removing the heavy burden of government taxes and levies on the peasants or, more explicitly, of removing the burden of expenditure for the revolutionary army. However, the exorbitant levies imposed on the peasants when the local bullies and bad gentry dominated rural administration, for example, the surcharge on each *mu* of land, have been abolished or at least reduced with the rise of the peasant movement and the downfall of the local bullies and bad gentry. This too should be counted among the achievements of the peasant associations.

12. *The Movement for Education*

In China education has always been the exclusive preserve of the landlords, and the peasants have had no access to it. But the landlords' culture is completely created by the peasants, for its sole source is the peasants' sweat and blood that they plundered. In China, *more than* 90 percent of the citizens have had no access to culture,[104] and of these the overwhelming majority are peasants. The moment the power of the exploiting class[105] was overthrown in the rural areas, the peasants' movement for education began. See how the peasants who hitherto detested the schools are today zealously setting up evening classes! They always disliked the "foreign-style school." When I was going to school and saw[106] that the peasants were against the "foreign-style school," I, too, used to identify myself with the general run of "foreign-style students and teachers" and stand up for it, feeling always that the peasants were "stupid and detestable people."[107] Only in the 14th year of the Republic, when I lived in the countryside for half a year,[108] did I realize that I had been wrong and the peasants' reasoning was *extremely* correct. The texts used in the rural primary schools were entirely about urban things and unsuited to rural needs. Besides, the attitude of the primary school teachers toward the peasants was very bad and, far from being helpful to the peasants, they came to be disliked by the peasants. Hence the peasants preferred the old-style schools (the so-called[109] "Chinese classes") to the modern schools[110] and the old-style teachers to the ones in the primary schools. Now the

---

104. The citizens *(guomin)* have had no access to culture *(wei shou wenhua)* → The people *(renmin)* have no education or culture *(wei shou wenhua jiaoyu)*.

105. The exploiting class → The landlords

106. Saw → Went back to the village and saw

107. "Stupid and detestable people" → Were somehow wrong

108. Half a year → Half a year, and was already a Communist and had acquired the Marxist viewpoint

109. The so-called → Which they called

110. Schools → Schools (which they called "foreign classes")

peasants are enthusiastically establishing evening classes, which they call "peasant schools." Some have already been opened, others are being organized, *and on the average there is one school for every township peasant association.* The peasants are very enthusiastic about setting up these *evening* schools and regard them, and only them, as truly their own. The sources of funds for the evening schools come from the local "public revenue from superstition," from ancestral temple funds, and from other idle public funds or property. The *xian* education boards wanted to use this money to establish national primary schools (that is, "foreign-style schools" not suited to the needs of the peasants), while the peasants wanted to set up peasant schools. Inevitably, there were clashes between the two sides, and the result was generally that both got some of the money, though there were places where the peasants got it all. The development of the peasant movement has naturally resulted in raising their cultural level. Before long, several[111] schools will have sprung up in the villages throughout the province; this is quite different from the empty talk about "universal education," which the intelligentsia and the so-called "educationalists" have been bandying back and forth and which after all this time remains an empty phrase.

13. The Cooperative Movement

The peasants really need cooperatives, especially consumers', marketing, and credit cooperatives. When they buy goods, the merchants exploit them; when they sell their farm produce, the merchants cheat them; when they borrow money or rice, they are fleeced by the usurers; and they are eager to find a solution to these three problems. During the fighting in the Yangtse valley last winter, when trade routes were cut and the price of salt went up in Hunan, a great many peasants organized cooperatives for salt. When the landlords deliberately stopped lending, there were many attempts by the peasants to organize credit agencies because they needed to borrow money. A major problem is the absence of detailed, standard rules of organization. In all localities, many of these spontaneously organized peasant cooperatives fail to conform to cooperative principles; as a result, the comrades engaged in the peasant movement are always eagerly enquiring about "rules and regulations." Given proper guidance, the cooperative movement can spread everywhere along with the growth of the peasant associations. *Because the term* hezuo *is not at all familiar to the peasants, [the idea] could also be rendered as* hehuopu.[112]

---

111. Several → Tens of thousands of

112. *Hezuo* (cooperate, literally "work together"), and *hezuoshe* (cooperative) have been the standard Chinese terms since the 1920s. The alternative that Mao suggests, *hehuopu*, means literally "joint goods shop." It is in fact this coinage which he used for "cooperative" in the title of this section of his report in the original version.

14. Building Roads and Embankments

This, too, is one of the achievements of the peasant associations. Before there were peasant associations the roads in the countryside were terrible. Because roads cannot be repaired without money, and the wealthy were unwilling to dip into their purses, the roads were left in bad shape. If there was any road work done at all, it was done as an act of charity; a little money was collected from families "wishing to gain merit in the next world," and a few narrow, skimpily paved roads were built. With the rise of the peasant associations, orders have been given specifying the required width—three, five, seven, or ten feet, according to the requirements of the different routes—and each landlord along a road has been ordered to build a section. Once the order is given, who dares to disobey? In a short time many good roads have appeared. This is no work of charity but the result of compulsion, and a little compulsion of this kind is not at all a bad thing. The same is true of the embankments. The ruthless landlords were always out to take what they could from the tenant-peasants and would never spend even a few copper cash on embankment repairs; they would leave them to dry up and the tenant-peasants to starve, caring about nothing but the rent. Now that there are peasant associations, they can be bluntly ordered to repair the embankments. When a landlord refuses, the association will tell him very affably:

"Very well! If you won't do the repairs, you will contribute grain, a *dou* for each workday." As this is a bad bargain for the landlord, he hastens to do the repairs. Consequently many defective embankments have been turned into good ones.

The fourteen deeds enumerated above have all been accomplished by the peasants under the command[113] of the peasant associations;[114] would the reader please consider and say whether any of them is bad? Only the local bullies and bad gentry, I think, will call them bad. Curiously enough, it is reported from Nanchang that Chiang Kaishek, Zhang Jingjiang, and other such gentlemen do not altogether approve of the activities of the Hunan peasants. This opinion is shared by Liu Yuezhi and other right-wing leaders in Hunan, all of whom say, "They have simply gone Red." But where would the national revolution be without this bit of Red? To talk about arousing the masses of the people day in and day out and then to be scared to death when the masses do rise—what difference is there between this and Lord She's love of dragons?[115]

---

113. The command → The leadership

114. Here the revised text inserts: in their fundamental spirit and revolutionary significance, . . .

115. The reference is to an anecdote in the *Xin xu* (New Prefaces) of Liu Xiang (76–5 B.C.), *zi* Zizheng, a descendant of Liu Bang. Lord She professed such a love of dragons that he decorated his whole palace with drawings and carvings of them. Pleased by this report, a real dragon paid him a visit and frightened Lord She out of his wits.

Letter to the Provincial Peasant Association

(March 14, 1927)[1]

I beg to state that I have recently read reports in the newspapers of Changsha about Jimei Publishing House's reprinting of *Collected Writings on the Peasants*.[2] These books were originally made available for reference to our institute's[3] students and to special representatives of the peasant movement from different provinces and were not for sale.[4] If it is necessary to reprint them, the following three conditions must be met: (1) your honorable association[5] must examine the matter and exclude from publication such dated items as, for exam-

---

This note was first published in the *Hunan minbao* on March 14, 1927. Our source is the text as reproduced in *Mao Zedong ji. Bujuan*, Vol. 2, p. 275.

    1. In the only existing version of this text, Mao's note is incorporated into a letter from the peasant association to the Public Security Bureau and to the publishing house concerned, asking them to take note of his views. March 14 is the date this composite document was published in *Hunan minbao*. The peasant association states that Mao's letter was received "yesterday," so it was probably written on March 12 or shortly before. Otherwise the association's letter adds nothing to Mao's and is omitted here.

    2. I.e., the series to which Mao's article of September 1, 1926, "The National Revolution and the Peasant Movement," constituted the introduction. For details regarding its contents, see above, the text of September 1, 1926, and the notes thereto. In this letter, Mao uses the title *Nongmin congkan* (Collected Writings on the Peasants) rather than *Nongmin wenti congkan* (Collected Writings on the Peasant Problem) as in 1926. The new title also appeared on the only version available to us, published by the Wusan (Five-three) Publishing House in Shanghai in May 1927. Since the Jimei Publishing House was located in Changsha, this is obviously not the reprint to which Mao is referring. The Shanghai edition does not include Mao's preface of September 1926 and omits many of the authors' names, no doubt as a result of the situation created by Chiang Kaishek's break with the Communists in April 1927. It was presumably yet another unauthorized reprint of a work on what was then an extremely fashionable topic.

    3. I.e., the Peasant Movement Training Institute in Guangzhou, which Mao had headed from May to September 1926.

    4. According to the editorial note accompanying Mao's preface to this series as reproduced in *Nongmin yundong* (see above, the text of September 1, 1926), the volumes were for sale by the Guoguang shuju. Probably they could be purchased only by persons working with the peasant movement and/or Guomindang members, and not by the general public.

    5. I.e., the Hunan Provincial Peasant Association, which Mao addresses politely as *gui hui*. We have omitted the "honorable" in translating the term on its subsequent appearances below.

ple, *Current Tactics for the Peasant Movement in Hunan;*[6] (2) prices must not be too high; only the cost of printing and paper may be charged;[7] [the reprints] must be checked by the association, and no mistakes are permitted. Otherwise, reprinting is not permitted. I authorize your association to handle this matter on my behalf.

---

6. This must have been either a reprint in pamphlet form of a document thus titled of August 1926, or a longer treatment along the same lines. This text has been attributed to Mao in the *Mao Zedong ji*, but his authorship is not recognized by the editors in Beijing. The line laid down in this document was a very moderate one, which clearly would not have been suitable in the context of the impending rupture with Chiang Kaishek. Mao's injunction that it be dropped apparently carried weight, for this text does not appear in the May 1927 edition. Perhaps it was replaced by the voluminous materials from the December 1926 Hunan Provincial Peasants' Congress, which (as indicated in the notes to the text of September 1, 1926) were added at the end of Volume IV.

7. This requirement, too, appears to have been met. The selling price of the four-volume set was 2 *yuan*, not excessive for a work of over 800 pages in fairly large format, bound in "foreign style."

Resolution on the Peasant Question

Resolution of the Third Plenum of the Second Central Executive Committee of the Chinese Guomindang[1]

(March 16, 1927)

In October of the 15th year of the Republic, the Joint Session of the Central Committee of our party and of the various provincial party organs passed several resolutions on improving the conditions of the peasants. In the five months since then, the struggle in the countryside between the oppressed peasants and their oppressors (such as landlords, the gentry, local bullies, and corrupt officials) has developed even more widely. But everywhere the resolutions of the Joint Session have remained largely a dead letter. Although peasant associations have tried to implement such resolutions, they have often encountered fierce resistance or even retaliation from those who control political power in the countryside. Since the government and party organizations are occupied with military operations, they have been unable to protect the organizations of peasants, let alone provide active support to enable peasants to establish their autonomous governments and use the leverage of the power of the autonomous governments to defeat their enemies. As a result of the victory of the Northern Expedition, many [provinces] have been placed under the rule of the national government; four million peasants have joined peasant associations and are struggling hard for their own liberation. At the same time, the enemies of the peasantry are doing their utmost to suppress the development of the peasant movement and to obstruct the realization of our party's resolutions. These enemies of the peasantry, the so-called power holders in the countryside, are also the enemies of the national revolution. All these forces left over from the feudal system must be eliminated in order for the national revolution to succeed. These remnant feudal forces are the root cause of the miseries of the peasantry. They are also the basis for the existence of

---

This document was published in the Hankou *Minguo ribao* on March 18, 1927. Our translation is based on the text as reproduced in *Mao Zedong ji. Bujuan*, Vol. 2, pp. 259–63.

1. This plenum, which met March 10–17, 1927, in Wuhan, was an important episode in the breakdown of relations between Chiang Kaishek and the Left Guomindang. The key posts occupied by Chiang as head of the party and of the national government were abolished in favor of a collective leadership. Two Communist Party members became ministers in the Wuhan government, and Mao played a significant political role, which is documented in many of the texts translated below.

the warlords and of imperialism in economically backward China. Therefore, our party and the national government must do their best to protect and develop the peasant organizations and see that the decisions of the Joint Session are carried out.[2] These resolutions represent the first step by our party toward the liberation of the Chinese peasants. If our party is unable to take such a step, the national revolution will face great dangers, and it will certainly lose the support of the peasantry, that is, the support of the overwhelming majority of the Chinese people. If our party must work hard to develop the peasant movement, it is not only for the sake of enabling the majority of peasants to intensify their struggle against the warlords and imperialists. In representing the interests of the great majority of the peasants, our party must also expand the peasant movement at all times in order to help the oppressed peasants reach their goal of seeking their own liberation, thanks to the power of their own organizations and struggle. In order for our party to ensure the liberation of the peasantry, our party must develop the organizations of the peasants so that they may use their own strength to struggle against all the oppressive forces under any political conditions. Only this will make the victory of the national revolution the victory of the peasantry. Therefore, in order to establish a unified democratic polity, to ensure that the Three People's Principles truly begin to be put into practice, and to make the peasants understand that our party is their friend and protector, our party should adopt the following resolution during the current plenum of the Central Executive Committee.

Immediately implement all the decisions concerning the peasant question adopted by the Joint Session of the Central Committee and provincial party organs in the areas newly liberated from under the iron feet of the warlords. In particular, the methods of implementing the decisions must be devised by investigating the actual demands of the peasants. In order to reach this objective, the Third Plenum of the Central Executive Committee recommends to the national government that it set up a Ministry of Peasant Affairs. Its responsibility should include the implementation of land reform, as well as economic and political reforms and construction demanded by peasants. Moreover, in order to achieve these goals, the Third Plenum of the Central Executive Committee has adopted the following ten points, which the government, the party, and revolutionary mass bodies must immediately [apply]:

> 1. The government must immediately start establishing self-governing organs for districts, townships, and villages, which are to be organized by rural

---

2. The texts of the Joint Session translated above do not include separate resolutions dealing specifically with the peasant movement, but Articles 24 through 31 of the "Basic Program" adopted on October 27, 1925, do provide guarantees to the peasants, from standardizing the land tax and prohibiting usury to the right to establish peasant associations. In particular, Article 24 calls for the 25 percent reduction in rent stipulated, below, in point 4 of this resolution.

residents in accordance with the laws of self-government for districts and townships. [These organs] are to manage all the administrative, economic, financial, and cultural affairs in the districts and townships. Under the guidance of our party, peasant associations should become the center for organizing and guiding such organs of self-government. The law of self-government for districts and townships will be written separately.

2. Within district organs of self-government, land committees should be established (when necessary, they should also be set up within township organs of self-government) and organized by the officials sent by the governing administrative agency of the [Ministry] of Rural Affairs and by the representatives of peasant associations. These committees are to make preparations for land reform and implement the various methods stipulated by the government on the rectification of land [ownership] and the use of land.

3. All rural armed groups that do not belong to the military forces of the government must be placed under the control of district or township organs of self-government. Those who refuse to comply must immediately be handled according to the provisions for dealing with counterrevolutionaries. District and township organs of self-government should have the power to reorganize such armed groups so that they may genuinely protect the people in the countryside and become the armed forces of the rural people and the armed forces necessary for the protection of the rural people. If it is felt that there is a lack of rifles and guns, the government must try to provide assistance.

4. Our party should carry out completely, within this year, the Joint Session's decision regarding a 25 percent reduction of rent. Rental and lease contracts should be registered with the township self-governing bodies. The township organs of self-government and peasant associations monitor and determine the maximum amount of rent in the local areas that may not be exceeded. The township organs of self-government and peasant associations should annul all the unreasonable provisions either within or outside rental contracts. The government should issue decrees to allow tenants to have a permanent right to the use of land. The land may not be rented to another tenant unless the landlord takes back the land and tills it personally. When tenants willingly return the land, or if the land has been improved when the landlord takes it back to till it himself, [the tenants] should receive appropriate compensation.

5. The government should issue decrees to take back the public land belonging to districts and townships and the properties of temples, and turn them over to district and township organs of self-government to manage. As for the produce of the temple estates of various clans, the clan leaders or a small number of [X][X] elements should be forbidden to keep the control of these assets to the detriment of the poor members of the clans.[3]

6. The government should severely punish corrupt officials, local bullies and bad gentry, and all counterrevolutionaries. It should also confiscate their

---

3. At the session of the Third Plenum on the previous day, Mao had declared: "If the property of the temples is not confiscated, it will be impossible to strike a forceful blow against the clan system." (*Nianpu* 1, p. 187)

land and assets according to law. Such land and assets belong to the districts and townships and should be regarded as belonging to the people.[4]

7. The old system of land taxation is a genuinely unreasonable and unfair system of taxation and should be reformed immediately. As for the various levies and taxes imposed on the peasantry at the moment, those that hurt the economy of the peasantry should be gradually abolished. The government should quickly stipulate a unified tax rate that meets the needs of local areas. Other taxes levied on land and rural products must be abolished without exception. Only this can reduce the burdens on peasants. All tax collection agencies should be transferred to the district and township organs of self-government and placed in charge of the special officials sent by financial administrations. The bad gentry and local bullies must be banned from controlling [these agencies]; [these agencies] must be completely reorganized.

8. In order to reduce, for the peasantry, exploitation through usury, the government should issue explicit ordinances to ban exploitation through usury and set interest rates below 20 percent per annum and 2 percent per month. It should also ban the compounding of interest on the old debts owed by peasants. The Ministry of Peasant Affairs of the national government should quickly devise means to relieve peasants of their sufferings caused by debts; it should also immediately try to set up peasants' banks and make loans to them at an annual interest rate of 5 percent.

9. In order to guard against landlords' and speculative businessmen's raising of food prices and to provide relief to peasants in the event of natural disasters, the government should authorize district and township organs of self-government to request the responsible agency of the [Ministry] of Peasant Affairs to grant them the special power to administer the export of food and keep certain quantities of food in reserve.

10. The national government should step up its preparations [to deal with] the following issues to be raised at the next plenum of the Central Executive Committee. (1) The payment of rent must be handled through township and village organs of self-government; how can the government deduct land taxes from the rent payment? (2) Creating *xian* governments based on a democratic system. (3) Organizing an independent, democratic judiciary to solve the land-related problems and other problems. (4) Concrete methods for solving the land problem for poor peasants. The Plenum of the Central Executive Committee believes that the above measures constitute only the first step in the struggle for the liberation of the Chinese peasantry. In order for such a struggle to expand its victories, we must rouse the peasants themselves to action and receive the full support of the government.

The Plenary Meeting of the Central Executive Committee firmly believes in the implementation of the above measures. It confidently thinks that, as the only

---

4. During the discussions on March 15, Mao had declared: "Local bullies and bad gentry must be dealt with by revolutionary methods. There must be courts adapted to the revolutionary situation. The best method for dealing with them is through direct action by the peasants; peaceful methods cannot serve to overthrow the local bullies and bad gentry." (*Nianpu*, 1, p. 187).

strong foundation for the national revolution, the tens of millions of Chinese peasants will support our party, the national government, and the National Revolutionary Army, and will struggle together with us. The Plenum firmly believes that this united front will certainly be able to liberate China from the oppression of imperialism, destroy all warlords, and eliminate obstacles to the development of agriculture. It will also deal with all the decadent phenomena in society, such as unemployment and banditry. For if we cannot liberate the 300 million peasants or improve their lives, then China's industry and commerce can certainly not be revived, and we will continue to be dependent on the imperialists. The above reform plans are the only method for establishing a new social order. The Plenum of the Central Executive Committee will certainly fight anyone who obstructs or sabotages such a united front and the development of the peasant movement, or anyone who obstructs the implementation of the revolutionary policies of the national government to liberate the peasants and China as a whole.

In addition, the Third Plenum of the Central Executive Committee takes the following further decisions. (1) At the next plenum, the government should provide a report on the results of the implementation of the above measures. (2) We call on all members of our party to arise together and propagate this resolution so as to make all the peasants of China understand it; in every township, village, military unit, and organization, they should use either printed materials or the method of reading to illiterates, so that everyone may understand this resolution.

Declaration to the Peasants

Resolution Passed at the Third Plenum of the Second Central Committee of the Chinese Guomindang

(March 16, 1927)[1]

Agricultural activities occupy the greater part of the lives of the citizens in economically backward and semicolonial China, and more than 80 percent of the population are peasants. The Chinese peasants suffer the three-fold exploitation of the imperialists, the warlords, and the landlord class, and their misery has reached an extreme. As a result, they are very eager to seek their own liberation. The major objective of the Chinese national revolution is therefore to help liberate the peasants. If the peasants do not gain liberation, it is absolutely impossible to complete the national revolution. As the largest political party leading the national revolution, the Guomindang assumes the mission of completing the national revolution. When this party was being reorganized in January of the 13th year of the Republic, the First National Congress promulgated a declaration that gave special attention to the peasant problem. The Second National Congress, held in January of the 15th year of the Republic, once again adopted guidelines regarding the peasant movement. At the Central and Provincial Joint Session held in October of the same year, new political programs were announced, among which twenty-two were in support of the peasants' interests. For the past three years, the members of our party have been engaged in the peasant movement, organizing the peasant associations and leading the broad peasant masses to join in the national revolution to promote the peasants' own interests. The organizations are so widespread that they cover almost every part of the country. This makes the revolutionary upsurge extremely broad and the revolutionary process extremely favorable. All this results from the fact that the peasants have suffered the most, so they are the most eager to seek liberation. Moreover, it is only because our party has properly supported the peasants' interests, expanded the peasant organizations, and led their actions that such a result has been achieved.

This document appeared in the Hankou *Minguo ribao* on April 1, 1927. Our translation is based on the text as reproduced in *Mao Zedong ji. Bujuan*, Vol. 2, pp. 267–71.

1. In some sources, this document is dated March 19, 1927, but the *Nianpu* (Vol. 1, p. 188) indicates that it was adopted by the Third Plenum on March 16, at the same time as the resolution translated above.

Recently the peasant uprisings everywhere have taken on an extraordinarily swift and violent aspect. In the three provinces of Hunan, Hubei, and Jiangxi especially, great progress has been made within a short period of time. With the advance of the Northern Expeditionary Army, the peasants in the lower valley of the Yangzi River and in the northern provinces are bound to rise rapidly and to become the main force in support of the revolution. In addition to participating in the war to help the revolutionary army achieve victory, the first action taken by the peasants after they join the revolution is to knock down the local bullies and bad gentry and to overthrow the privileges of the feudal landlord class in the villages. This feudal landlord class is a special class that directly exploits the peasants the most fiercely. All the imperialists, the warlords, and the corrupt officials depend on this special class to attain their goal of exploiting the peasants. Consequently, the feudal landlord class is the true basis of the imperialists, the warlords, the corrupt officials, and all the other counterrevolutionaries. Unless the power of this special class is overthrown, the imperialists, the warlords, the corrupt officials, and all the other counterrevolutionaries may suffer formal defeats, but the solid basis that enables them to exist is by no means destroyed, and they will constantly have the opportunity to change the nature of the revolution. As far as the peasants are concerned, for several thousand years they have been under the rule of the political power of the feudal landlord class. Without overthrowing the political power of the feudal landlord class in the villages, all the economic struggles, such as the struggle for reducing rent and interest, are simply out of the question. Thus what the revolution demands is a profound change in the countryside. There must be a great change in every rural area, so that the activities of the local bullies and bad gentry, of the lawless landlords, and of all the other counterrevolutionaries can be completely eliminated by their fear of the peasants. Village government must be taken from the hands of the local bullies and bad gentry, the lawless landlords, and all the other counterrevolutionaries and placed in those of the peasants, and democratic organs of the self-government, led by the peasants, must be established in the villages. This is the only way to bring about democratic politics. Our party has the strongest resolve to lead this struggle to ultimate victory.

If our party is to lead the peasants, who represent the democratic forces, in the struggle against the local bullies, bad gentry, and lawless landlords who represent the feudal forces, and to guarantee the victory of this struggle, one of the important conditions is that the peasants should obtain arms. The peasants must have military organizations for the purpose of self-defense. The military organizations of the feudal landlord class, such as the militia and the defense corps, must be disarmed, and the weapons must be handed over to the peasants. In addition, our party must seek ways to help the peasants buy weapons at low prices. In a word, we must make sure that the peasants have enough weapons to defend their own interests. This is the real guarantee of the victory of the agrarian revolution, that is, of the victory of the democratic forces in overthrowing the feudal forces.

After the peasants achieve victory in the political struggle, the economic struggle immediately follows. The significance of the peasants' economic struggle lies in their opposition to exploitation by the imperialists, the warlords, and especially the landlord class. The total of this exploitation amounts to more than 50 percent [of the peasants' income]. The task of our party is to lead the peasants to oppose this exploitation. The political program adopted at the Joint Session of our party includes the following clauses: (1) a reduction of the land rent of the tenant-peasants by 25 percent; (2) a ban on extortion by usurers and a limit to annual interest of no more than 20 percent; (3) a ban on [collecting] rent from the previous period; (4) a ban on levies of money and grain in advance; and (5) a ban on the contract letting system. At this Plenum, it has also been decided that the tenant-peasants should have the right to work the land, and that the land tax laws are to be reformed. It has moreover been decided that the organs of peasant self-government should have overall authority over local economic matters. All this constitutes the program for the initial economic struggle by the peasants. Our party must exercise the leadership in this struggle and carry it to victory in the aftermath of the political struggle. In areas ruled by the national government, we must use political power to help the peasants reach this goal.

Not only this, but with the progress of the revolution the peasants' demands have been developing rapidly from the initial stage to the second stage, and serious land problems have already emerged in many places. In the nature of the case, China's peasant problem is, as regards its content, a problem of the poor peasants. The number of the poor peasants has been constantly increasing down to the present. The utterly impoverished peasants who have no property at all, and the less impoverished peasants who have a little property but not enough to make a living, account for the majority of the whole peasantry. The existence of this broad poor-peasant class is the cause of all the instability and turmoil. At the same time, they are the key element in the motive force of the revolution. Unless the poor-peasant problem is solved, all the instability and turmoil will not subside, and the revolution will go on for a long time without reaching completion. The core issue of the poor-peasant problem is the issue of the land. Now in the provinces under jurisdiction of the national government—especially in Guangdong, Hunan, and Hubei, where the peasant movement is well developed—the demands of the poor peasants for land are becoming quite urgent. The land problem for the poor-peasant masses in the North is also very serious. The Director General of our party, Mr. Sun, had a deep insight into this and pointed out twenty years ago that "equalization of land ownership" is a revolutionary program. The Declaration of the First National Congress mentions that "the state should provide land to those peasants to plow, who have lost their land and become tenant-peasants." Moreover, in his lectures on the Principle of People's Livelihood, the Director General put forward the slogan of "land to the tiller," because he understood profoundly that the ultimate demand of the peasants is to have land. The peasants will not support the revolution until its final victory unless they are given land. Consequently, our party has resolved to support the peasants in their struggle for land, and will never cease to do so until the land problem has been completely solved.

Not only do the poor peasants have no land, but they have no capital either. As a result of the progress of the revolution, the well-to-do classes in the villages become extremely reluctant to lend money. In many places the relationship between the lender and borrower is almost broken off. This puts the society of poor peasants in a constant state of anxiety. Unless we develop some concrete policies, we will not be able to solve this problem of lack of capital. In the manifesto of the First National Congress of our party we read: "Because of lack of capital, the peasants have borrowed money at exorbitant rates of interest and become heavily in debt all their lives. The state will help create the coordinating institutions, such as the peasants' bank, to provide for these deficiencies."[2] The Political Program of the Joint Session of Central and Provincial Organs also lists the establishment of the peasant bank in a separate article and stipulates that the loans will be provided to the peasants at an annual interest of 5 percent.[3] Our party should ask its government to work hard in the areas where the revolutionary forces are spreading, to establish the peasants' bank and other lending institutions with favorable conditions within the shortest period of time in order to solve the problem of lack of capital.

In a word, the completion of the national revolution depends on the rising up of the peasants all over the country. Our party always stands for the interests of the peasants and represents the peasants in the struggle. Our party always supports every reasonable struggle of the peasants. We must make sure that all the special classes who exploit the peasants lose the means to do so; that the degree of their exploitation is reduced; and that every oppressed peasant is truly liberated. This is the historic mission of our party. We will carry out this mission without the slightest hesitation.

Proposed by: Deng Yanda,[4] Chen Kewen, and Mao Zedong

Members of the Standing Committee of the
Central Peasant Movement Committee

---

2. The quotation is from the section of the manifesto dealing with the Principle of People's Livelihood.

3. In fact, the "Basic Program," translated above, which had been adopted on October 27, 1926, did not contain a separate article on a peasant bank. Article 11 stipulated in part, however: "Establish a national bank. Develop agricultural, industrial, and commercial enterprise through minimal interest rates."

4. Deng Yanda (1895–1931), *zi* Zesheng, was a native of Guangdong. After participating in the 1911 Revolution, he graduated from Baoding Military Academy, and by 1922 had risen to the rank of regimental commander. In 1924 he helped create the Huangpu Academy, and at the Second Congress in January 1926 he was elected an alternate member of the Guomindang Central Executive Committee. During the Northern Expedition, he served as director of the general political department of the National Revolutionary Army. By the time of the Third Plenum of March 1927, Deng had sided firmly with the Wuhan leftists against Chiang Kaishek, and became head of the party's Peasant Department.

Remarks at the Meeting to Welcome Peasant Representatives from Hubei and Henan Provinces

(March 18, 1927)

(Special dispatch to this newspaper)[1] At seven o'clock on the evening of the 18th, the Committee for the Peasant Movement of the Central Committee, and the Central Peasant Movement Training Institute, jointly held a meeting to welcome the peasant representatives from Hubei and Henan provinces. The place of the meeting was at the Central Peasant Movement Training Institute in Wuchang. More than a thousand people attended the meeting, including the representatives from the two provinces, members of the Central Committee, the whole of the Central Peasant Movement Training Institute, and invited guests. The chairman, Chen Kewen, declared the meeting open; participants bowed three times to the national flag, the party flag, and the portrait of the late Director General. After the Director General's political testament was read, the chairman made opening remarks (omitted here). Then Mao Zedong, member of the Central Committee, gave the following remarks:

The interests of the peasants clash with those of the landlords. A group of Guomindang comrades in Hubei advocate the interests of the peasants. The most important resolution passed by the Central Committee plenum during the last few days is the regulation for punishing local bullies and bad gentry.[2] If we want to overthrow the local bullies and bad gentry, we must support this group, which advocates the interests of the peasants.

These remarks appeared in the Hankou *Minguo ribao* on March 22, 1927. Our translation is based on the text as reproduced in *Mao Zedong ji. Bujuan*, Vol. 2, p. 265.

1. I.e., the Hankou *Republican Daily*.

2. The reference is obviously to paragraph 6 of the Resolution on the Peasant Question adopted on March 16, 1927.

Speech at the Mass Meeting Convened by the Central Peasant Movement Training Institute in Memory of the Martyrs from Yangxin and Ganzhou[1]

(March 26, 1927)

Even within this domain[2] of the revolutionary forces, events involving the tragic slaughter of peasants and workers are constantly being acted out. This clearly demonstrates that the remnants of the feudal forces are accumulating strength and sharpening their weapons to fight their last struggle against us! From today on, we must have one resolve: to attack the forces of these reactionary elements, and to reach our true goals. This is the duty we should assume at today's memorial service. (Balance omitted.)

This summary was published in the Hankou *Minguo ribao* on March 31, 1927. Our source is the text as reproduced in *Mao Zedong ji. Bujuan*, Vol. 2, p. 273.

1. When this summary of Mao's remarks was first published on March 31, 1927, it was preceded by a lengthy editorial note of which the only available text contains many missing characters. We give here a translation of the more legible and significant portions of this introduction:

> In the wake of the tragic murders of the revolutionary comrades in Yangxin and Ganzhou, all the comrades in the Central Peasant Movement Training Institute began a period of mourning for the martyrs; in addition, they engaged in various activities to express their resolve. Because of the urgency of the present trend in party affairs, all the students of the institute went especially to the Central Party Bureau to present a petition on the day of the memorial service. . . . They urged that all the reactionaries be purged in order to protect the peasants and the workers. . . . Representatives handed the written petition to the Central Executive Committee. . . . In addition to issuing a telegram to the whole country calling for saving the party, they also issued a telegram condemning Chiang Kaishek and stating their positions. At six o'clock in the afternoon, the memorial service was held. Invited guests and all the students gathered in the stadium, their heads held high. . . . After the ceremony . . . Mao Zedong made a speech, the gist of which was as follows.

2. Two characters are missing here in the text as reproduced in the *Bujuan*; they have been supplied from the extract contained in *Nianpu* 1, pp. 189–90.

An Example of the
Chinese Tenant-Peasant's Life

(March 1927)[1]

Place: Xixiang, Xiangtan, Hunan
Time: The fifteenth year of the Republic

A hypothetical case: A hard-working and capable tenant-peasant in his prime rents 15 *mu*[2] of land (the amount of land that can be tilled with the manpower of one tenant-peasant) plus a sizable vegetable plot, a hilly area in which to collect firewood, and a thatched hut to live in. Both of this tenant-peasant's parents are dead, and he has only a wife and a son. The wife cooks and raises pigs for him, and the son of twelve or thirteen looks after the oxen for him. This tenant-peasant is able to till the 15 *mu* of fields he has rented without any hired help. Because he is poor, he rents the land from a dealer, so there is no rent deposit to be paid, and the rent, according to the general rule in this area, is 70 percent of the crops.

Part I: Expenditure

1. Food grain. The annual grain consumption of the tenant-peasant and his wife is 7 *dan* 2 *dou*[3] each. The child's grain consumption is 3 *dan* 6 *dou*. The total amount of grain consumed by all three is 18 *dan*. Grain is currently priced at 4 *yuan* per *dan,* so the total cost of food is 72 *yuan* (in silver, as below).

This document was first published as a separate booklet in a series put out by the Central Peasant Movement Training Institute in March 1927. Our source is the text as reproduced in *Mao Zedong nongcun diaocha wenji*, pp. 28–34.

1. Here the Chinese text has simply the year, 1926, when the data were collected. We have preferred to place it in the chronological sequence of Mao's writings under the date of first publication.

2. A *mu* is an area of 0.167 acre (0.0667 hectare).

3. *Dan* and *dou* are units of dry measure for grain. A *dan* (represented by the character also meaning "stone," read *shi* in other contexts) is equivalent to one hectoliter, a *dou* to one decaliter. A different character, also read *dan*, and commonly referring to a unit of weight, occurs in paragraph 10f below. A note in the Chinese edition warns, however, that the usage of these two terms is not consistent or uniform throughout this text.

2. Lard. Three people consume at least 1 *jin*[4] of lard a month, which makes 12 *jin* a year. At 25 *fen*[5] per *jin,* the total cost is 3 *yuan.*

3. Salt. Three people consume at least 2 *jin* of salt a month, 24 *jin* a year. At 13 *fen* (430 cash[6] in copper coins) per *jin,* the total cost is 3.12 *yuan.*

4. Lamp oil. At least 1 *jin* of kerosene a month, 12 *jin* a year. At 7 *fen* per *jin* (230 cash), the total cost is 84 *fen.*

5. Tea. At least 10 *jin* a year. At 20 *fen* per *jin,* the total cost is 2 *yuan.*

6. Wages. Thirty-six *yuan.* (If this peasant did not rent land to till, he could work for someone else and earn a wage of 36 *yuan* a year. By not working [for others] he loses this wage.)

7. Seed. Four *sheng*[7] per *mu* of land, 6 *dou* for 15 *mu,* worth 2.4 *yuan* in silver.

8. Fertilizer. One *yuan* in silver buys 2,400 *jin* of ox dung to cover one *mu* of land, so the cost of manure for 15 *mu* is 15 *yuan.* (If he uses pig manure, 1 *yuan* buys 2,000 *jin* to cover 1 *mu,* for a total cost of 15 *yuan.* If he uses soya beans, the price is 9 *yuan* per *dan,* and each *dan* of unhulled beans yields 3 *sheng.* One *mu* of land needs 6 *dan* of unhulled soya beans for a yield of 1 *dou* 8 *sheng* of beans. At 9 *fen* per *sheng,* the total cost is 1.62 *yuan,* and for 15 *mu* of land it would come to 24.30 *yuan.* If he uses dried vegetable, or rapeseed bricks, 1 *yuan* buys 40 *jin* at 2.5 *fen* per *jin.* Each *mu* uses 50 *jin* of this, which costs 1.25 *yuan.* The total cost for 15 *mu* of land is 18.75 *yuan.* But a tenant-peasant who rents 15 *mu* of land would not be able to afford soya beans or rapeseed bricks anyway.) In addition, for 15 *mu* of land it is necessary to spread 1,500 *jin* of lime, which costs 2 *yuan* per 1,000 *jin,* for a total cost of 3 *yuan.* These two items added together make a total cost of 18 *yuan.*

9. Draft animals. To rent oxen with a rice seedling guarantee (which means a guarantee to plow until the land is ready for rice seedlings to be transplanted) costs one *yuan* per *mu* of land, from which 24 *fen* must be deducted for the cost of manpower. (The cost of the manpower should properly be included in the oxen rental fee, but for the purposes of this hypothetical case we have assumed that no extra help is in fact hired. So this tenant-peasant must go to someone else's house to do odd jobs to compensate for this plowhand cost, while labor costs have been excluded from the oxen rental fee.) This comes to 76 *fen* per *mu,* totaling 11.4 *yuan* for 15 *mu* of land. Generally speaking, a tenant-peasant renting 15 *mu* of land raises an ox himself and has that ox provide him with manure,

---

4. In recent times, a Chinese pound or *jin* has been equal to half a kilogram, or 1.1 pounds avoirdupois, but Mao may have been using a more traditional measure, which was somewhat heavier.

5. The term *fen* refers to a modern-style currency unit equivalent to .01 *yuan.*

6. Here Mao gives the equivalent in *wen,* the traditional copper coins for which we have used the standard English equivalent of "cash." Throughout the present text, the rate of exchange is assumed to be approximately 3,300 cash for 1 *yuan.* This is stated most clearly in paragraph 10e, but in the present example, it will be seen that 430 divided by .13 yields a ratio of 3308.

7. A *sheng* is a unit of dry measure for grain equivalent to 0.1 *dou* (1 liter).

so why doesn't he do so? Let's do the calculations on the assumption that he raises one ox. An ox of medium quality would require a capital outlay of 40 *yuan*. At the current local interest rate of 8 *dan* of grain a year for 100 *liang* of pure silver, 40 *yuan*, equivalent to 30.7 *liang* of silver (1.3 big foreign dollars equals one *liang* of silver) would attract interest of 2.456 *dan* of grain a year. At a price of 4 *yuan* per *dan* of grain, the total cost is 9.824 *yuan*.[8]

10. Farm tool expenses

a. Two plows. Two plows a year are needed to till 15 *mu* of land. The plow crescents cost 10 *fen* apiece. Another 10 *fen* goes for the plow bottom, plowtail, and plow head. To make the parts into a plow, you need a carpenter, for whom the pay and food cost is 34.4 *fen*. (A carpenter is paid 1 *yuan* for 7 units of work. Each unit of work costs 14.3 *fen* plus 20 *fen* for food.) Plowshare and moldboard cost 40 *fen*. To treat the plow you use half a *jin* of tung oil, which costs 15 *fen* (30 *fen* per *jin*). The total cost of one plow is 1.093 *yuan*, and two plows come to 2.186 *yuan*.

b. An iron rake. Costs 6 *yuan* and can be used for 10 years, making an average annual expense of 60 *fen*.

c. Two rake heads. Each one weighs 5 *jin*, and one *yuan* buys 4 *jin* at 25 *fen* per *jin*. Thus each rake head costs 1.25 *yuan*. Two rake heads cost 2.50 *yuan*. They can be used for 3 years, making the average annual expense 83.3 *fen*.

d. Three hoes.

i. One digging hoe, which weighs 5 *jin*. One *yuan* buys 4 *jin* at 25 *fen* per *jin*. Thus 5 *jin* costs 1.25 *yuan*. It can be used for 10 years and must be reinforced once a year with steel, which costs 7 *fen* (230 cash), or 70 *fen* for 10 years. This makes a total outlay of 1.95 *yuan*, which, averaged over a period of 10 years, comes out to 19.5 *fen* per year.

ii. One farming hoe, which weighs 3.5 *jin* and costs 87.5 *fen*. It can be used for 5 years and must be reinforced with steel once a year at a cost of 7 *fen* (230 cash), which comes to 35 *fen* for 5 years. The total outlay for 5 years is 1.225 *yuan*, making an average annual cost of 24.5 *fen*.

iii. One pick hoe weighing 1.5 *jin* and costing 37.5 *fen*. It can be used for 2 years, the average annual cost coming to 18.75 *fen*.

The total annual cost of these three hoes is 62.75 *fen*.

e. One threshing bucket. The wood costs one *yuan*, and nails and

---

8. The *liang* (Chinese ounce, or "tael") of silver was a traditional unit of accounting. Regarding "big foreign dollars," see the relevant note to Mao's report of May 19, 1926. The practice of charging interest in kind on loans to the peasants was common at this time in the Chinese countryside. The rate of interest in monetary terms can easily be calculated from the data in this paragraph, and comes to 24.56 percent. This is consistent with the figure of 2 percent a month given below by Mao in his note to paragraph 10.

pincer cost one *yuan*. The carpenter's pay is 1.14 *yuan* for 8 units of work (at 7 units of work for one *yuan*). The carpenter's food money for 8 units of work is 1.60 *yuan*. Three *jin* of tung oil for treating [the wood] costs one *yuan*. One threshing shield (inclusive cost 5 strings of cash,[9] calculated at 3 strings 300 per *yuan*), 1.50 *yuan*. The total cost is 7.24 *yuan*. The bucket can be used for 20 years, so the average annual cost is 36.2 *fen*.

f. Six *Dan*[10] of bamboo baskets. At 3 *Dan* for 1 *yuan*, 6 *Dan* cost 2 *yuan*. They can be used for 20 years, making an average annual cost of 10 *fen*.

g. Six *Dan* of webs. Each *Dan* costs 100 coppers, making a total of 600 coppers, which is equivalent to 18 *fen*. They can be used for only one year.

h. Four *Dan* of winnowing fans. Two *Dan* are "Chang Xie" and 2 *Dan* are "Gou Suo." Each costs 10 *fen*, for a total of 40 *fen*. They can be used for one year.

i. Three picking fans. One is for pulling the grain, one for drying the grain, and one for containing grain. The total cost is 1 *yuan*. They can be used for 10 years, making the annual average 10 *fen*.

j. One windmill. The cost is 6 *yuan*. It can be used for 60 years at an average annual cost of 10 *fen*.

k. Grain-drying tools. One sifter, one smoothing harrow, and two toothed harrows cost a total of 1.50 *yuan*. They can be used for 10 years at an average annual cost for each year of 15 *fen*.

l. One *nanpan*. It can be used for 5 years at an average annual cost of 20 *fen*.

m. Two rice sifters. Two *yuan*, to be used for 10 years at an average annual cost of 20 *fen*.

n. One shovel. Two *yuan*, to be used for 4 years at an average annual cost of 50 *fen*.

o. One tilt hammer. Two *yuan*, to be used for 30 years at an average annual cost of 6.7 *fen*.

The total annual expenditure for the 15 types of farm tools listed above each year is 6.655 *yuan*.

Note [by Mao]: The expenditure for farm tools is certainly a large one, but interest on loans to buy them is an even bigger expense. The total of these 15 farm implements is 39.556 *yuan*. At a monthly interest rate of 2 percent, the interest comes to 9.49 *yuan* a year. The cost of the tools themselves is high

---

9. One "string" of copper cash traditionally consisted of 1,000 such coins, strung together through the hole in the middle.

10. Here, as noted above under paragraph 1, the character *dan* which normally refers to a unit of weight is employed. We capitalize this term to distinguish it from the unit of volume pronounced in the same way.

enough, but if interest were added into the calculations of the total expenditures it would come to a startling sum. Interest has not been figured into this article.

11. Miscellaneous expenditures. Customary gifts for seasonal festivities and for weddings and funerals, wine and cigarettes for entertaining visitors, plus other miscellaneous expenditures come to at least 1 *yuan* a month, or 12 *yuan* a year.

The total cost for the 11 items above is 167.3655 *yuan*.

Note: As for clothing, three people need at least six *zhang* of cloth each year (that is, two bolts). Excluding the cost for dying and tailoring, this comes to 4.80 *yuan* at 8 *fen* per *chi*.[11] In the case of ordinary poor peasants, however, their clothing is made by the women [in the family] and rarely is any money spent on cloth. Therefore this item of expenditure is not included in the above calculations.

Part II: Income

1. Receipts from the land. Each *mu* yields 4 *dan* of grain (paddy rice) annually, and 15 *mu* yield a total of 60 *dan* of grain. Rent is paid with 42 *dan* (70 percent), leaving 18 *dan* for the peasant himself. At 4 *yuan* per *dan*, the total is 72 *yuan*.

2. Raising pigs. Forty *yuan* a year (a minimum of 3.30 *yuan* a month).

3. Cutting firewood or working as a porter during the winter season. Twenty *yuan* can be earned in the course of a winter.

4. Savings in wages and food money. Because the peasant goes out to cut firewood or to work as porter during the months of September, October, and November and does not eat and work at home, food money and wages for one person should be deducted from the previous items of expenditure. The cost of food each month is 2.74 *yuan* (2.40 *yuan* for 6 *dou* of grain, 25 *fen* for 1 *jin* of oil, and 9 *fen* for 11 *liang* of salt). The total for 3 months is 8.22 *yuan*. Wages are 2.50 *yuan* a month, making a total of 7.50 *yuan* for 3 months. These two items add up to a total of 15.72 *yuan*.

The four items listed above add up to a total of 147.72 *yuan*.

Part III: Conclusion

Calculating income against expenditure leaves a shortfall of 19.6455 *yuan*.

Even an annual income of 147.72 *yuan* is possible only provided the following six conditions are met:

1. Absolutely no natural calamities of any kind such as flood, drought, wind-

---

11. One *zhang* consisted of 10 *chi* or Chinese feet. The official equivalent at this time was 141 English inches, but the exact length varied substantially with time and place.

storms, hailstorms, insect blight, and plant disease

2. Robust health, and absolutely no illness that would affect one's ability to work
3. Being shrewd and good at adjusting (the local way of saying "good at calculating" is "good at adjusting")
4. No disease and death amongst the pigs and oxen raised
5. Sunny days and no rain during the winter season
6. Hard work all year round, with no holidays whatsoever

Actually it is very rare that all six conditions are met, especially numbers 3 and 5. There are always more simple and honest ones than shrewd ones among the poor tenant-peasants.

In the countryside today, where the competition for survival is very fierce, this factor is of crucial importance to a peasant's rise or fall. Moreover, there is often an unbroken spell of wet and windy weather over the winter, which causes more suffering among poor tenant-peasants, greatly reducing their income from cutting wood and working as a porter. As to the first condition of natural calamities, the second of illness, and the fourth of animal diseases, all of them are basically inevitable. The sixth condition shows that a Chinese tenant-peasant lives a worse life than that of an ox, for an ox gets some rest during the year, while a man gets none at all. But in reality not every tenant-peasant can work so hard all year with no rest, and as soon as one so much as slacks off for a moment, a loss of income immediately follows. This is the real reason why, living a worse life than that of the tenant-peasants in any other country in the world, many Chinese tenant-peasants are being forced to leave the land and become soldiers, bandits, or vagrants.

Under the present system of heavy rents in China, such a life for the tenant-peasant—in which he earns a small amount of his income from his main occupation and the greater part of his income from sidelines, and at the end of the year suffers a large loss—is extremely widespread. It is only because the tenant-peasants themselves frequently do not count their wages in their own calculations that many of them exert their utmost efforts all year to struggle for survival through what they earn from side jobs, yet feel they are just managing to make ends meet and not suffering any great loss.

(This article is based on an interview with Mr. Zhang Lianchu, a tenant-peasant).

Yellow Crane Tower[1]

(To the Tune of "Bodhisattva Barbarians") [2]

(Spring 1927)

Endless and vast, the nine branches[3] flow through the land,
Deeply etched, one thread[4] cuts through from north to south.
In the blue haze of mist and rain,
Tortoise and Snake[5] shackle the Great River.
The yellow crane has gone who knows where,
Only this travelers' resting place remains.[6]
A libation of wine I pour to the surging torrent,
The tide of my heart rising high as its waves.

This poem was first published in *Shikan*, January 1957. We have translated it from *Shici duilian*, pp. 18-20.

1. Yellow Crane Tower is located near present-day Wuhan. Legend has it that an immortal once flew over the spot on a yellow crane and stopped there to rest, and that a tower was first built there during the Three Kingdoms period. Yellow Crane Tower has been a favorite subject of classical Chinese poetry since the Tang dynasty.

2. On the convention of "tune title" (*cipai*), see the note to Mao's 1923 poem addressed to his wife.

3. This refers to the tributaries that run into the Yangzi River at this point. The word Mao uses here for "branch" (*pai*) may also imply schools of thought, ideologies, contending forces.

4. This refers to the Beijing-Hankou Railway to the north and the Guangzhou-Hankou Railway to the south. It may also imply the northern and southern warlord forces.

5. These are two hills that face each other on opposite banks of the Yangzi River. The tortoise and the snake are both powerful creatures in Chinese lore. In addition, metal locks in the shape of the tortoise and snake were traditionally used on gates to important places.

6. These two lines echo the opening lines of a poem (also entitled "Yellow Crane Tower") by Cui Hao (d. 754) of the Tang dynasty: "Men of old rode off on the golden crane/All that's left here is Yellow Crane Tower./The golden crane is gone, never to return/White clouds drift in the void for a thousand years."

Telegram from the Executive Committee of the All-China Peasant Association on Taking Office

(April 9, 1927)

The Central Party Headquarters in Wuhan, the national government, the National Federation of Labor Unions, all provincial party headquarters, all provincial governments, all provincial peasant associations, all provincial federations of labor unions, all provincial associations of businessmen, all provincial federations of student unions, all provincial federations of teachers, officers and soldiers of the national revolution, and all newspapers:

The development of the peasant movement throughout the country has gathered enormous momentum. Five provinces have already established provincial peasant associations; more than ten provinces have set up preparatory offices for provincial peasant associations. There are already more than 10 million organized peasants in the whole country. A central national organization is urgently required in order to unite the front of the peasants across the whole country. On March 30, representatives from the peasant associations in Guangdong, Hunan, Hubei, and Jiangxi, and from the Henan Armed Peasants' Self-Defense Army, held a joint conference in Wuchang, and elected Deng Yanda,[1] Mao Zedong, Tan Yankai,[2] Tan Pingshan,[3] Xu Qian,

---

This telegram appeared in the Hankou *Minguo ribao* on April 17, 1927. Our source is the text as reproduced in *Mao Zedong ji. Bujuan*, Vol. 9, pp. 219-20.

1. On Deng Yanda, see the note to the text of March 19, 1927.

2. On Tan Yankai, see the note to Mao's letter of December 3, 1920, and Mao's discussion of his role in the text of July 1, 1923, translated above, "Hunan under the Provisional Constitution."

3. Tan Pingshan (1887–1956) was a native of Guangdong. After graduating from Beijing University in 1920, he participated in the organization of the Socialist Youth League in Guangzhou, and by 1923 he was a leading figure in the Guangdong branch of the Chinese Communist Party, which he represented at the Third Congress. At the First Congress of the Guomindang in January 1924, he was one of three Communists elected a full member of the Central Executive Committee. In November 1926 he went to Moscow as Chinese Communist Party delegate to the Seventh Plenum of the Executive Committee of the Comintern. On his return, he left Guangzhou for Wuhan, where at the time of the Third Plenum he was elected to the presidium of the Political Council and took charge of the Ministry of Peasant Affairs [*Nongzheng bu*]. This organ is often referred to as the Ministry of Agriculture, but as the Resolution on the Peasant Question of March 16, 1927 (translated above), which announced its establishment, makes plain, it was concerned with satisfying the demands of the peasants.

Sun Ke,[4] Tang Shengzhi,[5] Zhang Fakui,[6] Peng Pai,[7] Yi Lirong,[8] Lu Chen, Xiao Rengu, and Fang Zhimin as interim executive committee members to form the provisional executive committee of the All-China Federation of Peasant Associations and to carry out its duties. The conference also appointed Deng Yanda head of the Propaganda Department, Mao Zedong head of the Organization Department, and Peng Pai secretary general. The misery of the peasants in our country is caused entirely by the aggression of international imperialism and the oppression of the domestic feudal classes. The liberation of the peasants represents the success of the national revolution. That is why, with the progress of the forces of the national revolution, the peasantry is also becoming organized. We all deeply believe in this as an unvarying principle; we pledge ourselves to take a revolutionary stand and to lead the peasants of the whole country to struggle hard to complete the national revolution. We humbly lay this telegram before you in the hope of receiving your instruction regarding this final struggle against all imperialists and feudal classes.

The Provisional Executive Committee of the All-China Federation of Peasant Associations (Official Seal)

---

4. On Sun Ke, see above the note to the "Basic Program" dated October 27, 1926. In 1926, he was regarded as a member of the Guomindang right, but having gone to Wuhan with a delegation appointed by Chiang Kaishek, he threw in his lot with the left and became one of the key figures in the Wuhan régime.

5. On Tang Shengzhi, see above, the note to Mao's Hunan Peasant Report.

6. Zhang Fakui (1896–1980), zi Xianghua, was a native of Guangdong. After obtaining a military education, he rose steadily in rank in the forces supporting Sun Yatsen. In 1926, as a divisional commander, he distinguished himself in the Northern Expedition. In the summer of 1927, he led Wuhan's Second Front Army in a campaign against Chiang Kaishek. At that time he was regarded as a Communist sympathizer, but when the Nanchang Uprising took place on August 1, 1927, he attacked the rebels, retreating thereafter to Guangzhou.

7. Regarding Peng Pai, see above, the note to Mao's "Analysis of All the Classes among the Chinese Peasantry" of January 1, 1926. Peng had joined both the Chinese Communist Party and the Guomindang in 1924, and had served as secretary of the Peasant Department of the Guomindang Central Executive Committee. Thereafter, he returned to Haifeng to continue his work among the peasants, and published in 1926 the "Report on the Peasant Movement in Haifeng." In March 1927, he came to Wuhan, where he became, as indicated below, the secretary-general of the All-China Peasant Association, and participated in the Fifth Congress of the Chinese Communist Party. He was arrested and executed in Shanghai in 1929.

8. Regarding Yi Lirong, see above, the note to Mao's letter of January 28, 1921, to Peng Huang.

Remarks at the First Enlarged Meeting of the Land Committee[1]

(April 19, 1927)

I

The question of political power is merely a formal question. It will be sufficient to carry out effectively the resolutions of our party, and we will be able to extend the organization of the peasant associations, and then there will be no problem about the political power of the peasants. I have some views about the land question. In my opinion, there should be a set of principles regarding this question, to wit:

1. The significance of resolving the land question. When we are certain of this significance, we should propagate it energetically.
2. How shall we resolve the land question? That is to say, what should be the criteria for confiscating the land, and how should it be distributed? These points are the crux of the question.
3. The [relation] between the political power of the peasants and the land question, that is to say, what organ should be used to carry out confiscation and distribution.
4. Once the land has been confiscated and the tiller has his land,[2] should buying and selling be prohibited? Thus the problem of prohibiting buying and selling the land and of the nationalization of the land arises.
5. The problem of the land tax, or how to collect the land tax. This question is also extremely complicated.

II

The significance of the solution of the land problem includes the following points: (1) Bring about the liberation of the peasantry. The elimination of exploi-

---

We have translated these remarks from *Mao Zedong wenji*, Vol. 1, pp. 42–45, where the text is followed by the indication "based on the record of the First Enlarged Meeting of the Guomindang Central Land Committee."

1. The Land Committee had been established by the Standing Committee of the Central Executive Committee at its Fifth Enlarged Session on April 2, 1927. The other members, apart from Mao, were Deng Yanda, Xu Qian, Gu Mengyu, and Tan Pingshan. Its purpose was to be "deciding on measures for giving land to the peasants," and "creating a revolutionary phenomenon throughout the countryside, so as to permit the subsequent overthrow of the feudal system." (*Nianpu* 1, p. 191)

2. *Gengzhe you qi tianle*—in other words, when Sun's slogan "Land to the tiller" has been carried out.

tation and oppression by the landlords and all oppressing classes is truly the main significance of the subject under discussion. (2) If the land question is not resolved, the economically backward countries will not be able to increase their productive force, will be unable to resolve the problem of the misery of the peasants' lives, and will be unable to improve the land. According to the [agrarian] survey of the Russian comrades,[3] the productive capacity of our country's land is constantly falling, and the productive forces of the whole country have already encountered a great crisis. If this crisis is not resolved, an extremely great famine will undoubtedly arise. If the land question is not resolved, the peasants will be incapable of improving the land, and production will certainly continue to decline. Thus, the second significance lies in increasing production. (3) Safeguarding the revolution. Although the revolutionary forces are developing at present, they have also reached a crisis, and if in future no fresh troops arrive, we will certainly be defeated. If we wish to increase the new forces to safeguard the revolution, it cannot be done without solving the land question. The reason for this is that, once the land question has been resolved, the problems of finance and of soldiers can both be resolved. Whether or not soldiers can continue indefinitely to participate in the revolution will also be determined by the solution of the land question, because if the peasants want to protect their land, they will be obliged to fight bravely. These three points represent the great significance of resolving the land question.

III

Now we can add the following three points regarding the significance of resolving the land question: (4) Eliminate the feudal system, (5) Promote China's industrialization, (6) Raise the cultural level.

---

3. The reference is to a survey carried out in Guangdong in 1926 by two experts, M. Volin and E. Yolk, who were attached to the mission of Soviet advisers. The report containing their results ran to nearly 1,000 pages. It was indicated by Vera Vishnyakova-Akimova in her memoirs (see the translation by Steven Levine under the title *Two Years in Revolutionary China 1925–1927* [Harvard University Press, 1971], p. 222) that this work was destroyed by the rightists in 1927. In fact, it survived, and was one of the sources used by Karl August Wittfogel in writing his major work, *Wirtschaft und Gesellschaft Chinas* (Leipzig: Hirschfeld, 1931). According to Wittfogel (p. xi of the preface), a very few copies of this document were taken safely back to Moscow after the break between the Communists and the Guomindang. It is manifestly still available there, for the Soviet China specialist L. P. Delyusin refers to it in his book *Agrarno-krestiyanskii Vopros v Politike KPK (1921–1928)* (The peasant and agrarian question in the politics of the Chinese Communist Party, 1921–1928) (Moscow: Izdatel'stvo "Nauka," 1972). In his bibliography, he lists it among "foreign-language" documentary sources, as follows: *The Peasant Movement in Kwangtung (Materials on the Agrarian Problem in China).* Prepared by M. Volin and E. Yolk. Under the editorship and with a preface by M. Borodin. Part 2, Collection of materials. Canton: Canton Gazette Publishing Co., 1927.

IV

I strongly approve of the chairman's ideas.[4]

In my opinion, the Ministry of Peasant Affairs of the National Government should establish a committee on rural self-government to deal exclusively with the matter of organs of rural self-government. As for the political power of the peasants, there are two stages: (1) The period of the peasant associations. At the time of revolution in the countryside, political power is concentrated in the peasant associations. (2) Once the revolution is over, rural governments should come under a national government system. Originally, the peasant associations and the government belong to different systems, and in the exercise of this kind of peasant political power each province needs a few core *xian* as models. Hunan has already proclaimed regulations regarding district, township, and village self-government,[5] Hubei may also start, so Guangdong is an exception. In these articles, the most important thing is to lay down what sort of people are not permitted to participate in the organs of self-government. At present, we must recognize the political power of the peasants and develop it.

V

1. The problem of the political power of the peasants may constitute a separate problem.
2. The matter of reinforcing the organs for land distribution should be added to the above principles for resolving the land question.

---

4. The reference is to remarks by the chairman of the meeting, Deng Yanda, who had said, "The problem of the political power of the peasants should be viewed through the eyes of those at the lower levels. (1) Negatively, the feudal forces must be annihilated. (2) Positively, organs of peasant self-government should be created. But all self-government organs at the level of the township, district, or *xian* should have the guarantee of peasant armed forces. Hence, it is crucially important to resolve the problem of arms for the peasants. The first step should be to discuss a law regarding the organization of organs of self-government at the township, district, and *xian* levels. The second step should be to get arms for the peasants; the revolutionary party and the revolutionary government must find a way to get arms for the peasants. We should adopt a resolution requesting the Central Committee to hand over 5 or 10 percent of the output of the armaments factories to the peasants. The third step is for the Ministry of Peasant Affairs, on the basis of the resolutions, to adopt and promulgate a decree regarding the organization of township, district, and *xian* self-government." See *Mao Zedong wenji*, Vol. 1, p. 45.

5. The reference is to the "Circular regarding how to realize democratic political power in the villages" and the "Regulations regarding District and Township Self-Government in Hunan" appended to this document, adopted on February 16, 1927. (*Mao Zedong wenji*, Vol. 1, p. 45.)

Explanations at the Third Meeting of the Wuhan Land Committee

(April 22, 1927)[1]

What has been decided now is political confiscation of land owned, for example, by local bullies, bad gentry, warlords, and so on. This is the first step. The next step is the confiscation of all land that the owners do not till but rent out to others; this is economic confiscation. Economic confiscation is no longer a problem in Hunan. There the peasants themselves have already divided up the land. Fiscally speaking, there is no solution or way out if the land problem is not solved. The warlords in Hunan exploit the peasants. The national government, after establishing itself in Hunan, has also been unable to eliminate this exploitation completely. Because of the war, the old fiscal policy has to be continued. This situation is in contradiction with today's revolution. If no way out can be found, the revolution will certainly end in defeat. If under the present fiscal régime even the registration tax cannot be collected, and there are many cases in which land tax goes unpaid, the various sorts of exorbitant taxes and levies are even more impossible to collect. It is in the interest of the revolution as a whole to solve the land problem. If the current fiscal policy is continued in Hunan, annual revenue will amount to only slightly more than 10 million. (In 1925 it was between 15 and 20 million.) If the land problem were solved, a rate of 10 percent would bring in 56 million, and moreover, the rate could even be increased to 15 percent. Thus the financial difficulties could be immediately

---

We have translated this text from *Mao Zedong ji. Bujuan*, Vol. 9, 233–34, where it is reproduced from Jiang Yongjing, *Baoluoting yu Wuhan zhengquan*. The same text is excerpted and paraphrased in *Nianpu*, Vol. 1, pp. 195-96. Although Jiang Yongjing had full access to the Guomindang archives, there is reason to believe that this passage is far from complete, but it conveys something of the tenor of Mao's remarks.

1. On this occasion, the draft resolution regarding the land question elaborated by the five members of the Land Committee was presented for discussion by those attending. According to *Nianpu*, Vol. 1, pp. 195–96, it was Deng Yanda who gave the initial report on behalf of the committee as a whole. The present text is an extract from the supplementary explanations Mao put forward in the course of the meeting. Not surprisingly, in the light of Mao's call for expropriating rich peasants, even if they constituted half the population, Wang Jingwei observed that this might be political confiscation in theory, but that it was in reality economic confiscation. The upshot was that the resolution was handed over for revision to a Committee of Enquiry of fifteen members, including Wang, Tan Yankai, and other senior leaders, as well as Mao and the original five.

solved. Therefore, without making a decision on the land problem, there is no way out of the financial difficulties. The land of owner-peasants and middle peasants is not subject to confiscation; the land of rich peasants is. For example, if five out of ten households are rich peasants, we must redistribute the land of the rich peasants to the other five households. The peasants in Hunan are now redistributing the land themselves. They have meetings to redistribute the land. Therefore, with special reference to the situation in Hunan, it is not enough to rely on the mode of political confiscation. But generally speaking, only political confiscation can be used. That is why the national government should explicitly promulgate such regulations (generic types), while at the same time issuing specific ones (such as those applying to Hunan). Hubei cannot be compared to Hunan; Henan cannot be compared to Hubei, either. The solution [of the land problem there] is, of course, different. Therefore, to complete economic confiscation in one step is often incompatible with objective conditions. . . .[2] You may read the Survey of Land Distribution in China;[3] this table is relatively accurate and may be used for reference.

---

2. Suspension points in the original text.

3. The reference is not to the voluminous survey by Volin and Yolk (see above, the note to the text of April 19, 1927), but to a brief document providing an overview of the question in the whole country. This text clearly emanated from the work of the Land Committee, but its precise authorship is uncertain. Jiang Yongjing states that Mao was "one of the drafters." (Jiang, *Baoluoting yu Wuhan zhengquan*, p. 289.) Hofheinz concludes that it was mainly the work of the Russian expert Tarkhanov. (See Roy Hofheinz Jr., *The Broken Wave. The Chinese Communist Peasant Movement 1922–1928*, Cambridge, Mass.: Harvard University Press, 1977, p. 37.) (For a biographical sketch of Oskar Sergeevich Tarkhanov see V.I. Nikiforov, *Sovetskie istoriki o problemakh Kitaya* [Soviet Historians on the Problems of China], Moscow, Izdatel'stvo "Nauka," 1970, p. 139.) Tarkhanov, who had been studying land distribution in Guangxi while Volin and Yolk were working on Guangdong, did indeed speak at a meeting on April 23 regarding the differences in patterns of landholding across China, but he may not have written the document cited by Mao.

Circular Telegram from Members of the Guomindang Central Committee Denouncing Chiang

(April 22, 1927)

To party organizations in every province and special municipality, overseas party general branches, and for transmittal to party organizations at all levels, all provincial governments, government agencies at all levels, commanders in chief of all the army groups of the National Revolutionary Army, commanders of each front army, the commander in chief of the navy, commanders of every army, all officers and soldiers of each army, the general political department, political departments at all levels, all newspapers in the country, to be passed on to all organizations of the popular masses:

We have just read Jiang Zhongzheng's[1] clever telegram and realized that he has shifted from opposing the Central Committee to illegally setting up his own central committee. We have been aware of this conspiracy of Chiang Kaishek for a long time because he has been routinely treating the Central Committee as his puppet. When he saw that the Central Committee's action did not advance his self-interest, he began to convene meetings after the fashion of warlord cliques to demonstrate his defiance. Then he went on to call meetings like the Western Hills Conference to plot in favor of splits. Although all we colleagues have long been aware of this conspiracy of Chiang Kaishek, and it is too late to seek reconciliation, only when this ultimate split descended on us today did we begin to contemplate preventive solutions. We feel, indeed, deep remorse. Through the tone and rhetoric of the telegram, Chiang Kaishek sounded as if he deserved all the credit. Shall we ask whether, since the Northern Expedition began, countless comrades have lost their lives and shed their blood in order that Chiang Kaishek alone may claim fame and credit? For example, the likes of Wu Peifu and Zhang Zuolin used their military adventures to manipulate the government and caused Beijing to fall into a state of anarchy. Chiang Kaishek is attempting to emulate

---

This telegram was published in the Hankou *Minguo ribao* on April 22, 1927. We have translated it from the text reproduced in *Mao Zedong ji. Bujuan*, Vol. 9, pp. 221–22.

1. Here and throughout this document, Chiang is referred to politely as Jiang Zhongzheng. In accordance with our normal usage, we have changed this to Chiang Kaishek in all subsequent appearances of the name.

them, but the revolutionary masses cannot be deceived twice. This only shows that Chiang is blind to this reality. We now wish to call on the revolutionary popular masses: Chiang Kaishek's betrayal of the Central Committee and his establishment of a separate central committee are the result of the compromise he first made with the imperialists since his arrival in Shanghai. He would go so far as to inherit the mantle of disgrace from Wu Peifu, Sun Chuanfang, Zhang Zuolin, and Zhang Zongchang; he used anti-Communist slogans in order to curry favor with the imperialists; he did not even hesitate to butcher people as his tribute to them. He clearly knows that such acts are forbidden by the Central Committee; that is why he has no alternative but to embark on a course of rebellion against the Central Committee. He used the office of commander in chief to deceive those justice-loving troops disloyal to the traitors into doing battle, and cut off their supplies, leaving their fate to the enemy. He arrested, imprisoned, and murdered at will political workers in the army. He ordered his running dogs to persecute party members in the party organizations of provinces and cities. After he has purged his opposition and formed his own power base, he brazenly and recklessly sets up his own central committee. Then, all the tools of the imperialists have converged under his flag to engage in counterrevolution, while all the revolutionary elements have been eliminated on charges of being Communist or colluding with the Communist Party. This has already begun now and will certainly intensify in the future. The revolutionary base in the southeast has thus been dismantled by him. The revolutionary popular masses will soon be exterminated. All our popular masses and our comrades, especially our armed comrades, as well as those who do not want to see the pending victory of the revolution fall into the hands of Chiang Kaishek, must carry out the orders of the Central Committee and get rid of this traitor to the Director General,[2] the scum of this party, and the swindler of the people. With deep respect, we [X] all the national revolutionary armies to issue telegrams to voice their outrage. We [X] wish [X]. Members of the Central Executive Committee, alternate members of the Central Executive Committee, members of the national government, members of the Military Affairs Commission: Wang Jingwei, Tan Yankai, Sun Ke, Xu Qian, Gu Mengyu, Tan Pingshan, Chen Gongbo, Wu Yuzhang, Tang Shengzhi, Deng Yanda, Song Ziwen, Chen Qian, Zhu Peide, Zhang Fakui, Song Qingling, He Xiangning, Lin Zuhan, Wang [X][X], Chen Youren, Jing Tingyi, Yu Shude, Yang Baoan, Yun Daiying, Pang Zeming, Mao Zedong, Xu Suhun, Xiao Xi, Huang Shi, Dong Yongwei, Zhan Dabei, Wang Leping, Chen Qi'ai, Zhu Jiqing, Gao Yuhan, Chen Bijun, Jian Hao, Deng [X]xiu, Xie Jin, Kong Geng.

---

2. I.e., to Sun Yatsen.

Remarks at the Enlarged Meeting of the Committee on the Peasant Movement

(April 26, 1927, 7 P.M.)[1]

Chairman [Deng Yanda]: Central Committee members! Comrades! Today we are holding an enlarged meeting of the Central Peasant Movement Committee of the Central Party Bureau. The Central Peasant Movement Committee has been organized on the instructions of the Central Executive Committee in order to study our party's tactics toward the peasant movement. Only after we have such tactics and policies can we determine what the peasant movement should do and what its responsibilities should be. . . .

. . . During its first period, the Northern Expedition created a military autocracy, the dictatorship of an individual.[2] The victory of the revolution was a purely military victory and not a victory of the popular masses. Only when the peasants of Hunan and Hubei arose was there a turning point in this danger of

---

The source for this text is the papers of Professor C. Martin Wilbur, which have been deposited in the Rare Book and Manuscript Library of Columbia University. These files contain a complete copy, in Chinese, of the minutes of both sessions, made from the Guomindang archives, together with Professor Wilbur's translations. Our version of Mao's remarks is based on his, with some editorial modifications.

1. Two meetings were held on April 26. The first, convened at 4 P.M., was the Fifth Enlarged Meeting of the Land Committee. Chen Duxiu and Borodin had been specially invited to attend on this occasion, and they set the tone for the day's discussions. Of the two, Chen Duxiu was slightly less reticent about carrying out land reform. Chen himself summed up the difference by saying that, while Borodin advocated taking action only after the People's Assembly had adopted a land reform policy, he would be satisfied with the approval of the Provincial Party Office and the Provincial Peasants' Association. Both agreed that, while the peasants should have political power, matters could not be handled "carelessly" in areas controlled by the national government, and detailed procedures were required. The principle of "political confiscation" should be applied, and the land of small landlords and Revolutionary Army men exempted from confiscation. All the draft resolutions, including that on "The Significance of Solving the Land Problem," for which Mao was responsible, were to be revised and submitted to a subsequent enlarged meeting of the Land Committee, and to the Central Executive Committee. Mao sat through this first session in silence, but he spoke at some length during the second meeting, held at 7 P.M., which took the form of an enlarged session of the recently created Committee on the Peasant Movement. We have translated all of Mao's utterances, together with brief extracts from the chairman's opening remarks and from other people's contributions to put Mao's statements in context.

2. I.e., of Chiang Kaishek.

personal despotism. . . . In the revolution at present, the peasants are not only waging a political struggle, they are also seeking to resolve economic problems. This marks a new stage in the revolution. Now the movement for party power has already completed a phase, and the second Northern Expedition has begun.[3] This Northern Expedition is different from the first Northern Expedition. It advocates . . . on the one hand waging war, and on the other hand liberating the peasants. This is the important significance of the current Northern Expedition and the fundamental difference as compared to the first period of the Northern Expedition . . .

. . .

. . . Now, as we discuss together how to deal with the problem of liberating the peasants, we must be resolute and accept the demands of the new era in order to seek [their] liberation. This is the significance of Central's welcome to all you comrades. As we fraternal delegates report to all you comrades, we also await your instruction in order to achieve an excellent result.

. . .

Mao Zedong: Formerly, there was no All-China Peasants' Association. Only at the end of March did delegates from the provincial Peasants' Associations of Hunan, Hubei, Jiangxi, and Guangdong hold a meeting and organize it. The Henan delegates did not arrive, so armed peasants took part [in their place]. Why was it necessary to organize this organ now? It was because we thought that virtually all provinces had peasant movements, and if we did not have this national organization, our battle against the enemies of the peasant movement could not be unified. The All-China Peasants' Association elected Deng Yanda, Tan Yankai, Tan Pingshan, Xu Qian, Tang Shengzhi, Yi Lirong, Mao Zedong, Sun Ke, Zhang Fakui, Peng Pai, Lu Chen, Xiao Rengu, and Fang Zhimin, thirteen persons, as a temporary Executive Committee, and chose five among them as Standing Committee members. There are organization and propaganda departments, and a secretariat.[4] These are the general circumstances of the establishment and organization [of the All-China Peasants' Association]. As regards our work, there are two important items at present:

1. The convening of the First National Congress of Peasants' Delegates. Because the workers already have a very good organization, and the peasants'

---

3. "The Second Northern Expedition" was the term used in Wuhan, in April and May 1927, for a military thrust northward, with the aim of joining up with the forces of Feng Yuxiang, then regarded as favorable to the revolution. See Warren Kuo, *Analytical History of the Chinese Communist Party* (Taibei: Institute of International Relations, 1968), Vol. 1, pp. 310–12.

4. As indicated above, in the telegram of April 9, 1927, Mao himself headed the Organization Department; Deng Yanda was head of the Propaganda Department, and Peng Pai was general secretary.

organization is still deficient, we have decided to call a conference in Hankou on July 1, with 680 participants, of which 620 will be peasant delegates and 60 will be soldier delegates. The announcements have already been sent out.[5] The significance of this is very great. The demands of various provincial peasants' associations are limited to particular localities, and the demands of the peasants of the whole country have not yet been expressed. At present, the peasants' demands are to obtain political power and to solve economic [problems]. So it is necessary to convene this National Congress of Peasant Delegates.

2. Secondly, active attention should be paid to the peasant movement in the North. In areas under the national government, peasant movement work can easily be carried out and encounters no obstacles. But now the Northern Expedition is under way, and the peasant movement in the North is extremely important. If we do not obtain the sympathy of the northern peasants, the army of the Northern Expedition will struggle on its own.[6] Therefore provincial peasant associations should quickly be established in the three provinces of Zhili, Shandong, and Henan. It is also important that they be established in Shaanxi, Anhui, Sichuan, and Gansu. But particular importance attaches to the North, especially the regions occupied by Zhang Zuolin and Zhang Zongchang.

Time is short today, so the All-China Peasants' Association will limit itself to this one important aspect of our work in reporting to you comrades.

. . .

Chairman: [We need the support of the peasants in order to overthrow the feudal system, the warlords, and the imperialists, and to get it we must give them land. But at the same time, the troops are showing themselves unwilling to unite with the peasants.]. . . Today,[7] the discussions of the Land Committee have completed one phase. There are very large numbers of small landlords in China, and many of the Revolutionary Army men come from these families, so small landlords must be protected; this principle has already been laid down. Under the national government, a specialized committee has been established, and in particular there is the Ministry of Peasant Affairs. As regards the present Northern Expedition, in fighting for the liberation of the oppressed peasants in the North, we must first solve the problem of the peasants' political power . . .

. . .

Mao Zedong: The special work of the Northern Expedition is very important. Only Henan has peasant associations, but Shandong and Zhili still do not have

---

5. This had been done on April 18, but because of the worsening situation, the congress was in fact never held.

6. Here Mao is, of course, repeating the point he had made a year earlier, on March 30, 1926.

7. I.e., at the 4 P.M. meeting.

them. Henan is within the sphere of the enemy and must have a special organization, such as a Committee for the War Zone. Today time presses, and I fear there is no time to organize a detailed discussion. Could we not designate certain people to organize it? Personal opinions from all relevant points of view, such as the Central Peasant Movement Committee, the All-China Peasants' Association, the General Political Department, the Fourth Army, the Henan Provincial Party Office, the Henan Peasants' Association, students from the Central Peasant Movement Training Institute, the Peasant Self-Defense Army, and the Soldiers' Consolation Corps, should all join in, making rather a large number of people. Before Henan has been occupied, [affairs there] could be directed by the Committee for the War Zone. Shandong could be treated similarly. There are sixty or seventy students from Henan and Shandong in the Central Peasant Movement Training Institute who could follow along to the front to work. If there are students who want to go, there is no need to restrain them. As to details of organization and expenditure, we can discuss it further.

Yi Lirong: Comrade Mao has proposed a concrete method. Although we cannot decide on every item today, the situation is very pressing. Can we not do as Comrade Mao proposes? I fear, though, that it would be difficult to take detailed decisions today.

Li Xiyi: In the main, I approve of Comrade Mao's proposal. I am concerned, however, about [his suggestion that] we should wait until the army has arrived in Zhili and Shandong to organize in those areas. When military action is under way, it will certainly not be possible to do things in such an orderly manner. Moreover, I do not think we should necessarily wait to organize until the military contingency arises.

Mao Zedong: My idea was not that at present we would only organize in Henan. It is that, wherever the army arrives, and whatever province we enter, we should expand outward from there.

Chen Kewen: Comrades Mao and Li have discussed organization in the war zone. We must, however, consider how to manage propaganda materials and expenses in the rear after the front has moved forward. Could we not have part of the people remain in the rear? This is also a matter of organization, which I request you comrades to consider.

. . .

Chairman: Summing up, [the issues are]: (1) name, (2) composition, and (3) scope of the work. Adopting this order, let us first discuss terminology.

Resolved: that we retain the name of Peasant Movement Committee for the War Zone.

Chairman: Who should comprise the personnel?

. . .

Resolved: that all comrades in the peasant movement of every province who wish to join may do so.

. . .

Mao Zedong: Students from the Central Peasant Movement Training Institute should be added.

. . .

Chairman: . . . Now we should appoint the members of a preparatory committee, to hold its first meeting tomorrow. It is resolved to appoint Chen Kewen, Mao Zedong, Zhou Yili, Guan Xuecan, Zhang Bojun, and Peng Zexiang, with Mao Zedong as chairman.

. . .

Because the time is too short to discuss the third and fourth items on the agenda, I will explain these two items: (1) The Peasant Movement Committee does not exist only at the Center; each province should also organize one. (2) The work of the peasant movement is different in the various provinces: in some it is open, in others semi-open, and in others it is secret. It should be organized, and plans determined accordingly.

Mao Zedong: The peasants' associations are mass organizations. Now we must bring about intimate relations between the organizations of the popular masses and the party. The peasants' association of each province should also have relations with the provincial party headquarters and the provincial Peasant Department. Formerly most of them did not have links. All comrades should take responsibility for discussing this, and after taking a decision, issue a circular as to how the relations among the party headquarters, the Peasant Department, and the peasants' association of each province can be made close.

Chairman: The meeting is adjourned.

Report of the Land Committee

(May 9, 1927)

The land problem is not merely a problem that must be solved in terms of revolutionary theory; in reality, it has now also reached a point where it cannot be left without a solution. The peasants in Hunan have spontaneously mobilized to confiscate and redistribute the land. Every one of the provincial congresses of peasant associations in Guangdong, Hubei, Jiangxi, and other provinces has expressed an urgent demand for solving the land problem. Even the peasants in Zhili, who are oppressed by the Fengtian warlords, have caused countless conflicts and bloody incidents because of the issue of "turning official land into people's land." Moreover, from a political perspective, the revolutionary movement has now definitely undergone considerable development. But at the same time, it is fraught with enormous contradictions and dangers. There is no way to solve the fiscal problem, and questions have arisen with respect to the numbers and quality of the armed forces. A way out of these contradictions and dangers can only be sought through the solution of the land problem. In order to lead the masses and protect the revolution, our party has especially organized the Land Committee to take responsibility for discussing this critical issue, which demands urgent solution. Since the formation of the Land Committee, many meetings have been convened, and significant conclusions have been reached on the methods of solving this problem. Here is a brief report on the course of the discussions:

Three meetings have been convened since the formation of the Land Committee. It was felt that the problem was so important and complicated that a solution could not be found without collecting data from individual provinces and views from all sides. Therefore, after three meetings were convened, enlarged meetings were called; altogether five such enlarged meetings were called. Later, for the sake of facilitating discussion, special committees were organized to be in charge of examining individual draft resolutions; altogether four such meetings were called. The number of people who attended the enlarged meetings was between more than forty, at its highest, and a little over ten, at its lowest. The first enlarged meeting took place on April 19; the fifth and last

---

Our source for this text is the version in *Mao Zedong ji. Bujuan*, Vol. 9, pp. 235–39, which is reproduced from a documentary collection published by the Institute of International Relations in Taibei in 1973.

took place on May 6. The comrades who attended these meetings represent fifteen provinces. There were four reports and seven draft resolutions. Although no perfect methods were found to solve the land problem, considerable responsibility can be said to have been exercised in the course of the revolution. Here is a separate description of the course of these meetings:

1. Number of meetings
    a. three meetings of the Land Committee itself
    b. five enlarged meetings
    c. four meetings of special deliberative committees
2. Comrades who attended
    a. members of the Land Committee
    b. members of the Central [Executive] Committee
    c. leading comrades of provincial and district party organizations
    d. comrades in charge of the peasant movement in provinces and districts
    e. leading comrades in the military (army and divisional commanders, directors, or secretaries of the political departments)
3. Regions represented by the participants
       Hunan, Hubei, Guangdong, Henan, Zhili [Hebei], Shandong, Anhui, Jiangsu, Zhejiang, Fujian, Rehe, Fengtian, Chaha'er, Jilin, and Shanxi
4. Reports
    a. report by Russian Comrade Tarkhanov on the Russian experience of solving the land problem
    b. an overview of land distribution in the whole country[1]
    c. report by the party organization of Zhili Province on land distribution in that province
    d. report by the Rehe provincial party organization on land distribution in that province
    e. reports by comrades of other provincial party organizations on the land situation in their provinces
5. Central issues discussed:
       In the course of the meetings, it was generally recognized, on the basis of the reports and investigations from various places and on the needs of the revolution at the moment, that the land problem urgently required solution. But many debates were held regarding the method of solution: whether to confiscate and nationalize all available land immediately, or to confiscate part of the land. In the end it was agreed that, in theory, all land should, without a doubt, be confiscated and nationalized. But the current objective situation, the political environ-

---

1. This is presumably the brief survey, possibly by Tarkhanov, referred to by Mao in his remarks of April 22, 1927, translated above.

ment in the country as a whole and the strength of the peasants themselves do not permit the nationalization of all land. In the present objective circumstances, we can carry out only political confiscation (partial confiscation). The land of small landlords and of revolutionary soldiers should all be preserved. The system of landlords and tenants cannot be completely destroyed. The methods for a fundamental solution of the land problem cannot be specified in detail by meetings of the Central Committee. The Central Committee can only lay down principles; detailed methods should be formulated by the provinces themselves according to their actual conditions. Therefore, as a result of the meeting, the following resolutions were produced:

6. Resolutions

    a. resolution: "Program for Solving the Land Problem"
    b. resolution on the significance of solving the land problem
    c. resolution on the political power of the peasants and the solution of the land problem
    d. resolution on the law for the protection of tenants
    e. resolution on regulations to protect the land of revolutionary soldiers
    f. resolution on regulations for disposing of the properties of traitors
    g. resolution on solving the land problem

The above is the course of discussion on the land problem by the Land Committee. The Land Committee regards all the resolutions, especially items d. to g., as adapted to our party's current strategies and the needs of objective reality; they should be made into laws and regulations by our party for promulgation and implementation. We respectfully await your opinion on this.

The committee has verified the content of the above.
To the Central Executive Committee.

Enclosures:

(1) seven resolutions
(2) a volume containing the minutes of these meetings

For the Land Committee:

Deng Yanda, Tan Pingshan, Mao Zedong, Xu Qian, Gu Mengyu

May 9, 1927

Draft Resolution on Solving the Land Question

(April 1927)[1]

I. Principles:

(1) In the course of the national revolution, the land problem must be solved. This means the redistribution of the land of large landlords, government land, public land, and abandoned land to landless peasants and peasants with not enough land to make a living. The national government should protect the land of small landlords and the land of the fighting men who have worked hard for the revolution.

(2) In order to solve the land problem, we must see to it that the peasants have enough strength to gain and safeguard political power. Consequently, the national government should aid the peasants in the countryside in their struggle against the big landlords and all the other feudal forces.

II. Methods of implementation:

(3) The national government should immediately issue organizational regulations for organs of self-government in townships, districts, and *xian*, and also select and dispatch personnel specializing in peasant affairs to individual townships, districts, and *xian* to guide and support them in organizing.

(4) The national government should urge individual provincial governments to implement concretely all of our party's resolutions on the peasant issue, particularly the resolutions of the Joint Session of the center and the provinces, and those of the third plenum of the Central Executive Committee.

(5) Party organizations in all provinces should quickly work with the peasant

---

This resolution has been translated from the text in *Mao Zedong ji. Bujuan*, Vol. 9, pp. 225–26, which reproduces the version given in Jiang Yongjing, *Baoluoting yu Wuhan zhengquan.*

1. The available versions of this resolution are dated simply April 1927. It is probably a text drawn up in late April, adopted at the Sixth Enlarged Meeting of the Land Committee on May 6, and submitted by the Land Committee to the Central Executive Committee with their Report of May 9, translated above. As explained in the Introduction to this volume, none of these resolutions were in fact put into force, because the top leaders in Wuhan regarded them as too radical.

associations in their provinces to formulate, on the basis of the above principles and according to the practical conditions in their provinces, concrete methods of implementation for solving the land problem, and report them to the central party organization for approval before the national government orders provincial governments to implement them.

(6) In order to root out the feudal forces in the countryside and prevent reactionary forces from attacking the peasants, all provincial party organizations, governments, peasant associations, and the civic groups designated by provincial party organizations must organize popular tribunals to punish severely local bullies, bad gentry, and all the reactionary elements who harm the interests of the people.

(7) Agencies manufacturing weapons that are under the jurisdiction of the national government should set aside between 5 and 10 percent of their products to be supplied to peasants for them to form peasant self-defense forces; matters related to the maintenance and distribution of weapons are to be dealt with by the "People's Armed Forces Committee" to be organized by the Central Party Bureau.

(8) The national government should quickly survey the climate, water and land resources, and amounts of harvest in all the areas, and fix the criterion for small landlords as having no more than roughly 50 *mu* of fertile land per person and no more than 100 *mu* of poor-quality land per person. Land ownership rights may be enjoyed within such limits.

(9) The national government should immediately issue laws protecting tenants.

(10) The land currently owned by the officers and soldiers of the National Revolutionary Army should be protected by the national government; those without land should be given land to till by the national government after the end of the revolutionary war. The details are to be spelt out by laws.

(11) The propaganda program for the land problem should be determined by the Land Committee and approved by the Central Party Bureau.

III. Appendix:

The land to which this resolution refers is farming land. Such land as is used for cattle raising, forests, mines, houses, and workshops does not come within the scope of this resolution.

Important Directive of the All-China Peasant Association to the Peasant Associations of Hunan, Hubei, and Jiangxi Provinces

(May 30, 1927)[1]

The Chinese revolution has already developed to a new stage. At the beginning of this new stage, if we only point out the errors of the past from a negative perspective, we are bound to fail in leading the masses to push the revolutionary movement forward. New policies must be adopted to meet the needs of this new stage. For this purpose, the All-China Peasant Association today issues an important directive which points to the inevitability of certain phenomena in the early stage of the peasant movement and suggests some positive measures to deal with these problems. It instructs the peasant associations of Hunan, Hubei, and Jiangxi to implement these measures thoroughly. It is expected that, from now on, all the reactionary activities of sowing dissension will completely disappear, and the peasant movement will make great progress. Moreover, with these measures, the Chinese revolution will receive a real guarantee. This directive is not only of great importance to the peasant movement at present, it will also become the most illustrious chapter in the annals of the Chinese revolution. This newspaper made a special effort yesterday to obtain the original text of this directive, which is as follows:

More than 80 percent of the Chinese population are peasants, who have suffered the most severe political oppression and economic exploitation (the burdensome land rent and exorbitant levies commonly take more than 65 percent of their crops). Their revolutionary demands, therefore, are the most pressing. The facts of the past have already fully proved that, in order to get rid of exploitation, the peasants are very enthusiastic about joining the revolution, and they become the main force of the national revolution. The mission of the peasant associations is to lead this main force in achieving the liberation of the peasants, and thereby the success of the national revolution. For the significance of the national revolution lies in overthrowing the rule of imperialism and the feudal forces and in creating a democratic political power. To reach this goal, it is objectively necessary that

---

This directive was published on May 30, 1927, in the Hankou *Minguo ribao*. Our translation has been made from that text, as reproduced in *Mao Zedong ji. Bujuan*, pp. 249–53.

1. The date given here is that of publication. The introductory paragraph which precedes the directive was supplied by the newspaper in which it appeared.

we ultimately put into practice the principle of "land to the tiller," for only then can we overthrow the economic basis of imperialist exploitation in the Chinese countryside, and the political basis of the warlords, and thereby liberate the popular masses of all China, allowing the productive forces of the Chinese economy, as well as industry and commerce, to develop freely and fully.

Since the reorganization of the Guomindang in the thirteenth year of the Republic, when the policy of supporting the peasants and workers was adopted, this policy has been confirmed several times by the directives, resolutions, and declarations of the Guomindang and the national government. More and more concrete proposals are made to accept the peasants' demands for reducing land rent and for establishing village self-government. As a result, peasants all over the country, especially in Fujian, Hunan, and Jiangxi provinces, have supported the Guomindang and the national government wholeheartedly. In fighting against all the counterrevolutionary forces, the revolutionary forces are advancing from the Pearl River valley to the Yangtze valley, and they will advance further to the Yellow River valley, and the whole of China. With the development of the national revolutionary forces, the peasants in Hunan, Hubei, and other provinces have gained a considerable amount of freedom. They have recognized even more clearly that overthrowing the warlords means not only knocking down those individuals who have established spheres of influence by armed force, while colluding with the imperialists and oppressing the masses of the people, but in destroying root and branch the basis of the warlords—the local bullies and bad gentry. It is known to all that the local bullies and bad gentry in the countryside are nothing but small warlords in the villages, and they are often the lackeys of the big warlords. So when the National Revolutionary Army is fighting fiercely against the warlord troops of Wu Peifu and Zhao Hengti on the battlefields, it is also the time when the peasants are fighting fiercely against the local bullies and bad gentry in the villages. By waging vigorous attacks on the local bullies and bad gentry, the peasants are actually performing their tasks as the main force of the national revolution. The local bullies and bad gentry clearly know that such a struggle is of crucial importance, so they use all sorts of cruel means to resist stubbornly, and their hands are spattered with the blood of the peasants of every province. In order to survive and to protect the freedom bestowed on them by the national government, the peasants have no alternative but to use revolutionary means to respond to the attacks by the local bullies and bad gentry. These are the necessary measures that must be taken in the initial period of the peasant liberation movement. They are also the necessary means by which the national government can take the first steps toward people's rights. These measures are similar to the military emergency measures taken during the revolutionary wars by the national revolutionary army, and indeed they are beyond reproach.

The more the revolutionary forces develop, the fiercer the struggle becomes between revolution and counterrevolution. The imperialists, along with the old and new warlords, have spared no effort to support the local bullies and bad gentry in destroying the peasant movement. The peasants, however, because they could not immediately get strong support from the national government, have suffered greatly from these cruel attacks. In addition, Chiang Kaishek and the local bullies and bad gentry have gone all the way in sowing dissension, mudslinging, and rumormongering. All this has further aroused the indignation of the peasants and forced them to adopt even more violent means of resistance in order to survive. Moreover, the peasants' struggle in the past was limited to the local areas, and not closely linked to the revolutionary process in all of China, so the general situation on the revolutionary front is confusing. In the past the national government and National Revolutionary Army did not implement the declarations and resolutions concerning the peasants in timely fashion and failed to make every peasant understand that the national government and Revolutionary Army are fighting for the interests of the peasants. As a result, before the order of the national government was issued to protect the property of the revolutionary soldiers, a few peasants' actions sometimes unavoidably hurt the interests of the revolutionary soldiers. Chiang Kaishek and the local bullies and bad gentry seized the chance to spread rumors and sow dissension. First they blamed this on leftist agitation, and later they defamed the peasant movement. After the initial emergency measures of military style were taken, we should begin a new period of construction now that the revolutionary forces are indeed prevailing. The same is true of the peasant movement. Otherwise, if we go on in this way for a long time, it would obstruct the progress of the peasant movement. The reactionaries will also take advantage of this to endanger the consolidation of the revolutionary united front.

Already the Chinese peasant movement has made considerable progress, especially in Hunan and Hubei. New policies must be adopted to fit the new environment. The essential part of this new policy is to continue to organize the peasant associations and to create organs of self-government in the districts, villages, and *xian*, thus establishing democratic and autonomous governments there. In the village, for example, such a democratic government will have the peasants as its core, although the rest of the masses can also participate fully in the villagers' council and in the organ of political power in the village. This includes the middle class, the small landlords, middle and small merchants, intellectuals, and all those who are not local bullies and bad gentry or counterrevolutionaries. The same is true of the districts and the *xian*.

In the course of establishing organs of democratic self-government in the villages, we must, first of all, deal a severe blow to all the counterrevolutionaries and their policies of sowing dissension. We must make sure that the political power of the peasants can be fully exercised through such organs. All matters concerning arrests and fines must be dealt with, according to the laws and rules of the national government, by the judicial organs set up by these organs of self-government truly representing the interests of the majority of the people.

Second, as regards the small landlords and the families of the revolutionary officers, the majority of them are at most small landlords. They must, like the peasants, receive economic liberation; politically, they must, like the peasants, take their standing on the front fighting against counterrevolution. Naturally, they should support the peasants in setting up democratic political power. The peasant associations must therefore instruct the peasants to seek cooperation with them so that the organs of self-government in the villages may be able to provide real protection for them. Third, to establish the democratic organs of self-government in the village is an effective method for arousing the peasants and safeguarding the victories achieved by the revolution. On the one hand, such organs of self-government, under the direction of the national government, can continue the fight against the local bullies and bad gentry, and control and repress these elements, preventing them from engaging in violent and murderous actions. On the other hand, such organs of self-government in the villages will certainly provide a much deeper and wider social basis for the national government, for such self-governments are under the control of the national government administrative system. Fourth, in order to establish the democratic political power of the peasants in the villages, it is necessary to disarm the local bullies and bad gentry, to arm the peasant masses, and to provide a unified command, so as to protect the interests of the peasants. Moreover, with the establishment of organs of self-government in the villages, the peasant defense army can become the sole military force authorized by the national government to maintain law and order in the villages, while other military organizations in the villages, such as the militia,[2] should not be allowed to exist. Fifth, it is also one of the main tasks of the organs of village self-government, after they are established, to improve the living standard of the poor peasants. From the organs of self-government in the villages up to the national government, every effort should be made to find a concrete solution to this problem. Methods may include: setting up peasant cooperatives and the Peasants' Bank, seeking ways to help those who have no land or little land to make a living and to get some land, and providing capital and farm implements to the peasants. In this way, we can break through the economic blockade of the counterrevolutionaries and promote agricultural production. Regulations regarding the confiscation of the land of the local bullies, bad gentry, and big landlords must be in accordance with the policies of the national government. Sixth, because there was no good way to solve the problem of food grain in the past, and the profiteers and local bullies manipulated the prices, the peasants often had to resort to the method of blocking the grain from being sent out of their area in order to guarantee that they would not starve. From now on, this problem must be solved by the organs of self-government in the villages, or by the producers' cooperative and the consumers' cooperative jointly. For such organs can more easily produce a careful calculation of the grain requirements of

---

2. I.e., the landlord-controlled militia or *mintuan*.

the villages. Special efforts should be made to provide as much rice as possible for the use by the revolutionary army. Also, the flow of food and grain should be smoothed as much as possible so as to activate local finance and to enable the village people to buy the daily necessities, provided that such flow will not jeopardize the food supply of the local people. Seventh, after the organs of self-government are established in the villages, it is particularly important to carry out the laws protecting the interests of the tenant-peasants and the farm laborers and to maintain their living standards.

If we want to accomplish these tasks fully, we must now tighten up the organization of the peasant associations and take measures to consolidate the peasant movement. We should combine the local peasant movement with the process of the national revolution in the whole country and strengthen the revolutionary united front, thus building a strong revolutionary fortress for overthrowing imperialism and all the reactionary forces, safeguarding the victories achieved by the revolution, realizing the principle of "land to the tiller," and finally reaching the goal of liberating the people of all China. Otherwise, if we allow the primitive phenomena of the peasant movement during the initial stage of the revolution to continue, not only can the revolutionary victories already achieved by the peasants not be safeguarded, but they may even be manipulated and destroyed by the reactionaries, or suffer big setbacks.

All the above measures are of great significance for the future of the peasant movement. We therefore instruct the peasant associations of the three provinces to implement them accordingly and also to tell every *xian*, district, village, and locality to help the peasant masses understand the present new policy thoroughly, so as to work diligently. It is important that the provincial peasant associations report to this association on the implementation of these measures.

Tan Yankai, Tan Pingshan, Deng Yanda,
Mao Zedong, Lu Chen

Members of the Standing Committee of the
Provisional Executive Committee of the
All-China Peasant Association

Opening Address at the Welcome Banquet for Delegates to the Pacific Labor Conference

(May 31, 1927)

It is of extremely great significance that the Pacific Labor Conference is held this time in Hankou. For this reason, the All-China Peasant Association and the Provincial Peasant Association hosted a welcome banquet in the Pu Hai Chun Restaurant in Hankou on May 31. The peasant associations of Wu[chang], Yang[xin] and Xia[kou] *xian* also participated. About one hundred people attended the welcome banquet, including Mao Zedong from the All-China Peasant Association; Chen Yinlin, Fu Xiangyi, Guo Shuxun, and Deng Yasheng from the Provincial Peasant Association; and representatives from Wu, Yang, and Xia *xian*. Twenty-eight delegates to the Pacific Labor Conference were invited to attend the banquet as guests. It began with an opening address by Mao Zedong, the chairman [of the banquet]. The gist of his remarks was as follows:

The Chinese revolution is a part of the world revolution. In the past, this was no more than an empty slogan, but the welcome banquet today has already given substance to it. The international imperialists, in an attempt to oppose the Chinese revolution, have already fabricated the Second World War. The workers along the Pacific Rim are the first to raise the banner of righteousness and to oppose this cruel massacre. The Chinese peasants should become even more united and follow the workers in their fight to the death. The Chinese peasant movement is the main force in the revolutionary process. They should especially go hand in hand with the working class of the whole world and rely deeply on the influence and guidance of the workers' movement. This demonstrates that the workers have quite naturally become the leaders of the peasants. It will truly be of immeasurable benefit to the future of the revolution that the Chinese peasants are able today to receive guidance from the leaders of the international proletariat.

This report first appeared in the Hankou *Minguo ribao* on June 6, 1927. We have translated it from that text as reproduced in *Mao Zedong ji. Bujuan*, Vol. 2, p. 277.

New Directive of the All-China Peasant Association to the Peasant Movement

(June 7, 1927)[1]

This directive is to be strictly observed. Not long ago, Chiang, Xia,[2] and other renegades defected one after another, and all of them used the slogan of opposing the movement of peasants and workers as their banner. Although this has always been the slogan of the reactionary faction, it is not really a matter of whether or not the movement of peasants and workers has made any so-called mistakes. Yet, on one hand, due to the rapid upsurge of the revolutionary tide, the primitive manifestations of the early stage of the peasant movement have not been altogether eliminated, and on the other hand, the leadership capacity of the upper-level organizations does not match current needs—these are indeed undeniable facts. The Chinese peasant movement has entered a new stage, and new policies must be adopted. To facilitate their implementation, five issues are addressed below. It is hoped that all provincial peasants' associations will make sure to transmit them to the peasants' associations at all levels and act on them effectively.

(1) Pay attention to strengthening the organization and to strict discipline.

Because of overly rapid development in the past, peasants' associations at all levels unavoidably have had bad elements such as local bullies and bad gentry seize the opportunity to worm their way in so as to try to undermine the peasant movement. They invariably use the name of the peasants' associations to take all

---

This directive was published on June 8, 1927, in the Hankou *Minguo ribao*, and on June 11, 1927, in *Nongmin yundong*, No. 27. It is reprinted from the second of these sources in *Zhōnggong zhongyang wenjian xuanji*, Vol. 3, pp. 613–16. Both versions are included in *Mao Zedong ji. Bujuan*, Vol. 9, respectively pp. 285–88 and 305–09. We have taken as our source the text in *Zhonggong zhongyang wenjian xuanji*, which includes the names of the five authors.

1. This is the date of one of the two available versions of this document; the other is dated simply June 1927.

2. Xia Douyin had served earlier in Hunan. (See above, the section on the armed forces in "Hunan under the Provincial Constitution" of July 1, 1923.) At this time he was based in his native province of Hubei, where a few days after the Horse Day Massacre of May 21, 1927, in Hunan, his troops went on the rampage against the peasant associations, killing several thousand people and devastating entire villages. His action was believed to have been instigated by Chiang Kaishek.

kinds of actions that are harmful to the interests of the majority of peasants and to the reputation of the peasants' associations. To correct this adverse state of affairs, a majority of peasants must actively participate in the peasants' associations at all levels. The peasants' associations in all townships and districts in particular should, where possible, call representative meetings to review past work and oversee the actions of the members. If bad elements are discovered, revolutionary discipline must be implemented immediately and severe sanctions must be imposed. In order to carry out the new policies, the peasants' associations at all levels should convene representative meetings immediately, elect more new staff workers, and add new leadership positions. At the same time, the poor peasants, tenant-peasants, hired laborers, and self-employed peasants who till the fields should be enabled to become the solid social foundation for the peasants' associations.

(2) Pay attention to the interests of the allies of the revolution.

Small merchants in the countryside are the key elements in financial circulation, and they are in the same oppressed position as the peasants. The peasants' associations should lead the peasants as well as establish close revolutionary alliances with [the small merchants]. Brewing wine and making sugar and other commercial goods are in the interests of chambers of commerce, but they have to do with the rural economy as well and must be protected by the peasants' associations. As for grains in the countryside, before rural self-rule organizations come into being, the peasants' associations should be responsible for calculating grain needs and work hard to circulate surplus grain, avoid inconveniences to small landlords and rich peasants, and supply plenty of grain to the troops. Other important rural produce should also have good economic links with the commerce of cities so as to enable small and medium merchants to develop their businesses unimpeded. In the past there were places where, because of taxes and levies in goods and money, and for other reasons, the relations between the commerce of the cities and the countryside deteriorated gradually. In the future, such situations should be corrected and the development of commerce should be assisted in an organized way to prevent excessive exploitation by unscrupulous merchants. With regard to relatives and properties of revolutionary soldiers, this association's provisional order No. 1 has already stated explicitly that the peasants' associations at all levels should guide the peasants and provide effective protection to them. At present, this work in particular should be stepped up simultaneously with the movement of greeting, comforting, relieving, and aiding revolutionary soldiers.

(3) Pay attention to measures for changing old customs in the countryside.

In the countryside, the movements to forbid feasting, to forbid making food offerings and burning incense and candles [to the spirits], to oppose all superstitious and patriarchal old customs, to improve the status of women in the country-side and so on, are all actions necessary in order to smash the bad habits of feudal society, but only when they are preceded by prolonged propaganda efforts so that ordinary people understand them and the cultural level of society has been raised can they be carried out unimpeded. If actions are taken hastily, they will not only fail to yield good results, but will enable the reactionaries to use these backward ideas to spread rumors and stir up confusion, attack the progressive peasant movement, and destroy the revolutionary alliance in the countryside.

(4) Begin the task of construction in the countryside.

The establishment of rural organs of self-government is an important task in suppressing the reactionary feudal forces, consolidating the victories already won by the peasants, eliminating the state of anarchy in the rural areas, and adapting the peasant movement to the needs of the new revolutionary environ-ment. This association has already requested in writing that the national govern-ment promulgate regulations on rural organs of self-government as soon as possible. The peasants' associations at all levels should make contacts with the revolutionary common people at once and work hard to set up rural organs of self-government within the shortest possible time. Peasants' banks, consumers' cooperatives, and other construction enterprises should be built up jointly by the peasants' associations at all levels and the revolutionary common people.

(5) Step up propaganda work.

Since the peasant movement has achieved considerable development, local bul-lies, bad gentry, and other feudal forces have concentrated their efforts on brutally killing peasants, buying over running dogs, fabricating false accusations and rumors, and stirring up confusion. Having gained some measure of freedom for the first time, the poor peasants have no experience in organizing associations. They are bound to act in naive ways. The local tyrants and evil gentry then blow the thing out of proportion to shock the public. Since Renegade Xia's betrayal, their actions have been even bolder. The propaganda work of the peasants' associations at various levels in the past has been very lax, allowing the local bullies and bad gentry to spread propaganda that confused black and white and spread it all over cities and the countryside. Even revolutionary comrades were influenced by them and doubted the peasant movement. In the future, the peasants' associations at all levels should fully and effectively expose to revolu-tionary comrades and the revolutionary masses the facts of how cruelly the local bullies and bad gentry oppress and persecute the peasants, so as to disarm the local bullies and bad gentry of their biggest offensive weapon against the peas-ants. In addition, detailed facts about the peasant movement should be revealed as much as possible to enable the peasant associations to guide their work and correct their mistakes at all times. Regarding this association's provisional order No. 1, a broader propaganda effort should be conducted for a period of time, so that ordinary peasants may thoroughly understand the new direction of the peasant movement and so that they will actively work hard to follow the road pointed out by this association.

All five issues are essential matters for the consolidation of the revolutionary alliance and promotion of the national revolution. The peasants' associations in all provinces must lead the peasants' associations at all levels in effectively implementing them. Cases of lax implementation or of public compliance but private opposition shall be sanctioned by this association in accordance with revolutionary discipline, and such associations shall be reorganized immediately. If reactionaries use the name of the peasants' associations to stir up trouble or fabricate false accusations, the peasants' associations at all levels should request that the government eliminate them at once. It is imperative not to let them spread. This order must be carried out thoroughly.

Members of the Standing Committee of the Provisional Executive Committee of the All-China Peasant Association:
> Tan Yankai, Tan Pingshan, Deng Yanda, Mao Zedong, Lu Chen

Latest Directive of the
All-China Peasant Association

Resist the Armed Attack of Local Bullies and Bad Gentry

(June 13, 1927)

This directive is to be strictly observed. In the past, because the peasant movement developed too rapidly, its organization was not sound. If you add to this the fact that the local bullies and bad gentry have launched a fierce counterattack, thus causing the struggle in the countryside to become more and more intense, and that the leadership from above has often been far from perfect, it was inevitable that some disorganized actions would take place. This committee has already issued clear instructions in orders Nos. 1 and 2 of the provisional series to the peasant associations at all levels urging them to rectify these actions most forcefully, and to ensure that the peasants in every locality are under the command of the peasant associations and are continuing their struggle against all the local bullies and bad gentry, as well as other reactionary feudal forces, in an organized and planned way. Thus our peasants can fulfill their responsibility of overthrowing the economic foundation for imperialist exploitation of the Chinese countryside and the political basis of warlord rule, in the course of the revolutionary process. We have also pointed out that the present goal for the peasants' struggle everywhere is to fight for the autonomy of the villages. At present, according to reports from various quarters, the local bullies and bad gentry in the three provinces of Hunan, Jiangxi, and Hubei have launched an extremely violent attack on the peasants. In Jiangxi on June 5, after the authorities dismissed the staff involved in political work in party affairs, the local bullies and bad gentry everywhere all seized the opportunity to make trouble. The bad gentry in Jishui, in cahoots with vagabonds,[1] attacked the peasant associations and went into the villages to capture people; in the area of Nanchang, the bad gentry detained executive committee members; in Xinjian, the local bullies and bad gentry placed under arrest members of the peasants' association

---

This directive was published in the Hankou *Minguo ribao* on June 15 and 17, 1927. Our source is this text as reproduced in *Zhonggong zhongyang wenjian xuanji*, Vol. 3, pp. 617–20. The version previously available, which appears in *Mao Zedong ji*, Vol. 2, pp. 9–10, contains only the introductory paragraph and the concluding section, but not the graphic description of atrocities visited on the peasants.

1. *Liumang.*

and took away draft oxen belonging to the peasants; in Tonggu, all revolutionary organizations were destroyed; in Yiyang, the reactionary army carried out an even larger-scale massacre of peasant association staff members; in the fourth district in Taihe, not only was the peasant association destroyed by the reactionaries, but two executive committee members were arrested. In Hunan on the day of the May 21 Incident,[2] Xu Kexiang[3] murdered more than thirty people, including comrades from the provincial peasant association, the provincial labor union, the Workers' Movement Training Institute, and friends among the workers and peasants. After the incident, troops were sent to attack the masses in the *xian* of Xiangtan and Changde, and the total number of peasants who were killed or injured was close to 10,000. In addition, they beheaded the chief of the Xiangtan general labor union and kicked his head about with their feet, then filled his belly with kerosene and burned his body. Among the popular masses who watched all of this, there was no one who was not filled with the utmost rage. In Hubei they were particularly vicious. In Hubei the local bullies and bad gentry of the various *xian* allied themselves not only with local bandits but also with corrupt leaders of the secret societies in brutally murdering the peasants. For example, in Yangxin[4] the local bullies and bad gentry used kerosene to burn nine peasants alive; in Mianyang the bullies and gentry allied themselves with the "Hard Belly Society" and brutally killed more than fifty peasants; in Tianmen the bullies and gentry got together with the local bandits and brutally killed more than twenty peasant friends; in Zhongxiang the local bullies and bad gentry, in league with the "Hard Belly Society," brutally killed more than ten peasant friends; in Hanchuan the local bullies and bad gentry allied with vagabonds to kill and injure more than ten peasant friends; in Macheng the local bullies and bad gentry, in league with the "Red Spear Society," the "Black Spear Society," and the "White Spear Society," brutally murdered more than a hundred peasant friends and burned down people's houses to the extent of several dozen villages. Furthermore, they made use of the reactionary army's forces in an attempt to wipe out the peasant movement completely, and thereby shake the foundations of the revolutionary base area. The traitors Xia [Douyin], Yang [Sen], Xu [Kexiang], Zhang [Liansheng], and Yu [Xuezhong] have defected one after the other, and everywhere they go they release the local bullies and bad gentry who are under detention, using them to lead the renegade troops in committing massacres everywhere. In Jiayu more than thirty peasants were killed; in Xianning and Wuchang, more than fifty people were killed in each place; in Tianmen more

---

2. The editors of the *Zhonggong zhongyang wenjian xuanji* have corrected this date, which appears as May 2 in the text as originally printed. The incident of May 21, 1927, which took place in the vicinity of Changsha, is also known as the "Horse Day Massacre."

3. Xu Kexiang was the commander of the Thirty-third Independent Regiment of the National Revolutionary Army's Thirty-fifth Army, stationed in Changsha.

4. The editors of the *Zhonggong zhongyang wenjian xuanji* have corrected this place name, which appears with the two characters transposed in the original.

than 300 peasant houses were burned and over twenty people were killed; in Gongan, several dozen people were killed by branding; in Zaoyang, over 500 people were brutally murdered; in Mianyang, more than twenty people were murdered; in Xuandu, several dozen people were killed; in Macheng and Yanxiang, with arrests and killings, burning of houses, and raping of women, a total of more than 500 people were killed; in Sui *xian* at various times over 1,000 people were killed; in Lutian more than sixty people were brutally murdered; in Huang'an over 100 people were murdered; in Zhongxiang Wang Rutang, a member of the bad gentry, actually occupied the *xian* town, went from door to door, and cruelly massacred more than 200 people. Elsewhere in various *xian* including Xiakou, Huanggang, Yingshan, Yingcheng, Qichun, and Jianglin, the despotic gentry have without exception launched attacks on the peasants. The brutal punishments inflicted on the revolutionary peasants by the despotic gentry includes such things as gouging out eyes and ripping out tongues, disembowelment and decapitation, slashing with knives and grinding with sand, burning with kerosene, and branding with red-hot irons. In the case of women, they would run string through their breasts and parade them around naked in public, or simply hack them to pieces. Already four or five thousand peasants have been killed or injured, and the massacre continues in *xian* such as Xingmen, Songzi, and Xuanchang. In Wuhan, the capital of the nationalist government, only a dozen or so *li* from the *xian* town of Hanyang, there inevitably broke out an incident of the local bullies and bad gentry surrounding and killing peasants. The entire province of Hubei is completely enshrouded in white terror. In the three provinces of Hunan, Jiangxi, and Hubei, the total of party members, peasants, and workers who have sacrificed their lives is well over 10,000. They [i.e., the local bullies and bad gentry] are actively pursuing venomous schemes for driving an emotional wedge between the revolutionary soldiers and the peasants. Frequently, they make up stories, or call a stag a horse, or exaggerate the seriousness of a matter, in an attempt to bring about severe clashes between the soldiers and the mass organizations, set the soldiers against the people, break up the united front, sabotage the three great policies, and overthrow the party and the state. They do not scruple to do these evil things even though they know quite well that what they are trying to do will cause sufferings for the people and bring about the loss of our country and the extinction of our nation. At the same time, corrupt officials have arisen to work in concert with the local bullies and bad gentry, and together they cook up rumors to smear the peasants and attempt to sow discord in the relationship between the government and the people. For instance, the peasant association in Huanggang was not engaged in digging soft coal at all, but still the corrupt officials there filed a misleading report to the central government demanding an explanation. Now, having learned of the vicious plot whereby the imperialists, the warlords, the corrupt officials, the local bullies and bad gentry, the compradors, and other slaves of the foreigners, and all the reactionaries will launch a joint attack on the national government at the time when we are fully engaged in the Northern Expedition and in the fierce battle against the Fengtian Army, the Military Committee of the national government hereby orders all comrades in the armed forces to investigate all the misrepresentations and exaggerated rumors, and not to fall victim to the plots of the reactionaries. In recent days, however, the trend according to which the local bullies and bad gentry in various places collude with bandits and stragglers from disbanded armies to massacre the peasants is becoming even worse. Plots by corrupt officials to sow dissension between the government and the people are also constantly emerging. Recently, every organ has received at least several slanderous plaints against the peasants every day. Under such grave circumstances, the peasant associations at all levels should all unanimously urge the national government to do the following: (1) Issue explicit orders to protect the workers' and peasants' organizations, the workers' pickets, and the peasants' self-defense army, and also punish all reactionaries who murder workers and peasants and disrupt the rear area; allow labor unions, peasant associations, the Communist Party, and other revolutionary organizations complete freedom to unite the revolutionary forces and carry out a punitive expedition against Chiang Kaishek. (2) Eliminate the local bullies and bad gentry in various *xian* of Hubei who collude with rebel armies and bandits to massacre the peasants and workers, and punish severely Chiang Kaishek's agents and all other reactionaries who fabricate rumors and sow dissension, so as to consolidate Wuhan. (3) Issue explicit orders to punish Xu Kexiang, Qiu Ao, Peng Guojun, and Xiao Yukun; disband their reactionary organs, such as the Committee for Saving the Party and the Committee to Purify the Party; restore the Hunan provincial government, the provincial party committee, the provincial labor union, the provincial peasant association, and all the other revolutionary bodies that have been destroyed; accept the petition presented by the Hunan Petition Delegation; and order Tang [Shengzhi], the chairman of the Hunan provincial government, to crack down swiftly on the counterrevolutionaries in Hunan. (4) Issue explicit orders to curb any actions in Jiangxi to drive out the Communist Party and the leaders of the workers and peasants, and severely punish reactionaries who massacre the popular masses. As for the peasant associations themselves, they should step up their efforts to unite with the peasants, tighten their organization, and arm themselves for self-defense, so that they may resist the armed attacks of the local bullies and bad gentry, and put down any attempts by the reactionary feudal forces to provoke dissension. For if the arrogance of the local bullies and bad gentry is not stamped out, it will become simply impossible to establish autonomy in the countryside, and to set up democratic political power, let alone to achieve anything in the way of economic construction. Thus the foundations of the national government cannot be consolidated. It is so ordered.

> Members of the Standing Committee of the Provisional Executive Committee of the All-China Peasant Association: Tan Yankai, Tan Pingshan, Deng Yanda, Mao Zedong, Lu Chen
> June 13

Bibliography

In the first volume of this series, Mao's citations were drawn largely from the corpus of Chinese historical and literary writings over the centuries. For the most part, the references in the notes therefore gave only the title, and on occasion the volume or *juan* number of the work in question, so as to enable those with a knowledge of Chinese to locate the relevant passages. To have listed all those names and titles alone would have taken an inordinate amount of space, and would have been of limited utility. Consequently, we included in the "Bibliographic Note" only those works in Chinese for which a specific edition was cited in the notes, as well as items in Western languages, and translations of Chinese texts.

In the period covered by this and subsequent volumes, beginning with the 1920s, Mao alluded to a much wider range of contemporary writings, both Western and Chinese, which the title alone does not suffice to identify. In addition, his own works appeared in a variety of publications, briefly mentioned in the source notes to each text, regarding which appropriate bibliographic information is provided here. As a result, this section of the book has grown from a note to a full-fledged bibliography. For the convenience of the reader, we include here the short titles used for certain works, which are likewise given on the first appearance of each entry in the notes.

Analects, in Legge, Vol. I.

Atwell, Pamela, *British Mandarins and Chinese Reformers*. Hong Kong: Oxford University Press, 1985.

Bailey, Paul, "The Chinese Work-Study Movement in France," *The China Quarterly* no. 115 (September 1988), pp. 441–61.

Barman, Geneviève, and Dulioust, Nicole, "La France au miroir chinois," *Les Temps modernes* no. 498 (January 1988), pp. 32–67.

Bergère, Marie-Claire, "The Chinese Bourgeoisie, 1911–37," *The Cambridge History of China*, Vol. 12, pp. 721–825.

Book of Historical Documents, in Legge, Vol. II.

Book of Poetry, in Legge, Vol. IV.

Cai Hesen wenji (Collected Works of Cai Hesen). Beijing: Renmin chubanshe, 1980.

Chang Kuo-t'ao [Zhang Guotao], *The Rise of the Chinese Communist Party, 1921–1927: Volume One of the Autobiography of Chang Kuo-t'ao*. Lawrence, Kansas: The University Press of Kansas, 1971. (Short title: Chang, *Autobiography*.)

Chen Duxiu, "Beijing zhengbian yu Guomindang" (The Beijing Coup d'État and the Guomindang). *Xiangdao zhoubao* (The Guide Weekly) no. 31/32 (July 11, 1923), pp. 229–30.

Ch'en Kung-po [Chen Gongbo], *The Communist Movement in China*, edited with an introduction by C. Martin Wilbur. New York: Columbia University East Asian Institute, 1960. [Master's essay submitted in 1924]. (Short title: Ch'en, *Communist Movement*.)

Cherepanov, Aleksandr Ivanovich, *Zapiski voennogo sovetnika v Kitae (1924–1927)* (Notes of a Military Adviser in China, 1924–1927). Vol. 1. Moscow: Izdatel'stvo "Nauka," 1964. Abridged English translation of this volume, and of the second volume, A.I. Cherepanov, *As Military Adviser in China*. Moscow: Progress Publishers, 1982.

Chesneaux, Jean, *Le mouvement ouvrier chinois de 1919 à 1927*. Paris: Mouton, 1962. (Short title: Chesneaux, *Mouvement ouvrier*.)

Chesneaux, Jean, *Les syndicats chinois, 1919–1927*. Paris: Mouton, 1965.

Couvreur, Séraphin, *Les quatre livres*. Paris: Cathasia, n.d.

Dalin, Sergei Alekseevich, *Kitayskie memuary 1921–1927* (Chinese Memoirs 1921–1927). Moscow: Izdatel'stvo "Nauka," 1975.

Dangde wenxian (Documents of the Party), No. 1, 1989. Beijing: Zhonggong zhongyang wenxian yanjiu shi, 1989.

Day, M. Henri, *Máo Zédōng 1917–1927. Documents*. (Stockholm: University of Stockholm, 1975) (Skriftserien för Orientaliska Studier no. 14)

Delyusin, Lev Petrovich, *Agrarno-krestiyanskii vopros v politike KPK (1921–1928)* (The Peasant and Agrarian Question in the Politics of the Chinese Communist Party, 1921–1928). Moscow: Izdatel'stvo "Nauka," 1972.

Deng Zhongxia, *Zhongguo zhigong yundong jianshi (1919–1926)* (Brief History of the Chinese Labor Movement, 1919–1926). Originally published in Moscow in 1930. Reprinted Beijing: Renmin chubanshe, 1949.

Eudin, Xenia, and North, Robert, *Soviet Russia and the East 1920–1927*. Stanford: Stanford University Press, 1957. (Short title: Eudin and North, *Soviet Russia and the East*.)

Fairbank, John K. (ed.), *The Cambridge History of China*, Vol. 12, *Republican China 1912–1949, Part I*. Cambridge: Cambridge University Press, 1983.

Fung Yu-lan, *History of Chinese Philosophy*, translated by Derk Bodde. 2 vols. Princeton: Princeton University Press, 1952.

Galbiati, F., *P'eng P'ai and the Hai-Lu-feng Soviet*. Stanford: Stanford University Press, 1985.

Glunin, V.I., "The Comintern and the Rise of the Communist Movement in China (1920–1927)," in *The Comintern and the East*. Moscow: Progress Publishers, 1979, pp. 280–344.

Graham, A.C., *Poems of the Late T'ang*. Harmondsworth: Penguin, 1965.

Hofheinz, Roy, Jr., *The Broken Wave. The Chinese Communist Peasant Movement, 1922–1928*. Cambridge, Mass.: Harvard University Press, 1977.

Hunan jinbainian dashi jishu (Hunan shengzhi diyi juan) (An Account of Important Events in Hunan during the Past Hundred Years [vol. 1 of the Hunan Provincial Gazeteer]), edited by the Hunan Provincial Gazeteer Editorial Committee, 2nd ed. Changsha: Renmin chubanshe, 1979. (Short title: *Jinbainian*.)

Hung, William, *Tu Fu: China's Greatest Poet*. Cambridge, Mass.: Harvard University Press, 1952.

Jiang Yongjing, *Baoluoting yu Wuhan zhengquan* (Borodin and the Wuhan Régime). Taibei: Zhongguo xueshu zhuzuo jiangzhu weiyuanhui, 1963.

"Jingren," "Beijing zhengbian yu laodong jieji" (The Beijing Coup d'État and the Laboring Class). *Xiangdao zhoubao* (The Guide Weekly), no. 31/32 (July 11, 1923), pp. 234–35.

Kuo, Warren, *Analytical History of the Chinese Communist Party*, Vol. 1. Taibei: Institute of International Relations, 1968.

Legge, James, *The Chinese Classics*. Vol. I, *Confucian Analects, The Great Learning, The Doctrine of the Mean*. Vol. II, *The Works of Mencius*. Vol. III, *The Shoo king [shujing] or the Book of Historical Documents*. Vol. IV, *The She King [shijing] or the Book of Poetry*. Reprinted Hong Kong: Hong Kong University Press, 1960.

Li Chien-nung [Li Jiannong], *The Political History of China, 1840–1928.* Stanford: Stanford University Press, 1956. (Short title: Li Chien-nung, *The Political History of China.*)

Li Jui [Li Rui], *The Early Revolutionary Activities of Comrade Mao Tse-tung.* Tr. Anthony W. Sariti (from first Chinese ed). White Plains, N.Y.: M.E. Sharpe, 1977. (Short title: Li Jui, *Early Mao.*)

Li Rui, *Mao Zedong tongzhi de chuqi geming huodong* (The Early Revolutionary Activities of Comrade Mao Zedong). Beijing: Zhongguo qingnian chubanshe, 1957. Third ed.: *Zaonian Mao Zedong* (The Young Mao Zedong). Shenyang: Liaoning remin chubanshe, 1991.

Li Yongtai, *Mao Zedong yu da geming* (Mao Zedong and the Great Revolution). Chengdu: Sichuan renmin chubanshe, 1991. (Short title: Li Yongtai, *Mao and the Great Revolution.*)

Ma Yuqing and Zhang Wanlu, *Mao Zedong gemingde daolu* (Mao Zedong's Revolutionary Way). Xi'an: Shaanxi renmin chubanshe, 1991. (Short title: Ma and Zhang, *Mao's Way.*)

Mao Zedong, "Ruhe yanjiu Zhonggong dangshi" (How to Study the History of the Chinese Communist Party), in *Dangshi yanjiu* (Research on Party History) No. 1, 1980, pp.2–7.

Mao Zedong, *Selected Works of Mao Tse-tung,* Vols 1–4. Peking: Foreign Languages Press, 1960–1965.

Mao Zedong ji (Collected Writings of Mao Zedong), ed. Takeuchi Minoru. 10 vols. Tokyo: Hokubōsha, 1970–1972; second edition, Tokyo: Sōsōsha, 1983

Mao Zedong ji. Bujuan (Supplement to the Collected Writings of Mao Zedong), ed. Takeuchi Minoru. 10 vols. Tokyo: Sōsōsha, 1983–1986

Mao Zedong nongcun diaocha wenji (Collected Writings of Mao Zedong on Rural Investigations). Beijing: Renmin chubanshe, 1982.

Mao Zedong shici duilian jizhu (Annotated Edition of Mao Zedong's Poems and Couplets). Changsha: Hunan wenyi chubanshe, 1991. (Short title: *Shici duilian.*)

Mao Zedong shuxin xuanji (Selected Correspondence of Mao Zedong), ed. Zhonggong zhongyang wenxian yanjiu shi. Beijing: Renmin chubanshe, 1983.

Mao Zedong wenji (Collected Writings of Mao Zedong), ed. Zhonggong zhongyang wenxian yanjiu shi. 2 vols. (January 1921–June 1937 and August 1937–December 1942). Beijing: Renmin chubanshe, 1993.

Mao Zedong xinwen gonzuo wenxuan (Selected Writings by Mao Zedong on Journalistic Work). Beijing: Xinhua shudian, 1983.

Mao Zedong xuanji (Selected Works of Mao Zedong), Vol. 1. First edition, Beijing: Renmin chubanshe, 1951. Second edition, Beijing: Renmin chubanshe, 1991.

McDonald, Angus W., Jr., *The Urban Origins of Rural Revolution. Elites and the Masses in Hunan Province, China, 1911–1927.* Berkeley: University of California Press, 1978. (Short title: McDonald, *Urban Origins.*)

Mencius, in Legge, Vol. II.

Mif, Pavel Aleksandrovich [Mikhail Aleksandrovich Fortus] (ed.), *Strategiya i taktika Kominterna v natsional'no-kolonial'noi revolutsii na primere Kitaya* (The Strategy and Tactics of the Comintern in the National-colonial Revolution, on the Basis of the Chinese Example). Moscow: Institute of International Economics and International Politics, 1934. (Short title: Mif, *Strategy and Tactics.*)

Minguo ribao (Republican Daily) (Guangzhou).

Nongmin congkan (Collected Writings on the Peasants). 4 vols. Shanghai: Wusan shudian, May 1927.

Nongmin yundong (The Peasant Movement [organ of the Peasant Department of the Guomindang Central Executive Committee]), No. 8, September 21, 1926.

Pang Xianzhi (ed.), *Mao Zedong nianpu. 1893–1949* (Chronological Biography of Mao Zedong, 1893–1949). 3 vols. Beijing: Zhongyang wenxian chubanshe, 1993. (Short title: *Nianpu*.)

Saich, Tony (ed.), *The Origins of the First United Front in China. The Role of Sneevliet (Alias Maring)*. 2 vols. Leiden: E.J. Brill, 1991. (Short title: Saich, *Origins*.)

Saich, Tony, *The Rise to Power of the Chinese Communist Party. Documents and Analysis, 1920–1949*. Armonk, N.Y.: M.E. Sharpe, 1995. (Short title: Saich, *Rise to Power*.)

Schram, Stuart R. (ed.), *Mao's Road to Power: Revolutionary Writings, 1912–1949*. Vol. I, *The Pre-Marxist Period, 1912–1920*. White Plains, N.Y.: M.E. Sharpe, 1992.

Schram, Stuart R., *Mao Tse-tung Unrehearsed, Talks and Letters: 1956–71*. Harmondsworth: Penguin Books, 1974. American edition: *Chairman Mao Talks to the People, Talks and Letters: 1956–71*. New York: Pantheon, 1974.

Schram, Stuart R., and Carrère d'Encausse, Hélène, *Marxism and Asia: An Introduction with Readings*. London: Allen Lane The Penguin Press, 1969.

Shaffer, Lynda, *Mao and the Workers. The Hunan Labor Movement, 1920–1923*. Armonk, N.Y.: M.E. Sharpe, 1982. (Short title: Shaffer, *Mao and the Workers*.)

Shiji (Records of the Historian). Translations of extracts: Burton Watson, *Records of the Grand Historian of China*. New York: Columbia University Press, 1961; Yang Hsien-yi and Gladys Yang, *Records of the Historian*. Hong Kong: The Commercial Press, 1974. (Short title: *Records of the Historian*.)

Siao-yu [Xiao Zisheng, Xiao Xudong], *Mao Tse-tung and I Were Beggars*. Syracuse: Syracuse University Press, 1959.

Snow, Edgar, *Red Star Over China*. London: Gollancz, 1937.

Sun Yatsen, *San Min Chu I. The Three Principles of the People*, (tr. Frank W. Price). Shanghai: China Committee, Institute of Pacific Relations, 1927.

Torr, Dona (ed.), *Marx on China 1853–1860: Articles from the* New York Daily Tribune. London: Lawrence and Wishart, 1951.

Vishnyakova-Akimova, Vera Vladimirovna, *Two Years in Revolutionary China 1925–1927* (tr. Steven Levine). Cambridge, Mass.: Harvard University Press, 1971.

Volin, Mikhail [Semen Natanovich Belen'kii], review of Mao's "Analysis of the Classes of Chinese Society" as published in *Zhongguo nongmin* No. 2, February 1, 1926. Volin's article originally appeared in *Kanton* (Canton), the journal of the Soviet advisers in Guangzhou, no. 8/9, 1926; it was reprinted in *Voprosy Filosofii* (Questions of Philosophy) no. 6, 1969, pp.130–36.

Watson, Burton (tr.), *The Complete Works of Chuang Tzu*. New York: Columbia University Press, 1968.

Wilbur, C. Martin, *The Nationalist Revolution in China, 1923–1928*. Cambridge: Cambridge University Press, 1984. (First published in 1983 as chapter 11 of *The Cambridge History of China*, vol. 12.) (Short title: Wilbur, *Nationalist Revolution*.)

Wilbur Papers in the Columbia University Rare Book and Mansuscript Library.

Wittfogel, Karl August, *Wirtschaft und Gesellschaft Chinas*. Leipzig: Hirschfeld, 1931.

Xiangdao zhoubao (The Guide Weekly [organ of the Chinese Communist Party]). Nos. 1–201, September 13, 1922–July 18, 1927. (Short title: *Xiangdao*.)

Xinmin xuehui ziliao (Materials on the New People's Study Society), ed. Museum of the Chinese Revolution and Hunan Provincial Museum. Beijing: Renmin chubanshe, 1980. (*Zhongguo xiandai geming shi ziliao congkan*)

Zhang Guotao, "Wode huiyi" (My Memoirs) Chapter 6. *Ming bao* Vol. 1, no. 10 (October 1966), pp. 78–92.

Zhang Yunhou et al., *Liufa qingong jianxue yundong* (The Work-study Movement in France). 2 vols. Shanghai: Shanghai renmin chubanshe, 1980, 1986.

Zhonggong zhongyang wenjian xuanji (Selected Documents of the Central Committee of the Chinese Communist Party). Vol. 1, 1921–1925; Vol. 2, 1926; Vol. 3, 1927. Beijing: Zhonggong zhongyang dangxiao chubanshe, 1989. (Short title: *Central Committee Documents.*)

Zhengzhi zhoubao (Political Weekly) (Guangzhou [Organ of the Guomindang Propaganda Department]). Issues nos. 1–4, which appeared between December 5, 1925, and January 10, 1926, were edited by Mao Zedong. Beginning with issue no. 5, published on March 6, 1926, it was edited by Mao Dun (Shen Yanbing).

Zhongguo gongchandang huiyi gaiyao (A Summary Account of Chinese Communist Party Meetings), ed. Jiang Huaxuan et al. Shenyang: Shenyang chubanshe, 1991. (Short title: *Party Meetings.*)

Zhongguo Guomindang quanguo daibiao dahui huiyilu (Minutes of the [First] National Congress of the Chinese Guomindang). Guangzhou: Zhongguo Guomindang zhixing weiyuanhui, 1924. Repr. Washington, D.C.: Center for Chinese Research Materials, 1971.

Zhongguo Guomindang dierci quanguo daibiao dahui huiyi jilu (Minutes of the Second National Congress of the Chinese Guomindang). Guangzhou: Zhongguo Guomindang zhixing weiyuanhui, April 1926.

Zhongguo Guomindang diyi, er ci quanguo daibiao dahui huiyi shiliao (Historical Materials on the First and Second National Congresses of the Chinese Guomindang). 2 vols. Yangzhou: Jiangsu guji chubanshe, 1986.

Zhongguo nongmin (The Chinese Peasant). Guangzhou: Peasant Department of the Central Executive Committee of the Chinese Guomindang, 1926.

Zhonghua nongxuehui bao (English title on cover: "The Journal of Agricultural Association of China"), No. 52. Shanghai: Agricultural Association of China, November 1926.

Zou Lu quanji (Complete Works of Zou Lu), Volume 9. Taibei: Sanmin shuju, 1976.

Index

Agricultural Association of China, xlvii, 386

All-China General Labor Union, 114, 330, 334

All-China Peasant Association, lii, liv, lv, 434n15, 485–86, 509, 514–17; founding of, 495; and local associations, 504–8; and Peasant Movement, 510–13

All-Hunan Federation of Labor Organizations, xxvi, 132, 133, 139, 147, 149, 151, 153, 174

America: anti-communism of, 276; democratic revolution in, 320; elections in, 41, 209; imperialism of, xxxv, xli, 159, 180–81, 189–90, 231, 239, 240, 246; labor rights in, 111; missionaries from, 171, 216n5; as model, 69; strikes in, 171, 343; study in, 77; universities in, 287, 288; writings on, 383; and Zhili clique, 242

Anarchism: and labor, 136; of Mao, xvi, xxv, 7, 8, 11, 35, 68; New People's Study Society on, 67, 69

Anfu clique, 231, 241, 242, 245, 292n6, 294; propaganda of, 268, 317, 357

Anhui clique, 149, 158, 159, 166. See also Anfu clique

Anyuan labor movement, 109n2, 121, 174, 176, 251n13

Association of Chinese Spinning Mill Owners, 180n9

Bai Chongxi, 364

Bai Shan. See Li Lisan

Bai Yu, 28

Baldwin, Stanley, 275

Bandits, 461, 471, 514, 515, 517

Banking Associations, 181, 389

Banks, 394, 475, 507, 512

Bansong Park meeting (May 1920), 11, 26, 37n1, 63

Barbers' Union, 133, 138–39, 140, 175, 177

Basic Program (on rural problems), xlviii

Bebel, August, 381

Beijing, xxii, xxvi, xxxvi, xxxviii, 30, 94, 291, 374; newspapers in, 311, 374. See also Cao Kun; Duan Qirui; Western Hills conference

Beijing-Hankou railroad, xxviii, 147n2, 241

Beijing-Wuhan railroad, 149, 151, 151n2, 153, 259

Beiyang faction, 166

Bin Bucheng, 175, 176

Blacks, 382

Bolshevism, 69, 70. See also Communism

Bolshevization (chihua), 276, 293

Boot and Shoe Craftsmen's Union, 133, 140, 175

Borodin, Mikhail Markovitch, xxxv, xxxviii, xxxix, xl, xlv, 284, 287, 297, 494n1; biography of, 284n1

Bourgeoisie: among peasants, 305, 306; class nature of, 250, 252–56, 260, 261; and factions, 235, 324; and landlords, 304; Mao on, xxx, xxxiv–xxxv, xl, xli, xliv, 237; and proletariat, 7, 10, 253, 391; propaganda of, 318; and revolution, 320, 321, 322, 323, 325, 326; Stalin on, xxxix, liv

Britain, 94, 171, 216n5, 276, 280n2, 383; democratic revolution in, 320; factions in, 235; Mao on, xxxv; as model, 69, 135; propaganda against, 437, 457; universities in, 287, 288. See also British imperialism

British and American Tobacco Company, 190

British imperialism, xl, xli, 159, 186; collusion with, 264; and Guangdong, 236; opposition to, 246, 269, 326; and taxes, 189–90; and warlords, 231, 232, 233, 239, 240, 242, 243, 244; and Weihaiwei, 186–88

British Labor Party, xl, 235

Bukharin, Nikolai Ivanovich, 285

Bu Lici, 420

525

About the Editor

Stuart R. Schram was born in Excelsior, Minnesota, in 1924. After graduating from the University of Minnesota in physics, he took his Ph.D. in political science at Columbia University. From 1954 to 1967, he conducted research at the Fondation Nationale des Sciences Politiques in Paris, and from 1968 until 1989, he was Professor of Politics with reference to China at the School of Oriental and African Studies, University of London. Since 1989, he has worked at the Fairbank Center, Harvard University, on the edition of Mao Zedong's pre-1949 writings of which this is the second volume.

His research has dealt with Leninist theories and their application in Asia, Chinese history and politics in the twentieth century, and the influence of the Chinese tradition on the theory and practice of the state in China. His works include *Mao Tse-tung* (1967), *The Political Thought of Mao Tse-tung* (1969), *Marxism and Asia* (in collaboration with Hélène Carrère d'Encausse) (1969), *Ideology and Policy in China since the Third Plenum, 1978–1984* (1984), and *The Thought of Mao Tse-tung* (1989). He has also edited a volume entitled *Foundations and Limits of State Power in China* (1987). *Mao Tse-tung* and *The Thought of Mao Tse-tung* have been translated into Chinese and published in Beijing.

About the Associate Editor

Nancy J. Hodes was born in Philadelphia in 1946, and spent her formative years in Beijing, China, where her father taught physiology at the Chinese Academy of Medical Sciences. After graduating from Radcliffe College in Far Eastern Languages, she edited the *Bulletin of Concerned Asian Scholars*, taught Chinese, and worked as a freelance translator. She returned to China in the 1970s to teach English and work on *A Chinese-English Dictionary* at the Beijing Foreign Languages Institute (#1). Later she taught Chinese at Tufts University and Harvard Summer School, worked as a translator for M. E. Sharpe's translation journals and the Mao's Writings Project at Brown University, and served as Assistant Editor of the *Harvard Journal of Asiatic Studies*. After receiving her Ph.D. in Chinese literature from Harvard University, she taught East Asian Civilizations and Chinese at Boston College, and has been working since 1991 with Stuart R. Schram on the present edition of Mao Zedong's pre-1949 writings. She serves concurrently as Associate Director of the Boston Research Center for the 21st Century, founded in 1993 by Soka Gakkai International President Daisaku Ikeda.

DATE DUE

APR 2 8 2008			
MAY 1 5 2008			